The Changing Party Elite in East Germany

The MIT Press
Cambridge, Massachusetts, and London, England

The Changing Party Elite in East Germany

Peter C. Ludz

Originally published in 1968 by Westdeutscher Verlag, Cologne and Opladen under the title *Parteielite im Wandel,* as part of the series "Schriften des Instituts für politische Wissenschaft"
Copyright © 1968 by Westdeutscher Verlag, Cologne and Opladen

Translation published under the auspices of the Research Institute on Communist Affairs, Columbia University in the City of New York
Translated by Israel Program for Scientific Translations

English translation Copyright © 1972 by
The Massachusetts Institute of Technology

This book was designed by The MIT Press Design Department.
It was set in Linotype Times Roman
by Monumental Printing Co.
printed on Mohawk Neotext Offset
by The Colonial Press, Inc.
and bound in Columbia Milbank vellum
by The Colonial Press, Inc.
in the United States of America.

ISBN 0 262 12053 4 (hardcover)

Library of Congress catalog card number: 76-162918

Contents

Foreword

It gives me great pleasure to write a few words of introduction to Professor Ludz's classic study of the Communist Party elite in East Germany. This study first appeared in German in 1968 and was immediately recognized as a contribution of lasting importance not only to our understanding of East German politics but to political science and political sociology itself. Accordingly, the Research Institute on Communist Affairs, Columbia University, with which Professor Ludz has been associated over the years, undertook to make this study accessible in the English language to interested scholars in this country and elsewhere.

Professor Ludz's study is impressive on three different levels. First of all, it provides a politically significant theoretical framework for the analysis of the role of political elites in a Communist-type political system. In so doing, Professor Ludz casts new light on the nature of modern bureaucratic organization and on the role of the elite as a key element in the political system. Second, Professor Ludz's study is a significant source of information on the gradual shaping of the East German Communist elite, its political and ideological evolution, and the relationship between the foregoing and social-economic change. As such, it widens our understanding of the historical development of the East German regime and provides an effective analytical point of departure for judgments concerning that political system's developmental prospects. Third, on the basis of the first two levels, Professor Ludz's study represents also an important contribution to our understanding of the role of ideology in the East German Communist political system. Indeed, I would go further than that and suggest that his study is in itself a significant contribution to our appreciation of the evolution of Communist ideology when applied to the social-economic conditions of a relatively advanced and modernized society.

In recent years students and scholars of Communist affairs have hotly debated the prospects of further political change in Communist systems. Professor Ludz's discussions of the relationship between the cybernetic systems concept and the Marxist theory of organization is a particularly important contribution to that debate. The value of his study thus goes beyond the confines of the East German regime; no informed student of Communist affairs will henceforth be able to discuss the possibilities of change in the Soviet system without reference to the issues and ideas with which Ludz's study has been concerned. Toward the end of his study Professor Ludz notes that "the profound changes in the Marxist-Leninist ideological system of the GDR may be interpreted variously as decay, inertia, or finally, a refunctionalization of the ideological dogma. Analysis of differences and conflicts in various interpretations of historical and dialectical materialism was included in this study, since these differences paralleled trends perceived in the organizational and social spheres." Given the wide-ranging and probing character of his study, both political science and Communist studies are richer because of the existence of Professor Ludz's pioneering study.

Zbigniew Brzezinski

Introduction to the American Edition

For nearly twenty years of its short history the German Democratic Republic (GDR) was popularly assigned the status of a Moscow satellite in West Germany and in other Western countries. This image served both as the basis for West German policy toward the former Soviet Zone of Occupation and for West German studies on the GDR's political and social system. While the former was dominated by the so-called Hallstein doctrine, the latter conceived of the GDR as a totalitarian system of the Stalinist type. Cold-war narrowmindedness and academic misconceptions in each part of divided Germany concerning the other were in the foreground.

However, toward the middle sixties the political as well as the academic image of the GDR began to change in the West. In politics, the Hallstein doctrine became increasingly undermined, and gave way to political forces that sought cooperation with the GDR rather than confrontation or total disregard of the second German state. GDR research, basing its statements more and more on newly gathered empirical data, helped to bring about this new era in politics while it underwent considerable changes by rendering its previously basic methodological concept, namely totalitarianism, obsolete.

The new evaluation of the GDR was developing on the grounds of changes in GDR society itself. These changes, evident since at least 1963, are not commonly known in the West. Thus it is one of the main purposes of this book to communicate new observations to a partly uninformed public—a public that may still be biased in some degree as well. This study intends to contribute to a better and more realistic understanding of what was and is going on in that part of Germany which in 1949 named itself "Deutsche Demokratische Republik."

The methodology is taken from sociology and political science. Both disciplines are increasingly concerned with phenomena of closely interrelated changes in political and social structures; their efforts in this respect are interwoven. Trends of change and structural transformations in political and societal systems are, however, frequently accompanied by phenomena indicating stability and immobility. Consequently, social change induces both latent and manifest conflicts which have been studied by political scientists as well as sociologists.

A variety of social-science studies have proved that political and social change is not restricted to advanced Western societies or developing countries. Indeed, the dynamics of change in traditional structures are now evident in the Soviet Union and other countries of Eastern Europe, just as they are in East Germany. These processes are accelerated in the economic sphere by the principle of functional efficiency, now supported by the overwhelming majority of Communist leaders in Eastern Europe.

This study represents an attempt to document this changing situation in Eastern Europe via the analysis of one particular sociopolitical system, that of the GDR, where the forces of change and immobilism find themselves in a particularly stark confrontation. Society there displays many characteristics of a dynamic industrial society, on the one hand; on the other, it is still marked by bureaucratic controls of the nonpluralistic type, even though the very forms of controls have been altered too. Because this society's structure is so self-contradictory in its multiple stratifications, it is a highly stimulating subject for the political analyst.

Naturally, the whole of society of East Germany *per se* could not be the object of a single case study. Our sample thus was limited to change and differentiation covering about one decade in the politically most important subsystem of this new society, the Socialist Unity Party of Germany or SED.

Although numerous concepts of social and political change have been advanced by sociology and political science in recent years, no definitive theory has yet been formulated. Case studies are thus more likely to clarify interdependencies of phenomena, or to emphasize major points of reference and elaborate indices, which—via the analysis of change in partial structures—lay open entire social orders to scientific research. This work thus consolidates systematically organized data on the SED—not generally available in the West—collected since the earlier studies by the German political sociologists Carola Stern and Ernst Richert. It is, however, far more than a mere compilation of materials. An interpretative framework has been established, since only studies that have a methodological point of departure permit differentiating between reliable and unreliable data and expanding the range of theoretical insights. Additionally, this kind of study allows greater scope for serious speculation on the future of a political and social system. The dynamics of change invariably encompass the past, present, and future of a society. There is therefore an equal need for historical, sociological, and political description and analysis as well as prognosis.

Conceived within the range of comparative political science and sociology, the theoretical framework developed for this study intends to relate questions, concepts, and categories pertaining to several dimensions of one sociopolitical subsystem so as to make them comparable (cf. Chapter One). By this method it was possible to grasp certain corresponding trends in the SED's organization, its social structure, and its ideology. For example, it was possible to establish certain facts to document the existence of an institutionalized counter elite within the SED which not only is characterized by certain biographical data and status criteria but also holds specific positions within the SED's hierarchy and has developed ideological concepts of its own.

The raw materials on which this study is based and, correspondingly, the techniques used differ in accordance with the very dimensions investigated:
1.
The social-structure analysis (cf. Chapter Three).
The members and candidates of the Politburo, the Central Committee secretaries, and the other members and candidates of the SED Central Committees from 1954 through 1966/1967 have been empirically studied with specific characteristics in mind. These characteristics were so compiled as to furnish a biographical data profile for each person studied. The systematization of heterogeneous biographical material led to a series of correlations which not only allowed a more precise re-examination of confirmed knowledge but also provided new insights into the sociopolitical reality of the GDR. By extrapolation of hierarchical and functional changes within the leadership groups of the GDR, further characteristics can undoubtedly be added to our data structure in future analyses. These data can also serve as a basis for comparative elite studies, particularly between the GDR and the Soviet Union, but also for the SED and similar party structures of Eastern Europe.
2.
The organizational analysis (cf. Chapter Two).
The case study on the SED leadership's social structure has been juxtaposed to a more or less descriptive treatment of changes in the

organizational structure of the party apparatus. The focus of this investigation was on the Central Committee, the Politburo's committees and commissions formed in 1963, and the *Bezirk* secretariats as well as the workers' and peasants' inspectorates (ABI) and the production committees.

3.

The ideological analysis (cf. Chapter Four).

The theory of ideology (as developed by scholars on the basis of Karl Mannheim's sociology of knowledge) has provided the instruments for Chapter Four. Selected aspects of the ideological system, especially the newer tenets of revisionism, were emphasized. The East German philosophical discussions on alienation were singled out, as were some epistemological problems in dialectical materialism resulting from the acceptance of certain idioms and concepts developed by Western schools of thinking (such as the philosophy of science and cybernetics).

For the three areas investigated here—the SED's organizational system, its social structure, and its ideology—we could establish that the very pictures in the early sixties differed widely from those in the fifties. To a notable degree the SED elites have proved capable of steering the processes of modernization in East German economy and society. They have also succeeded in insulating the power center from the forces of change and mobility. Thus, modernization of the socioeconomic system has been achieved by evading liberalization of the political system.

How long the SED can hold this course is a question still to be answered. In the last three years, which followed the first publication of this book in West Germany, the GDR has moved toward further economic and social consolidation. The dynamics set free in the early sixties are more or less channeled by now; the political system, however, is still vulnerable.[1] With Erich Honecker, who replaced Walter Ulbricht in May 1971, as its First Secretary, the SED is still laying the burdens of modernization on the shoulders of the institutionalized counter elite. However, the party at present is favoring technicians who are also devoted party members more explicitly than before. While in the early

[1] For further details, cf. my booklet *The German Democratic Republic from the Sixties to the Seventies* (Harvard University: Occasional Papers in International Affairs, No. 26, November 1970).

sixties, when Ulbricht introduced the "new economic system," technocrats and other experts from various societal sectors, especially economists, gained ground, Honecker has chosen qualified party ideologists and organizers as well as other party experts to help him direct the processes set in motion a decade ago.[2] Or to put it otherwise, compared to the early sixties, the institutionalized counter elite is now less describable by the label "counter" and more by the adjective "institutionalized." However, it still holds a counter position insofar as, compared to the strategic clique, it is better equipped for the GDR's long way toward modernization.

The present book is a translation of the German *Parteielite im Wandel,* which was first published in 1968; it is an abbreviated and revised, although not updated, version of the German original. This M.I.T. edition would not have existed if I had not been assisted generously by several institutions and individuals. In the first place, I want to thank Professor Zbigniew Brzezinski and the Research Institute on Communist Affairs, Columbia University, New York. Between 1968 and 1972 I was awarded various short-time RICA fellowships which gave me the opportunity of supervising this translation. I am also indebted to Professor William E. Griffith, who acted as additional sponsor. My further thanks are directed to all those who were engaged in the translation process: Mr. D. Ben-Jaakov in Tel-Aviv, who prepared the draft translation of the German text; Miss Deborah A. Stone and Mr. Edward L. McGowan, who—thanks to generous arrangements made by Professor Brzezinski—showed an exceptional understanding for the manuscript while assisting me in revising the translation.

Peter C. Ludz
Berlin
November 1971

[2] Cf. my article "Continuity and Change Since Ulbricht," *Problems of Communism,* March-April, 1972. This article gives an assessment also of the SED's 8th Party Congress (June 1971).

List of Abbreviations

ABI
Arbeiter und-Bauern-Inspektion
(Workers' and Peasants' Inspectorate)

AGF
Archiv für gesamtdeutsche Fragen
(Archives for All-German Affairs)

AGL
Abteilungsgewerkschaftsleitung
(Union Executive of a Section [in large enterprises], subdivision of the BGL)

APO
Abteilungsparteiorganisation
(Party Organization of a Section [in large enterprises], subdivision of the BPO)

BFN
Büro für Neuererwesen
(Bureau for Innovation)

BGL
Betriebsgewerkschaftsleitung
(Factory Union Executive)

BPKK
Bezirksparteikontrollkommission
(*Bezirk* Party Control Commission)

BPO
Betriebsparteiorganisation
(Factory Party Organization)

BRD (FRG)
Bundesrepublik Deutschland
(Federal Republic of Germany)

CC
See ZK

CEMA
See RGW

COMECON
See RGW

CPCC
See ZPKK

CPSU
See KPdSU

CSSR/CSR
Ceskoslovenská Socialistická Republika
(Czechoslovak Socialist Republic)

DDR (GDR)
Deutsche Demokratische Republik
(German Democratic Republic)

DFD
Demokratischer Frauenbund Deutschlands
(Democratic Womens' Association of Germany)

DRK
Deutsches Rotes Kreuz
(German Red Cross)

DSV
Deutscher Schriftstellerverband
(German Writers' Union)

DTSB
Deutscher Turn- und Sportbund
(German Gymnastics and Sports Association)

FDGB
Freier Deutscher Gewerkschaftsbund
(Free German Trade Union Association)

FDJ
Freie Deutsche Jugend
(Free German Youth)

FRG
See BRD

GBl
Gesetzblatt
(Law Register, i.e., the official government publication for all regulations having the force of law)

GDR
See DDR

GST
Gesellschaft für Sport und Technik
(Association for Sport and Technology)

IG
Industriegewerkschaft
(Industry-wide Union)

IWE
Informationsbüro West
(Information Bureau West)

JP
Junge Pioniere
(Young Pioneers)

KB
Kulturbund
(Cultural Association)

KdT
Kammer der Technik
(Chamber of Technology)

KJV
Kommunistischer Jugendverband
(Communist Youth Association)

KPD
Kommunistische Partei Deutschlands
(Communist Party of Germany)

KPdSU (CPSU)
Kommunistische Partei der Sowjetunion
(Communist Party of the Soviet Union)

KPÖ
Kommunistische Partei Österreichs
(Communist Party of Austria)

LDPD
Liberal-Demokratische Partei Deutschlands
(Liberal Democratic Party of Germany)

LPG
Landwirtschaftliche Produktionsgenossenschaft
(Agricultural Cooperative)

MTS
Maschinen-Traktoren-Station
(Farm Machines' and Tractors' Station)

ND
Neues Deutschland
(New Germany, the SED's leading daily newspaper)

NDPD
National-Demokratische Partei Deutschlands
(National Democratic Party of Germany)

NEC
See VWR

NF
Nationale Front
(National Front)

NÖSPL
Neues ökonomisches System der Planung und Leitung der Volkswirt-
schaft
(New Economic System of Planning and Direction of the National
Economy)

NSDAP
Nationalsozialistische Deutsche Arbeiterpartei
(German National Socialist Workers' Party, "Nazi Party")

NVA
Nationale Volksarmee
(National Peoples' Army)

PUWP
(Polish United Workers' Party)

RGW (COMECON) (CEMA)
Rat für gegenseitige Wirtschaftshilfe
(Council for Mutual Economic Aid)
(Council for Economic Mutual Assistance)

RSDRP
Rossiiskaia Sotsial-Demokraticheskaia Rabochaia Partiia
(Russian Social Democratic Workers' Party)

SBZ
Sowjetische Besatzungszone
(Soviet Zone of Occupation)

SDAPR
Sozialdemokratische Arbeiterpartei Russlands
(Russian Social Democratic Workers' Party)

SED
Sozialistische Einheitspartei Deutschlands
(Socialist Unity Party of Germany)

SPD
Sozialdemokratische Partei Deutschlands
(Social Democratic Party of Germany)

UdSSR (USSR)
Union der Sozialistischen Sowjetrepubliken
(Union of Soviet Socialist Republics)

UTP
Unterrichtstag in der Produktion
(i.e., indoctrination day in an industrial enterprise or agricultural cooperative)

VdgB
Vereinigung der gegenseitigen Bauernhilfe
(Peasants' Mutual Aid Association)

VDJ
Verband Deutscher Journalisten
(Association of German Journalists)

VEB
Volkseigener Betrieb
(Nationally Owned Enterprise)
VEG
Volkseigenes Gut
(Nationally Owned Farm)
VVB
Vereinigung Volkseigener Betriebe
(Association of Nationally Owned Enterprises)
VWR (NEC)
Volkswirtschaftsrat
(National Economic Council)
WMW
Werkzeugmaschinen und Werkzeuge
(Toolmaking Machines and Machine Tools)
WTZ
Wissenschaftlich-Technisches Zentrum
(Scientific-Technical Center)
ZK (CC)
Zentralkomitee
(Central Committee)
ZKSK
Zentrale Kommission für Staatliche Kontrolle
(Central Commission for State Control)
ZPKK (CPCC)
Zentrale Parteikontrollkommission
(Central Party Control Commission)

Note:
Since different terms for the GDR administrative units are in use in the English language, the German names for the administrative units below the State (National or Central) level were not translated.

Bezirk
The second (or, compared to the USA, state) level of administration (in other publications referred to as "district" or "county").

Kreis
The third (or, compared to the USA, county) level of administration (in other publications translated as "county" or "district"). There are *Stadtkreise* (cities) and *Landkreise* (regions).

Stadtbezirk and *Gemeinde*
The fourth administrative level, the former comparable to municipal boroughs, the latter to rural communities in the USA.

In this study, *Kreise, Stadtbezirke,* and *Gemeinden* are sometimes referred to as "local" levels of administration.

1

The Theoretical Frame of Reference

1. The Problem Posed

As an empirical and systematic study of recent changes in the political system and social order of the German Democratic Republic (GDR), this work focuses primarily on the organizational and social composition of the decision-making groups: the Central Committee of the Sozialistische Einheitspartei Deutschlands (Socialist Unity Party—SED), the Politburo, and the Central Committee Secretariat. Since approximately 1956-1957, change within the SED and many other East German social groupings has become increasingly evident. Signs of this phenomenon have appeared in the organizational structure of the party and in the social composition both of the leading bodies and the elites active in them. Change can also be seen in fundamental Marxist-Leninist ideology as well as in the field of "operational" ideology.

From the broad spectrum of perceptible change in the SED apparatus and in East German society the following theses have been formulated:

1. In contrast to earlier periods of its history, GDR society is now undergoing increasing differentiation as a result of the industrialization process. Certain political and social conflicts generated by these developments are becoming dominant.[1]

2. The ruling party in the GDR is also an integral component of society, although—at least for its top echelons—it is relatively isolated from that society. The party's monopoly on the exercise of power, plus its artificially preserved distance from society, produce conflicts that radiate throughout the social order. Although these conflicts are precipitated and usually

---

[1] This analysis of East German society will concentrate on the general theme of conflict, rather than that of integration. Conflicts are invariably social, as well as political. For the sociological analysis of social conflicts, see Ralf Dahrendorf, "Die Funktionen sozialer Konflikte," in his *Gesellschaft und Freiheit. Zur soziologischen Analyse der Gegenwart* (Munich, 1961), pp. 112 ff; and Lewis A. Coser, *The Functions of Social Conflict* (Glencoe, Ill.: The Free Press, 1956). For recent Marxist concepts of conflicts, see Jaroslav Klofáč and Vojtěch Tlusty in *Soziale Welt* 16, no. 4 (1965): 309 ff.

controlled by the party leadership, they, being of a generally social nature, invariably rebound to spread within the ranks of the SED itself.

3. The SED, rooted in the tradition of political secret societies, is additionally influenced by endemic conflicts, which can be understood only within the context of the party's historical development. Two types of conflict are basically intrinsic to the tradition of the secret society: those directed "outward" toward a society regarded as "hostile" and "alien," which can be described as adaptational conflicts of a specific type; and those that can be directed "inward," which by contrast with conflicts in other groups have quite unique characteristics. The organization of the *Bund* is not only characterized chiefly by the interdependence of the ideology of the leaders and the organization of its members, but also by tension and adaptational conflicts in the stricter sense. The classic sociological definition of the *Bund* is that of a social unit functioning between primary groups and larger social organizations. As such, it embodies two organizational principles: a more democratic strain based upon the ideology of friendship (*Freundschaft*), and a more authoritarian one, resulting from the prerequisites of secrecy. The latter principle is particularly applicable to the political secret societies of the eighteenth and the early nineteenth centuries in Europe, like the *Bund der Freien Männer* in Jena (1794-1798), the *Tugendbund* in Prussia (1808-1809), and the craftsmen's and students' leagues (e.g., the *Bund der Gerechten* [1832] and the *Bund der Geächteten* [1835] in Paris). Both inward- and outward-directed conflicts are reflected in the ideologies, or critical and Utopian programs, of the secret societies, as well as in the specific forms of organization adopted by them. But it often happened that ideological programs and organizations were not explicitly linked. Though Wilhelm Weitling and Karl Marx were generally aware of these relationships, it was V. I. Lenin who made them explicit for all Communist parties. He was the first to emphasize the necessity for constantly coordinating the program of the small (secret) group with its organizational forms.

4. Thus, conflicts within a Communist party are diverse in origin and are expressed both in the organizational and ideological spheres. Their consequences also become manifest in the changing social structure of the party leadership. The connection between internal and external conflict is

a complex one. The structure and outer organizational limits of the SED are not solely determined by conflicts with "outgroups" of East German society. Indeed, the conflicts arising from the SED's tradition, grounded both in German and Russian history, have particular significance as examples of "ingroup" conflicts.

5. The groups embodying these conflicts can be defined with relative clarity. On the whole, the older generation can be distinguished as a social group separate from the postwar generation that grew up in the Communist society of the GDR. Conflicts are produced by the coexist-ence and competition of different behavior patterns, guiding ideals, and social mores. In East German society certain ideals and norms are closely associated with certain generations, but "new" ideals cannot automatical-ly be attributed to the younger generation, nor can traditional norms be viewed as belonging exclusively to their elders.

6. With regard to the internal development of the SED itself, two groups that embody major strains of conflict have emerged: the leading political group, which remains bound to the traditions of a secret society, and is characterized as "insulated" on the margin of East German society; and the party experts who exercise decisive, day by day influence on economic and social decisions. Even within the party appartus these experts are relatively more open-minded toward modern organizational solutions and more committed to the criteria of pure "performance" *(Leistung)* in the sense in which it is universally accepted within capitalist systems.

7. The combined "general" and "partial" nature of social conflicts within the SED is reflected by the continued hegemony of the older generation alongside the rise of a new elite. All party oligarchies—particularly those in Communist systems—tend toward superannuation. The generation problem in East Germany in general, and the SED in particular, corroborates this general observation. Furthermore, mutually competitive behavior patterns, ideals, and social mores—characteristic of the gener-ation gap—are intertwined with specific social developments, perhaps unique to East German society. The postwar industrialization drive, the growth of vast bureaucracies, the general trend toward functional ration-alization, as well as a new ideological and professional outlook on the part of the younger generation, have not just produced different behavior

patterns, ideals, and social mores; they have also given rise to new patterns for achieving success and new criteria for upward mobility within and without the SED party apparatus. Supported, in a sense, officially by the party and because of its own professional outlook, the younger generation in East Germany has great incentives to opt for integration into the system rather than for voluntary exclusion from society. This development corresponds to increased upward professional mobility for the experts and trained functionaries, paralleled by decreasing competitiveness and downward mobility patterns for untrained functionaries.

8. The growth of vast bureaucracies in the GDR is accompanied by divergence of outlook and increased competition, particularly between the apparatus of the SED and that of the state (including the economic and scientific apparatuses). The traditional interchangeability of positions in the party and state apparatuses (i.e., horizontal functional mobility) for top SED functionaries has not yet been formally abrogated. However, in practice this trend appears to be on the decline.

9. An institutional basis for the rising new elite has been provided by the relatively greater autonomy of the great bureaucracies—particularly those of the state and the economy—vis-à-vis the party apparatus.

10. An analysis of these contradictions and conflicts in the organizational, sociological, and ideological sectors, as well as an adequate definition of the structural changes underlying these conflicts, could provide a basis for establishing the regularities observed in changing industrial societies under Communist rule.

These postulates can be summarized in a unifying hypothesis: Under conditions of political, social, and intellectual change, the originally totalitarian SED has tended to develop into an authoritarian party. Since Stalin's death, such changes have been evident throughout Eastern Europe, though they developed more slowly in the GDR. Certain features of this new authoritarian rule clearly distinguish it from totalitarian rule: First, although authoritarian rule requires a comprehensive ideology similar to that of totalitarian systems, there is one important difference between the two ideologies. Authoritarian ideologies precede the founding of movements, are regarded as eternal "givens," and thus need not be continually redefined or sustained by permanent terror.[2] Furthermore, authoritarian (versus totalitarian) rule is characterized by greater flexibility within the system of control and higher adaptability of its various organizational systems to scientific and technical progress. Whereas totalitarian rule requires a relatively rigid system of control, the authoritarian framework includes more flexible means to coordinate and coopt. A more highly differentiated control system is supplemented by new patterns of communication.

Authoritarian rule is not based largely on mass terror, but on a specific form of group identification achieved by the increasingly differentiated organizational structure of the party, state, and economy. It rests on a certain "shared consciousness" and an openness toward the solution of certain new tasks. Finally, in an industrial society with a Communist political system, authoritarian rule is characterized by the political leadership's recognition, or at least toleration, of genuine social conflicts. Conflicts are no longer regarded as necessarily dysfunctional to the stability of the political system but, in Lenin's words, as "motors of development." Nevertheless, the recognition or toleration of conflicts is limited. Although conflicts or conduct that diverge from the behavior patterns of the party leadership are now permissible in East German society, they cannot aim at establishing an independent political organization in opposition to the SED. The conflicts acknowledged by the party leadership are those which can be "integrated," i.e., subjected to centralized control. It is difficult, however, to decide a priori which conflicts are so regarded, since the party leadership itself is still trying to make such distinctions.

Recognition or toleration of conflicts within these limits marks a change in the Politburo's policy. The SED's strict exercise of pure totalitarian power during the first two periods of its construction (from the time it seized power until 1952, and 1952–1958) was motivated largely by its need to secure its claim to legitimate political primacy through tightened controls and strict sanctions. Party power has assumed

[2] See Martin Drath, "Totalitarismus in der Volksdemokratie," Introduction to Ernst Richert, *Macht ohne Mandat—Der Staatsapparat in der Sowjetischen Besatzungszone Deutschlands,* 2nd ed. (Cologne and Opladen, 1963), p. xxvii and passim.

essentially new traits in the period since completion of the consolidation stage, that is, since 1963. Presently, economic and social administration and guidance are the goals assigned top priority by the regime. The militant use of power that characterized the first historical phases of SED rule is now on the wane. The party's claim to rule is increasingly based on new forms of communication—more persuasion combined with less coercion.

Soviet and East European party leaderships are still confronted by the need to control the dynamics of scientific and technical progress, especially in the economic sphere. Since the Twentieth CPSU Congress, the major trend in patterns of control has been toward reduced mass terror. Even when one looks back at the heyday of Stalinism, terror and control cannot be regarded as inseparable, although such forms of compulsion were then more closely associated than at present. Control by the ruling party in an industrial society, with its requirements of functional efficiency, implies the replacement of terror by a broadly designed, finely calibrated system of institutionalized social controls.

If the change in methods of control observed in recent years is found to be structural in nature, the general concept of the totalitarian party may have to be re-evaluated. In principle, such a reappraisal would have to treat two problems: first, a firm definition of the "safety barriers" of the party's exercise of power—i.e., a definition of the limits to which the party, without losing its monopoly of control, can prevent the centralized exercise of political power from being dysfunctional to the industrialization process; and, second, the determination of the means by which the party's power techniques of control can be constantly adapted to rapid change in a highly industrialized society. This study aims to provide clearer answers to these two questions.

A basic hypothesis with regard to the qualitative distinction between totalitarian and authoritarian rule may now be formulated: Totalitarian rule becomes authoritarian when the features of an industrial society— primarily the prevalent organizational model—are implicitly or explicitly recognized by the party elite. Scientific and technical progress liberates forces associated with conflicts which may be functional or dysfunctional to the maintenance of the ruling system. Economic progress encourages a functional differentiation within the political leadership and gives rise to new, competing elite groupings. Consequently, the total interpenetration of a society by the ideological will of one party is substantially decreased and oscillation in the application of sanctions by the leadership becomes almost inevitable.[3]

In addition, our basic hypothesis presumes that society as a whole exists outside the immediate object of our research since the latter (i.e., the party and especially its leading groups) constitutes only a part of this whole. The "whole of society" in turn constitutes both actual social reality in the GDR and the "ideal society" (society as it *should* be) as subjectively conceived by the SED leadership. This methodological assumption seems indispensable for the investigation of elites in Communist systems. Their social outlook in itself is an important component of actual social reality.

The theoretical framework of this study of elites encompasses the preconditions and consequences of change in the organization, social structure, and ideology of the party elite and its impact on East German society. The narrower traditional framework of studies of elites is thus greatly expanded. In the context of the larger society, the party is regarded primarily as an organizational subsystem, with its own inner contradictions, operating on the officially proclaimed principle of "democratic centralism." "Society" is taken to mean the comprehensive social system, i.e., the overall correlation and interdependence of all social subsystems. The term "elite," in this work, covers the members of policy-making leadership groups in the SED. The problems associated with the preconditions and consequences of social mobility and change in one section of the party are thus considered indicators of problems of change in East German society as a whole. If changes in the party elite are indeed fundamental in nature and not merely ephemeral, they will likewise be evident in the other areas of society to which their effects extend.

Based on this assumption, the following questions can be formulated: How, and to what extent, is the restructuring of the SED's system of control connected with changes in the social structure of the party elite and modifications of ideological dogma?

---

[3] For details, see Peter Christian Ludz, "Entwurf einer soziologischen Theorie totalitär verfasster Gesellschaft," in Peter Christian Ludz, ed., *Studien und Materialien zur Soziologie der DDR (Kölner Zeitschrift für Soziologie und Sozialpsychologie,* Special Issue 8) (Cologne and Opladen, 1964), pp. 19 ff.

Are the processes in these three areas parallel or divergent—or do they run parallel but with a time lag associated with additional conflicts, in turn caused by this "delay" effect?

To what extent does the differentiation of the SED's control system limit the political and organizational power potential of its leading groups?

Under what conditions can the political elite reject or accept adaptation to presently mandatory new roles and modes of behavior?

How are the principles of a cadre and mass membership party—both embodied historically in the SED—affected by the pressures of new technology, industrialization, and specialization?

To what extent has the political elite withdrawn from positions of control in all spheres of state, economic, and cultural affairs to several "commanding heights," thus creating for competing groups within and without the party the opportunity to raise their social status and exert greater influence upon political decisions?

How and to what extent is the criterion of performance (in the sense of economic rationalization and efficiency) applied in the recruitment of new cadres?

Have new elites with specific career patterns developed in the GDR?

What indices can be used to measure the social rise of new elites in the GDR?

What is the relationship between the old and new elites?

These questions will be examined in three subdivisions, briefly outlined below. Since the Sixth SED Congress (January 15–21, 1963), widespread changes in the structure of the party apparatus have become apparent. These changes were directly connected to structural reforms in the party and state administrations of the Soviet Union. The restructuring of the East German party, state, and economic apparatuses appears to have been modeled on Khrushchev's "great administrative reform" of November 1962. The organizational reforms of the East German bureaucracies were motivated primarily by political considerations. As in the Soviet Union, by the end of November 1962 East German moves to ensure a further fusion between party, state, and economic bureaucracies were widely heralded. In addition, these bureaucracies were to move closer to economic and social "practice."[4]

There was one trend that remained relatively unaltered by this politically conditioned adaptation to changes in the Soviet Union. Since 1963 the East German party apparatus has shown far greater recognition of the economic and technical developments inherent in modern societies, a trend acknowledged in the program for the "New Economic System of Planning and Direction of the National Economy" (NÖSPL). Control of the economy by the Council of Ministers and its subsidiary organs has since been supplemented by the so-called party "operational directives" to be put into immediate practice. It will be shown that this adaptation has not remained entirely without consequences for the structure of various organizational systems in the GDR.

Although many of Khrushchev's reforms have been reversed in the Soviet Union since his fall in October 1964, Ulbricht only partially followed the Soviet example. In the wake of the September 1965 Plenum of the CPSU, the National Economic Council was dissolved and its former industrial departments changed to independent industrial ministries.[5] However, the SED leadership did not dissolve the Ideological

---

[4] By contrast, in Czechoslovakia discussion on restructuring the party organization within the framework of changes in the economic system began later than in East Germany. Cf. Jan Skalond, Vice-President of the Bratislava University Law Faculty, "The Party and Management Theory" *Predvoj*, August 5, 1965.

[5] Cf. Walter Ulbricht's report to the Eleventh Plenum of the Central Committee of the SED, "Probleme des Perspektivplanes bis 1970," *Neues Deutschland*, December 18, 1965. An Industrial Ministry did not succeed every department of the National Economic Council. As of January 1, 1963, some sixteen departments were under the NEC control: power; coal; iron metallurgy; nonferrous metal industry and potash; foundries and forges; the State Geological Commission; chemistry; heavy machinery construction; general machinery construction; electrical engineering/electronics; machine tools and automation; research and development institutions directly subject to machinery construction; textiles, garments, leather; wood, paper, and polygraphy; glass and ceramics; and foodstuffs. (See Herbert Kusicka and Wolfgang Leupold, *Industrieforschung und Ökonomie. Zu einigen Problemen der Ökonomie geistig-schöpferischer Arbeit und der materiellen Interessiertheit in Forschung und Entwicklung in der Industrie der DDR* [Berlin 1966], p. 39.) Following the Eleventh Plenum of the SED Central Committee in December 1965, only nine new industrial ministries were created for basic industries, mining and metallurgy,

Commission until the end of 1966, though in the Soviet Union this was done as early as March 1965. Furthermore, the East Germans proclaimed their "new economic system" before the Soviets did.[6] These examples demonstrate that in recent years the SED leadership has exhibited some independence from the Soviet line, at least with regard to certain domestic, social, economic, and organizational questions. This becomes particularly evident if we consider the complementary relationship between ideology, policy decisions, and the leading institutions and organizations in a Communist system. Changes in the institutional sphere invariably indicate a new political line, as do changes in ideology (understood, in its broadest sense, as a set of quite general programmatic guidelines).

Changes in the organizational structure of the party elite and increasing differentiation in the ideological sphere have been—as previously indicated—accompanied by extensive social recomposition of the party elite, as well as of its rank-and-file membership. Ulbricht himself described this transition at the Sixth SED Congress: "It is now the turn of the young technicians and engineers" and "It is important that the leading party cadres should also be trained experts."[7] These statements illustrate a problem central to this study: the replacement of the old guard in the SED leadership by a new, younger elite. Restratification, along with the gradual supplanting of the old leadership, and the open conflict of social norms and behavior patterns are naturally accompanied by tension. Paradoxically, this transitional process is constantly facilitated and at the same time impeded by changes in the party's organizational patterns. It is facilitated to the extent that the party leadership begins to perceive and adapt to the requirements of an industrial society, with a

---

chemical industry, electrotechnical industry and electronics, heavy machinery and installations, machine building and vehicles, light industry, *Bezirk*-directed and food industries, and material economy. For details see Chapter Two, *infra*.

[6] See Karl C. Thalheim, "Liberalisierungstendenzen im Ostblock?" in *Der Osten auf dem Wege zur Marktwirtschaft*, Wirtschaft und Gesellschaft in Mitteldeutschland, Vol. 6 (Berlin, 1967), p. 40.

[7] Cf. Ulbricht's speech to the Sixth SED Congress, "Das Programm des Sozialismus und die geschichtliche Aufgabe der SED," *Protokoll der Verhandlungen des VI. Parteitages der SED. 15. bis 21. Januar 1963 in der Werner-Seelenbinder-Halle zu Berlin*, 4 vols. Vol. 1 (Berlin, 1963), p. 207 (hereafter cited as *Protocol of the Sixth SED Congress*).

concomitant growing dependence upon professionally trained party functionaries—a process that began in 1958, following Khrushchev's reforms
of 1956–1957 in the Soviet Union.[8] On the other hand, the process is
impeded insofar as the party leadership must also take into account those
endemic pressures within the party organization which, in resisting the
inherent dynamics of an industrial society, develop a momentum of their
own. These built-in pressures are largely of two kinds: first, the traditional structure and *raison d'être* of the party apparatus which until 1963 was
overwhelmingly devoted to the political control of society, but not to its
functional streamlining; and, second, the traditional political mores and
outlook of veteran functionaries who hitherto secured and administered
party power at the very foundations of society, particularly during the
period 1945–1963.[9]

In addition to these interrelated changes in the organizational and
social structure of the top party groups, comprehensive sociological
analysis reveals changes in the "ideological field" and a similar interdependence between these changes and the other two general transitional
trends. In recent years a "refunctionalization" of ideology has taken
place. "Refunctionalization" does not necessarily mean the disintegration
of Marxist-Leninist ideology, but rather the broadening of its scope so as
to assume new and more effective functions of control and guidance. This
process presupposes the "rationalization" or "positivization" (in the
epistemological sense) of ideology. To some degree, Marxist-Leninist
ideology has adapted to the imperatives of rationalism and positivism.
First, the ideological system has been adapted to take into account
numerous elements, concepts, and categories from modern theories of
cognition and logic, the natural sciences, cybernetics, and empirical
sociology. Second, numerous relevant socioeconomic facts are absorbed
into the dogma but, by contrast with the past, are not elaborated
ideologically. An unmistakable feature of this process is that the range of
"operational ideology"—utilized to initiate and control the ongoing
campaigns of the party leadership—is expanded and simultaneously

[8] For the Soviet Union, cf. Boris Meissner, *Russland unter Chruschtschow* (Munich,
1960), pp. 198 ff.
[9] For details up to 1956–1957, see Carola Stern, *Porträt einer bolschewistischen
Partei. Entwicklung, Funktion und Situation der SED* (Cologne, 1957), pp. 284 ff;
up to 1963, Richert, *Macht ohne Mandat*, Chapter Two.

shifts its focus away from the original ideological core concepts. Consequently, positivization exacerbates the process of ideological disintegration, though this does not proceed at the same rate at all levels (basic axioms, official ideology, operating ideology) and in all fields (historical materialism, dialectical materialism, political economy). The question arises whether the uncoordinated transformation of basic ideological doctrines enhances the process of decay and/or encourages its proponents to further adapt to the society they rule, since they can thereby enlarge their potential for control. As the SED leaders regard ideological unity and stabilization of their power bases as inseparable operational principles, they are bound to regard a shift in key dogmatic tenets as a weakening of their positions of power. However, this absence of conscious coordination in the refunctionalization of basic ideological dogma —or the tailoring of dogmatic axioms to fit operational situations—permits party ideologues to control the necessary adaptation of the party to the behavior patterns and norms of other social groups. Thus, a mutual adaptation between party and society and a consequent—at least partial—identity of interests can come into being, to the extent that the norms and ideals of social groups and strata begin to permeate the ideological system throughout the process of transformation.

PRELIMINARY LIMITATIONS ON THE SCOPE OF THIS STUDY

The initial presentation of the issues investigated by this study should include certain basic definitions. One group serves to explicate the subject matter examined; the other deals with the information used, the periods selected for examination, and the methods and techniques employed herein. Some comment on our terminology falls into the second group of definitions; such comment will be dealt with as a separate topic in each chapter. At this point we are concerned only with definitions of the first type.

Although reference will be made to major events in the history of the SED, this study is not intended to be a history of the party (as, for example, Carola Stern's for the period 1946–1957[10]). The influence of foreign policy considerations on developments within the SED (especially with regard to the influence of the CPSU on the SED) has been for the

[10] Stern, *Porträt*.

most part ignored. Naturally, our social and political analysis includes East German government and society, but only certain sectors of the system over a limited period of time will be examined. This study does not aim at a general, in-depth analysis of the East German system's responses to other specific domestic issues (as, for example, that of Ernst Richert or Dietrich Storbeck[11]).

Although we shall repeatedly encounter problems associated with internal information and communication within the SED apparatus, the flow of information within the party cannot be traced with full certitude. There is simply not enough information in the West—a regrettable state of affairs since this lack of information also precludes an exact discussion of the actual process of political decision-making in the SED leadership bodies. Analysis of the decision-making process is further impeded by the lack of precise knowledge of the interrelations among the party apparatus, the state apparatus (which includes the economic, educational bureaucracies, etc.), and the mass organizations. An analysis of the decision-making process in the ruling system of the SED presupposes an exact knowledge of functions and positions in all these bureaucratic structures. These processes, however are at present not open to really thorough investigation. Although some analysts have succeeded in drawing useful conclusions regarding the inner workings of the ruling system of the GDR,[12] the data available do not suffice for an exhaustive empirical study.

Given these limitations, it was necessary to conceive this study on a different methodological level. Its aim is to relate the processes of change that we have posited to a theoretical frame of reference, buttressed by empirical data. In Chapter Two some of the major, more obvious organizational changes in the SED apparatus since the Sixth SED Congress are traced and compared with the organizational structure of the party prior to 1963. In addition, in Chapter Three the members of

---

[11] Richert, *Macht ohne Mandat;* and *Das zweite Deutschland. Ein Staat, der nicht sein darf* (Gütersloh, 1964); also Dietrich Storbeck, *Soziale Strukturen in Mitteldeutschland. Eine sozial-statistische Bevölkerungsanalyse im gesamtdeutschen Vergleich* (Berlin, 1964).

[12] See especially Richert, *Macht ohne Mandat,* passim; and Siegfried Mampel, *Die Verfassung der Sowjetischen Besatzungszone Deutschlands, Text und Kommentar* (Frankfurt-on-the-Main and Berlin, 1966, 2nd ed. expanded), passim.

the SED leadership bodies are classified according to certain biographical characteristics in order to obtain a preliminary profile of changes in the social structure of the party leadership. The resulting composite portrait of the party elite should not be regarded as an exact image of the SED in the photographic sense. Nevertheless, the transitional processes within the leadership bodies of the SED provide some valid insights into the situation of the party and of society in East Germany.

In Chapter Four, a description of changes in the organizational and social structure of the SED is supplemented by analysis that aims at establishing changes in the ideological sphere. There is a question as to whether, and to what degree, shifts in the organizational sphere are reflected in the self-image of the party ideologists. Coverage of the entire spectrum of interpretations of historical and dialectical materialism in the GDR, or even a fuller historical review of ideological problems, is beyond the scope of this study. Since the Twentieth CPSU Congress, the systematization and differentiation of Marxist-Leninist dogma in the Soviet Union, and the consequent amalgamation of polycentric and revisionist tendencies in Eastern Europe, have assumed such proportions that any attempt to trace them, even in one nation, is beyond the scope of a single work.

2. Introductory Problems of Metatheory

A systematic, empirical study of social structure in a given country should be complemented by a number of metatheoretical considerations. A study that covers selected aspects of a Communist political and social system must deal primarily with three problems of metatheory, now predominant in sociological and political discussions in the field of Sovietology. These problems are in turn associated with the problems of defining "totalitarianism" and "reproach of positivism," as well as with questions concerning the specific, empirical qualities of political and social data on a Communist society, seen through Western eyes.

TOTALITARIANISM

No concept in Sovietology is as unequivocal in its general tenets as that of totalitarianism. Two approaches in nearly all social or political research on Communist societies—namely, the politically motivated, value-charged, "involved" view, on the one hand; and the "objective," thus allegedly "uninvolved" attitude on the other—have converged to form an almost inseparable core within the concept of totalitarianism.

Research on totalitarian systems must take into account the fact that the phenomena examined are almost invariably political, though on the surface this would not seem to be the case. This holds equally for Nazism, Fascism, or Communism and their attendant social and political phenomena. Like all political systems, those of the totalitarian type are invariably value systems, which elicit from the researcher "loaded" interpretations. The fact is that any object of empirical investigation in a Communist system also has an actual political dimension which cannot be concealed without prejudice by a scientifically substantiated, or even unsubstantiated value judgment. Research on totalitarianism during the early 1950s provides many examples of this. Communist social systems, considered by their leaders as thoroughly politicized, were seen by the West as "hostile" agglomerations threatening the very existence of parliamentary democracy.[13] This attitude was conducive to distortions and uncritical value judgments. Particularly in the sphere of research on the GDR, personal involvement, combined with an uncritical—or at best, idealized—view of existing parliamentary democracies, has made otherwise useful works of dubious intellectual value.[14]

Since the cognitive and evaluative functions are nearly always inseparably fused in the concept of totalitarianism, a theoretically based empirical analysis which uses this concept uncritically must be rejected. The weakness of the concept of totalitarianism is further emphasized by the fact that it works with an ideal type (in the sense used by Max

[13] The "defense effect" (*Abwehr-Effekt*) has played an essential role in discussions of totalitarianism for decades, probably until the development in the Soviet Union characterized by Khrushchev's reform program of September 1962. Cf. Otto Stammer, "Aspekte der Totalitarismusforschung," in his *Politische Soziologie und Demokratieforschung—Ausgewählte Reden und Aufsätze zur Soziologie und Politik* (Berlin, 1965), p. 259.

[14] This holds true, for example, for the work of Siegfried Mampel (ftn. 12) as well as for Karl Valentin Müller, *Die Manager in der Sowjetzone—Eine empirische Untersuchung zur Soziologie der wirtschaftlichen und militärischen Führungsschicht in Mitteldeutschland* (Cologne and Opladen, 1962). Mampel labors under a concept of liberty that is uncritically absolutistic, while Müller distorts his analysis by his specifically stratified theory of abilities.

Weber), and does not take into account the fact that the Weberian ideal type cannot be subjected to empirical verification in the strict sense.[15] Research, with its controllable hypotheses and methods, is a priori impeded when dealing with systems that are manifestations of such an ideal type. These impediments did not affect the less empirically oriented, traditional research on totalitarian societies. There are many reasons for this orientation. One possible cause is the absence of empirical data, compounded by the attitude of emigré scholars who were engaged primarily in ideological and political controversy with totalitarianism. Furthermore, the general development of the social sciences must also be taken into account, as well as the fact that in the forties and fifties interconnections between sociology, political science, and research on totalitarianism had hardly been developed.

Consequently, totalitarianism has been rejected as the leading concept in the theoretical frame of reference of this work.[16] Even the term "totalitarian–organized society,"[17] used by the author at an earlier date, is of value here only insofar as the type of authoritarian rule that can now be observed in the GDR developed from a specific historical situation (namely, the so-called Stalin era), generally described as "totalitarian" in the literature. Rejection of the pure totalitarian concept for our purposes is justified by the fact that an empirical study devoted to organizational theory, elite theory, and an analysis of ideology does not require such a normative theory. Rather than evaluating, accusing, or drawing hasty conclusions, we will attempt to analyze and systematize empirical results. We will not attempt to compare ideals and norms embodied in the constitutions, political structures, and social orders of Eastern and Western systems. Indeed, it is our intent to exclude the social and political structures from our subjective evaluations; instead, we shall describe them and fit them into an empirical pattern. Our rejection of the totalitarian concept also takes into account the changing aims of the SED leadership since 1963. Consequently, it is no longer meaningful to speak of *the* ideology of the party leadership. Two

[15] See also Judith Janoska-Bendl, *Methodologische Aspekte des Idealtypus. Max Weber und die Soziologie der Geschichte* (Berlin 1965), pp. 76 ff.
[16] Alfred G. Meyer also tends to renounce the totalitarian concept in *The Soviet Political System. An Interpretation* (New York, 1965), p. 470; see also p. 298.
[17] Ludz, "Entwurf einer soziologischen Theorie totalitar verfasster Gesellschaft."

advantages are thus gained. First, our view of the actual social and economic structure; standards, ideals, and behavior patterns; examples of vertical and horizontal mobility; and the actual nature of the political decision-making processes is not colored by prejudice. Thus, there is less emphasis on the ideological aims of the SED leadership and more on the changing social system of the GDR. This approach in social science allows a more realistic, undistorted scanning of the facts. The second advantage is that it remains possible to deal suitably with the attempts of a Communist leadership—in this case, the SED Politburo—to maintain a comprehensive bureaucracy, ideological stereotypes, moral invocations, and ideals under changing conditions.

To conclude with a brief survey of the present state of research in this sphere: Carl Joachim Friedrich, William Kornhauser, Richard Löwenthal, and Alfred G. Meyer describe Communist systems—often the Soviet one—as totalitarian, since specific characteristics of the ruling apparatus preclude the limitations placed upon the exercise of political power by parliamentary democracies—i.e., limitations ensured by means of separation of powers, guarantees of civil liberties and personal rights, and the rule of law. In this context, Hans Kelsen mentions the "extreme étatism" of ruling Communist party systems.[18] Friedrich essayed a structural classification of "étatism," citing six characteristics typical of a totalitarian system, based on phenomena observed in such systems, which have since received frequent treatment in the literature. They are: an official ideology, a single mass party typically led by one man, a terroristic police apparatus, a monopoly of information and arms for the party, and a centrally controlled and directed economy.[19] Alfred G. Meyer places the main emphasis upon centralized control in all spheres of the economy and society by the party. He also stresses the CPSU's attempt to organize and politicize all human relationships so as to establish a new system of social values. The bureaucratization of Soviet rule constitutes the actual core of Communist rule for Meyer.[20]

[18] Hans Kelsen, *The Political Theory of Bolshevism: A Critical Analysis* (Berkeley and Los Angeles, 3rd ed. 1955), p. 6.
[19] Cf. Carl Joachim Friedrich and Zbigniew K. Brzezinski, *Totalitarian Dictatorship and Autocracy*, 2nd ed. revised by Carl J. Friedrich (Cambridge, Mass.: Harvard University Press, 1965), pp. 15–22.
[20] Meyer, *The Soviet Political System*, pp. 470 ff.

Kornhauser, in his more general treatment of "the mass society," advances similar arguments in distinguishing "totalitarian societies" from "mass societies." He also emphasizes "totalitarian control" in elaborating the structural characteristics of such a society.[21] In this sense, "total" or "totalitarian control" is closely connected with control of society by a "permanent revolution from above," as conceived by Richard Löwenthal.[22]

In further pursuing the disagreement with these academic approaches which the present author has expressed on various occasions,[23] we shall merely state in this connection that the social changes initiated on a large scale by the party leadership have already developed an inherent dynamism within the narrow confines of the party elites. Admittedly this dynamism is not powerful enough to seize control of the hierarchical system away from the one-party rulers. Yet on the other hand it has given rise to phenomena which in fact constitute a limitation of control and thus of the monopoly rule enjoyed by the leadership.

A systematic empirical analysis that is not restricted to cataloging the structures and forms of compulsion avoids the problem of comparing terror, total control, and total planning "from above," on the one hand, and the absence of such compulsions, on the other. Indeed, by defining the "safety barriers," i.e., the minimum limits within which the party's power must be maintained in the face of encroaching demands for functional efficiency within the social system, such an investigation must concentrate on the intermediate range between total compulsion and total freedom. This range would seem to constitute the present operating reality of these systems. Accordingly, the concept formulated by Friedrich, Löwenthal, et al., must be modified and adapted to fit the situation

[21] William Kornhauser, *The Politics of Mass Society* (Glencoe, Ill.: The Free Press, 1959), pp. 67 and 180. He describes the second characteristic of a totalitarian society as "total mobilization" (p. 62).
[22] Richard Löwenthal, "Stalins Vermächtnis. Zur Interpretation seiner letzten Schrift," *Der Monat* 5, no. 55 (April 1953): 16 ff, and "Totalitäre und demokratische Revolution," ibid. 13, no. 146 (November 1960): 29 ff.
[23] Peter Christian Ludz, "Totalitarismus oder Totalität? Zur Erforschung bolschewistischer Gesellschafts- und Herrschaftssysteme," *Soziale Welt* 12, no. 2 (1961): 129 ff, "Offene Fragen in der Totalitarismus-Forschung," *Politische Vierteljahresschrift* 2, no. 4 (1961): 319 ff, and "Entwurf einer soziologischen Theorie totalitär verfasster Gesellschaft."

in the GDR as follows: All-inclusive, total rule by the SED leadership, with terror as its keystone, has been replaced in broad areas by measures necessitated by the need to balance quasi-pluralistic social and political forces. The "permanent revolution from above," consisting in conscious, centrally manipulated changes of the social structure, has given rise to an inherent dynamism in the social and structural development of the SED itself and in its major political ramifications, the Politburo, the Secretariat of the Central Committee and the Central Committee. This dynamism exhibits a tendency to veer away from totalitarian rule to a form of rule characterized by central guidance of social change. "Central guidance"— or, in recent cybernetic terminology, "regulation"—could be defined as the decisive characteristic of authoritarian rule in this context. The various forces that have contributed to changes in the system have been conducive to its replacement only in the sense that "every Soviet system destroys itself by its own success" (A. G. Meyer).

WESTERN EMPIRICAL RESEARCH ON COMMUNIST SYSTEMS
Besides the aforementioned pitfalls of adopting the theory of totalitarianism a second, perhaps more difficult, problem is the impossibility of directly gathering empirical data (interviews, questionnaires, etc.) in the East European countries while working in the West. This constitutes an a priori limitation on the scientific value of investigations into the problems of rule and society in Communist systems. Correspondingly, all empirical social scientists advance the view that the available sources, i.e., newspapers; journals; books; protocols and speeches; published decisions of party, state, and economic apparatuses as well as mass organizations; and, finally, the self-images conveyed by the ideological terms, are relevant to the contemporary historian, but in no way supplant methodologically obtained data and direct observation. The social sciences regard these sources as secondary data of somewhat dubious value. These criticisms against East European studies, advanced by scholars doing empirical research, are weighty. Nevertheless, they should not deter us from attempting empirical studies of East European countries since, at present, information can be gathered from a variety of available, although mostly secondary, sources (e.g., biographical information, information on organizations and institutions, or sectors of the "ideological

field"—which can often be translated into empirical data). In particular, some parts of the chapters on the SED's organizational system and the social structure of its leadership bodies demonstrate that empirical methods can now cast light on relatively large segments of a Communist political and social system.

Analysis of Communist systems is further facilitated by one practical consideration in the evaluation of empirical data: the decisive importance of the written word—or legal codifications—for all such social systems.[24] In contrast to the character of the written word in parliamentary democracies, these verbal formulations are of considerable value for analysis of the Communist political system. The political secret societies of eighteenth and early nineteenth century Germany, Italy, and France, and the revolutionary conspiracies in Russia, e.g., those formed during Nicholas I's reign and later the RSDRP, invariably attempted to formulate a succinct view of themselves and the world. To this end, they drew up ideological and/or Utopian programs, combined with very specific operative executive directions. Analogously, protocols of SED congresses, discussions at Central Committee plena and economic conferences, and the justification of decisions by the party leadership can be regarded as attempts by a partly insulated organization to develop an identity and to formulate a universalist ideology. Thus, the protocols of party congresses, conferences, etc., constitute major empirical sources for establishing, for example, the degree of self-isolation attained by the SED in East Germany over a given period of time. In principle, they can be decoded by semantic and content analyses.

A REPROACH OF POSITIVISM

Proponents of Hegelian–Marxian dialectical or critical sociology have frequently advanced a "reproach of positivism,"[25] maintaining that a frame of analysis using a terminology and certain fixed concepts determined by specific historical, political, and social conditions cannot be uncritically imposed on a completely different political and social system. They contend that in addition to ignoring the problem of value judgment

[24] Ludz, "Entwurf," pp. 22 ff.
[25] See Theodor W. Adorno, "Soziologie und empirische Forschung," in Klaus Ziegler, ed., *Wesen und Wirklichkeit des Menschen. Festschrift für Helmuth Plessner* (Göttingen, 1957), pp. 245 ff.

or uncritical acceptance of the status quo, or of merely registering bare facts, the use of this type of analysis leads to the risk of forming a distorted political perspective.

Werner Hofmann was the first German scholar to apply the arguments of critical sociology to these problems. In connection with his criticism against applying the class concept—a concept derived from Western industrial societies—directly to the Soviet Union, Hofmann raised the question of how to correctly measure changing socioeconomic structures in Communist social systems.[26] In view of the process of "positivization," which can be observed in official Marxist-Leninist ideology, the controversy with the reproach of positivism can be gathered from the following questions: What language can be used to analyze Communist social systems, taking into account changes in the Marxist terminology in which these societies endeavor to describe themselves? This question cannot be answered in the same way for every aspect of a given social system. Above all, differences in the organizational and social structure on the one hand, and in the ideological sphere on the other, must be considered. Western sociology is presently more capable of dealing with the first two dimensions.[27] An empirical analysis of ideology must devote more attention to basic Marxist-Leninist terminology, on the assumption that ideology fulfills functions in the social and political spheres and that its analysis leads to a better understanding of the total system. The problem of analysis of ideology in its proper frame of political sociology has thus been treated only in passing.[28]

Empirically oriented research on Eastern Europe meets with criticism from another school of social science: that which espouses a normative political philosophy. In analyzing Communist systems the proponents of dialectical sociology are implicitly or explicitly guided by the assumptions of German idealistic philosophy, especially those of Hegel and/or the young Marx. Proponents of normative philosophy frequently base their analyses on ideal conceptions of parliamentary democracy taken from the classical theory of democracy. That there are similarities in dialectical sociology and normative political philosophy

[26] Werner Hofmann, *Die Arbeitsverfassung der Sowjetunion* (Berlin, 1956), p. 501.
[27] See pp. 26-53, *infra.*
[28] See pp. 53-66, *infra;* also T. D. Weldon, *The Vocabulary of Politics* (London: Penguin Books, 1953), especially Chapter Three.

may seem surprising at first. But, from the point of view of the sociology of knowledge as well as of the philosophy of science, both schools work with underlying ideological assumptions derived not from the actual object under examination, but from working models derived from preindustrial societies. Thus, the normative basis of dialectical sociology, i.e., the Utopian vision of man (harking back to the young Marx), is in many points comparable to the concept of man (looking back to the ideal of the "common man"[29]) on which normative political philosophy is grounded. Consequently, both schools may fail to cover the total range of their selected objects of research, and may also overlook the interdependencies and historical significance of social and political phenomena. Furthermore, both dialectical sociology and normative political philosophy tendentiously blur the difference between political philosophy and empirical political theory. If political theory is to be conceived as the attempt to explain social and political facts by establishing regularities, using scientific methods, with the purpose of making predictions, then this concept of theory is different from that applied by normative political philosophy. Therefore, theory cannot be understood in the sense of providing mandatory guidelines for the selection of one's practical political aims. Neither can it be regarded as a philosophical system in which all that exists—as it is and as it ought to be—is indiscriminately preserved. This makes it clear that in normative political philosophy "theory" and "philosophy" are inextricably intertwined or, in terms of the philosophy of science, confused one with the other. Such an identification of theory with philosophy is probably less of a problem when dealing with global and/or generally comparative descriptions of intellectual and political situations, various political systems, etc. However, this identification impairs empirical analysis, since moralistic and uncritical political biases cannot fail to influence the progress and distort the results of an empirical and systematic investigation.

The reproach of positivism, voiced by both normative political philosophers and dialectical sociologists, cannot be discussed in detail here. However, the arguments advanced by some proponents of normative political philosophy, primarily those who advocate a philosophy of

[29] Cf. Carl Joachim Friedrich, *The New Image of the Common Man* (Boston: Beacon Press, enl. ed. 1950).

the "common weal,"[30] deserve the following reply: Empirical research in our sense distinguishes between factual evidence and value judgments, without disregarding the latter. This study can in no sense be described as a "value-free" analysis; constant re-evaluation takes into account the inner dynamics of the East German system as well as its self-evaluations. Proponents of the reproach of positivism who wish to make an immanent interpretation of these societies—i.e., an interpretation based solely on the self–image and terminology developed within the societies under investigation—should be answered as follows: In both earlier and contemporary Communist area studies, insights have been possible which could not have been obtained by purely immanent observations. Of course, the relevance of these insights is dependent on how carefully they are interpreted, i.e., related to internal developments within the Communist systems.

These considerations lead us to synthesize the major elements of dialectical sociology's critique and *our* methods of empirical research—i.e., toward what may be called a "critical-empirical" approach. "Critical-empirical" and "positivist" approaches are distinguished as follows: The critical-empirical approach excludes the speculative, Utopian dimension of the object under examination without ignoring its qualitative factors, i.e., the intellectual, historical and social contexts. Karl R. Popper regards the critical-empirical method as the method of "tentative solutions," or open-ended conclusions. Here, however, empirical science is not regarded as a "system of statements which satisfy certain logical criteria, such as meaningfulness or verifiability." On the contrary, the distinctive characteristic of empirical statements is seen in their "susceptibility to revision—in the fact that they can be criticized." Consequently, "falsifiability," not "verifiability," is taken as a "criterion of demarcation."[13] Critical-empirical and, for that matter, any systematic investigation seems to require this kind of methodological outlook because its findings must constantly be subjected to proof. Although we do not intend to continue this line of speculation, we should state here that we are especially committed to the axiom of "open-endedness," which is ensured

[36] For example, Otto Heinrich von der Gablentz, *Der Kampf um die rechte Ordnung. Beiträge zur politischen Wissenschaft* (Cologne and Opladen, 1964).
[31] Karl R. Popper, *The Logic of Scientific Discovery* (New York: Science Editions, Inc., 1961), pp. 40–41, and 48.

in our theoretical approach by permanent intersubjective testability. This commitment lies at the base of our empirical analysis.

The qualitative side of the critical-empirical nature of this study is expressed also in our analysis of ideology. For example, the study of conflicts in East German society takes into account the "theory of contradictions," as it is understood by the political leadership of the SED. (The approach of conflict research is also applied to our empirical findings.) To give another example, the study of different social patterns within the framework of Marxist-Leninist terminology will not neglect the different interpretations of alienation contained in recent Marxist social theory in the GDR. Likewise, the analysis of integrational tendencies does not disregard the harmonistic ideal underlying the political elite's concept of organization. The resonance of this ideal is evident not only in the Marxist concept of organization but also in the expression the latter finds in cybernetic terminology. Following the tenets of our critical-empirical approach to ideology, we have investigated the organizational pattern of East German society both "qualitatively" and "quantitatively." A substantial part of the SED's social structure must of necessity be examined when using this approach. Finally, the analysis of the social structure of the SED also proceeds on both a quantitative and qualitative level: Biographies of the party elite are not merely used as "data"—i.e., in quantitative fashion—but are also taken into account qualitatively, as regards their respective social contexts. The tools of empirical analysis "from without" are thus combined with a perspective "from within." Nevertheless, the author is aware that he has not solved the more general methodological problems involved, but has only made an attempt to cope with them within the narrow context of this study.

Given the dimensions of the subject and the methodological intentions of the author, this study of necessity combines a variety of research designs within its broader critical-empirical approach.

3. Some Aspects of the Research Strategy

Our study is a contribution to the field of empirical elite research, a type of field research[32] in which factual evidence is heavily emphasized.

---

[32] Abandoning Parsons' structural–functional theory, sociologists are increasingly adopting the field concept, borrowed from physics (Einstein) that Lewin

Consequently, the data will not be elaborated primarily by the descriptive historical method, but subjected to systematic analysis by means of various methodological formulas. Concepts developed within the field of organizational sociology, the study of elites, and the theory of ideology, used to prepare and systematize our material, were chosen in order to furnish a basis for further comparative work in these fields. Formulated in the language of Lewin or Lasswell, this constitutes an attempt to use a clearly limited empirical field for designing a "systematic context system," which renders individual sectors of this field comparable.[33] However, in keeping with the character of a systematic empirical study, we cannot carry this abstract principle so far as to make our study a purely analytical one. It still moves largely in the systematizing, descriptive area and its degree of abstraction is relatively low. In René König's[34] terms, this study extends via the "determination of regularities" only to the stage of constructing "ad hoc theories," i.e., to a level of abstraction at which recognized regularities are put into the context of theoretical propositions. Only the frame of reference constructed below could allow work in the dimension of "middle range theories." Accordingly, classifying concepts, rather than "categories," are used in the analysis to follow.

Thus, we make no claim here to construct a comprehensive theory of Communist political systems or societies. Global normative interpretations—such as the thesis of convergence or divergence of Eastern and Western systems—play an even lesser role. However, we attempt to include the historical dimension of the subject matter. In accordance with the formal frame of reference, the changes and rigidity of the system, and

---

transferred to psychology. Although the clearer term "field" (as opposed to "structure") does not yet adequately characterize this concept, it is clarified in the process of comparison. See also Harald Mey, *Studien zur Anwendung des Feldbegriffs in den Sozialwissenschaften* (Munich, 1965), passim.

[33] Harold D. Lasswell, "The Qualitative and the Quantitative in Political and Legal Anaysis," in Daniel Lerner, ed., *Quantity and Quality: The Hayden Colloqium on Scientific Method and Concept* (New York: Free Press, 1961), pp. 103 ff.

[34] René König, "Grundlagenprobleme der soziologischen Forschungsmethoden," in Friedrich Karrenberg and Hans Albert, eds., with the collaboration of Hubert Raupach, *Sozialwissenschaft und Gesellschaftsgestaltung. Festschrift für Gerhard Weisser* (Berlin, 1963), p. 32 and passim.

the inner "regularities" and transformations of the ideological dogma over a period of time are taken into account. Although hypotheses about the processes of change and rigidity are formulated, their predictive value is relatively low. Historical regularities become apparent only through comprehensive analysis of events over a long period of time. Consequently, the period covered by this study—1954 to 1963–1964, and, for some data, up to 1966-1967—seems to allow only short-term prognoses.

SELECTED PERTINENT ASPECTS OF ORGANIZATIONAL THEORY

The principal line of questioning to be pursued in this study is directed toward the changes in the organizational structure of the SED. By "changes in the organizational structure" we naturally do not mean this or that change in the party apparatus, this or that improvement of the organizational effectiveness that may have been introduced within the past few years; rather we are concerned with fundamental party transformations that go down to the very roots of party power politics, the party's gradual and controversial dissociation from the organizational schemes of the secret groups that had been formed in the days of preindustrial society, and the adaptation and absorption of such groups into the dynamics of industrial society.[35]

The development of the "production principle," propagated as a principle of organization by the party leadership since 1963, occupies the center of our attention. The SED leadership launched a campaign to reorganize the party at the beginning of 1963, for the stated purpose of bringing industry and agriculture closer to ideal production efficiency. This new organizational structure was a mixed type, combining elements of both the territorial and production principles.[36] Not completely novel, this modified party structure was really a continuation of the old Bolshevik tradition of organizing the party in "production groups," thus establishing a closer connection with purely industrial organizational forms. Nevertheless, for decades the Marxist-Leninist theory of organization remained in the grip of the secret society mentality. Here we refer primarily to the hierarchical principles of such societies, which can be

---

[35] This frame of reference is a theoretical concept not open to complete empirical verification in the following chapters.

[36] For a discussion of the "production principle," see pp. 92 ff, *infra*.

classified largely in terms of the rituals of their "initiation" processes and the degree to which they determine access to information on the part of the membership. The veiling of the "secret," ideological distortion, and the "revelation" of reality result in the familiar conspiratorial nature of all political secret societies, with the world divided into "good" and "evil." Georg Simmel was the first sociologist to observe that the forms of organization in such societies reflect the dominance of the sense of secrecy—i.e., the ritual of acceptance, the esoteric nature of membership, symbolic designation of various rungs of the hierarchy and, above all, the leading clique's self-isolation from the rank-and-file members. In his theory of the revolutionary party, Lenin developed this correspondence between ideology and organization. He classified members of the Social Democratic Workers' Party of Russia (RSDRP) by the degree of organization in general and the degree of conspiracy in particular. The party rank-and-file were divided into "organizations of revolutionists" and "organizations of workers" in the factories. The revolutionists—the actual core of the party—were to form a "close" and "conspirative" organization that would be able to act independently of the workers' organizations.[37] This simultaneous duality and unity rendered the party, in the eyes of Bolshevik theoreticians, the "highest" organizational type not only of all "class organizations," but also of future Communist society. On the other hand, the Bolshevik revolutionaries and their successors, the party bureaucrats, repeatedly attempted to apply the principle of a small conspiratorial group, comprised of the actual core of the party leadership, to individual functional areas of party organization. Communist parties that have seized and consolidated political power in an industrial society are only loosely connected with Lenin's tradition. The production principle—as well as the territorial principle—developed from the requirements of a large industrial organization, though it retained some of the specific characteristics of both the Bolshevik and West European types of secret societies.

Some major questions now arise. What is the meaning of "organization" in the sense used here? How can the heterogeneous structural elements of contemporary Communist organizational systems be distin-

[37] V. I. Lenin, "What Is To Be Done?," *Collected Works*, Vol. IV (New York: International Publishers, 1929), pp. 207 ff.

guished? Can Max Weber's thesis of the fundamental similarity of state and industrial bureaucratic organization be applied to a Communist party? To answer these questions we must first examine the structure of the organizations we deal with. Organization, as used here, has three, very different dimensions, representing three approaches that must intersect in order to describe the complex structure of an authoritarian party organization in a changing society.

The organization of the SED, originally a socially marginal type of party whose structure was based on that of the political secret societies of the eighteenth and nineteenth centuries, must be regarded primarily as a *historical* phenomenon. Its Utopian ideology must be related to its social integration or disintegration, here reduced to a formula that necessitates abbreviating the historical process: Revolutionary ideology and/or Utopia corresponds to the complete social disintegration (i.e., the completely marginal social position) of its ideologists, the revolutionary intelligentsia. The destruction and subsequent "refunctionalization" of the ideology or Utopia corresponds to the full integration of its ideologists, and thus to the formation of a new social stratum.[38] Currently, the latter relationship between ideology and integration can be observed in the SED party organization. As detailed in Chapter Four, a process of "refunctionalizing" ideology that "reflects" increasing social integration is evident in the GDR.

Second, the organization of the SED can be *sociologically* defined. Industrial sociology maintains that all structures that are described as organizations share the characteristic "that a multiplicity of persons cooperate for the attainment of a specific aim or a limited number of specific aims in a conscious and rational fashion."[39] Barnard defines organization as a "system of consciously coordinated personal activities or forces."[40] Like Renate Mayntz, he holds that organization is determined

---

[38] See Peter Christian Ludz, "Ideologie, Intelligenz und Organisation. Bemerkungen über ihren Zusammenhang in der frühbürgerlichen Gesellschaft," *Jahrbuch für Sozialwissenschaft* 15, no. 1 (1964): 85.

[39] Renate Mayntz, "Die Organisationssoziologie und ihre Beziehungen zur Organisationslehre," in Erich Schnaufer and Klaus Agthe, eds., *Organisation* (Berlin and Baden-Baden, 1961), p. 30.

[40] Chester I. Barnard, *The Functions of the Executive* (Cambridge, Mass., 1951), p. 72.

by three characteristics: communication, willingness to serve, and a commonly held aim.[41] The characterization of industrial society as a type of organization itself is linked to the sociological definition of large modern organizations. By developing the concept of "industrialism," Clark Kerr et al. attempted to transfer the organizational concept from industrial sociology to sociology proper. Industrialism reduces all social organizations—governments and labor and management organizations—to a single, general type: the "industrial relations system."[42] This view of "organizations" is closely tied to the concepts of "interaction" and "communication." Large organizations, such as present-day Communist parties, can thus be regarded from the point of view of comprehensive systems of interaction and communication.

Finally, Communist parties can be viewed as *political* organizations or systems. Political systems analysis defines a party as a system of political interactions between various sociopolitical groups. Although based on phenomena observed in Western parliamentary societies, the concepts of "political interaction" and "political group" can be used in this context, since political groups that interact externally and internally can also be distinguished in nonparliamentary industrial societies. Those political groups regarded by Arthur F. Bentley and David B. Truman as constituent elements of the "political process"[43] are themselves embedded in an all-encompassing, total society. The "political system" can be separated analytically from society, viewed as the "all-embracing

[41] Ibid., p. 82.
[42] Clark Kerr et al., *Industrialism and Industrial Man: The Problems of Labor and Management in Economic Growth* (Cambridge, Mass., 1960), pp. 292 ff.
[43] Arthur F. Bentley, *The Process of Government: A Study of Social Pressures* (Evanston, Ill., 1949), pp. 200 ff; and David B. Truman, *The Governmental Process: Political Interests and Public Opinion* (New York, 1951), pp. 23 ff. The group concept is also used in sociology from the point of view of the "ideological group." See Vladimir C. Nahirny, "Some Observations on Ideological Groups," *The American Journal of Sociology* 67, no. 4 (January 1962): 400; and David W. Minar, "Ideology and Political Behavior," *Midwest Journal of Political Science* 5, no. 4 (November 1961): 317 ff. Werner Sombart's concept of the "intentional corporate group" (*intentionaler Verband*) is a predecessor of the "ideological group" concept. See Werner Sombart, "Grundformen des menschlichen Zusammenlebens," in Alfred Vierkandt, ed., *Handwörterbuch der Soziologie* (Stuttgart, 1931), pp. 233 ff.

suprasystem." According to Easton,[44] political interactions are distinguished from other kinds of social interactions by their "relevance to the authoritative allocation of values for a society." Although the concept of the "political system" is analytic in character, this tool enables us to broaden the concept of organization, as defined by (functional) organizational sociology. For political interactions, as defined by Easton, may take place in various kinds of organizations, one aspect of which is their "parapolitical system."

Small groups, parties, and bureaucracies, as well as entire societies, can thus be conceived of as "systems." According to Dwight Waldo, W. Richard Scott et al., these "systems" are to be regarded as " 'entities' which are more or less autonomous and composed of mutually dependent elements."[45] This concept of a system retains traces of functionalist views and must be supplemented by the concept of "openness." Systems are regarded as "open" insofar as "the behavior of the system depends on already 'integrated' as well as on 'external factors'."[46] Following the model conceived by Ludwig von Bertalanffy, this concept of the political system is now used primarily by David Easton, Karl W. Deutsch, Kenneth E. Boulding et al.[47] A uniform terminology to describe elements and relationships in various social orders enhances the analytical usefulness of organizational theory. The behavioral trend in political science, which defines "political life as a system of behavior" (Robson), has added to the utility of the systems approach. System theoreticians assume that behavior in various types of systems is conditioned, at least by "analogous"—if not "homologous"—processes.[48] Within the framework of this approach, the concept of "system" can be regarded as fundamental, in both sociological and empirical political theory. Indeed, it is primarily conceived in this fashion by Easton and Deutsch. Although the theory of systems has been formulated to a higher degree

[44] David Easton, *A Framework for Political Analysis* (Englewood Cliffs, N.J., 1965), p. 38 and pp. 50 ff.
[45] Dwight Waldo, "Zur Theorie der Organisation. Ihr Stand und ihre Probleme," *Der Staat* 5, no. 3 (1966): 294.
[46] Peter Nettl, "The Concept of System in Political Science," *Political Studies* 14, no. 3 (October 1966): 307.
[47] Easton, *A Framework for Political Analysis*.
[48] For example, Easton, ibid., p. 16.

of abstraction than organizational theory—or the theory of elites—the boundaries are nevertheless fluid. Consequently, this study proposes to link the concept of organization to systems analysis and thus broaden it.

Returning to the problem of ruling Communist parties in advanced, industrialized societies we find three determinant characteristics of party organization: the "marginality" of the leadership group, inherited from the tradition of the secret society; behavioral norms that gradually diverge from those of a revolutionary party of the Leninist type, and slowly become more rationalized and stereotyped; and political interactions conditioned by conspiratorial attitudes and primary group loyalties, combined with "bureaucratic" attitudes characteristic of mass party organizations. These three characteristics reflect the basic conflicts between the functional requirements of the industrial system and the requirements postulated by leadership groups in order to preserve political power. To delineate further these basic conflicts, it is necessary to describe in some detail the process of adaptation or integration of the original party organization, whereby it develops into an organization suited to the demands of running a contemporary industrial society.

Adaptation, or integration to industrial society may be defined as the adoption by the party of the general operational principles that commonly characterize a large industrial organization—a definition consistent with the formulations of organizational sociology. Four interconnected, major features are characteristic of a large industrial organization: (1) bureaucratic rationality;[49] (2) expanded bureaucracies, resulting from the processes of rationalization and specialization of labor, as well as from competition between organizations;[50] (3) typical features of charismatic authority (as redefined by R. Bendix from the Weberian model), with clear manifestation of coercion and "utility" as techniques, combined with an advance of "functional authority"[51] based on the premium alloted to expertise; (4) the "belatedness" of large-scale organi-

---

[49] Robert Presthus, in *The Organizational Society: An Analysis and a Theory* (New York, 1962), pp. 52 ff, cites five characteristics common to the rationalization phases in large industrial complexes.

[50] Cf. Wilbert E. Moore, *The Conduct of Corporation* (New York, 1962), p. 128.

[51] Heinz Hartmann, *Funktionale Autorität. Systematische Abhandlungen zu einem soziologischen Begriff* (Stuttgart, 1964), passim.

zations, i.e., the fact that large-scale organizations historically spring from and systematically rank behind small groups (*Gemeinschaften*) and secret societies.

Given the intrusion of these elements of wide social groups and large industrial organizations into the party structure, a whole series of conflicts arises: The party leadership, with its overriding compulsion to maintain its power base, finds itself forced to preserve a system of rule which at least partially neglects the principle of functional authority. The organizational form of Communist parties is designed for permanence of power; it is based on hierarchical authority, with executive power overconcentrated in the top echelons. Consequently, developments requiring the recognition of "functional authority" cannot be opposed without threatening the power position of the political elite. Such developments involve increased mobilization of the entire society and accelerated circulation within the major leadership groups. This risk becomes greater as functional efficiency is emphasized (especially if we recall that authoritarian parties carry certain built-in counter tendencies).

The party elite must keep intact a residue of its "marginality"[52]— or exclusiveness—in order to preserve a certain distance from its rank and file, as well as from society as a whole. This principle is an essential ingredient of the exercise of political power. The complete social marginality originally characteristic of the leadership group derives its ultimate legitimacy from the eschatological, or Utopian, dimension of its ideology, as has been abundantly illustrated in the history of Marxism. Concomitant to the refunctionalization[53] of the ideology, this marginality has developed into the more typical "social distance" required by all political leadership groups. Nonetheless, some residue must be and is, in effect, preserved. This enables the leadership of the GDR to rely, as the case may demand, on each and every technique of knowledge for the sake of domination, amplified by various elements of Marxism-Leninism, to legitimize its authority. The party is, therefore,

---

[52] The concept of "marginality" was taken from Everett V. Stonequist, *The Marginal Man: A Study in Personality and Culture Conflict* (New York, 1961).
[53] I.e., bringing its tenets closer to the reality of the moment (cf. pp. 11-12 *supra.*).

constantly compelled to limit the free flow of information in society. Unquestioning acceptance of the existing system and a belief in the legitimacy of the ruling party diminish in direct proportion to the extent to which information becomes freely available to all members of society.

This phenomenon is typical in the history of Communist parties. Reviving and clarifying Marx's and Lenin's concepts for application to contemporary society, Georg Lukács emphasized the "total fearlessness with regard to the existing system" as the decisive characteristic of a party operating illegally in the twentieth century.[54] He established "functional illegality" and conspiratorial attitudes as the criteria of a party's capacity to act. Unquestioning acceptance of the given situation, combined with conscious limitation of information, were the indispensable operational techniques of a revolutionary party operating within a bourgeois society, no longer accepted uncritically by all its members. The usefulness of these techniques became more questionable after Communist parties gained power. At this point (particularly in the case of the SED), we are dealing with a "social distance" maintained by a group which, at least purportedly, does not regard the entire society as "hostile" in principle. However, under these circumstances unquestioning belief in what exists, coupled with the careful rationing of information, remains functional for the leadership. Thus, the operational principles of illegality have not, and still cannot be jettisoned entirely.

A dogmatic, operational theory of illegality was never a basic concept of Marxist-Leninist ideology. Nevertheless, like all Communist leaderships, the SED elite constantly reverts to an illegality (as defined by organizational theory[55]) facilitated by the relatively restricted membership of the Politburo and its position which shelters it from the party rank and file, as well as from society as a whole. The development of rationalization, increased formalization of procedures, and functional speculation in bureaucratic organizations, plus greater opportunity for open discussion and criticism, is thus counterbalanced by artificial insulation of the power nucleus within the executive decision-making

[54] Georg Lukács, *History and Class Consciousness, Studies in Marxist Dialectics* (Cambridge, Mass.: M.I.T. Press, 1971), p. 263.
[55] For an organizational-sociological explanation of illegality, see Niklas Luhmann, *Funktionen und Folgen formaler Organisation* (Berlin, 1964), pp. 304 ff; and p. 313.

group. As emphasized by Bendix and Lipset,[56] this artifical insulation also places limits on the general process of industrialization and the complementary processes of social mobility, as well as opportunities for public or internal criticism of the party—a common feature of East European and Soviet political systems. For example, Khrushchev had attempted (since 1961–1962) to encourage expert criticism of the system "from the grass roots," though he made it quite clear that the Politburo would continue to exercise its monopoly in matters of power and interpretation of ideology.[57]

On the whole, the crucial conflict lies between the rigidity of the insulated leadership bodies (i.e., their maintenance of an impassable zone between themselves and society) on the one hand, and their adaptation to and metamorphosis into industrial organization forms, on the other. Marginality, or distance from society, thus appears to be a "constant" for Communist political systems, even under the conditions imposed by an industrial society.

Additional insights may be found in examining the above-mentioned phenomenon of belatedness (*Nachträglichkeit*). Herman Schmalenbach was the first to confirm that, historically, in all societies or "secondary groups" (*Gesellschaften*), individuals precede the corporate group (*Verband*). He utilized the perceptions of Ferdinand Tönnies and Max Weber. In secondary groups, social formation is invariably "belated" (*nachträglich*); in "primary groups" (*Gemeinschaft, Bund*), individual members are bound together as an "organic whole" from the very beginning.[58] Consequently, the social orientation of primary group members is still determined by charismatic and traditional forms of authority—or, as Shils puts it, by a "primary group loyalty," which in present-day Western parliamentary systems is limited largely to military units.[59]

[56] Seymour Martin Lipset and Reinhard Bendix, *Social Mobility in Industrial Society* (Berkeley and Los Angeles, 1959), p. 280.
[57] Cf. Zbigniew Brzezinski and Samuel P. Huntington, *Political Power: USA/USSR* (New York: Viking Press, 1965), pp. 51–52.
[58] Herman Schmalenbach, "Die soziologische Kategorie des Bundes," in *Die Dioskuren. Jahrbuch für Geisteswissenschaften* I (Munich, 1922) 71.
[59] Cf. Samuel A. Stouffer et al., *The American Soldier; Combat and Its Aftermath*, Studies in Social Psychology in World War II, Vol. 2 (New York, 1949); and Rolf R. Bigler, *Der einsame Soldat. Eine soziologische Deutung der militärischen Organisation* (Frauenfeld, 1963), especially p. 134 ff.

Having postulated the interpenetration of Communist party organizations by belated organizational principles, and keeping in mind that these groups have also preserved certain features of primary group organization, we pose the following questions: How has primary group (or "elementary") behavior, derived from nineteenth-century secret societies and revolutionary parties, changed or been preserved in the course of restructuring the party apparatus? Have the elementary forms of behavior been institutionalized and/or divorced from the conditions which generated them—thus losing their original meaning? How, and to what extent throughout society (i.e., non–Communist party organizations), are new and informal groups emerging as a reaction to overorganization? Are new forms of organization (e.g., an increasingly bureaucratic organizational system) developing in the leadership groups (the Politburo, etc.)? Do these crypto-organizations in turn generate new forms of competing elites, *politically*, but not *organizationally*, integrated? Are counter elites, which may be regarded as "institutionalized," necessary major features of a Communist social system undergoing increasing differentiation?

To answer these questions it will be helpful to examine current opportunities for spontaneous association in the party organization. According to Homans and Luhmann,[60] the types of elementary behavior referred to above—solidarity and constantly invoked faith in a common aim—do not necessarily denote the forms of direct or indirect personal contact embodied in normal "informal" group interactions or charitable group activities, but may be looked upon as constitutional characteristics of secret societies.

There are indications that these traditional norms and ideals have been maintained in the leadership groups of the SED. Two subgroups of the East German political elite—Ulbricht's Politburo group and the veteran functionaries in the Secretariats of the SED *Bezirk* (District) executives—have maintained solidarity vis-à-vis the rise of a new organizational type. As organizations within the SED organization, these elite subgroups constitute "strategic cliques."[61] As leadership groups of

[60] Cf. Luhmann, *Funktionen und Folgen,* p. 331.
[61] Ibid., pp. 327 ff. In the following, the terms "strategic clique," "strategic leadership group," and "strategic decision-making elite" are used synonymously. Although the concept of the strategic clique has been drawn from industrial sociology, and designates primarily a specific type of informal group within

a Communist party undergoing adaptation to and integration into a new organizational type, each subgroup may be adequately described as a "strategic clique." Such cliques resemble similar ones in social or industrial organizations: Both are small groups that enjoy preferential positions in the system by virtue of their high offices. By its very nature, the clique maintains a boundary between its members, the party apparatus, and society in general. This is the residual marginality essential for the maintenance of power within a political group.[62] Marginality of the leaders vis-à-vis the other members is characteristic of secret political societies (such as the *Bund der Geächteten* and the *Bund der Gerechten,* which may be regarded as forerunners of the political parties established in the nineteenth or the twentieth century). A further characteristic of secret political societies, the maintenance of an internal hierarchy, may also be parallel to the SED's strategic clique. The internal hierarchy established by Ulbricht's group has kept Politburo candidates (insofar as they are technical and economic specialists) within the institutionalized counter elite of the SED leadership groups.[63] Even while secretaries of the Central Committee, Politburo candidates like Apel, Mittag, and Jarowinsky occupied a secondary rank. On the other hand (in accordance with the theories of Kingsley Davis and W. E. Moore), members of the strategic clique are dependent on those Politburo candidates who are at the same time technical and economic specialists.

---

economic enterprises, we have chosen to apply it to political leadership groups. The term "strategic clique" seems to best describe the residual "marginality" enjoyed by the veteran functionaries in the SED, particularly in the Politburo and the Secretariats of the district and local (*Kreis*) executives. Lucian W. Pye, in "The Non-Western Political Process," *The Journal of Politics* 20 (1958): 486 ff. goes so far as to characterize the political process in "non-Western" societies as a predominance of cliques. Similar concepts are finding acceptance in research on elites and parties. See Susan Keller, *Beyond the Ruling Class: Strategic Elites in Modern Society* (New York, 1963), who uses the concept of "strategic elites." Cf. also C. Wright Mills, *The Power Elite* (New York: Oxford University Press, 1956), p. 278, who speaks of the military clique; and Maurice Duverger, *Die politischen Parteien,* Siegfried Landshut, ed. and trans. (Tübingen, 1959), p. 167, who uses the term cammarilla" under comparable conditions.

[62] At an early stage Mosca emphasized the "distance" between the "ruling class" and the masses. See Gaetano Mosca, *The Ruling Class* [Elementi di scienza politica], Hannah D. Kahn, trans. (New York and London: McGraw-Hill, 1939), pp. 55 ff.

[63] Cf. also pp. 288-289 of this work.

Concepts taken from industrial organization models can be used both to describe strategic cliques within Communist parties and leadership bodies, and to focus on conflicts existing within Communist organizations. To borrow from the language of industrial sociology, SED leading cliques include "line executives" and "staff executives." Although neither term is defined clearly in contemporary industrial sociology, there is one basic distinction useful for our purposes: Compared with the "fixed line" organization of an enterprise (i.e., its hierarchical structure), the "staff" (or functional) organization can be regarded as a major source of social conflict. Conflicts often arise when limitations on competence are insufficiently coordinated with management aims. For example, can the staff cancel or change incorrect decisions made by line personnel? How do staff executives formulate alternate decisions? How do staff executives obtain information on which to base their decisions? How far can those in line positions evaluate or check the relevance of staff information? To solve these problems many large enterprises have combined staff and line systems into "task forces" or "task groups" (Eldersveld). Task forces are composed of staff and line executives with interchangeable spheres of competence. Here, staff and line functions interact and are to some degree interchangeable, since task group members who seek out and elaborate problems can occasionally put their knowledge into practice and thereby assume actual executive functions.

It is not easy for an authoritarian party organization to accept the task force concept; such a staff system threatens the strategic clique's base of power. Nevertheless, a task force system was created in the course of the post–1963 reorganization of the SED party apparatus. Full members of the Politburo and the first secretaries of the *Bezirk* executives represent the hierarchial "line" structure that determines the aims and tasks of the organization and supervises the execution thereof. This "line" finds itself increasingly broken by scientific, technical, and economic specialists—functional representatives of the staff organization—who are integrated either directly, as Politburo candidates, or in an advisory capacity, as specialists consulted in Central Committee plena. Organizational theory of industrial enterprises continues to emphasize that the competence of such specialists is less clearly defined than that of line executives (the latter may be termed "generalists").

This phenomenon led Max Weber and others either to over- or underestimate the competence or power of staff executives.[64] Research on the GDR contains numerous examples of such erroneous estimates of function; in light of our findings they will be treated later.

Even within the SED's organizational system, the need to recognize functional authority to some degree has given experts in the party the right to make decisions, endowing them with considerable power. This decision-making power exercised by functional authorities (Mittag, Jarowinsky, and others) is exceptionally important for the final implementation of decisions made by the strategic clique. As functional authorities attain such power, that of the strategic clique is inevitably reduced (H. Hartmann speaks in this sense of the "emancipation of expertise"[65]) and its exclusive status is threatened. Thus, the ambivalent attitude of political power cliques toward changes in the organizational structure and the rise of the experts within their own ranks is understandable. Nevertheless, the strategic clique has constantly maintained the original order of internal ranking (i.e., the formal character of the line) in the East German political system.

The SED's strategic clique has succeeded in preserving a careful balance between concealment and revelation, accessability and inaccessability to knowledge and information, characteristic of political elites in all Communist systems, particularly those of the Communist-authoritarian type. One form of this balance, rarely recognized by outsiders, is the combination of clearly and vaguely defined aims and executive instructions issued by the strategic clique. In this context, vague aims and instructions can be regarded as a function of the stabilization of political power. The strategic clique may choose to include or exclude rising technical and economic experts (whether or not they belong to the Communist party) in or from the decision-making process. Acceptance by the strategic clique involves the accumulation of formal functions (*Ämterkumulation*), as well as obligatory surrender of control in the spheres of technical and economic expertise. This implies

[64] For problems in industrial society, see Joseph A. Litterer, *The Analysis of Organizations* (New York, London, and Sydney, Australia, 1965), Chapters XVI–XVIII.
[65] Heinz Hartmann, "Bürokratische und voluntaristische Dimensionen im organisierten Sozialgebilde," *Jahrbuch für Sozialwissenschaft* 15, no. 1 (1964): 126.

a loss by the new cadres of the qualifications that the ruling clique regards as simultaneously desirable and dangerous.[66] For example, after Günter Mittag was accepted as a full member of the Politburo in September 1966, his influence in the staff section of the Central Bureau of Industry and Construction, of which he was director from its creation in 1963 until its dissolution, diminished. As a full member of the Politburo he has assumed "generalist" political responsibilities to a far greater degree than heretofore. Another example of the operational concepts of the strategic clique, rarely understood by analysts of the "new economic system," is illustrated by the frequently oscillating attitude of the SED elite when introducing reforms. This ambivalence toward innovation can be regarded as a function of a political system of rule in flux.

In Chapter Two we shall attempt to substantiate the application of the terms used by organizational sociology to structural change in the organization of the SED and the power pyramid that it controls. The usefulness of applying the sociological theory of industrial organizations to the phenomena of change in a large party organization will become evident. At this early stage, essential structural elements of the East German system can be fitted into a uniform theoretical pattern. Applying the distinction between authoritarian and totalitarian rule elaborated in section two of this chapter, we shall try to fit the concept of authoritarian rule into a framework of organizational sociology.

A prominent theory of authoritarian systems is Boris Meissner's concept of authoritarianism as a type of rule in which only certain sections of society are subject to comprehensive, thoroughgoing planning and control. Meissner sees authoritarianism as a species of totalitarianism.[67] This study will extend this definition to reinterpret authoritarian rule as a transitional political system that was originally totalitarian. This

[66] Similar processes and behavior patterns have been observed in large American concerns. See Victor A. Thompson, *Modern Organization* (New York, 1963), p. 143. Furthermore, the literature of organizational sociology has long dealt with the problem of maintaining inner-organizational hierarchy by controlling upward professional mobility. See Alvin W. Gouldner, *Patterns of Industrial Bureaucracy* (Glencoe, Ill., 1954), pp. 166 ff.

[67] Boris Meissner, "Wandlungen im Herrschaftssystem und Verfassungsrecht der Sowjetunion," in Erik Boettcher, Hans-Joachim Lieber, and Boris Meissner, eds., *Bilanz der Ära Chruschtschow,* (Stuttgart, Berlin, Cologne, and Mainz, 1966), pp. 141 ff.

interpretation follows the conceptual scheme developed by Rensis Likert, and applied for the first time by A. G. Meyer in an analysis of the Soviet political system. We choose to regard totalitarianism and totalitarian rule as outmoded concepts particularly as we test their relevance through the perspective of organizational sociology.

Likert makes the basic distinction between "authoritative" and "participative" organizational systems. The former are subdivided into "exploitative authoritative" and "benevolent authoritative" types. Occupying a place between the authoritative and participative systems, there are systems of the "consultative" type.[68] Likert sets up his system types on a continuum and gives numerous characteristics for each type. Interpreting his scheme for the purpose of our investigation, we would find associated with an exploitative authoritarian system traits of terror, a rigid military–hierarchical structure, and only outward acceptance of the declared aims of the power clique on behalf of the ruled. The benevolent authoritarian type may be described as a modified form of the first species. In contrast, the use of terror has been greatly reduced in consultative systems of organization and the beginnings of noncoercive methods of cooperation and coordination can be observed. Participative systems are a further permutation of consultative ones.

Interpreting Likert's continuum in this way, we find ourselves in accord with A. G. Meyer. He has further developed Likert's scheme in applying its categories to Communist political systems. Meyer distinguishes four types of "political authoritarianism": "exploitative," "benevolent," "consultative," and "participative."[69] There are a series of characteristics or parameters for these four types, some of which are now detailed for the sake of precision. In agreement with Likert, we find it useful to emphasize the following traits: for exploitative authoritarianism (type A) a striving for physical security; for benevolent authoritarianism (type B) a striving for status security; for consultative authoritarianism (type C) the openness toward new experience and, finally, for participative authoritarianism (type D) an increase in this openness. Another dimension involves some basic characteristics of interaction and communication within organizations. Likert connects desirable/undesirable in-

---

[68] Rensis Likert, *New Patterns of Management* (New York, Toronto, and London: McGraw-Hill, 1961), pp. 222 ff.
[69] Meyer, *The Soviet Political System,* p. 243.

teraction or communication with the attainment of the particular aims of the organization. Within the sequence of system types, Likert gives the following answers: "very little," "little," "quite a bit," and "much" with both individuals and groups. The question of the character of the interaction–influence process is posed in terms of "fear" or "confidence." Whereas fear predominates in type A and confidence is a negligible factor, the situation changes for types B and C. In type D the fear factor has almost disappeared and confidence notably increased.

Some further operating characteristics in which these four types are distinguishable are: the decision-making process or, more specifically, the levels at which decisions are made and the extent of technical and scientific knowledge required for making decisions, as well as the downward, respectively upward, flow of information. This analysis also takes into account system parameters, which indicate whether individuals or groups make given decisions, and whether decisions were taken in the optimal fashion. Finally, the parameter of the character of control processes in these four system types must also be included. The extent of control is to be determined as well as the level at which it is exercised. Likert has supplemented his findings for these questions by still further differentiations, which yield a series of parameters permitting further distinctions between the systems concerned. In particular, the consultative and participative types of authoritarian rule are characterized by a higher incidence of delegated controls, widespread feeling of responsibility, teamwork, increasing realization of and need for scientific and technological knowledge, a high premium placed on functional authority, etc. Correspondingly, growing elite competition is present in all variants of the consultative and participative types.[70]

By applying this scheme to political systems, we obtain a consistent framework for analyzing the development from "totalitarian" to "authoritarian" rule. Sociological differentiation within Communist political systems repeatedly called for by writers in this field is now possible, because social change and social conflicts can be included in our analysis. At this stage the rooting of political rule in the soil of society is our subject of analysis. In principle, this interconnection allows us to pursue a comparative analysis for a given political system over different segments of time.

[70] Likert, *New Patterns of Management,* pp. 230 ff.

Following A. G. Meyer's distinctions, we may characterize "exploitative authoritarianism" and "benevolent authoritarianism" as forms of what is traditionally known as totalitarian rule. This shift in perspective permits us to include the historical dimension, i.e., the waxing and waning of Stalinism in the GDR. The terms "consultative" and "participative" authoritarianism may also be utilized. They enable us to give a more exact description of the situation in the GDR since 1961–1962. Since this date—but particularly since the introduction of the New Economic System in the spring of 1963—elements of consultative authoritarianism can be perceived in wide sectors of the state and economy, and also in the party itself. On the other hand, the concept of participative authoritarianism is not applicable to the past or present realities of the GDR. It may, however, provide us with a major point of reference: It may indicate the stage of advancement toward which the system could be developing if a series of "if–then" hypotheses were verified, e.g., the following: if decisions are made by groups, then interaction and communication increase not merely within these groups, but in the entire system (as compared to a situation in which decisions are made only by individuals). However, taking into account additionally the technical and economic development in Western industrial societies, we can assume that participative authoritarianism is no longer a purely theoretical concept in application to the GDR and the other highly industrialized countries of the Eastern bloc. The growing primacy attached to technical progress cannot permanently operate to exclude participation in the general sense. Indeed, a growing demand for education and training associated with technical progress leads to a rapid increase in a demand for participation.[71] Trends of consultative authoritarianism can be perceived in the GDR insofar as experts are increasingly consulted in the bureaus of industry and construction—but primarily in the Central Committee and the secretariats of the SED *Bezirk* executives.[72] Since 1963 an increasing number of expert subcommittees has been affiliated, permanently, with these latter named bodies.

In summary, differentiations in the organizational definition of

[71] See Kerr et al., *Industrialism*, pp. 287 ff and passim, where these processes are described as phenomena of "industrialism."
[72] For details regarding the Bureau for Industry and Construction, and the Workers' and Peasants' Inspectorate (ABI), see pp. 97 ff. and 156 ff, *infra*.

changing totalitarian systems are possible; by determining the various major characteristics of a given system, we can pinpoint specific phenomena of change. Properly applied, the Likert pattern permits the observation of changes in a totalitarian system along a continuum—i.e., changes over the course of time. In addition, it allows a systematic examination of the complex process associated with changing phenomena in the political system and society. Finally, this concept allows us to make a more precise political evaluation of the forces of change and rigidity in the system under observation.

SOME ASPECTS OF ELITE THEORY

Elements of organizational sociology and elite theory are combined in the theoretical concept to be developed in this section. At first sight, this statement seems inconsistent; the theory of systems hardly encompasses elite groups and "membership systems" in general. Elites cannot just be divided into separate segments. However, they can be conceived of as "control units" "that specialize in the cybernetic functions of knowledge processing and decision making and in the application of power."[73] This definition contains two elements important for the systems approach utilized here: "control" over and "integration" into larger units or "supra-units." Up until now, this concept has seldom been applied in empirical elite studies. Rather, elite studies attempt largely to classify elites empirically, usually by analyzing political and professional career patterns, as well as so-called career mobility (see Eldersveld). Empirical career research based on extensive biographical data shows promise of becoming one of the most important branches of elite studies. This raises closely connected methodological questions. In elite studies, as in many branches of political science research, behavioral analysis is counterposed to analysis of institutions, functions, or positions. The institutional approach generally uses the so-called positional method (Dahrendorf, Zapf); the behavioral approach uses criteria of prestige, or decision analysis (see the work of E. K. Scheuch). Position analysis assumes that incumbents in top positions can, and actually do, make the relevant decisions they are formally responsible for making. The corresponding

[73] See Amitai Etzioni, *The Active Society: A Theory of Societal and Political Processes* (London: Collier–Macmillan Ltd.; New York: The Free Press, 1968), p. 668.

"function" of the incumbent is deduced from his leadership "position." A correspondence between positions and functions can be established primarily by noting changes in the membership of an elite, as well as by investigating the social biographies of its members. In contrast, behavioral analysis, in the narrower sense, denies the connection of top positions with the decisions actually made.[74]

Contemporary schools of behavior research in political science (V. O. Key, Jr., A. Campbell, S. J. Eldersveld, etc.) have rediscovered that political institutions and organizations—particularly political parties—are the dominant "frame[s]" of the behavior of political elites.[75] Eldersveld, for example, regards parties, as well as communications systems, as organizational systems. The most recent developments in research on party systems promise to combine both aspects: the institutional factor with prestige, or the decision-making function. However, contrasted with bureaucratic organizations, parties are in principle regarded as "open," "personalized" systems in which the informal element plays an essential role. The type of hierarchy found in parties should also be distinguished from that found in other bureaucratic organizations. Following Lasswell and Kaplan, Eldersveld uses the term "stratarchy" instead of hierarchy. Despite these differences, recent research on parties shows a trend generally similar to the development of comparative politics. The comparison of social structures *within* specific systems and *between* differing systems is now regarded as being more precise and meaningful when a positional or behavioral approach, rather than a purely descriptive institutional approach, is applied.

In the following passages, the elite theory approach is detached from the theoretical and organizational section of this study and systematically examined in detail. Both approaches—the organizational

[74] See Erwin K. Scheuch, "Führungsgruppen and Demokratie in Deutschland," *Die neue Gesellschaft* 13, no. 5 (September-October, 1966): 362 ff. The author clearly wishes to attribute these valuable suggestions in the field of elite theory to Wolfgang Schluchter.
[75] See, for example, Dankwart A. Rustow, "The Study of Elites: Who's Who, When, and How," *World Politics* 18, no. 4 (July 1966): 695. For recent behavioral party research, see Samuel J. Eldersveld, *Political Parties: A Behavioral Analysis* (Chicago, 1964), Part III, *The Party As an Organizational System,* pp. 331 ff; and Angus Campbell, "Recent Developments in Survey Studies of Political Behavior," in Austin Ranney, ed., *Essays on the Behavioral Study of Politics* (Urbana, Ill., 1962), pp. 31 ff.

and that of elite theory—attempt to examine aspects of "government" (in the sense of its institutionalized forms) and "society."[76] Institutional analysis is frequently one-sided; to avoid this pitfall, our two approaches will include the most decisive conditions of social dynamics as they affect government, with particular consideration given to the concurrence of political power and social status.[77]

However, *different* elites in authoritarian systems and differences in criteria for their selection, their social and/or political rise, their "basis" groups (Jaeggi), or their "mother" groups (Stammer) will not be investigated here. Nor will all the important elites in a political system or a society (i.e., political parties and their leaders, formal legislative and executive elites, interest groups and interest elites, influential editors and publishers, etc.,) be covered, as was done by Edinger and Deutsch for West Germany.[78] Indeed, an empirical description of the various East German elite groups would be impossible now. Our sole concern is with the political elite in the narrower sense—the leadership bodies of the SED.

The following characteristics for the members and candidates of the SED Central Committee have been taken into account: age, sex, social origin, political biography, occupation and mobility, and guiding ideological norms.[79] Their positions and functions are examined. With respect to the changes in the GDR's system, the investigation centers on the question of how different groupings within the political elite can be related to the process of increasing the functional efficiency of the system. A positional elite concept is used which deviates from Edinger's earlier investigations, but is in accord with what he discusses in a later article on "political science and political biography."[80] Indeed, this close

[76] Also Robert Dahl, "A Critique of the Ruling Elite Model," *The American Political Science Review* 52, no. 2 (June 1958): 464.
[77] Cf. Herbert Goldhamer and Edward A. Shils, "Power and Status," in Lewis A. Coser and Bernard Rosenberg, eds., *Sociological Theory: A Book of Readings* (New York and London, 2nd ed., 1964), pp. 134 ff.
[78] Karl W. Deutsch and Lewis J. Edinger, *Germany Rejoins the Powers: Mass Opinion, Interest Groups, and Elites in Contemporary German Foreign Policy* (Stanford, Cal., 1959), passim.
[79] For details, see Chapter Three.
[80] Lewis J. Edinger, "Post-Totalitarian Leadership: Elites in the German Federal Republic," *The American Political Science Review* 54, no. 1 (March 1960): 58 ff. Apparently, Edinger is conscious of these problems in his empirical elite

association of position and function seems valid for the political leadership groups in GDR society. East German incumbents in political elite positions exercise functions to which actual power and influence can be ascribed to a far greater degree than in parliamentary democracies. Political upheaval in the GDR is still a relatively recent phenomenon, and the positions of power of the SED leading groups are not so secure that the party elite can afford to leave their incumbents without the appropriate allocative functions.

Furthermore, within the above limitations, all explicitly or implicitly normative elite concepts (as can be seen in theories of democratic systems even in recent periods[81]) are beyond the scope of this study, as is the concept and idea of the normative ("value forming") elite. Finally, the concept of the *functional elite* used by Stammer and Dahrendorf[82] is acceptable only in modified form, since it contains a "normative and descriptive double function" in the sense used by Topitsch. According to Stammer, functional elites are intended, on the one hand, to protect parliamentary systems from being dominated by privileged minorities; they thus exercise a protective, or indirect normative, function. On the other hand, functional elites themselves formulate the ideological norms of the system. Conceived by Stammer as "active minorities" in a democracy, functional elites provide alternatives for the molding of the value system of their society. Functional elites, based primarily in the political parties, provide the basis for political pluralism in a parliamentary democracy. While the concept of functional elites is thus intended to describe very specific social structures, it is also used to establish norms for "correct" social behavior. In other words, functional elites have a directly normative, or ideological, function. Therefore, the

---

studies, primarily in his identification of elites and the holders of key positions. See his "Political Science and Political Biography: Reflections on the Study of Leaderships," *The Journal of Politics* 26, 2 and 3 (May and August 1964): 423 ff and 648 ff.

[81] See V. O. Key, *Public Opinion and American Democracy* (New York, 1961); and criticism of it by Jack L. Walker, "A Critique of the Elitist Theory of Democracy," *The American Political Science Review* 60, no. 2 (June 1966): 285 ff.

[82] Otto Stammer, "Elite und Elitenbildung," in Wilhelm Bernsdorf and Friedrich Bülow, eds., *Wörterbuch der Soziologie* (Stuttgart, 1955), p. 110; Stammer, "Das Elitenproblem in der Demokratie," in his *Politische Soziologie,* pp. 63 ff; and Dahrendorf, *Gesellschaft und Freiheit,* p. 174.

concept of functional elites can be used here only if the normative element is omitted and elites are regarded as functional in a "system neutral" way. Without necessarily being bound to democratic traditions, we may call elites "functional" when they serve a system.

A third concept frequently used is that of the "power elite." In the relevant literature (e.g., C. W. Mills, Lasswell, Kaplan, and Bottomore), its various formulations are based on a conception of power characterized by three parameters. The first is a general social focus that includes, but goes beyond, the pattern of political power. (See Max Weber. In his sense, power requires no legitimacy and is sociologically an amorphous category.) The second is the presence of specific connections between the elite and the society. A power elite sees society predominantly as a framework for selection and upward occupational mobility.[83] The third is the reduction of the political process to decisions involving sanctions.[84] A main criticism of the concept of the power elite is that it seems to ignore many aspects of social differentiation that condition the fundamental conflicts over power and decision-making prerogatives. Even when they have been accounted for—as by Bendix and Lipset[85]— the idea of power is so general that a theoretical concept can hardly apply it fruitfully. Conditions and opportunities to exercise "power" change with the forms of organizations. New groups rise within a political system as it moves from a traditional type, based on the norms of a secret society, toward a modern organizational type. Politically, the new groups are bound to the same "basis groups" as the veteran political leadership. Socially, they originate from various "basis groups" within and without the party. With regard to specific problems of upward social mobility and selection, criteria must be applied to new groups different from those applied to the traditional political elites within whose ranks they ascended.

[83] This was pointed out by Wolfgang Schluchter in his critique of Hans P. Dreitzel's *Elitebegriff und Sozialstruktur* (Stuttgart, 1962). See Wolfgang Schluchter, "Der Elitebegriff als soziologische Kategorie," *Kölner Zeitschrift für Soziologie und Sozialpsychologie* 15, no. 2 (1963): 250 ff.

[84] For the definition of power as decision making, see Harold D. Lasswell and Abraham Kaplan, *Power and Society: A Framework for Political Inquiry* (London, 1952), pp. 174 ff. "Power" is regarded as participation in the making of decisions, and "decision" is understood as a policy involving severe sanctions.

[85] Lipset and Bendix, *Social Mobility in Industrial Society*, p. 276.

Given these distinctions, it becomes clear that the concept of "decision making" has to be be still further refined. This holds true even more for general and long-term political decision making by the leadership group in a given system. Consequently, the difference between the creation of a general political framework and the actual transformation of a general strategy into specific and detailed instructions of economic policy, finance, or education cannot be described by a decision concept that has not been historically or empirically derived. Global interpretations must be avoided and the conceptual structure brought closer to reality. The idea of the *political elite* is an obvious solution. Dahrendorf and Zapf define a political elite as a group of persons "in a position from which they can proceed to make laws."[86] In this way Zapf attempts to bypass the distinction between leaders and nonleaders. He and Dahrendorf feel that persons occupying leading positions in a society actually make the relevant social decisions. This may apply to a greater degree to the GDR; since the reconstruction of government and society implemented by the SED leadership, only those persons occupy leading political positions who actually make the relevant command decisions.

But who makes the laws, who sets standards in the GDR—the members of the Politburo, the Secretariat of the Central Committee, the Central Committee, the State Council, or the Council of Ministers? Apparently different laws are prepared and promulgated by various subgroups in these bodies. However, these subgroups are internally differentiated and represent very different "trends" within the larger organization, the SED. Therefore, our analysis of the political decision-making process must be closely tied in with a career study of the decision makers and, if need be, with the elaboration of a composite career pattern for the political elites.[87] Careless use of the concept of political elite is thus avoided since it appears useful only in a general analysis which, for example, seeks to distinguish between administrative, intellectual and economic or managerial elites. Bethusy-Huc's definition of political elites as influencing only the formation of political will is not

[86] Wolfgang Zapf, *Wandlungen der deutschen Elite. Ein Zirkulationsmodell deutscher Führungsgruppen, 1919-1961* (Munich, 1965), pp. 18 ff. He is in agreement with Dahrendorf here.
[87] Donald R. Matthews, *The Social Background of Political Decision-Makers* (New York, 1954).

fully satisfactory here. The same applies to the term "industrializing elite" used by Kerr et al.[88] From the starting point of comparative industrial studies, these authors define an industrializing elite as the "leaders of the industrialization process," lumping together the very elites that we propose to distinguish from one another.

For the purposes of this study, the concept of a political elite is defined as follows: Political elites in the GDR comprise the leading cadres in the SED, as well as the leading functionaries in the apparatuses of the state, economy, agriculture, mass organizations, and military and cultural elites. Political elite in the narrower sense refers only to the top functionaries of the party apparatus—the party elite. If we look at the party elite from the perspective of their political and social upward mobility and, in addition, examine the differences in their professional training and functional areas, two subgroups are clearly distinguishable: first, the party bureaucrats, headed by the strategic clique of veteran functionaries who constitute the political decision-making group. These functionaries have often risen via work in the party apparatus of the KPD/SPD/SED and they fulfill almost exclusively political leadership and control functions in the Politburo, the Secretariat of the Central Committee, or the Secretariats of the SED *Bezirk* executives. The second group is comprised of the younger functionaries. Most of these men have not risen through the party apparatus but, after completing technical or scientific studies, have worked in industry or economic management positions. They mostly occupy posts in the functional areas of economics and social policy, without wielding real political power in the strict sense. These functionaries may be described as a subgroup of what has been called an "industrializing elite." This group of younger functionaries includes those within the party who are entrusted with economic and agricultural tasks. Together with the full-time economic and agricultural functionaries in the state apparatus, they exercise political influence typical for that of the younger generation. The overall social relevance of the functional areas which those groups oversee makes them an important component of the GDR's political system. In the large bureaucracies of party and state, older functionaries used to administrative work are counterbalanced by younger functionaries who

[88] Kerr et al., *Industrialism and Industrial Man,* pp. 47 ff.

occupy positions which typically require professional training. Whereas the older functionaries, on the whole, owe their present position to membership in unintegrated, more or less oppositional groups which trace their origins to the twenties and thirties, the group of younger experts attained influence via integration into a political ruling system which set the society's standards in all spheres.

These differentiations between the two subgroups of the party elite can be expanded into a distinction between two types of elites, in tacit, but intense competition with each other. This, however, need not be manifested, especially not in the political sense. The endorsement of the critical role of expertise by the political decision-makers, possibly compounded by the dynamics of the social system, remains highly qualified. The strategic clique endeavors to exploit and integrate expertise to a certain degree, but inwardly strives to retain control over these developments. The experts are to be consulted, but fenced off from the actual control arena of power. In this context, the concept of the *counter elite,* introduced by Lasswell and Kaplan and originated by Max Weber[89] may be recalled. Lasswell and Kaplan (as do many other authors, such as Edinger) repeatedly speak of counter elites as a political alternative to the decision-making elite in the general sense. Accordingly, in the classical interpretation of totalitarian systems, the concept of a counter elite has frequently been used to characterize latent or openly oppositional trends.[90] This also holds for the thesis advanced by Lange, Richert, and Stammer, namely, that the rising intelligentsia's readiness to support the system is reduced in direct proportion as it gains increased professional knowledge.[91] This variant of the counter elite concept appears meaningful only in the case of a socially and politically unstable system—e.g., the GDR up to the 1956-1957 period. In this

[89] Max Weber, *The Theory of Social and Economic Organization,* trans. A. M. Henderson and T. Parsons (New York: Free Press; London: Collier-Macmillan, 1968), p. 338; and Lasswell and Kaplan, *Power and Society,* p. 266.
[90] See Edinger, "Post-Totalitarian Leadership," p. 76.
[91] Max Gustav Lange, Ernst Richert, and Otto Stammer, "Das Problem der 'neuen Intelligenz' in der Sowjetischen Besatzungszone. Ein Beitrag zur politischen Soziologie der kommunistischen Herrschaftsordnung," in *Veritas, Justitia, Libertas. Festschrift zur 200–Jahrfeier der Columbia University, New York,* submitted by the Free University, Berlin, and the Deutsche Hochschule für Politik, Berlin (1953), p. 235.

early phase of GDR society, Wolfgang Harich and his followers (the historians, economists, and others, who were condemned as revisionists in 1956–1957) could have been characterized as counter elites in this classic sense. However, it is highly doubtful whether Robert Havemann, acting as an "individualist" in 1964–1965, can be identified as a member of the counter elite in our restricted sense.

Consequently, Lasswell's definition of the counter elite as a politically articulated opposition group in a totalitarian or authoritarian system is a highly restricted concept which cannot fully account for the phenomenon of an "institutionalized" counter elite. The "institutionalized counter elite," as defined here, is a part of the "political elite" as defined in the broader sense; in many areas it overlaps with the political elite in the narrower sense. Within this counter elite two subgroups are distinguishable, representing, respectively, the "counter" and the "institutionalized" aspects of our definition. The first group comprises those party philosophers and ideologues who are the present proponents of a specific kind of ideological revisionism.[92] A second major subgroup within the framework of an institutionalized counter elite is comprised of the party experts. As members of the political elite in the narrower sense, these men hold political positions but do not hold strategically decisive ranks, inasmuch as that they do not determine but merely oversee the implementation of actual guidelines of policy. Furthermore, this group is affiliated with a socially important group outside the narrower organizational confines of the party, namely those administrative and economic experts who, though in a sense integrated in the existing political system, occupy a tacit position counter to that of the strategic clique. Their alternative outlook originates in career patterns and social norms that diverge from those of the strategic clique and former economic functionaries.

Concepts of social norms and society can also differ. Whereas the social outlook of the institutionalized counter elite can be determined as more dynamic in the sense of an "ordered dynamic,"[93] that of the

[92] For details concerning this version of the institutionalized counter-elite concept cf. the arguments in the ensuing sections of this chapter as well as in Chapter Four.
[93] Richard F. Behrendt, *Dynamische Gesellschaft. Über die Gestaltbarkeit der Zukunft* (Berne and Stuttgart, 1963), p. 70.

strategic clique contains more pronounced conservative elements of rigidity. The institutionalized counter elite has at its core mostly younger party experts and revisionist party philosophers. But its spectrum of outlooks, backgrounds, and personalities is broad: it includes many ambitious careerists and trained scientists, plus functionaries in the fields of culture, economy and agriculture. In its basic functional groupings and the depth of its reserves of new blood, the institutionalized counter elite is more stratified and at the same time broader than the strategic clique.

We must now give our exegesis of the concept of "counter position." Party functionaries entrusted with technical and economic tasks represent the principle of functional authority and thus mobilization and vitalization of the party organization, which could in the long run permanently undermine the residual exclusivity of the political decision makers. Mobilization and vitalization are processes that invariably imply an open, spontaneously expanding cooptation of experts into the elite. This relative openness of admission into the ranks of the institutionalized counter elite contrasts starkly with the relative exclusivity of the strategic clique. What opportunities for rejuvenation have been engendered by the strategic clique, which at the same time wishes to preserve its distinct position vis-à-vis experts within the party? Have alternative career patterns been created which can compete in practice with those of the counter elite? How attractive are party careers in the SED to young adults at present?[94] These problems are dealt with in Chapters Two and Three of this study.

Furthermore, the conception of a counter elite in an authoritarian system from the sociological perspective would appear to verify in our given context the models for elite competition in parliamentarian democracies noted by Stammer. However, if we utilize Stammer's distinction between rivalry aimed at barring an opposing group from the crucial central area of power and competition with counter groups in issue areas,[95] we should remember that the given opposition groups act within larger elites. Rivalry and competition, in our context, occur among various groups within an authoritarian party, the SED. This

---

[94] This question, applied to the CPSU, also occupied Borys Lewytzkyj in his "Die Führungskräfte des sowjetischen Parteiapparates," *Osteuropa* 15, no. 11–12 (November–December 1965): 749 ff.

[95] Stammer, "Das Elitenproblem in der Demokratie," p. 87.

approach accounts for differences within the SED; on the other hand, we have qualified the concept of elite competition in its normal meaning. At present, both latent and manifest conflicts exist within the SED between the numerous efficiency-oriented institutionalized counter elites and the strategic clique. Such conflicts exist between representatives of the various functional organizations within the SED itself, of various political backgrounds, and of various age groups, among all of whom, however, there is a basic, fundamental consensus of political aims. Consequently, the conflict, as posed here, exists between groups basically integrated in their society. Our concept of the counter elite is thus grounded in the appearance of different patterns of social mobility and different views of the total society and its mores, but not in an assumption of the existence of a priori fundamentally different political goals, or for that matter "Utopias"—to recall our discussion of comparable (ideological) features of secret political societies.

With regard to the GDR, "counter position" designates more a social than a political conflict situation. Furthermore, this conflict pattern can be regarded as functional to the SED's political stability, derived from the drive for continuity of its innate power aspirations. Our interpretation naturally concurs with our previous definition of the strategic clique's rationale that it is the "given" legitimate ruler of East Germany.

SOME THEORETICAL ASPECTS OF IDEOLOGY

Some reflections on ideology and the role of the theory of ideology naturally follow any exegesis of organizational and elite theory, particularly in the analysis of transitional patterns for a party elite schooled in Marxist-Leninist dogma. Dynamic social and political change within an authoritarian party elite devoted to the tradition of Marxism-Leninism invariably finds a particular expression in the given party's ideology. Problems that arise in this connection are related to one's definition of "ideology" and its specific connotations in political science; it is also necessary to determine strictly the specifically "ideological" components in the process of change under investigation. More precisely, we here deal with the following questions for the empirical political scientist: What theory of "ideology" is meaningful if one's analysis is both theoretical and empirical? Furthermore, how can we link the concept of "ideology" to those of organization and elite in a strict methodological fashion?

These questions bring us, perforce, back to methodological considerations. Recent empirical research on ideologies (S. H. Barnes, H. McClosky, R. E. Lane, D. Minar, etc.) distinguishes between political behavior systems and political ideologies.[96] In this view, Marxist-Leninist ideology is a relatively consistent system of basic axioms and codified operational strategies of the ruling elites. These axioms and strategies are applied differently by different groups in different specific settings. Thus, ideologies are also conceived as systems which must be subdivided into their component "units." This interpretation of ideology requires a further analysis of terminological systems, codified dogma, etc., as parts (subsystems) of a comprehensive whole: the "ideological system." We can now draw a correlation between organization, elite, and ideology: All three are seen as complex systems composed of various subsystems. Our previous assertion that ideologies, propagated by elites, become politically operational only if given organizational form can thus be processed theoretically.

Our examination will be supplemented by a brief review of the concept of ideology in the history of ideas. Starting with Bacon, the French Enlightenment, and Marx,[97] the concept of ideology is found to contain three constituent elements: a claim to absolute "truth," an analytical–cognitive element, and an element of "false consciousness." The "truth" component may be seen in the commonly shared faith of the philosophers of the Enlightenment and the Utopian Socialists and Marxists in the power of "reason," in a just rule, and in an egalitarian society. Society is to liberate itself from ideological delusion by progressive self-enlightenment. The "self-evident" process of the masses' liberation is defined by the "initiates," i.e., the intelligentsia which represents, classically speaking, the critical and Utopian element in society.

[96] Samuel H. Barnes, "Ideology and the Organization of Conflict: On the Relationship Between Political Thought and Behavior," *The Journal of Politics* 28, no. 3 (August 1966): 524.

[97] For the best description of concepts of the function of ideology from Bacon to Marx and Nietzsche, see Hans Barth, *Wahrheit und Ideologie* (Erlenbach, Zurich, and Stuttgart, 2nd enl. ed., 1961).

The ideological concept is both analytical and cognitive insofar as it claims to identify the bases of political power in given societies at given stages. Basically, this involves individuals or social groups defining the function which a political elite, deluded by a distorted self-image, has in a society. H. J. Lieber has defined ideology as "a prevailing social self-image, continuously projected by the ruling group in order to secure and consolidate its power."[98] This analytical-cognitive dimension of ideology must be seen as having its origin in concepts of the mechanistic and mathematical natural sciences of the sixteenth and seventeenth centuries.[99] A mechanical, or causal, element has been preserved in the theories of both dogmatic Marxism-Leninism and the thought of numerous revisionists, from Bernstein to Havemann. Indeed, it is now being revived by both dogmatists and revisionists as they attempt to incorporate more recent phenomena, particularly the experiences of an industrial society, into the ideology.

In our opinion, an element of "false consciousness" is closely interwoven with the cognitive character of the ideological concept. Consciousness is "false" if it serves to stabilize the power of ruling elites through the mechanisms of delusion, revelation, justification, and promise. Consciousness is "cognitive" as well as "false," since the dissipation of the magical aura surrounding elites is tied up with the projection of a new understanding of man, society, and the world. This Utopian promise gradually becomes detached from its original component of reason, disguising the latter in turn.[100] Marx was able to avoid this fate for the ideological concept by defining "reason" in such a way that he did not need to strip it of its transcendental qualities. For him, reason in its concrete form in societies makes the historical process proceed toward a

[98] Hans-Joachim Lieber, *Philosophie—Soziologie—Gesellschaft. Gesammelte Studien zum Ideologieproblem* (Berlin, 1965), p. 61.

[99] For details, see Otto Brunner, "Das Zeitalter der Ideologien: Anfang und Ende," *Die Neue Rundschau* 65, no. 1 (1954): 145.

[100] "Utopian" is used here in Mannheim's sense: "Only those orientations transcending reality will be referred to by us as utopian which, when they pass over into conduct, tend to shatter, either partially or wholly, the order of things prevailing at the time." See Karl Mannheim, *Ideology and Utopia: An Introduction to the Sociology of Knowledge,* Louis Wirth and Edward Shils, trans. (New York: Harcourt, Brace & World, Inc., A Harvest Book, 1962), p. 192.

goal that is teleologically determined. He thus tied in his criticism of the capitalistic system and its repressive tendencies with the ending of man's alienation, which he took to be identical with the salvation of mankind. Marx's way of defining this transcendence has remained unique. Although many Marxists have followed him in anchoring reason in society, they have remained unable to preserve his concept of alienation in a convincing form; they have not been able to revive the transcendental point of reference which has disappeared over the hundred years of Marxist thought.

The theory of ideology corresponds to this briefly outlined structure of the concept of ideology. Thus, it may be defined as "insight into the social determination of structures, the contents of the human consciousness and their social and political functions."[101] On the basis of this definition, it may be stated that the theory of ideology is separate from given social contexts, for example, from the Workers' Movement or from a revolutionary political group. Although generalized thought not specific to any single group or class is already included in Marx's concept of ideology, the theory of ideology has developed into the sociology of knowledge only in the twentieth century.[102] The sociology of knowledge is distinguished from the theory of ideology primarily by the fact that the former is an instrument of research within the social sciences and not a universal tool to examine systems of thought. Concerning this basic postulate there is hardly any difference of opinion between various schools and approaches influenced by the sociology of knowledge. Using Mannheim's distinction between the theory of ideology and sociology of knowledge, other writers have limited ideology to the status of a historical and political phenomenon, established the interdependence of ideology and organizations, and tried to determine the functions of ideologies for specific social groups, organizations, and institutions.[103]

[101] Lieber, *Philosophie*, p. 83.

[102] Ideological criticism is to be distinguished from the sociology and knowledge, at least since Karl Mannheim published his *Ideologie und Utopie* in 1929.

[103] See especially Reinhard Bendix, *Work and Authority in Industry: Ideologies of Management in the Course of Industrialization* (New York: Harper & Row, 1963); and "Industrialization, Ideologies, and Social Structure," *The American Sociological Review* 24, no. 5 (October 1959): 613 ff. See also Seymour M. Lipset, Martin A. Trow, and James S. Coleman, *Union Democracy: The Internal Politics of the International Typographical Union* (Glencoe, Ill., 1956); C.

By elaborating this distinction and by incorporating the positive elements of Mannheim's sociology of knowledge,[104] they developed the term ideology and the theory of ideology for research in the disciplines of political sociology and political science.

Various representatives of Popper's "logic of scientific discovery" approach and those influenced by it in the field of sociology also have applied the theory of ideology to their research[105] (for example, Barrington Moore, Jr., Alfred G. Meyer, et al.). However, different in detail, all these schools have one thing in common: They use terms like "criticism," "analysis," "function," etc., in a different sense from that used in the classical theory of ideology. While the latter invariably aims at the "totality" of society and traces "the whole" in all its parts, the theory of ideology applied in the framework of the philosophy of science analyzes distinct individual strata and elements—the various

---

Wright Mills, *The Power Elite* (New York: Oxford University Press, 1956); David E. Apter, ed., *Ideology and Discontent* (London, 1964); and Hans Gerth, Die sozialgeschichtliche Lage der bürgerlichen Intelligenz um die Wende des 18. Jahrhunderts. Ein Beitrag zur Soziologie des deutschen Frühliberalismus (Diss. phil., Frankfurt-on-the-Main, 1935).

[104] The author refers to Karl Mannheim, "Beiträge zur Theorie der Weltanschauungs–Interpretation," in his *Wissenssoziologie. Auswahl aus dem Werk,* introduced and edited by Kurt H. Wolff (Berlin and Neuwied, 1964), p. 137.

[105] See also Theodor Geiger, *Ideologie und Wahrheit. Eine Soziologische Kritik des Denkens* (Stuttgart and Vienna, 1953); Donald G. MacRae, "Class Relationships and Ideology," *The Sociological Review* 6, no. 1 (1958): 261 ff; Ernst Topitsch, "Das Verhältnis zwischen Sozial- und Naturwissenschaften. Eine methodologisch-ideologiekritische Untersuchung," in Ernst Topitsch, ed., *Logik der Sozialwissenschaften,* Neue wissenschaftliche Bibliothek, Vol. 6 (Cologne and Berlin, 1965), pp. 57 ff; Arne Naess, *Democracy, Ideology, and Objectivity: Studies in the Semantics and Cognitive Analysis of Ideological Controversy* (Oslo and Oxford, 1956); Gustav Bergmann, "Ideology," *Ethics* 61, no. 3 (1951): 205 ff; David D. Comey, "Marxist–Leninist Ideology and Soviet Policy," *Studies in Soviet Thought* 2, no. 4 (1962): 301 ff; Joseph M. Bocheński, "The Three Components of Communist Ideology," *Studies in Soviet Thought* 2, no. 1 (1962): 7 ff; Ervin Laszlo, "Dynamics of Ideological Change in Eastern Europe," *Inquiry* 9, no. 1 (1966): 47 ff; Robert E. Lane, *Political Ideology: Why the American Common Man Believes What He Does* (New York and London, 1962); Barrington Moore, Jr., *Soviet Politics. The Dilemma of Power. The Role of Ideas in Social Change* (Cambridge, Mass.: Harvard University Press, 1959); and Zbigniew K. Brzezinski, *The Soviet Bloc, Unity and Conflict* (Cambridge, Mass.: Harvard University Press, rev. and enl. ed., 1967).

fields of an ideological system. The theory of ideology developed by Marx equated theory, analysis, and criticism and invariably interpreted any phenomenon in terms of its revolutionary potential; the theory of ideology influenced by the philosophy of science conceives of theory and criticism in a purely analytical sense. Empirical statements and value judgments are clearly distinguished from each other. Ideology is investigated through the approaches of causality, sociological behavior research, psychological and sociological motivation analysis, and semantics.[106] The quest of the proponents of the classical theory of ideology for "the" truth is thereby eliminated, and a distinction is made between "absolute" and "scientific" truth.[107] The proponents of the "logic of scientific discovery" claim that, since the search for truth in classical ideology was invariably associated with the investigation of changes in the respective political and social position of individuals or groups, thought could not attain objectivity in the sense of Kant, and, later, Popper. Popper's intersubjective verifiability and control were not possible in this classical type of thought. They argue further that only scientific truth played a role for the cognitive action. The theory of ideology, as conceived by the proponents of the philosophy of science, is bound to scientific truth by the disclosure—in Mannheim's terms—of the social or existential determination of thought.

The framework of this study requires a discussion of the historical and empirical dimensions of ideology. For this purpose, the term "ideology" has to be reformulated. If we apply the theory of ideology as conceived by the philosophy of science, ideology can be delineated as follows: The "fields" and "processes" of official ideology and the modes of its interpretation by various groups (e.g., within the CPSU or the SED) can in principle be separated into distinct "units," much as in an organizational system. The units in both types of systems (ideological or organizational) can be formulated similarly in the semantic sense. Furthermore, the "formalization" and "hierarchization of Marxist-Leninist ideology lend themselves to this analytic approach. The innate formalization and hierarchization indicate that the ideological dogma of Marxism-

---

[106] Naess, *Democracy, Ideology, and Objectivity*, pp. 147 ff.

[107] Ernst Topitsch, *Sozialphilosophie zwischen Ideologie und Wissenschaft* (Neuwied, 1961), p. 28.

Leninism never basically departed from the critical–rational traditions of Marx and the German philosophical idealists.

Research in the social sciences has as its task the exegesis of this tradition. It will also help to show that the core of this tradition has been transposed, or transmuted, from the official ideology into the individual variants of modern East European revisionism. Using this approach of empirical political science, we shall attempt to establish parallel conflicts between "idea" and "reality" in the hierarchical structure of party and society on the one hand, and within the ideological system itself on the other.[108] Empirical political science—endeavoring to establish the interdependence of ideology, elites, and organizations at various points in time—will thereby be enabled to handle the historical dimension. Of course, it will have to exclude an understanding of ideology, or the theory of ideology which applies the image of democratic societies in analyzing authoritarian political systems. In other words, empirical political science cannot pursue empirical research work and at the same time contribute to the process of self-enlightenment in a society. A critical–empirical approach, as used in this study, implies consideration of the fundamental nature of an historical and/or empirical object no longer subject to our direct experience. Furthermore, in such an approach we must separate from the analysis itself those philosophical reflections which do not apply strictly to the object of research.

In accordance with the concepts of organization and elites used in our study, the entire ideological range of Marxism-Leninism is described as a "system." This system encompasses the official dogma (i.e., historical and dialectical materialism), political economy, and "scientific socialism," as well as various interpretations of the dogma elaborated by the political elite, and certain modifications of those interpretations conceived by the institutionalized counter elite. An initial point of departure is thus indicated: Ideological dogma is not regarded strictly as such; we have taken into account its transformation into politically relevant thought and its application by one or more political groups. Acceptance of ideological axioms by a Communist elite is never a purely

---

[108] Cf. Hans-Joachim Lieber, *Individuum und Gesellschaft in der Sowjetideologie* (Wolfenbüttel, 1964), p. 18 and p. 34.

philosophical issue; such axioms must also be analyzed from the point of view of their transformation into actual everyday politics.

Following the scheme of Barrington Moore, Jr., and Zbigniew Brzezinski, we propose to discuss the sociological implications of the ideological concept for the categories of "official ideology" and "operating ideology." The operating ideology of the party leadership can be regarded as the "open-ended" component of the official ideology. The normative nature and consequent rigidity of official ideology leaves operating ideology as the only sphere retaining some flexibility over a long period of time.[109] Briefly, we adopt the distinction made by Brzezinski in defining official ideology as "doctrine" and operating ideology as an "action program."[110] Official ideology or doctrine refers to the theory of Marxism-Leninism, including its concrete formulations in party statutes and programs.[111] Changes of emphasis, as expressed in the operating ideology of the Communist party leadership, will seep into the area of doctrine and affect it only with the passage of time. There is, in addition, a converse interdependence of doctrine and the changing action programs of the party leadership. The axioms and theories of official ideology are frequently taken over into the sphere of operating ideology. A reverse process also takes place. For example, slogans like "the construction of Socialism is completed," or "the Socialist conditions of production have now been fully realized," appear in speeches by the party leadership as aspects of operating ideology and only subsequently are codified within official ideology.

Besides this interdependence of doctrine and action program, there exists a process of transmission of ideological statements. For example, the statements codified in the party statutes or programs are first made public in speeches by members of the strategic clique. They are then incorporated into laws, directives, and decrees (for example, after the Ulbricht speech at the Sixth Party Congress, into the "Guideline for the

[109] Moore, Jr., *Soviet Politics,* p. 420; and Brzezinski, *The Soviet Bloc,* pp. 386 ff.
[110] In discussion of the political relevance of the ideological concept, operating ideology is frequently summarized under the confusing term "propaganda." Cf. Karl Loewenstein, "Über das Verhältnis von politischen Ideologien und politischen Institutionen," *Zeitschrift für Politik* 2, no. 3 (October 1955): 197.
[111] Both party statutes and programs pertain to the doctrine as well as to operating ideology. Thus their classification is problematical.

New Economic System of Planning and Direction of the National Economy"). The formulations are passed further down to the SED *Bezirk* executives, where they are included in the various expositions of policy made by the *Bezirk* secretaries. Finally, after being processed into directives of the VVB (*Vereinigung Volkseigener Betriebe*) and VEB (*Volkseigener Betrieb*) managements on the one hand, and of the BPO (*Betriebsparteiorganisation*) and BGL (*Betriebsgewerkschaftsleitung*) secretaries on the other, they reach the lowest stage of transmission—the stage of their direct application as economic and social policy. A field analysis of ideology would be required to follow this transmission process whereby official ideology is transformed into concrete economic decisions, or to relate its actual results to the original intentions of the party elite. Such an analysis would require a semantic approach and is thus not a component part of the theoretical concepts in our analytic scheme; it would imply a much higher theoretical level of analysis. Instead, this study will concentrate on that middle range of deliberations which we have chosen to examine. Given the restrictions of an outsider's perspective, we again focus on the question of how substantive ideological change can be adequately detected. We will attempt, as well, to fit changes in the ideological field into a wider theoretical frame of reference.

Various components of ideological doctrine and the changing operating ideology can be distinguished. These are: directives to act; manipulation, or "reinterpretation," of facts (including historical traditions); justification of decisions made; criticism of the "enemy"; and the vision projected of the "promised" society. These five characteristics fulfill varying functions within the framework either of the ideological doctrine, or the operating ideology. Using these characteristics as basic determinants, we can identify the following functions of ideology: an activating and directive function; a function of articulating a self-image and a world view, which includes the major function of controlling information; a legitimizing and integrating function; and a critical and Utopian function.[112] This differentiation of the functions of ideology

[112] Richard V. Burks, using a historical perspective, has pointed out that the personal ideology of the party elite invariably includes a "theory of society." Cf. Richard V. Burks, "A Conception of Ideology for Historians," *Journal*

allows us to integrate the study of ideology with political science. Since different groups of the political elite utilize the above five functions in various combinations, processes of differentiation within the ideological and the political spheres can be related to each other. In this way, manifestations of revisionism can be investigated in their full complexity. The polycentric nature of communism has shown that, in recent years, apart from the actual political decision makers, other groups are pressing to articulate their respective views of society and politics within the range permitted by Marxism-Leninism. This articulation need not be understood primarily as a phenomenon of political opposition, although it implies to a high degree the existence of social and political alternatives, manifested in the writings of Adam Schaff, Leszek Kołakowski, Georg Klaus, Karel Kosík, Robert Havemann, Wolfgang Heise, et al.[113]

To relate the above to our treatment of elite theory—particularly the concept of the institutionalized counter elite—we may term the views of many oppositional philosophers and ideologues "institutionalized revisionism."[114] By revisionism is meant a combination of criticism aimed at the very core of the official ideology, with a certain exegesis, which claims to be true and correct, of the historical heritage; a comprehensive social and world view within the framework of the tradition now viewed differently; and a de-emphasis, with only limited preservation, of the postulate of political "praxis" and the consequent recourse to, and re-emphasis upon, the subjectivism of the Enlightenment. The characteristics of the classical pre-Marxist ideological con-

---

of the History of Ideas 10 (1959): 187. Comey distinguishes three functions of ideology: the "masking function," the "authenticating function," and the "directive function." See Comey, "Marxist–Leninist Ideology and Soviet Policy," p. 315.

[113] Adam Schaff, *Marx oder Sartre? Versuch einer Philosophie* (Vienna, Cologne, Stuttgart, and Zurich, 1964); Leszek Kolakowski, *Der Mensch ohne Alternative. Von der Möglichkeit und Unmöglichkeit, Marxist zu sein* (Munich, 1960); Georg Klaus, *Kybernetik und Gesellschaft* (Berlin, 1964); Karel Kosík, *Die Dialektik des Konkreten. Eine Studie zur Problematik des Menschen und der Welt* (Frankfurt-on-the-Main, 1967); and Robert Havemann, *Dialektik ohne Dogma? Naturwissenschaft und Weltanschauung. Hat Philosophie den modernen Naturwissenschaften bei der Lösung ihrer Probleme geholfen?* (Reinbek, 1964).

[114] This term would appear to have been coined by Richard V. Burks.

cept—demystification and mystification—thus remain in modern Eastern European revisionism. A puristic view of mankind and society, combined with recourse to a specific tradition (differently interpreted), criticism of its distortions, and, finally, rejection of the pragmatic element characterizing reformism marks these revisionist formulations.

Institutionalized revisionism differs from this form of revisionism in its attempt to adapt official ideology and operating ideology to the dynamics of an industrial society; at the same time it does not seek to transform dogma into a new revolutionary philosophy.[115] Commensurate with the change in the perceived "objective situation," this adaptation is not effected by decree "from above," or by the application of sanctions by the strategic clique, but from "below"—originating in the social and universalist views of individual thinkers. Beyond its pragmatic adaptation to industrial society—i.e., its openness towards the experience of the modern world—this revisionism is institutionalized insofar as it adheres to a special form of dogmatism that seeks to retain its original ideological heritage. Adherence to dogmatism indicates that the adaptation of institutionalized revisionism to the experience of an industrial society always seems only partially successful. The mode of its criticism and the "intensity" of the model of Utopia that it projects indicate its high degree of adaptation to the systems in which it has appeared. The Utopian-eschatological element of dogma and the power techniques of control of the strategic clique are sometimes ignored and, in any event, only partially criticized. Finally, this revisionism is institutionalized insofar as its bearers stand upon the foundations of the given political and social system and regard themselves as true Marxists or Communists. This conviction is, *inter alia,* expressed by ambition for, or occupation of, high political and/or scientific offices, and by an apparent desire to rise further in the political and social system as it is presently constituted. However, over time the route of ascent has changed. Competitive selection in an established system has replaced the former revolutionary "capture" of the commanding height in politics and society. The last-named feature of institutionalized revisionism—the acceptance of political office by its bearers—applies to the representa-

[115] In line with the analysis of Brzezinski and Huntington, *Political Power: USA/USSR,* p. 123.

tives of two groups within the institutionalized counter elite: on the one hand, party experts like Erich Apel, Günter Mittag, Werner Jarowinsky; on the other, party philosophers and ideologues like Georg Klaus and Adam Schaff. For example, in the period investigated, Apel, Mittag, and Jarowinsky either are or were candidates of the Politburo and secretaries of the Central Committee. Adam Schaff was, until late 1968, a member of the Central Committee of the Polish United Workers' Party and, until the summer of that year, a director of the Institute for Philosophy and Sociology at the Polish Academy of Sciences. Kołakowski was dismissed from his post as professor of social philosophy and history of philosophy at Warsaw University in late 1966 or early 1967. (He has now emigrated from Poland.) For many years, he was also chief editor of the journal, *Studia filosoficzne,* and a member of the editorial staff of the literary journal, *Nowa kultura.* However, even while he occupied that position, he could not remain a politically influential editor. His Utopian-revisionist outlook developed more and more into a variant of Marxist neopositivism[116] and, later, into a kind of mysticism. Even in his case, the position and function of a professor of philosophy was best suited to someone who, though at the very edge of the political system, was still—albeit to a certain minimal degree—"in."

The thought of institutionalized revisionism is especially characterized by the fact that its proponents wish to revitalize or give a more attractive cast to the operating ideology. The party experts also endeavor to render the party's bureaucracy and the state and economic apparatuses more efficient and flexible. The revisionists discussed here seek to confront the empty formulas[117] of historical and dialectical materialism (manipulated capriciously by the strategic clique) with the direct experiences and current problems of an industrialized world. They seek to restore the role of historical and dialectical materialism and political

---

[116] Cf. Leszek Kołakowski, "Ist der verstehende Materialismus möglich?," in Frank Benseler, ed., *Festschrift zum achtzigsten Geburtstag von Georg Lukács* (Neuwied and Berlin, 1965), pp. 270 ff.
[117] For the concept of "empty formulas," see particularly Ernst Topitsch, "Über Leerformeln. Zur Pragmatik des Sprachgebrauchs in Philosophie und politischer Theorie," in Ernst Topitsch, ed., *Probleme der Wissenschaftstheorie. Festschrift für Victor Kraft* (Vienna, 1960), pp. 236 ff. Alfred G. Meyer describes the empty formulas of ideological indoctrination in the Soviet Union. See his *The Soviet Political System,* pp. 354 ff.

economy so that their thought may serve as a firm ideological perspective on which to formulate actual political and economic decisions. However, they also aim at a theory of cognition consonant with the requirements of philosophy of science and, finally, a philosophy of man.

As part of the entire ideological system, with various distinct elements and strata, institutionalized revisionism can refer either to the dogma's positive or negative features (thus, incidentally perpetuating the "we—they" juxtaposition of the conspiratorial secret political society).[118] In Kołakowski's thought the "negative" forms are criticized. For example, Kołakowski distinguishes true "intellectual" Marxism from its degenerate, intellectually atrophied, "institutionalized" form.[119] Havemann identifies sterile ideological dogma with its institutional—i.e., bureaucratic—manifestations in the political system. His criticism draws on the classical version of the theory of ideology: "Consequently, the name 'Ideological Commission' for the body seeking to develop social consciousness would be a *contradictio in adjecto* since the very aim of the Communist movement is the abolition of all (formalized) ideology."[120]

The "positive" reference to dogma is found in the works of both Adam Schaff and Georg Klaus. Schaff calls for an absolute "ethical historicism." Referring to the utter absence of a philosophy of man within the current conspectus of Marxism-Leninism, he demands that this state of affairs be terminated.[121] To give another example, the cybernetic model of society, which the philosopher of science, Klaus, has been developing, is explicitly conceived of as a positive expansion of some basic axioms in historical and dialectical materialism. Klaus returns repeatedly to the central problem posed, which for him consists in "applying cybernetic knowledge to the further development of historical materialism and other aspects of the Marxist social studies. . . ."[122] Institutionalized revisionism thus inherently combines both positive and negative evaluations of official ideology, as we have defined it. This

---

[118] Cf. Leopold Labedz in his "Introduction" to *Revisionism,* ed. by L. Labedz (New York: Praeger, 1962).

[119] Kołakowski, *Der Mensch ohne Alternative,* p. 17 and passim.

[120] Havemann, *Dialektik ohne Dogma?,* p. iii.

[121] Schaff, *Marx oder Sartre?,* p. 16.

[122] Klaus, *Kybernetik und Gesellschaft,* p. ix.

characteristic synthesis of positive and negative dogmatic elements in revisionism, which have become more and more apparent since the Polish October and the Hungarian Revolution in 1956, must be regarded as tendencies toward more open-ended views. In fact, this is an ambivalent, hesitant openness vis-à-vis the concrete, existential experiences of an industrial society. This ambivalence can be noted in the outlooks of thinkers of quite different predictions, such as Klaus and Schaff on the one hand, and Kołakowski on the other.

2

Trends of Continuity and Change in the SED Organization

1. Introductory Remarks

Chapter One presented in conceptual terms the conflict between the strategic clique and the institutionalized counter elite in a highly industrialized Communist society. This question will be examined in greater detail through the investigation of selected centers of the party organization. The actions of the strategic clique are aimed largely at securing its position of power and thus at controlling the processes of organizational change in society. The party experts, on the other hand, seek organizational developments within the SED which would permit maximum adaptation to a changing industrial society. However, attaining power and seeking adaptation to economic and technical progress need not be mutually exclusive.

This study focuses mainly on the Central Committee of the SED. The transformation of this institution from an exclusively acclamatory and declaratory organ to a cooperative, transmittable and—above all—consultative assembly is sketched below in order to prepare an empirical analysis of its social composition in Chapter Three. The Central Committee had certain coordinating and transmittable functions before 1963, but with the institution of the "new economic system" these tasks have assumed priority. We shall also document the high value placed on expertise by party experts and functionaries insofar as it has been expressed in organizational measures. Discussion will further include the earliest indications of the ideological phenomena discussed in detail in Chapter Four.

2. The Party Congresses of the SED between 1954 and 1963

Three party congresses took place between 1954 and 1966–1967: the Fourth Congress, March 30–April 6, 1954; the Fifth, July 10–18, 1958; and the Sixth Congress, January 15–21, 1963. (See Appendix 1 for the Seventh Congress, April 17–22, 1967.) In addition, the Third Party Conference was held March 24–30, 1956. This section will emphasize only those decisions and events relevant to the SED's development of social policy.[1] Changes in the social policy of the SED leadership are documented by speeches and decisions made at the party congresses and conferences. The dynamics inherent in East German society, the rise of new elites, and the functionalization of the upward mobility processes are reflected in these SED self-images. The party leadership sought to cope with the problems arising from this situation in its decisions at the congresses.*

    The Fourth Congress of the SED was held under the rubric of the "new course" of 1953. Malenkov's fall in February 1955 brought this to a halt—at least in the economic and social spheres. Despite emphasis on the "class struggle directed inward," the Fifth Congress served as preparation for the pragmatic direction of the economic sphere evident at the Sixth Party Congress. In 1954 the strategic clique was not yet able to administer and control society and the economy competently. The "building of Socialism," proclaimed in 1952, had hardly gone beyond state expropriation of industry and agriculture and the seizure of the "commanding heights" in politics, as well as in the economic and social spheres. The problem of power in the GDR was decisively resolved by

---

* Editor's note: Party conference (Parteikonferenz) must be distinguished from party congress (Parteitag). In comparison with the congress which takes place once in every four years (cf. Fourth SED Statute, article 34), the conference will only be summoned at special occasions (cf. Fourth SED Statute, article 47). Up to 1971 the SED has organized eight party congresses (in 1946, 1947, 1950, 1954, 1958, 1963, 1967, 1971) and three party conferences (in 1949, 1952, 1956). *Plenary sessions* (or plenums; in German *Tagungen, Plenen*) of the Central Committee take place between party congresses at least once every six months (cf. Fourth SED Statute, article 40). The plenary sessions between two congresses are given numbers (i.e. first plenum, second plenum etc); the counting starts again after each congress held (thus, there is a first plenum in 1963 as well as in 1967).

[1] For historical background of the development of the SED, see: for the years 1945-1949 Hans Müller, *Die Entwicklung der SED und ihr Kampf für ein neues Deutschland (1945 bis 1949)* (Berlin, 1961); for the period until 1956, Carola Stern, *Porträt einer bolschewistischen Partei. Entwicklung, Funktion und Situation der SED* (Cologne, 1957); and Stefan Dörnberg, ed., *Beiträge zur Geschichte der Sozialistischen Einheitpartei Deutschlands* (Berlin, 1961), published on the occasion of the fifteenth anniversary of the SED. On the twentieth anniversary (1965) appeared the proceedings of party conferences under the title *Im Bündnis fest vereint, 1945-1965* (Berlin, 1966). See also Werner Horn, ed., *20 Jahre Sozialistische Einheitspartei Deutschlands. Beiträge.* (Berlin: Karl Marx Party Institute of the SED's Central Committee, 1966).

the intervention of Soviet troops on June 17, 1953. The country's traditional social structure had already been considerably changed, although privately controlled industry and agriculture were still contributing an essential part to the national output and had even visibly recovered under the influence of the "new course." Since the party leadership had been made insecure by the riots of June 17, 1953, Malenkov's fall, and the failure of central economic planning, new experiments were proclaimed with some hesitation. This situation permitted the continuation of more traditional social norms among the populace. At that point the norms posited by the party had very shallow rooting in East German society.

As the first East German reaction to the Twentieth CPSU Congress, the Third SED Conference displayed self-contradictory currents. On the one hand the "Directive for the Second Five-Year Plan of the National Economy in the GDR 1956–1960" demanded more rapid nationalization of private industry and agriculture. On the other, Soviet criticism of Stalin visibly affected the self-confidence of many important SED functionaries, such as Karl Schirdewan. An overall evaluation of the SED's performance during the years 1952–1954 was drawn up by the party leadership only at the Fifth Party Congress in 1958. However, largely because of the rigorous purges in the SED in the spring of 1958, the overall situation in the party remained unresolved at the Fifth Congress. By contrast, the Sixth Congress inaugurated a period of drastic rationalization in the apparatus of the party, state, and economy. Only since early 1963 have the conflicts in the organizational, social, and ideological sectors of the SED apparatus covered by this study emerged.

THE FOURTH CONGRESS OF THE SED (MARCH 30–APRIL 6, 1954)
The "new course" theme continued to dominate the proceedings of the Fourth Congress. Full reversion to Stalinism was not as yet obvious. Instability in the ranks of the SED had been heightened by the Zaisser-Herrnstadt crisis of 1953.[2] At the Fourth Congress reexamination

---

[2] Wilhelm Zaisser, Minister of State Security and member of the Central Committee and the Politburo since 1950 and Rudolf Herrnstadt, since 1949 editor-in-chief of *Neues Deutschland* and since 1950 member of the Central Committee and candidate of the Politbüro, were ousted from the Central Committee and

of SED membership status was central to the discussions on the party's future line as outlined in Ulbricht's report to the Central Committee and the reports delivered by Hermann Matern and Alfred Neumann. Criticism of Zaisser and Herrnstadt accompanied demands to organize the SED as a "revolutionary avant-garde" rather than a mass party.[3] Soon after Schirdewan was to emphasize the "revolutionary" character of the party, citing the statute adopted on that occasion.[4]

This reference to the party statute deserves attention if only because it indicates the equivocal attitude of the party leadership toward the social policy to be adopted. Greater differentiation among party members is one of the major goals. Apart from the functionaries, we meet for the first time rank-and-file individuals among nominees to member and candidate status in the SED. The time requirements for candidacy indicated the social structure of the party sought by the SED. Article 21 of the statute fixes the duration of candidacy at six months "for blue-collar workers active in industry or agriculture for at least five years before the date of application, for young workers in industry or agriculture, for members of the German Peoples' Police and the National Peoples' Army, who have met one of these conditions before enlisting in these units,"; one year "for all other workers, foremen and other subordinate technical cadres, for members of agricultural cooperatives, for members of the German Peoples' Police and the National Peoples' Army, who met at least one of these conditions before their enlistment"; two years "for white-collar employees, working small farmers, artisans, members of the intelligentsia and all others."[5] The strategic clique was undoubtedly attempting to form a solid cadre

---

the Politburo in July 1953 because of "antiparty factionalism," and relieved of their functions. For the background of the Zaisser–Herrnstadt affair and its connection with the events of June 17, 1953, see Carola Stern. *Ulbricht: A Political Biography* (New York: Praeger, 1965), p. 141.

[3] Hermann Matern in the report of the Central Party Control Commission in *Protokoll der Verhandlungen des IV. Parteitages der SED, 30 März bis 6, April 1954 in der Werner-Seelenbinder-Halle zu Berlin*, 2 vols. (Berlin, 1954) (cited hereafter as *Protocol of the Fourth SED Congress*) 1: 206 ff., 208.

[4] Karl Schirdewan, "Nach dem IV. Parteitag," *Neuer Weg* 9, no. 8 (April 1654): 3.

[5] Third Statute of the Socialist Unity Party of Germany, in Protocol of the Fourth SED Congress, II: 1124 ff.

nucleus within the SED and raise the proportion of workers in its membership.

These measures must be viewed against the background of the party leadership's weakened authority, especially in the economic sphere. The leadership sought to compensate for this shortcoming by granting, in accordance with Article 70 of the Third Party Statute, party organizations the right of control "in activities of management," particularly in enterprises engaged in production, trade, transport, and communications. This policy aimed at creating the organizational prerequisites for removal of the considerable shortcomings in planning and the losses in nationalized enterprises. The measure was accompanied by initial reductions in planned targets. This development was a harbinger of the relative independence of the enterprises, equally hoped for and feared by many party functionaries.

This hardened line in the industrial economy reached a further peak six months after the Fourth SED Congress at the Twenty-First SED Central Committee Plenum, November 12–14, 1953. The measures invoked included increased participation by the FDGB *(Freier Deutscher Gewerkschaftsbund),* expansion of the production councils, creation of activist commissions in the enterprises, and the introduction of socialist competition in a permanent mass campaign (e.g., the Frida Hockauf movement and the Wilhelm Pieck campaign among the trade unions). At the Twenty-First Central Committee Plenum, Ulbricht demanded "spontaneous" increased output by workers in mass competition:

The previous methods of competition bear the character of personal obligations. True competition consists of competing for the fulfillment of specific production tasks, the lowering of costs and material-consumption norms from man to man, brigade to brigade, and division to division.[6]

On the other hand, the SED regarded mass competition as an effective step in the further consolidation of the social order. With specific consideration for June 17, 1953—assessed as a reversal within the framework of "the achievement of Socialism"—"Socialist construction" was to be sought in the phase of stabilization in 1954. The mass

[6] Walter Ulbricht, *Zur sozialistischen Entwicklung der Volkswirtschaft seit 1945* (Berlin 1959), pp. 235 ff.

competition campaign was regarded by the SED as an integral component of this "construction" process.

SED activity in the factories was accompanied by an ever more rigid position vis-à-vis the rural populace. Although no major disturbances occurred in the countryside as a result of June 17, 1953, migration and flight of independent farmers and agricultural workers forced the SED to strengthen its historically weak position in rural districts. The party was forced to increase rapidly its influence in the countryside and create "bases of support." In this context we cite some of the most important measures taken by the strategic clique. At the beginning of 1954, the Seventeenth Plenum of the Central Committee decided to introduce "country Sundays" in all rural districts to ensure more effective mass agitation. Special functionaries for agitation were appointed in SED *Kreis* (subdistrict) executives for these country Sundays to explain the policy of the party and stimulate an increase in agricultural production.[7] The strengthening of the SED's position in the countryside also served to accelerate the campaign for the formation of agricultural cooperatives (LPG). This campaign was further intensified during 1954–1955. By comparison with 1960, the year of "full collectivization" with more than nineteen thousand cooperatives and one million members, there were only some five thousand cooperatives with 160,000 members in 1954.[8]

Emphasis on the cadre principle, the decreed improvement of the party functionaries' positions in the economic sphere, and increased agitation in the countryside were accompanied by a series of measures in the field of social policy, which need not be mentioned in detail at this point. The gap between party and society was widened by the SED's cadre policy.[9] Although Ulbricht in his Congress speech sharply attacked the "bureaucratism" of the party functionaries, he nevertheless

[7] For the introduction of the "country Sundays," see the Central Committee Resolution of January 23, 1954 (Seventeenth Plenum), "Über die Entfaltung der politischen Massenarbeit im Dorf und die nächsten Aufgaben in der Landwirtschaft," in *Dokumente der Sozialistischen Einheitspartei Deutschlands,* vol. 5 (Berlin, 1956): 50.

[8] For 1954, see *Statistisches Jahrbuch der Deutschen Demokratischen Republik* (Berlin 1956) 1: 197. For 1960, see ibid. (Berlin, 1961) 6: 422.

[9] See Joachim Schultz, *Der Funktionär in der Einheitspartei. Kaderpolitik und Bürokratisierung in der SED* (Stuttgart and Düsseldorf, 1956). See Chapter Fourteen, pp. 364 ff.

placed "Marxist-Leninist knowledge" decisively above "expert knowledge" in the schooling of young cadres.[10] The bureaucratic directives of the leadership naturally served to insulate the party from the people. A visible expression of this withdrawal by the party into itself was its resolute retreat from the "block" policy cultivated during the "new course" in 1953, after the fall of Malenkov in the spring of 1955. This picture was completed by many other details, such as the affront to the churches administered by the so called "youth consecration" to party ideals.[11]

The period of 1954–1958 was marked by the uncertainty and eclecticism of the measures pursued by the strategic clique. Nevertheless, the SED further consolidated its position, not just in the economic and agricultural bureaucracies, but in the whole of East German society. Despite internal shocks, the party survived the two serious crises of June 1953 and the Twentieth CPSU Congress.

THE FIFTH CONGRESS OF THE SED (JULY 1958)

Official history has represented the Fifth Congress as a decisive step in the historical development of the GDR. Indeed, a significant development seems to have occurred then, since, following the Soviet model (and basing itself directly on the Second Party Conference of July 1952) the program proclaimed the onset of the "building of Socialism in

[10] Walter Ulbricht, "Die gegenwärtige Lage und der Kampf um das neue Deutschland," in *Protocol of the Fourth SED Congress*, 1: 181.

[11] With the establishment of the Central Board for Youth Consecration on November 14, 1954, this ceremony—the secular equivalent of confirmation and communion—was introduced in the GDR as a "social institution supplementing in a variety of ways and methods the socialist education and acculturation work carried out by the parents, the secondary schools, the Ernst Thälmann Pioneer Organization, and the FDJ and helping to prepare the fourteen-year-olds for their entry into the community of laborers." The proportion of youngsters taking part in the ceremony rose from 17.7 percent in 1955 to 44.1 percent in 1958, 80.4 percent in 1959, and 90.7 percent by 1962. See Heinz Frankiewicz et al., *Pädagogische Enzyklopädie*, 2 vols. (Berlin, 1963) 1: 482 ff.

[12] Walter Ulbricht, "Die gegenwärtige Lage und die neuen Aufgaben der SED" in *Protokoll der Verhandlungen der 2. Parteikonferenz der SED, vom 9. bis 12. Juli 1952 in der Werner-Seelenbinder-Halle zu Berlin* (Berlin, 1952) (hereafter cited as *Protocol of the Second SED Conference*), pp. 61 ff.

the GDR."[12] Since the two periods of "transition"—1945 through October 1949, when the GDR emerged as an independent state, and 1949 through the middle of 1952, when the economic foundations of the new social order were created—the SED leadership has increasingly emphasized the irreversible nature of Germany's partition. Accordingly, party history records the "new" situation from the summer of 1952 onward: "The struggle is now consciously directed, and socialist transformation has commenced in all spheres."[13] This formula implied an increased effort by the SED to "overcome the relics of capitalism embedded in the thinking and the habits of people," particularly since the Fifth Congress.[14]

For the Politburo, the primary objective of the Fifth Congress was the justification of the policies followed since the Second Party Conference in 1952.[15] The period of transition from capitalism to socialism was thought over.[16] Despite the fact that the party leadership's political concepts were still guided largely by the "inward-directed class struggle" (though modified),[17] it nevertheless recognized the widening of the gap

[13] Werner Horn, *Die Errichtung der Grundlagen des Sozialimus in der Industrie der DDR, 1951 bis 1955* (Berlin, 1963), p. 162. See Stefan Doernberg, *Kurze Geschichte der DDR* (Berlin, 1964), p. 196.

[14] Ibid., p. 324.

[15] See the resolution of the Fifth Party Congress of the SED "Über den Kampf um den Frieden, für den Sieg des Sozialismus, für die nationale Wiedergeburt Deutschlands als friedliebender, demokratischer Staat," in *Protokoll der Verhandlungen des V. Parteitages der SED, 10. bis 16, Juli 1956 in der Werner-Seelenbinder-Halle zu Berlin,* 2 vols. (Berlin, 1959) (hereafter cited as *Protocol of the Fifth SED Congress*)2: 1338 ff.

[16] See Walter Ulbricht, "Der Kampf um den Frieden, für den Sieg des Sozialismus, für die nationale Wiedergeburt Deutschlands als friedliebender, demokratischer Staat," in *Protocol of the Fifth SED Congress,* 1: 39ff. For the dogmatic foundations of the thesis on the termination of the transition period from capitalism to socialism, see especially Fred Oelssner, *Die Übergangsperiode vom Kapitalismus zum Sozialismus in der Deutschen Demokratischen Republik* (Berlin, 1956). This is a reprint of a lecture delivered by Oelssner at the Theoretical Conference of the Economic Institute of the German Academy of Sciences in Berlin on March 11, 1955.

[17] The modification of the class struggle thesis as compared with 1952–1953 is particularly apparent in the party leadership's new assertion that it had ever since 1949, and especially since 1952, sought the cooperation of the broadest possible strata of the population in "socialist reconstruction." For particulars, see Carola Stern, "Der V. Parteitag der SED. Die DDR soll Schaufenster des Ostblocks werden," *SBZ-Archiv,* vol. 9, 16 (August 1958): 242 ff.

between this concept and political and economic reality, particularly as regards the behavior and orientation of most social groups. The previous approach was criticized with some disquiet in the leadership bodies of the SED. However, this self-criticism did not lead immediately to a more realistic assessment of the overall economic and political situation.

The main outlines of the political program adopted by the Fifth Congress can be summarized as follows: Because of the increase in international economic competition, the third five-year plan, originally scheduled to end in 1965, demanded the "overtaking of West Germany in per capita consumption of the population." Socialist competition was now to become *de rigueur* in all industrial enterprises. In addition, the party leadership made its first attempt to strengthen the hitherto reduced authority of management in the economy which had been undermined by the party itself for years. This attempt was, however, accompanied by further measures which might well have the opposite effect. In his report to the Fifth Congress Ulbricht demanded the obligatory introduction of "innovative methods" in all nationalized enterprises.[18] These methods were intended to produce an increase in the labor-intensive production of highly processed goods, in accord with decisions of the Conference of the Communist and Workers' Parties of May 1958 and the subsequent Ninth Convention of COMECON in June 1958. Actually, these measures further weakened management and authority in the factories down to the level of foreman.[19] Finally, the SED intruded extensively into other organizational spheres, particularly in the state apparatus. This authority had to be constituted to counter excessive bureaucratization and isolation from society and the economy. In Ulbricht's words, the state apparatus was now to assume its primary "function as the main

[18] Ulbricht, "Der Kampf um den Frieden": 100. On the evolution of the innovators' movement (*Neuererbewegung*) within the "new economic system," see particularly the work of Rudi Weidig, based on sociological studies, *Neuerer in der technischen Revolution* (Berlin, 1965).

[19] Of the extensive literature on the so-called "foremen's debate," see Herbert Dönitz, "Die Stellung und die Aufgaben des Meisters in der sozialistischen Produktion," *Einheit* 13, no. 11 (November 1958): 1621 ff. and the summarizing conclusions of Fritz Hörning, "Mehr Unterstützung den Meistern!" *Einheit* 17 no. 2 (February, 1962): 60 ff. Under the "new economic system" the function of the plant foreman seems most significant. See Kurt Pöschel and Joachim Tripoczky, *Probleme der Kaderarbeit in der sozialistischen Industrie* (Berlin, 1966), particularly p. 25.

instrument of socialist construction."[20] The legal basis was provided by the "Law on the Improvement and Streamlining of Work in the State Apparatus of the GDR," February 11, 1958.[21] Although the efficiency of the state apparatus was not at first enhanced, Apel and Mittag retroactively and correctly regarded this law as the true beginning of the "New Economic System of Planning and Direction of the National Economy."

The structure of the state apparatus and the core of the state's direction were adapted to the development of the forces of production and the state of consciousness of our people. As a result of this process the guidelines of the states' activities have been largely established. These now provide a foundation for the transition to the new economic system of planning and direction of the national economy.[22]

The most important regulations concern leading economic bureaucracies. After the dissolution of the previous National Economic Council (VWR), the State Planning Commission under Erich Apel became the "central organ of the Council of Ministers for planning and guiding the national economy, as well as for the control of plan implementation."

Two innovations significant for future economic developments in the GDR were the establishment of "economic councils" in the *Bezirk* (district) councils[23] and the Associations of Nationally Owned Enterprises (VVB) as "leading economic organs" of the centrally directed national enterprises. The formation of economic councils on the *Bezirk* level signaled the initial phase of decentralization, as well as increasing differentiation. The principle of locating decison-making powers where practical was first put into practice during this period, albeit hesitantly.

---

[20] Ulbricht, "Der Kampf um den Frieden," p. 56.

[21] "Gesetz über die Vervollkommnung und Vereinfachung der Arbeit des Staatsapparates der DDR," in *GBl der DDR* (1958) 1: 117 ff.

[22] Erich Apel and Günter Mittag, *Ökonomische Gesetze des Sozialismus und neues ökonomisches System der Planung und Leitung der Volkswirtschaft* (Berlin, 1964), p. 28.

[23] According to Article 12 of the "Gesetz über die Vervollkommnung und Vereinfachung der Arbeit des Staatsapparates," p. 120, "economic councils of the *Bezirk* councils shall be established for the standardized management of the economy in the *Bezirk*. These councils operate under the auspices of the *Bezirk* councils as well as of the State Planning Commission in order to plan and control the economy in the *Bezirk*." At the end of 1961 their name was changed to *Bezirk* economic councils.

Despite the formation of these two economic chains of organization, power was, on the whole, further concentrated in the State Planning Commission. Most VVBs were subject to the respective departments of this authority and the newly formed economic councils were not only subject to *Bezirk* councils, but also to the State Planning Commission. The sphere of this Commission's power was further widened by other organizational measures. Following dissolution of the eight industrial ministries, as well as of the State Secretariat for Local Economy and the Council of Ministers' Advisory Board for Construction, their duties largely devolved upon the State Planning Commission.

These changes were paralleled by a restructuring in many other areas of society, especially education. In July 1958 polytechnic education was reorganized and extended. From the beginning of September 1958, 450,000 pupils of the seventh to twelfth grades in the comprehensive polytechnical secondary school were to be familiarized for three to four hours a week with the basic problems of industrial environment in a nationalized or cooperative enterprise.[24] Although at this time there were no generally accepted and specific curricula[25] and each school administration had to work out the content of the student work program in agriculture or industry independently, the basic aim of these new directives was clear from the beginning: a return to and simultaneous narrowing of universalistic-Utopian concepts determined by the Marxian philosophy of man. The UTP program was designed to give a general insight into the foundations of technology and production, without professionalization of school training. Professionalized training was only instituted after the expansion of the principles of the "new economic system" in education by decision of the Politburo and the Council of Minis-

[24] See the Education Ministry's directive of July 30, 1958, "Zur Durchführung des Schuljahres 1958–1959," extracts of which were reprinted in: Siegfried Baske and Martha Engelberg, eds., *Zwei Jahrzehnte Bildungspolitik in der Sowjetzone Deutschlands. Dokumente,* 2 vols. (Berlin, 1966) 1: 397 ff. See also Kurt Hager's report to the Fourth Plenum of the Central Committee in January 1959 (which contains the first analysis of results): "Die weitere Entwicklung der polytechnischen Schule in der DDR," *Neues Deutschland,* January 21, 1959.
[25] The first curriculum for a comprehensive polytechnical secondary school was published by the Ministry of Education on June 20, 1959. An abstract was published in *Zwei Jahrzehnte Bildungspolitik,* 2: 29 ff.

ters in July 1963.[26] The program of the SED and the innovations called for by the Fifth Party Congress were based on an already differentiated social concept; principles with a pragmatic orientation—primarily in economic policy—were recognizable, as was the retention of a dogmatic philosophy of man. The Fifth Congress can thus be described as a point of departure for the SED leadership's concept of society—a concept governed by ideological dogmatism even after 1963, but influenced to a greater degree by a pragmatically operating ideology. Despite retention of the basic axioms of historical and dialectical materialism, the beginnings of a concept more in tune with social reality (in the sense of organizational policy) can be traced from the spring and summer of 1958. The decisions of the Fifth Congress can be regarded as the genuine precursors of the "New Economic System of Planning and Direction of the National Economy," introduced at the Sixth Congress.

Continued uncertainty on the part of the SED leadership in the ideological sphere and its reversion to dogmatism became evident in the policy toward party cadres. Despite the introduction of polytechnical education in 1958, the training system for party cadres was not reformed. Instead, the rigid guidelines of cadre training established during 1950–1952 were retained at the Thirty-Third and Thirty-Fifth Central Committee Plenums of October 1957 and February 1958, respectively. These should be regarded as decisive historical dates, for the elimination of the last political alternative to the Ulbricht group within the SED (composed of the Politburo members Schirdewan, Wollweber, and Oelssner) was underway or had been decided upon. Like Vieweg in agriculture, Oelssner wished to encourage rationalism in the economy at a point which Ulbricht's strategic clique deemed premature for securing its power base.

Schirdewan's wish to "democratize" the SED was perceived as a

[26] "Gemeinsamer Beschluss des Politbüros des Zentralkomitees der SED und des Ministerrats der DDR über die Grundsätze der weiteren Systematisierung des polytechnischen Unterrichts, der schrittweisen Einführung der beruflichen Grundausbildung und der Entwicklung von Spezialschulen und -klassen," of July 3, 1963, in *Zwei Jahrzehnte Bildungspolitik,* 2: 278 ff. For interpretation, see Siegfried Baske, "Das Experiment der polytechnischen Bildung und Erziehung in der DDR," in Peter Christian Ludz, ed., *Studien und Materialien zur Soziologie der DDR* (Cologne and Opladen, 1964), pp. 195 ff.

threat. He and Oelssner may be classified as members of the classical political, rather than institutionalized, counter elite (as the term is used in this study). After a decisive struggle against the counter elite, in 1958 the strategic clique succeeded in re-establishing its positions of power. The struggle was waged, in typical fashion, in the ideologically determined field of politics. The contrast that has emerged since 1962–1963 between the highly ideological and technocratic conceptions of social processes which heralded the rise of the institutionalized counter elite—played no role at this time in the exclusion of Oelssner, Vieweg, Schirdewan, and Wollweber.[27] The downgrading of the opposition was followed by a widespread purge that affected all fifteen SED *Bezirk* executives, as well as the SED *Gebiet* executive Wismut.[28] The extent of this purge indicates the bitterness of intraparty conflicts—a bitterness that certainly must have continued to exist in latent form since the Twentieth CPSU Congress. In the eyes of the strategic clique the purge was indispensable, since Schirdewan had for many years been chief of SED cadres and had gained considerable influence on cadre policy. However, from a historical and political perspective the question arises whether this shakeup among the ranks of the *Bezirk* executives was

[27] Karl Schirdewan (born in 1907), a secretary of the Central Committee and director of the Section for Party and Mass Organization since 1952, became a member of the Politburo in 1953 and, with Ernst Wollweber (1898–1967), who succeeded Zaisser in 1953, was ousted from the Central Committee in February 1958. Schirdewan lost all his positions and became director of the State Archives' Administration in Potsdam. The criticism leveled against Wollweber and Oelssner (born in 1903), at one time the economic expert of the party, as well as against Vieweg by the party leadership, has been summed up in Erich Honecker's Report to the Politburo of the Thirty-Fifth Plenum of the Central Committee, *Neues Deutschland*, February 8, 1958. The points of the program of the Schirdewan–Wollweber faction have been summed up by Heinz Brandt, *Ein Traum der nicht entführbar ist. Mein Weg zwischen Ost und West,* with an introduction by Erich Fromm (Munich, 1967), p. 328 ff. For an interpretation, see Hans Schimanski, 'Die Revolution in Glaspalast. Der Kampf der Reformer gegen Ulbricht," *SBZ-Archiv,* 9, no. 4 (February, 1958): 50 ff. For the dispute between the party leadership and the agronomist Kurt Vieweg (born in 1911), see Peter Christian Ludz, "Revisionistische Konzeptionen von 1956/57 in der DDR," *Moderne Welt,* 2, no. 4 (1960–1961): 360 ff.

[28] See in particular Stern, *Ulbricht,* pp. 107 ff.; and Martin Jänicke, *Der dritte Weg. Die antistalinistische Opposition gegen Ulbricht seit 1953* (Cologne: 1964), p. 185 ff.

not intended to provide an initial opportunity for opening up positions in the SED for rising experts. This question appears to be all the more justified since Schirdewan cooperated mainly with veteran Communists and nonemigrants within the party. The causes and effects are certainly closely intertwined in this case as well: Ideological uncertainty necessarily compelled the retention of a "party of cadres," in principle insulated from outside forces and isolated within its own society. This compulsive reaction must have played a preponderant role during the purge. For example, in the spring and summer of 1958 ideological training of cadres was again given first priority in party affairs[29] (mostly through Alfred Neumann's influence). As a result of the crisis within the party, dogmatic ideological indoctrination (especially of *Bezirk* and *Kreis* secretaries) and retention of the rigid traditional norms and mores of the KPD and the SED were made obligatory. The repercussions of this training in the social and economic spheres in effect legitimized a bureaucratic style of leadership, as well as a monolithic, centralized party apparatus largely territorial in structure. This not only prevented reconstruction of and differentiation within the party apparatus, but continued to impede the development of a more realistic approach toward ongoing tasks in the economic sphere.

THE SIXTH CONGRESS OF THE SED (JANUARY 1963)

The Sixth Congress should be viewed within the context of two major events that created a basically new situation in the GDR: first, "protection of the border" (i.e., the building of the Wall); and second, the ending of the forced collectivization of agriculture during 1960–1961. Given this situation and the example of Soviet administrative reform in the fall of 1962, Ulbricht, in his speech to the Sixth Congress, voiced a changed political outlook based on a more realistic assessment of the economic situation and the hitherto unexplored economic potential of the GDR. The highlight of Ulbricht's speech was the proclamation of "The New Economic System of Planning and Direction of the National

[29] Schirdewan himself, as head of the CC cadre section, is supposed to have worked out training guidelines as early as 1955–1956. His scheme was to provide a well-rounded vocational college education, mainly through correspondence courses, to all members of the Central Committee and the SED *Bezirk* executives.

Economy."[30] As he did at the Fifth Congress in 1958, Ulbricht criticized the shortcomings of the economy, especially planning procedures and the price structure. Moreover, his criticism projected a relatively realistic picture of the tense economic situation in the GDR. Compared with the unrealistic goals of the economic program of 1958—among others, that of attaining the per capita consumption level of West Germany within a few years—economic and social aims were formulated in a far more cautious, restrained fashion.

In some areas of policy the changed attitude of the SED was already evident. For example, nationalization of private enterprises between 1958 and 1963 continued, sometimes rigorously, but, except for agriculture, no longer systematically. As reported by the Central Committee at the Sixth SED Congress, the proportion of private enterprises dropped from 7.8 percent in 1958 to 3.1 percent in 1961. In 1958 private craftsmen's shops still comprised 93 percent of all enterprises in those branches; in 1961 their proportion dropped to 67 percent. By the same token the number of craft production cooperatives rose from 1304 in 1958 to 4090 in 1962. Membership in these bodies likewise increased from 61,567 in 1958 to 170,243 in 1962.[31] Private enterprises in commerce and the handicraft and trade industries were directly subordinated to the planning system, but more in the technical–economic than in the sociopolitical sphere. In this context it is worth marking the formation of "product groups"[32] as well as the financial participation of the state in private enterprises.[33]

[30] Walter Ulbricht, "Das Programm des Sozialismus und die geschichtliche Aufgabe der SED," in *Protokoll der Verhandlungen des VI. Parteitages der SED. 15. bis 21. Januar 1963 in der Werner-Seelenbinder-Halle zu Berlin,* 4 vols. (Berlin, 1963) (hereafter cited as *Protocol of the Sixth SED Congress*), 1: 28.

[31] According to the Report of the Central Committee to the Sixth SED Congress in *Protocol of the Sixth SED Congress,* 4: 5 and 157-159.

[32] Product groups are "groups of related plants (or production departments in major plants) within a given industry, which produce technologically similar or technically associated products, semifinished products, structures or parts," quoted from Jochen Theel, *Technische Revolution und Erzeugnisgruppenarbeit,* (Berlin: 1965), p. 83. For a discussion of resulting problems that existed in the "new economic system" until the beginning of 1964, see Peter Christian Ludz, "Widersprüche im Neuen Ökonomischen System. Organisatorische Probleme der Erzeugnisgruppen," *SBZ-Archiv,* 15, no. 7 (April 1964): 101 ff.

[33] On the basis of the resolution passed at the Twenty-Fifth Plenary Meeting of

This more realistic assessment was accompanied by a shift of emphasis in the ideological sphere. At the Seventeenth Central Committee Plenum in October 1962 Ulbricht was no longer speaking of the imminent victory of socialism, but of the "victory of socialist production conditions" in the GDR.[34] These formulations also modified the "class struggle" thesis. The line adopted at the Fifth SED Congress was thus rendered more flexible vis-à-vis the populace. Khrushchev's formula of "class struggle directed inward," which he stated in his address to the Sixth SED Congress, was to be channeled in particularly flexible and "sensitive" directions in the GDR. The First Secretary of the CPSU went on to say that "the class struggle in the German Democratic Republic often assumes acute forms." Having made such veiled allusions to the SED leadership's more sophisticated policy toward the rank and file of society, Khrushchev proceeded to expressly emphasize the "broad front of all patriotic, progressive, and democratic forces" forged by the SED.[35] In light of measures introduced under the "new economic system" and the social policy of the party leadership since 1963, it would be correct to say that the theme of the class struggle directed inward has been muted rather than sharpened. In his comments Khrushchev confirmed that the Stalinist thesis of an increasing intensification of the class struggle had been jettisoned, even in the GDR.

The introduction of the new economic system was accompanied by a basic organizational restructuring of all East German bureaucratic institutions. In the party apparatus the hitherto dominant "territorial principle" was replaced by the "production principle," a measure which

the Central Committee of the SED in October 1955 on "The New Situation and the Policy of the SED (Preparation for the Third Party Conference)," (supplement to *Neues Deutschland,* November 1, 1955), state participation in private firms was first introduced. The share of the so-called seminationalized enterprises in the GNP rose steadily from 1956 (0.2 percent) to 1964 (6.6 percent) while at the same time the share of the private enterprises receded from 40.6 to 6.9 percent. For the period 1956–1962, see *Statistisches Jahrbuch der Deutschen Demokratischen Republik,* vol. 9 (Berlin, 1964), p. 27. For the period after 1960, see ibid., vol. 11 (Berlin, 1966), p. 37.

[34] Walter Ulbricht, "Die Vorbereitung des VI. Parteitages der Sozialistischen Einheitspartei Deutschlands," *Neues Deutschland,* October 6, 1962.

[35] N. S. Khrushchev in his address to the Sixth SED Congress in *Protocol of the Sixth SED Congress,* 1: 296.

paralleled developments in the Soviet Union at the time. Khrushchev impetuously invoked a greater consideration for the production principle in his address to the Sixth SED Congress:

By adapting the party organization and its leading organs to the production principle we are endeavoring to shape the direction of the national economy by the party in a more expert, concrete, and objective fashion, so as to bring it closer to the factories, construction enterprises, cooperatives, and state farms.[36]

Although the territorial and production principles existed side by side in the SED before the Sixth Congress, the territorial structure of the party was predominant. In his major address to the Sixth Congress Ulbricht tied the adaptation of the party, state, and economic apparatuses to the introduction and future consideration of such economic factors as profit, price, profitableness, etc.: ". . . new tasks demand the consistent realization of the production principle in the guidance of the economy and in connection with this the conversion of the Associations of Nationally Owned Enterprises to the principle of cost accounting."[37] The connection between party reorganization and economic considerations can be established only by taking into account the restructuring of the VVBs.

The most important elements of the new economic system—slated for full development in the new seven-year plan (1964–1970)—are the new role of the VVBs and the modification of the "system of economic levers" detailed by Ulbricht. The new "socialist concerns" (i.e., the VVBs) are to be responsible for technical and commercial development. Previously, the VVBs served as links between the Council of Ministers and the VEB; they have now become relatively independent units designed to guide the total development of individual branches of industry, according to each one's productive potential. Concern for presently available productive capacities on the part of the SED leadership was also expressed by the introduction of the production principle in the top management echelons of the VVBs.[38] Accordingly, the decision-making roles of VVB general directors were strengthened

---

[36] Khrushchev "Address to the Sixth SED Congress," p. 293.

[37] Ulbricht, "Das Programm des Sozialismus," p. 112.

[38] This has been pointed out by Erich Apel and Günter Mittag, *Wissenschaftliche Führungstätigkeit. Neue Rolle der VVB* (Berlin: 1964), p. 41 and passim.

and the sphere of their obligations widened. Their future responsibilities were to include profit-and-loss accounting, the balance sheet, organization of the administrative and socially important cooperative relations in their respective branches of the economy, and—to a certain extent—marketing of products. The managing directors of the VVB were now held responsible for supervising the introduction of modern methods of consumer research, and were further entrusted with establishing closer relations between their factories and industrial research institutes and all branches of scientific research. These measures applied primarily to the following branches of industry: chemicals (particularly the petrochemical industry), electrical engineering, metallurgy (at the final processing stage), machine building (particularly textile machinery), power, and transport.

The guiding considerations of the "new economic system" cited by Ulbricht were not limited to price, cost, profit, or profitableness. A "system of economic incentives" for the individual worker was proclaimed. Instead of relying on pure ideological incentives to increase production, the new system appealed to the material interests of the individual. Some examples of these new incentives are the linking of bonuses to wages while taking into account "efficient performance," and the awarding of extra time off for high productivity.[39] The most important suggestions of the economist Jevsei Liberman of Charkov were thus incorporated into the new economic system. Liberman called for an improvement in planning procedures through strengthening planning and guidance at the enterprise level. Furthermore, he advocated premiums based on real production figures and demanded that profitableness be made the decisive criterion for assessing the productivity of an enterprise or individual employed there.

The decisions adopted at the Sixth SED Congress thus followed the economic course first—albeit hesitantly—adopted by the Fifth Congress. From 1963 through the spring of 1967 there occurred no fundamental deviation from these concepts, particularly in the economic and political fields. Cultural policy, however, constitutes an exception to

[39] Ulbricht, "Das Programm des Sozialismus," p. 101 ff; for detailed comparison, see Karl C. Thalheim, *Die Wirtschaft der Sowjetzone in Krise und Umbau* (Berlin, 1964), p. 82.

the rule; here, the attitude of the East German Communist leadership appears to have hardened, as in the Soviet Union, Poland, and Czechoslovakia.[40]

3. Domestic Social Consequences of the New Economic System

The introduction of the "new economic system" ushered in social consequences for East Germany that extended beyond simple economic policy or the reorganization of the economic, state, or party bureaucracies. The reorganization of the party on the basis of the production principle broke down many of the barriers that had existed between East German society and the SED since the SED's assumption of political power. Indeed, the SED's "secret society" features were already undergoing erosion by virtue of the fact that the SED had been a mass party from its inception. However, the party organization and methods of selecting candidates, both characteristic of a secret society, were present until the early 1960s. With the advent of the "new economic system" and consequent reforms in the party apparatus, the SED's conspiratorial nature became restricted to the top echelons of party leadership. Since then, the characteristics of a secret society and those of a large mass organization have obviously coexisted in the SED. The consequences of this new situation cannot yet be assessed in detail. There are indications within GDR society of a "spontaneous" mobilization not directed by the party leadership, albeit initiated from the top. Nevertheless, the basic trends of this mobilization are clearly recognizable. They are characterized principally by the either open or tacit approval of previously taboo social conflicts by the strategic clique. For this reason the theses reported in Chapter One concerning the phenomenon of social conflicts in totalitarian systems will be taken up once more in this context and in a more concrete form. Simultaneously, some of the social conflicts characteristic for the general political situation in the GDR around the middle of 1963, that have actually made their appearance, will be outlined both here and in following sections.

---

[40] On the exacerbation of the cultural and political situation in the German Democratic Republic, see the contributions of Kurt Hager, Alfred Kurella, Christa Wolf, and Hanna Wolf at the Eleventh Plenary Session of the Central Committee in December, 1965, in *Neues Deutschland,* December 19, 1965.

For the first time in the history of the SED the idea of "nonantagonistic contradictions,"[41] propagated by Mao Tse-Tung and elaborated by Stalin, was liberated from its arid schematism and brought into closer contact with political reality. This principle is now the subject of intense controversy in the Soviet Union. Significant conflicts between the party and society, between the vast bureaucracies of the party, state, and economy, and between party functionaries and factory managers were for the first time not merely explicitly identified, but also recognized as having a possibly positive function for the political stability of the entire system. This did not apply to the attitude toward *all* social conflicts. The party leadership's emphasis on the "system of economic levers" does indicate increased individual incentives. But the system was, and is, invariably "directed to eliminate all contradictions between the basic interests of society and the material interests of the individual in the narrower sphere of everyday life."[42] This formulation indicates that the SED's effective adaptation of wage policy to the desire for incentives and to the productive capacities of the individual is still subject to economically set limits. The SED leadership thus admits the existence of social and organizational conflicts, but continues to claim the right to declare them either capable of solution or socially dysfunctional. The strategic clique does not permit free and open resolution of these conflicts, but repeatedly creates new organizational channels into which they are to be diverted.

Although the strategic clique took greater account of social tensions, the classic conflict between party leadership and factory managers assumed new dimensions in the GDR. Over the first eighteen postwar years party functionaries in enterprises were engaged primarily in passing on and supervising the implementation of administrative directives. However, with the introduction of the production principle, they have assumed executive functions in the socioeconomic sphere. This does not seem to have perceptively intensified the conflict between the

---

[41] For particulars, see Peter Christian Ludz, "Widerspruchsprinzip und Soziologie" in Erik Böttcher, Hans-Joachim Lieber and Boris Meissner, eds. *Bilanz der Ära Chruschtschow* (Stuttgart, Berlin, Cologne, and Mainz: 1966), pp. 307 ff.
[42] Erich Apel and Günter Mittag, *Planmässige Wirtschaftsführung und ökonomische Hebel* (Berlin, 1964), p. 55.

party secretaries in enterprises and management. On the contrary, the conflict appears to have been dampened by an increase in the influence of experts on party policy in enterprises in the wake of the creation of bureaus of industry and construction at the *Bezirk* and *Kreis* levels of the SED apparatus. Furthermore, the decision-making powers of VVB general directors and managers of large enterprises have broadened so much since 1963 that representatives of the SED at the enterprise level have actually been deprived of some of their politically based authority. Thus, Bendix's model of East German society[43] has been outstripped by reality. Incessant pressure, compulsion, terror, and the enforcement of party authority at any price can no longer be regarded as fundamental characteristics of this society. Beside the securing and consolidation of power, economic and technical efficiency of the system are now assigned top priority.

As Victor Thompson has stated, the supplanting of an organizational principle rooted and legitimized in an authoritarian system by the criteria of functional authority does not invariably lead to an intensification of traditional conflicts or the generation of new ones, even in other (e.g., Western) societies. Leadership groups and those occupying other positions in large bureaucratic organizations on the whole tend to deny the existence of incipient social conflicts or blame them upon incompetent individual functionaries, but not on the system per se.[44] This idea seems the more applicable to the situation in the GDR, since recognition of intra- or interorganizational conflicts by the party leadership would legitimize the principle of diverse aims within and among the various organizations and thus officially reduce the authority of the party-leadership phenomenon. The transferral of general political or pure power conflicts to the social sphere discussed in Chapter One is thus confirmed.

A further consequence of the institution of the "new economic system" is the fact that progressive opening up of the SED to social currents has increasingly impressed the features of a career-oriented society upon the GDR. A highly industrialized social system based on

[43] Reinhard Bendix, *Work and Authority in the Course of Industrialization* (New York: John Wiley & Sons, 1956), pp. 434 ff., p. 443.
[44] Victor A. Thompson, *Modern Organization* (New York: 1963), p. 123.

functional efficiency must—in accordance with modern developmental trends—produce an ever greater number of academically trained personnel and patterns of increasingly specialized professionalization, with careers planned far in advance, in order to remain competitive or even viable. Such a trend was initiated by the leadership when it introduced the "new economic system" and the accompanying processes of differentiation and rationalization in the functional areas of the party, state, and economy. This trend has developed a relatively powerful and inherent dynamism all its own, largely characterized since 1963 by the increasingly evident rise in the upward social mobility of new elites.

The rise of a technocratic elite in the economy is shown by the general directors of the VVB. This elite has not necessarily gone through the cadre training of the SED apparatus. Available biographical data on the general directors of the VVB and the managers of the VEBs permit the assumption that even in East Germany the attainment of leading economic positions is increasingly predicated on an institutionally predetermined training program.

The following career pattern seems to apply to a large number of economic leaders. After completing their studies in the natural or technical sciences or economics (in many cases at the Technical University of Dresden, the Mining Academy in Freiberg, or the University of Economics in Berlin–Karlshorst) these future economic leaders enter the upper-middle level of the industrial pyramid as managerial assistants, engineers, etc., in one of the large industrial combines, such as the VEB Leuna-Werke "Walter Ulbricht," the VEB Elektrochemisches Kombinat Bitterfeld, or the VEB Chemische Werke Buna in Schkopau. After a successful probationary period, they tend to rise rapidly to top executive positions at these enterprises. The flight of many leading economists to West Germany up to mid-1961, attrition among the pre-War generation in enterprises, plus the need to replace executives who have been "kicked upstairs" since 1945 can be regarded as additional contributory causes of professional mobility in the economy, as well as the declared intention of the strategic clique to rejuvenate their leadership cadres, especially at the top and middle levels.

The preceding indicates that the economic and social policy implemented since the Sixth SED Congress has led to or has been accelerated by internal social change. Explicit recognition of social conflicts by the strategic clique and its approval of the social rise among new elites have released new forces with a strong inherent dynamism in East German society. Social policy, reflected in the measures of the strategic clique, is thus characterized by two phenomena: First, the party leadership groups were apparently interested in accommodating rising social elements both within and outside their own ranks. Second, the party leadership appears to have succeeded—although in limited fashion—in linking the professional destiny of rising nonparty elites to its own fate by offering them opportunities of advancement, rather than by fiat or compulsion. This has certainly narrowed the gap between the party and the people since 1963. However, new possibilities of conflict exist, since the strategic clique can permit a challenge to its political power by competing elites only to a limited degree.

4. Changes in the Organizational System of the SED

THE PARTY STRUCTURE AT VARIOUS STAGES (A SCHEMATIC COMPARISON) Compared to 1958, the organizational structure of the SED had changed greatly by 1963. The restructuring affected the party's organs at the central, *Bezirk,* and *Kreis* levels as well as its primary organizations. The Fourth Party Statute of 1963 and the Politburo decree of February 26, 1963 define the outline of the new order.

A glance at Figures 1 and 2 reveals that the organizational structure of the SED in 1963 was characterized primarily by separation of functions among "line" and "staff" executive bodies at all levels. Certain functions were removed from the party's "line" organizations (i.e., the Central Committee Secretariat and the secretariats of the *Bezirk, Kreis,* and *Stadt* executives) and taken over by the newly established "staff" organizations (i.e., the bureaus, commissions, and departments). The central and regional party control commissions and the revision commissions at all levels remained unaffected; they had existed side by side with the secretariats (or bureaus) in 1958 and before.

The new "staffs" were organized on the production principle. The following production branches were affected by the changes: industry

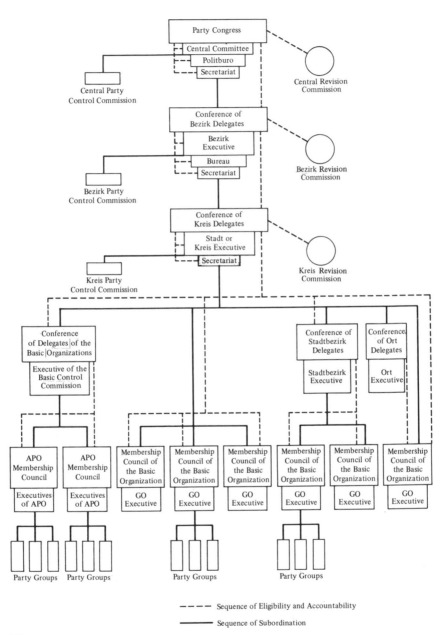

Figure 1.
Organizational scheme of the SED in 1958 (according to article 3 of the Fourth SED Congress, as amended by the Fifth SED Congress). Source: *20 Jahre Sozialistische Einheitspartei Deutschlands,* Werner Horn, ed. (Berlin, 1966), p. 388.

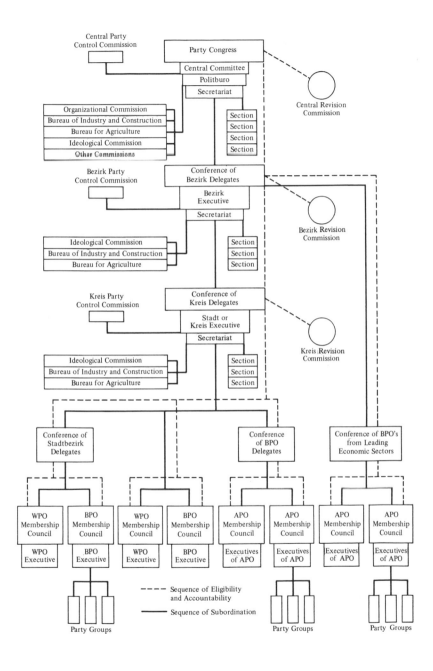

Figure 2.
Organizational scheme of the SED in 1963 (according to article 4 of the Sixth **SED** Congress). Source: *Ibid.*, p. 389.

and construction, transportation, trade and supply, agriculture, ideology, agitprop, and party organization. It appears that the executive organs of the "line" organizations that had existed until the end of 1962—primarily on the *Bezirk* and *Kreis* levels—had failed to meet the requirements of a differentiated economic and social system. For example, numerous factories could not fulfill their planned quotas because unwieldy party organizations interfered with production. The new policy, emphasizing "staff" formation, was accompanied by a tightening up within the "line" organizations themselves. For example, the bureaus and secretariats at the *Bezirk* level that existed up to February–March 1963 were now consolidated into secretariats with greatly reduced membership.

In contrast to the organizational structure of the SED from 1958 to 1962, party organizations in important enterprises of the centrally directed industries were now subordinated to the bureaus of industry and construction at the *Bezirk* level. Party organizations in agriculture were analogously structured. However, the actual pattern of subordination is not made clear in the decree of the Politburo. The decree could be interpreted as in Figure 2, taken from an official publication of the strategic clique: the bureau of industry and construction on the *Bezirk* level is in contact with its associated *Betriebsparteiorganisationen* (BPO—i.e., party organization in each factory) only via the secretariat of the *Bezirk* executive, and there is no direct influence by the Central Bureau of Industry and Construction on its *Bezirk* branch. Representatives of the counter elite tend toward a different interpretation; they regard the bureaus of industry and construction as relatively more independent entities at all levels vis-à-vis the "line" organization, and as more closely associated with each other.

THE INTRODUCTION OF THE PRODUCTION PRINCIPLE

The 1963–1964 renovation of the organizational structure of the SED apparatus followed the Soviet model, replacing the territorial principle with that of production. At the November 1962 plenum of the CPSU Central Committee, Khrushchev announced that in the future the party would be organized on the production principle—a major administrative reform, interpreted by Boris Meissner as a "revolutionary departure in the prevailing administrative structure of the Soviet Union," and "the most fundamental alteration of the organizational structure in the party since the October Revolution."[45] Special executive party organs were to be formed for industry and agriculture. The numerous lower-level party organizations of the CPSU, previously responsible for both industrial and agricultural affairs, were to be dissolved and replaced by separate party committees. However, the Central Committees of the CPSU and the Soviet republics were less affected by this reorganization. The Central Committee structure was merely supplemented by bureaus for industrial and agricultural production, as well as by an ideological commission.

In accordance with the reform demanded by Khrushchev, the Politburo of the SED underwent additional reorganization at the upper levels. The Sixth Party Congress made it clear that the SED had not blindly followed the Soviet model. The territorial principle remained fully valid. The secretariats of the SED *Bezirk* and *Kreis* executives continued to direct the work of respective bureaus and commissions. The emphasis on the production principle since the beginning of 1963 seems to have involved the creation of separate suborganizations for specific functional areas of the party apparatus. The principle of division of labor was introduced in the larger organizations of the SED. Accordingly, article 25 of the Fourth Party Statute, adopted at the Sixth SED Congress, states: "The party is constituted on the production and territorial principles. Its guiding activity is organized on the principle of production."[46]

The territorial principle shaped the party's structure to a considerable extent until the spring of 1963. Starting with the Politburo, the Central Committee Secretariat, and the Central Committee apparatus, the party was organized by *Bezirke* (districts), *Kreise* (counties), *Städte* (cities), and *Orte* (towns and villages), as well as *Betriebe* (enterprises) and *Verwaltungen* (administrations). Establishing the BPOs beside the other party bodies (in enterprises and administrations)

---

[45] For instance Boris Meissner, "Die grosse Verwaltungsreform Chruschtschows," *Osteuropa,* 13, no. 2–3 (February–March 1963): 87 and 91.

[46] Fourth Statute of the Socialist Unity Party of Germany, in *Protocol of the Sixth SED Congress,* 4: 419. The restructuring of the SED party organizations according to the production and territorial principle has become apparent since the Fourth Party Congress. See Section 27 of the Third Statute of the SED, p. 1126.

violated the territorial principle. The production principle classifies the party apparatus along lines of "spheres of production." In the form introduced in the GDR in 1963 the "spheres of production" are still largely amalgamated at the territorial level. The most important of these are industry, construction, agriculture, and ideology. The division of the economy and society along the lines of spheres of production affects the work of the party organizations in the apparatus of the state and the economy, as well as that of the basic-level party organizations in all industrial and agricultural enterprises. Production spheres are thus those sections of the social system from which the economic pattern can be more directly and efficiently planned, guided, and controlled by the SED. By applying the production principle, or by classifying economy and society in terms of spheres of production, economic planners intend to organize East German society along the lines of the desired or existing socioeconomic structure. The decisive effects of the production principle on the organizational structure of both the party apparatus and the SED youth organization, *Freie Deutsche Jugend* (FDJ), indicates the importance attributed to this organizational principle by the party leadership and the close relationship between the FDJ and the SED.

Richard Herber (then and now a section head in the Central Committee apparatus) justified the introduction of the production principle as follows:

Since economic tasks have become greater and more complex, new, higher standards must be applied; therefore, it has become necessary to improve the party's guidance of the economic development of the GDR. The previous forms of guidance no longer suffice; a change in leadership activity and the creation of corresponding organizational forms are needed to meet these new requirements. The leadership activities of the party are therefore organized on the production principle, which guarantees a more concrete, systematic, and objective guidance, together with improved consideration for the special requirements of industry and agriculture. Higher quality personnel work is correspondingly necessary.[47]

Erich Honecker, a Politburo member and Central Committee Secretary for Security, explained the introduction of the production principle in a speech to the Sixth SED Congress:

The claims of various *Bezirk* and *Kreis* executives to the effect that their

[47] Richard Herber, "Zur Leitung der Parteiarbeit nach dem Produktionsprinzip," *Einheit,* 18, no. 5 (May 1963): 4.

agricultural tasks often do not permit them to solve industrial problems contain some truth. Let us turn to the Halle district for an example. This is the site of our chief chemical industries, so important to the development of our national economy and of great significance to the entire Socialist camp. Moreover, other important enterprises for machine building, mining, light industry, etc., are located there. This *Bezirk* is also an important producer of agricultural products. If the *Bezirk* executive were to retain the present methods of [economic] direction, it would be difficult to maintain firm control of both industry and agriculture while attaining the necessary pace of development.[48]

Indeed, organizational control of economic matters had become particularly difficult in "mixed" districts for the secretariats of the SED *Bezirk* and *Kreis* executives.[49]

The SED leadership attempted to solve four major problems with the increased application of the production principle. First, the previously inadequate organization of the party apparatus was to be strengthened and improved. The complicated mechanism of a differentiated industrial society could no longer be administratively controlled, let alone directed, by territorially organized groups. In particular, the bureaus in the *Bezirk* and *Kreis* executives were prevented by their size and bureaucratic style from imparting the necessary impulse to the GDR's economy. The territorial principle was therefore to be supplemented by a form more suitable to the modern economy. Second, the style of the party bureaucracy was to be adapted to the requirements of a dynamic industrial society. Third, information gathered by the party at various levels was not to be evaluated primarily by the central apparatus, but was to be applied in more effective fashion at the lower levels.[50]

[48] Erich Honecker, "Das Parteistatut der Sozialistischen Einheitspartei Deutschlands," *Protocol of the Sixth SED Congress,* 2: 158.

[49] It should be noted here that the production principle, the enforcement of which was entrusted mainly to the Bureau for Industry and Construction was not confined to the party apparatus but also played a decisive role in the organization of the Associations of Nationally Owned Enterprises (VVBs). Apel and Mittag (*Wissenschaftliche Führungstätigkeit,* p. 41) have clearly formulated the expanded application of the production principle to the core industries.

[50] Regarding the effectiveness of the decisions, we may, according to Karl W. Deutsch, distinguish between two systems of decision making: those able to utilize the information they require and those unable to do so. See Karl W. Deutsch, *The Nerves of Government. Models of Political Communication and Control* (London: 1963), pp. 161 ff. The question of whether, and to what extent, the "mixed" organizational systems of the Communist parties belong to Deutsch's second category is beyond the scope of this study.

A more rapid and objective flow of information was sought. The leading economic experts of the SED clearly recognized that "it was impossible to control centrally the complex multiplicity of the production process in all its detail."[51] Fourth, the production principle permitted the entry of younger, properly trained party functionaries whose élan and dynamism made it possible for them to rise quite rapidly within the ranks of the party apparatus.

Analysis of the social structure of the Central Committee (to be discussed in Chapter Three) indicates a shift of emphasis since 1963 from predominantly political aims—i.e., maintenance of political power—toward economic and social priorities. The party leadership originally aimed at attaining, solidifying, and maintaining political power. Since the end of the 1950s—particularly after the Sixth SED Congress—the construction of a functionally efficient economic and social system (called for as early as the Second SED Conference in 1952) has received high priority. However, the realization of this aim has long met with almost insuperable resistance.

After acknowledging the primary importance of functional efficiency, the Politburo expanded its guiding social principle. It became increasingly apparent to the strategic clique that in a highly industrialized and specialized economy and society it was no longer feasible to lump all the desirable leadership qualities in one supreme decision-making body. A gap between functional expertise and the political savoir-faire of the power seekers became evident. A party leadership which continued to ignore this gap would eventually lose its alleged unity. Therefore, the traditional, hierarchical line of the party—which served to ensure continuity—and the associated type of bureaucratic authority had to be adapted to the conditions of a dynamic industrial society. To acknowledge objective–functional, as opposed to ideological–functional, criteria for authority was to intrude an "alien" order into the established order of a large organization. Such a development could lead to a reduction in the authority of the established group, though not necessarily of the political system. This process, which threatens the strategic clique, the accepted style of leadership, and the staffing of the

[51] Apel and Mittag, *Planmässige Wirtschaftsführung,* p. 53.

top party bodies, can be observed in the Soviet Union and is a result of growing stability. During the early revolutionary stages in the Soviet Union power and functional expertise could be united only in one person. The heroic image of Lenin pushed by party propaganda originated during this period. The Soviet and East German practice of identifying political with functional expertise disregards actual historical circumstances. The inefficiency of the organizational structure of both parties, the phenomenon of the personality cult, etc., is a result of this incorrect assertion, as well as the leadership's insistence upon structural unity and uniformity in the party system.

THE BUREAUS AND COMMISSIONS OF THE POLITBURO

At the end of February 1963,[52] and shortly after the Sixth SED Congress, four "bureaus," or "commissions," were organized in the Politburo: the Bureau of Industry and Construction, the Bureau of Agriculture, the Ideological Commission, and the Agitprop Commission. These organizations were established at the Central Committee level and, except for the Agitprop Commission, extended down to the *Kreis* level. The *Kreis* executives were required to organize along lines corresponding to the economic structure of their respective areas—i.e., either a bureau of industry and construction or a bureau of agriculture, and in every case an ideological commission, was appointed. This was not a sudden step. Ulbricht had announced "certain structural changes in the work of the party executive" at the Seventeenth Central Committee Session in October 1962.[53] He went on to state "that the production principle will in the future be applied to the activities and structure of the leading party organs."

[52] According to the Resolution of the Politburo of the Central Committee of the SED, February 26, 1963, "Über die Leitung der Parteiarbeit nach dem Produktionsprinzip," *Dokumente der Sozialistischen Einheitspartei Deutschlands,* vol. IX (Berlin, 1965), pp. 331–335.

[53] Cf. the second part of Walter Ulbricht's speech to the Seventeenth Central Committee Session, "Die Vorbereitung des VI. Parteitages der Sozialistischen Einheitspartei Deutschlands," *Neues Deutschland,* October 14, 1962. For analysis, see Hans Schimanski, "Parteiaufbau nach Produktionsprinzip. Die SED wird nach sowjetischem Muster reorganisiert," *SBZ-Archiv,* 14, no. 8 (April 1963): 119 ff.

While an Ideological Commission and an Agitprop Commission already existed under the aegis of the Politburo, the new bureaus and commissions, organized on the production principle, were "staff" rather than "line" organizations. Thus, the Politburo Decree of February 26, 1963 states that "the activity of the bureau is largely independent." The consequent organizational independence of these new bodies was counterbalanced by the way in which they were staffed. Commissions and bureaus at the Politburo level were headed by full or candidate members. For example, Kurt Hager, a Politburo member, is Chairman of the Ideological Commission and Albert Norden, likewise a Politburo member, is Chairman of the Agitprop Commission. Günter Mittag, a candidate member of the Politburo, took over the Bureau of Industry and Construction. Gerhard Grüneberg, another candidate member, was appointed Director of the Bureau of Agriculture. Thus, members of the strategic clique occupied the functional areas in ideology and agitprop, while supervision of the economic and technical fields fell to representatives of the institutionalized counter elite, at least in the Bureau of Industry and Construction.

For our analysis, the Bureau of Industry and Construction and the Ideological Commission are the most relevant.[54] The two leading SED economic experts, Erich Apel and Günter Mittag, jointly worked out the guidelines for the activities of the bureaus of industry and construction at all levels, and developed the principal outlines of the future economic policy of the party. Directors and functionaries of these bureaus may be

[54] The Bureau of Agriculture and the Commission for Agitprop Affairs could be excluded. Among other things, the Bureau of Agriculture is in charge of the basic-level organizations of the SED in the Agricultural Council (established at the Council of Ministers). The Agricultural Council has replaced the Ministry of Agriculture and Foresty, which was dissolved early in 1963 and is responsible for the implementation of the agricultural plans decided upon by the Politburo. In line with the organizational structure of the Bureau of Industry and Construction and the Ideological Commission, agricultural bureaus were also set up in the *Bezirk* executives of the SED in the rural areas. The *Bezirk* and *Kreis* agricultural bureaus are in charge of party organizations in the agricultural institutes, the LPGs (agricultural cooperatives) and VEGs (nationally owned farms). Together with the Agricultural Council, the Bureau of Agriculture is required to carry out a current analysis of the economic position of the LPGs and VEGs and in collaboration with the Bureau of Industry and Construction, to coordinate the "development problems of agriculture" with industrial development.

regarded as representatives of the technocratic group. It is they who will have to implement the new pragmatic style of leadership that has been called for.

The Politburo Decree of February 26, 1963 bestowed comprehensive power on the bureaus of industry and construction and the secretariats of the SED *Bezirk* executives attached to it:

The Bureau concentrates its activity primarily upon implementation of the party decrees for a more rapid rise in labor productivity through scientific and technical advances, and will elaborate new problems in the fields of politics, ideology, economy, and organization. It will also propagate the best achievements of party work in the various branches of the economy and in the various *Bezirke*. The Bureau will assume the political leadership of socialist mass competition in order to attain high levels of scientific and technical achievement, particularly in the leading branches of the national economy. In this context, the Bureau is also responsible for the development of effective production propaganda, for agitation work, and for the furtherance and development of the cadres in areas of functional responsibility.[55]

Apel's and Mittag's concepts regarding the future tasks of the Bureau of Industry and Construction were from the very beginning directed toward the fulfillment of economic tasks. The organizational guidelines of the bureaus were conceived along these same lines:

The basic-level party organizations of economically important enterprises in centrally directed industries, as well as those of the leading enterprises, are directly controlled by the bureaus of industry and construction in the *Bezirk* executive bodies. The bureaus of industry and construction within *Kreis* executive bodies are responsible for party work in several centrally directed enterprises that do not belong to the leading branches of the national economy, as well as in basic-level organization of *Bezirk-* and *Kreis-*directed economy, insofar as these are not pilot plants [*Leitbetriebe*].[56]

Also,

In establishing these activities to be carried out by the bureaus of industry and construction and the party executives in the VVB, we are reaching the completion of the process whereby the party organizations

[55] Politburo Resolution of February 26, 1963, p. 331. For analysis of the resolution, see Herber, "Zur Leitung der Parteiarbeit," p. 15. Herber seems to put even greater stress than the Resolution on the "organic integration of the economic and organizational with ideological political work."

[56] *Das funktionelle Wirken der Bestandteile des neuen ökonomischen Systems der Planung und Leitung der Volkswirtschaft,* publication of the Bureau for Industry and Construction (Berlin, 1964), p. 11.

and their executives are placing a concrete emphasis upon economic aspects. . . .[57]

Despite emphasis on the economic and organizational tasks of the central bureau, there was some consideration of mass political activities at the beginning of 1963. Accordingly, Ulbricht, in his speech to the Sixth SED Congress, characterized the area of responsibility of the bureaus of industry and construction as "comprehensive." He stated that the proper direction of party work is guaranteed only if it proceeds essentially according to the principle of production. This means that the bureaus of industry at the Central Committee, at the *Bezirk* executives, and at the *Kreis* executives are in command of the party organization in the economic councils, the VVB, and the institutions, as well as of the basic organization within the industrial enterprises.

A few paragraphs later this point is made in even clearer terms. "These bureaus are obliged to guide work in their sphere of activity in all aspects—i.e., political, economic, and cultural."[58]

The different conceptions of how the Bureau of Industry and Construction were to function illustrate the divergence in outlook between the institutionalized counter elite and the strategic clique. Apel and Mittag, as representatives of the counter elite, emphasize economic efficiency and the need for a party apparatus adapted to an industrialized society. Ulbricht, representing the established strategic clique, sees the party apparatus exercising political, ideological, and economic influence without any necessity for restructuring the system from within. Thus, the representatives of the counter elite postulate a more independent role for these bureaus than does the strategic clique. However, both Ulbricht's statements at the Sixth Congress and the Politburo decree of February 26, 1963 were equivocal enough to permit the representatives of the counter elite to reach their own interpretations. Apel, Mittag, and other leading party experts appeared to neglect ideological tasks during 1963–1964. SED technocrats concentrated on drawing experts into party work. They dealt very little with mass politics, i.e., the continual organization of mass meetings of basic-level party organizations in the

[57] Günter Mittag in his contribution to the debate of the economic conference of the Central Committee of the SED and the Council of Ministers of the German Democratic Republic, "Durchsetzung des Produktionsprinzips in der Parteiarbeit," *Die Wirtschaft* 18 no. 26 (1963): 27.

[58] Ulbricht, "Das Programm des Sozialismus," pp. 233 and 245.

factories. Instead, they called for conventions of party activists in various branches of industry.

Such conventions, based on similiar concrete conditions in the respective branches of industry whose enterprises are faced by similar problems and economic tasks, permit a thorough discussion of the tasks of party work. Generalized discussion cannot predominate at such conventions. Discussions are limited to the concrete problems of the branch in an objective, considered tone, motivated by a sense of high political responsibility.[59]

Apel and Mittag not only rejected traditional forms of mass agitation and production propaganda as of minimal worth, but also attempted both to restructure the SED from its basic-level organizations by convening party activist meetings in the various industries, and to introduce a new working style in the basic-level party organizations. (The strategic clique's unequivocal reaction to these measures, as the growing economic decision-making power of the Bureau of Industry and Construction became apparent toward the end of 1963, will be discussed below.)

It may be assumed that the newly constituted bodies associated with the Politburo were formed with the intention of creating an organizational form with its own structure of authority and working style. This type of organization, necessitated by increasing differentiation and rationalization of socioeconomic control, constitutes a first attempt at integrating a genuinely "alien" structure of authority—i.e., the functional authority that can be identified in industrial enterprises—into the organizational structure of the party apparatus. The accompanying dangers and possibilities of the SED's rapprochement with society were perceived clearly by several leading SED functionaries. As early as March 1963, before the Second Economic Conference of the Central Committee and the Council of Ministers in June, Richard Herber was trying to conceal the structural conflict between party functionaries and party experts.

. . . this does not mean that the party leadership is assuming operative leadership of production. The production principle brings the party closer to production, not from the standpoint of administrative control, but in the political sense, as the leading representative of the workers.[60]

[59] Apel and Mittag, *Ökonomische Gesetze des Sozialismus,* p. 128.. Since the beginning of 1966 at the latest, the party activs again were called upon by the secretariats of the *Bezirk* executives to "reinforce the line."

[60] Herber, "Zur Leitung der Parteiarbeit," p. 7.

In his characterization of "operative* leadership" Herber did not seek to emphasize the previously discussed two-sided nature of the SED's rapprochement with the people. Rather, he had in mind the various "leadership styles," such as political direction by party functionaries and executive functions of party experts—primarily in the economic sphere— so as to establish the by now defunct uniform leadership style.

Operative leadership, already a classic element in Communist organizations, is described by Stammer as a "dynamic bureaucracy."[61] The meaning of operative leadership changed over the years without losing the dynamic character of its organizational style. A constant factor of this operative style was a merely postulated direct involvement with the objects of bureaucratic behavior (Stammer). Joachim Schultz had already stated that during 1950–1956 bureaucratization within the leadership bodies was to be overcome constantly by attitudes of close involvement with targets of party work.[62] This involvement was regarded as achieved when practiced in the political or agitprop field. Throughout 1963–1964 political and agitprop work was accorded secondary priority with respect to operative leadership style, especially in the activities of the Bureau of Industry and Construction. The operative style currently propagated by the party experts has two new characteristics: concentration upon the principal economic and technical aspects of work, and carefully planned utilization of professionally trained party instructors and instructor brigades in the economy.[63]

With the establishment of an ideological commission on the level of the Bureau of Industry and Construction, the strategic clique and the SED indicated that they were by no means willing to abrogate their power. However, the establishment of an organization to deal with ideological affairs should not be considered only as a means of guaranteeing the

---

* Editor's note: By operative is meant the ideological and effective supervision of work processes.

[61] Otto Stammer, Introduction to Schultz: *Der Funktionär in der Einheitspartei*, pp. 9 ff. For the bureaucratization of a Communist organizational system, also see Alfred G. Meyer *The Soviet Political System, An Interpretation* (New York: 1965), passim.

[62] Schultz, *Der Funktionär in der Einheitspartei*, pp. 191 ff.

[63] Reinhold Miller and Günther Hoppe, eds., *Arbeit, Gemeinschaft, Persönlichkeit, Soziologische Studien* (Berlin, 1964), pp. 149 ff.

party's position of power. Rather, its situation of competition with the Bureau of Industry and Construction brought the ideological commission into association with the general economic policy of the party. The Politburo resolution of February 26, 1963 states that

It is the task of the [ideological] Commission to elaborate and deal with the basic questions of the theoretical, scientific, and ideological work of the party, including its cultural policy. The Commission will be concerned with the questions of implementing the general economic policy of the party, together with the fulfillment of specific economic plans; with problems of Marxist-Leninist theory and the development of the social sciences; with the development of a uniform system of education . . . ; with the content, forms, and methods of ideological and propagandistic work, including the activity of party schools; with questions of culture, and the work of our cultural institutions and organizations.[64]

It is clear that in the sphere of production propaganda the tasks of the Bureau of Industry and Construction and those of the Ideological Commission overlap. While reorganizing the party apparatus the strategic clique made use of a historical organizational technique to preserve its power—a deliberately vague delineation of spheres of responsibility in order to facilitate intervention in internal party matters and social situations and processes.

THE REFORM OF THE PARTY APPARATUS AT THE *Bezirk* LEVEL

The introduction of the production principle created many organizational problems for the party, primarily within the SED *Bezirk* and *Kreis* executive organs. In late February 1963 their bureaus were dissolved and replaced by greatly reduced secretariats. The expansion of previously existing bureaus between 1959 and 1962 was halted temporarily. Prior to the reorganization each bureau in the fifteen SED *Bezirk* executives[65] employed some fifteen to twenty persons: the first and the second secretaries of the *Bezirk* executive; one secretary each for economics, agriculture, agitprop, education, and culture; the chairmen of the *Bezirk* council, economic council, and planning commission; a *Bezirk* chairman of the FDGB, a first secretary of the SED Stadt executive in the *Bezirk* capital; a first secretary of the SED *Kreis*

[64] Politburo Resolution of February 26, 1963, pp. 332–333.
[65] The fifteen *Bezirk* executives do not include the *Gebiet* (area) executive of Wismut; cf. note 66, p. 289.

executive for the rural area under the administration of the *Bezirk* capital; plant directors or first secretaries of the industrial party organizations for important enterprises and/or secretaries of one or several larger LPGs; a chairman of the *Bezirk* Party Control Commission; and a *Bezirk* director of the Ministry for State Security.

Because of their size and composition, these bureaus could not effectively reach or implement adequate decisions. It is not surprising that they were reproached repeatedly by the party leadership for an "administrative style of leadership." Consequently, during 1963 the bureaus were reduced to secretariats, in accord with the restructuring of the party apparatus at the *Bezirk* level. The new secretariats appear to have only five secretaries: a first secretary; a director of the division of party organizations (a position sometimes filled by the second secretary); a director of the bureau of industry and construction; a functionary responsible for agriculture; and a director of the ideological commission. No agitprop commissions were established either at the *Bezirk* level or in the secretariats of the *Kreis* executive bodies. The number of members and candidates in the *Bezirk* executives of the SED has changed little since 1963. For example, in June 1960 the SED *Bezirk* executive for Dresden consisted of sixty-four members and seventeen candidates. In June 1964 it had sixty-five members and seventeen candidates.[66] These relative ratios persisted in the spring of 1967 during the elections for the SED *Bezirk* executives.[67] However, the membership of the SED *Bezirk* secretariats expanded greatly in the spring of 1967. At the Eighth Conference for Delegates in March 1967 six permanent functionaries were elected and sixty-seven additional mem-

[66] See *Sächsische Zeitung,* June 15, 1960, and June 22, 1964. Also compare the following data about other SED *Bezirk* executives elected in 1960 and 1964 at the Fifth and Seventh Conferences of Delegates. The Potsdam executive, for instance, consisted of 68 members and 17 candidates in 1960, and 65 members and 17 candidates in 1964 (*Märkische Volksstimme.* July 25, 1960, and June 22, 1964). In the *Bezirk* executive of Halle, 65 members and 17 candidates were elected in 1960 and its numerical composition was not changed in 1964 (*Freiheit,* June 20, 1960, and June 22, 1964).

[67] In each of the *Bezirk* executives of Magdeburg, Neubrandenburg, and Potsdam, for instance, 65 members and 17 candidates were elected. In the Schwerin *Bezirk* executive a total of 80 members and candidates were represented. See *Neues Deutschland,* March 20, 1967.

bers appointed to the secretariats. After the "silent transformation" initiated at the beginning of 1966 (when the bureaus of industry and construction were dissolved) the 1967 secretariats contained the following staff members: first and second secretaries; one secretary each for economics, agriculture, agitprop affairs, and one for scientific, educational, and cultural affairs. The expanded secretariats also have the following representatives for various functional spheres: chairman of the *Bezirk* council; chairman of the *Bezirk* economic and agricultural council; director of the *Bezirk* planning commission; first secretary of the SED *Stadt* (city) executive in the *Bezirk* capital; first secretary of the FDG *Bezirk* executive and—with the exception of the SED *Bezirk* executive for Halle—chairman of the FDGB *Bezirk* board.[68]

These new line positions require the secretary for economic affairs to assume the duties performed in 1963 by the director of the Bureau of Industry and Construction. The spring 1967 reorganization of the secretariats does not appear to involve any surrender of the functions reallotted when the "new economic system" was instituted. Although the changes of 1967 appear to have re-emphasized the territorial principle, there does not seem to be any prospect of restoring the former bureaus, since neither the present size nor composition of the secretariats resembles that of the bureaus. Furthermore, the list of their major responsibilities and activities is derived from the 1963 resolutions governing the secretariats.

The primary task of the bureaus or secretariats of the SED *Bezirk* executives was and is the implementation of party decisions. Like the bureaus dissolved in 1963 the secretariats must coordinate party work at the *Bezirk* level—a function that has been emphasized increasingly since the institution of the production principle. The secretariats of the *Bezirk* and *Kreis* apparatuses will concentrate their attention on defining the basic problems of the *Bezirk* or *Kreis*; they coordinate the work of the bureaus and commissions; thus the gradual assumption of leadership of centrally directed enterprises by the bureaus of the *Bezirk* executives is

---

[68] For the Berlin *Bezirk* executive, see *Berliner Zeitung,* March 13, 1967; for the Frankfurt-on-the-Oder, *Neuer Tag,* March 13, 1967; for the Schwerin, *Schweriner Volkszeitung,* March 20, 1967; for the Suhl, *Freies Wort,* March 20, 1967.

effected in a more thorough fashion.[69] The secretariats direct and control the newly created bureaus and commissions even at the *Kreis* level by means of "work plans." Such control was necessary because of the low degree of coordination, evident in recent years, between the *Bezirk* and *Kreis* executive bodies.

Despite the increased function of the secretariats, their sphere of authority, compared with that of the former bureaus, was restricted between 1963 and 1966. Major leadership tasks in industrial and agricultural enterprises instead fell to their associated bureaus for industry, construction, and agriculture, undoubtedly narrowing the range of the SED's decision-making powers at the level of its line organizations. It is thus at least possible that the reduced competence of the secretariats was eventually to be reversed in the course of their transformation and enlargement in the spring of 1967.

The 1963 reorganization of the bureaus in the secretariats had been preceded by personnel changes (initiated at the Fifth Party Congress) during 1959–1960. While this turnover affected nearly all SED *Bezirk* executive bodies its primary effects were on the spheres of secretaries for economics, agricultural and agitprop affairs as well as that of the second secretary. Most of the first secretaries of the bureaus of the *Bezirk* executives remained at their posts in 1963, i.e., they took over direction of the newly formed secretariats. The former section chiefs, some of whom were appointed in 1959–1960, headed the new staff positions after reorganization of the bureaus—i.e., the bureaus and commissions— except where replaced by new cadres. For example, former economic or agricultural secretaries assumed direction of the bureaus of industry and construction respectively for agriculture. The *Bezirk* secretaries previously responsible for agitprop activities now headed the ideological commissions.

Whereas the social characteristics of the executive functionaries of ideological commissions resembled those of the second *Bezirk* secretaries, the directors of the bureaus of industry and construction and agriculture bore the unmistakable general characteristics of the institutionalized counter elite. The directors of the Bureau of Industry and

[69] Rudolf Wettengel, "Das Produktionsprinzip bewährt sich. Zu einigen Ergebnissen der Bezirksleitungssitzungen," *Neuer Weg* 18, no. 18 (September 1963): 817 ff.

Construction of the SED *Bezirk* executives for Rostock, Neubrandenburg, Schwerin, and Halle belonged almost exclusively to the generation
born between 1920 and 1929, or between 1930 and 1939. They had
either completed economic studies, or had previously occupied responsible functional positions in the economy. The second of the two groups
distinguished here in the secretariats of the SED *Bezirk* executives are
the second secretaries. Compared with the first secretaries they represent
and still retain the characteristics reflecting the general mobility processes. They can be regarded as the rising generation of the strategic
clique at the *Bezirk* level. Most of the second secretaries remained in the
same positions after the reorganization of the party apparatus in 1963,
or were entrusted with the direction of the party organization sections by
1964 at the latest. At present, when many of the former directors of
bureaus and commissions of the secretariats have again assumed the
leadership of the respective sections, the function of the second secretary
has been reintroduced in the organizational structure of these bodies.[70]

[70] Naturally, not all functionaries of the bureaus and commissions dissolved in
1966 and 1967 were thereafter entrusted with similar functional responsibilities.
However, the number of those who assumed former functions under a different
title is very high. Tables of functions for the secretariats of the *Bezirk* executives
of Berlin and Schwerin are given as an example:

Secretaries of the Berlin *Bezirk* Executive in March 1967	Function in March 1967	Function in June 1964
Verner, Paul	1st Secretary	1st Secretary
Naumann, Konrad*	2nd Secretary	Director of the Section for Party Organization
Wagner, Hans	Secretary of Economic Affairs	Director of the Bureau of Industry and Construction
Stein, Ernst	Secretary of Agriculture	Director of the Bureau of Agriculture
Bauer, Dr. Roland	Secretary of Science, Education, and Culture	Director of the Ideological Commission
Modrow, Dr. Hans	Secretary of Agitprop Activities	————

Source: *Berliner Zeitung,* March 13, 1967 and June 17, 1964.
* In 1963 Naumann still held the post of 2nd secretary of the FDJ Central
Council. The 2nd Secretary of the SED *Bezirk* Executive of Berlin in 1963 was
Hans Kiefert, who died in 1966.

The group of second secretaries in the *Bezirk* executives is also composed of younger party functionaries. However, for the most part they have risen in the ranks of the party apparatus (and in the ranks of the state or mass organizations). The second secretaries now have a representative in the supreme party body in the person of Horst Dohlus, formerly second secretary of the SED *Bezirk* executive for Cottbus. He is now the director of the party organization section in the Central Committee apparatus and—after the Fifth Plenum of the Central Committee in February 1964—director of the Commission for Party and Organizational Questions attached to the Politburo.

The third group of functionaries to be singled out in this context are the first secretaries of the SED *Bezirk* executives. They remained untouched by the restratification initiated at the Sixth Party Congress. They have been and remain a factor of political stability in the party organization. Many of them were exercising their functions at the beginning or the middle of the fifties. The changes made in three first

Secretaries of the Schwerin *Bezirk* Executive in March 1967	Function in March 1967	Function in June 1964
Quandt, Bernhard	1st Secretary	1st Secretary
Raskop, Hans*	2nd Secretary	Director of the Section for Party Organization
Gröbel, Rudi	Secretary of Economic Affairs	Director of the Bureau of Industry and Construction
Ulbrich, Erich	Secretary of Agriculture	Director of the Bureau of Agriculture†
Wandt, Hans	Secretary of Agitprop Activities	Director of the Ideological Commission
Ramming, Gerhard	Secretary of Science, Education, and Culture	————

Source: *Schweriner Volkszeitung,* March 20, 1967 and June 22, 1964.
* In 1963, before the party organizations section was established, Hans Raskop was 2nd Secretary of the *Bezirk* Executive.
† The Schwerin Bureau of Agriculture appears to have been established long after the bureaus in other districts. Because Schwerin is mostly an agricultural district, the entire executive bears "full responsibility for party work in agriculture. Consequently, no bureau of agriculture has been formed." (Quoted from *Das funktionelle Wirken der Bestandteile des neuen ökonomischen Systems,* p. 11.) According to an IWE report of July 13, 1964, the Bureau of Agriculture of the Schwerin executive was transformed into a department of agriculture in 1964.

secretariats in *Bezirk* executives at the beginning of 1963 involved no real social changes, in contrast with those made in the departmental bodies. With two exceptions, the SED *Bezirk* secretary for Berlin and the first secretary of the *Gebiet* (territorial) executive for Wismut, the sixteen first secretaries of the *Bezirk* executives in 1963 were either members or candidates of the Central Committee.[71] In 1967 the three first *Bezirk* secretaries who had not yet been coopted into that body also became members. They include Central Committee candidate and veteran Communist Kurt Kiess, first secretary of the SED *Gebiet* executive of Wismut, who can be regarded as a member of the strategic clique. Of the two new full Central Committee members in the group of first secretaries, Werner Wittig (forty years old, with a graduate degree in the social sciences), first secretary of the *Bezirk* executive of Potsdam, can be regarded as belonging to the younger ranks of party functionaries. He replaced the present chairman of the ZRK Kurt Seibt, who resigned "for reasons of health." Johannes Chemnitzer, first secretary of the SED *Bezirk* executive of Neubrandenburg, holds degrees in the agricultural and social sciences. He falls into the group of party experts. Four of the first *Bezirk* secretaries also belonged to the Politburo in 1963: Paul Fröhlich, first secretary of the Leipzig *Bezirk;* Erich Mückenberger, first secretary of Frankfurt-on-the-Oder; and Paul Verner, simultaneously secretary of the Central Committee and first secretary of the Berlin *Bezirk,* were all full members. Horst Sindermann, first secretary of the Halle *Bezirk,* was a candidate Politburo member. In the Politburo elected by the Seventh SED Congress these functionaries, now full members, continue to represent the group of first *Bezirk* secretaries. As will be clarified by empirical analysis in Chapter Three, the first secretaries of the *Bezirk* executives in 1963 (as in 1967) bear the characteristics typifying members of the strategic clique.

The reduction of the secretariats required increased cooperation between the representatives of the strategic clique, party functionaries of the younger generation, and the representatives of the institutionalized

---

[71] Kurt Kiess, first secretary of the SED *Gebiet* executive of Wismut, and Johannes Chemnitzer, first secretary of the *Bezirk* executive of Neubrandenburg, were not members of the Central Committee in 1963. For a survey of first secretaries of the *Bezirk* executives, see Chapter Three.

counter elite, i.e., the young party experts. This increased potentials for conflict within the secretariats. The regional decision-making bodies were better organized in the functional sense after the Sixth Party Congress, since now they had only one representative each for the most important social areas. Nevertheless, this had reduced their potential as centers of conflict. Because they were much less homogeneous in their composition conflicts had multiplied. The possibilities for conflict were not limited to the overlapping of responsibilities and spheres of activity; their primary source was precisely the social composition of these bodies. Possibilities of conflict arose between the generations and between the strategic clique of the first *Bezirk* secretaries and the younger party functionaries (e.g., second secretaries). In our analysis the conflict between party experts and the two groups of party functionaries must be distinguished from the clash between generations. It is probable that the reorganization of the secretariats in the spring of 1967 was not effected with the purpose of precluding such conflicts. To be sure, the clash between representatives of the production and territorial principles, caused by overlapping functional responsibilities, was to be reduced. However, it seems that the smoother functioning of bodies that operated according to the territorial principle—i.e., in the traditional style of leadership and organization—was a decisive factor. This interpretation is born out by the fact that in the Soviet Union the organization of the CPSU along the lines of the production principle has again assumed low priority.

A discussion of the conflicts that could arise as a result of the social composition of the secretariats should not overlook the relative freedom of action available as early as the spring of 1963 to the representatives of the strategic clique at the level of the *Bezirk* executives. At that time the first secretary could himself choose the directors of the bureaus of industry and construction and of agriculture, or cast the decisive vote for their selection. However, there is some breakdown in the insulation of the strategic clique at the level of the *Bezirk* executive secretariats. This is due to the fact that they have fewer opportunities than the Politburo to create boundaries between themselves and the SED rank and file. The supreme policy-making body of the strategic clique retains the power to freeze representatives of the institutionalized counter elite in candidate positions in the top echelon of the party. The secretariats of the *Bezirk* executives organized in 1963 could not avail themselves of this opportunity, since the directors of the bureau were always full members of the secretariat.

The social composition and political leadership of the secretariats in SED *Bezirk* executive bodies in 1958, 1963, and 1967 differed from *Bezirk* to *Bezirk*. Apart from secretariats which were formed for the most part in 1963, incorporated representatives of the younger or intermediate generations, and were occupied by party experts (Rostock), there existed "mixed" secretariats (Neubrandenburg). In the latter, younger and older party functionaries and experts were represented. Also, there were and still are secretariats in which members of the strategic clique predominate (Halle, Frankfurt-on-the-Oder, Schwerin). The SED *Bezirk* executive of Rostock is an example of the entry of the institutionalized counter elite—the party experts— into the *Bezirk* secretariats. By contrast, the example of the Halle secretariat exemplifies the entrenched position of the strategic clique at the local level.

In 1963 the SED *Bezirk* executive of Rostock absorbed a high proportion of professionally and economically trained younger functionaries. Even the First Secretary, Harry Tisch, a member of the Central Committee since 1963, had received training as a skilled worker (construction mechanic). The directors of the Bureaus of Industry and Construction and of Agriculture, Dr. Gerhard Buchführer and Bruno Lietz, completed economic and agronomic studies and can be regarded as representatives of the institutionalized counter elite. This applies only marginally to the director of the Ideological Commission, Prof. Herbert Luck, who has degrees in economics and the social sciences.[72] Only Ernst Timm, secretary of the Section for Party Organization, came from the FDJ apparatus and has no professional training.

[72] Prof. Dr. Herbert Luck (born in 1923) received his Ph.D. in economics after having completed his apprenticeship as a toolmaker. Since 1956 he has been a full professor of economics at Rostock University. In 1957 he was dean of the faculty of economics at that university, when he engaged in a controversy with the "revisionist" economist, Fritz Behrens, through his article, "Bemerkungen zum Artikel von Behrens 'Zum Problem der Ausnutzung ökonomischer Gesetze in der Übergangsperiode'," *Wirtschaftswissenschaft*, 5 (1957), special issue no. 3: 95 ff.

The 1963 secretariat of the SED *Bezirk* executive of Halle was particularly notable for its strong "political incumbency in composition." The central strategic clique appointed veteran Communist Horst Sindermann from among their midst (previously a candidate, then [since 1967] a full member of the Politburo and [since 1958] a member of the Central Committee) as first secretary of the *Bezirk* executive and made Central Committee member Gerhard Frost his second secretary. Franz Mellentin, director of the Bureau of Agriculture, also worked in the Politburo's Bureau of Agriculture. Franz Bruk, director of the Ideological Commission,[73] can also be classified as a member of the strategic clique. Only one member of the secretariat seems to fall into the institutionalized counter elite category: the economist Heinz Schwarz (member of the Central Committee), who is director of the Bureau of Industry and Construction.

This analysis of the expanded spheres of competence of the secretariats created in 1963 and their personnel composition is to be concluded by a study of the Bureau of Industry and Construction, and of the Ideological Commissions attached to the *Bezirk* secretariats. The regional bureaus of industry and construction at the *Bezirk* and *Kreis* levels (as conceived in the spring and summer of 1963) were responsible for the tasks of the primary organizations of the SED in the VVB and VEB, and also for the primary organizations in the centrally and locally directed enterprises of trade, transport, and construction. They had to work out the specific implications of the planned guidelines given them by the secretariats of the SED *Bezirk* executives, coordinate them with the projected plans of their associated enterprises, and return them to the central Bureau of Industry and Construction. The central bureau (in the SED Politburo or Central Committee) then coordinated those plans that had to do with economic problems with the State Planning Commission and, until the end of December 1965, with the National Economic Council. Since 1967 the functions formerly exercised by the

---

[73] Franz Bruk (born in 1928) was relieved of his functions as early as February 1966. Together with Dr. Siegbert Löschau, he also resigned from the *Bezirk* executive. He was replaced by Werner Felfe, who interestingly enough had already been elected secretary for agitprop activities. See *Freiheit*, February 19, 1966.

National Economic Council have been assumed by the relevant industrial ministries.

In 1963 the regional bureaus of industry and construction were also made fully responsible for "political life in their respective primary organizations"—a responsibility that extended to political, ideological, economic, and organizational work in the enterprises. The director of the Bureau of Industry and Construction of the SED *Bezirk* executive of Berlin, Rudi Rubbel, reconfirmed in August 1963 that the directives and controls of these bureaus referred to the "all-round party work of their associated enterprises and institutes." Rubbel emphasized control of "political and ideological mass effort."[74] This included the organizational tightening up of party work in the enterprises (primarily APO and BPO), as well as organization of intra-factory competition, improvement of production propaganda (in factory journals), and the direction and control of mass organizations in the enterprises. Under the terms of the "new economic system," control and partial assumption of responsibility of mass political tasks in the enterprises, performed by the Chamber of Technology (KdT), was given highest priority.

These multiple functions were fulfilled by a number of leading officials. In 1963 the bureaus of industry and construction in the secretariats of the *Bezirk* executives had ten to fifteen members. Of these, approximately 50 percent had completed university or technical college training, usually in chemistry, machine construction, electrical engineering, the textile or construction industries. The other members of the bureaus of industry and construction had undergone extensive training, usually in the *Bezirk* party schools of the SED.[75] Leading functionaries were first concentrated in the various "sectors" of the bureaus. In 1963 the particularly large Bureau of Industry and Construction in the secretariat of the SED *Bezirk* executive of Berlin consisted of sectors for machine construction, electrical engineering,

---

[74] See an interview with Rudi Rubbel, "Büro für Industrie und Bauwesen organisiert Parteiarbeit nach dem Produktionsprinzip," *Die Wirtschaft*, 18, no. 33 (1963): 5.

[75] For data on the SED *Bezirk* executive of Gera, see Horst Dohlus, "Produktionsprinzip erfordert höheres Niveau der Organisationsarbeit," *Neuer Weg*, 18, no. 21 (November 1963): 965.

chemical industry, etc. There existed also a sector for agitprop affairs despite the fact that the Ideological Commission was in the process of being established. The individual enterprises controlled by the bureaus were then further subdivided into "groups." For example, in the machine-construction sector, groups were established for toolmaking machines, vehicle construction, metallurgy, instrument making, etc. Each of these groups was the responsibility of a leading functionary from a corresponding sector at the bureau of the secretariat. He was active in the technically most advanced enterprise of the "group" and at that time collaborated extensively with nonsalaried appointees. This parallelism was continued in the organizational sense, when at the beginning of 1964 various *Bezirke* of the GDR (e.g., Karl-Marx-Stadt) went over to organizing the working groups in the bureaus of industry and construction of the *Bezirk* executives by product groups rather than enterprises, which had already gained organizational importance at this period. Every leading functionary of these working groups thus became directly responsible for eight to twelve basic-level SED organizations in the various industrial enterprises, which came under the rubric of the same product group.

In practice, a member of the bureau of industry and construction was usually responsible for one or several sectors or groups. In each case the representatives of the bureau of the SED *Bezirk* executives cooperated closely with the representatives of the corresponding industrial party organizations (BPO). To ensure cooperation the activity of the directors and members of the bureau's sectors had to be coordinated with the directives of party organizers of the Central Committee apparatus. Leading managers of the system, particularly Erich Apel and Günter Mittag, repeatedly emphasized the need for cooperation or subordination of the BPO in vital enterprises to the bureaus: "Direct responsibility for the work of the party organizations in the enterprise lies . . . with the bureaus of industry and construction of the *Bezirk* executives."[76] In the Berlin region, for example, party organizations of the electrical engineering enterprises were until September 1963 subordinated to the Bureau of Industry and Construction of the SED *Bezirk* executive. According to Rudi Rubbel, the party organizations of other

[76] Apel and Mittag, *Wissenschaftliche Führungstätigkeit*, p. 43.

important enterprises in the Berlin area were to be similarly subordinated by autumn 1963.[77]

It has already been stated that the leading party functionaries directing "sectors" and "groups" of the bureau were to be augmented and supported largely by nonsalaried aides. The SED's campaign to recruit these people can be seen as meaning any one of a variety of things. On the one hand, the directors and members of the bureaus attempted to concentrate expert builders, technicians, and economists who did not belong to the SED into small groups under their direct supervision, where they would be vulnerable to easy surveillance. This measure consolidated their own power, both at the level of the enterprise and the secretariats of the *Bezirk* executives. Simultaneously, the technically inexpert party leadership had expert knowledge readily at hand for reaching decisions. They were thus able to secure expert evaluation of political decisions outside the actual policy-making bodies of the party, and to apply expert decisions in the political sphere. The last aim was served by numerous measures, e.g., the establishment of the nonsalaried bodies of "new technology" in large enterprises.

In contrast to the nonsalaried working groups in the enterprise, these bodies constituted a more solid organizational structure and permitted the directors of the bureaus of industry and construction to exercise greater influence upon the inefficient Bureaus for Innovation (BFN) and the Scientific–Technical Centers (WTZ), as well as other similar institutions. The recruitment of nonsalaried personnel who were members of or newcomers to the SED also corresponded with the "opening of the party ranks"—a move that increasingly has characterized the policy of the Politburo vis-à-vis the populace since early 1963. However, nonsalaried activities of party members must be distinguished from those of nonmembers. Nonmembers were organized in bodies outside the party, but under its control (ABI, Production Committees, etc.). Nevertheless, intensified cooperation of this sort in many enterprises has blurred the heretofore frequently sharp separation between party members and nonmembers, and has decreased the obvious favoritism shown party members, with the constant conflicts produced by different social mores and behavioral norms. Finally, one of the major

[77] Interview with Rudi Rubbel.

declared aims of the SED, a permanent mobilization of party members and nonmembers, could be pursued here under circumstances different from the normal ones. For participating party members, nonsalaried activity may be seen as a new form of party "mission" under the conditions of the "new economic system." Whereas in the fifties party "missions" could only be assigned by appropriate party executives, assemblies, or the competent SED party secretary, the staff positions of the party apparatus were now endowed with the same responsibilities.[78] This change in the method of distributing party assignments undoubtedly rates attention in connection with the thesis concerning the intrusion of large organizational structures into the party apparatus.

Cooperation between the representatives of the bureaus of industry and construction of the SED *Bezirk* executives and the party organizers within the apparatus of the Central Committee and the BPO secretaries and the plant management often resulted in improved exchange of expert knowledge and a reduction in bureaucratic obstacles. As a result, in 1964 and 1965 the activities of SED basic-level organizations in many vital enterprises could be directly entrusted to the supervision of regional bureaus of industry and construction.[79] This applied particularly to the three most important industrial branches as defined within the COMECON agreements: the chemical, electrical engineering, and machine construction industries. For example, in the beginning of 1964 in the Karl-Marx-Stadt *Bezirk* some three hundred SED basic-level organizations within these industries were associated directly with the bureau of industry and construction of the *Bezirk* executive.[80] Together with these measures, which greatly revitalized the regional bureaus of industry and construction in the organizational sense, certain enterprises were declared

---

[78] See Manfred Tietze, "Direkte Anleitung bewährt sich. Erste Erfahrungen des Büros für Industrie und Bauwesen der Bezirksleitung Dresden mit ehrenamtlichen Kollektiven," *Neuer Weg*, 18, no. 14 (July 1963): 632 ff.

[79] See Erich Honecker's speech at the Fifth Plenary Session of the SED Central Committee, in *Neues Deutschland*, February 12, 1964. Thus, in the Dresden *Bezirk* the basic-level party organizations of the ten major electrical appliance and machinery plants were directly subordinated to the Bureau of Industry and Construction at the Dresden Party executive.

[80] According to Günter Erdmann, "Das neue ökonomische System der Planung und Leitung in der Praxis durchsetzen," *Neuer Weg*, 19, no. 4 (February, 1964): 153.

"consultative enterprises" (i.e., as regards optimal production standards) for the entire complex of VVBs. In the spring of 1966 one experimental enterprise of the SED, the VEB "Modul" in Karl-Marx-Stadt, was selected from forty-one similar enterprises with thirty-six thousand workers of the VVB for Toolmaking Machines and Machine Tools (WMW)[81] and designated as a "consultative enterprise." It was expressly stated that "the basic-level organizations of the other enterprises in this branch of industry should avail themselves of the example of this enterprise's experiences."[82]

However, particularly in the first half of 1963, this novel form of direct subordination caused many problems in setting boundaries of competence between those responsible for the bureaus of industry and construction within the concerned *Bezirk* and *Kreis* executives. These problems were to be solved in accord with several pertinent Politburo pronouncements, e.g., the directive "On Further Improvement in Performance of the Party's Work by [Implementing] the Production Principle" of July 17, 1963.[83] The document called for the bureaus of industry and construction of the *Kreis* executives to concentrate their activities upon enterprises directed by the *Bezirk* or *Kreis* administrations. Party work in the centrally directed enterprises was to be performed only by the bureaus of industry and construction at the *Bezirk* level. This Politburo decision led to lively discussions among leading functionaries of many SED *Kreis* executives, primarily those in the highly industrialized southern regions of the Republic: "If the centrally directed industries are withdrawn from the purview of our responsibility, what is left for the *Kreis* executive [to oversee]?"[84]

Difficulties caused by overlapping spheres of competence also arose in the functional relationship of the Bureau of Industry and Construction to the Ideological Commission. The newly established Ideological Commission had been assigned an important role in the "new economic

---

[81] The data on the VVB WMW are taken from *Sächsische Zeitung,* March 10, 1966.

[82] Erdmann "Das neue ökonomische System," p. 155.

[83] The resolution is not known to be published, but see Kurt Thieme, "Die Leitung nach dem Produktionsprinzip im Kreis," *Neuer Weg,* 18, no. 18 (September 1963): 823 ff.

[84] Ibid.

system." Its task was extended to the economic sphere, although only in indirect fashion. The Ideological Commission was entrusted with implementing the appropriate political and ideological line in enterprises. Werner Neugebauer, Central Committee member and former deputy director of the Ideological Commission for the SED *Bezirk* executive of Berlin stated: "We thus place economic problems at the center of our concern: planned increase in labor productivity, assuring scientific and technical progress, and the fulfillment of the national economic plan. These are the criteria of our work."[85] Correspondingly, activities of the Ideological Commission or the Commission for Agitprop Affairs which stimulated production in industry and agriculture occupied the foregound of concern: the supervision of mass competition, production propaganda, control of those party bodies in enterprises known as *Lektorate,*[86] and the editorial control of factory journals. Secondary attention was given to the control of professional training, adult education, and mass cultural activities within enterprises. Neugebauer greatly widened the sphere of competence for ideological commissions at the *Bezirk* level.

The Ideological Commission will institute comparable thoroughness of approach in its dealings with scientific institutes and their connections with production enterprises, in its political work, among youth (FDJ elections) and women's organizations as well as with the program of the theaters in Berlin, admissions to theaters, the tasks of the Association for the Propagation of Scientific Knowledge and the Higher Institute for Sculpture and Designing Arts. Naturally, preparations for the "Berlin Festival" days of May 1 and 8, for the workers' festival games, and for the new party-study year are also part of our planning.[87]

The program of the Sixth SED Congress had not envisaged such a comprehensive task for the ideological commissions at the *Bezirk* level. Nevertheless, the personnel of these commissions were greatly increased until the number approximated that of the bureaus of industry and

[85] "Ideologische Kommission begann mit ihrer Arbeit" (interview with Werner Neugebauer), *Neuer Weg,* 18, no. 9 (May 1963): 366.
[86] The so-called *Lektorate* (lectorates) have a standing parallel to that of the ideological commissions and the bureaus of industry and construction. In practice, however, owing to their small size, they are usually subordinated to the bureaus of industry and construction in charge of production propaganda within their area of jurisdiction. These offices have started to form "lectorates" for certain specific aspects—i.e, the so-called "branch lectorates" for technology, mechanics, etc.
[87] Interview with Werner Neugebauer, p. 367.

construction, or the bureaus of agriculture. For example, the Ideological Commission in the SED *Bezirk* executive of Berlin was staffed by the following functionaries: the director, his two deputies, two economists, and Werner Tzschoppe, the party secretary of Humboldt University, the first secretary of the *Bezirk* executive of the FDJ, the chairman of the *Bezirk* committee of the National Front, and the party secretary of the Stern Radio VEB, which is a particularly important, centrally directed enterprise. These officials were supplemented by several (at least four) propagandists and approximately three cultural functionaries.[88] Even with these fifteen or twenty members, such a grandiose program could scarcely be fulfilled. The ideological commission members thus had institutional and personal contact from the beginning—as in the bureaus of industry and construction—with numerous "nonsalaried consultative bodies" composed of party members and acting as task forces. For instance, East Berlin in the summer of 1963 had one collective each for press work, supervising the party's study year, mass propaganda, the visual media and the broadening of press readership, for questions of university-level educational policy, and literature. The Ideological Commission of the SED *Bezirk* executive of Berlin also supervised the work of the local Commission for Historical Research in Problems of the Workers' Movement and the permanent commissions of the municipal councilors' assembly, particularly those for educational and cultural affairs.

Analysis of the reorganization of SED *Bezirk* executive bodies in early 1963 has led to the conclusion that representatives of the strategic clique at the district level were almost always to be found in the position of first secretary—a trend that has intensified since the Seventh SED Congress in April 1967. On the other hand, the positions of second secretary and director of the bureaus and commission have been occupied since 1963 by an increasing number of younger, professionally trained personnel. This pattern has not changed substantially, even after reorganization of the *Bezirk* secretariats in 1967.

It has also been established that in 1963–1964 the position of the bureaus of industry and construction in the *Bezirk* executives assumed

---

[88] Ibid., p. 370.

well-nigh dominant positions, politically and economically. These bureaus overshadowed the *Bezirk* secretariats, where the bureau directors not only had equal prerogatives with the first and second secretaries, but also had a controlling voice in the ideological commissions. Whereas establishment of these bureaus had largely abolished the bureaucratic leadership style of the party, there was no notable reduction of possible conflict potential in the regional party bodies. The power leverage of the bureaus plus the organizational dynamics inherent in the pragmatically oriented functionaries in staff positions in fact engendered many additional conflicts within areas of competence. Consequently, the aggrandizement of power of the regional bureaus of industry and construction was gradually limited; this development culminated in their dissolution in 1966.

5. The Central Committee of the SED: Its Transformation to a Body of Coordination, Transmission, and Consultation

This analysis of the changing composition of SED leadership groups was aimed primarily at determining whether there has been any increase in the representation of economic and technical experts, a goal proclaimed by Ulbricht at the Sixth Party Congress; we wished thus to clarify the process of change within the social structure of the party itself. With this in mind, we have analyzed empirically the composition of the members and candidates of the Politburo, the secretaries of the Central Committee and the Central Committee's constituents for the periods of the Fourth, Fifth, and Sixth Party Congresses.

We wish to precede our analysis of changes in the social composition of the party elite with an investigation of the role of the Central Committee as the repository of the central party apparatus. From such an approach, changes in organizational structure can also be pinpointed. At the Third SED Congress (July 20–24, 1950) the Central Committee of the SED was established with its present status, along the lines of the party structure of the CPSU. Have the functions of the Central Committee changed in the intervening period (from 1954 to 1966–67)? Furthermore, is this functional change paralleled by changes in the social composition of the party elite? Did the gradual expansion of the Central Committee from 1954 to 1963—a phenomenon that could be observed within the CPSU Central Committee[89]—and the increased cooperation of experts strengthen or weaken this party institution?

THE ORGANIZATIONAL ROLE OF THE CENTRAL COMMITTEE
WITHIN THE PARTY APPARATUS

At the Third Party Congress in 1950 a total of 51 members and 30 candidates were elected to the Central Committee of the SED. At the Fourth Party Congress in 1954, 91 members and 44 candidates were elected. At the Fifth Congress in 1958 the comparable numbers rose to 111 full and 44 candidate members. After the Sixth Congress in 1963 the Central Committee had 121 members and 60 candidates. The Seventh Congress in April 1967 "returned" 131 members and 50 candidates.[90] Thus, over the past seventeen years the number of members and candidates in the Central Committee has more than doubled. This increase in membership closely duplicates developments within the CPSU.[91] However, some differentiation of functions in the role of the SED Central Committee can be regarded as parallel to the industrialization process. The expanded responsibilities of the Central Committee are paralleled by an increase in the functional responsibilities of numerous other top bodies, e.g., the Council of Ministers and the National Research Council.

A detailed elaboration of this thesis should begin with an examination of the officially documented self-image of the SED. Comparison of certain relevant paragraphs of various SED statutes is useful for this purpose. The Statutes of 1946, 1950, 1954, and 1963[92] identify the

---

[89] For particulars, see Merle Fainsod, *How Russia Is Ruled* (Cambridge, Mass.: Harvard University Press, revised ed., 1967), pp. 176 ff.

[90] See Appendix 2, pp. 443 ff.

[91] Brzezinski and Huntington present a survey of CPSU Central Committee membership from 1917 to 1961. The number of Central Committee members increased from 21 (at the Sixth CPSU Congress in 1917) to 175 (at the Twenty-Second CPSU Congress in 1961). See Zbigniew Brzezinski and Samuel P. Huntington, *Political Power, USA/USSR* (New York: Viking Press, 1964), p. 179.

[92] The First Statute of the SED, in *Protokoll des Vereinigungsparteitages der Sozialdemokratischen Partei Deutschlands (SPD) und der Kommunistischen Partei Deutschlands (KPD) am 21. und 22. April 1946* (Berlin, 1946), pp. 180 ff; Second Statute of the SED, in *Protokoll der Verhandlungen des III. Parteitages der SED, 20–24. Juli 1950, in der Werner-Seelenbinder-Halle zu Berlin*, 2 vols. (Berlin, 1951) (hereafter cited as *Protocol of the Third SED Congress*), 2, pp. 307 ff. Third

Central Committee as the "highest organ of the party," and the "deputy" of the party congresses held every four years. "The Central Committee implements the decisions of the party congress between congresses; it is the highest functioning organ of the party and directs its entire activity. . . ."[93] Although the number of full and candidate members of the Central Committee is formally decided upon by party congresses, it is in reality determined by the cadre sections of the central and regional party apparatuses. In 1950 only persons who had been party members for four years were eligible for election to the Central Committee; this requirement was increased to six years by the statutes of 1954 and 1963.[94] If we recall that in 1950 the SED had only existed for four years, the required period for acceptance by the Central Committee can be regarded as an index for the maintenance of the cadre principle in the traditional sense. However, membership in a Socialist or Communist workers' party was invariably counted toward longevity in the SED when the party was founded.

The formula whereby the Central Committee is the highest organ of the party between party congresses seems hardly ever to accord with the actual balance of power in the party's formal organization. In the SED, at least, the Politburo holds the greatest power, with the Secretariat in second place—at least since 1953–1954.[95] The Politburo and the Secretariat are staffed largely by members of the strategic clique. In the years from 1954 to 1966 the secretaries of the Central Committee were invariably members of the Politburo.[96] The institutionalized counter elite entered the strategic clique only after 1963, when Apel, Mittag, and

Statute of the SED of 1954 (cf. ftn. 5, p. 70); and Fourth Statute of the SED of 1963 (cf. ftn. 46, p. 93). The Third Statute was supplemented at the Fifth Party Congress in 1958; the same happened to the Fourth Statute at the Seventh SED Congress in 1967.

[93] Fourth Statute of the SED, Article 39.

[94] See Article 39c of the Third Party Statute of 1954, and Article 38c of the Fourth Statute.

[95] During 1950–1953 Ulbricht made increasing attempts to restrict the influence of the Politburo (founded in 1949) in favor of the Secretariat. See Stern, *Porträt*, p. 272.

[96] The 1967 elections were the first time that a secretary of the Central Committee was not simultaneously admitted to membership or candidature in the Politburo. Central Committee Secretary Werner Lamberz was nominated Secretary for Agitprop Affairs at the Seventh Party Convention. In the Politburo itself, Albert Norden has long been in charge of Agitprop Affairs.

Jarowinsky became candidates for the Politburo.[97] In spite of the fact that they enjoy only candidate status, these party experts are also Central Committee secretaries.

The Politburo and its comparable middle- and lower-level party organizations, the secretariats of the SED *Bezirk* and *Kreis* executives, were responsible for foreign policy, intra-German affairs, ideology, and direction and control of security matters. Yet the basic decisions in all spheres of East German social life were and still are made by the Politburo. The Central Committee Secretariat should be regarded as the "apex of the inner party executive."[98] It oversees and takes appropriate measures for the implementation of social and party policies dictated by Politburo decisions. In pursuing these functions the Politburo must cooperate closely with the various sections and commissions of the Central Committee apparatus.[99] Each secretary is responsible for individual sections of the Central Committee apparatus. These bodies draft both secretariat and "collegial" decisions that affect the time schedules of the *Bezirk* and *Kreis* executives.[100] Since the Central Committee secretaries have not invariably been members of the Politburo as well, the establishment of bureaus and commissions associated with that body could be regarded as an organizational tactic on the part of the Politburo to balance off these organs against the secretariat.

The opportunities to exercise power afforded the Politburo and Central Committee on the one hand, and the Central Committee Secretariat on the other, become more clearly apparent through comparing the tasks of the Central Committee stipulated in the party statutes with those which it actually performs. The *de jure* functions of the Central Committee in 1963 and 1967 had changed little from those of 1950 and 1958. According to the Fourth Statute of the SED (§§39–47), the Central Committee is to implement the "decisions of the party congresses" and to represent the SED, primarily as regards the bourgeois

---

[97] See pp. 288-289.
[98] Ernst Richert, *Macht ohne Mandat* (Cologne and Opladen, 1963), pp. 30 ff.
[99] For particulars, see ibid. See also Stern, *Porträt*, pp. 271 ff. For the relationship between the Politburo and the Secretariat of the Central Committee, also see Stern, *Ulbricht*, pp 112 ff, as well as Schultz, *Der Funktionär*, pp. 179 ff.
[100] See Wolfgang Arlt, "Der Kampf der Sozialistischen Einheitspartei Deutschlands um die Vervollkommnung des Arbeitsstils," in Werner Horn et al., eds., *20 Jahre Sozialistiche Einheitspartei Deutschlands*, pp. 220 ff; p. 255.

parties and the mass organizations. The Central Committee also appoints representatives to the "highest organs of the state apparatus and the economy" and approves the candidates of the SED for the Peoples' Chamber. The Central Committee controls "the work of the elected state and social organs of organizations through their party groups." The Central Committee—including its apparatus—is entrusted with the political control of economically preponderant organizations. In this context the primary task is the direction of party enterprises and the appointment of party organizers or the installation of party secretariats in the VVBs and large VEBs.[101]

Compared with the fifties, the scope of duties of the Central Committee undoubtedly has been expanded with the transference of these functions. By December 1957 the Central Committee had convened a conference to "improve the functioning of the party." Numerous members and candidates took a leading part in this intraparty conference.[102]

However, those functions not explicitly stipulated in the party statutes appear to be even more important. Primary directives are submitted to the Central Committee for its decision on their respective priorities. Previously, they were worked out jointly by the Politburo and the Secretariat, upon consultation with the relevant section of the Central Committee apparatus.[103] This pattern of decision making frequently led Western observers to conclude that the Central Committee functioned largely as a forum for "declamation and acclamation," in confirming previously adopted decisions. Accordingly, the Central Committee "had hardly any influence" and was politically "insignificant."[104] In view of the political and personnel issues which undoubtedly occupied the foreground until the sixties, the Central Committee is regarded as the "mock parliament" of the SED, a representative body without any real functions. This repeated assertion is further confirmed by taking into account the period between the plenary sessions of the Central Committee. The party statute of 1950 stipulated that plenary sessions be held every three

[101] Fourth Statute of the SED, Article 43.
[102] See Arlt's presentation, "Der Kampf," p. 260.
[103] Stern, *Porträt,* p. 268.
[104] This conception was put forward by Richert in *Macht ohne Mandat,* p. 30, and in *Das Zweite Deutschland* (Berlin, 1964), p. 70.

months; in fact sessions were held at more frequent intervals, particularly during 1957–1958 (§ 40). In 1954 this period was lengthened to four months (§ 41) and in the Party Statute of 1963 to six months, in accord with statutes of the CPSU (§ 40). The prolonged periods between plenary sessions would seem to indicate that the Central Committee was increasingly deprived of actual decision-making powers, particularly since the Politburo and the Secretariat of the SED continued to meet at least once or twice a week.

The present position of the Central Committee in the party apparatus and in East German society is highlighted by several new empirical phenomena. The latter seem to indicate that intraparty and general social change, with concomitant restructuring of major functional areas in the large bureaucracies, encompassed the Central Committee itself. For example, when we compare the draft of the Fourth Party Statute with its final version, we find that a greater preponderance is attached to the "principle of management by production," along with explicit endorsement of intervention of party bodies in the economic process. Furthermore, the party leadership's attempt to reduce the distance between the party and those segments of society directly engaged in production should be emphasized. The original draft of the preamble to the 1963 Statute also takes note of "other segments of the working population" beside workers, collective farmers, and the intelligentsia. Although this passage was deleted, together with the preamble—apparently to maintain an ideologically pure image—it nevertheless refers to the repeatedly noted conflict between the principle of a "cadre" vs. a "mass" party. There are numerous reasons to assume that this typically exaggerated conflict is being resolved in favor of a new, more effective combination of the traditional principles of a cadre and a mass party. The attitude of the strategic clique to party traditions is a typical indication. For example, in the 1963 Statute the reference made in 1954 to the traditions of the KPD embodied by Karl Liebknecht, Rosa Luxemburg, Ernst Thälmann, and the Spartakusbund has been omitted.[105]

[105] This has been pointed out by Klaus Westen in his commentary on the Fourth Statute of the SED, in Alois Riklin and Klaus Westen, *Selbstzeugnisse des SED Regimes. Das Nationale Dokument. Das erste Programm der SED. Das 4. Statut der SED* (Cologne, 1963), pp. 165 ff.

A more significant change is the reformulation of Article 40 of the 1963 Statute. Section II reads:

In accordance with the character of the questions to be discussed, the Central Committee can invite functionaries of party organs, mass organizations, state and economic organs, or scientists and the creative intelligentsia, innovators, production workers, and collective farmers to participate actively in its plenary sessions.

This passage does not appear in the Statutes of 1950 and 1954. Its insertion indicates that the plenums are to resume the character of working sessions which they possessed in 1953–1954 and occasionally in later years[106] (e.g., the Ninth Session of the Central Committee in July 1960, which was devoted to a discussion of technological developments in the machine-building industry and metallurgy). Furthermore, Central Committee members always have and still do participate in meetings of commissions and committees of the Politburo and the Central Committee apparatus.[107] In addition, since the Fifth Party Congress in 1958— but more so since the beginning of 1963—scientists, technocrats, managers, and leading functionaries of the central *Bezirk* and *Kreis* party apparatuses have been invited by the SED leadership for repeated or occasional consultations.[108] This is an institutional expression of the party leadership's stated goal of "expertization" of social planning and control. Certain features of the consultative authoritarianism described in Chapter One emerge in this pattern.

Article 40 of the Party Statute of 1963 goes even further than these principles of consultative authoritarianism: it appears to envisage a

---

[106] E.g., Carola Stern states: "Central Committee plenary sessions and their importance for party policy cannot simply be equated with that of party congresses and conferences. They have much more of the character of work sessions where experiences are exchanged, and the feeling of being *entre nous* leads to relatively more objective and open discussions than is the case at the party congresses, where the speakers are determined in advance and usually read their contributions from prepared texts that have been approved in advance by the *Bezirk* party bureaus." (*Porträt,* p. 268.)

[107] Relevant data in this connection may be found in Herbert Prauss, *Doch es war nicht die Wahrheit. Tatsachenbericht zur geistigen Auseinandersetzung unserer Zeit* (Berlin, 2nd ed., 1960), pp. 133 ff.

[108] This will be clarified in an analysis of the Economic Conferences jointly sponsored by the Central Committee and the Council of Ministers in 1961 and 1963, and the Rationalization Conference of 1966, pp. 132 ff.

significant change in the relationship between party and society. This article demonstrates that the Central Committee, as the "parliament" of the party, now constitutes a true representation of society's currents, one different from that projected by the party in the 1950s. The rigid, abstract, Utopian patterns of "class" and "class struggle," still being projected by the party leadership in 1958 at the Fifth Congress, have been replaced by a more realistic conception of social structures and functions. The traditional ideal of the relationship between state and society developed during the "early years of struggle" (1946-1949), retained up to 1952, and maintained through the first stage of "construction of Socialism in the GDR" until 1958, seems to have been replaced by somewhat more sober views in the Politburo. The social image of the party leadership itself has changed: the axiom of the "class struggle directed inward"—an elementary component of traditional dogma—has since 1962 faded into the background of the party's ideological action programs. This occurred somewhat later than in the Soviet Union and took place after popular outrage at the program for total collectivization of agriculture had been exacerbated by protest against the Berlin Wall and the artificial border in general.

In addition to these indicators of the Central Committee's changed position, as manifested within the party apparatus, another relevant factor should be considered. To cope with the exigencies of the new economic system the strategic clique requires more information and power of surveillance and control than it ever did before. The party leadership's need for information has manifested itself in various ways. Beginning in 1961, and increasingly since 1963 and 1964, both the Politburo and the Central Committee formed "working groups"—usually headed by Ulbricht or some other full Politburo member—in which many scientists participate.[109] The leadership's increasing need for information has led to more consultation with scientific and parascientific SED institutes about the direction and control of the economy and

[109] Wolfgang Berger and Otto Reinhold, *Zu den wissenschaftlichen Grundlagen des neuen ökonomischen Systems* (Berlin, 1966), report that shortly after the Sixth SED Congress in January 1963 a work group, including members of the Central Committee, the Council of Ministers, and numerous scientists, worked out the outlines of the "new economic system of planning and direction of the national economy." (pp. 25 ff.)

society. One example is the establishment of the Central Committee's Central Institute for Socialist Management[110] in 1965 and the Central Committee's Institute for Opinion Research in 1964. The expansion of the Central Committee's Institute for Social Sciences and last, but far from least, the foundation of a special sociological department within this Institute also deserve mention. The party leadership is interested more than ever in identifying and balancing conflicting group interests within and beyond party ranks. They must create organizational forms which permit the expression of divergent interests. In this context we once again refer to the characteristics of "consultative authoritarianism" in modern industrial societies.

As a result of reorganization in other functional areas of the party, state, and economic bureaucracies, and because of the demands of a highly industrialized system, the Central Committee is assuming more and more the character of a coordinating, transmitting, and consultative body within the party apparatus. Decisions and directives prepared by the Politburo are discussed in the Central Committee and, in the words of Paul Fröhlich, a Politburo member and First Secretary of the Leipzig *Bezirk* executive, the Central Committee assumes the function of a "leading executive" of the SED. Hermann Matern, also a Politburo member and Chairman of the Central Party Control Commission, regards the Central Committee as the strategic "leadership staff" for economic and social affairs.[111] Fröhlich evaluates this function of the Central Committee as a "positive" concomitant of the development of GDR society as an advanced industrial system.

The uniform process of overall social development requires uniform, centralized direction . . . making its decisions on the basis of an all-inclusive perspective, knowledge of all its interconnections, and based on criteria of actual social development.[112]

[110] Cf. also the address by Dr. Günter Mittag at the opening of the first year of studies at the Central Institute for Socialist Management of the Central Committee of the SED on March 24, 1966: *Zur Wirtschaftspolitik der SED in der Periode des umfassenden Aufbaus des Sozialismus in der DDR unter den Bedingungen der technischen Revolution* (Berlin, 1966).

[111] Paul Fröhlich, "Das Leben unserer Partei," *Einheit* 21, no. 4 (April 1966): 419; and Hermann Matern, "Die revolutionären Traditionen der deutschen Arbeiterbewegung leben im Kampf der Sozialistischen Einheitspartei Deutschlands," *Einheit* 21, no. 4 (April 1966): 433.

[112] Fröhlich, ibid., p. 419.

Such definitions of the Central Committee's function by leading party personalities indicate the position of this body in the SED's conception of itself. This change of self-image has been accompanied by moves to make party and state organs more similar in their functions: the directions agreed upon in the Politburo or Secretariat are "processed" by the Council of Ministers, the State Planning Commission, and the Research Council for effective, not merely programmatic, application.

The technical details contained in the major reports delivered by Politburo members and candidates—such as Neumann, Mittag, and Jarowinsky—and technical reports of Central Committee section heads— for example, Lothar Oppermann at the Eighth Plenum in February 1965[113]—require far more comprehension and specific technical knowledge on the part of the listener than was the case in 1959–1960. Party experts Apel and Mittag repeatedly emphasized the primary importance of expertise: "It can be said that expertise is the structure around which the capacities and properties of a leader in socialist society are molded."[114]

Only after the Sixth SED Congress did the expanded functions of the Central Committee become apparent. However, the trend toward more technical discussion was already evident at the Ninth Plenum of the Central Committee in July 1960 and during the Economic Conference of the Central Committee and the Council of Ministers in October 1961. These tendencies are especially evident when the subjects of discussion at various conferences are distinguished and compared. Central Committee plenums at which scientists, factory managers, and technicians participate must be distinguished from conferences organized jointly by the Central Committee and the Council of Ministers. The latter are carried out in closed sessions devoted principally to economic and domestic policy problems. Finally, the conferences organized by the Central Committee must be distinguished from occasions at which members of sections of the Central Committee apparatus participate in leading roles. The very multiplicity of conferences organized or sponsored by the Central Committee is an indication of the coordinating, transmitting, and consultative

[113] Lothar Oppermann, "Für höchste Qualität bei der Verwirklichung des Gesetzes über das einheitliche sozialistische Bildungssystem," *Neues Deutschland,* February 13, 1965.
[114] Apel and Mittag, *Wissenschaftliche Führungstätigkeit,* p. 91.

functions of this body. Many disparate social groups, interests, and goals must repeatedly be coordinated. This task is the more necessary, since current Central Committee plena have become arenas for sharp controversy. For example, at the Eleventh Central Committee Plenum in December 1965 different groupings, norms, and attitudinal mores were explicitly articulated. Hanna Wolf, Alfred Kurella, and Paul Fröhlich represented the strategic clique, while the writer Christa Wolf expressed a model of "dynamic order," characteristic of the institutionalized counter elite.[115] Christa Wolf apparently considered herself a representative of the "new morality" in East German society, and thus a critical authority vis-à-vis the party. Although advocates of the "new morality" must be distinguished from pragmatic representatives of the "dynamic order"— i.e., from the rising generation of managers and technocrats—both groups support the thesis of this order. The "dynamic order" is characterized by a relative openmindedness and flexibility of thought, the courage to experiment, and the search for rational decisions, primarily in the economic sphere. Despite criticism of the party, state, economy, and society, disciples of the "new morality" and pragmatic technocrats accept the prevailing system and do not challenge its basic principles.

Selected Central Committee meetings will be analyzed below, with particular emphasis on illustrations of the functional change in that organ's role. The discussion will begin with the Ninth Central Committee Plenum of July 1960, which functioned as a working session prior to the introduction of the new economic system.

THE NINTH PLENUM OF THE CENTRAL COMMITTEE, JULY 1960

The Ninth Central Committee had a total of 474 participants. According to *Neues Deutschland*,[116] 115 members and candidates of the Central Committee were augmented by 300 scientists, technicians, engineers, and functionaries of the regional party and mass organizations. The plenum

---

[115] Cf. the contributions to the debate published in *Neues Deutschland,* December 19, 1965.

[116] The communiqué of the Ninth Central Committee Plenum reads as follows: "The Central Committee convened July 20–23, 1960 with the participation of 474 guests who were scientists of various institutes and institutions of higher learning, laborers, technicians, and engineers from socialist enterprises, as well as party, state, and economic functionaries." *Neues Deutschland,* July 24, 1960.

was organized under the slogan, "Toward a scientific–technical optimum in machine construction and metallurgy through cooperative socialist labor." Based on "discussion papers" dispatched by Ulbricht to the Central Committee,[117] numerous professional lectures were given on the current stage of development of metallurgy, machine and machine-tool construction, electrical engineering, and the construction of chemical plants. Contributions to the discussion were for the most part limited to the topics covered in the principal speeches. National and regional situations in these branches of industry were discussed. The Central Committee paper placed the greatest stress on the demand "for the economical use of raw material and strictest measures of economy." This was the first meeting to deal comprehensively with problems of rationalization and standardization in important industries, which were to become increasingly important as topics of discussion after 1961. The discussion included organizational problems, mostly with reference to the VVBs. The plenum repeatedly called for expansion of VVB, production group, and WTZ activities and responsibilities.

The minutes of the Ninth Plenum list 54 speakers. From these it will be useful to distinguish four groups: (1) functionaries without professional training; (2) functionaries with professional training; (3) economists, scientists, and other experts; (4) persons with honorary functions.[118]

[117] Letter from Walter Ulbricht to laborers, foremen, technicians, engineers, and scientists in the industries and institutes for machine contruction and metallurgy, the universities, colleges and professional schools, the German Academy of Science, and the state and economic authorities, and the Central Committee on the economical utilization of raw materials and the greatest possible economy, in 9. Tagung des Zentralkomitees (Berlin, 1961), pp. 5 ff.

[118] The first group comprises functionaries of the party, state, and mass organizations, who have no economic–technical training or long-standing experience (i.e., functionaries without professional training). The second group consists of functionaries of the party, state, and mass organizations with an economic–technical education or long-standing experience (professionally trained functionaries). The economic functionaries in the narrow sense—i.e., those functionaries who do not serve in the state administration but in the economic enterprises, the VVB, VEB, LPG, etc., were not included within the group of state functionaries. They belong to the third group of economists, scientists, and experts. The group of "persons with honorary functions" includes those who have no direct bearing on the subject matter, usually subsidiary officeholders in various

If participants are classified into these groups, we find that the proportion of professionally trained people who addressed this plenum is quite high: 11 party functionaries with professional training (group 2) and 24 experts (group 3), as compared with 7 untrained functionaries (group 1) and 6 persons with honorary functions (group 4).[119] However, lectures and contributions to discussion by professionally trained persons dealt less with problems of machine construction and metallurgy than with questions of a more general ideological nature.

THE ECONOMIC CONFERENCE OF THE CENTRAL COMMITTEE
AND THE COUNCIL OF MINISTERS, OCTOBER 1961

A more precise analysis of the change and expansion of Central Committee functions is furnished by examining both the topics treated and the backgrounds of the participants at the Economic Conferences of 1961 and 1963, and the Rationalization Conference of 1966. Studied in connection with the events of the Ninth Plenum, these conferences further emphasize the increasing expertise of the Central Committee and the "pragmatic" nature of intraparty discussions.

At the Economic Conference in October 1961 the SED leadership drew its first conclusions from the two major policy initiatives that immediately followed the erection of the Berlin Wall in mid-August 1961: the campaign called "freedom from [economic] interference" on the part of the FRG (including Western shipments), and the "production campaign." As both campaigns were complex in character, an attempt to clarify briefly the political and ideological dimensions of these initiatives is in order. The production campaign was carried out over a relatively long period. That it was still the central topic of the party press in August 1962—twelve months after the Wall was built—indicates that East

---

social and economic spheres. This study is confined to the participants known through the publication of their opinions and statements at the discussions. In addition, the available information on acquired occupation and particular function, which was supplemented from the material of the Institute for Political Science at the Free University of Berlin and their published contributions to the debates were taken into account in this classification.

[119] For six participants we lacked biographical data for classification.

German society found itself in a particularly difficult economic situation at that time.[120]

The strategic clique started out with a broad range of ideological arguments. Agitprop activities were channelled "inward"—i.e., directed toward party members—and "outward"—toward the populace of the GDR, West Germany, Eastern Europe, and the rest of the world public. This ideological campaign put particular stress on social and economic concepts of great dimension: "In the plans of the Bonn regime to undermine and politically blackmail the GDR, sabotage of commercial relations between the two German states has played a not insignificant role."[121] The national emergency was portrayed with a sense of urgency suitable to a crisis situation. "In the present weeks and months we are passing through a period the significance of which will become apparent only in the future. Nevertheless, we all sense that we stand poised at a point in our development of decisive importance for the history of the future Germany."[122] In the fall of 1961 such proclamations served to distract the attention of the public from the burning issue of that period—the Berlin Wall.

Besides functioning as a call for solidarity in a situation of "national emergency," the production campaign allowed the SED's social planners to experiment with alternative solutions to the more general social problems confronting them: "The implementation of the production campaign raises old and new problems in an intensified form, not only with regard to the economy, but also with regard to the development of social life in our Republic."[123] Here, the party leadership was using a classic tactic of Communist tradition. Totalitarian leaders always attempt to adjust to the actual situation while aiming at further transformation of their societies. Among the unsolved problems that continue to confront the SED are the establishment of a "code of Socialist morality" and, in

[120] Cf. Harry Matthes, "Materielle Interessiertheit und Produktionsaufgebot," *Einheit* 17, no. 8 (August 1962): 13 ff.
[121] "Zur Umstellung der Produktion und Sicherung unserer Wirtschaft gegenüber der Störtätigkeit Bonns," *Einheit* 16, no. 10 (October 1961): 1470.
[122] "Das Produktionsaufgebot. Ausdruck der hohen politischen Erkenntnis unserer Werktätigen," *Einheit* 16, no. 10 (October 1961): 1464.
[123] Ibid., p. 1465.

connection with this, the elimination of factors which impede the workers from achieving high productivity.

The production campaign will be realized successfully not when decreed from above, but when the masses are truly drawn into the process, [i.e.] if by dint of expert political and ideological work the initiative comes from below—from the brigades and foremen—and if these [contractual] obligations are truly those of the workers and employees.[124]

The inconsistency of the party leadership's policy toward the rank-and-file membership was shown more clearly in its appeals of August–December 1961. However, the construction of the Berlin Wall, the campaign for freedom from interference in internal GDR affairs, and the production campaign were appropriate issues for appealing to the elite consciousness of party members. All SED members were to regard themselves as *the* political elite of East German society in an hour of danger. It was argued that the class-conscious worker had "power"; consequently "he and his class bear decisive social responsibility" for the consequences of events.[125] To dissipate growing insecurity in the SED's rank and file, the leadership constantly stressed the "absolute" and unassailable position of power of the party, as the legitimate heir of political power in the GDR: "The major significance of the GDR workers' confidence in their power is the fact that it is rooted in our objective situation and the nature of the worker-and-peasant state."[126]

The domestic political consequences of such ideological arguments indicated a return to the political traditions of the original Bolshevik Party, i.e., to the period of War Communism in Soviet Russia that existed from mid-1918 to the spring of 1921. During the fall of 1961 the SED repeatedly cited Lenin's speech to the Ninth Party Congress of March 1920. While Lenin spoke of the "class consciousness and perseverance of the working class," he also emphasized "tasks of peaceful economic construction," thus foreshadowing the New Economic Policy (NEP). Although the SED's references to the history of the CPSU were intended to bolster the waning confidence of its membership, this measure was not

---

[124] Ibid.
[125] Alfred Beau and Karl-Heinz Schulze, "Klassenbewusstsein und Produktionsaufgebot," *Einheit* 16, no. 11–12 (November–December 1961): 1697.
[126] Ibid., p. 1701.

quite consistent with a turn toward a more pragmatic economic policy.[127]

The ideological campaign initiated by SED agitprop cadres, based on references to the history of the CPSU, was clearly traditional in style. This kind of agitprop activity was only marginal to the new, more objective tone exhibited by the scientists, economic functionaries, and party theorists at the SED Economic Conference in the fall of 1961, which was devoted to newer, more rational solutions of concrete economic and social problems. In the midst of the agitprop campaigns, more realistic voices could be distinguished; the campaigns for production and freedom from outside interference in the economy facilitated rationalization of the tense relationship between the SED and the East German populace by emphasizing the economic reasons for this relationship.

When more workers realize that in the long run they cannot consume more than they have previously produced, that they cannot demand more from the State than they have given it, and when with ruthless honesty toward themselves, their class, and their country they evaluate their own performance and place the conscientious fulfillment of their duties and the maintenance of social interests in the foreground of their actions, they will change their attitude toward work.[128]

Such pronouncements seem to express a certain rapprochement between the SED and East German society, and at least a partial identity of interest between the two groups. The individual was to realize that he should work and at the same time relinquish his hostility toward or rejection of the party. In transcending mere postulated and ideological phraseology and posing rational arguments to the people, the SED leadership for the first time began to treat the masses as its partners.

That the East German people have taken pride in their performance since 1961, and even more so since 1963, is due to this change of approach. There is no real contradiction in the purposes of this new programmatic emphasis in the relationship between the party and the populace, since during the same period the new pride was exploited by the party far more skillfully than previously. Many letters to the edi-

---

[127] Cf., for instance, the arguments presented by Manfred Herold, "Der XXII. Parteitag der KPdSU und einige Fragen des sozialistischen Aufbaus in der DDR," *Einheit* 16, no. 11–12 (November–December 1961): 1589 ff.

[128] "Das Produktionsaufgebot," p. 1466.

tor,[129] articles, and pamphlets on the homeland, the state, and the national consciousness[130] were published. Moreover, even critical Western visitors and observers noted the formation of a new "GDR consciousness," particularly among the youth.[131] Pride in their accomplishments and "GDR consciousness" on the part of many social groups, especially those involved in the productive process, is accompanied by a relatively extensive rise in productivity. Although the application of the concept of efficiency in the production campaign was hampered by an essentially ideological outlook, some predictability of individual performance has been in evidence since 1963–1964. That it is possible for an individual to estimate his performance, and the attraction of increased social status, are operating factors at present. Thus, in agreement with findings for Western industrial societies, fixed rules of ascent presuppose

[129] Although the "letters to the editor" appear to have been manipulated by the party press, some of the more recurrent arguments are presented here. Thus, Robert Mühlberg on April 10, 1965 wrote a letter to the editor of *Neues Deutschland* under the heading "Is the German dualism to blame?" "To my mind many citizens of our state have from time to time had to face the question: should I change my place of residence, should I go to the West? Difficulties at work and family conflicts were often the underlying reason, and not a few have chosen this course. . . . Here nothing came to us gratis. Nobody gave us a dollar infusion, nobody opened the doors of the highly industrialized West European countries before us. We have paid our war debts, whereas West Germany evaded this accursed duty and obligation. I could give you many examples of the unspeakable difficulties that have arisen in our modern factories. Nobody can believe that we could ever forget the sweat we sacrificed. We think differently about our homeland, the German Democratic Republic, from the way the affluent citizen in the Federal Republic thinks of his. For us the concept of "Fatherland" —however much scholars may argue about its correct definition—is a term based on our actions. Our Fatherland is not that mystical Germany which in reality has no longer existed since 1945; it is the state we have built and in which we are living now. There are those who realize this fact consciously; others are only subconsciously aware of it."

[130] On the discussion about German national consciousness, see Ewald Schröder, "Frühes Werden, gutes Sein. Probleme bei der Erziehung von Staatsbürgern," *Sonntag* 21, no. 29 (1966): 3 ff; Gottfried Richter, "Patriotismus, schlechte Gewohnheiten, gute Atmosphäre," ibid., pp. 6 ff; and Johannes Zelt and Karl Reissig, *Patriotismus und Internationalismus heute* (Berlin, 1964).

[131] See the relevant passages in Amos Elon, *In einem heimgesuchten Land* (Munich, 1966), p. 137, and Günter Zehm, "Lebt der Mensch vom Brot allein? Heute jenseits der Zonengrenze: DDR-Bewusstsein und Nationalbewusstsein." *Die Welt,* January 7, 1967, Supplement *"Die Geistige Welt,"* p. 1.

the existence of an objective performance scale for East German society.[132] The party adjusted rapidly to the growing demands of numerous social groups for objective criteria for production performance, rise in social status, career, and professional patterns. For example, Ulbricht, at a mass rally of Berlin youth on September 25, 1963, made repeated demands for the immediate establishment of operative professional criteria in industry.[133] The SED leadership shows a more than passive concern for establishing a career-oriented society; in fact, it actively encourages this model of behavior.[134]

The series of campaigns inaugurated during 1961–1963 appear to fit into this general pattern in their organizational and educational outlines. Erich Apel's statements on differentiation, efficiency, and the creation of fixed standards—and, thus, the predictability of sanctions—in the economy and society exemplify the emphasis placed on economic and social factors in these campaigns.

Knowledge is required to apply science, and to develop, introduce, and preserve our new technology. Consequently, Comrade Ulbricht has demanded at the Economic Conference the creation of an atmosphere of reading and learning throughout our Republic.[135]

Ensuing organizational improvements and conversion to the principle of cost accountability in the factories, the introduction of new technological processes, rationalized investment procedures, and the emphasis on the selective development of certain production spheres were to constitute the immediate agenda. The production campaign and the drive to free the

---

[132] Friedrich Fürstenberg. *Das Aufstiegsproblem in der modernen Gesellschaft* (Stuttgart, 1962), p. 154.

[133] Walter Ulbricht, "Die Aufgaben der Jugend bei der Verwirklichung des neuen ökonomischen Systems der Planung und Leitung der Volkswirtschaft," in *Zum neuen ökonomischen System der Planung und Leitung* (Berlin, 1966), pp. 316 ff.

[134] The occupational profiles published in 1964 by the Ministry of Education and compiled in collaboration with the enterprises involved contain information about: (a) the significance of the occupation for the national economy; (b) the qualifications required in order to practice the occupation in question; (c) the contents and scope of the work area; (d) the preliminary requirements for learning the occupation; (e) the duration and means of training; and (f) opportunities for specialization and further training. See *Berufsbilder für Ausbildungsberufe,* publication of the Ministry of Education (Berlin, 1964).

[135] Erich Apel "Einige Grundfragen der Leitung unserer sozialistischen Volkswirtschaft," *Einheit* 16, no. 11–12 ((November–December 1961): 1624 ff.

economy from outside influences in the fall of 1961 can be regarded as initial steps in the implementation of the new economic system that was to be outlined more fully in 1963.

The final elaboration of the principles of the new economic system is linked to the First Economic Conference of the Central Committee and the Council of Ministers held in October 1961 in Berlin, as well as to the campaigns of 1961. Both the composition and number (3500) of the participants at the Conference indicated its "mobilizational" and predominantly agitational character. According to an editorial comment in *Die Wirtschaft,* the participants included

. . . leading workers from industry, transport, and construction; trade workers; foremen, engineers, and managers from enterprises and VVBs; academic personnel in research, teaching, and industry; representatives of the cultural sphere, party functionaries, officials from the government and various economic and social organizations.[136]

In addition, to judge from the speakers and participants in the discussions, the Economic Conference can be seen as a harbinger of the expansion of the organizations represented.

Two prominent features of the Economic Conference indicated that preparations for restructuring the party organization were underway. These were the strategic clique's ambivalent attitude toward rank-and-file party members, and the party and state apparatuses' preparations to implement policies within the general directives of the "new economic system" (which was influenced considerably by the Soviet model). Although the new economic system has been in effect only from the fall of 1963, the party had long envisaged the comprehensive reorganization of a differentiated economy and social system. These phenomena are indicative of the party leadership's reorientation, particularly in the organizational sphere.

The selection of speakers and participants, and the speeches and discussions at the Conference reflect the complex character of the consequent restructuring process. As at the Ninth Central Committee Session in 1960, four groups stand out: functionaries of the party, the state, or the mass organizations without (1) or with (2) technical training; economists, technologists, scientists, and experts (3); and speakers with purely honorary functions (4). Each group, especially the first

[136] See the lead editorial in *Die Wirtschaft* 16, no. 42–43 (1961): 1.

three, used divergent arguments. Ulbricht and the sixteen nonprofessional functionaries who spoke emphasized the political and ideological aspects of the situation that existed in the fall of 1961. Foreign policy statements were accordingly concerned mainly with the problem of linking the GDR in an economic community with the Soviet Union and the other East bloc states under the aegis of COMECON. After the speeches of Erich Apel, Alfred Neumann, and Karl Mewis, trained economists, technologists, and scientists took up three major domestic problems: (1) Economic planning was to be supplemented by "complex-territorial" planning. Previous planning according to branches and areas of industry was to be combined with that according to *Bezirke*. (2) On the national level of the state apparatus this economic restructuring involved the devolution of numerous functions to subordinate levels. (3) The State Secretariat for Research and Technology was established and the tasks of the Research Council and State Planning Commission were reformulated. Whereas the Research Council was made responsible for central planning and control mainly in the natural sciences, the Planning Commission, as the "central organ of the Council of Ministers," was to take future responsibility "for planning and proportional development in all branches of the economy." At the top level numerous new leadership bodies were established.

Intra-enterprise problems were also discussed. In addition to the problem of increasing productivity, the Conference dealt with the problems of a more exact consideration of objective economic criteria and conversion to work norms and "average" salaries. Implicit in this change in the wage structure were reductions in premiums. This was indirectly admitted at the conference by Gerhard Schürer, soon to be Erich Apel's successor as Chairman of the State Planning Commission and at that time Section Head for economic affairs in the Central Committee apparatus: "The production campaign . . . has served to correct several mistaken concepts in the principle of material incentives; that is to say, where the [incorrect] opinion has been held that material incentives may be obtained without really earning them."[137] In the discussion on problems of food supply, almost all of the party and

[137] Gerhard Schürer, "Neue Technik. Neue Vorgabezeiten," *Die Wirtschaft* 16, no. 44 (1961): 4.

government speakers advocated a hard-line approach (in contrast with the line taken in 1963). For example, Pupluschnik, head of trade and supply for the Halle *Bezirk* council, rejected all "egalitarian and leveling" methods of supplying the people with foodstuffs, demanding instead a "focal point" approach in food distribution.[138]

Published accounts of the conference list 17 functionaries without professional training, 7 functionaries with professional training, 13 economists, scientists, and other experts, and 11 persons with honorary functions.

THE ECONOMIC CONFERENCE OF THE CENTRAL COMMITTEE
AND THE COUNCIL OF MINISTERS, JUNE 1963

In contrast to the complex political, ideologic-agitatorial, and economic goals that have dominated the economic conference of the SED leadership in October 1961, the June 1963 conference can be classified as an almost apolitical technical meeting. The organizational-political tendency already manifested in the first economic conference of the Central Committee and the Council of Ministers becomes more pronounced in this second meeting. The change of the Central Committee from an acclamatory to a consultative body is even more evident in the general trend of discussion and the premature closing of the Economic Conference in June 1963. However, comparison of the number of participants at both Conferences indicates some change. The number of participants dropped from 3500 in 1961 to just under 600 in 1963.[139] A summary of the most important topics treated at the 1963 Economic Conference will be followed by a detailed analysis of the shift from the hortatory style of discussion employed at the 1961 Conference to the more dispassionate treatment of concrete issues in 1963.

Political arguments such as Ulbricht's 1961 emphasis on the ties between the GDR and the Soviet Union, which was aimed at buttressing the strategic clique's position, were relegated to the background in 1963. No explicit stress of the close ties to the Soviet Union or East Europe is to be found in any of the Conference's twenty-five published speeches and

---

[138] See his contribution to the debate of the Economic Conference in *Die Wirtschaft* 16, no. 42–43 (1961): 18.
[139] See *Die Wirtschaft* 16, no. 42–43 (1961): 1; and 18, no. 26 (1963): 3.

comments. The 1963 Economic Conference focused mainly on problems in the VVBs and VEBs, as well as on the situation in the food supply sector. Ulbricht devoted long sections of his speech to the production principle. He concluded his remarks with the statement that "the production principle encompasses the overall activities of the government." He also paid more attention to improving scientific research in the economy and proclaimed the establishment of a special advisory body for economic research, to be under the aegis of the State Planning Commission. Other problems covered were: increasing the autonomy of the VVBs—i.e., the socialist trusts—which in the central plan were called upon to take over full responsibility for planning, and the direction and control of subordinate VEBs; the creation of a functional guidance system in the factories; increased powers for general directors, chief economists, and the plant managers; in the VVBs, cooperation between factories, universities, and other research institutes; and, finally, changes in the factories brought about by the introduction of economic accountability and consideration of cost, price, and profit indices as the guiding economic factors.

In questions of food supply and in the attitude of the party leadership vis-à-vis the people considerable change was called for. Ulbricht called upon the party "to make the shopwindow the magnet of material interest."[140] In contrast to 1961, and for that matter to the restrictive repressive consumer policy followed by the Politburo since 1949, commerce henceforth was to "react in an operative way to changes of demand."[141] Criticism of the catastrophic supply situation of the preceding fifteen years, particularly with regard to consumer items of high quality, was comparatively free.[142]

The overall style of the 1963 Conference was determined largely by those party, government, and economic functionaries with professional training, along with technologists and scientists. The speeches of 25

[140] Walter Ulbricht, "Das neue ökonomische System der Planung und Leitung der Volkswirtschaft in der Praxis," *Die Wirtschaft* 18, no. 26 (1963): 18.
[141] Albert Dressel, "Ökonomische Hebel und bedarfsgerechte Warensortimente," *Die Wirtschaft* 18, no. 26 (1963): 41.
[142] See, for instance, the Conference statement of Zwarg, a staff member of the consumer cooperative of the city of Potsdam, "Wege zur besseren Versorgung der Bevölkerung," *Die Wirtschaft* 18, no. 26 (1963): 28-30.

functionaries were publicly reported. The group of speakers consisted of 6 functionaries without professional training, 4 functionaries with professional training, 13 economists, scientists, and other experts, and 2 persons with honorary functions.

THE ECONOMIC CONFERENCES OF 1961 AND 1963 COMPARED

A striking feature of the 1963 Economic Conference is that the number of professionally untrained participants among the speakers was far lower than in 1961. Press accounts and official published protocols indicate that this group shrank from seventeen in 1961 to six in 1963. Another index of increased professionalization and dispassionate discussion in the Central Committee is the decrease in the number of functionaries from lower level party *Kreis,* VEB, and VVB executive bodies who, although resembling the honorary participants, have not been included in that group. In 1961, 10 of the 24 representatives of party and state apparatuses or mass organizations belonged to this latter group. In 1963, only 1 of these persons can be regarded as a purely honorary participant. Examination of the speakers' roster of honorary functionaries yields further data essential to our analysis. While in 1961, 11 of the 48 speakers could be regarded as honorary, this category had shrunk to a mere 2 out of 25 in 1963.

However, in absolute terms, the other two groups—namely, party functionaries with professional training and scientists, technicians, and economists—have remained approximately equal in number for both Conferences. Of 48 speakers in 1961, 7 were party and state functionaries with training or experience, while 13 can be categorized as experts. In 1963, among the 25 speakers cited in the weekly *Die Wirtschaft,* 4 were functionaries and 13 experts. Thus, the ratio of experts to the other groups has risen considerably from that of 1961.

These conclusions are borne out when the group of party and scientific experts is examined with respect to the substance of their contributions to the discussion. At the 1961 Economic Conference, 3 of the 7 party experts spoke in quite general terms on ideological matters. Only 5 of the 13 economists dealt with specifically technical issues. In 1963, 3 of the 4 party experts at the Conference, Günter Mittag—then Secretary of the SED Central Committee for Economic Affairs—

Wolfgang Junker, Minister for Construction, and chief planner Erich Apel dealt exclusively with specific problems. Of the 13 experts who spoke at the 1963 Conference, 11 spoke exclusively on economic and financial policies and 2 on problems of contractual research, or the duties of the Chamber of Technology within the framework of the "new economic system."[143]

THE SEVENTH CENTRAL COMMITTEE PLENUM, DECEMBER 1964

While many representatives of the sciences, industry, and administration had been invited to participate at the Ninth Central Committee Plenum of July 1960, almost all participants at the Seventh Plenum of December 1964 were full and candidate members of the Central Committee.[144] The Ninth Plenum appears in retrospect to have represented the Central

[143] Contractual research has a long tradition in the GDR. As early as 1957 it was known as "Auftragsforschung." (See Fritz Selbmann "Neue Phase in der Forschungsarbeit der DDR," *Die Wirtschaft* 12, no. 34 (1957): 6.) From the beginning of 1963 its role continued to increase. Institutes of higher learning signed general contracts for "scientific-technical collaboration" with VVB and other nationally owned enterprises. A contract of this kind, concluded by the Martin Luther Universität in Halle with an unnamed VVB has been published in *Das Hochschulwesen* 13, no. 10 (October 1965): 649 ff. Evidently such contractual research was of still greater importance for the technical and trade colleges and the universities. Thus, the Commissary Director of the Institute for Process Technology at the Technical University of Dresden, who also is a member of the Scientific-Technical Council of the VVB Potash Works in Dresden, has stated: "Our contract is based on mutual advantage. Just as a project for the award of a degree or a diploma, where a student who is about to finish his studies carries out a scientific investigation for three months without renumeration, is to the industry's economic advantage, so the student also profits from it in that he becomes integrated within and accustomed to his future field of work without as yet bearing full responsibility. A research assistant who for purposes of promotion engages in concentrated fashion on a project relating to the potash industry saves that industry considerable work." Manfred Schubert "Verträge vermeiden 'Feuerwehreinsätze,' Probleme der sozialistischen Gemeinschaftsarbeit in der Wissenschaft," *Neues Deutschland,* October 16, 1965, Suppl. No. 42, p. 4. On the legal provisions governing contractual research, cf. in particular Such *et al.,* "Vertragssystem und Wissenschaflich-technische Arbeit," *Staat und Recht* 12, no. 1 (January 1963): 102 ff; Prof. Dr. Heinze, "Wirksamere Vertragsforschung," *Die Wirtschaft,* 18, no. 26 (1963): 26; Prof. Dr. Ing. Horst Peschel, "Komplexe Gemeinschaftsarbeit in der KdT," *ibid.,* p. 36.
[144] The proceedings of the Seventh Convention of the Central Committee of the SED, December 2–5, 1964 have appeared in a series of brochures (Berlin: Dietz, 1965); the volumes are not numbered. The reader is referred to the

Committee's coordinating functions; the Seventh Plenum's atmosphere was that of a closed executive session of the Central Committee.

The Seventh Session dealt with the experiences of the new economic system and subsequently concentrated on limiting the influence and independence of the exceptionally successful experts within the SED. Apart from organizational problems (in particular, those relating to the activities of the regional economic councils), the session focused mainly on emphasizing the SED's leading role. This line was promulgated and the spheres of responsibility for general directors of the VVBs were narrowed.[145] Indeed, since December 1964 the territorial principle and questions of SED organization have received increased priority, while the production principle has been correspondingly de-emphasized. Among the many speakers who reiterated this theme throughout the proceedings, Ulbricht, Hager, and Honecker pointed out that the SED and the mass organizations were political, not economic organizations. The speakers' roster underlines this point: Twenty-seven functionaries with no apparent technical training, as opposed to thirteen with such training, and three economists spoke. However, the honorary functionaries were almost entirely relegated to the background. Only one from this group spoke.[146]

---

following: Kurt Hager's report, *Bericht des Politbüros an die 7. Tagung des ZK der SED, 2. bis 5. Dezember 1964; Diskussionsreden zum Bericht des Politbüros an die 7. Tagung des ZK der SED;* Georg Ewald, *Die Anwendung des neuen ökonomischen Systems der Planung und Leitung der Volkswirtschaft. Referat;* Margot Honecker, *Der Volkswirtschaftsplan 1965 und die Aufgaben auf dem Gebiet des Bildungswesens. Referat;* Werner Jarowinsky, *Über die Durchführung des neuen ökonomischen Systems der Planung und Leitung der Volkswirtschaft im Binnenhandel in Verbindung mit der Verwirklichung des Volkswirtschaftsplanes 1965. Referat;* Horst Kaminsky, *Die sich aus dem Volkswirtschaftsplan 1965 ergebenden Grundfragen des Staatshaushaltsplanes und die Aufgaben der Finanz-, Bank- und Preisorgane bei der weiteren Durchführung des neuen ökonomischen Systems der Planung und Leitung der Volkswirtschaft. Referat;* Alfred Neumann, *Der Volkswirtschaftsplan 1965 in der Industrie und die weitere Durchführung des neuen ökonomischen Systems der Planung und Leitung der Volkswirtschaft. Referat; Zur Durchführung des Volkswirtschaftsplanes und des Staatshaushaltsplanes, 1965. Diskussionsreden. Schlusswort: Erich Apel;* and Walter Ulbricht, *Antwort auf aktuelle und ökonomische Fragen. Schlusswort zur Diskussion über den Bericht des Politburos an die 7. Tagung des ZK der SED, 2. bis 5. Dezember 1964.*
[145] Neumann, *Der Volkswirtschaftsplan 1965*, p. 7.
[146] A total of 44 speakers' names was ascertained by comparing *Neues Deutschland,* December 6, 1964, with the brochures listed in note 144.

THE CONFERENCE OF THE CENTRAL COMMITTEE AND THE COUNCIL OF
MINISTERS ON "SOCIALIST RATIONALIZATION AND STANDARDIZATION,"
JUNE 1966

Measures for rationalization of large sectors of the economy—primarily
that of investment—occupied the attention of the SED leadership after
the Eleventh Plenum of the Central Committee in December 1965. The
Politburo's grandiose plans to "free the economy of the GDR from
(external economic) interference" (i.e., from West Germany), were
evident in a series of extensive new investments made between 1961
and 1964. These created new functions which could not always be filled.
Simultaneously, other branches of industry which had been perennially
neglected, e.g., construction, the machine and agricultural machinery
construction industries, transport, light industry, agriculture, domestic
trade, and public health were now spotlighted in the discussions.

Moreover, these latter branches of industry were given special
consideration in the formation of working groups at the rationalization
conference. Other working groups were set up for the chemical, metal-
working and ore-mining, metallurgy, and potash industries. The details of
a comprehensive rationalization program, given in the speeches and
reports to the working groups, can be summarized briefly. Rationalization
and standardization must concentrate on the following problems: home
production of the means of production; reduction of the number of
vacant jobs and an increase in the work efficiency in occupied jobs;
reduction of stocks of goods; reduction of the excessive numbers of
product classifications (*standards*) (at present there are some 10,000
GDR standards and 20,000 branch-determined standards [*Fachbereichs-
standards*], the numbers of which are still on the rise). A further tightening up of administration in the VVBs and VEBs was demanded.
More than before, the State Planning Commission, the Ministries, the
State Secretariat for Research and Technology and the National Research Council along with the *Bezirk* economic councils were to be
made responsible for implementing the rationalization program.[147]

[147] Günter Mittag, "Komplexe sozialistische Rationalisierung—eine Hauptrichtung
unserer ökonomischen Politik bis 1970," in *Sozialistische Rationalisierung und
Standardisierung. Konferenz des Zentralkomitees der Sozialistischen Einheitspartei
Deutschlands und des Ministerrates der Deutschen Demokratischen Republik, 23.
und 24. Juni 1966 in Leipzig. Referate, Berichte, Schlusswort* (Berlin, 1966),
pp. 31 ff, particularly pp. 57 ff.

The problems elaborated at the June 1966 Rationalization Conference indicate the main bottlenecks in the GDR economy. This meeting may be of greater ultimate significance than the Economic Conferences of 1961 and 1963. Both the number and qualifications of the participants certainly lead to the conclusion that the Central Committee's sphere of functional activities had been expanded further. Several hundred participants,[148] of whom some 150 participated as lecturers and chairmen of working groups, commented in the discussions or submitted written contributions. One would further infer that the Central Committee was to fulfill numerous directing or controlling functions, which are to be coordinated with those of the Council of Ministers within the framework of the state apparatus. Available sources indicate that participants included 13 leading functionaries from the party and state apparatuses and mass organizations who had no technical training or extensive experience, 34 top functionaries with training, 77 technologists, managers, scientists, and experts, and two persons with purely honorary functions.[149] The experts, many of whom belong to the CC, occupied the center of the stage throughout the Conference.[150] The "professionalization" of the Central Committee's work style, recognizable since 1964, is thus apparent. Undoubtedly, the stature of the Central Committee and the Council of Ministers as consultative and transmissional bodies where important social decisions are worked out has gained as a result of this convention.

The foregoing (and partial) analysis indicates that since 1963 the Central Committee, the State Planning Commission, the Council of Ministers, the National Research Council, and other bureaucratic bodies seem to have changed both functionally and organizationally. The process of transformation in the party's organizations which led to

[148] Thus, according to a report of Johann Wittik, the working group on light industry, the food industry and *Bezirk*-directed industries alone comprised 240 members (See ibid., p. 106).

[149] Ascertained from the proceedings of the above Conference and the reports on the conference which appeared in the Supplements to *Die Wirtschaft* 21, no. 26–28 (1966). For lack of biographical data, 24 speakers and participants in the debate had to be excluded from our analysis.

[150] Cf. the minutes of the Conference in *Sozialistische Rationalisierung und Standardisierung. Konferenz* (cited in footnote 147) as well as in *Sozialistische Rationalisierung und Standardisierung. Konferenz . . . Diskussion zu den Referaten und zum vorgelegten Entwurf der Thesen*, 2 vols. (Berlin, 1966).

increasing adaptation to the dynamics of an industrial society had already been initiated by § 40 of the SED Statute of 1963. This process can be more accurately characterized as a trend toward "professionalization" and "functionalization" combined with the preservation of the political power of a strategic clique and an increase in the functional efficiency of an industrial society. The characteristics, coming increasingly into the foreground after 1963, of the "consultative" even if not of the "participative" authoritarianism greatly gain in profile by comparison with the speakers and participants at the plenums and economic conferences under study. Even though only a comparative analysis of the contents of the lectures and discussions held at the meetings investigated here can provide accurate information concerning changes in the function of the CC, it has already become clear that the CC, aided by economic-political pressures that develop an increasingly forceful inner dynamic, assumes more and more the functions of a center for coordination and transformation.

Despite the growing prominence of experts both within and outside the party ranks, analysis of the social composition of the Central Committee in 1963 (see Chapter Three) will prove that the experts do not yet directly influence the processes of political decision making. The technocracy of Veblen, the managerial regime of Burnham, or the meritocracy of Young—which even in the West reflect political and social reality only to a limited extent—have yet to replace the rule of the strategic clique in the GDR. Nevertheless, the SED's bureaucratic role is being weakened by experts in the functional spheres, in the party apparatus itself, and in the state and economy. While experts have staked out extensive areas of social and political power, they have not yet succeeded in penetrating the sphere of top political decision making in the GDR.

The entry of experts into the SED apparatus is accompanied by a phenomenon unique to East Germany—indeed, to all authoritarian ruling systems of this type. That is the fact that the distinction between the strategic clique and the party experts extends deep into the professional sphere. While binding designs for occupational positions appear to be on the increase for experts in all functional areas of society, crystallization and institutionalization of professional and career patterns has resulted in few standardized patterns for upward professional mobility for lower-level, nonexpert functionaries only. Since the establishment of the new economic system it is possible to speak of a decrease in precise occupational patterns for nonexpert SED functionaries.

6. Attitudes of Party Experts and Party Functionaries toward Expertise
The increase in the aspirations and self-confidence of SED experts —particularly economists—has coincided with a higher regard for expert knowledge and a concomitant devaluation of the roles of pure ideological and political theory. Apel's and Mittag's 1963–1964 speeches and writings put more emphasis upon the importance of the experts. Furthermore, comparison with statements of veteran functionaries of the strategic clique demonstrates explicitly the extreme tension between the strategic clique's and the experts' image of the correct conduct of human affairs. Such tension did not preclude the elaboration of a dynamic concept of production for the GDR; as a matter of fact, it seems to have facilitated the rise of the experts at the expense of the pure functionaries of the party. This concept was developed primarily in Georg Klaus's writings on the "philosophy of productivity."[151] Strict orientation toward production issues on the one hand, and the concept of a philosophy of productivity on the other reveal a high degree of collaboration between the representatives of the institutionalized counter elite in economic and political spheres and their ideological spokesmen, the institutionalized revisionists. This seems particularly remarkable, since the operating ideology of the strategic clique reveals a similar disposition toward a dynamic view of mankind and society. The strategic clique can no longer ignore the dynamics of technical progress. The struggle to formulate an effective social and political world view on the part of the leading groups in the SED seems extremely significant. The fact that different interpretations of ideological dogma can be openly published and discussed in the party press is clearer evidence of the structural conflict within the party apparatus—the clash between different social behavioral models and principles of organization among the members of the strategic clique. However, the "realism" of the party experts should not be misinter-

[151] See in particular Georg Klaus, *Kybernetik in philosophischer Sicht* (Berlin: 4th ed., 1965) and *Kybernetik und Gesellschaft* (Berlin, 1964).

preted. They do not desire a basic organizational and political change in the economic and social system of the GDR. Even the representatives of the institutional counter elite seek only a gradual evolutionary change of the status quo. The goal of establishing an efficient economic system requires the elimination of irrational social and political decisions based on outmoded dogmatic ideological tenets. The technological dynamics of an industrial society require a higher degree of individual freedom and social mobility, as well as a "pluralistic" differentiation of incentives and control. Such conditions do not require ideological dogma; rather they call for constant and pragmatic readaptation, in order to maintain the economy and the society—essentially regarded by the new planners as systems—in functioning order. The party experts, for the most part younger, are thus distinguished from the veteran functionaries by more realistic attitudes. The elaboration of many basic decisions in the leadership groups today presupposes no real direct confrontation of liberalism by dogmatism, or vice versa—and certainly not humanistic socialism by dogmatic socialism. The true clash is between pragmatic neoconservatism and the dogmatic conservatism of the SED veterans.[152] The different models sketched above are manifest (as in the discussions of 1956–1958) in the different views concerning the prerogatives of the plant manager and the degree of centralization or decentralization to be practiced by the State Planning Commission.[153]

Erich Apel and Günter Mittag, who represent the institutionalized counter elite, place the ability to make objective decisions at the very heart of their managerial concept:

Making decisions does not mean the distribution of arbitrary directives, but rather the selection and elaboration of scientifically prepared plans or issues with the aid of a high degree of expert knowledge and responsibility, as well as a timely start in preparations; furthermore,

[152] Clark Kerr et al. have observed that such conflicts are frequently found among executives in Western industry. See Clark Kerr et al., *Industrialism and Industrial Man. The Problems of Labor and Management in Economic Growth* (Cambridge, Mass., 1960), pp. 283 ff.

[153] As far back as 1956, Fritz Behrens und Arne Benary advocated greater autonomy of the plants and restriction of the authority of the central economic administration. See their contributions to the third special issue of *Wirtschaftswissenschaft* (Vol. 5, 1957), which appeared under the title *Zur ökonomischen Theorie und Politik der Übergangsperiode.*

required operational decisions must be rapidly and correctly made without excessive frequency of further corrective measures in the course of subsequent events.[154]

Apel and Mittag thus take a strong position against arbitrariness and indecisive instructions. They not only criticize the frequent lack of clarity in the directives of the strategic clique, but insist that instructions be unequivocal. Consequently, scientifically prepared decisions are a key element in the concept of the experts. A scientific approach to factory planning and management is the central characteristic of this modern operational style: "Without scientific planning there can be no modern leadership." This concept is closely connected with the establishment of the "exclusive domain of leadership activities," i.e., the demand for extensive autonomy for enterprise management.[155] Apel, Mittag, and many other scientists (e.g., the expert in constitutional law, Uwe-Jens Heuer) have repeatedly demanded the expansion of the "exclusive leadership sphere" and the restriction of central planning responsibility to the establishment of only the most general framework.

Central state planning is thus in transition toward assuming the obligation of providing the orientation and goals for independent activities of the VVB, enterprises, institutes, etc., and simultaneously widening the responsibility of the respective organs of economic leadership in the planning of their own sphere of activity.[156]

Clearly counterposed in the above discussion to the concept of *Führerprinzip* (i.e., the perfect leader principle) as propagated by the representatives of the strategic clique, are the "professional" and personal qualities, deemed indispensable for the new type of leader; this is not the case for his political capacities however:

The New Economic System of Planning and Direction of the National Economy requires a new type of leader possessing high personal and professional qualifications in responsible executive functions, particularly at the head of Associations of the Nationally Owned Enterprises and factories. The still occasionally encountered type of subordinate bureaucrat cannot fulfill these tasks.[157]

Consequently, "expert knowledge" is regarded as an indispensible qualifi-

[154] Apel and Mittag, *Ökonomische Gesetze des Sozialismus*, pp. 132 ff.

[155] Uwe-Jens Heuer, *Demokratie und Recht im neuen ökonomischen System der Planung und Leitung der Volkswirtschaft* (Berlin, 1965), p. 111.

[156] Erich Apel, "Technische Revolution und volkswirtschaftlicher Nutzeffekt," *Einheit* 19, no. 9–10 (September–October 1964): 47.

[157] Apel and Mittag, *Ökonomische Gesetze des Sozialismus*, p. 133.

cation for the factory manager. Personnel management, and knowledge of modern psychological methods in administration and problems of the atmosphere of work are the talents stressed most frequently for the manager.

Accordingly, Apel and Mittag view centralized decision-making power—a keystone of the strategic clique's tenets—with skepticism. The permanently dynamic, complex situation confronting managers of large industrial enterprises requires increasing delegation of power (just as in the West). With this in mind, Apel and Mittag call for different training even for junior staff members several rungs down the enterprise's hierarchy. This training is to be based on "unity" of economic and technical knowledge: "It is thus a decisive task systematically to train managerial talent well grounded in their knowledge of economic and technical matters, consonant with the requirements of the technical revolution."[158] This call is supplemented by the demand to "combine the art of human leadership" with the will and capacity for decision making: "The principal concept of training must include the systematic completion of qualifying courses as well as the development of both the capability of performing responsible tasks and the decision-making capacities."[159] "Unity of economics and politics" is repeatedly demanded by Ulbricht, Honecker, Fröhlich, Matern, Neumann, and other representatives of the strategic clique, but is barely mentioned in the speeches and writings of Apel, Mittag, Heuer, et al.

The evaluation of expert knowledge by the representatives of the strategic clique has also changed. It is by no means unequivocal. The ideal of the "professionally trained party functionary" has been established in such a way that it is open to varying interpretations, even within the ranks of the strategic clique itself. This can be explained on the one hand by the unsatisfactory evolution of cadre policy and planning within the SED, and on the other by the party's jargon, which is by now largely a string of "empty formulas" to be filled according to the requirements of the strategic clique. Cadre planning in the SED has been hampered since the beginning of the 1950s by the rigid maintenance of two parallel

[158] Erich Apel and Günter Mittag, *Fragen der Anwendung des neuen ökonomischen Systems der Planung und Leitung der Volkswirtschaft bei der Vorbereitung und Durchführung von Investitionen* (Berlin, 1965), p. 127.
[159] Apel and Mittag, *Wissenschaftliche Führungstätigkeit*, p. 92.

Leninist principles difficult to integrate in practice: "1. Can the comrade be politically trusted? 2. Is the comrade professionally qualified?"[160] However, the causes of the difficulties in the party leadership's policy on cadres have still deeper roots. The educational level of leaders in SED basic-level organizations, *Kreis* secretaries, and the leading functionaries in the *Bezirk* and *Kreis* executives, has improved since the beginning of the 1960s but does not yet fully meet the present requirements.

The result of this unsuitable personnel policy was a heavy turnover at lower party levels.[161] A further failing is the unsatisfactory preparation of "cadre development plans" in the bureaus or secretariats of the SED *Bezirk* and *Kreis* executives.[162] Apparently the desired systematic change of party leadership since 1965 in the factories and the state and party apparatuses had not yet been satisfactorily implemented at these levels.[163] The situation in the apparatus of the government and the economy is similar to that in the party ranks. Although in recent years the number of experts in the *Bezirk* and *Kreis* councils has risen greatly, both the Eleventh and Thirteenth Central Committee Plenums in 1965 and 1966 were forced to deal with cadre problems in the state and economic apparatuses.[164]

Ulbricht himself has repeatedly attempted to solve the cadre

[160] Lore Albrecht, "Über die marxistisch-leninistischen Prinzipien der Kaderentwicklung," *Neuer Weg* 9, no. 7 (April 1954): 7. See also Walter Hinrichs et al., "Fluktuation der Kader hemmt die Entwicklung und Festigung der leitenden Organe der Partei," *Neuer Weg* 9, no. 22 (November 1954): 16.

[161] According to reports published in *Neuer Weg* 9, no. 11 (June 1954): 35 ff, about 54 percent of all members and candidates of the SED *Kreis* executives, about 71 percent of all first and second secretaries (including senior headquarters staff), as well as 42 percent of all auxiliary staff were replaced in 1954. Alfred Neumann, in "Lehren des XXI. Parteitages der KPdSU und aktuelle Fragen der Parteiarbeit der SED," *Neuer Weg* 14, no. 6 (March 1959): 335, pointed out the insufficient educational qualifications of leading staff members of the SED *Bezirk* executives in Potsdam, Schwerin, Magdeburg, Halle, and Neubrandenburg.

[162] See Alois Pisnik, "Die Perspektiven des Siebenjahrplanes. Grundlage der Erziehung und Qualifizierung der Kader," *Neuer Weg* 15, no. 3 (February 1960): 258 ff.

[163] See the Central Committee Secretariat Resolution of February 17, 1965, *Neuer Weg* 20, no. 6 (March 1965): 341.

[164] See Walter Ulbricht, *Probleme des Perspektivplanes bis 1970. Referat auf der 11. Tagung des ZK der SED. 15. bis 18. Dezember 1965* (Berlin, 1966), pp. 11 ff.

problem. But even he was unable to differentiate this problem from zigzags in the social policy of the Politburo, and—last but not least—from the internal tensions building up in the party leadership. It thus seems natural that he himself has frequently adopted an eclectic and self-contradictory attitude. For example, at the Sixth SED Congress the First Secretary of the SED stated: "The general guidelines for political education are no longer sufficient; leading party workers must also be trained experts who both control and apply Marxist-Leninist theory."[165] On the other hand, in the wake of stronger emphasis on the territorial principle, at the Seventh Plenum of the Central Committee in December 1964 he announced the establishment of "groups for scientific-economic direction," consisting of party functionaries and economists.[166] At least in 1964 he appeared to regard cooperation between party functionaries and experts in the enterprises, government offices, and economic administrations as more likely to produce success than the constant proclamation of empty formulas, such as "unity of politics and economics" or "the most recent accomplishments of Marxist-Leninist science and modern technical knowledge."[167]

Present guidelines for cadre policy have been kept vague as the result of a lack of clarity in the social and political policies of the strategic clique:

The concept of cadre is the guiding force of experts and specialists, who differ substantially in regard to their activity, but have a single common characteristic: namely, that they must be developed in a planned and systematic fashion and applied in accordance with society's requirements.[168]

[165] Walter Ulbricht, speech at the Sixth SED Congress, in *Protocol of the Sixth SED Congress,* 1: 233.

[166] Ulbricht, in his concluding speech to the Seventh Plenary Session of the Central Committee, gave the following reasons for the establishment of "groups for scientific-economic management": "In order to improve the managerial capacity and training of the executive cadres, we consider it necessary that groups for scientific-economic management be set up at the national economic council, the agricultural council, the VVB, and the *Bezirk* councils, which will engage in managerial activities, the training of executives, and production economics." Ulbricht, *Antwort auf aktuelle politische und ökonomische Fragen,* p. 4.

[167] See Alfred Lange, *Die ökonomische Weiterbildung von Wirtschaftskadern. Erfahrungen—Probleme* (Berlin, 1965), p. 48.

[168] Richard Herber and Herbert Jung, *Wissenschaftliche Leitung und Entwicklung der Kader* (Berlin, 1964), pp. 12 ff.

This comprehensive but vague definition of the cadre concept, formulated in 1964, can be easily adapted to the selection criteria prevailing since the beginning of the "new economic system":

The selection of cadres must be carried out on the following criteria; 1. selection of cadres to fulfill the main tasks of socialist construction; 2. selection of cadres on the basis of their political and professional qualifications; 3. the appointment of both veteran and young cadres to the leading organs of the party and state.[169]

In particular, the last of the cited aspects introduces a new variable into the official discussion of the cadre problem. The intensified conflict between the generations in the party is not merely admitted, but treated as an established fact. The rise of new expert elites and junior political functionaries has given unprecedented pertinence to the problem of generation conflict in the SED, evident since 1962–1963. The strategic clique has been obliged to consider the dissatisfactions and demands of many veteran functionaries who have been relegated to the sidelines, without, however, surrendering the "new economic system," with its requirements for objectively qualified leadership. The cadre problem as outlined above had hardly changed up to the beginning of 1967. Along with a greater emphasis upon ideology and partisanship since the Eleventh Plenum of the Central Committee in December 1965, another theme, the "concrete conditions of the class struggle," has dominated discussions of cadre policy, as well as the beginning of the "new economic system":

The nature of socialist cadre work consists of effectively implementing the cadre policy of the working-class party as the leading force in the construction of socialism. It is successful when significant results are attained in implementing the decisions of the party and leadership of the state by the planned selection and correct use of and the qualified training and education of leaders and functionaries. By basing our entire cadre activities in the state and economic organs on the decisions of the party and the state on the scientifically objective requirements of social development, we simultaneously dissociate ourselves from all subjectivist views. In cadre work there can be no neutral positions separated from the concrete requirements of the class struggle and social necessities.[170]

Even this qualifying criterion for a party cadre, with its stronger

[169] Horst Wagner, *Die Verantwortung der leitenden Parteiorgane für die Kaderarbeit und die Parteierziehung* (Berlin, 1963), p. 15.
[170] Rudi Rost, "Die Kaderarbeit als Führungsaufgabe," *Staat und Recht* 16, no. 1 (January 1967): 5.

accentuation of the "concrete conditions of the class struggle," is quite different from the Stalinist image of a cadre, described by Georg Dimitroff as "the bureaucrat with the character of a complete Bolshevik." Dimitroff distinguished four characteristics of the complete Bolshevik:

. . . first, complete devotion to the cause of the working class, party loyalty tested in struggles, prisons, before the courts and the class enemy. Second, closest contact with the masses, a complete identification of interests with the masses, to feel the pulse of their life and know their moods and requirements . . . third, the capacity for independent orientation in every situation and assumption of responsibility for decisions taken. He who fears responsibility is no leader and he who cannot take the initiative is no Bolshevik . . . fourth, discipline and Bolshevik fortitude, both in the struggle against the class enemy and in an implacable attitude toward all deviations from the Bolshevik line.[171]

These guidelines of cadre policy are composed in the pathetic style of Utopian communism. They are suited to a small revolutionary party struggling for power and not to a large organization rooted in industrial society, which must control and direct many areas of the economy and society. Dimitroff's model of a cadre policy is thus only suited to developing a historical party tradition. The SED strategic clique is no longer so insulated from the populace as to declare such a cadre model operative either for the party rank and file or for the rest of society. On the other hand, the institutionalized counter elite's ideal of the party expert cannot be completely accepted by the strategic clique.

7. The Reorganization of Party Control and Structural Conflicts in the Party and Factories

The penetration of the large organizational principle into the party apparatus at the beginning of 1963 encountered resistance which had been building up since the beginning of February 1954. This policy was initiated by the strategic clique, with the primary aim of restricting the sphere of decisions in central and regional bureaus of industry and construction. This policy, which had no major effects on the principles of

[171] Georg Dimitroff in his paper presented to the Seventh World Congress of the Comintern, "Die Offensive des Faschismus und die Aufgaben der Kommunistischen Internationale für die Einheit der Arbeiterklasse gegen den Faschismus," in his *Ausgewählte Schriften*, 3 vols. (Berlin, 1956–1958) 2: 656 ff. See Herber and Jung, *Wissenschaftliche Leitung*, p. 45, for a reference to Dimitroff.

the "new economic system" involved four major measures: (1) In May 1963 a central organ as well as central and regional committees of the so-called Workers' and Peasants' Inspectorate (ABI) were formed. (2) Production Committees were established in many large enterprises. (3) Organs of inspection were installed in the central and regional bureaus of industry and construction and of agriculture for the duration of their existence, i.e., up to the beginning or middle of 1966. (4) Finally, the Ideological Commission was given higher status. These four measures initiated by the strategic clique must be seen in their full context. They were based on the Soviet model. In the Soviet Union the reorganization of bodies of inspection in the party and state apparatuses was decided upon at the 1962 November Plenum of the Central Committee of the CPSU. The measures taken by the SED also had the aim of ensuring control over the party and economy while simultaneously strengthening and ensuring the organizational security of the group of professionally untrained party functionaries. Consequently, these new authorities were fitted into the existing organization of the party and enterprises.

Restructuring of party organizations, ongoing since the Sixth Congress, was sidetracked, but not truly halted, by these measures, since such organizational corrections are inherent in the policy adopted for the restructuring of the party and economic apparatus along the lines of the production principle.

THE WORKERS' AND PEASANTS' INSPECTORATES

Perhaps the most important addition to the system of guidance and control established by the SED at the beginning of 1963 are the newly formed Workers' and Peasants' Inspectorates (ABIs). Like the bureaus and commissions these organizations are also based on the production principle. Accordingly, branches of the ABI were first established in the leading sectors of the economy, the chemical, electrical engineering, and machine construction industries, and later in nearly all sectors. Economic and social affairs were overseen by *Bezirk* and *Kreis* inspectorates, as well as by factory commissions in the VEB and the newly composed "Peoples' Control Committees" (see Figure 3).

These inspectorates were based largely on the Soviet "Committees for Party and State Control." The Soviet committees are simultaneously

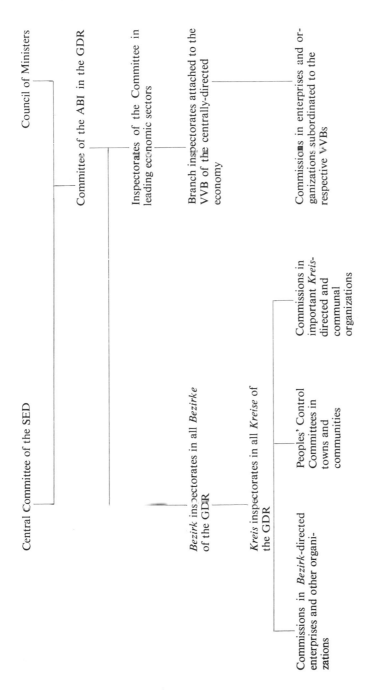

Figure 3
Organizational Structure of the Workers' and Peasants' Inspectorate and the Subordinate Relationship of the ABI Organs, the Factory Commissions, and the Peoples' Control Committee

Source: Kittner and Richter, *Arbeiter-und-Bauern-Inspektion,* p. 59; see note 173, p. 159.

responsible to the Central Committee of the CPSU and the Council of Ministers of the USSR. The regional committees in the USSR Republics are directly subordinate to the Central Committee. They are subdivided along the lines of the production principle according to their fields of activity (in industry or agriculture). The committees have been given extensive powers. They have the right to examine all documents in the factories under their observation. Already in mid-1963 the Committees for Party and State Control in the Soviet Union had three million honorary members.[172] In the Soviet Union the regional committees are subdivided into numerous commissions, each directed by a member. Every commission is responsible for a specific functional sphere, e.g., for technological problems in the factories, for labor safety, for finance and accounting, for price control, etc. The individual commissions frequently absorb worker correspondents and editors of factory journals, as well as members of the "lectorates" and divisions for production propaganda. This is designed to ensure greater public visibility for the committees. The worker correspondents have as their special task the publicizing of activities of the committee in the local press.

The establishment of these inspectorates was not dictated solely by the actual situation, either in the Soviet Union or in the GDR. This step harked back to the history of workers' control in the Soviet Union under Lenin and the workers' soviets in Germany after World War One. The Soviet principles of party and state control are based on Lenin's demand that the workers and peasants themselves exercise control and keep account in matters of production and distribution. In the Soviet Union these principles were first implemented by the establishment of a Workers' and Peasants' Inspectorate between 1924 and 1930. In the GDR party historians have established a connection with the Control Committee Movement initiated by the *Reichsrätekongress* in Weimar, Germany in 1922. In the 1930s the Soviet trade unions exercised inspection functions. They were expressly entrusted with this task at the Seventeenth CPSU Congress in 1943. In the USSR the trade unions have also overseen wholesale trade and construction since the 1930s and 1940s. After Khrushchev's great administrative reforms these

[172] According to H. Schindler, "Millionen arbeiten mit. Die Komitees für Partei- und Staatskontrolle in der UdSSR," *Die Wirtschaft* 18, no. 31 (1963): 29.

functions were taken over by the Committee for Party and State Control.

In the GDR these inspectorates also have an extensive history. The first "Peoples' Control Committees" were activated in the SBZ in 1946 as auxiliary organs of the German Peoples' Police,[173] i.e., organs of the state apparatus. At the beginning of the half-year plan in 1948 and the two-year plan in 1949 these committees were increasingly used to supervise the fulfillment of economic plans. By 1949 there existed some 4000 people's control committees with 27,000 members. The people's control movement was absorbed in 1952 by the "Central Commission for State Control" (ZKSK). In the decade between 1952 and 1963 this commission supervised the implementation of the laws, decrees, ordinances, and regulations of the Council of Ministers. The effective implementation of these decrees was newly regulated in the "Order on the Statute of the Central Commission for State Control" of May 1962. After September 1959 control of the state apparatus was increasingly extended to enterprises by the formation of party control organs.[174] However, conflicts between the competing control organizations soon arose. Since the autumn of 1960 the *Bezirk* and *Kreis* representatives of the Central State Control Commission have tried to improve relations with the labor control organs within the trade unions. However, overlapping spheres of responsibility and unsatisfactory adaptation to control tasks proliferated, primarily in the trade and supply sector. This was the last but not the least reason for the State Council's decree of February 1961, extending the activity of the Central Commission for State Control to nearly all spheres of state and economic administration to be channelled through auxiliary groups (*Helferaktivs*). The resolutions of the Fourteenth and Fifteenth Plenums of the Central Committee in autumn 1961 emphasized—in conjunction with the decisions of the Twenty-Second CPSU Congress—the necessity for increased control in the ranks of the party apparatus and mass organizations, primarily in the production sphere.

[173] Heinz Kittner and Karl-Heinz Richter, *Arbeiter-und-Bauern-Inspektion—neue Qualität der Kontrolle* (Berlin, 1963), p. 13.
[174] For the history of the workers' and farmers' inspection program in the GDR, see ibid., pp. 13 ff.

In accord with the decree on the statute of the Central Commission for State Control, the leadership bodies of all mass organizations cooperating with this commission (e.g., the Presidium of the National Board of the FDGB, the Secretariat of the Central Council of the FDJ, and the Secretariat of the DFD) resolved to improve their relations with this body. However, these measures could not overcome the overlapping of jurisdictions and the errors arising from the absence of a uniform control center responsible at the same time for the activities of the party, the state, and mass organizations.[175] This was the reason for the formation of the Workers' and Peasants' Inspectorates after the dissolution of the ZKSK in spring 1963.

The new instrument of control proclaimed by Ulbricht at the Sixth SED Congress (but not established until May 1963 after the initial experiences with the "new economic system") is subject to both the Central Committee and the Council of Ministers (see Figure 3). The supreme body and executive arm of the ABI is composed of the chairman, the first deputy, and six other deputies, as well as the directors of the bureaus.[176] Also represented on the committee are the directors of *Bezirk* and some *Kreis* inspectorates, the director of the Central Administration for Statistics, representatives of the FDGB, the National Front, the DFD, directors of the VVB and the VEB, and the chairmen of the LPG.

The Central Committee of the ABI meets every three or four months. Between May 1963 and July 1965 seven sessions were held.

[175] The Central Commission for State Control has been subject to growing criticism since the Twelfth Plenum of the Central Committee in March 1961. The shortages for which it was blamed were chiefly fragmentation of the mobilized "honorary auxiliary activs" and the lack of professional guidance in their tasks. Cf. Max Sens, "Initiative der Helfer auf örtliche Probleme lenken," in *Die Aufgaben zur weiteren ökonomischen Stärkung der DDR und zur Festigung der sozialistischen Demokratie. 12. Tagung des Zentralkomitees der SED, 16. bis 19. März 1961* (Berlin, 1961), pp. 172 f.

[176] Cf. "Beschluss des Zentralkomitees der SED und des Ministerrates der DDR über die Bildung der Arbeiter- und Bauern-Inspektion der DDR," of February 28, 1963, in *Dokumente der SED*, IX: 352 ff. The members of the Central Committee of the ABI in 1966 were Heinz Matthes (chairman), Hans Albrecht (first deputy chairman), Herbert Ebert, Kurt Hofmann, Günter Lewinsohn, Harry Schwermer, Heinz Stiebritz, and Günter Vogel. The Director of the Office was Fred Goldmann. All the committee members were affiliated with the SED.

Commissions of the Workers' and Peasants' Inspectorate were established in industrial enterprises, the construction industry, commerce, agriculture, education, and cultural organizations. Depending on the size of the enterprise, these bodies contain ten to twenty members whose main tasks are directed by the BPO.[177] The members of the top-level inspectorates are full-time functionaries. In the branch inspectorates membership in factory commissions and peoples' control commissions is mostly honorary. Women and youth representatives also participate. Experts have preference over people in other categories in elections. Candidates are drawn from scientists, technicians, engineers, and builders, as well as from activists and innovators in the enterprises. Since many scientists, technicians, and engineers do not belong to the SED or are politically passive, the SED assumes that work in the inspectorates will lead to the political activization of technical personnel.

To give some idea of the actual composition of a *Bezirk* workers' and peasants' inspectorate, the ABI members in the Erfurt *Bezirk* are listed as follows: Beside the director and his deputy, this ABI includes the following members: the Director of the Inspection Group for Industry, Construction, and Trade; the Director of the Inspection Group for Agriculture; the Inspector for Areas Outside Industrial and Agricultural Production of the *Bezirk* Inspectorate of Erfurt; the Director of the *Kreis* Inspectorate of the ABI of Erfurt; the First Secretary of the FDGB *Bezirk* Board; the Secretary of the National Front's *Bezirk* Committee; the Director of the Control Post Staff of the FDJ *Bezirk* executive; a member of the DFD *Bezirk* executive; the Deputy to the Editor-in-Chief of the local SED paper, *Das Volk;* the Director of the *Bezirk* Bureau of Statistics; a working group leader in the local management of the German National Bank; the Deputy Director of the *Bezirk* Branch of the German Peasants' Bank; a scientific research associate of the Institute for Agriculture in Neudietendorf; and the plant manager of an important local enterprise, VEB Fire Extinguishing Equipment "Apolda."[178] The composition of this body shows that the regional ABI is intended to function as an instrument of inspection in the spheres of

---

[177] Heinz Matthes, "Arbeiter-und-Bauern-Inspektion—das demokratischste Kontrollinstrument," *Neuer Weg* 18, no. 13 (June 1963): 581.
[178] *Das Volk,* July 10, 1963.

party and state apparatuses and the economic bureaucracy, as well as the mass organizations.

The workers' and peasants' inspectorates at the local level collaborate closely with the Arbitration and Conflict Commissions (*Schieds- und Konfliktkommissionen*) in the enterprises. To an even greater degree than the ZKSK these latter coordinate the various social controls primarily in the industrial sphere, not yet effectively integrated otherwise. This includes FDJ controls, workers' controls of the trade unions, the commissions for party control in the enterprises, and the previous "auxiliary committees" of state control. The sphere of duties for the ABI has been extensive from their founding. They are to cooperate in the unequivocal fulfillment of the SED program, to organize systematic control over the actual implementation of the party's decrees and directives, contribute to the perfecting of planning techniques and guidance in the economy, and reinforce national discipline as well as strengthen socialist society.[179] In economic practice, fulfillment of the "plan for new technology," implementation of "innovative methods," and the "rise in standards of quality" occupy the foregound of their activities.

However, between 1963 and 1966 the sphere of activities of the ABI has been continuously expanded to such tasks as reviewing the implementation of the Youth Law and overseeing both occupational counseling and the polytechnical courses. Further, together with the school inspector's offices, the ABIs in the summer of 1965 were responsible for the "mass political inspection" of the entire GDR educational system. The controllers then included not only full-time and honorary members of the ABI, but also teachers, school inspectors, and scientists. The working conditions for the teachers and the quality of educational materials were examined largely within the framework of this campaign. Mass control campaigns, particularly in agriculture, have become more frequent since 1964. For example, the regional ABIs carried out nineteen such drives in agriculture from February to June of 1964. Almost 120,000 persons were mobilized for this task.

In principle, industry and transport (mail, goods transport) is

[179] "Beschluss über die Aufnahme der Tätigkeit der Arbeiter- und Bauern-Inspektion der Deutschen Demokratischen Republik," in *GBl der DDR* (1963) II: 262.

controlled largely by the ABI. Fulfillment of export contractual obligations, the investment plans for industry and construction, implementation of industrial price reform, methods of raising productivity and rationalizing production are examined by the ABI. In this context the establishment by the ABI of the so-called "technically conditioned norms for the consumption and storage of materials" rates mention. The peoples' control commissions, together with members of the trade and supply commission of the *Kreis* and *Stadt* councils, also supervise price policies in cooperative and private trade.

The growing sphere of activities of the ABIs led to an increase in membership from 46,000 in December 1963 to approximately 112,000 in July 1966.[180] Such an expansion required special training for these members. As early as 1964 courses were organized and in July 1964 a training center for ABI members was opened at Halle University. During the three-month courses held biweekly after working hours in 1964–1965, questions dealing with the relationship of the ABI to the local representatives and to the managements of the VVB and VEB were discussed. With the institution of these courses the SED undoubtedly succeeded in including and mobilizing circles not previously under systematic control. The party's objective, which by now could almost be designated as traditional, to continuously undertake renewed attempts toward activization and mobilization, came into play here once more.

According to the decision of May 1963 factory commissions were formed and peoples' control committees reorganized within the framework of the ABI. The number of these bodies grew rapidly. In the summer of 1963 some 3000 factory commissions and approximately 2200 peoples' control committees had begun operations. In the autumn of 1963, 37 inspectorates in all branches of industry (VVB), *Bezirk* inspectorates in all 15 districts as well as 204 out of 214 *Kreis* inspectorates were active.[181] In May 1964 approximately 4500 factory commissions with some 25,000 members were active in industry, construction, and transport, in addition to some 4000 peoples' control

---

[180] This is evident from a table in *Neuer Weg* 21, no. 16 (August 1966): 786. According to *Neues Deutschland,* February 15, 1967, there were 2200 persons registered in February 1967 as honorary officers of the ABI in East Berlin.
[181] According to *Neues Deutschland,* October 2, 1963.

committees with approximately 45,000 members. In December 1965 the number of peoples' control committeees had risen to approximately 7000.

The factory commissions of the ABIs not only have the right to examine and investigate, but are also empowered to publicize shortcomings, particularly in the sphere of supply and storage. In some factories the results of inspection campaigns have been recorded in photographs, diagrams, etc., and exhibited in the enterprise's "Hall of Culture." (See the inclusion of editors of factory journals in control work according to the Soviet model.)

The factory commissions of the ABIs cooperate closely with the BPO and the secretariats of the SED (*Industrie-*) *Kreis* executive bodies. In part, the factory commissions take charge of the "right of control" of the basic-level party organizations in the factories, as established in the party statutes of 1963. In the spring of 1965 the local bureaus of industry and construction continued to evaluate regularly the control reports of the factory commissions or the *Kreis* inspectorates of the ABI—e.g., in the VEB Leuna-Werke "Walter Ulbricht." The close connection between the ABI factory commissions and the BPO has been emphasized repeatedly by the press. Despite formal guidance by the *Kreis* inspectorates, in practice the factory commissions frequently accept directions from the BPO. Thus the factory commissions have increasingly developed—separately from the production committees—as control organs of the SED. However, numerous problems of dividing up authority existed. As a rule the chairman of the ABI factory commission is also a member of the production committee. Must he also direct a working group of the production committee? The same applies to the director of the FDJ control post, who is also a member of both control bodies. In factories—e.g., in the VEB Heavy Machinery Works "Ernst Thälmann," Magdeburg—exchanging control findings has been a common practice of the production committee and the ABI factory commissions in recent years.

There are some similarities in the way the factory commissions of the ABI are now used by the BPO and the secretariats of the (*Industrie-*) *Kreis* executives as control organs, and the relationship of the peoples' control committees of the ABI to the local representations of the people (i.e., the *Bezirk* and *Kreis,* etc., assemblies). For

example, in autumn 1965 Minister Heinz Matthes, Chairman of the
Committee of the ABI, explicitly described the peoples' control committees as "control organs of the local peoples' representations." As before,
the committees concentrate mainly on the price of consumer goods, the
material economy in the small artisan sphere and the service professions
(repairs). Private enterprises, like artisans' and trade cooperatives, to a
considerable extent are embraced by this control system. The peoples'
control commissions cooperate closely with the local artisans' guild.

The comprehensive and growing role of the ABI in 1967 already
demonstrated that it is more likely to serve the SED in guiding and
governing socio-economic processes than to stimulate economic production. Given its structure and present sphere of competence, the ABI
must be regarded as the strongest link in a central control system that,
having emerged in the summer of 1963 and been greatly expanded since
early 1965, is the means by which the party elite is trying to harness the
dynamic changes in the economy and society. It is clearly the intention
of the Politburo to create a centrally guided, interconnected set of
controls, while striving for a rise in the production efficiency of many
(for the most part, the larger) enterprises. In this context the decree of
the State Council of July 2, 1965 is worthy of mention.[182] It stipu-
lates that the local councils must cooperate closely with the ABI in
order to ensure the "leading activity" of the *Bezirk, Kreis,* etc., councils.
Bezirk and branch inspectorates of the ABI must pass information to the
local councils. Thus, the ABIs and the production committees may be
designated as defensive mechanisms established by the strategic clique.

Since mid–1966 attempts have been made to coordinate the various
control systems, a project which despite all efforts had not been realized
by the end of 1965. The following institutions were affected:
the ABI as the "operative" organ of the Central Committee and the
Council of Ministers;
party control by means of the ideological commissions and the establishment of divisions for party organization and ideology in the regional
bureaus of industry and construction;

[182] "Erlass des Staatsrates der DDR über Aufgaben und Arbeitsweise der örtlichen
Volksvertretungen und ihrer Organe unter den Bedingungen des neuen ökonomischen Systems der Planung und Leitung der Volkswirtschaft," of July 2, 1965,
in *GBl der DDR* (1965) 1: 159 ff.

social control by the mass organizations, primarily the FDGB, the DFD, and the NF;

economic control by financial review and by banks; internal factory control by production committees in the larger VEBs

supervision by special state control authorities (price control, health inspection, etc.)[183]

In the following sections selected control bodies will be dealt with in detail: the production committees, the divisions for party organs and ideology at the regional level of the bureaus of industry and construction, and the Ideological Commission.

THE PRODUCTION COMMITTEES

At the end of October 1963 production committees were first formed, in some and eventually in all, large East German enterprises, in accordance with a decision of the Politburo.[184] Like the workers' and peasants' inspectorates, these committees followed the earlier Soviet organizational model. At the November 1962 Plenum of the Central Committee of the CPSU, Khrushchev called for the establishment of production committees in industry and construction. Their main purpose was the "inclusion of more workers in factory management."[185] The committees were to cooperate "in discussing the plans, checking on their fulfillment, setting work norms, and directing cadres." At the beginning of 1963 the first Soviet production committees were set up in certain Leningrad enterprises. Their activities were extensively covered in the Soviet and East German press.

At the beginning of 1964 the first production committees were set

---

[183] Following the theses set up by a working group at the Walter Ulbricht German Academy for Political Science and Jurisprudence. See "Probleme der wissenschaftlichen Führungstätigkeit der örtlichen Staatsorgane in der zweiten Etappe des neuen ökonomischen Systems der Planung und Leitung. Thesen," *Staat und Recht* 15, no. 4 (April 1966): 585.

[184] Resolution of the Politburo of the SED Central Committee, October 29, 1963: "Grundsätze über die Aufgaben und Arbeitsweise der Produktionskomitees in volkseigenen Grossbetrieben," in *Dokumnte der SED*, IX: 720 ff. At the fourteenth plenum of the SED Central Committee in December 1966, Gerhard Grüneberg stressed that henceforth "production boards [would be] established in *all* producer plants." (*Neues Deutschland*, December 16, 1966.)

[185] Khrushchev's report to the CPSU CC Plenum, November 19, 1962, reprinted in *Neues Deutschland*, November 21, 1962.

up on an experimental basis in the following large East German enterprises: the VEB Rayon Plant "Siegfried Rädel" in Pirna, the VEB Electrical Transformer Plant Oberschöneweide in Berlin, the VEB Heavy Machinery Plant "S. M. Kirow" in Leipzig, the VEB Chemical Fiber Plant "Friedrich Engels" in Premnitz, the VEB Modul in Karl-Marx-Stadt, and the VEB Lignite Combine in Lauchhammer. These production committees were to assist in the solution of various specific problems, such as formulation of plans for technological development, methods of rationalization, and investment policy decisions. In addition, they were to coordinate the various intra-enterprise control bodies, especially the "honorary commissions." Until the introduction of these new control bodies, some twelve or more "honorary" supervisory organizations worked simultaneously, often at cross purposes.[186] The new production committees were thus to represent the previously existing control organs of the party and the mass organizations in the enterprises. They were regarded by the SED and some social scientists (e.g., Uwe-Jens Heuer) as a step toward the "democratization of the production process." However, this theme did not become dominant in practice. Despite promising beginnings in 1963-1964, such democracy has since been defined (in 1967) as merely the efficient implementation of democratic centralism in nationally owned enterprises.[187] This definition raises prospects of further strengthening the role of the production committees, their expansion as a controlling instrument of the SED in the

---

[186] Werner Tippmann reported that "in most enterprises there were factory committees for modern technology, ABIs, permanent production councils, innovators' councils and activs, honorary construction bureaus, and other bodies consulted by the state managers. In addition, there are numerous commissions and activs for the management of the mass organizations, especially the trade unions, who collaborate under various aspects in solving problems and the shaping of working conditions. Last, but not least, the meetings of the mass organizations within the plant constitute a forum where questions of production and its development are considered, and appropriate measures are recommended to the state managers." (Werner Tippmann, "Die Bildung der Produktionskomitees in Grossbetrieben—ein wichtiger Bestandteil der Entwicklung der sozialistischen Demokratie," *Staat und Recht*, 13, no. 3 [March 1964]: 479.) See also "Was ist ein Produktionskomitee?," *Der Morgen*, January 17, 1964.

[187] Arno Lange et al., "Produktionskomitee anno 1967," *Forum* 21, no. 4 (1967): 10. Lange and the other authors are on the Faculty for Marxism-Leninism at the University of Economics in Berlin-Karlhorst.

large nationally owned enterprises, thereby consolidating the position of the strategic clique in the economy as well as in the party.

Ulbricht's famous October 1963 speech to the workers of the VEB Kirow Plant in Leipzig clarified the tasks of the production committee, but also revealed the structural ambiguity of their functions. The First Secretary of the Central Committee began by demanding that "the production committee . . . concentrate on basic questions of guidance and development [in the areas of production], i.e., on the elaboration of project planning plans." This could have meant that, together with the plant managers, the production committees were to exercise genuine executive functions consistent with the expansion of enterprise autonomy. However, Ulbricht went on to emphasize that the newly created organs in the factories "will occupy themselves with the basic facets of socialist competition and such important questions as cooperative relationships. The production committee ensures that the important economic issues will actually be discussed with the workers. . . ."[188]

Honecker set forth the tasks of the production committees even more explicitly at the Fifth Plenum of the Central Committee. "With the completion of the party elections, all members of our party must clearly understand that the party executive coordinates and consolidates, via comrades in the production committee, all forces of the state and its social organs, in order to solve the basic problems of production and enhance the economic development of the enterprises. The production committees will enable the trade unions to fulfill more successfully their functions as representatives of the workers' interest."[189] Honecker thus emphasized the activity of these committees as central control bodies of the SED in the factories. The production committees apparently were to become a type of organization in which the representatives of the party and the FDGB could cooperate. They were intended to prevent the factory party organizations from taking over all significant political tasks of the BGL and AGL, a frequent occurrence in the past.

The production committees, like the factory commissions of the

[188] Walter Ulbricht, Answers at an election rally in the VEB Kirow Works in Leipzig, in *Neues Deutschland,* October 17, 1963.
[189] Erich Honecker to the Fifth Central Committee Session, *Neues Deutschland,* February 12, 1964.

ABI, were conceived as controlling organs of the party. On the other hand, they were intended to relieve the BPO and initiate a more differentiated and rationalized system of guidance and supervision which, it should be noted, was supposedly readily accessible to surveillance. This program undoubtedly expressed the party elite's desire to exploit the potentials of modern economic organization and was bound to lead to a rationalization of party control in the enterprise. It likewise seemed an important development that the production committees replaced the permanent production councils (*Ständige Produktionsberatungen*), and assumed some of their functions. In contrast to these bodies, the production committees addressed themselves exclusively to basic technical and economic questions within the given enterprise.

The existence of those permanent production councils which had been subordinate to the BGL and AGL was not affected by the dissolution of the central permanent production councils. However, since the establishment of the production committees, the factory union executives have adhered to their guidelines. Despite the inevitable reduction of trade union functions in the factory, the production committees are not intended to render the FDGB completely superfluous.

All problems concerning the individual enterprise's production plan and production cycle have gradually come under the jurisdiction of the production committees, including problems peculiar to trade unions, such as workers' safety provisions. The BGL and AGL remained responsible for such traditional trade union tasks only when these did not concern issues affecting the entire enterprise. However, since the dissolution of the permanent central production councils, the influence of the permanent production councils under the BGL and the AGL has increased. Guided by the new committees they are entrusted with practically unbounded functional areas, primarily those involving the "struggle for daily plan fulfillment."[190] Consequently, far more people belong to these production councils—which exist in many more enterprise departments—than to the production committees. In the spring of 1955 the permanent production councils had some 380,000 members,

[190] Martin Berthold, BGL Chairman of the Eastern Iron Foundry Combine, "Unser Komitee hat sich bewährt," *Tribüne,* September 17, 1964.

while only 3500 persons were organized in the 160 production committees of larger enterprises.[191]

Establishment of the production committees undoubtedly created a
more efficient organ of control in the enterprises. This is clearly
expressed by the plant manager of the VEB Rayon Plant in Pirna:

Since the formation of the production committee, I have had more time
for general policy problems and prospective planning. Economic functionaries become more highly qualified through direct involvement in
working out our plans. Our production directives are better understood in the enterprise and accrue higher profits, since the suggestions of
the workers have been taken into consideration.[192]

The production committees usually meet twice a month; the plant
manager is permitted to sit in at the sessions. He can take into
consideration the recommendations of the committee, but also has the
right to submit his own proposals at meetings. There is no doubt that the
establishment of production committees has simplified the work of the
plant manager, since he now deals only with one instead of various
commissions. The plant manager quoted above also claims that not the
least advantage of the new system consists in dealing with a stable
group of people working together, instead of continuously changing
commissions.[193]

The size of the production committees in the enterprise varies.
Although the Politburo decreed a top limit of 25 members, in practice
membership exceeds this number occasionally. For example, in the VEB
Electrical Transformer Plant Oberschöneweide in Berlin, the production
committee had 30 members in 1964: 13 engineers, 3 executives, 5
economists, and 9 workers.[194] In the VEB Pentacon in Dresden, which
is the pilot plant for photography and cinematography within the VVB
Control Technique, Instrument Building and Optics, the production

---

[191] See Heinz Puder "Wie entwickelt sich mit dem neuen ökonomischen System
unsere sozialistische Demokratie weiter?" *Die Arbeit* no. 4 (1965): 37.

[192] Werner Goldstein, "Das Produktionskomitee. Erste Erfahrungen des Kunst-
seidenwerkes Pirna," *Neues Deutschland*, November 17, 1963.

[193] Ibid., and Arno Lange et al., "Das Produktionskomitee in System der Leitung
sozialistischer Industriebetriebe," *Die Wirtschaft* 19, no. 38 (1964): 21.

[194] The functions of the members of the production commitee are not known. The
data are taken from Wilfried Sieber, "Aus der Arbeit des Produktionskomitees.
Durch gute Leistungen Achtung erworben," *Berliner Zeitung*, September 5, 1964.

committee in autumn 1964 had 28 members, not counting the director and the secretary of the BPO. Of these, 21 had university, college, or professional school training, 2 were members of the FDJ executive in the factory, and 5 were workers.[195] In the VEB Rayon Plant "Siegfried Rädel" in Pirna (one of the enterprises in which production committees were formed in November 1963) there were only 13 members: 3 foremen, 7 engineers, 1 economist, and 2 workers.[196] This indicates that the production committees are small expert bodies, frequently under the guidance of the BPO secretary, who usually has a degree from a university, college, or professional school. In many cases this secretary is deputized by the chairman of the BGL. In this way the SED also established its leadership claim vis-à-vis the FDGB. There is little doubt that the production committees exerted more influence from the start than the trade union's control organs, despite the supposedly consultative functions of the former.

This analysis of the production committees demonstrates the truth of the "law" of specialization and differentiation—a process described by Werner Hofmann as "spontaneous self-regeneration of the bureaucracy."[197] Indeed, the production committees were originally conceived as the special organizational embodiment of the production principle within the enterprise and, consequently, as an instrument of uniform control. But since the Ninth Plenum of the Central Committee in April 1965, their functions have been continually expanded. For example, after the formation of the production committee in the VEB Chemical Fiber Plant "Friedrich Engels" in Premnitz in the fall of 1963, several existing control organs of the BPO and the BGL (e.g., the Committees on "New Technology") instead of being dissolved were restructured as independent suborganizations:

The former Commissions for Scientific and Technical Recruitment, the Innovators' Activs, and the Committees on New Technology are not replaced by different organs of the production committee, but are

[195] According to Siegfried Zugehör, "Die Skeptiker durch Tatsachen überzeugt. Alle gesellschaftlichen Kräfte unter einen Hut gebracht," *Junge Welt,* September 17, 1964.
[196] Goldstein, "Das Produktionskomitee."
[197] Werner Hofmann, "Die Arbeitsverfassung der Sowjetunion," *Volkswirtschaftliche Schriften,* 22 (Berlin, 1956): 515.

reincarnated as independent working groups of the production committee. This eliminates parallelism in work and expands the work of the commission beyond its narrow formal limits. At the same time, the work of the production committee can be qualitatively improved if it uses these working groups to prepare and evaluate its consultations. For specific questions ad hoc task forces are also formed.[198]

The trend toward expansion of the production committee's functions is also evident in the formation of numerous working groups under its control. In October 1964 Günter Mittag criticized the expanding authority of these newly created control organs. He warned of the dangers of new organizations with "separate functional organs" within the enterprises which might create difficulties in the gathering of information.[199] In 1967 discussions of the role of the production committee within the control system of the factory had not yet ended. The SED has apparently been trying to expand the authority of the production committees as an instrument of party control in the enterprise. This may be construed from suggestions that the production committee be integrated into the BPO:

The danger of developing separate control and organizational structures within the production committees is to be countered by (a) having the production committees of a section work under the guidance of the APO; and (b) coordinating the work of enterprise production committees and the production committee of sections in an enterprise with the mass organizations, under the guidance of the BPO.[200]

[198] Günter Rohrlack "Aus den Erfahrungen eines Produktionskomitees," *Einheit* 19, no. 8 (August 1964): 40.

[199] Mittag stated: "In practice several production committees have already formed permanent working groups to deal with those problems formerly dealt with by the innovators' councils and activs, etc. Thus, with the establishment of the New Technology work group by the production committee in the Flöha cotton-spinning mill, the question of whether the plant committee on New Technology should be abolished was considered. The development of the work of the production committee along these lines means that, in fact, it gradually assumes the character of an organization with separate functions. But we do not need any new organizations in our factories. The necessary organs already exist. The primary task of the production committee is to coordinate the operation of the existing organizations and bodies, so as to render them more effective." (Günter Mittag, "Die Rolle der Produktionskomitees bei der Ausarbeitung und Durchführung des Perspektivplanes und der Verwirklichung des neuen ökonomischen Systems," *Die Wirtschaft* 19, no. 40 (1964): 7.)

[200] Christa Duglos and Karl Wille, "Aufgaben und Arbeitsweise wichtiger institutioneller Formen der Einbeziehung der Werktätigen in die Planung und Leitung des Betriebes. Thesen," *Staat und Recht* 14, no. 8 (August 1965): 1317.

THE DISSOLUTION OF THE BUREAUS OF INDUSTRY AND CONSTRUCTION

The strategic clique directed yet another measure against the organizational bases of the institutionalized counter elite, the bureaus of industry and construction. They were to be brought under tighter control by the strategic clique, starting in 1965. Although modified, the pragmatic course in the economic sphere was not abandoned in principle.

The limitation on the application of the production principle—hinted at in the Politburo Decree of the Establishment of Production Committees—was organizationally reinforced at the Fifth Plenum of the Central Committee at the beginning of February 1964. Erich Honecker announced the creation of divisions for party organs and ideology in the central and regional bureaus of industry and construction as well as for agriculture:

In order to ensure that the bureaus of the Politburo and the *Bezirk* party organizations will be able to meet their responsibilities fully, sections for party organs and sections resp. divisions for ideological work are (forthwith) to be established. We also consider it necessary to form a Commission for Party and Organizational Affairs under the Politburo in order to improve party and organizational work.[201]

Honecker justified the establishment of divisions for party organs and ideology by stating that the bureaus of industry and construction had neglected their functions of direction and control, particularly vis-à-vis SED basic-level organizations, and thus had also neglected "mass political work" in the VEBs and VVBs. In their work they had used only professionally trained party members (technicians and experts).

The strategic clique attempted to restrict the authority of the party experts by placing these control organs within the structure of the SED. Since the beginning of 1964 the bureaus of industry and construction (and the bureaus of agriculture) were deprived of the right to make decisions binding on lower party organs. At the same time, the consolidation of the position of the secretariats of the SED *Bezirk* and *Kreis* executives vis-à-vis the bureaus in their respective areas was also evident. During 1964 the party organizations in important economic enterprises previously controlled by the bureaus of industry and construction at the level of SED *Kreis* executives were subordinated to the secretariats of the SED *Bezirk* executives. The de-emphasis of the

[201] Erich Honecker on preparation of the party elections, *Neues Deutschland,* February 12, 1964.

production principle and the strengthening of the "line" within the party organization was further stressed at the Seventh Plenum of the SED Central Committee in December 1964. In his "answers to contemporary political and economic questions" Ulbricht declared unequivocally:

Our party is not an economic party in the narrower sense. It guides the entire social life of the Republic. It is responsible for the entire complex of political, ideological, scientific, technical, economic and cultural work. It is thus necessary to apply the correct combination of the territorial and production principles."[202]

The territorial principle was cited before the production principle, not only by Ulbricht, but also by Hager and other members of the strategic clique (Albert Norden, Erich Mückenberger). This was hardly coincidental. Ulbricht had defined the need for guidance and control of the party apparatus by the principle of production at the Sixth Party Congress in comprehensive fashion, but in his speech to the Seventh Plenum he repeatedly stressed "tight control of political and ideological mass work."

Kurt Hager in his report to the Seventh CC Plenum focused on a further measure of the strategic clique to restrict the functions of the bureaus of industry and construction: "The Politburo deems it . . . necessary, that the Secretariat of the Central Committee or the secretariats of the *Bezirk* and *Kreis* executives assure closer coordination of the work of the ideological commissions, the bureaus of industry and construction and the bureau of agriculture." He justified this shift of emphasis. "It is known that previously we had to sacrifice the primacy of general political propaganda for the solution of purely economic problems. There are now indications that ideological work has been partly relegated to the background."[203] Honecker supported this line by referring to examples from party gatherings and *Kreis*-level party activist sessions in October and November, 1964.

At present, in the activity of the party, state, and economic organs—from the highest to the lowest levels—ideological work, explanations of the basic problems of our policy, and work with human beings does not

---

[202] Ulbricht, *Antwort auf aktuelle . . . Fragen*, p. 4.
[203] Report of the Politburo to the Seventh Session of the Central Committee (presented by Kurt Hager). *Neues Deutschland*, December 4, 1964.

occupy the important place demanded by the conditions of our struggle.[204]

Honecker expressed the fears of the strategic clique that discussion of economic problems was liable to take place at the expense of political indoctrination, thus leading to a reduction of political influence of the SED among the people.

It is the main task of the party to organize work with people. We must thus ensure that all party organizations strive to go beyond the narrow confines of mass political activity, frequently limited solely to the explanation of economic questions. Rather, they should concentrate on talking with the people in a simple and lively fashion, making it clear that the economic establishment of our German Democratic Republic is of decisive political significance for securing peace, the solution of national problems, and the improvement of our living conditions.[205]

The appointment of Horst Dohlus, a party functionary, not professionally trained, as director of the new Politburo Commission for Party and Organizational Affairs is a further indication that the strategic clique will endeavor to secure its position against party experts as far as is possible. Like Mittag, Dohlus was born in 1926. Before 1954 he was for several years the first resp. second secretary of the *Gebiet* Party executive of Wismut—especially important in the 1950s since uranium was produced there. From 1956 to 1958 he was the secretary of the *Kombinat* Party Executive "Schwarze Pumpe," near Hoyerswerda, and after mid-1958, the second secretary of the SED *Bezirk* executive for Cottbus. Since the Sixth SED Congress he has been the director of the Section for Party Organs of the Central Committee apparatus.[206] Although this party functionary has some experience in the field of economics, he rose within the party apparatus and must be regarded as a protégé of the strategic clique from the younger generation. Responsibility for internal control was not relegated only to veterans such as Kurt

---

[204] Honecker in his contribution to the Seventh Plenary Session of the Central Committee, "Anforderungen an führende Rolle der Partei wachsen," *Neues Deutschland,* December 5, 1964.

[205] Ibid.

[206] On the occasion of the Seventh SED Congress, Dohlus was again presented as "Director of the section for Party Organs of the Central Committee," or as "Section Head of the Central Committee." (See *Neues Deutschland,* April 18 and 23, 1967.) Presumably, thereafter the Commission for Party and Organizational Affairs at the Politburo no longer exists.

Hager, but was also parceled out among younger party functionaries. This development indicates that the conflict of generations in the SED cannot simply be equated with that between party functionaries and experts. The appointment of Dohlus by Ulbricht demonstrates that the strategic clique in the SED intends to emphasize the attractiveness of a party career, even though the rules of ascent are not clearly defined.

The bureaus of industry and construction were dissolved without public announcement throughout 1966. Actually, their functions had been gradually curtailed over a long period before. A further measure of the strategic clique, designed to reinforce its power position in the "new economic system," was the strengthening of the Ideological Commission of the Politburo. The strategic clique placed a greater emphasis on ideology and agitprop matters, and simultaneously tightened internal party control—a combination of tactics frequently used by Communist leaderships. The structuring of the Ideological Commission (responsible for codifying doctrine and setting forth operating ideology) reflects the deliberate and increased application of pure techniques of power by the strategic clique. Tighter party control and increased ideological pressure were also intended to restore the distance between the strategic clique on the one hand and the party apparatus and "society," on the other—a distance which had diminished during the course of the "new economic system." An integral component of this endeavor was the emphasis in mass agitation upon self-justification and self-legitimization of the strategic clique.

To achieve these aims, the Politburo initiated a bureaucratic reorganization of the Ideological Commission. Within the framework of the new 7-year plan (1964–1970) this commission was responsible for drawing up the prospective plans in ideological work, and this plan was declared obligatory for future party work:

The prospective plan in ideological work must be a unified scheme, indicating the trend for the Ideological Commission and for the ideological divisions of the bureaus; in addition it serves as a guideline for ideological work in the organs of the state and the economy. It must be the common foundation of the work for all leading party organs, not just a matter of concern to the Ideological Commission.[207]

[207] Report of the Politburo to the Seventh Session of the Central Committee (cf. footnote 203), p. 5.

When working out and establishing this prospective plan, the divisions for party organs and ideology (newly established in the bureaus) coordinated their task with the Ideological Commission of the Politburo.

That the organizational strengthening of the Ideological Commission was already taking place in autumn 1964 is evident from the fact that "mass political work" once again moved into the foreground of party activity. "Prospective plan discussions" in enterprises revealed a shift of emphasis from economics to agitprop activities: "The plan discussion covers not only questions of production, but our entire social life."[208] Journals and factory broadcasting facilities were used for production propaganda purposes.

The trend, which continued until the dissolution of the Ideological Commission in late 1966, was expressed at an early stage in the principles of cadre policy:

Since the last party elections in 1962, many party executive organs were strengthened by the closer cooperation of scientifically and technically trained cadres. This positive development led to success in party work. It became evident, however, that some of these cadres still lacked experience in political leadership activities.[209]

As early as October 1964, some BPO secretaries (factory party secretaries), as representatives of the "line," ruthlessly criticized the experts:

Discussion of the plan is an expression of our Socialist democracy. This does not mean that a few experts should merely discuss dry statistics, but that all workers should define the outlines of our society for future years. It is thus most important that in every enterprise all opportunities for workers' participation be exploited and developed.[210]

There is no doubt that the countermeasures of the strategic clique during 1965–1967 were effective in controlling the growing power of the party experts. Indications of this trend to date include. the establishment and expansion of the ABI and the production committees; the restriction of the authority of the bureaus of industry and construction, followed by their gradual and unannounced dissolution; the reorganization and broadened power of the central Ideological Commission; and the

[208] "Wie bereiten wir die Mitgliederversammlungen zum Perspektivplan vor? ND-Gespräch mit Parteisekretären," *Neues Deutschland,* October 23, 1964.
[209] Franz Müller, "Lehren einer Parteiaktivagung im Industriezweig Chemieanlagen," *Neuer Weg* 19, no. 5 (March 1964): 230.
[210] *Neues Deutschland* interview with party secretaries, October 23, 1964.

establishment of a Commission for Party and Organization Affairs. The deletion of the passage referring to the "production principle" from the statutes of the SED at the Seventh Party Congress in April 1967 is a further sign of the present relative power situation within the SED.[211] The conflict between functionaries and experts has not been decisively solved by these measures. On the contrary, it has become a structural conflict inherent in the system, since the strategic clique must be assured of the cooperation of the experts more than ever before. In addition, the organizational principles of large social organizations (cf. Chapter One) are now so deeply ingrained in the apparatus of state and economy that the desuetude of these principles would affect the power basis of the party itself.

8. The Main Characteristics of Change in the SED's Social Structure

The changing social structure of the party features some striking trends, which have been briefly dealt with earlier. They are analyzed more fully below.

Since 1961 the SED has clearly developed from a "cadre" to a "mass" party, as well as from a cadre party of the traditional type to one of a new (cadre) type. Indeed, since its foundation in 1946, the SED has tended to combine the original Bolshevik tradition of the cadre party with older socialist traditions of a mass party. This trend was initiated by the entrance of many former members of the SPD into the new party. From 1961 on, the SED has increasingly become a large and differentiated body, more and more adapted to the pressures of a dynamic industrial society, and increasingly bearing the hallmarks of a large organization.

This development is illustrated by fluctuations in the membership of the SED. According to official data released at party congresses and

[211] Article 25, section 1, of the Fourth Statute of the SED (1963) states: "The party is organized according to the production and territorial principle. Its principal activities are organized according to the production principle." The new version of this section, decided upon at the Seventh SED Congress, reads "The party is organized according to the territorial and production principle." The reasons given for this change are: "The version in force up to now, that the party organizes its main activities according to the production principle, should be deleted. This change results from the Resolutions of the Seventh Session of the Central Committee." (See *Neues Deutschland*, April 22, 1967.)

conferences, the SED had nearly 1.3 million members in what was then the Soviet Zone of Occupation when the KPD and the SPD united on April 21, 1946. Of these, nearly 680,000 (52 percent) had previously belonged to the SPD. In January 1949 at the First Party Conference, this membership had risen to almost 1.8 million. In April 1950, 1.75 million persons still held party cards. In September 1953, after the first major purges and intensification of "political emigration," membership had dropped to 1.2 million, according to Ulbricht's address to the 16th Plenum of the Central Committee. Since 1954 there has been an almost unbroken rise in membership: in April 1954 there were 1.4 million members; in December 1957 nearly 1.5 million; and at the end of December 1963 nearly 1.68 million members and candidates. The total membership remained unchanged during 1964, rose in 1965 to 1.7 million, and at the end of December 1966 reached nearly 1.8 million members and candidates.[212] Thus, by spring 1967, the SED had regained its membership level of January 1949.

By the end of 1966 the social composition of the party was as follows:[213]

Blue-collar workers	807,312 = 45.6%
Cooperative farmers	112,998 = 6.4%
Members of the intelligentsia	217,796 = 12.3%
White-collar employees	285,066 = 16.1%
Members of production cooperatives	15,029 = 0.8%
Students and pupils	28,323 = 1.6%
Independent artisans, horticulturists, fishermen, tradesmen, and government-supported businessmen	12,218 = 0.7%
Housewives	77,121 = 4.4%
Pensioners	214,049 = 12.1%

[212] For the period until 1954 Carola Stern, in *Porträt einer bolschewistischen Partei,* has compiled and processed the official data on the membership drive (pp. 282 ff.). For later data, see *Protocol of the Fifth SED Congress,* 2: 1608 ff.; *Protocol of the Sixth SED Congress,* 4: 252 f.; and *Neues Deutschland,* April 17, 1967, p. 12, resp. *Protokoll der Verhandlungen des VII. Parteitages der SED, 17. bis 22. April 1967 in der Werner-Seelenbinder-Halle zu Berlin,* 4 vols. (Berlin, 1967) (hereafter cited as *Protocol of the Seventh SED Congress*), 4: 226 f.

[213] *Neues Deutschland,* April 17, 1967, p. 12. The social composition of the party at the subsequent dates mentioned may be derived from the sources cited in note 212.

This list constitutes the most highly differentiated socio-structural breakdown ever published by the SED. For the first time "cooperative farmers" are listed immediately after blue-collar workers and not after white-collar employees and members of the "intelligentsia." Further, the group which in earlier years was always described as "miscellaneous" was specified. Compared with the social composition of the party in earlier periods, the proportion of workers has greatly risen. By the end of 1961, the percentage of workers was only 33.8.[214] The concern of the strategic clique in 1961 for legitimizing the SED as a workers' party can be perceived mainly in the explanatory remarks in the "Report to the Central Committee at the Seventh Party Congress": "The character of our party as a party of the working classes is also expressed by the fact that 61.6% of the members and candidates were workers upon entrance into the party. A large proportion of these comrades now exercise leading functions in the party, state, economy, and armed forces; many have become qualified members of the intelligentsia or technicians."[215]

Between 1961 and 1967 the proportion of the intelligentsia among all members rose from 8.7 to 12.3 percent. This high rate of increase confirms a trend previously emphasized in this study: even in the SED qualified persons are represented in increasingly higher proportions. The number of white-collar employees dropped markedly: from 32.6 percent at the end of 1961 to 16.1 percent at the end of 1966. The number of cooperative farmers rose little: from 6.2 percent at the end of 1961 to 6.4 percent in 1966. No comparative figures were available for the representation of other social groups at the Seventh Congress. They had hitherto

---

[214] This is the lowest proportion of blue-collar workers in the party that has ever been reported. Their share in the total membership of the party since 1947 shows the following development:

May 1957   47.9%
January 1949   44.5%
April 1950   41.3%
April 1954   39.1%
December 1957   33.8%

[215] Report of the Central Committee to the Seventh SED Congress, extracts of which published in *Neues Deutschland,* April 17, 1967. (Complete reprint in *Protocol of the Seventh SED Congress*).

appeared as "miscellaneous" and amounted to between 15 and 20 percent of the total membership.

At the end of December 1966 the composition by age of the party was:[216]

up to 25 years old	145,121 = 8.2%
26 to 30	214,527 = 12.1%
31 to 40	443,384 = 25.1%
41 to 50	305,217 = 17.2%
51 to 60	286,079 = 16.2%
61 to 65	147,304 = 8.3%
over 65	228,280 = 12.9%

The high proportion of members in the 31 to 40-year-old group is quite notable: it constitutes more than 25 percent of the total SED membership. This age group plays a decisive role in the party, as in all other fields, particularly the economic. Here, comparison with earlier periods would be instructive. Because neither the Fourth, Fifth, nor Sixth SED Congresses published comparable figures, comparison was possible only with data from 1950. For this period the age composition was:[217]

up to 25 years old	8.8%
26 to 30	11.0%
31 to 40	18.7%
41 to 50	27.6%
over 50	33.9%

If a group of those 50 and over is selected for 1966 the proportion is 37.4 percent (compared with 33.9 percent in 1950), which makes this the largest single age group. Between 1950 and 1966 its proportion rose only slightly. While the proportion of party members aged 41 through 50 dropped sharply, the proportion of those between 26 and 30 and 31 to 40 has risen considerably. The changing proportion of the youngest group (persons under 25) seems significant. The total proportion of this group in the SED membership from 1950 to 1960 changed as follows:[218]

[216] *Neues Deutschland,* April 17, 1967.
[217] Stern, *Porträt,* p. 284.
[218] For 1950, see ibid; for 1954 and 1957, see *Protocol of the Fifth SED Congress,* 2: 1609; for 1961, *Protocol of the Sixth SED Congress,* 4: 253; and for 1966, *Neues Deutschland,* April 17, 1967, p. 12.

Summer 1950	8.8%
End of 1954	5.4%
End of 1957	7.7%
End of 1961	9.8%
1966	8.2%

The rise of the younger group between 1954 and 1961 and their proportionate drop between 1961 and 1966 deserves note.

A further indication of changes in the SED's social composition appears in the "Report of the Central Committee to the Seventh Party Congress."

Our party has many members who have actively participated in revolutionary transformations for 15 to 20 years, and who have gained rich experience both from the anti-Fascist-democratic change and the implementation of the Socialist revolution. This applies to 41.2% of all party members and candidates. Our party has approximately 120,000 comrades—6.9%—who were already members of the KPD or the SPD before 1945, who proved their mettle in the class struggle before 1933 as well as during the period of Fascism, and who have rich party experience.[219]

In 1967, 40 to 50 percent of the SED members can be regarded as old comrades. The number of veteran functionaries from the KPD and SPD has however, shrunk to some 7 percent (about 120,000 members).

A demand for the "opening" of the party and its transformation to a ruling, all-embracing party was made in the 4th Party Statute of 1963. In response to this demand, the period of candidacy was reduced to and uniformly fixed at one year and the guarantor requirements were simplified. An attempt to "integrate" groups of the "working intelligentsia" into society, through their social participation even when they do not belong to the SED, is also evident.

The concern of the party elite that workers might become a minority social group in the SED was still obvious in 1963. The importance of a workers' majority was still maintained by Honecker at the Seventh Party Congress in April 1967. The gradual implementation of the collectivization in agriculture in spring 1960 (preceded by an intensified campaign of transferring "the industrial worker to the countryside" and the establishment of party organizations in new and existing LPGs) encouraged a more traditionally oriented recruitment policy.

[219] *Neues Deutschland,* April 17, 1967, p. 12.

This policy was then threatened by the ensuing influx of younger experts into the Party.

The second feature of the changing social structure of the party elite is the considerable increase in the group of party members and candidates with university, college, technical, trade, or other professional school training. The number of trained party members and candidates rose by the middle of 1964 to 57,100 university and college trained experts and 132,500 experts with technical or other professional school training (as far as can be determined from Western sources). According to Honecker's report at the Fifth Central Committee Plenum in 1964, this is almost double the 1962 total, though some significant differentiations should be noted. Whereas in the central apparatus of the Central Committee in 1963 some 75 percent of all members had completed university, college, or professional school training, this figure was only 50 percent for the SED *Bezirk* executives, 30 percent for the political functionaries of the party apparatus as a whole, and 25 percent for the *Kreis* executives.[220]

Executives in the central state apparatus (primarily in the Council of Ministers and the various ministries) are increasingly apt to be professionally trained. Whereas in 1958 only 38 percent of the leading members of the central and local state apparatus had university, college, or professional school degrees, in 1963, 57 percent had these same qualifications.[221] According to data given by the director of the Bureau of the Council of Ministers, State Secretary Dr. Rudi Rost, since the Sixth SED Congress 637 of the 808 (79 percent) top functionaries (state secretaries, chief section directors, and section directors) had

[220] According to Erich Honecker, in *Protocol of the Sixth SED Congress,* 2: 181. Evidently the position of the SED improved considerably from 1963 until 1966–1967. The report of the Central Committee to the Seventh SED Congress mentions that 33.7% of the executive members elected into the basic and departmental party organizations before the Seventh Congress were graduates of institutions of higher learning. At present 83 percent of the first and second secretaries of the SED *Kreis* executives belong to this category; this number includes, however, graduates of party colleges, such as the Institute for Social Sciences of the Central Committee of the SED. About 64 percent of the *Kreis* secretaries have attended the "Karl Marx" Party College. See *Neues Deutschland,* April 17, 1967.

[221] According to Willi Stoph "Gradmesser der Leistung ist der Nutzeffekt," *Neues Deutschland,* January 18, 1963.

university degrees. The educational level of personnel in the state apparatus thus slightly exceeded that of the party apparatus in 1963. This also applies to *Bezirk*-level personnel.[222]

Compared with the leadership bodies of the party (the Politburo, Central Committee Secretariat, the Central Committee, the *Bezirk* executives) and with the entire party apparatus, the proportion of members and candidates with university, college, or other professional training in the SED as a whole is considerably lower: it amounts to some 190,000 out of 1.68 million in 1963 (11.3 percent). The proportion of academically or professionally trained party functionaries rises particularly noticeably near the upper echelon of the party apparatus.

There is a third notable characteristic of the changing social structure of the SED: relative constancy of the number of women among the members and candidates of the SED. The proportion of women in the total membership of the SED has hardly changed since 1957: In 1966, women represented 26.5 percent of the total membership—some 450,000 members and candidates of the party.[223] The proportion of women in the SED on the whole thus approximately corresponded to the proportion of female members and candidates elected at the lower levels of the party apparatus and the SED *Kreis* executives.[224]

9. Conclusions
The analyses in this chapter reinforce a basic theme of our study: the conflict-ridden transformation from an insulated leadership group still

---

[222] According to Rost "Die Kaderarbeit," p. 6. Although he speaks only about "college graduation," his figures may be used as a comparison.

[223] *Neues Deutschland*, April 17, 1967, p. 12, The proportion of women in the SED has fluctuated as follows:

May 1947	23.9%
1954	20.0%
End of 1957	23.5%
End of 1961	24.0%
End of 1966	26.5%

For 1947, see Stern, *Porträt,* p. 284; for 1954 and 1957, see *Protocol of the Fifth SED Congress,* 2: 1609; for 1961, *Protocol of the Sixth SED Congress,* 4: 253; and for 1966, *Neues Deutschland,* April 17, 1967, p. 12.

[224] Already in 1963 their share stood at about 25%. See Wagner, *Die Verantwortung der leitenden Parteiorgane,* p. 22.

largely committed to models of preindustrial societies into a complex and comprehensive modern social organization. This development in the case of the SED can hardly be explained by traditional models of conflict in Leninist parties, i.e., conflicts between ideology and organization, or between functionaries and intelligentsia. Rather, the change in the party organization of the SED should be regarded as a transformation which reflects and influences a corresponding transformation of the GDR's society itself.

The detailed analysis of structural conflicts in central and regional leadership bodies of the SED establishes several wider political patterns and processes: the attitudes both of members in the strategic clique and the rival institutionalized counter elite have over the years blurred and overlapped in several major policy areas. Major inconsistencies in the patterns of applying sanctions would seem to have become the norm since the introduction of the "new economic system." Power instrumentalities of the traditional totalitarian type (mass terror, lack of predictability in social norms, etc.) have become combined with the techniques of consultative authoritarianism (the rational considerations of an industrial society and response to group interests). As a result of this changed situation, the instruments of totalitarian power themselves have undergone continuous transformation. With the shift to "economic competition" in the East-West conflict and the emphasis on the functional requirements of the economy some at least partly rational economic and organizational considerations have governed the decisions of the strategic clique. The pattern of conflict and cooperation typical of large economic organizations in general can be seen in the party organization of the SED since 1963. This has compelled the strategic clique to be somewhat more than a mere isolated secret conspiratorial society.

An analysis of change, as we have been careful to define it, must take into account the clash of the forces of dynamism and those of continuity and describe the structural conflicts between and interdependencies of these forces. Such conflicts have been demonstrated on three levels of the party's apparatus: at the level of the Central Committee of the SED, a clash between archetypes of organization and those patterns based on requirements of a modern industrial system. In the Central Committee the acclamatory and declamatory functions have declined increasingly while coordination, transmissional and consultation functions have assumed greater importance. Even the newly established control organizations in the party apparatus are tailored to the model of a large social system. After their establishment they have not changed along the pattern of the traditional organizational patterns of the SED, but were rather grafted upon an organizational system already functioning according to the production principle. Even after the territorial principle regained its former preeminence, there was no question of abandoning the basic elements of the production principle.

The "operational" work of the SED in the economic sphere has also been studied. The members of the bureaus of industry and construction appear to have represented the social norms of party experts rather than functionaries. Even after these bureaus were dissolved, the process of differentiation along the same lines (i.e., experts vs. untrained functionaries) within the SED has continued with the same momentum. A tendency so embedded in the general process of social change cannot very well be negated by measures of a purely political organization. Finally, an important conflict reflected in social changes has become obvious in our findings of this chapter: party functionaries of the older and younger generations are confronting party experts represented largely by the younger generation.

These conflicts and organizational changes in the SED had not yet reached fruition by 1963-1964. Organizational comparison therefore yields only limited hypotheses for future development: the boundary drawn by a formerly dictatorial party changing to a large organization so as to maintain its far-reaching power is no longer rigid, but in the case of the SED at least must be regarded as shifting. The shift is not merely one toward new forms of totalitarian rule; the shift in power boundaries also involves the need for recognition of the party's relatively increased adaptation to, and integration in, society. "Adaptation" however must not be equated with a renunciation of guidance and control: the differentiation of controls and the will to perfect the functional efficiency of the social system have, however, softened the basic totalitarian features of the SED.

3

Trends of Continuity and Change in the Social Composition of the SED Leadership Bodies

1. Introduction

The organizational analysis of the Central Committee and the process of restructuring within the SED apparatus observed since 1962–1963 that were covered in Chapter One are here followed by an empirical evaluation of the social statistics for the Central Committee in 1954, 1958, and 1963. Such an expansion of our research formula is necessary to illustrate clearly the change in the SED leadership. In Chapter Four this analysis of comprehensive restratification will be complemented by a study of change and continuity in the ideological sphere.

NOTE ON THE COLLECTION AND EVALUATION OF DATA
Our study includes all 275 full and candidate members of the Central Committees in 1954, 1958, and 1963. (In some cases relevant biographical data have been recorded through the end of 1966 or early 1967. These data do not appear in the tables. When absolutely essential to the analysis they have been included in the text and footnotes.) A personal file was established for each full and candidate member, which contains notes on his membership in the Central Committee, the Central Committee Secretariat, and the Politburo in 1954, 1958, 1963 (and sometimes in 1966 and 1967) as well as the following data:

Sex.
Date of birth.
Place of birth (country).
Father's profession.
Completion of education or professional training.
Acquired profession.
Date of entry into the KPD/SED or other parties.
Political training.
Residence in the Soviet Union.
Politically relevant activity or residence between 1933–1945.
Membership in the Peoples' Chamber (1954, 1958, and 1963).
Membership in the Council of Ministers (1954, 1958, 1963, and 1965).

Membership in the State Council (1960 and 1963).

Actual occupation (primary function) during comparable periods: 1954, 1958, and 1963.

Secondary functions in selected mass organizations during comparable periods: 1954, 1958, and 1963.

The study is based on individual data contained in biographies. Correlation of characteristics and overall assessments are affected only at the evaluation stage—a practice in keeping with the general purpose of this study, which is to work closely with the available empirical data. Data collection was facilitated by both East and West German sources of which the following were consulted:

From the GDR:

The Protocols of the Fourth, Fifth, and Sixth SED Congresses in 1954, 1958, and 1963.

The Handbooks of the Peoples' Chamber for the Second, Third, and Fourth Election Periods (1954, 1958, and 1963).

The Statistical Yearbooks of the GDR for 1958, 1959, 1963, and 1964.

The Yearbooks of the GDR for 1958, 1959, and 1960.

The Handbook of the German Democratic Republic (1965).

The Yearbooks of the German Academy of Sciences in Berlin, 1954, 1958, and 1963.

University catalogs as available in West Germany.

Biographical sketches and announcements, primarily from *Neues Deutschland,* the weekly *Die Wirtschaft,* and the SED local press.

From West Germany:

SBZ Biographie, all editions, including the 3rd ed. (1964).

SBZ von A bis Z, all ten editions, 10th ed. (1966).

Wer ist wer? Das Deutsche Who's Who. 14th ed. of Degeners *Wer ist's?,* II (1965).

Kürschners Deutscher Gelehrtenkalender (1961).

Relevant information and material in the SBZ Archive.

Biographical data from the *Mitteilungen* and *Handbuch der Sowjet-zonen-Volkskammer, 2. Legislaturperiode,* II (Berlin: 1955–1957), both published by the Informationbüro West (IWE).

The personnel files of the Institute for Political Science at the Free University of Berlin.

Material from the Personnel Files of the Archives for All-German Affairs (AGF), Bonn.

Data from the author's files.

Data from the Institute of Journalism at the Free University of Berlin.

Information on "Die Mitglieder das Zentralkomitees (1954)," in Carola Stern, *Porträt einer bolschewistischen Partei. Entwicklung, Funktion und Situation der SED* (Cologne: 1957): 297 ff.

"Personalien," in *Der FDGB. Erfüllungsgehilfe der SED,* published by the National Board of the German Trade Union Association (DGB), 3rd enlarged ed. with supplements (Düsseldorf: 1964).

Ehemalige Nationalsozialisten in Pankows Diensten, compiled and published by the Investigation Committee of Liberal Jurists (Untersuchungsausschuss Freiheitlicher Juristen), 4th enlarged ed. (Berlin: 1962).[1]

Careful comparison and coordination of our data guarantees a high degree of accuracy; however, certain circumstances prevented the establishment of ultimate reliability in many cases. Particular problems that arose in the coordination of different materials are specifically discussed in the present introduction as well as in special sections.

The culled and processed data were transferred to hand tabulation cards after codification. These cards were first counted linearly (for the three Central Committees), with a distinction preserved between members and candidates.[2] Some of these results have been taken over directly in tabular form (see Tables 1, 2, 3, 5, 7, 8, 9, 10, and 12). Linear counting revealed that differences in age, training, or acquired and actual occupation of Central Committee members between 1958 and 1963 are more marked than those for 1954 and 1958. For this reason special counts have been made only for the Central Committees of 1958 and 1963 under the categories of, inter alia, training as differentiated by age groups, acquired and actual profession, and the ascent/descent or fluctuation analysis. A record already saturated with data was not to be further overladen with evaluation results.

In keeping with the primarily descriptive character of this empirical section, the following analysis has been utilized to treat individual data. Naturally, an overall description could not include every possible item. The survey cites only such findings as could be incorporated meaningfully into the total compilation.

[1] Further sources and literature are cited in the footnotes.
[2] Considerable significance is attached to the candidacy period, also on the basis of the Fourth Statutes of the SED of 1963. Hence, this chapter tries, as far as possible, to make a distinction between members and candidates of the Central Committee. However, this could not be done with regard to all biographical data.

PROBLEMS OF SOURCES

Since members and candidates of the Central Committee represent a supraregional group in an exposed social position, biographical sources are plentiful. Furthermore, mutually independent information was secured, both for Western and Eastern materials. Thus, it was possible to form a highly reliable biographical data profile for each member or candidate of the Central Committee, based primarily on age and actual occupation for various periods. Political and biographical data and other information on training and primary occupations could not be secured with equal precision.

Sources on the social origin of Central Committee members and candidates are unreliable, contradictory, and incomplete. Although collection was limited to the father's occupation, available data were not satisfactory even for this modest purpose.[3] In many cases there simply are none at all, or those available could well prove unreliable.

Communist functionaries sometimes attempt to deny "bourgeois origin." Consequently, it was impossible to verify the father's real occupation in cases where "worker" had been declared—particularly since complete analysis would have to establish the respective period during which the father was allegedly thus employed. Here it must be recalled that many who had been Nazis, either temporarily or for a longer period, became "workers" after 1945, and their children may now claim "pure" worker parentage. Empirical verification of such data is almost impossible since direct inquiry from the West is precluded. Furthermore, the social origin of fathers of full and candidate members of the Central Committee might be lower-middle or lower class; thus, their origin cannot be determined by methods used in elite studies (e.g., listing in telephone books). Therefore, it was necessary to omit a social characteristic important to the overall context of this study. Nonetheless, this omission is not serious, since the study does not cover social changes within the political leadership of the GDR after World War II but concentrates mainly on the limited field of change in segments of the leadership for the period 1954–1963 and 1964.

Research is much more fruitful in the field of political biography of Central Committee members and candidates, although here not all gaps

[3] See the discussion following Table 4.

can be filled. The date of entry into the SPD and the KPD for functionaries belonging to either party cannot always be pinpointed. East German sources are often of no help, since the SED regards itself as the Socialist Unity Party of Germany formed from the KPD and SPD. Western sources (primarily the publications of the Federal Ministry for All-German Affairs) on the whole give the appropriate distinctions; therefore, except where other material indicates to the contrary, these data were accepted. They were subject to verification in cases where the party member participated in Central Conventions of the KPD, SPD, etc., for which transactions and, most important, lists of the participants were published. However, the status of the majority of full and candidate Central Committee members could not be determined by this method. Information on the lives of Central Committee members and candidates between 1933 and 1945, as well as on their residence in the Soviet Union, is also of doubtful worth. Exact data on the duration of the respective residencies or activities are unavailable. Many of the biographical details had to be gathered from widely scattered sources, such as memoirs, obituaries, documentation, monographs, etc. Despite our relatively rough criteria for these categories, full clarity could not be established for many biographies between 1933 and 1945.

Data on the occupational situation of Central Committee members and candidates could not always be accepted at face value. This problem was compounded by our codification system. To characterize a given man's professional situation, we selected completion of highest level of education, acquired profession, and actual occupation in 1954, 1958, and 1963. Whereas available data on given individuals' occupations are reliable and could be repeatedly confirmed by cross checking, the situation for determining completion of education and acquired occupation is less satisfactory. Available data thus allow only rough classifications (Tables 9 and 10). Although main educational profiles of the Central Committee could be determined with comparative reliability, data—such as those given by Karl Valentin Müller[4]—on those who were educational drop-outs were impossible to find. Thus, in some cases

---

[4] See Karl Valentin Müller, *Die Manager in der Sowjetzone. Eine empirische Untersuchung zur Soziologie der wirtschaftlichen und militärischen Führungsschicht in Mitteldeutschland* (Cologne and Opladen, 1962), p. 50.

for high-school, public-school, and technical- or trade-school pupils their incomplete education may be represented as complete. However, this does not apply to a particularly important group—that encompassing university graduates and graduates of technical, trade, and other colleges, since this group includes only Central Committee members and candidates, the completion of whose studies were amenable to verification.

A further limitation on our data for education and acquired occupation is occasioned by the fact that information available for those attending trade or graduate schools is not available for public-school pupils; the same applies to those who became skilled workers through training courses in the factories. It can be assumed that many full and candidate Central Committee members received some comparable form of adult education. In the GDR, political and educational training are closely linked. Furthermore, since 1963, party training can certainly be regarded as a professional qualification in view both of the strong tendency to place a high premium on scientific training, and the trend toward "professionalization."

Data for "acquired occupation" are also of uneven reliability. Data on a skilled worker and an artisan, or on skilled, trained, and unskilled workers cannot always be distinguished. We have tried throughout this analysis to exclude politically motivated distortions. The criterion "acquired occupation" is thus of secondary importance. Our systematization hews closely to the categories given in the original source (see Table 11). This approach does, however, take into account the overall context of our study by admitting valid distinctions between various types of economic functionaries.

PROBLEMS OF CODING AND ANALYSIS

Problems of codification arose in considering actual occupation and later in analyzing occupational mobility. Since the people for whom we have reliable data constitute (according to the SED statute) the "supreme" SED body between Party Congresses—which normally take place every four years—its members must be considered a part of the political elite of GDR society. On the other hand, since the party as a whole also constitutes a part of this society, this larger group includes within itself a wide spectrum of functions. The primary functions of Central Committee candidates and members in 1954, 1958, and 1963 have thus been taken into account in order to include their occupational characteristics. These years were selected as recording periods, so as to permit comparison with the respective membership/nonmembership ratio in the Central Committee. Systematizing the primary function made a new framework of analysis necessary. According to our formula in Chapter Two, the analysis of occupational situation in this study is not tied to the commonly used social criteria, "worker," "employee," etc., or "upper-middle," "lower-middle," "upper-lower class," etc., as would be justified for large area or intergeneration analysis.[5] Indeed, in the given context a more narrow occupation concept concentrating on the positional aspects must be used. Furthermore, only one of the most important occupational positions held or functions fulfilled could be retained at the given periods for the Central Committee members and candidates. In determining "primary function" we considered, on the one hand, the socioeconomic sphere in which it is exercised (apparatus, functional area), and on the other, the position occupied by the respective functionary in the hierarchy of the apparatus. The following functional areas were distinguished: party, state, the economy and agriculture, mass organizations, cultural and educational training institutions, NVA, international organizations, and finally all other organizations. Within these functional areas a hierarchical structure was established along the lines of the following distinctions: top, upper-middle, middle-middle, etc.[6] These differentiations could be based only on known data pertain-

---

[5] For German postwar society, see the stratification models elaborated by M. Janowitz, H. Moore, G. Kleining, and E. K. Scheuch for the Federal Republic of Germany, which are represented and discussed comprehensively by Karl Martin Bolte et al., *Soziale Schichtung* (Opladen, 1966), p. 52 et seq; Ralf Dahrendorf, *Gesellschaft und Demokratie in Deutschland* (Munich, 1965), p. 94 et seq; and Dieter Claessens et al., *Sozialkunde der Bundesrepublik Deutschland* (Düsseldorf and Cologne, 1965), p. 258 et seq. For the GDR, see the calculations by Kurt Lungwitz, *Über die Klassenstruktur in der Deutschen Demokratischen Republik. Eine sozialökonomisch-statistische Untersuchung* (Berlin, 1962). Even though the frequencies given by Lungwitz for the individual groups may no longer apply, his general social stratification model still seems valid. For a critical review of stratification models from the point of view of Marxist social theory, see Stanislaw Ossowski, *Die Klassenstruktur im sozialen Bewusstsein* (Neuwied and Berlin, 1962).

[6] See code on pp. 226-227; also note 35.

ing to the respective organization. By contrast, apart from some special cases—e.g., the classification of prominent writers—the actual (as opposed to formal) influence of the respective incumbents had to be disregarded in our rankings.

The key used in codifying data on primary function assumed each of the different socioeconomic areas to be a hierarchical system, as the term is normally used in organizational sociology. This concept proved equally useful in our analysis of occupational mobility. We define occupational mobility as the movement of Central Committee members and candidates from one occupational position to another. These positions have been determined for the respective Central Committees of 1954, 1958, and 1963. In contrast to the mobility concept generally used in sociology, we have limited ourselves to mobility in the strict occupational sense and have applied the concept only to a period covering four years.[7] As in most mobility studies, we distinguish between horizontal fluctuation and vertical ascent/descent movements. Analysis of professional mobility for the members and candidates of the Central Committee centered upon the problem of developing a comparative ranking scheme between the various hierarchical structures: e.g., Can the chairman of a mass organization (and furthermore, every mass organization, or which of them?) be placed on the same level as a Central Committee secretary? Can the editor-in-chief of *Neues Deutschland* and the managing director of a VVB be attributed equal status? Is the chairman or deputy chairman of a district council equal to a full professor? Such questions can only be clarified by a sociological analysis of all segments of the GDR. The answers have assumed that a basic comparability exists between positions regarded as "top" and "upper-middle," etc., within individual socioeconomic areas. This is based on the view that the incumbent in such positions within the hierarchy of the apparatus exerts a degree of influence equal to the power exercised by a comparable incumbent at the same level in another apparatus.

However, consideration of overall social influence can hardly be determined by using this formula. Though in general we have assumed the basic comparability of various positions, it was deemed suitable to go

[7] We shall therefore speak neither of social mobility nor of intragenerational mobility.

back to individual biographical data when analyzing ascent and descent. Significant distinctions which may have been omitted during codification could thus be highlighted.[8]

Because analysis of social mobility and other factors treated in this chapter concentrate on a small social segment of society—the members and candidates of the Central Committee—during a ten- to twelve-year period, there is no question here of analyzing political elites within the framework of the comprehensive social changes now underway in the GDR. Indeed, the period selected would be inadequate for this purpose. Analysis of the development of political elites in the GDR, compared to their historical predecessors, or comparable political leadership groups in West Germany, is beyond the scope of this study, which is limited to an analysis of change and stability in the social composition of the Central Committee and the associated political bodies during the period 1954 to 1963.

2. Statistical and Demographic Data on Central Committee Members and Candidates in 1954, 1958, and 1963

Evaluation of the empirical material at hand begins with the results obtained in preparing statistical and demographic data on Central Committee members and candidates for 1954, 1958, and 1963. These are lists by sex, age, and place of birth (see Tables 1, 2, and 3). Age is the only factor considered in the following sections as it alone is related to the analysis. Father's profession (see Table 4) is not generally included in the demographic data. Where it has been included, this was because it—like sex or birthplace—is not taken into account in the later sections.

SEX

Comparison between the Central Committee members and candidates for 1954 and 1958 by sex reveals that the proportion of male to female remained almost unchanged: 13.3 percent of members and candidates in 1954 and 13.5 percent in 1958 are female. However, the proportion of female candidates in the Central Committee dropped from 13.5 percent

[8] This can be verified in detail from Tables 22, 23, 26 and 27.

Table 1
The Members and Candidates of the Central Committee (1954, 1958, and 1963) by Sex

Sex	1954 Central Committee								1958 Central Committee								1963 Central Committee							
	Members		Candidates		Total		of these not in CC in 1958		Members		Candidates		Total		of these not in CC in 1963		Members		Candidates		Total		of these new in 1963	
	abs %		abs %		abs %		abs %		abs %		abs %		abs %		abs %		abs %		abs %		abs %		abs %	
Male	82	90.1	35	79.5	117	86.7	36	94.7	100	90.1	34	77.3	134	86.5	46	82.1	106	87.6	55	91.7	161	89.0	73	89.0
Female	9	9.9	9	20.5	18	13.3	2	5.3	11	9.9	10	22.7	21	13.5	10	17.9	15	12.4	5	8.3	20	11.0	9	11.0
Total	91	100.0	44	100.0	135	100.0	38	100.0	111	100.0	44	100.0	155	100.0	56	100.0	121	100.0	60	100.0	181	100.0	82	100.0

Table 2
The Members and Candidates of the Central Committee (1954, 1958, and 1963) by Age

Age group	Year of Birth	1954 Central Committee				1958 Central Committee				1963 Central Committee			
		Members	Candidates	Total	of these not in CC in 1958	Members	Candidates	Total	of these not in CC in 1963	Members	Candidates	Total	of these new in 1963
1	prior to 1890	8	0	8	1	7	0	7	3	4	0	4	0
2	1890–1899	14	4	18	4	16	3	19	7	11	1	12	0
3	1900–1909	33	9	42	8	42	7	49	15	38	5	43	9
4	1910–1919	20	6	26	4	23	11	34	9	30	10	40	15
5	1920–1929	8	11	19	1	17	17	34	10	37	37	74	50
6	1930–1939	0	0	0	0	0	0	0	0	1	7	8	8
x	No data	8	14	22	20	6	6	12	12	0	0	0	0
	Total	91	44	135	38	111	44	155	56	121	60	181	82

Table 3
The Members and Candidates of the Central Committee (1954, 1958, and 1963) by Place of Birth

Place of Birth	1954 Central Committee				1958 Central Committee				1963 Central Committee			
	Mem-bers	Candi-dates	Total	of these not in CC in 1958	Mem-bers	Candi-dates	Total	of these not in CC in 1963	Mem-bers	Candi-dates	Total	of these new in 1963
Germany now GDR	26	11	37	6	34	15	49	17	45	24	69	37
Germany now FRG	21	4	25	5	25	4	29	10	20	6	26	7
West & East Berlin	13	3	16	1	18	7	25	5	20	7	27	7
Germany (1939) now other region	12	6	18	4	14	7	21	6	19	6	25	10
Abroad (West)	2	0	2	0	4	0	4	2	2	0	2	0
Abroad (East)	2	0	2	0	3	0	3	1	3	3	6	4
No data	15	20	35	22	13	11	24	15	12	14	26	17
Total	91	44	135	38	111	44	155	56	121	60	181	82

Table 4
Social Origin of Selected* Members and Candidates of the Central Committee (1954, 1958, and 1963)

Occupation of Father	Central Committee in 1954				Central Committee in 1958				Central Committee in 1963			
	Members	Candidates	Total	of these not in the CC in 1958	Members	Candidates	Total	of these not in the CC in 1963	Members	Candidates	Total	of these new in 1963
Upper-Class Occupation	3	0	3	0	5	0	5	3	3	0	3	0
Middle-Class Occupation	11	5	16	2	15	7	22	4	21	2	23	6
of these:												
Craftsman	7	1	8	2	9	2	11	1	9	0	9	1
Farmer	1	2	3	0	1	2	3	2	3	1	4	3
Lower-Class Occupations	30	6	36	4	43	6	49	12	45	3	48	11
of these:												
Worker	28	6	34	4	39	6	45	11	42	3	45	11
Farmer, hired farm hand	1	0	1	0	1	0	1	1	0	0	0	0
No data	4	7	11	4	5	7	12	3	6	16	22	17
Total	48	18	66	10	68	20	88	22	75	21	96	34

* The members and candidates selected were the bearers of primary functions 11, 12, 21, 22 and 41 while they were full or candidate members of the respective Central Committee (see Table 12).

of 155 members and candidates in 1958 to 11 percent in 1963, despite numerical enlargement of the Central Committee.

In all three Central Committees the absolute number of female members and candidates is so low that differences by sex are of minimal value as characteristics collected for this study (see Table 1). This confirms (at least for the development of the Central Committee from the Fourth to the Fifth and Sixth SED Congresses) the incorrectness of the SED leadership's frequent claim that the proportion of women in the political decision-making bodies of the GDR is not only higher than that of West Germany, but has also constantly grown.[9]

AGE

Table 2 gives the age structure of Central Committee members and candidates for 1954, 1958, and 1963, and provides much more evidence of change than Table 1. The age factor merits particular attention in testing the thesis of a "changing of the guard" in the political leadership of the GDR, and will often be cited in the following section.

Table 2 outlines the rapid rejuvenation of the Central Committee of 1963, which is particularly salient compared to 1958. Even though some data for the Central Committees in 1954 and 1958 are missing, this conclusion seems valid. In 1958 age groups 4 and 5 showed an absolute and relative rise compared with figures for 1954, which remained far below the ratios for 1958 and 1963, both in absolute and relative changes within age groups 5 and 6. Out of the total of 49 members and candidates of the Central Committee in 1958 from age group 3 (born between 1900 and 1909) 15 were not readmitted to the 1963 CC (a loss of 30.6 percent). In 1963 only 9 in this age group were elected. The situation is reversed for age group 4 (those born between 1910 and 1919): 9 former members and candidates from 1958 left the Central Committee in 1963, while 15 in this age group were newly elected. In age group 5 (those born between 1920 and 1929), 10 former members

[9] In 1958–1963 the proportion of women in the Peoples' Chamber (house of representatives) rose both in absolute and relative terms: of the 466 members in 1958, 114 or 24.5 percent were women, compared with 137 or 27.4 percent of the 500 members in 1963. These data taken from *Die Volkskammer der Deutschen Demokratischen Republik. 4. Wahlperiode* (Berlin, 1964), p. 125.

dropped out and 50 new members entered. Finally, a group not represented in the 1958 Central Committee—age group 6 (those born between 1930 and 1939)—for the first time was represented by 8 members in 1963.

This rejuvenation from 1958 to 1963 becomes even more evident if we consider that the 99 functionaries remaining in this period have aged by four to five years. In spite of this, the average age of the Central Committee for 1963 is lower (47.2 years) than the average age of the Central Committee in 1958 (48.2 years).[10] Moreover, 58 persons from the group born between 1920 and 1939 (i.e., 71 percent of the total 82 members and candidates of these years) are new entries in the 1963 Central Committee. In 1958 this age group had a total of 34 members and candidates and in 1954, a mere 19. This is particularly noteworthy in view of the fact that in all three Central Committees the number of members is smaller than that of candidates for these two age groups alone. The ratio for age group 6 in the Central Committee of 1963 is also notable, since there are now seven candidates for one full member.

The strategic clique has tended over some years to give as many younger party members as possible a chance for advancement. It is evident that this changing policy toward personnel is not just biologically conditioned, but is a consciously planned change of generations in the higher party echelons. Ulbricht himself, at the beginning of 1963, co-opted representatives of the younger party experts such as Erich Apel, Günter Mittag, and Werner Jarowinsky into the Central Committee Secretariat and Politburo as candidates.[11]

---

[10] In this context, two phenomena should be noted: (1) The average age of members and candidates of the Central Committee in 1954—as far as can be calculated in view of the high drop-out rate—was less than in 1963 (about 46). Between 1954 and 1958 the average age seems to have risen rather than declined. (2) Compared with political leadership groups in other regimes, particularly the German Federal Republic, the average age of the Central Committee is low. Zapf has calculated an average of 53.9 years for the political elite (ministers, heads of state, parliamentary and party leaders) of the Weimar Republic in 1925. The average age of the political elite under Hitler was 50.3 in 1940; under the Bonn regime the political elite had an average age of 56.2 in 1955. (Wolfgang Zapf, *Wandlungn der deutchen Elite. Ein Zirkulationsmodell deutscher Führungsgruppen, 1919–1961* [Munich, 1965], p. 170.)

[11] See note 2.

The second general phenomenon illustrated by Table 2 is the turnover in the younger party cadres. Such changes among those holding key positions cannot be regarded as the result of mere attrition, since increasing differentiation within GDR society is accompanied by transformations within its organizational structure. Rationalization of the organizational system does, however, imply a higher degree of interchangeability of functions and, thus, functionaries; such a transformation has had its effect as well on the organizational forms of the SED, which originated in a preindustrial society. Of the 34 Central Committee members and candidates in 1958 born between 1920 and 1929 (age group 5), 10 (29.4 percent) were dropped from the Central Committee in 1963.[12] This corresponds approximately to the figures for those born between 1900 and 1909 (15 out of 49, or 30.6 percent). Furthermore, in both age groups the number of those dropping out for natural causes (i.e., by death or for reasons of health) is approximately equal. For both groups the number of members who left between 1958 and 1963 exceeds that for candidates (by approximately 2:1).

PLACE OF BIRTH

The criterion of place of birth is a statistically determinable item useful as an indicator of the demographic insulation of the GDR and the self-isolation of the SED vis-à-vis the West. Our preparatory categories were selected with this in mind, and Table 3 makes a distinction between members and candidates born in the area of the present GDR and the present Federal Republic, etc. However, its value is somewhat reduced by the fact that for a good many members and candidates in all three Central Committees no place of birth is listed. Nevertheless, the relative and absolute numbers of members and candidates born in the GDR has risen for the period observed, although the youngest among those in the sample were born prior to the establishment of the GDR. In the 1954 Central Committee, 37 out of a total 135 members and candidates (27.4 percent) were born within the present boundaries of the GDR, whereas of the 155 members and candidates in 1958, 49 (31.6 percent) were born in East Germany. In 1963 the proportion of

[12] Comparison with the members and candidates who left the Central Committee in 1954 is impossible, because the age of too many is unknown.

members and candidates born in the GDR rose to 38.1 percent (69 of a total 181 members and candidates).[13]

FATHER'S OCCUPATION

Only an approximate distinction has been made between upper, middle, and lower level occupations—a differentiation based on the assumption that the social structure in Germany during the lifetime of these fathers can be described relatively exactly by using these three criteria.[14] It was not possible to include all members and candidates because for many data were unavailable. No data on the father's profession appeared for 58 (42.9 percent) of the total 135 Central Committee candidates and members in 1954. This information was missing for 51 (32.9 percent) of the total 155 members and candidates in 1958, and for 71 (39.2 percent) of the total 181 for 1963. Consequently, Table 4 includes data only for those functionaries who, at the time of their entry or reentry into the Central Committee in 1954, 1958, or 1963, occupied leading positions in the party, state, and mass organizations (primary function: 11, 12, 21, 22, 41), and for whom data is much more readily available. Data on the father's profession are missing for 11 of the 66 (approximately 16 percent) in 1954, for 12 of the 88 (approximately 14 percent) in 1958, and for 22 of the 96 members and candidates (approximately 23 percent) in 1963.

With regard to the social position determined by the father's occupation, as given in Table 4, there is virtually no difference in the

[13] Similar results for the members of the German Academy of Sciences in Berlin were obtained by Arthur M. Hanhardt. (See Arthur M. Hanhardt, "Die ordentlichen Mitglieder der Deutschen Akademie der Wissenschaften zu Berlin (1945 bis 1961). Ergebnisse einer empirischen Untersuchung," in Peter Christian Ludz, ed., *Studien und Materialien zur Soziologie der DDR* (Cologne and Opladen, 1964), pp. 248 ff.

[14] In this statement we are reverting to Theodor Geiger's monograph (first published in 1930), "Zur Theorie des Klassenbegriffs und der proletarischen Klasse," in his *Arbeiten zur Soziologie. Methode—Moderne Grossgesellschaft—Rechtssoziologie—Ideologiekritik*, selected and introduced by Paul Trappe, *Soziologische Texte*, Vol. 7 (Neuwied and Berlin, 1962), in particular pp. 243 and 235 ff. Geiger distinguished between the capitalist, the proletarian, and the middle class. The subdivision into capitalists, old middle class, new middle class, proletaroids, and proletariat that appeared in his 1932 study *Die soziale Schichtung des deutschen Volkes*, p. 73, does not seem applicable in the present context.

composition of the Central Committees of 1954, 1958, and 1963.[15] Table 4 shows an unequivocal predominance of the category "worker." However, such information should be accepted with reservations. Some mistrust seems justified, since "worker" was not further specified as unskilled, skilled, specialist, etc. Furthermore, in Table 4 the complete absence of functionaries at the upper levels whose fathers were peasants or agricultural workers is particularly notable. Only three members and candidates of the Central Committee in 1954 and 1958 have described their fathers as "farmers" or "middle peasants," in contrast to the presence of four farmers' sons in the Central Committee of 1963. Smaller (here, *not* independent) peasants and agricultural laborers appear even less frequently. Data on peasant origin appears more reliable than that for "workers." In the first place, these categories did not serve, as could the term worker, to hide the originally bourgeois professions of the fathers. Second, it seems far less probable that a peasant or agricultural laborer's origin should be kept concealed or altered. On the whole, the evidence of these reduced compilations of the father's occupation yields such a low correlation that it seemed best to forego this important sociostructural criterion for purposes of the analysis.

3. Some Observations on the Political Biography of Central Committee Members and Candidates in 1954, 1958, and 1963

From Table 2 it is evident that the 1963 Central Committee changed greatly in its composition by age, compared with those of 1958 and

[15] Interesting differences are revealed, however, when comparing the social structure of the Central Committee with that of the Peoples' Chamber where there are far more deputies of bourgeois or peasant parentage. For the official data, see *Die Volkskammer der Deutschen Demokratischen Republik. 4. Wahlperiode*, p. 127. Arthur M. Hanhardt and his coworkers at the University of Oregon in Eugene are preparing a comparative study of the German Bundestag (parliament) and the Peoples' Chamber which, as far as the unpublished material indicates, may also serve as a reference. Wolf Mersch has made a stratification analysis of the deputies of the two Houses according to the model of Morris Janowitz. (Wolf Mersch, "Volksvertreter in West und Ost. Das Sozialprofil von Bundestagsabgeordneten und Delegierten der Volkskammer." in Wolfgang Zapf, ed. and comp., *Beiträge zur Analyse der deutschen Oberschicht* (Munich, 2nd exp. ed., 1965), p. 34. The comparison shows that the two are widely divergent with respect to the social position determined by the father's occupation.

1954. Selected information from the political biographies of the members and candidates illustrates further changes. For purposes of statistical analysis of the political biographies the following data have been selected: political activities as party members (Tables 5 and 6), politically relevant activity or residence between 1933 and 1945 (Table 7), and residence and/or training in the Soviet Union or in the GDR (Table 8).

PARTY AFFILIATION

These patterns were documented primarily by data on entry into various parties. Because of problems connected with the collection of this data (discussed in the introduction to this chapter) the categories in Table 5 are limited to the following: "entry into the KPD/CPSU or other Comintern parties before 1933,"[16] "entry into the KPD/CPSU in 1934–1944," and "entry into the KPD/SPD or SED between 1945 and 1951," etc.[17] The most difficult questions to determine were entry into the KPD/CPSU between 1934 and 1944, and if so, when. During this period many European Communist parties were illegal. Given Central Committee members were placed in this group only when entry into the party for this period was corroborated by various sources. Finally, Central Committee members and candidates who had been members of the SPD before 1933, and whose political careers were rooted in SPD tradition, were considered separately (Table 6).

Two groups dominate Table 5: the "veteran Communists," persons who had belonged to the KPD, the CPSU, or other Comintern parties before 1933; and those who joined the SED after 1945 but before

[16] Thus, Alois Bräutigam and Rudolf Dölling, both members of the Central Committee of 1958 and 1963, were members of the Communist Party of Czechoslovakia (KPC). Alois Pisnik, likewise a member of the Central Committee in 1958 and in 1963, was a member of the Communist Party of Austria.

[17] Here admission into the youth organizations of the parties in question was taken into account. As far as is known, none of the members or candidates of the Central Committees examined was affiliated with any of the bourgeois parties before 1933. This may, however, be due to the omission of data from the material available. On the other hand, it is known that some members and candidates of the Central Committee were members of the NSDAP (the Nazi party). Apart from the two SS members shown in Table 7 (Prof. Dr. Karl-Heinz Bartsch, born in 1923, who held the post of Chairman of the Agricultural Council of the DDR, became a member of

1952—that is to say, before the Second Party Conference of the SED.[18] Due to the rejuvenation of the Central Committee, the proportion of the first group is naturally lower in 1963 than in 1954 and 1958. It dropped from 47.7 percent in 1958 to 37 percent in 1963. It is rather remarkable that in 1963, 15 percent of the group of older party members were dropped and replaced by a like number. However, this addition did not compensate for the reductions in their ranks, either in absolute or relative terms: 17 of 74 (approximately 23 percent) of the group of veteran Communists left the Central Committee in 1963. The increase did not suffice to reestablish a numerical preponderance of veteran Communists in the Central Committee for 1963. The political influence

the 1963 Central Committee but resigned from it in February 1963 because of his National-Socialist past; and Ernst Grossman, born in 1911, who until 1959 was Chairman of the agricultural cooperative "Walter Ulbricht" in Merxleben, was a member of the Central Committees of 1954 and 1958, until he was ousted in 1959 because of his SS membership), the following Central Committee members who were entrusted with senior state functions had been affiliated with the NSDAP: Dr. Herbert Weiz, born in 1924, member of the SED since 1946, member of the 1958, 1963, and 1967 Central Committees, for many years State Secretary for Research and Technology, and since July 1967 Deputy Chairman of the Council of Ministers; Prof. Dr. Erich Rübensam, born in 1922, member of the SED since 1951, candidate of the 1954 and 1958 Central Committees, and member of the 1963 and 1967 Committees, former deputy head of the agricultural section of the SED Central Committee, and at present first vice-president of the German Academy of Agricultural Sciences and director of the Institute for the Cultivation of Field Crops and Plants at the German Academy of Agricultural Sciences in Müncheberg. Heinz Matthes, now a minister and Chairman of the Committee of the Workers' and Peasants' Inspectorate, who is likewise frequently cited as a prominent member of the NSDAP, was born in 1927 and was not yet 17 years old when he joined the Nazi Party in April 1944. As far as is known, excluding those born in 1925 or after, there were nine persons between 1954 and 1963 who had been former members of the NSDAP, including one (Mette) who was a member of the National Socialist Motorists' Corps. In the 1954 Central Committee there was one member (Grossman) and one candidate (Rübensam); in the 1958 Committee three members (Grossmann, Mette, Weiz) and one candidate (Rübensam); in the 1963 Committee four members (Bartsch, M. Ewald, Rübensam, Weiz) and three candidates (Jäckel, Krussk, Sakowski).

[18] At the Second Party Conference (July 9–12, 1962) the commencement of the "Construction of Socialism in the DDR" was officially announced. This date is generally reckoned as the end of the postwar period and the beginning of the determined effort of the SED leadership to build its own social and political system in the DDR.

Table 5
The Members and Candidates of the Central Committee (1954, 1958, and 1963) by Date of Entry into the Party

Entered the Party	Central Committee in 1954				Central Committee in 1958				Central Committee in 1963			
	Members	Candi-dates	Total	of these not in the CC in 1958	Members	Candi-dates	Total	of these not in the CC in 1963	Members	Candi-dates	Total	of these new in 1963
Entry into the KPD/CPSU, etc., before 1933	51	10	61	9	61	13	74	17	59	8	67	10
Entry into the KPD/CPSU, etc., 1934–1944	0	0	0	0	1	0	1	0	2	1	3	2
Entry into the KPD/SPD or SED 1945–1951	25	16	41	5	36	20	56	20	55	42	97	61
Entry into the SED after 1952	0	1	1	0	0	2	2	0	2	9	11	9
Data only on entry into the SPD	5	3	8	5	3	0	3	0	3	0	3	0
No data	10	14	24	19	10	9	19	19	0	0	0	0
Total	91	44	135	38	111	44	155	56	121	60	181	82

Table 6
Former Long-Term Veteran SPD Members in the Central Committee

1954 Central Committee	1958 Central Committee	1963 Central Committee
Members	Members	Members
R. Alt	E. Baumann	J. Balkow
E. Baumann	O. Buchwitz	E. Baumann
O. Buchwitz	F. Ebert	O. Buchwitz
F. Ebert	O. Grotewohl	F. Ebert
O. Grotewohl	K. Kern	O. Grotewohl
K. Helbig	K. Krüger	K. Kern
K. Kern	H. Lehmann	K. Krüger
K. Krüger	E. Mückenberger	E. Mückenberger
H. Lehmann	F. Wehmer	F. Wehmer
E. Mückenberger		
H. Schlimme		
E. Schuppe		
F. Wehmer		
Candidates	Candidates	Candidates
G. Grauer	G. Grauer	—
A. Kupke		
H. Redetzky		

of the older party functionaries in the Central Committee also seems not to have been substantially increased by these new entries. Most of the ten veteran Communists who entered the Central Committee in 1963 are not party functionaries in the strict sense: four are prominent writers or artists, one a senior jurist, one an economist, and only one a functionary in the state apparatus. Three can be described as veteran party officials.[19] Consequently, the new members and candidates from the group of veteran Communists are prominent representatives of East German society rather than the SED. The second group, composed of

[19] These were Lea Grundig, Maxim Vallentin, Walter Kaiser-Gorrish, Max Zimmering, Josef Streit, Lorenz Lochthofen, Otto Gotsche, Marianne Lange, Paul Roscher, and Richard Herber.

Table 7
Politically Relevant Activity or Residence of Members and Candidates of the Central Committee (1954, 1958, and 1963) between 1939 and 1945

Politically Relevant Activity/Residence	Central Committee in 1954			Central Committee in 1958			Central Committee in 1963		
	Members	Candidates	Total	Members	Candidates	Total	Members	Candidates	Total
Emigration to the Soviet Union	18	3	21	21	1	22	19	0	19
Emigration to Western Countries	8	2	10	8	3	11	12	5	17
Illegal Antifascist Activity	6	1	7	8	2	10	10	1	11
Nazi Concentration Camps and Prisons	16	2	18	17	2	19	14	1	15
Residence in Germany (Membership in the SS)	1	0	1	1	0	1	1	0	1
Residence in Germany (Nonpolitical)	17	9	26	17	8	25	14	3	17
Participation in World War II as Members of the German Army	6	5	11	15	8	23	20	17	37
Not Applicable (born in 1925 or later)	2	5	7	5	8	13	17	22	39
No data	17	17	34	19	12	31	14	11	25
Total	91	44	135	111	44	155	121	60	181

Table 8
Residence in the Soviet Union and Political Training of CC Members and Candidates (1954, 1958, and 1963)

Residence/ Political training	Central Committee in 1954				Central Committee in 1958				Central Committee in 1963			
	Mem-bers	Candi-dates	Total	of these not in the CC in 1958	Mem-bers	Candi-dates	Total	of these not in the CC in 1963	Mem-bers	Candi-dates	Total	of these new in 1963
Residence and/or Training in the USSR before 1945	22	4	26	5	24	2	26	7	21	2	23	4
of these: Additional training in the GDR	0	0	0	0	1	0	1	1	0	0	0	0
Not in the USSR before 1945	48	24	72	10	63	29	92	26	86	50	136	70
of these: Training in the USSR after 1945	5	4	9	0	7	7	14	3	12	4	16	5
Training in the GDR	11	8	19	2	20	6	26	11	21	2	23	8
Training in the USSR after 1945 with Additional Training in the GDR	1	1	2	0	0	3	3	0	2	3	5	2
No Data on Training after 1945	31	11	42	8	36	13	49	12	51	41	92	55
No Data	21	16	37	23	24	13	37	23	14	8	22	8
Total	91	44	135	38	111	44	155	56	121	60	181	82

candidates and members who entered the party after 1945, comprises some 60 percent of the new 1963 entries. While in 1954 they constituted less than a third of the Central Committee, and in 1958 a bare third of the members and candidates in the Central Committee, in 1963 approximately half of all the members and candidates fall within this group.

In 1954 and 1958, the veteran Communists dominated numerically. However, in 1963 the rate of entry for the postwar generation was six times that of veteran Communists. Younger SED members who had not grown up in the Comintern tradition thus gained greatly in numerical weight. It is not clear, however, that their political influence grew commensurately. The political stability of the veteran Communist group appears to have been little affected: of the 74 members and candidates in the Central Committee in 1958 who entered the KPD before 1933, 57 (77 percent) retained their positions in the Central Committee in 1963, whereas of the 56 members and candidates in 1958 who had belonged to the SED between 1945 and 1952 only 36 (some 64 percent) were elected to the Central Committee in 1963. In addition, analysis of the Politburo and the Central Committee Secretariat leads to the conclusion that the major positions of political power in the party apparatus continue to be staffed largely by the older generation.

This table proves, at least numerically, that the younger SED Central Committee members represent a generation with novel and different political experience, as well as new social norms and mores. The strategic clique's aim to reduce the generational conflict, plus the policy of equalization between old and new "comrades," has thus led to results in personnel and organizational policy, the concrete expressions of which in organizations have been repeatedly noted in this and the previous chapter. Younger party experts have occupied important socioeconomic positions since 1963, primarily in the Central Committee Secretariat, the Council of Ministers, and in the State Planning Commission.

Compared with the members and candidates of the Central Committee who began their careers in the KPD or the CPSU, the proportion of former veteran SPD members is negligible. Their names appear in Table 6. The low proportion of former SPD members in the Central Committee in 1954, 1958, and 1963 reflects a trend which had reached its zenith in 1954. Of the approximately 680,000 former SPD members who were collectively accepted into the SED in 1946 (the total number of SED members in 1946 approximated 1.3 million, including those with dual party memberships), some 280,000 had left by autumn 1953.[20] The findings in Table 6 do not allow us to perceive a conflict between former KPD and longtime SPD members in the Central Committees of 1954, 1958, and 1963. However, this conclusion holds true only in a relative sense, since the comparative disunity of the German Communist Party in the 1920s fostered many different orientations on the part of subgroups in the KPD, including those of social democratic origin. The ideological conflict between the SPD and the KPD is thus indicated in the composition of party membership to only a limited degree. Detailed investigation of this problem is beyond the scope of this work.

POLITICAL ACTIVITIES OR RESIDENCE FOR THE YEARS 1933–1945
The political activity between 1933–1945 of those investigated in our sample casts further light upon the political biographies of Central Committee members and candidates in 1954, 1958, and 1963. However, numerous problems hampered the preparation of relevant data. Gaps and inexplicable contradictions for the period between 1933-1945 appeared in many biographies. Incomplete and frequently unreliable information made detailed analysis impossible. Furthermore, available data for the years 1933–1938 are so inaccurate that compilation was not attempted. Yet relative reliability of biographical data for 1939–1945 was established by setting up eight groups of characteristics (see Table 7). Invariably, each full and candidate member of the three Central Committees was associated with one of these groups. Where several characteristics applied to any one person, classification was effected only within that group related to the longest temporal segment of the given person's biography between 1939–1945. (Differences with Table 8 can be explained via this processing.)

The eight criteria are:
Emigration (residence) to the Soviet Union including participation in World War Two as a member of the Red Army.

[20] For particulars, see Joachim Schultz, *Der Funktionär in der Einheitspartei. Kaderpolitik und Bürokratisierung in der SED* (Stuttgart and Düsseldorf, 1956), pp. 247 ff.

Emigration (residence or internment) to Western countries, including those temporarily occupied by the German Army (e.g., Denmark, Sweden, Norway).

Illegal antifascist activity. This group contains members and candidates of the Central Committee whose biographies indicated illegal activity in Germany and/or German-occupied territory during this period, so that no regular employment could be engaged in.

Nazi concentration camps and prisons.

Residence in Germany (membership in the SS).

Residence in Germany (nonpolitical). This group includes individual members and candidates of the Central Committee who may have engaged in illegal activities, but not to the same extent as the group classified under "illegal antifascist activity."

Participation in World War Two as members of the German Army. This group includes members and candidates of the Central Committee who served in Punishment Battalion 999 and those who engaged in illegal activity while serving in the Army.

Nonapplicable (those born in 1925 and later).

Table 7 clearly proves that the structure of the Central Committee has changed greatly in the course of its rejuvenation. Biographical characteristics influenced by life under Nazi rule are especially relevant. The following facts are indicative: The proportion of Central Committee members and candidates residing in the Soviet Union from 1939 to 1945 dropped only slightly in 1963, compared with 1958 and 1954. While 21 were former emigrés in 1954, and 22 in 1958, there were 19 left in 1963.[21] Furthermore, of the 19 who belonged to this group in 1963, 14 were Central Committee members in 1954 and only one joined the Central Committee in 1963 (Vallentin).The number of emigrés to the Soviet Union in the Central Committee membership (including candidates) has scarcely fluctuated over the years. This group consists largely of former collaborators in the National Committee "Free Germany," including two members of the "Ulbricht Group" (Maron, Winzer) plus Ulbricht himself. This characteristic differs for the proportion of those emigrating to Western countries. The enlargement of the Central Committee led to a relatively minor—but not insignificant—absolute rise in the proportion of Central Committee members and candidates who are former emigrants to countries in Western and Northern Europe, the United States,

---

[21] In these and the following comparisons based on Table 7 it should be noted that there was a different dropout rate in the various committees which, in addition to the general dropout rate. might further distort the results.

and South America. The comparatively high number of Western emigrants in the 1963 Central Committee indicates formal recognition of
their political rehabilitation. Of these seventeen Western emigrants, nine
were in the Central Committee in 1954. Following Yugoslavia's expul-
sion from the Cominform in 1948, a number of high political functionaries were ousted from the SED or were compelled to surrender their
formal party functions for alleged Titoism. This excuse was often used to
eliminate Western emigrants, troublesome functionaries, etc. Nevertheless, many functionaries sympathized with the most important credo of
Titoism, that of an "independent path to socialism." The demotion of
Paul Merker and Bruno Goldhammer in 1950 is an indication of the
strategic clique's resulting feelings of insecurity. Table 7 also shows that
the group of Western emigrants contains more candidates than that of
former Soviet emigrants. The 1963 Central Committee lists 5 of the 17
Western emigrants as candidates. To specify acquired occupations the
group consists of one journalist (Geggel), one writer (Zimmering), one
natural scientist (Lappe), one musicologist (E. H. Meyer), and a
government official (Plenikowski).

Finally, we come to the group of those who saw military service
between 1939 and 1945. With 37 members in 1963, this group is
relatively and absolutely much larger than it was in 1954 (11 persons)
and 1958 (23 persons). In contrast to this group, the group of those
imprisoned between 1939 and 1945 has dropped from 18 in 1954 and
19 in 1958 to a mere 15 in 1963.

The findings in Table 7 make it clear that the SED Central
Committee has been since 1963 (i.e., since the beginning of the "new
economic system") a kind of melting pot for disparate sociopolitical
groupings who were originally hostile or mutually isolated. In the
present phase of one-party rule—influenced largely by the GDR's
industrial dynamism—allowances must be made for traditional conflicts,
as well as for the appearance of new differences in outlook. Consequently, the strategic clique must endeavor to adapt functionally both these
trends to their political and social system.

RESIDENCE IN THE SOVIET UNION AND POLITICAL TRAINING

Table 8 presents a general political profile based on the criteria of residence and/or study and political training in the Soviet Union and in the GDR of full and candidate members of the Central Committee. Training is defined as participation in political courses given by party institutes or comparable political institutions. (This definition does not include regular study of the social sciences [political economy] at the university, college, or technical college level.) For the pre-1945 period it was considered advisable to include persons who had lived some time in the Soviet Union, although their political training could not be established definitely in each case. It could, however, be assumed that all persons coming from "capitalist-fascist" Germany were required to undergo indoctrination courses.

Within the limits of the material Table 8 proves that, with the passage of time, the proportion of Central Committee members and candidates who had lived in the Soviet Union before 1945 and received political training dropped from 19 percent in 1954 and 17 percent in 1958 to only 13 percent in 1963. This implies that the proportion of members and candidates who had not emigrated to the Soviet Union before 1945 and/or were not indoctrinated there has risen. In 1954 the "non-Soviet group" in the Central Committee consisted of 72 members and candidates (approximately 55 percent), and in 1958 of 92 (or approximately 60 percent). By 1963, there were 136 members and candidates (approximately 75 percent) who had not been in the Soviet Union for an extended period prior to 1945. These figures further reflect a changing of the Guard.

Furthermore, hardly any of those residing and/or politically trained in the Soviet Union before 1945 underwent similar training in the GDR. Consequently, the category "residence and/or political training in the Soviet Union before 1945" is especially suitable for distinguishing two groups in the Central Committee, and may well coincide with the age division. The proportion of cadres trained in the Soviet Union after 1945 fluctuated very little: 11 (9 and 2) of the 135 members and candidates in 1954, 17 (14 and 3) of the 155 members in 1958, and 21 (16 and 5) of the 181 in 1963. (Numbers in parentheses refer to categories listed in Table 8.) In contrast, the proportion of members and candidates who received political training in the GDR after 1945 dropped from 14 percent in 1954 and 17 percent in 1958 to only 13 percent in 1963. However, the latter findings could be occasioned by the fact that increased professional training in the GDR could be combined with political education or that such training for Central Committee members and candidates is such an obvious prerequisite today that it no longer rates mention in biographies. The high number of those who were not in the Soviet Union prior to 1945 and for whom no data with regard to indoctrination courses in the GDR is available could also reflect this professionalization trend.

THE GENERATIONAL CONFLICT IN THE LIGHT OF POLITICAL
BIOGRAPHICAL DATA

Like the data on entry into the party given in Tables 5 and 6, the results given in Tables 7 and 8 become clear only if it is kept in mind that the generation gap manifested in the composition of the Central Committee in 1954, 1958, and 1963 frequently indicates other differences, such as in social ideals and mores. The contrast is not only between those whose political formation occurred in the 1920s (and later, when the party went underground during Nazi rule) and those whose political formation occurred after 1945, but these two main age groups also exhibit differences within themselves. In the older generation widely differing experiences and sociopolitical norms of behavior clash among the former members of the KPD, the SPD, and the CPSU. These differences are accentuated by the variety in the fortunes of these men between 1933 and 1945. Another differentiation appears in the occupational and political experience under SED rule. The image of society held by party members active largely in party and state administration is likely to differ from that of functionaries engaged mainly in economic, cultural, and educational careers. True to Lenin's adage, politically tested and reliable veteran functionaries were selected to take over the state apparatus at the beginning of the East German regime (1945–1946). By contrast, younger Central Committee members have tended to specialize in economic and technological occupations.

The conflict between generations may be characterized by the following four major criteria:

1. The norms of behavioral patterns of so-called veteran Communists

and younger members and candidates of the Central Committee whose roots are not in the KPD or Comintern tradition stand at opposite poles from each other.[22]

2. Among members of the veteran group differences in outlook go back to the disunity and factional struggles that took place within the Marxist parties during the 1920s, as well as their different experiences between 1933 and 1945.

3. The norms or behavioral patterns of the younger experts and party cadres clash with those of older functionaries, since the former group had to confront the problems of modernization of GDR society and derived their experience only from this society.

4. Within the younger party cadres social distinctions exist along the following functional lines: between economic experts, technicians, and educators, on the one hand, and barely trained party functionaries on the other, there are clear differences in outlook.

Available biographical data for members and candidates of the Central Committee neither confirm nor contradict the above four theses. Extrapolation from Tables 7 and 8 permits the limited conclusion that the younger generation in the Central Committee has been formed in a different political mold.

4. The Vocational Situation of Central Committee Members and Candidates in 1954, 1958, and 1963

The vocational training of Central Committee members and candidates is analyzed below in order to determine more exactly the differences in the social composition of the Central Committee in 1954, 1958, and 1963. The following are regarded as important criteria in determining that general situation: completion of training (Table 9), acquired vocation (Tables 10 and 11), and occupation upon entry into the Central Committee (Tables 12, 13, and 14). In addition, the available material permits a study of the vocational situation specific to each age group (Tables 15-21).

---

[22] This conflict was most clearly expressed at the Eleventh Plenary Session of the Central Committee of the SED in December 1965 in the speeches of Hanna Wolf and Christa Wolf. See *Neues Deutschland,* December 19, 1965.

Table 9
CC Members and Candidates (1954, 1958, and 1963) by Completion of Education

Completion of Education or Training	Central Committee in 1954				Central Committee in 1958				Central Committee in 1963			
	Members	Candidates	Total	of these not in the CC in 1958	Members	Candidates	Total	of these not in the CC in 1963	Members	Candidates	Total	of these new in 1963
Elementary School (*Volksschule*)	39	9	48	5	50	13	63	16	55	18	73	26
Secondary School (*Realschule, Mittlere Reife*)	4	0	4	1	5	0	5	1	4	0	4	0
High School, College (completed by the *Abitur*)	2	0	2	0	3	2	5	0	5	1	6	1
Trade or Technical School (*Fachschule*)	9	10	19	3	15	6	21	5	21	6	27	11
Trade or Technical College (*Fachhochschule*) or University	15	6	21	5	18	8	26	7	26	18	44	25
No Data	22	19	41	24	20	15	35	27	10	17	27	19
Total	91	44	135	38	111	44	155	56	121	60	181	82

Table 10
CC Members and Candidates (1954, 1958, and 1963) by Acquired Occupation

Acquired Occupation	Central Committee 1954			Central Committee 1958			Central Committee 1963		
	Mem-bers	Candi-dates	Total	Mem-bers	Candi-dates	Total	Mem-bers	Candi-dates	Total
11 Technical Occupations in State, Economics, Agriculture	61	18	79	66	18	84	72	36	108
Of these:									
111	4	0	4	5	2	7	8	10	18
112	41	13	54	48	13	61	51	22	73
113	16	5	21	13	3	16	13	4	17
12 Administrative Occupations in State, Economics, Agriculture	11	4	15	14	8	22	23	9	32
Of these:									
121	1	1	2	1	4	5	6	4	10
122	10	3	13	13	4	17	17	5	22
2 Service Occupations	2	3	5	4	1	5	5	2	7
3 Educational Occupations	4	5	9	5	3	8	8	7	15
4 Free Occupations	7	4	11	10	5	15	11	5	16
No Data	6	10	16	12	9	21	2	1	3
Total	91	44	135	111	44	155	121	60	181

Table 11
Complete List of Data Collected for the Criterion "Acquired Occupation" of Central Committee Members and Candidates (1954, 1958, and 1963)

	CC 1954	CC 1958	CC 1963
1 Technical and administrative occupations in state, economy, and agriculture			
11 Technical occupations			
111 Leading functions			
Engineer with diploma	1	2	4
Engineer-economist with diploma	—	—	1
Mechanical engineer	—	1	2
Electrical engineer	1	2	1
Construction engineer	—	—	1
Engineer graduated from a technical school	—	—	2
Chemist with diploma	1	1	4
Agronomist with diploma	1	1	2
Certified agronomist	—	—	1
112 Middle functions (artisan, skilled worker, farmer)			
Fitter	6	6	10
Machine fitter	7	9	11
Auto mechanic	1	1	2
Construction fitter	—	—	1
Mechanic	1	1	—
Mason	4	11	7
Concrete specialist	1	—	—
Plasterer	—	—	1
Carpenter	5	4	2
Construction carpenter	—	1	4
Blacksmith, blacksmith-mechanic	1	2	0
Tinsmith, plumber	—	—	3
Electrician, electrical mechanic	2	2	2
Roofer	3	2	2
Furnace repairman	1	1	1
Heating fitter	—	—	1
Foundry worker	1	—	—
Woodworker	1	—	—
Lathe operator	1	—	—
Cast iron worker	1	—	—
Metal grinder	1	1	—
Metal extruder, former	2	3	2
Iron worker	—	1	1
Toolmaker, lathe operator	—	2	3
Machine mechanic, technician	1	—	1
Aviation mechanic	—	1	—
Riveter	1	1	1
Welder	—	—	1

Ship mechanic	1	2	2
Printer	2	2	4
Typesetter	4	3	1
Glassblower	1	—	—
Tanner	1	1	1
Butcher	—	1	1
Weaver	—	—	1
Decorator	1	1	2
Piano maker	—	1	2
Dairyman	3	—	—
Farmer	—	1	1
Agricultural technician	—	—	1
Surveyor	—	—	1

113 Lower functions

Blue-collar worker	4	3	3
Metalworker	3	4	3
Woodworker	—	1	1
Transport worker	2	1	1
Small farmer, smallholder	2	—	—
Farm hand	5	4	6
Miner	3	3	3
Boatman	1	—	—
Sailor	1	—	—

12   Administrative professions

121 Leading functions

Railway inspector	—	1	1
Manager with diploma in economics	2	4	9

122 Medium and lower functions

White-collar employee	2	2	2
Commercial white-collar employee	4	6	10
Insurance salesman	1	1	1
Administrative employee	—	—	1
Commercial assistant	1	1	1
Bank employee	1	2	1
Bookkeeper	2	2	1
Stenotypist	2	3	3
Agricultural machinery salesman	—	—	1
Forester	—	—	1

Table 11 (continued)

		CC 1954	CC 1958	CC 1963
2	Service occupations			
	Hairdresser	1	1	1
	Tailor	2	2	3
	Cook	2	2	2
	Pastry maker	—	—	1
3	Educational professions			
	University teacher of natural sciences	1	3	5
	University teacher of agricultural sciences	1	1	2
	Other university teachers	2	1	4
	Schoolteachers	5	3	4
4	Free professions			
	Physician	1	1	2
	Lawyer	1	1	1
	Writer	1	3	2
	Journalist	1	1	1
	Editor	1	1	1
	Artist	—	1	1
	Sculptor	1	1	—
	Architect	2	3	1
	Commercial painter	1	—	1
	Actor	2	3	5
	Stage director	—	—	1

COMPLETION OF EDUCATION OR PROFESSIONAL TRAINING

The proportion of members and candidates with elementary education[23] remained approximately the same or rose slightly in 1963 (73 out of 181 or 40.3 percent) compared with 1958 (63 out of 155 or 40.6 percent) and 1954 (48 out of 135 or 35.6 percent). The proportion of new members and candidates in 1963 with no schooling beyond the

[23] No data on attendance at vocational and higher education facilities were available. With the official announcement of the members and candidates of the Central Committee in 1967, considerably more accurate occupational data were published, which also indicate graduation from school and other training institutions. For particulars, see Appendix 1, esp. pp. 426 ff.

elementary level is relatively high (26 out of 73 or 35.6 percent). It contrasts with the proportion of 25.4 percent for candidates and members with elementary schooling who were not elected to the Central Committee in 1963 or who died in the meantime.

The total number of members and candidates who completed at least ten years of primary and secondary education is astonishingly low for all three Central Committees. This is certainly no accident, since such lengthy primary and secondary education involves training for the most part at a (trade) school and, to a lesser extent, at a (technical) college or university. Those members and candidates who completed their training in a trade or technical school (*Fachschule*), a trade or technical college (*Fachhochschule*), a technical university (*Technische Hochschule, Technische Universität*), or university (*Universität*) rate special attention. The absolute and relative proportion of this group increased in the 1963 Central Committee (71 out of 181 or 39 percent) compared with 47 out of 155 or 30 percent in 1958, and 40 out of 135 or 30 percent in 1954. For the first time in the 1963 Central Committee this group is nearly as strongly represented as graduates of elementary schools: 71 members and candidates completed a trade or technical school, college, or university. Of these 36—i.e., approximately half— were newly elected to the Central Committee in 1963. Among the latter, those with a completed higher education are clearly more numerous than the elementary school graduates.

Although the figures for Table 9 include a relatively high proportion of persons for whom no data were available—and the reliability of our information must not be overestimated—a continuing improvement in the educational level of Central Committee members can be posited. Indeed, a general rise in the educational level is evident throughout GDR society. Whereas in 1950 a mere 0.5 percent of the adult population had completed college, this had risen to 1.3 percent at the time of the national and occupational census of December 31, 1963. At that time 84 percent of all university level graduates had begun their studies after 1945.[24]

A special census of Central Committee members and candidates

[24] Karl Dieter Seifert, "209,000 Männer und Frauen mit Hochschulbildung." *Neues Deutschland,* November 13, 1966.

Table 12 (See the key on page 226.)
Primary Functions of CC Members and Candidates (1954, 1958, and 1963) at the Time of Their Admission into the Central Committee

Primary function	Central Committee in 1954				Central Committee in 1958				Central Committee in 1963			
	Members	Candidates	Total	of these not in the CC in 1958	Members	Candidates	Total	of these not in the CC in 1963	Members	Candidates	Total	of these new in 1963
1 In the party apparatus	22	11	33	6	40	13	53	13	41	14	55	20
of these:												
11	8	2	10	4	14	2	16	0	13	0	13	1
12	10	3	13	0	17	6	23	6	18	10	28	13
13, 14, 10	4	6	10	2	9	5	14	7	10	4	14	6
2 In the state apparatus	23	11	34	6	29	13	42	10	42	12	54	16
of these:												
21	15	5	20	4	21	5	26	4	30	7	37	12
22	6	4	10	0	5	4	9	4	3	1	4	1
23, 24	2	2	4	2	3	4	7	2	9	4	13	3
3 In the economic apparatus	16	2	18	6	12	2	14	7	9	10	19	14
of these:												
31	1	1	2	0	2	1	3	0	5	5	10	8
32	6	1	7	3	7	1	8	5	3	2	5	3
33, 34	9	0	9	3	3	0	3	2	1	3	4	3

35 In the agricultural apparatus	8	6	14	10	6	3	9	4	5	5	10	7
of these:												
351	8	5	13	9	6	3	9	4	5	5	10	7
353	0	1	1	1	0	0	0	0	0	0	0	0
4 In mass organizations	11	5	16	4	11	3	14	8	12	5	17	9
of these:												
41	9	4	13	2	11	3	14	8	11	3	14	7
42	2	1	3	2	0	0	0	0	1	2	3	2
5 In culture and education	8	5	13	2	9	5	14	7	10	11	21	14
of these:												
51	2	1	3	0	3	1	4	2	5	2	7	3
52	6	1	7	2	5	1	6	3	3	3	9	8
53, 50	0	3	3	0	1	3	4	2	2	3	5	3
6 In the National Peoples' Army	2	0	2	0	0	1	1	0	0	2	2	2
7 In international organizations	0	0	0	0	0	0	0	0	2	1	3	0
8 In other organizations	1	0	1	0	1	0	1	1	0	0	0	0
No data	0	4	4	4	3	4	7	6	0	0	0	0
Total	91	44	135	38	111	44	155	56	121	60	181	82

Extract of the Key Used in Codifying the Primary Functions

1 Primary function in the party apparatus

10 No detailed data

11 Upper:
CC secretary; director of the SED's Institute for Social Sciences; editor-in-chief of *Neues Deutschland*

12 Upper middle:
Full-time functionary in the CC or CPCC; section head; 1st or 2nd secretary of a *Bezirk* executive

13 Middle middle:
Head of subdivision (sector) in CC section; department head at the Institute for Social Sciences; secretary in a *Bezirk* executive; chairman of a BPKK; 1st or 2nd secretary of a *Kreis* executive; 1st or 2nd secretary of a BPO (large enterprises) or similar institutions

14 Lower middle:
Secretary in a *Kreis* executive; secretary or instructor in a BPO (large enterprise); 1st or 2nd secretary of a BPO (medium or small enterprise)

2 Primary function in the state apparatus

20 No detailed data

21 Upper:
Prime minister, minister, deputy minister, state secretary (incl. comparable positions in comparable state institutions, such as chairman or deputy chairman of the State Planning Commission); other member of the Council of Ministers; ambassador to an important country (Soviet Union or China)

22 Upper middle:
Head of (main) department; leading official in the central administration; ambassador to a smaller country (Czechoslovakia); lord mayor of Berlin

23 Middle middle:
Chairman or deputy chairman of a *Bezirk* council, a *Bezirk* economic or agricultural council; head of a *Bezirk* ABI committee; *Bezirk* school commissioner or health officer

24 Lower middle:
Chairman or deputy chairman of a *Kreis* council, a *Kreis* economic or agricultural council

3 Primary function in the economic apparatus

30 No detailed data

31 Upper:
General director (formerly director general) of a VVB; manager (director) of a VEB (large enterprise)

32 Upper middle:
Commercial or technical director in a VVB or VEB (large enterprise); manager (director) of a VEB (medium or small enterprise)

33 Middle middle

34 Lower middle:
Brigade leader; (chief) foreman

34 Lower middle:
Brigade leader; technical assistant

35 Primary function in the agricultural apparatus

350 No detailed data

351 Upper, upper middle:
Chairman of a LPG or MTS

353 Middle, lower middle, lower:
Brigade leader, member of a LPG

4 Primary function in mass organizations

40 No detailed data

41 Upper:
1st or and secretary resp. chairman or deputy chairman of a presidium; chairman of a section group (such as the Union of Scientists within the FDGB) provided he is also member of the presidium of the superior organization

42 Upper middle:
Secretary, functionary in the central apparatus of a mass organization; chairman of a section group who is not member of the presidium of the superior organization; executive secretary on the *Bezirk* level; chairman of a BGL

5　Primary function in culture and education

50　No detailed data (students included)

51　Upper:
President of an important organization, such as the Construction Academy, the Central Institute of Pedagogy; broadcasting director, editor-in-chief of an important publication; prominent author or artist

52　Upper middle:
Director of an institute (university or academy level); director of a smaller, independent institution; director of the German State Opera; director of a *Bezirk* theater

53　Middle middle:
Full professor; high school principal; artists and authors of less prominence

54　Lower middle:
Lecturer at a university or college

6　Primary function in the National Peoples' Army

60　No detailed data

61　Upper

62　Upper middle

7　Primary function in international organizations (such as COMECON)

8　Primary function in other organizations (such as the German Red Cross)

Table 13
Distribution of Primary Functions for CC Members and Candidates (1954, 1958, and 1963) upon Entry into the Central Committee in the Various Functional Areas

Functional Area		CC 1954 Members/ Candidates absolute %		CC 1958 Members/ Candidates absolute %		CC 1963 Members/ Candidates absolute %	
1	Party Apparatus	33	25	53	34	55	30
2	State Apparatus	34	25	42	27	54	30
3	Economic Apparatus	18	13	14	9	19	10
35	Agricultural Apparatus	14	10	9	6	10	6
4	Mass organizations	16	12	14	9	17	9
5	Cultural Affairs	13	10	14	9	21	12
6, 7, 8	Others	3	2	2	1	5	3
No Data		4	3	7	5	0	0
Total		135	100	155	100	181	100

Table 14
Positions of CC Members and Candidates in the Hierarchy at Various Functional Areas

Position within Functional Area	CC 1954 Members/ Candidates absolute %		CC 1958 Members/ Candidates absolute %		CC 1963 Members/ Candidates absolute %	
Top	61	45	72	46	91	50
Upper Middle	40	30	46	30	49	27
Middle and Lower Middle	27	20	28	20	36	20
Not Accounted for	7	5	9	4	5	3
Total	135	100	155	100	181	100

Table 15
CC Members and Candidates from Age Groups 3, 4, 5* (1958 and 1963) According to Their Highest Completed Level of Education or Training

Completion of Education or Training	Central Committee in 1958 Members and Candidates							Central Committee in 1963 Members and Candidates							Central Committee in 1963 New† Members and Candidates						
	Age group* 3	4	5	Total of Age groups 3,4,5	Total for 1958 CC	of these M‡	C	Age group 3	4	5	Total of Age groups 3,4,5	Total for 1963 CC	of these M‡	C	Age group 3	4	5	Total of Age groups 3,4,5	New Total	of these M	C
Elementary School (Volksschule)	18	19	14	51	63	50	13	16	24	25	65	73	55	18	3	8	14	25	26	9	17
Secondary School (Realschule, Mittlere Reife)	1	0	2	3	5	5	0	1	0	1	2	4	4	0	0	0	0	0	0	0	0
High School, College (completed by the Abitur)	2	3	0	5	5	3	2	3	3	0	6	6	5	1	0	1	0	1	1	0	1
Trade or Technical School	9	4	2	15	21	15	6	8	8	4	20	27	21	6	1	2	6	9	11	6	5
Trade or Technical College (Fachschule)	8	5	8	21	26	18	8	9	3	26	38	44	26	18	3	2	16	21	25	10	15
Trade or Technical College or University (Fachhochschule)	11	3	8	22	35	20	15	6	2	18	26	27	10	17	4	3	11	18	19	4	15
No Data																					
Total	49	34	34	117	155	111	44	43	40	74	157	181	121	60	11	16	47	74	82	29	53

* See Table 2.
† Refers to the 82 members newly elected to the CC in 1963.
‡ M = member; C = candidates.

Table 16
CC Members and Candidates from Age Groups 3, 4, 5* (1958 and 1963) by Acquired Occupation

Acquired Occupation**	Central Committee in 1958 Members and Candidates							Central Committee in 1963 Members and Candidates							Central Committee in 1963 New† Members and Candidates					
	Age group* 3	4	5	Total of Age groups 3,4,5	Total for 1958 CC	of these M‡	C	Age group 3	4	5	Total of Age groups 3,4,5	Total for 1963 CC	of these M	C	Age group 3	4	5	Total of Age groups 3,4,5	New Total M	C
11 Technical Occupations in the State, Economic, & Agricultural Apparatus	31	21	17	69	84	66	18	27	26	39	92	108	72	36	5	11	29	45	51 18	33
of these:																				
111	3	4	0	7	7	5	2	2	2	4	15	18	8	10	1	2	9	12	15 5	10
112	20	13	16	49	61	48	13	19	19	24	62	73	51	22	4	9	15	28	31 12	19
113	8	4	1	13	16	13	3	6	3	6	15	17	13	4	0	0	5	5	5 1	4
12 Administrative Occupations in the State, Economic, & Agricultural Apparatus	6	4	8	18	22	14	8	7	4	18	29	32	23	9	1	0	11	12	13 5	8

of these:

121	0	1	4	5	5	1	4	0	1	8	9	10	6	4	0	0	4	4	5	2	3
122	6	3	4	13	17	13	4	7	3	10	20	22	17	5	1	0	7	8	8	3	5
2 Service Occupations	1	2	2	5	5	4	1	1	2	4	7	7	5	2	0	0	2	2	2	0	2
3 Educational Occupations	3	0	3	6	8	5	3	4	2	8	14	15	8	7	2	2	5	9	9	4	5
4 Free Occupations	5	4	1	10	15	10	5	3	6	3	12	16	11	5	1	2	2	5	6	2	4
No Data	3	3	3	9	21	12	9	1	0	2	3	3	2	1	0	0	1	1	1	0	1
Total	49	34	34	117	155	111	44	43	40	74	157	181	121	60	9	15	50	74	82	29	53

* See Table 2.
† This includes the 82 members newly elected to the CC in 1963.
** For the detailed coding of the occupational categories, see Table 11.
‡ M = members; C = candidates.

Table 17
CC Members and Candidates from Age Groups 3, 4, 5* (1958 and 1963) by Primary Functions upon Entry into the Central Committee

	Central Committee in 1958 Members and Candidates							Central Committee in 1963 Members and Candidates							Central Committee in 1963 New† Members and Candidates						
Main function upon entry in the CC**	Age group*			Total of Age groups 3,4,5	Total for 1958 CC	of these		Age group			Total of Age groups 3,4,5	Total for 1963 CC	of these		Age group			Total of Age groups 3,4,5	New Total		
	3	4	5			M‡	C	3	4	5			M	C	3	4	5			M	C
1 In the party apparatus	17	15	14	46	53	40	13	7	19	25	51	55	41	14	0	5	15	20	20	8	12
of these:																					
11	5	6	2	13	16	14	2	3	4	4	11	13	13	0	0	0	1	1	1	1	0
12	9	6	7	22	23	17	6	3	9	13	25	28	18	10	0	2	11	13	13	4	9
13, 14, 10	3	3	5	11	14	9	5	1	6	7	14	14	10	4	0	3	3	6	6	3	3
2 In the state apparatus	15	9	5	29	42	29	13	9	18	20	47	54	42	12	2	3	11	16	16	6	10
of these:																					
21	9	4	3	16	26	21	5	8	11	12	31	37	30	7	2	3	7	12	12	6	6
22	3	3	1	7	9	5	4	2	0	1	3	4	3	1	1	0	0	1	1	0	1
23, 24, 20	3	2	1	6	7	3	4	6	1	6	13	13	9	4	0	0	3	3	3	0	3
3 In the economic apparatus	5	3	2	10	14	12	2	4	3	7	14	19	9	10	2	2	7	11	14	4	10
of these:																					
31	0	1	2	3	3	2	1	2	1	4	7	10	5	5	2	0	4	6	8	3	5
32	4	2	0	6	8	7	1	1	1	2	4	5	3	2	0	1	2	3	3	1	2

33, 34, 30	1	0	0	1	3	3	0	1	1	1	3	4	1	3	0	1	1	2	3	0	3
35 In the agricultural apparatus	2	1	4	7	9	6	3	1	0	7	8	10	5	5	0	5	5	5	7	3	4
of these: 351	2	1	4	7	9	6	3	1	0	7	8	10	5	5	0	5	5	5	7	3	4
4 In mass organizations	2	2	7	11	14	11	3	2	4	8	14	17	12	5	0	3	5	8	9	4	5
of these: 41	2	2	7	11	14	11	3	1	2	8	11	14	11	3	0	1	5	6	7	4	3
42	0	0	0	0	0	0	0	1	2	0	3	3	1	2	2	2	0	2	2	0	2
5 In culture and education	7	3	1	11	14	9	5	8	4	7	19	21	10	11	5	2	6	13	14	4	10
of these: 51	3	1	0	4	4	3	1	2	1	3	6	7	5	2	0	3	3	3	3	1	2
52	3	0	0	3	6	5	1	4	2	2	8	9	3	6	3	2	2	7	8	2	6
53, 54, 50	1	2	1	4	4	1	3	2	1	2	5	5	2	3	2	1	1	3	3	1	2
Others (6, 7, 8)	0	1	0	1	2	1	1	1	1	2	4	5	2	3	0	0	1	1	2	0	2
No Data	1	0	1	2	7	3	4	0	0	0	0	0	0	0	0	0	0	0	0	0	0
Total	49	34	34	117	155	111	44	43	40	74	157	181	121	60	15	50	74	82	82	29	53

* See Table 2.
† This refers to the 82 members newly elected to the CC in 1963.
** See code on pp. 226-227.
‡ M = members; C = candidates.

Table 18
The Proportion of Younger Top Functionaries in the Party and State Apparatus

Year of Birth	CC members and candidates Main function: 11* (Upper level party apparatus)		CC members and candidates Main function: 21* (Upper level state apparatus)	
	1958	1963	1958	1963
1900–1909 (Age Group 3)	5	3	9	12
1910–1919 (Age Group 4)	6	4	4	8
1920–1929 (Age Group 5)	2	4	3	11
Total Incumbents	16	13	26	37

* See code on pp. 226–227.

Table 19:
The Proportion of Younger Functionaries Holding "Upper Middle" Positions in the Party and State Apparatus

Year of birth	CC members and candidates Main function: 12* (Upper middle party apparatus)		CC members and candidates Main function: 22* (Upper middle state apparatus)	
	1958	1963	1958	1963
1900–1909 (Age Group 3)	9	3	3	2
1910–1919 (Age Group 4)	6	9	3	0
1920–1929 (Age Group 5)	7	14	1	1
Total Incumbents	23	28	9	4

* See code on pp. 226–227.

Table 20
The Proportion of Younger Functionaries in the Various Functional Areas

Functional Area ("Apparatus")	Central Committee 1958		Central Committee 1963	
	Members and Candidates with Main Functions in the . . . Apparatus Total	Of these, born between 1920 and 1929	Members and Candidates with Main Functions in the . . . Apparatus Total	Of these, born between 1920 and 1929
Party Apparatus	53	14	55	25
State Apparatus	42	5	54	18
Economic Apparatus	14	2	19	7
Agricultural Apparatus	9	4	10	7
Mass Organizations	14	7	17	8
Cultural Affairs	14	1	21	7
CC Total	155	34	181	74

Table 21
The Proportion of Older Functionaries in the Various Functional Areas

Functional Area ("Apparatus")	Central Committee 1958		Central Committee 1963	
	Members and Candidates with Main Functions in the . . . Apparatus Total	Of these, born between 1900 and 1909	Members and Candidates with Main Functions in the . . . Apparatus Total	Of these, born between 1900 and 1909
Party Apparatus	53	17	55	7
State Apparatus	42	15	54	20
Economic Apparatus	14	5	19	4
Agricultural Apparatus	9	2	10	1
Mass Organizations	14	2	17	2
Cultural Affairs	14	7	21	8
CC Total	155	49	181	43

with professorial titles in 1958 and 1963 confirms the thesis that cadres were becoming increasingly highly qualified. While only 2 of 18 professors in the 1958 Central Committee were properly academically qualified[25] (i.e., had passed the *Habilitation* examination) and 5 had earned their Ph.Ds, 4 of the 20 professors in the 1963 Central Committee were fully qualified academically (*habilitiert*) while 5 others had earned their doctorates.[26]

In summary, it can be stated that among the 1963 Central Committee groups with individuals having graduated trade or technical schools, colleges, or universities are for the first time clearly on the increase, whereas members and candidates with only elementary schooling appear in approximately equal numbers for 1954, 1958, and 1963. However, a further distinction should be made between those graduating from the various schools, colleges, and universities: The increase in the number of trade or technical school graduates in 1963, compared with that for 1954, is far less impressive than the increase in the number of graduates of technical or trade colleges or universities. In

[25] The data on academic qualification were taken from the following reference works: *Kürschners Deutscher Gelehrtenkalender; Jahrbuch der Deutschen Akademie der Wissenschaften zu Berlin; Biographischer Index der Mitglieder der Deutschen Akademie der Wissenschaften zu Berlin*, Kurt H. Biermann and Gerhard Dunken, eds. (Berlin, 1960). The relevant lecture schedules available from the various colleges and universities were also consulted, particularly those of the winter terms 1958–1959 and 1963–1964.

[26] Lappe and Rompe, insofar as may be ascertained from the corresponding lecture schedules, received their Ph.D. degrees only between 1958 and 1963. The same presumably also applies to Rübensam, while Schirmer received his as early as 1954. The data on Rompe and Rübensam conflict somewhat. According to Western sources he was awarded a doctorate by the University of Bonn as far back as 1942, but this could not be confirmed from university records. In the *Jahrbuch der Humboldt-Universität zu Berlin 1963* (Berlin, 1964) (press deadline, December 31, 1963) Rompe is listed both as Prof.Dr., Dr.-Ing.e.h. (p. 81) and as Prof.Dr.phil.habil., Dr.-Ing.e.h. (p. 86). The Humboldt University's lecture schedules list him as Prof.Dr.phil.habil. since the academic year 1963–1964 (the press deadline for the schedules was May 31, 1963), while in connection with the Seventh SED Congress he is presented as Prof. Dr. (See *Neues Deutschland*, April 23, 1967). Rübensam, who graduated in 1950 from the Faculty of Agriculture of Rostock University, is likewise listed in the lecture schedule as Dr.agrar.habil. since the academic year 1963–1964; this does not, however appear in the data published by *Neues Deutschland* on the occasion of the Seventh SED Congress.

addition, for the latter two categories changes among those who were Central Committee candidates should be emphasized: the number of candidates among cadres with college or university training in the Central Committee of 1963 had more than doubled in comparison with the 1958 Central Committee candidate membership. This increase is thus considerably higher than that for full members with comparable training.

These facts once again highlight the probationary function of candidacy for graduates of technical colleges and universities within the party apparatus. Whereas for elementary school graduates the ratio between members and candidates in the 1963 Central Committee is approximately 3:1, that for graduates of technical or trade colleges and universities is approximately 3:2. If we take into account the special opportunities for manipulation available to the party leadership in establishing the composition of the Central Committee,[27] the interest of the strategic clique in strengthening the proportion of qualified personnel becomes clear.

ACQUIRED OCCUPATION

The limited value of this criterion was noted in the introduction to this chapter. Consequently, we made no correlations for acquired occupation and completion of education. However, since the variable of "acquired occupation" cannot be completely disregarded, a code was prepared for classifying individual vocational data, which follows the material as closely as possible and takes into account both technical and economic occupations (see Tables 10 and 11). Those included in the categories the code appear in Table 11.[28]

In Tables 10 and 11 the occupations of (industrial) artisan, skilled worker, and small farmer, which we have designated 112, clearly dominate. This combined group is approximately equally represented in all the Central Committees investigated. For the 1954 Committee it

[27] See Schultz, *Der Funktionär in der Einheitspartei*, p. 41.
[28] For those few members and candidates of the Central Committee who have been trained in two or more occupations, only the one closest to the occupation practiced currently was taken into account. With regard to the 1967 Central Committee, totally new problems arose. See Appendix 1, esp. pp. 426 ff.

comprised 54 out of 135 (or 40 percent) members and candidates, in 1958, 61 out of 155 (39 percent) members and candidates, and in 1963, 73 out of 181 (or 40 percent) members and candidates. No notable deviations occur in the respective Central Committees.

The second category, workers and agricultural workers (code category: 113) rates attention for its comparative smallness. In the 1958 and 1963 Central Committee it constitutes approximately one quarter of the artisan group. The proportion was found higher only among the 1954 Central Committee full and candidate members: 21 workers and agricultural workers against 54 artisans.[29]

Members of these two professional groups (112 and 113) belong to the lower and lower-middle social strata and their representation in the Central Committees of 1958 and 1963 is approximately the same. In contrast, a notable difference was found for middle and upper-middle groups. Technical occupations for leading economic and agricultural functionaries (occupational category 111) were pursued by 4 Central Committee members and candidates in 1954, 7 in 1958, and 18 in 1963. A similarly rapid increase appears for the leading administrative occupations (category 121). By contrast, there is hardly any proportional deviation for this period within the range of medium and lower administrative positions. Comparison of the Central Committee of 1963 with those of 1954 and 1958 shows a considerable increase in the number of full and candidate members in the educational profession. Compared to organizations of political leadership in Western societies, the free professions are relatively rarely encountered in the Central Committee—a reflection of the decrease in the number of free professionals active in East Germany (i.e., those officially designated "inde-

[29] The difference between the designations of craftsman and laborer are hazy, since in the DDR it is unusual to designate someone who has learned a trade or profession as a laborer. Thus, in the Handbooks of the Peoples' Chamber the categories "skilled industrial laborer" or "skilled agricultural laborer" have been established. Both undoubtedly comprise occupations which in the present classification—in the absence of information about the actual training received by the respective members and candidates of the Central Committee—come under craftsmen (code No. 112), but should possibly have been included under laborers (code No. 113). For the social composition of the Peoples' Chamber, see *Die Volkskammer,* 4. Wahlperiode, p. 128. See also Mersch, "Volksvertreter in West und Ost," pp. 30 ff.

pendently occupied outside the area of material production").[30]

The most marked changes in the composition by occupation of the three Central Committees again appear between those of 1958 and 1963. They occur primarily for leading technical, administrative,[31] and educational[32] occupations. Twenty members of these groups before 1958 stand in clear contrast to 43 in 1963. Analysis of Table 10 thus leads to the conclusion that the structure of the Central Committee in 1963, with regard to the categories of acquired occupation or training for members or candidates, has changed in two directions, compared with 1958, if the results of Table 9 and the comparatively great amount of missing data for the Central Committee of 1958 are taken into account: First, "professionalization" of political functionaries in the party apparatus has increased, compared with the situation in 1958; and second, functionaries with leading technical and administrative occupations are more numerous in 1963 than in 1958. Finally, educational professions are more prominent. This phenomenon can be interpreted as an expression of the relatively greater "opening" of the SED toward society; it constitutes at least a partial rapprochement between the party and the people after the building of the Berlin Wall in 1961. This conclusion is further supported by the findings in Table 11, which lists all the occupations recorded in our analysis of the Central Committees of 1954, 1958, and 1963.

As regards occupations represented overall, in the 1963 Central Committee in contrast to the 1958 and 1954 data, a wider variety is evident. Eleven occupations occur for the first time in the 1958 Central Committee, as compared with seventeen in 1963. Compared with the Committee of 1954 that of 1963 contains twenty-eight new occupations not limited to a single specific stratum. By contrast, five occupations in 1963 as compared with 1958, and ten compared with the number for 1954, are no longer represented. An analysis of technical occupations for persons in leading functions in 1954, 1958, and 1963 makes it clear

[30] See *Statistisches Jahrbuch der Deutschen Demokratischen Republic,* Vol. 11 (Berlin, 1966), p. 68. It lists only 38,854 persons under this heading out of a total of 7.67 million persons employed in 1965.
[31] Index code Nos. (see Table 10, p. 219) 111,121 comprised a total of 12 in 1958 and of 28 in 1963.
[32] Index code No. 3 included a total of 8 in 1958 and of 15 in 1963.

that those active in occupations classified as "vital" since the Seventh
COMECON Convention (in East Berlin, May 18–25, 1956) have
entered the party apparatus only in 1963.[33] This group includes primarily
engineers holding a college degree, particularly electrical and construction engineers. The party leadership is also especially interested in
graduate chemists and professionally trained agronomists.[34] Table 11
indicates that these professions are more strongly represented in 1963
than in 1958 and 1954.

A comparison of "medium-level functions" (artisans, skilled workers, and farmers) in 1954, 1958, and 1963 demonstrates that these
traditional occupations are still prominent among the occupations represented in the Central Committee despite a noticeable rise and differentiation within the vocational scale on the whole. Individuals with a "wide
professional profile," an ideal propagated by the party since approximately 1962–1963, have hardly begun to enter the Central Committee.
These occupations include primarily the middle level of the metal,
construction, chemical, ceramics, and glass industries, as well as mining
and the electrical industry, including power; but also transport, light
industries, and the food industry. The rapid expansion of representation
for the technical occupations—also in political bodies—is still rare at the
middle level; this also holds true for the highly specialized technical
occupations (e.g., surveyor).

ACTUAL OCCUPATION AT THE TIME OF ENTRY INTO
THE CENTRAL COMMITTEE

Here, "actual occupation" is defined as the primary function upon
acceptance into the Central Committee or directly thereafter. In Table
12, the material has been prepared with this in mind. The key for
codifying these primary functions has been constructed to permit analysis of professional mobility, both vertically and horizontally. The code

[33] For the outcome of the Seventh Convention of the Council for Mutual Economic Aid, see Konstantin Pritzel, *Die wirtschaftliche Integration der Sowjetischen Besatzungszone Deutschlands in den Ostblock und ihre politischen Aspekte*
(Bonn and Berlin, 2nd revised and augmented ed., 1965), pp. 81 ff.
[34] Nineteen agricultural occupations (occupational profiles) are known for 1966,
all of which require graduation from college, vocational college, or vocational
school. See *Berufsbilder für Ausbildungsberufe* (Berlin, 1964), p. 471.

has been alluded to in the introductory remarks in this chapter[35] and appears in tabular form on pp. 226–227. A comparison of primary functions for members and candidates at the time of their election to the Central Committee in 1958 and members and candidates who entered this body in 1963 reveals that the relative distribution in the various functional areas has scarcely changed. In contrast, the 1954 Central Committee has quite a different structure. For the sake of clarification, this result from Table 12 is included in Table 13.

In the 1958 and 1963 Central Committees, members and candidates with functions in the party and state apparatus clearly predominate. (They amount in both cases to some 60 percent.) Although these

[35] The code was worked out on the basis of the material here presented, that is the information available about the members and candidates of the Central Committee on their occupational position/function at various dates. It does not claim to be valid beyond the scope of this study. All the positions/functions specified were represented by the material or proved necessary to differentiate between existing positions. The positions held by the members and candidates of the Central Committee in 1954 also had to be consulted for the mobility study. It is in the nature of a classification index of this kind that those social domains in which Central Committee members or candidates were not represented to any major degree (35 Agriculture, 6 NVA [National Peoples' Army] 7 International organizations) should show fewer subdivisions than the party (1) and state (2) apparatus. Moreover, for most domains a lower limit had to be defined. The code, as stated at the beginning of this chapter, is constructed in such a way that positions formally included in the same category, though in different apparatuses, should basically be comparable. Such a formal subclassification is, however, unsatisfactory for the sociologist who is interested in general social spheres of competence and authority. It is not enough merely to determine the position of a given member or candidate of the Central Committee within a certain hierarchy when questions of occupational rise and decline are at stake. On the other hand, it is impossible, on the basis of the information available at present, to present more specific data on the sphere of authority of individual positions in different social institutions of the DDR on an overall social basis. Extensive empirical studies would be required, for instance, to assess, from the point of view of the society at large, the relationship between the authority of the head of the State Planning Commission (top level of the state apparatus) and the Central Committee Secretary of Economics (top level of the party apparatus), or one of the cabinet ministers in the economic sphere (top level of the state apparatus). For this reason, we adhered largely to the formal classification, which was, however, reviewed in each case according to the individual's occupational rise or decline. Any deviations from the formal classification are noted in the corresponding tables (22, 23, 26, and 27).

groups still predominate in the 1954 Central Committee (50 percent), representatives of other social spheres are more noticeable than previously. The ratio of party to government functionaries in the 1954 and 1963 Central Committees is approximately equal, whereas in 1958 party functionaries predominate.[36]

Differences among the three Central Committees can also be established in connection with positions occupied by members and candidates in various functional areas (see Table 14). Here it becomes clear that during the period observed the number of members and candidates coopted into the Central Committee who occupy top positions in the relevant apparatuses have increased, whereas the proportion of those in middle and lower positions dropped slightly.

A comparative analysis cannot, in the context of this study, limit itself to establishing bare percentage proportions of occupations in the various social spheres for all the main functions represented in the Central Committees of 1954, 1958, and 1963. Shifts in the absolute numbers must also be taken into account. While 34 members and candidates occupied positions in the state apparatus in 1954, and 42 in 1958, by 1963, there were 54 in this occupational category. Of these 54 functionaries, 37 (compared with only 26 in 1958 and 20 in 1954) are in top-level positions in the state apparatus (ministers, deputy ministers, state secretaries, etc.). Twelve in these positions entered the Central Committee only in 1963.

From these observations it is possible to draw two conclusions, the implications of which appear somewhat contradictory. First, in 1963 the influence of the party in the state apparatus had increased, compared with the situation in 1958 and 1954. Furthermore, the group of younger technologists and managers (with no previous SED or KPD career) usually enter the party apparatus via the state apparatus (most often via the Council of Ministers and the State Planning Commission). This second conclusion is evident only from later interpretations of data[37]

---

[36] Apparently in this respect the social structure of the Central Committee differs greatly from the top-level party bodies in the USSR, where the party apparatus is still pre-eminent. See Zbigniew Brzezinski and Samuel P. Huntington, *Political Power: USA/USSR* (New York: Viking Press, 1965), pp. 172 and 181. For the changes that have taken place in the GDR since the Seventh SED Congress, see Appendix 1.

[37] See Section 8, p. 292, of this chapter.

and comparative analysis of some biographical data for twelve new members and candidates who were admitted to the Central Committee in 1963 and who had previously occupied top positions in the state apparatus.[38]

In addition, a count of secondary governmental functions exercised by 1958 and 1963 Central Committee members in top positions of the party apparatus has been made in order to illustrate the peculiar interlocking relation between the party and the state apparatus. In 1958, of the 31 Central Committee members holding top party positions (primary functions 11, 12) 26 also belonged to the Peoples' Chamber. Of these 26, 5 were members of other state organs: Ulbricht, member of the Council of Ministers and later the State Council; Matern, member of the Peoples' Chamber Presidium; Hager, member of the Research Council; and Mewis and B. Koenen, members of the State Council. The findings for 1963 were similar: Of 31 Central Committee members and top functionaries, 26 also belonged to the Peoples' Chamber. Of these 26, 6 belonged to other government bodies as well.[39] Probably the most important finding brought to light by this count is the fact that top party functionaries do indeed occupy other high positions, but rarely assume leading posts in the actual professional bodies of economic and agricultural affairs. The low number of secondary functions occupied by top party functionaries in 1958 and 1963 in the Council of Ministers, the State Planning Commission, the Agricultural Council, and the Research Council is particularly noteworthy in comparison with the earlier period.[40] These findings lead to the further conclusion that there

[38] See Section 6, pp. 276 ff., of this chapter.

[39] In this context mention should also be made of the Central Committee members and candidates who held principal or part-time positions in the hierarchy of the NVA. There were six such members in the 1958 Committee (Dölling, Hoffmann, Kessler, Mielke, Sägebrecht, and Stoph) and one candidate (W. Verner). In the 1963 Committee there were six such members (Dölling, Hoffmann, Kessler, Mielke, Stoph, and W. Verner) and three candidates (Beater, Ernst, Marschner). Dölling, Ernst, and Marschner were not reelected to the Central Committee at the Seventh SED Congress, and no representative of the NVA came in their stead.

[40] Only official and formal subsidiary functions could be taken into account here. The inofficial or informal influence of full-time party functionaries on the authorities of the state through the innumerable boards and commissions has scarcely been investigated. We may, however, join Ernst Richert in asserting that the principle according to which the SED influences the state apparatus through "the fusion of the top echelons of the party institutions and state authorities"

is a tendency toward divergence between functional areas in the state and economic apparatus, on the one hand, and functional areas within the party on the other; in short, a differentiation within the leadership group of the GDR is observable.

THE VOCATIONAL SITUATION OF VETERAN CENTRAL COMMITTEE MEMBERS AND CANDIDATES AS COMPARED WITH THAT OF THE YOUNGER GROUP
In addition to comparing the occupational situation of Central Committee members and candidates for 1958 and 1963, this study differentiates between age groups within the sample. This has been done in order to verify one of the main theses of our study, namely, that younger party experts have increasingly come to occupy sociopolitically relevant power positions in the GDR. The criteria selected for professional position were formal education (Table 15), acquired occupation (Table 16), and actual occupation upon entry into the Central Committee (Table 17).

Only those Central Committee members and candidates born between 1900 and 1929 have been taken into account. Subdivision by decades was effected along the lines of the criteria used in Table 2. The three groups distinguished are those born between 1900–1909 (age group 3), those born between 1910–1919 (age group 4), and those born between 1920–1929 (age group 5). In 1958, 117 (75 percent) of the total 155 members and candidates fell within these three groups. In 1963, 157 from a total of 181 members and candidates fell within these categories. Of the 82 new members and candidates who entered in 1963, 74 (90 percent) belonged to these three groups.

Table 15 supplements the results of Table 9[41] by revealing that the proportion of Central Committee members and candidates in 1958 and 1963 with only elementary schooling greatly exceeds the overall proportion in the case of the 1910–1919 age group. Forty percent of the 1958 Central Committee were elementary school graduates. Altogether 19 of 34—i.e., somewhat more than half—of the members and candidates in 1958 born between 1910–1919 (age group 4) completed only elemen-

has been relaxed. See Ernst Richert, *Macht ohne Mandat. Der Staatsapparat in der Sowjetischen Besatzungszone Deutschlands* (Cologne and Opladen, 2nd ed., 1963), pp. 47 f.
[41] All the reservations made for Table 9 apply here as well.

tary school. In the 1963 Central Committee the (medium) age group 4, with 60 percent of elementary school graduates, considerably exceeds the overall proportion of some 40 percent for this Central Committee. In both Central Committees this holds true even more for members than for candidates. When the proportion of members and candidates who completed their education at the elementary level is taken together, there are hardly any differences between the Central Committees of 1958 and 1963, even with distinctions by age groups. Differences become clear only when the new members and candidates elected in 1963 are analyzed separately. Comparison of the corresponding columns in Table 15 shows that within age group 5 (born between 1920 and 1929) the proportion of elementary school graduates among members and candidates dropped: in 1958, 14 out of 34 (41 percent) members of the younger generation completed elementary school only; in 1963 there are 25 out of 74 (34 percent) and, among the new members accepted in 1963, 14 out of 50 (28 percent). This finding is not clearly reinforced by the proportion of elementary graduates in the 1900–1909 age group, but neither is it contradicted: In the 1958 Central Committee, 18 out of 49 (37 percent) members and candidates of age group 3 had no further schooling beyond the elementary level. In the 1963 Central Committee there are 16 out of 43 (37 percent) and among the 9 new members and candidates of this age group elected in 1963 there are 3 (i.e., 33 percent) with elementary schooling only.

Another important finding in support of this thesis is the fact that the proportion of graduates from trade or technical, etc., schools, trade or technical, etc., colleges, and universities has risen in both absolute and relative terms in 1963 by comparison with 1958. This trend is already evident in Table 9. As outlined in Table 15, it applies primarily to age group 5 (those born between 1920 and 1929). In this group the proportion of members and candidates who completed their training in trade or technical schools, colleges or universities reached about 40 percent in 1963. At first glance this result appears less notable, since in age group 3 the proportion of college and university graduates for 1963 is also higher (some 40 percent). However, the proportional increase of members and candidates with technical and university education between 1958 and 1963 is greater for age group 5 than for age group 3.

The previously emphasized, now more clearly substantiated trend associating rejuvenation of the Central Committee with professionalization becomes particularly clear when the proportion of elementary school graduates is compared with that of graduates of trade or technical schools, colleges, etc., for the different age groups. For the older age group (number 3), the proportion of elementary school graduates in the Central Committees of 1958 and 1963 equals approximately that of graduates of trade or technical schools, colleges, and universities. In age group 4 (1910–1919) elementary school graduates clearly predominate in 1958 as in 1963; however, among the younger functionaries (those born between 1920–1929) the proportion of graduates from trade or technical schools, colleges, and universities exceeds that of the elementary school graduates for the 1963 Central Committee.

Extrapolation from the findings in Tables 10 and 11 leads to the conclusion that from Table 16 the differences in the composition of the Central Committee for 1958 and 1963 according to "acquired occupation" show a correlation with age differences. The top-level technical, administrative, and educational professions show a stronger representation in 1963 than in 1958; this is particularly the case for those born between 1920 and 1929. This fact is especially noticeable for leading technical functions: whereas in the 1958 Central Committee none of group 5 occupied a leading technical position (code category 111), in 1963 of the 18 persons in this functional area 9 had such positions. These 9 younger technical cadres admitted for the first time in 1963 represent a preponderant segment of the 15 persons within this occupational group who were newly admitted. This difference within the group of leading administrative occupations is not quite so extreme (see code category 121). In 1958, 4 of the total of 5 persons born between 1920 and 1929 held such positions, and, in 1963, 8 of the 10. A similar picture holds true for the educational professions: Of those born between 1920 and 1929 only 3 of the 8 were active in education, whereas in 1963, 8 of the 15 members and candidates held educational positions.

In the middle functional areas (mainly on the level of [industrial] artisans and skilled workers, code category 112) considerable differences arise between the 1958 and 1963 Central Committees on the basis of age classification. In the group born between 1900 and 1909 (age group 3) the proportion of artisans, etc., is approximately equal for 1958 and 1963 (in 1958, 41 percent and in 1963, 44 percent). In the group born between 1910 and 1919 the proportion has risen noticeably, from 38 to 48 percent, and for the group born between 1920 and 1929 it falls from 47 to 32 percent. In the 1963 Central Committee the proportion of artisans, etc., for the younger age groups (age group 5) is less than for the older age groups 3 and 4. Nevertheless, a drop in age in the group of artisans, etc., is evident: 16 of the 61 members in this class for 1958 (26 percent) belonged to the younger generations; in the 1963 Central Committee these comprise 24 of the 73 (33 percent) and for newly accepted members and candidates for 1963 15 out of 31 (roughly 50 percent).

It is evident that the proportion of younger Central Committee members and candidates in age group 5 who have entered leading technical and economic occupations (code category 111) has risen in inordinate proportion. Whereas the number of younger incumbents in the technical professions (code category 11) has more than doubled (a rise from 17 to 39), the 1963 Committee for the first time contains no less than 9 younger members and candidates who had entered leading technical professions. In no other age group of the 1963 Central Committee was the proportion of technical professions so high as for group 5.

The interpretation of Table 12 by age groups (Table 17) confirms certain trends established earlier. The proportion of younger top functionaries has grown both in the party and government (cf. Table 18).

The number of younger top functionaries in the party (primary function 11) and the state (primary function 21) has risen greatly in 1963 compared with 1958; in the party apparatus there are twice as many members and candidates in the 1920–1929 group occupying top positions in 1963 compared with 1958. In the state apparatus the difference is even more clear-cut; here the number has almost quadrupled. Regarding the total number of respective incumbents the difference between 1958 and 1963 is also noteworthy; in 1958 two of the 16 incumbents in the highest party functions (cf. 4 out of 13 in 1963) were born between 1920 and 1929. The change in top positions of the state apparatus is similar. The replacement of the old guard is still more obvious in the party apparatus, if we consider positions at the upper-middle level (see Table 19).

The proportion of those born between 1920 and 1929 in the Central Committee rose from 30 to some 50 percent at the upper-middle echelon of the party apparatus (primary function 12) between 1958 and 1963. This development deserves attention: Of the 14 functionaries from the 1920–1929 generation in 1963, 11 entered the Central Committee in 1963 (3 as members and 8 as candidates). These include the four first secretaries of *Bezirk* executives; Werner Krolikowski (Dresden), Albert Stief (Cottbus), Harry Tisch (Rostock) and Herbert Ziegenhahn (Gera). The seven other functionaries are all full-time functionaries in the Central Committee or Politburo.

From a study of the composition of the Central Committee, it is apparent that the age of members tends to become lower. However, the first *Bezirk* secretaries analyzed as a group show no such turnover.[42] In this case, the trend is one of stability. The trend toward regionalism and the formation of "dynasties" for first *Bezirk* secretaries long in office cannot be disregarded.[43] For upper-middle functionaries of the central party apparatus no similar information is available, as their composition and number are not presently known.

A drop in average age is also evident for Central Committee members and candidates who occupy top positions in other social spheres, such as the economy, agriculture, and cultural affairs (see Table 17). This is particularly evident in agriculture, where 7 of a total of 10 Central Committee members and candidates in 1963 belong to the 1920–1929 age group.[44]

Analysis of Central Committee members and candidates occupying high positions in mass organizations—primarily the FDGB, FDJ, and DFD—yields a somewhat different image. The younger generation already constitutes a comparatively high proportion in 1958: 7 of the 14 incumbents in the 1958 Central Committee were born between 1920 and 1929; in the 1963 Central Committee 8 out of 17 were in a comparable category. Of the 7 younger functionaries active in the

[42] See Section 7 of this chapter, pp. 289-292.
[43] This tendency was noted in Chapter 2, pp. 106 ff.
[44] For particulars, see pp. 276 ff.

central apparatus of mass organizations in 1958, 4 belonged to the FDJ or the Young Pioneers (Hertwig, Modrow, Namokel, and Steinke).[45] The representatives of the mass organizations in the Central Committee thus constitute the only group for which rejuvenation is hardly noticeable (compare Table 20). It will be shown in section 8 of this chapter that the following is in accord with the general findings of this study: The mass organizations have increasingly lost their representation in the Central Committee, due to the "professionalization" of young Central Committee members.

The trend toward rejuvenation is associated with a corresponding decrease or persistence of veteran functionaries. This thesis will be verified by a summary table drawn from Table 17 (cf. Table 21). In the 1963 Central Committee the proportion of those born between 1900 and 1909 has generally dropped. Going into details, we must emphasize that the proportion of Central Committee members and candidates from the party apparatus has dropped greatly in this age group: If in the 1958 Central Committee there remained 17 of a total of 53, in 1963 this number dropped to 7 out of 55. Furthermore, there are hardly any changes in this respect among Central Committee members and candidates from the state apparatus; these changes are comparatively minor for the mass organizations too.

5. The Occupational Mobility of Central Committee Members and Candidates in 1958 and 1963

Analysis of the occupational situation of Central Committee members and candidates at the time of their entry into this body should be complemented by that of occupational changes before and after membership in the Central Committee. To this end we have established the primary functions in 1958 and 1963 for members and candidates in

[45] This is explicable on the grounds that the Free German Youth (FDJ) should be regarded as a reserve for the "cadres" of the SED. In this context it should be noted that the Bureau of the Central Council of the Free German Youth, which in 1958 comprised a total of 21 members, included, apart from the 5 members and candidates of the 1958 Central Committee (3 of them candidates!), three younger functionaries who were admitted to the Central Committee in 1963: I. Lange, W. Lamberz, and K. Naumann. There are no comparative data for the FDGB and the DFD.

those years. Additionally, the primary functions for 1954 were established for the 1958 members and candidates. These are accurately correlated below, in order to analyze occupational mobility,[46] i.e., occupational ascent and descent and horizontal mobility between the various functional areas of the party, state, and economy, etc.[47] These correlations are limited to the Central Committees of 1958 and 1963 and address themselves to two main questions.

First, the ascent or descent and horizontal mobility of members and candidates for the 1958 Central Committee are compared with those for 1963, i.e., their occupational situation four years prior to entry into the Central Committee was compared with that directly after entry. For the 1958 Central Committee we are correlating the primary functions for 1954 and 1958 (Table 22), and for the 1963 Central Committee the primary function for 1958 and 1963 (Table 23). The comparison is aimed primarily at establishing whether the 1958 Central Committee constitutes a more homogeneous group than that of 1963 from the perspective of professional ascent/descent and horizontal mobility.

The relationship between Central Committee membership[48] and occupational changes will also be examined. To secure the relevant answers we have used a comparison between primary functions in 1958 and 1963 exercised by the members and candidates of the 1958 Central Committee (Table 26) and related this to our previously elaborated findings. In addition, examination of the group of new members elected in 1963—possibly due to their occupational situation—further complements our analysis (Table 27). Analysis of those belonging to the Central Committee in 1958 (but not in 1963) may also provide equally valuable evidence.[49] The following questions should be posed within the framework of our main question: Does occupational ascent occur before

[46] On the concept of mobility adopted here and the methodological problems that arose in the mobility study, see p. 194 above.

[47] As explained in note 35, we have abstained from giving a general rank order of the various functional areas. The positions in the various social areas are regarded as comparable. Whenever differentiation is required in individual instances, this has been specially noted.

[48] In the following, unless otherwise specified, Central Committee members and candidates are treated as being of equal rank.

[49] There seemed to be no justification for arranging data on this group in tables, since for too large a number of them no occupational data are available.

or after entry into the Central Committee?[50] Is horizontal mobility greater before or after entry into the Central Committee? Are occupational ascent and entry into the Central Committee directly correlated? What is the relationship, if any, between occupational descent and being dropped from the Central Committee?

The respective primary functions of the full and candidate members of the Central Committee were classified in accordance with the code tabulated on pp. 226-227, which indicates functional area and position within this area. Correlation according to functional area permits us in this context to analyze horizontal mobility (cf. Tables 24, 25, 28, 29). Correlation by functional area and position will permit the inclusion of occupational ascent and descent, i.e., vertical mobility (cf. Tables 22, 23, 26, 27).

OCCUPATIONAL MOBILITY OF CENTRAL COMMITTEE MEMBERS AND CANDIDATES IN 1958 AS COMPARED WITH THAT IN 1963

A look at Tables 22, 23, 24, and 25 clearly proves that the occupational mobility of Central Committee members and candidates in 1958 was lower between the periods compared (1954 and 1958) than for the 1963 Central Committee (between 1958 and 1963). In the 1958 Central Committee a total of 97 members and candidates are represented whose occupational positions did not, or did not notably, change in 1958 compared with 1954 (see Table 22); the same group totals 99 for the 1963 Central Committee (see Table 23). The others are distributed as follows:

1958 CC	1963 CC	
30	46	Ascending members and candidates
4	13	Descending members and candidates
15	15	Members and candidates transferred to a different apparatus at the same level
9	8	Members and candidates for whom detailed data are not available

[50] "Before," according to the design of the study, means four years before admission or reelection to the Central Committee. "After" means four years after the respective Central Committee was set up. Changes in the occupational position that took place immediately before or after election or reelection to the Central Committee are not specifically included, but constitute the chief current function.

Table 22
Vertical Occupational Mobility of CC Members and Candidates in 1958 (1954–1958)†

Main Function 1958	Main Function 1954 Top							Upper Middle						Middle/Lower Middle				X
	11	21	31	351	41	51	61	12	22	32	42	52	82	13, 14, 10	23, 24, 20	33, 34, 30	53, 54, 50	X
Top																		
11	6	2					2	6	4			1			1			
21		19	2						1					1; 2	1			
31			2															2
351				6							1							
41					11									1; 2				
51						3						1						
61		1																
Upper Middle																		
12								15	1	1	1			1; 4	1		1; 1	
22								1	6	1					1; 1			
32									1	4					1; 1	2		
42													1					
52												6						
82													1					
Middle/Lower middle																		
13, 14, 10					1					1	1			11	1	1	1	
23, 24, 20					1					1	1			2	1; 1	1; 1	1	
33, 34, 30															3	3		
53, 54, 50																	3	
X								1										6

	Berg Matern Mücken-berger Schön Ulbricht Wolf, H.	Abusch Becher Benjamin Buchwitz Grotewohl Handke Kosel Kramer Leuschner Pieck Rau Rübensam Wittkow-ski	Ermisch Schirmer	Gross-mann Grünert Schröder, W. Schubert Wittig Wulf	Biering Hertwig Lehmann, H. Reichert Steinke Svihalek Thiele Warnke, Herb. Wehmer	Collein Lieb-knecht		Buchheim Florin Fröhlich Lange, Ernst Mewis Pisnik Quandt Seibt Sens Steffen	Ebert Heiden-reich Kern Säge-brecht Scholz	Bönisch Fabian Gsell Zierold		Burghardt Naumann, R. Rienäcker Rompe		Baum Baumgart Krause Lange, Emil Nimz Rent-meister	Warnke, Hans	Eydam Kassler	Arnold Lange, Erich Minetti	
minor changes		Dölling Hoffmann Koenen, W. Plenikow-ski Stoph Winzer			Lehmann, O. Tille	Bredel		Funke Kiefert Reuter Sinder-mann Weihs	Hennecke			Rodenberg Wende	Molt-mann	Holz-macher Knolle Schneikart Thieme Vielhauer		Weber		
		Apel Norden Verner, W					Kessler Maron	Schneide-wind	Koenen, B. Baade	Götzl	Schumann			Albrecht Wolf, E.		Meinhardt Krüger	Erler*	
					Honecker*			Axen Grüneberg Hager, K. Mittag Neumann Verner, P.	Dahlem Honecker-Feist Mielke Rumpf Weiz		Modrow	Kurella Barthel		Konzack Lehmann, R. Namokel Baumann Bräutigam Frost Neuge-bauer	Jendretz-ky Deutsch-mann Schuckert Grauer*	Wenig Wirth	Dohlus* Mette	
					Felfe Kirchner*					Riemer	Brandt							

remained in same function — transferred — promoted — demoted — X no data

* Dohlus—was a student in 1954.
Erler—exact function not ascertainable for 1958; but it is known that E. Erler was a female student in 1954 and subsequently active in the party apparatus.
Grauer—rose from 24 (Chairman of the Hoyerswerda *Kreis* Council) to 23 (Deputy Chairman of the Cottbus *Bezirk* Council).
Honecker—ascent: from a code number 41 (Chairman of FDJ) to number 11 (Secretary of CC).
Kirchner—delegated for study leave.
† For codifying primary functions see code on pp. 226–227.

Table 23
Vertical Occupational Mobility of CC Members and Candidates in 1963 (1958–1963)†

Axen Grünecker Honecker Matern Norden Schön Ulbricht Verner, P. Wolf, H.	Abusch Buchwitz Dahlem Dölling Gehring Grotewohl Kessler Koenen, W. Kramer Maron Mielke Plenikow- ski Rumpf	Ermisch Rödiger	Dallmann Rieke Schröder, W. Sternberg Thoma Wulf	Lehmann, R. Naumann, K. Thiele Warnke, Herb. Wehmer	Adameck Barthel Bredel	Bräutigam Florin Frost Funke Herber Koenen, B. Lange, Ernst Pisnik Quandt Seibt Süss	Ebert Kern	Bönisch Weng	Kuron Meier	Kayser Lappe Meyer, E. H. Rompe Valentin	Baumgart Brandt Lange, M. Lassak Meinhardt	Krüger Wolf, E.	Eydam Fischer		Grundig Kaiser- Gorrish Lange, Erich Minetti
minor changes	Hager, K. Mittag	Balkow Gotsche Hoffmann Honecker Feist Stoph Winzer Wittkow- ski		Döhler	Heintze Hertwig	Neuner	Döhlus Müller, F. J. Sinder- mann	Henneke				Baum Diehl Holz- macher Lietz	Albrecht Oerter	Strauss		
	Apel Neumann Berg	Rübenagen Weiß Schirmer Ewald, M. Jendretz- ky Kosel Leuscher					Verner, W.		Heynisch			Thieme	Schwerz Sakowski			Marsch- ner*
			Grünert* Wittig*	Lange, I.*			Mewis Schumann	Jarowin- sky Scholz	Gallerach Hager, W. Löschau Markgraf		Bartsch Roden- berg Burghardt Wolf, Ch.	Ernst	Ewald, G. Schürer Solle Streit Wyschof- sky Müller, F. H. Juch Knolle Krolikow- ski Roscher Tiedke Tisch Ziegen- hahn	Beater* Matthes Wittik Warnke, Hans Brasch Jäckel Felfe* Krusak*	Locht- hofen Traut* Walther*	Waak* Hempel	Müller, M.* Berger* Mäde
Kurella Mückenberger	Heinrich				Lamberz Modrow	Geggel Zimme- ring	Neuge- bauer Pöschel Baumann Kiefert		Heiden- reich	Wirth						

remained in same function   [ ] transferred   ▦ promoted   ▨ demoted   X no data

* Beater—...act function in 1958 unknown.
Berger—S...dent in 1958.
Felfe—ascent from 24 (Chairman of Zschopau Kreis Council) to 23 (Chairman of Karl-Marx-Stadt Bezirk Council).
Grünert—ascent from 351 (LPG Chairman in Worin) to 23 (Chairman of the Agricultural Coun-cil in the Frankfurt-on-the-Oder Bezirk).
Krusak—...se from 24 (Kreis school councillor) to 23 (Bezirk school councillor).

Lange, I.—ascent: from 41 (FDJ Secretary) to 12 (Chairman of the Women's Commission of the Politburo).
Marschner—exact function in 1958.
Müller, M.—Student in 1958.
Traut—exact function in 1958 unknown.
Waak—exact function in 1958 unknown.
Walther—exact function in 1958 unknown.
Wittig—ascent from 351 (LPG Chairman in Kauern t= 23 (Chairman of the Agricultural Coun-cil for the Gera Bezirk).

† For codi...ring primary functions see code on pp. 226–227.

Table 24
Horizontal Occupational Mobility of CC Members and Candidates in 1958 (1954←1958)

Functional Area in 1958	Functional Area in 1954								
	1 Party	2 State	3 Economy	35 Agriculture	4 Mass Organizations	5 Culture/ Educ.	6 NVA	8 Other Organizations	x No Data
1 Party	42	3	2		3	3			
2 State	3	33	2		1	1	2		
3 Economy		3	11						
35 Agriculture	1			6					2
4 Mass Organizations	2				12				
5 Culture/Education					1	13			
6 NVA		1							
8 Other Organizations								1	
x No Data	1								6

Table 25
Horizontal Occupational Mobility of CC Members and Candidates in 1963 (1958←1963)

Functional Area in 1963	Functional Area in 1958								
	1 Party	2 State	3 Economy	35 Agriculture	4 Mass Organizations	5 Culture/ Educ.	6 NVA	7 International Organizations	x No Data
1 Party	46	4			3	1			1
2 State	11	35	2	2		2	1		1
3 Economy		1	14						4
35 Agriculture				8		1			1
4 Mass Organizations	2	3		1	9	1			1
5 Culture/Education		3	1			17			
6 NVA							2		
7 Internat. Organizations	1	1	1						
x No Data									

Differences between members and candidates in the 1958 and 1963 Central Committees are thus primarily evident in their vertical mobility. Here, further noteworthy distinctions have been found. Contrary to the overall trend, the leading group in the party apparatus (primary function 11) has proven more stable in 1963 than in 1958. Only 6 (slightly more than a third) of the total 16 Central Committee members in 1958 who occupied function 11 in that year also occupied this function in 1954 (cf. Table 22). The following rose hierarchically, or were transferred to top positions in the SED: Apel, Axen, Grüneberg, Hager, Honecker, Kurella, Mittag, Neumann, Norden, and Paul Verner. In the 1963 Central Committee, of the total of 13 top party functionaries all but 2 (the agronomist Rübensam and the economist Jarowinsky) had already occupied top positions in 1958. All top functionaries of the 1958 Central Committee remained in the 1963 Central Committee. However, three were transferred to other positions: Erich Apel and Alfred Neumann to the state apparatus, and Helene Berg (long-time director of the SED Central Committee's Institute for Social Sciences) to the editorial board of the journal *Probleme des Friedens und des Sozialismus*. Two top functionaries from the 1958 Central Committee suffered hierarchical demotions between 1958 and 1963: Alfred Kurella and Erich Mückenberger.[51]

[51] There is no clear official information in the West for the reasons of their downgrading. The Politburo Commission for Cultural Affairs, directed by Alfred Kurella since its establishment in 1957, was dissolved when the production principle was introduced at the Sixth Party Congress. Its duties were partly transferred to the Ideological Commission (Director: Kurt Hager) of which Kurella remained a member. Kurella lost his post as a candidate of the Politburo but remained a candidate member of the Central Committee, which status he retained at the Seventh Party Congress. In 1963 he succeeded Stefan Hermlin as secretary of the section for the cultivation of poetry and linguistics of the German Academy of Arts. Two reasons can be cited for the possible elimination of Kurella from the first rank of party functionaries: (1) his failure as director of the Commission for Cultural Affairs. He did not succeed in organizing unanimous support of artists for the cultural line of the party. See Heinz Kersten, "Die Defensive der Dogmatiker. Kulturpolitische Auseinandersetzungen vor und nach dem VI. Parteitag der SED," *SBZ-Archiv* 14, no. 5 (March 1963): 71. (2) Under the aegis of the "new economic system" the Party was not anxious to push Kurella, an old functionary and Stalinist (he was active as editor and writer in the Soviet Union from 1934 until 1954), too far into the foreground. The reasons for this are highly complex. The SED leaders may very well have been anxious to emphasize their independence toward the Soviet Union, especially in connection with the

Developments within the echelons of leading state functionaries represented in the Central Committee are the exact opposite of the leadership situation in the party apparatus. Mobility for this group in the 1963 Central Committee is considerably greater than that in 1958: when the 1958 Central Committee was constituted, only 7 top state functionaries (primary function 21) augmented the 19 who had already occupied such positions in 1954. By contrast, of the 37 incumbents of leading state positions in the 1963 Central Committee only 21—i.e., slightly more than half—had already occupied such positions in 1958. Four were coopted to state leadership positions by transfer (Apel, Neumann, Weiz, and Waldemar Verner). The other 12 rose as follows:

From the upper-middle level of the party apparatus: Mewis.

From the upper-middle level of the state apparatus: Scholz.

From the upper-middle level of the cultural apparatus: Bartsch and Rodenberg.

From the middle/lower-middle level of the party apparatus: G. Ewald, Schürer, Sölle, Streit, and Wyschofsky.

From the middle/lower-middle level of the state apparatus: Beater, Matthes, and Wittik.

Among the 1963 Central Committee members and candidates who rose to high state functions, 7 are entrusted with economic or agricultural responsibilities: Scholz, Schürer, Sölle, Wyschofsky, Wittik, Bartsch, and G. Ewald. All were born between 1920 and 1929. Three more can be classified as state functionaries in the narrow sense (Mewis,

---

controversy about Stalinism. But beyond this, the area of ideology was evidently to be under the leadership of a younger functionary, more familiar with conditions in the GDR, now that a new development phase had been initiated with the introduction of the "new economic system."

Erich Mückenberger, who since 1953 had been secretary for agriculture at the CC, and who since 1950 was a candidate and since 1958 a full member of the Politburo, was replaced late in 1959 or early in 1960 by Gerhard Grüneberg, who took over the secretaryship. In August 1961 Mückenberger became first secretary of the SED *Bezirk* executive in Frankfurt-on-the-Oder and retained his membership in the Politburo. So far as is known, his demotion was due to professional incompetence. This conclusion is based on two IWE reports. On December 19, 1957, the IWE reports that agricultural scientists had opposed him on technical grounds in connection with discussions concerning the "square-nest" planting method for potatoes in 1957. Furthermore, according to an IWE report dated August 24, 1961, Mückenberger is said to have been sent to Moscow for an extended period of indoctrination after his replacement by Grüneberg.

Beater, and Matthes), as well as two who assumed specific functions (Rodenberg and Streit). Among them only Heinz Matthes (born in 1927)—now chairman of the Workers' and Peasants' Inspectorate—can be regarded as a younger, technically trained functionary. Thus, the trends of rejuvenation and professionalization, observable for the Council of Ministers, has had consequences for the composition of the Central Committee. This is not true, however, for the top level of the party apparatus in the narrower sense, i.e., the full-time top party functionaries. Rejuvenation and professionalization were thus restricted to the top state functionaries in the Central Committee.

With regard to mobility the 1963 Central Committee is a less homogeneous group than that of 1958. However, mobility has affected the top party functionaries very little. Instead, a marked stability for this group can be noted in the 1963 Central Committee compared with 1958. As for the concept advanced in Chapter One regarding the relative stability of the "strategic clique," trends toward continuity constitute the major characteristic of the leading bodies of the SED. The party elite, which in the early years of the GDR (as shown by the composition of the 1958 Central Committee) was characterized by considerable mobility and exceptional ascent and descent, has now been partly insulated from these processes and consolidated. The capacity for stability among top party functionaries can be regarded as the fundamental determinant for GDR society at present.

VERTICAL OCCUPATIONAL MOBILITY AND CENTRAL COMMITTEE
MEMBERSHIP

Career curves usually level off after entry into the Central Committee. In effect, vertical mobility has largely ended after candidacy or membership in entering the Central Committee. This is confirmed by Tables 26 and 27. The fields on Table 26 that show mobility between 1958 and 1963 for members and candidates of the 1958 Central Committee are far less occupied than the fields on Table 27 which indicate mobility between 1958 and 1963 for those members and candidates newly admitted to the 1963 Central Committee. Some results of Tables 26 and 27 have been summarized in order to support this thesis. In the 1958 Central Committee the proportion of incumbents on the three stages

Table 26
Vertical Occupational Mobility of CC Members and Candidates in 1958 (1958—1963)†

Primary Function 1963	Primary Function 1958 Top							Upper Middle					Middle/Lower Middle				X
	11	21	31	351	41	51	61	12	22	32	52	82	13, 14, 10	23, 24, 20	33, 34, 30	53, 54, 50	
Top																	
11	11	1	1					1									
21	2	18	1		1			1						1			
31			1														
351				4													
41		1			7 1			2								1	
51						3											
61																	
Upper Middle																	
12	2							12					1	1			
22								4		1 5							
32									1								
42					1						4						1
52																	
62																	
Middle/Lower middle																	
13, 14, 10					4 1	1 1		4 3	1	1			9 1	1 3 1			
23, 24, 20				2	1			1						1			
33, 34, 30				1	1					1					3		
353				1													
53, 54, 50									1	1			3			3	
X				1	2			1	1	1		1					
Deceased		4		1	1			1				1					
Retired						1							3				6

	Remained in the same function (minor changes)													
Remained in the same function	Axen, Grüneberg, Hager, K., Honecker, Matern, Mittag, Norden, Schön, Ulbricht, Verner, P., Wolf, H.	Abusch, Benjamin, Buchwitz, Dahlem, Dölling, Grotewohl, Kessler, Koenen, W., Kramer, Maron, Mielke, Plenikowski, Rumpf	Ermisch	Konzack, Schröder, W., Thoma, Wulf	Biering, Lehmann, R., Thiele, Warnke, Herb., Wehmer	Barthel, Bredel, Collein	Bräutigam, Florin, Fröhlich, Frost, Funke, Koenen, B., Lange, Ernst, Pisnik, Quandt, Seibt	Ebert, Kern	Bönisch, Gsell, Schuckert, Wenig, Zierold	Naumann, R., Rienäcker, Rompe, Wence	Brandt, Baumgart, Erler*, Meinhardt	Wolf, E., Krüger	Eydam, Kassler, Weber	Arnold, Lange, Erich, Minetti
minor changes	Hoffmann, Honecker-Feist, Stoph, Winzer, Wittkowski	—			Lehmann, O., Hertwig	—	Dohlus, Sindermann	Hennecke, Schneidewind			Baum, Holzmacher, Rentmeister, Schneikart, Vielhauer	Albrecht		
Transferred at the same level	Apel, Neumann, Berg	Rübensam, Jendretzky*, Kosel, Leuschner — Weiz, Schürmer					Verner, W.	Mette*	Baade		Thieme			
Ascent				Grünert*, Wittig*			Mewis, Buchheim*, Schumann	Scholz		Roderich, Burghardt	Knolle	Warnke, Hans, Riemer, Grauer, Felfe*		Kirchner*
Descent	Kurella, Mückenberger			Grossmann	Reichert*, Steinke, Mosdrow, Tille		Neugebauer, Reuter, Steffen, Welhs, Baumann, Götzl, Kiefert	Heidenreich	Wirth					

Legend:

▓ Remained in the same function   ▯ Transferred at the same level   ▤ Ascent

minor changes   ▨ Descent   X no data

* Buchheim—first promoted and then "shelved" on the promotion level from 12 (1st Secretary of the SED *Bezirk* executive Karl-Marx-Stadt) in 1959 to 41 (deputy chairman of the National Board of the FDGB), and then, from 1961 on, also at the 41 level (chairman of the People's Solidarity).
Erler—exact function in 1958 unknown.
Felfe—rose from 24 (chairman of the Zschopau *Kreis* Council) to 23 (chairman of the Karl-Marx-Stadt *Bezirk* Council).
Grünert—achieved ascent: from 351 (LPG chairman in Worin) to 23 (chairman of the Agricultural Council in the Frankfurt-on-the-Oder *Bezirk*).
Jendretzky—descent: from 21 (deputy Minister of the Interior and State Secretary for Local Councils) to 41 (member of the Secretariat of the FDGB National Board).
Kirchner—was a student in 1958.
Mette—retired, but not stripped of all of his University functions.
Reichert—descent, since he was demoted from 1st to 2nd Chairman of the DTSB.
Wittig—ascent: from 351 (LPG Chairman in Kauern) to 23 (Chairman of the Agricultural Council in the Gera *Bezirk*).
† For codifying **primary** functions see code on pp. 226-227.

Table 27
Vertical Occupational Mobility of Members and Candidates Newly Admitted to the Central Committee in 1963 (1958–1963)†

Primary Function 1963	Primary Function 1958 Top					Upper Middle						Middle/Lower Middle						X
	21	31	351	41	51	12	22	32	42	52	62	13, 14, 10	23, 24, 20	33, 34, 30	353, 350	53, 54, 50	60	X
Top																		
11																		
21	3	1										5	3					1
31			4											2	1			1
351				2			1	4		1	1	1	1		1	1		2
41	1			2	2											1		
51					2					1	1							
61																		
Upper Middle																		
12				1	1	3						6	1					1
22																		1
32									2					1				2
42									2									
52					1			1		4			1		1	1		
Middle/Lower Middle																		
13, 14, 10						1						4	1 1					
23, 24, 20	1												1	2				1
33, 34, 30																		
353, 350																		
53, 54, 50													1			2		
60																	1	

	Gehring	Rödiger	Dallmann / Rieke / Sternberg	Neumann, K.	Adameck	Herber / Stief			Kuron / Meier	Kayser / Lappe / Meyer, E. H. / Vallentin		Lange, M. / Lassak		Fischer		Grundig / Kaiser-Gorrish	
minor changes	Balkow Gotsche	—	Döhler	Heintze	Neuner	Müller, F. I.	—		—			Diehl Lietz	Oerter	Strauss			Marschner*
	Ewald, M.							Heynisch					Schwarz Sakowski			Müller, M.* Berger* Mäde	
	—		Lange, I.*					Jarowinsky	Gallerach Hager, W. Löschau Markgraf	Bartsch Wolf, Ch.	Ernst	Ewald, G. Schürer Sölle Streit Wyschofsky Müller, F. II. Juch Krolikowski Roscher Tiedke Tisch Ziegenhahn	Beater* Matthes Wittik Brasch Jäckel Krussk*	Lochthofen Traut* Walther*	Waak* Hempel		
	Heinrich		Lamberz		Geggel Zimmering	Pöschel											

▥ Remained in the same function in 1958.

▤ Transferred at the same level.

▰ Ascent

▨ Descent

X No Data

* Beater—exact function unknown in 1958.
Berger—Student in 1958.
Krussk—rose from 24 (*Kreis* school councillor) to 23 (*Bezirk* school councillor);
Lange, I.—ascent: from 41 (FDJ Secretary) to 12 (Chairman of the Women's Commission at the Politburo).
Marschner—exact function in 1958 unknown.
Müller, M.—Student in 1958.
Traut—exact function in 1958 unknown.
Waak—exact function in 1958 unknown.
Walther—exact function in 1958 unknown.
† For codifying primary functions see code on pp. 226–227.

Table 28
Horizontal Occupational Mobility of CC Members and Candidates in 1958 (1958→1963)

Functional Area in 1963	Functional Area in 1958									
	1 Party	2 State	3 Econ-omy	35 Agri-cul-ture	4 Mass Or-gani-za-tions	5 Cul-ture/ Educ.	6 NVA	7 Inter-nat. Or-gani-za-tions	8 Other Or-gani-za-tions	x No Data
1 Party	39	2			1					
2 State	7	28	3	2	1	1	1			
3 Economy		1	9							
35 Agriculture				5						
4 Mass organi-zations	2	2			8	1				1
5 Culture/ Education		2				11				
6 NVA					1					
7 International Organizations	1	1	1							
8 Other Organizations										
x No Data	3	1	1	1	2					6
y Deceased	1	4		1	1				1	
z Retired		1				1				

"upper," "upper-middle," and "middle/lower-middle" in all functional areas concerned (party, state, economy, agriculture, mass organizations, culture and education, NVA and international organizations) remained comparatively constant between 1958 and 1963 (cf. Table 30).

In contrast, there is a marked trend toward ascent for members and candidates who were newly admitted to the Central Committee in 1963: whereas in 1958 only 18 members and candidates fulfilled functions at the top level of the party, state, economy, etc., we find 39 in 1963, while the number of incumbents in the middle/lower-middle has dropped from 38 to 15 (cf. Table 30). The same difference established by Tables 26 and 27 (indicating vertical mobility) cannot be found in Tables 25, 28, and 29 (indicating horizontal mobility). When the horizontal mobility between various functional areas in Table 28 is compared with that of Table 29 the differences are not so great—compared to the variations noted in Tables 26 and 27. One hundred of a total 155 Central Committee members and candidates in 1958, as well as 10 of those who

Table 29
Horizontal Occupational Mobility of Members and Candidates Newly Admitted to the Central Committee in 1963 (1958—1963)

| | Functional Area in 1958 | | | | | | | |
| | 1 | 2 | 3 | 35 | 4 Mass Or- gani- za- tions | 5 Cul- ture/ Educ. | 6 | x |
Functional Area in 1963	Party	State	Econ- omy	Agri- cul- ture			NVA	No Data
1 Party	14	2			2	1		1
2 State	5	9				1		1
3 Economy			10					4
35 Agriculture				5		1		1
4 Mass organizations	1	2		1	4	1		
5 Culture/Education		2	1			11		
6 NVA							2	
x No Data								

Table 30
Vertical Occupational Mobility and Entry into the Central Committee

Position	Central Committee 1958				Central Committee 1963 (new)			
	1958		1963		1958		1963	
	abso-lute	%	abso-lute	%	abso-lute	%	abso-lute	%
Top	73	47	70*	45	18	22	39	47
Upper Middle	47	30	37*	24	19	23	28	34
Middle/Lower Middle	28	18	34	22	38	46	15	19
Reference No.	155	100	155	100	82	100	82	100

* Members and candidates of the Central Committee who died or were retired between 1958 and 1963 were included as incumbents. These consisted of 7 persons occupying a top position and 3 in the upper middle category.

died or were retired between 1958 and 1963 (all told 71 percent)[52] were in the same functional area in 1958 as in 1963. Of the 181 members and candidates in 1963 a total of 131 (72 percent)[53] did not change their functional area. For newly admitted members and candidates in 1963 the corresponding percentage is 67 percent.[54] A further conclusion that can be drawn from this is the rare dependence between horizontal mobility and membership in the Central Committee. There is, however, a greater dependence between ascent and descent on the one hand, and membership in the Central Committee on the other.

OCCUPATIONAL DESCENT AND ELIMINATION FROM
THE CENTRAL COMMITTEE

This section deals with downward professional mobility and its relationship to Central Committee membership. The results of Table 26 are therefore interpreted for members and candidates not re-elected to the Central Committee in 1963 (cf. Table 31). The primary finding is that the occupational position of individual members and candidates and their position in the Central Committee are not in full accord. Table 31 also

[52] Omitting 20 members and candidates for whom no data for 1963 are available.
[53] With 9 dropouts. ·
[54] With 7 dropouts.

Table 31
Departure from the Central Committee in 1958 and Occupational Position

Departure/ Occupational Position	Members		Candidates	
	No.	Name	No.	Name
Departure with simultaneous occupational demotion				
a) Because of Nazi past	1	Grossmann	0	
b) "Unfit for the higher tasks of Socialism"	1	Steffen	0	
c) No reasons available	5	Buchheim Götzl Reichert Reuter Tille	2	Steinke Weihs
Departure with simultaneous upward occupational mobility	0		3	Grauer Kirchner Riemer
Departure without noticeable change in occupational position				
a) Remained in the same position	9	Gsell Kassler Konzak R. Naumann Rienäcker Schuckert F. Weber Wende Zierold	4	Arnold Biering Collein (Erler)*
b) Change of position without demotion	2	O. Lehmann Schneikart	4	Baade Rentmeister Schneidewind Vielhauer
Departure and occupational change for "natural" reasons				
a) Death	8		0	
b) Health reasons, retirement	3		0	
No Data	8		6	

* In parentheses, since exact data on occupational position in 1958 were not known.

shows that—contrary to Wolfgang Zapf's thesis—comparatively "normal" resignations also occur in Communist party apparatuses.

Of the 56 members and candidates who left the Central Committee after 1958, 11 were "natural" departures, due to death and old age. For 9 a simultaneous downward mobility was established, whereas 19 remained in the same positions or merely changed these, without incurring demotion. Even when taking into account the 14 members and candidates for whom no further data were available, the number of those who left the Central Committee and simultaneously suffered professional demotion is comparatively low. Furthermore, not all 16 members and candidates of the 1958 Central Committee who occupied lower positions in 1963 were excluded from the Central Committee elected in that year.[55]

This finding is further verified if we refer to the biographical[55] data for some whose occupational positions did not change or changed imperceptibly: Walter Biering belongs to the group for whom no change in professional level occurred. He was born in 1898, started life as a mason, and later became a farmer. From 1954 until his death in 1964 he was deputy chairman of the Peasants' Mutual Aid Association (VdgB). Günther Rienäcker (born in 1904) professor of chemistry at Humboldt University in Berlin since 1954, remained director of the Institute of Chemistry at the University after leaving the Central Committee. Since 1957 he has also become secretary-general of the German Academy of Sciences in Berlin. However, the loss of his secondary political function may very well be connected with his resignation from the Central Committee. In 1959 Rienäcker left his post as first chairman of the Central Board of the Union of Scientists. Six members and candidates occupied comparable—or up to a certain point, even the same—positions after leaving the Central Committee. For example, Kurt Schneidewind, born in 1912, was a senior SED functionary since 1945 and served as special ambassador to North Korea from 1959 to 1963. He is now director of the Far Eastern Department in the Ministry

[55] Despite occupational downgrading, Baumann, Heidenreich, Kiefert, Kurella, Modrow, Mückenberger, Neugebauer, and Wirth remained on the Central Committee.

of Foreign Affairs. These two positions can be regarded as equivalent.[56] Among the three who rose professionally was Central Committee candidate Rudolf Kirchner, a writer born in 1919. For many years he was a member of the Presidium and Secretariat of the National Board of the FDGB. From 1959 to 1962 he was delegated for further training and was only deprived of his functions in the FDGB apparatus for this period. At the Sixth Congress of the FDGB (November 1963) he again became a member of the Presidium and Secretariat of the National Board. However, he did not return to the Central Committee, even in 1967.

The thesis that Central Committee membership and occupational position are not clearly inseparable can be further confirmed by citing the eight members and candidates who experienced professional demotion, but nonetheless remained in the Central Committee. We have selected only two examples: the biographies of Alfred Kurella and Erich Mückenberger. Alfred Kurella was for a long time director of the SED Politburo's Commission for Cultural Affairs. He lost this major position in the party apparatus in 1963 when he was expelled from the Politburo, but remained in the Central Committee. Since March 1963 his main occupation has been secretary for Poetry and Linguistics at the German Academy of Arts. Erich Mückenberger was Central Committee Secretary for Agricultural Affairs from 1953 to 1960. Since 1958 he has been a full member of the Politburo and since 1950 a member of the Central Committee. He lost his post as Central Committee secretary and became first secretary of the SED *Bezirk* executive for Frankfurt-on-the-Oder in August 1961, without leaving the Politburo and Central Committee.[57]

[56] His change of position might possibly be interpreted as a promotion, especially considering that in Bolshevist systems the posts of ambassadors and emissaries are frequently kiss-off positions (very much like the position of judge in America). Thus, the ambassadorial appointments of Molotov, Pervuchin and others are interpreted by Brzezinski and Huntington as demotions. (See Brzezinski and Huntington, *Political Power: USA/USSR*, p. 149). In the GDR this definitely applies to Karl Mewis, who lost his post as Minister and Chairman of the State Planning Commission in January 1963 and has served as ambassador to Poland since April 1963.

[57] See note 51.

UPWARD OCCUPATIONAL MOBILITY AND ENTRY INTO
THE CENTRAL COMMITTEE

Examining the other side of the coin, i.e., the situation with hierarchical promotions, we find likewise that there is no exact parallel between Central Committee membership and occupational ranking. Among the 82 new members and candidates in the 1963 Central Committee (with the exception of 7 for whom we had no data) the following applies:

Twenty (9 members, 11 candidates) occupied equivalent hierarchical positions throughout the period 1958-1963.

Ten (4 members, 6 candidates) showed minor changes in their ranking within the same functional area between 1958 and 1963; their mobility was largely in a slight upward direction.[58]

Four (1 member, 3 candidates) remained in the same position, but were transferred to a different functional area.

Thirty-six (14 members, 22 candidates) experienced occupational ascent.

5 (all candidates) underwent demotion.

If we also include among the 36 Central Committee members and candidates who were promoted professionally the ten whose positions became slightly higher between 1958 and 1963 upon entry into the Central Committee, entry coincided with a rise in position for 46. This comprises slightly more than half of the newly elected members and candidates in 1963. In contrast, there were 20 newcomers whose positions had not changed and 4 who experienced horizontal mobility between 1958 and 1963. In summary, 24 persons—i.e., somewhat less than a third—of the newly elected Central Committee members and candidates exhibited no notable change in profession when they entered the Central Committee. To these should be added those who were demoted between 1958 and 1963 (cf. Table 32).

Following our investigation into the members and candidates newly accepted into the CC in 1963—of whom roughly one half rose in rank respectively enjoyed some minor improvement in their professional status, while one third remained unaffected by their acceptance and 4% descended—we shall now take a closer look at the 36 professionally ascended members and candidates who joined the CC in 1963. Of these, 22 were promoted within their functional areas between 1958 and 1963,

---

[58] As from Deputy Minister to Minister.

Table 32

Members and Candidates Newly Admitted to the Central Committee in 1963 Whose Occupational Ranking Fell*

Name		Primary Function 1958		Primary Function 1963
Heinrich	21	Deputy State Secretary for Registration and Procurement of Agricultural Products	23	Chairman of the Agricultural Council Schwerin *Bezirk*
Lamberz†	41	1st Secretary of the FDJ Central Council for Culture	12	Working group director and member of the Commission for Agitation of the Politburo
Geggel	51	Director of Broadcasting	12	Section director of the Central Committee, Secretary of the Commission for Western Affairs
Zimmering	51	Secretary of the German Writers' Union	52	Director of the Institute for Literature "J. R. Becher"
Pöschel	12	Deputy Director of the Machine-Building Section at the Central Committee	13	Chief of Task Force for Research and Development, and investment policy attached to the Central Committee

* "Descent" in the sense of the main function model derived from criteria of formal position (cf. Table 12).

† The functions assumed by Lamberz in 1963 must be regarded as transitory in nature. As early as 1966 Lamberz rose to the post of director of the Agitprop Section of the Central Committee and then in April 1967 (at the Seventh Party Congress) became a secretary of the Central Committee.

6 within the party apparatus, 4 in the state apparatus, 7 in the economy, 1 in agriculture and 2 each in education and the NVA. Six members and candidates entered the state apparatus as a result of this promotion, and 8 were promoted while simultaneously experiencing horizontal mobility, e.g., between state and party, between party and mass organizations, and so on.

The incumbents in "'middle-middle" positions in party and state accounted for the highest proportion of professional ascents. Of the total of 20 members[59] and candidates in the 1963 Central Committee who

[59] The holders of positions 14 and 10, who were lumped together with position 13 in Table 23 solely for reasons of space, have been deducted.

Table 33
New CC Members and Candidates in 1963 Who Rose from "Middle-Middle" Positions in the Party Apparatus*

Name	Year of Birth	Main Function 1958	Main Function 1963
Promoted within the party apparatus			
H. Juch	1920	Functionary of the CPCC	Functionary and member of the CPCC
W. Krolikowski	1928	Secretary for Agitprop of the SED *Bezirk* executive for Rostock	1st Secretary of the SED *Bezirk* executive for Dresden
P. Roscher	1913	2nd Secretary of the SED *Bezirk* executive for Erfurt	1st Secretary of the SED *Bezirk* executive for Karl-Marx-Stadt
K. Tiedke	1924	Functionary of the CC Apparatus	Director of the CC Propaganda Section
H. Tisch	1927	Secretary for Economic Policy of the SED Rostock *Bezirk* executive	1st Secretary of the SED *Bezirk* executive for Rostock
Promoted from the party apparatus to positions in the state apparatus			
G. Ewald	1926	1st Secretary of the SED *Kreis* executive Rügen	1st Chairman of the Agricultural Council at the Council of Ministers
G. Schürer	1921	Sector chief for planning in the Planning and Finance Section of the CC	1st Deputy Chairman of the State Planning Commission
H. Sölle	1924	Sector chief for Foreign Trade in the Section for Trade, Supply and Foreign Trade of the CC Apparatus	Under State Secretary and 1st Deputy Minister in the Ministry for Foreign and Domestic Trade
J. Streit	1911	Functionary of the CC Apparatus	Attorney-General
G. Wyschofsky	1929	Functionary of the CC Apparatus	Deputy Chairman of the State Planning Commission
Those who rose from the party apparatus to positions in mass organizations			
F. Müller II	1918	Secretary for Agriculture of the SED *Bezirk* executive for Erfurt	1st Chairman of the Central Board of the Farm and Forestry Laborers' Union

* "Ascent" in the sense of the main function model derived from criteria of formal position (cf. Table 12).

occupied middle-middle positions in the party for 1958, more than half, i.e., 11, rose in position. These individuals, all functionaries newly admitted to the Central Committee in 1963, are named in Table 33.

PATHS OF ASCENT

Two main paths of ascent can be ascertained for those in the 1963 Central Committee: a rise within a given apparatus and ascent, plus horizontal cooptation, from the party apparatus to state positions. However, these are not typical for those in the 1958 Central Committee; for this group ascent within the ranks of a single given apparatus predominates (cf. Table 34). First, let us note the number of those who were promoted within their respective functional areas for both Central Committees. Of the 26 members and candidates in 1963 who rose on the occupational ladder between 1958 and 1963, in all 7 were promoted within the party apparatus, 7 in the economic apparatus, 6 in the state apparatus, 3 in cultural positions, 2 in the National Peoples' Army, and 1 in agricultural administrative work. By comparison, 10 members and candidates of the 1958 Central Committee rose in the party echelons between 1954 and 1958, 7 in the state apparatus, 2 in the economic apparatus, and 1 each in the cultural and mass organizational hierarchies. The number who advanced within the party apparatus in the 1963 Central Committee has thus dropped compared with that of 1958. This is all the more surprising, inasmuch as the self-image of the SED leadership demands that the elite of the party apparatus be represented

Table 34
Paths of Ascent of CC Members and Candidates (1958 and 1963)

	CC 1958 1954←1958	CC 1963 1958←1963	CC 1963 (newly-elected) 1958←1963
Ascent within a given apparatus	21	26	22
Ascent from . . . to the state apparatus	1	8	6
Ascent from the party apparatus to positions in mass organizations	2	2	1
(Others, all of which occur for single individuals)	(6)	(10)	(7)

in the Central Committee and rise automatically in their occupational status upon cooptation to the Central Committee. The number of those who rose within the party apparatus in the 1963 Central Committee contrasts not only with 13 who rose in economic or state positions, but in addition with 8 more individuals who changed from the party to the state apparatus in their upward mobility. In this context the recurrent phenomenon, whereby party functionaries lose ground in the Central Committee to cadres occupying positions in the state and economic apparatuses, is once again confirmed in our findings.

HORIZONTAL OCCUPATIONAL MOBILITY AND CENTRAL COMMITTEE
MEMBERSHIP

The correlations that have been made to analyze horizontal occupational mobility (cf. Tables 24, 25, 28, and 29) clearly confirm that a preponderant majority of Central Committee members and candidates retained their primary occupations in the same functional area through-out the period observed. This applies even more to members and candidates of the 1958 Central Committee, which was observed between 1954 and 1958 (cf. Table 24), than to the 1963 members and candidates whose occupational situation between 1958 and 1963 was contrasted (Table 25). As with vertical mobility, differences in horizontal mobility were more pronounced in the 1963 group than in that of 1958. It is apparent that horizontal mobility does not cease upon entry into the Central Committee to the same degree as vertical mobility. Analysis of the 1958 Central Committee *after* its formation reveals a rate of horizontal mobility (cf. Table 28) similar to that which prevailed among full and candidate members of the 1963 Central Committee *before* their entrance into this body (cf. Table 29). For the 1958 Central Committee this horizontal movement has even increased slightly since that year (cf. Table 28) in comparison to the situation which obtained in 1954 (cf. Table 24). However, from these correlations it emerged that at most only a third of the Central Committee members and candidates had changed their functional areas.

These findings permit the conclusion that when the career paths of individual Central Committee members and candidates are traced, functional areas ("apparatuses") are relatively insulated from each other with respect to interchange of personnel. It may be stated that the frequently alleged interchangeability among occupational positions in totalitarian societies[60] hardly prevails under conditions of change to authoritarian forms of political rule. The model of consultative authoritarianism is associated with a remarkable proliferation of consultative and controlling bodies. The number of persons active within these bodies increases in direct proportion to this proliferation. A rising differentiation and specialization within formal organizations is accompanied by the demand that those incumbent in these bodies have, by virtue of education or practical experience, very specific career paths. Thus, it may be concluded with a high degree of certainty that the rate of interchangeability between economic and party functionaries is lower for this period than for the early 1950s.

Horizontal mobility is especially observable within the party and state apparatuses. For the period observed, more functionaries were dismissed from than accepted into the party. The state apparatus constitutes a sort of repository for functionaries from other organizations; it therefore exhibits a higher overall rate of turnover in personnel. On the basis of our findings, the economic apparatus and agricultural administration may be regarded as relatively closed spheres. The educational and mass organizations display greater "openness." Consequently, compared to top party functionaries, representatives of the state apparatus have tended to become increasingly important in the Central Committee. This finding is confirmed by analysis of patterns of horizontal and vertical mobility, although it could have been postulated on the basis of the results in Table 12. Even though a far from significant proportion of promotions occurred in the lateral direction from party apparatus to state functions, it will be demonstrated that state—and primarily economic—officials are clearly gaining ground in disproportion

[60] See, for instance, Zbigniew K. Brzezinski, *The Permanent Purge. Politics in Soviet Totalitarianism* (Cambridge, Mass., 1956), p. 19. An example in support of this thesis is the testimony of Wolfgang Leonhard, *Die Revolution entlässt ihre Kinder* (Cologne and Berlin, 1955), p. 308: "It is generally customary in the Stalinist apparatus for a functionary to be assigned another new task by the party leadership after one and a half to three years." Ernst Richert objected to this thesis although he failed to disprove it. (See *Macht ohne Mandat*, pp. 260 ff and 276 ff.)

to others. Our analysis of mobility has already established that the advance of economic functionaries runs parallel to stabilization and consolidation of the SED leadership group.

6. Representation of Economic Functionaries in the Central Committee

In the preceding sections of this chapter various data have been used to establish the point that the social composition of the 1963 Central Committee differed from those of 1958 and 1954. To recapitulate the most important findings regarding these differences:

1. Age: Compared with the Central Committees of 1958 and 1954, an inordinate drop in age, or rejuvenation, is noticeable in that of 1963.

2. Data derived from given individuals' political profiles: The increasingly higher profile of the younger generation is accompanied, at least in absolute numbers, by the replacement of functionaries whose social and political experiences date from the pre-World War Two period.

3. Occupational situation classified by age groups: It was established that, compared with the Central Committees of 1958 and 1954, in that of 1963 the group of younger functionaries had graduated from trade, etc., schools, and technical and trade colleges and universities to an increasing degree. With respect to acquired occupation, younger cadres who were better qualified for technical and economic leadership positions had a higher representation in the 1963 Central Committee. Furthermore, with the sole exception of mass organizations, the proportion of younger functionaries in top positions increased in all organizations for the 1963 Central Committee.

4. Analysis of mobility: It was established that changes for the period 1958–1963 affected primarily those Central Committee members and candidates whose primary occupation was in the state apparatus, rather than those who belonged to the SED leadership group in the stricter sense. Thus, trends of change in top state bodies are balanced by continuity at the highest echelons of the party.

These findings give rise to a question basic to this study. What is the representation in the 1958 and 1963 Central Committees of younger economically and agriculturally trained functionaries, or those entrusted with technical and administrative tasks in these fields?[61] In this section,

---

[61] Briefly referred to below as economic or agricultural functionaries.

Central Committee members and candidates are differentiated by their general biographies and respective primary functions, rather than by their individual characteristics. The following groups can be distinguished as pertaining more or less to the institutionalized counter elite, along the lines of the theoretical frame of reference developed in Chapter One: (1) economic functionaries in the narrower professional sense; and (2) economic functionaries in the broader sense, including party officials with economic agricultural tasks of a technical or administrative nature, and state officials with agricultural tasks of a technical or administrative nature.

Within these groups composition by age and changes for the period 1958–1963 will be considered, and further possible differentiations between these groups will be given. However, the results of our analysis of the institutionalized counter elite can be properly evaluated only when the groups which we have distinguished from this elite—party and state functionaries who are not holding economic or technical functions—are subjected to comparable analysis. (On the basis of our findings, the Politburo and the first secretaries of the SED *Bezirk* executive bodies should be distinguished from economic functionaries in both the narrower and broader professional sense. Therefore, a later subsection deals with trends of stability for forces traditionally rooted in the Central Committee.)

ECONOMIC FUNCTIONARIES IN THE NARROWER PROFESSIONAL SENSE

Here, analysis is limited to *economic functionaries,* in the strict sense, since those active in agriculture would not really add anything to the analysis, but would only broaden the area of discussion. Furthermore, the GDR has developed to the point where it is the second industrial power after the Soviet Union within COMECON. Consequently, agriculture is much less relevant than economy. In addition, the group of agricultural functionaries in the Central Committee is smaller than that of the economists. In the 1958 Central Committee there were altogether 12 members and 2 candidates who could be regarded as economic functionaries in the narrower sense (cf. Table 35).

Two economic functionaries in the 1958 Central Committee belonged to the younger generation: Wolfgang Schirmer, born in 1920, and

Table 35
Economic Functionaries* in the 1958 Central Committee

Name	Primary Function
Upper level:	
Luise Ermisch	Plant Director of the Garment VEB in Mühlhausen
Prof. Dr. Wolfgang Schirmer	Plant Director of the VEB Leuna-Werke "Walter Ulbricht" in Merseburg
Dr. Herbert Weiz	First Deputy Plant Director of the VEB "Carl Zeiss" in Jena
Upper middle:	
Prof. Dipl.-Ing. Brunolf Baade	Technical Director of VVB for Aviation Construction in Dessau
Fritz Bönisch	Plant Director of the Lignite VEB in Pfännerhall or Geiseltal-Mitte
Wolfgang Fabian	Plant Director of VEB "Karl Marx" in Magdeburg
Wilhelm Gsell	Plant Director of the VEB for Power Supply in Magdeburg
Walter Schuckert	Plant Director of the VEB for Loading and Transportation in Leipzig
Josef Wenig	Personnel Director of the General Management Board, Wismut
Erich Wirth	Director of the Patent Bureau for the VEB Aviation Plant in Dresden
Kurt Zierold	Plant Manager of the VEB for Anthracite "Deutschland" in Oelsnitz
Middle/Lower middle:	
Kurt Eydam	Foreman in the VEB "Modul" in Karl-Marx-Stadt
Berthold Kassler	Divisional Director in the VEB DEFA Copying Works in Berlin
Fritz Weber	Foreman in the VEB Construction Union in Leipzig

* Ascription to the various levels of the economic hierarchy was determined in accordance with the code on pp. 226-227.

Herbert Weiz, born in 1924. Both have completed formal professional schooling. Dr. Weiz is an engineer and economist and Prof. Dr. Schirmer achieved his *Habilitation* in chemistry. Schirmer and Weiz represent two of the biggest industrial enterprises in East Germany, the VEB Leuna-Werke "Walter Ulbricht" in Merseburg and the VEB "Carl Zeiss" in Jena. Of the group of economic functionaries only these two left the Central Committee between 1958 and 1963, and they may have been transferred to more responsible positions. In 1963 Wolfgang Schirmer was appointed as first chairman of the COMECON's Permanent Commission for Chemical Industry in Berlin. Herbert Weiz became State Secretary for Research and Technology. In addition, both Schirmer and Weiz act as deputies to the Chairman of the Research Council.

The successor to Wolfgang Schirmer at the VEB Leuna, Dr. Siegbert Löschau, and the new first deputy Plant Manager of the Zeiss-Werke, Ernst Gallerach (graduated in economics), were elected to the 1963 Central Committee as candidates. The Leuna and Zeiss plants were the only two enterprises represented in the 1958 and 1963 Central Committees by their directors or deputy directors, regardless of the person representing them (cf. Table 36).

Of the total of 19 economic functionaries in the 1963 Central Committee, 10 belong to the younger generation (born 1920–1929) or to our youngest group, that born after 1929. They are particularly noticeable in the group of leading economic functionaries (primary function 31). Only four economic functionaries of the 1958 Central Committee were taken into that of 1963 in the same occupational capacity: Bönisch, Ermisch, Eydam, and Wenig. Two others were transferred: Schirmer and Weiz, and one was transferred and descended professionally: Wirth. The other seven left the Central Committee without changes in their occupational careers.[62]

This indicates that with respect to the selection of economic functionaries for the 1963 Central Committee, different principles apparently applied than in 1958. Although the group of economic

[62] Except Wolfgang Fabian, about whose occupational position in 1963 no data could be obtained. The six remaining members and candidates holding equal or comparable positions who left the Central Committee in 1963 are Baade, Gsell, Kassler, Schuckert, Weber, and Zierold.

Table 36
Economic Functionaries* in the 1963 Central Committee

Name	Primary Function 1963†
Upper level:	
Luise Ermisch	Plant Director of the Garment VEB in Mühlhausen
Ernst Gallerach	1st Deputy Plant Manager of the VEB "Carl Zeiss" in Jena
Dr. Werner Hager	Plant Director of the VEB Petroleum Processing Plant Schwedt/Oder
Lorenz Lochthofen	Plant Director of the VEB Office Machinery in Sömmerda
Dr.-Ing. Siegbert Löschau	Plant Director of the VEB Leuna-Werke "Walter Ulbricht," Merseburg
Martin Markgraf	General Director of the VVB Regulating Technique, Instruments, and Optics, Berlin
Günter Prey	Director of Chemical Fibre Combine, Guben
Kurt Rödiger	General Director of the VVB Potash, Erfurt
Herbert Traut	General Director of the VVB Glass, Grossbreitenbach
Hans Warnke	Director of the Rostock Port Authority
Upper middle:	
Fritz Bönisch	Plant Director of the Lignite VEB, Geiseltal-Mitte
Renate Credo	Plant Director of the Potash Chemistry VEB, Berlin
Elisabeth Walther	Plant Director of the VEB United Hosiery Works "Esda," Auerbach/Erzgebirge
Joseph Wenig	Personnel Director of the General Management Board, Wismut
Friedrich Wesselburg	Workshop Director in the Roller Works VEB, Hettstedt
Middle/Lower middle:	
Kurt Eydam	Foreman in the VEB "Modul," Karl-Marx-Stadt
Martin Fischer	1st Smelter in the VEB Refined Steelworks, Freital
Peter Kamps	Chief Fitter in the VEB Bergmann Borsig, Berlin
Paul Strauss	Foreman in the VEB Residential Construction Combine, Rostock

* Ascription to the various levels of the economic hierarchy was determined according to the code on pp. 226-227.
† Changes in position after 1963, e.g., for Luise Ermisch, Ernst Gallerach, Siegbert Löschau, and Renate Credo, were not given.

functionaries in the Central Committee as such rose only from 14 members and candidates in 1958 to 19 in 1963, some changes are worth noting: (1) the above-mentioned rejuvenation; (2) the previously mentioned high fluctuation (of 14 economic functionaries in the 1958 Central Committee, 7 are no longer represented in 1963, whereas 14 were newly elected in 1963);[63] (3) the fact that the group of economic top functionaries (primary function 31) in particular has increased considerably from 3 to 10 Central Committee members and candidates in 1963; and (4) the shift in the ratio between members and candidates is as follows: among the 14 economic functionaries in the 1958 Central Committee there were 12 members and only 2 candidates, while 10 candidates and only 9 members represented this group in 1963.

This is supplemented by a few qualitative changes: The economic spheres represented by the relevant functionaries in the Central Committee differ. Apart from the representatives of the Leuna and Zeiss plants, who belonged to both Central Committees, the other functionaries in the 1958 Central Committee (insofar as they represent important branches of industry) come for the most part from heavy industry and the power industry: lignite (Bönisch), anthracite (Zierold), uranium mining (Wenig), power supply (Gsell), as well as the aeronautics industry, which was still regarded as having a future in the late fifties (Baade and Wirth).

In contrast, the selection of economic functionaries in 1963 proves that other spheres of the economy have been given higher priority. Some of the vital industries which were within the framework of COMECON agreements sent one or more representatives to the Central Committee: potash chemistry (Rödiger and Credo); control techniques, instrument making, and optics (Markgraf); office machines (Lochthofen); synthetic fibers (Prey); and steel processing (Wesselburg and Fischer).

The proportion of functionaries from the raw materials and heavy industries has dropped. The ranks of those representing the lignite industry (Bönisch) and uranium mining (Wenig) were augmented in 1963 only by Werner Hager, who represented the Petroleum Processing Works at Schwedt, and Peter Kamps from the VEB Bergmann-Borsig.

---

[63] A similarly high turnover is noticeable only among the agricultural functionaries.

Only three of the 80 VVB general directors[64] are represented in the 1963 Central Committee. This fact, plus the selection of an apparently limited number of representatives from important branches of industry by the SED, lead to the general conclusion that top economic functionaries need not necessarily be personally associated with the Central Committee.

The thesis of this study that, apart from educators and government functionaries, the proportion of economic officials has grown remarkably in the 1963 Central Committee must thus be modified. The increasing significance of economic functionaries in the Central Committee does not mean that the composition of the Central Committee has become more "economic." It should not be regarded even as a rough representational model, to the degree that the party includes all senior functionaries responsible for policy toward economic and social tasks in the Central Committee. Rather, the following questions should be asked: What is the representational concept implicit in the present social composition of the Central Committee? Do the members and candidates of the Central Committee largely reflect the social composition of the SED itself, the various elites within the framework of the ruling system, or the key groups in GDR society as a whole? These problems have already been touched upon in Chapter Two. With regard to changes in the social composition of the SED, we find that the Central Committee must represent all these groups. In addition, the most important economic spheres should be represented.

ECONOMIC FUNCTIONARIES IN THE BROADER PROFESSIONAL SENSE

Table 37 shows the proportion of party and state functionaries fulfilling economic and agricultural tasks while represented in the Central Committee. A comparison between 1958 and 1963 reveals practically no changes on all levels of the party apparatus. For a slight rise in the proportion of party functionaries in the Central Committee, an equally slight rise of economic functionaries can be noted. With respect to the biographies of party functionaries entrusted with economic and agricultural tasks, a comparison between 1958 and 1963 does not contradict

[64] In 1968, so far as is known, there were about 110 to 120 VVBs (Associations of Nationally Owned Enterprises).

Table 37
Economic and Agricultural Functionaries (in the Broader Sense) in the Central Committee (1958 and 1963)

Position* Party/State functionaries with . . . sphere of activity	Central Committee 1958				Central Committee 1963			
	Top	Upper Middle	Middle Middle	Total	Top	Upper Middle	Middle Middle	Total
Party functionaries	16	23	8	47	13	28	12	53
of these:								
entrusted with party administration (party functionaries in the narrow sense)	7	18	6	31	6	22	6	34
with professional party task	9	5	2	16	7	6	6	19
of these:								
with economic tasks	2	1	0	3	2	1	1	4
with agricultural tasks	2	0	1	3	2	0	1	3
State functionaries	26	9	5	40	37	4	11	52
of these:								
with administrative tasks (officials in the narrow sense)	14	5	2	21	16	1	5	22
with professional tasks	12	4	3	19	21	3	6	30
of these:								
entrusted with economic tasks	6	2	3	11	10	2	1	13
with agricultural tasks	1	0	0	1	2	0	3	5

* See the code on pp. 226-227.

this thesis. Among party functionaries with economic tasks in 1958, Erich Apel and Günter Mittag belonged to the younger generation with acquired professional training: Apel graduated as a machine construction engineer with the degree of Dr. rer. oec. in 1960 from the Economic Faculty of Humboldt University. Mittag is a railway expert and a graduate economist of the Transport Academy "Friedrich List" (Dresden 1958) with the title of Dr. rer. oec. Compared with Apel, Mittag, who is ten years younger, is more strongly entrenched in the party apparatus. A third economic functionary in the party apparatus is Ernst Lange, long-time director of the Section for Commerce, Supply and Foreign Trade in the Central Committee. Born in 1905, he is a veteran party functionary apparently distinguished by his professional success. Mittag and Lange remained in their posts in 1963, while Apel was appointed Chairman of the State Planning Commission. The Economic Commission of the Politburo previously directed by Apel was taken over by Mittag as director of the Bureau of Industry and Construction as well as Central Committee Secretary for Economic Affairs.

The following persons for the first time entered the group of economic experts from the party apparatus in the Central Committee of 1963: Werner Jarowinsky as Secretary for Commerce and Supply (also a qualified member of the younger generation as a graduate economist with the degree Dr. rer. oec.), and Bruno Baum as Director of the Bureau of Industry and Construction of the SED *Bezirk* executive for Potsdam, by occupation an electrician who acquired his training while occupying various positions in the party and state apparatus. At the Seventh SED Congress in April 1967 he was introduced as an electrical engineer.

Economic tasks at the top level of the party apparatus have been—as regards the members and candidates of the Central Committees between 1958 and 1963—clearly delegated to younger experts. A similar trend, with certain limitations, can be noted for the agricultural sphere since 1963. This became pronounced after Erich Mückenberger's exit from the Central Committee apparatus. Gerhard Grüneberg and Erich Rübensam, who were entrusted with agricultural tasks in the Secretariat of the Central Committee and the Politburo in 1963, also belong to the younger generation. In contrast to Rübensam, who is qualified (Dr. agrar. habil.) and has taught agricultural science at Humboldt University for some years, Grüneberg did not complete any studies.

Table 37 shows that the proportion of state officials who are given economic (agricultural), technical, and administrative responsibilities and are members and candidates of the Central Committee is considerably higher in 1958 and in 1963 that that of party officials. In addition, the absolute number of state functionaries simultaneously belonging to the Central Committee did increase greatly, but the relationship of functionaries with economic and agricultural tasks to other officials—primarily at the top level of the government apparatus—has not changed substantially.

If we examine the biographies of the respective incumbents, we find that quantitative data do not suffice to determine the extent of this development. The six leading state economic functionaries of 1958 all belong to the generation born before 1910. Only two appear in the 1963 Central Committee in the same positions, Erwin Kramer and Willy Rumpf. This functional area was further represented in 1963 by five members of the younger generation (Scholz, Schürer, Sölle, Wittik, Wyschofsky), as well as by Erich Apel (born in 1917), Alfred Neumann from the party apparatus, and Julius Balkow, who appears in the Central Committee for the first time in 1963. The group of those Central Committee members and candidates occupying high economic or agricultural offices in the state became much younger in the wake of the Central Committee's enlargement from 1958 to 1963.

The professional qualifications of the group have also risen. However, the changes in this respect are not so obvious as in the highest state body, the Council of Ministers. The thesis which is proved in section 8 of this chapter may be formulated here: when the highest functionaries of the state apparatus represented in the Central Committee are compared with top state officials who belong to the SED—but not to the Central Committee—the established trend toward change is less pronounced for the Central Committee group. Nevertheless, the trends of change that have been established are confirmed for the group of Central Committee members and candidates occupying top positions in the state. However, the total dynamism of this process becomes apparent only through detailed analysis of changes in the Council of Ministers.

Compared with the economic functionaries in the party apparatus, those in the state and the economy are clearly in the majority. This trend was further reinforced in 1963, compared to 1958, even though Mittag and Jarowinsky (the sole exponents of the party apparatus) have more influence than the leading state officials. Numerically speaking, the entry of younger and professionally trained economic functionaries into the Central Committee takes place more often via the state and economic apparatuses than the party. This thesis will be analyzed below with particular attention to the trend toward rejuvenation and professionalization in two key policy-making groups of the party apparatus: the Politburo and the first secretaries of the SED *Bezirk* executive.

7. Tendencies toward Stability in Groups Traditionally Based in the Central Committee

THE POLITBURO

It may be assumed that since Stalin's death in March 1953 and the Fifteenth Plenum of the SED Central Committee in the summer of 1953, actual political decision making has been concentrated in the Politburo.[65]. Therefore, that body, rather than the Central Committee Secretariat, will be examined here. Table 38 illustrates changes in the composition of the Politburo.

In 1963 the Politburo was composed of 14 members and 9 candidates; all of the latter were newly appointed that year. If we disregard the two members of the Politburo who died in 1958 and 1963 respectively, Heinrich Rau and Wilhelm Pieck, changes took place only at the candidate level. Of the 14 members 10 had belonged to this body for many years and 4 were already members or candidates of the Politburo in 1958.

None of the 14 members was born after 1920 and all are veteran functionaries of the KPD or SPD. Only two were entrusted with economic policy: Neumann and Leuschner. (The latter died in 1964.)

[65] See Carola Stern, *Porträt einer bolschewistischen Partei. Entwicklung, Funktion and Situation der SED* (Cologne, 1957), p. 272.

Table 38
Members (M) and Candidates (C) of the Politburo (1954–1963)

Name	Politburo		
	1954	1958	1963
Apel			C
Axen			C
Bartsch			C
Daumann		C	
Ebert	M	M	M
Ermisch		C	
Ewald, G.			C
Fröhlich		C	M
Grotewohl	M	M	M
Grüneberg			C
Hager, K.		C	M
Honecker, E.	C	M	M
Jarowinsky			C
Kurella		C	
Leuschner	C	M	M
Matern	M	M	M
Mewis		C	
Mittag			C
Mückenberger	C	M	M
Müller, M.			C
Neumann	C	M	M
Norden		M	M
Oelssner	M		
Pieck	M	M	
Pisnik		C	
Rau	M	M	
Schirdewan	M		
Sindermann			C
Stoph	M	M	M
Ulbricht	M	M	M
Verner, P.		C	M
Warnke, Herbert	C	M	M

Both were active mainly in the state apparatus. Neumann, formerly Chairman of the National Economic Council, has been Minister for the Supply Economy since the end of 1965 or the beginning of 1966.

The candidates differ markedly from full members. The oldest, Horst Sindermann, was born in 1915. He can be regarded as a party functionary of the middle generation with his roots in the apparatus. Hermann Axen (born in 1916) is a career functionary of the middle generation, while Erich Apel (born in 1917) belongs to the intermediate generation of technicians, who joined the SED at a relatively late date (after 1952). The candidates include the economic triumvirate that emerged between 1963 and 1965: Apel, Jarowinsky and Mittag; as well as Karl-Heinz Bartsch, an agricultural expert active in the state apparatus who had been deprived of his offices as early as February 1963. Finally, there are two agricultural functionaries rooted in the party apparatus: Georg Ewald and Grüneberg.

In this context, various criteria that characterize the Politburo as a strategic clique in the sense defined in this study can be set forth.

Within the group there exists a formal hierarchic differentiation based on the traditions of a secret society—a differentiation essential for understanding many of the present-day Communist parties. The members of the Politburo appear to constitute the actual political core. They form a politically decisive subgroup within the strategic clique, distinct from the Politburo candidates. The members of the Politburo should be regarded as a relatively homogeneous group, not with respect to their political outlook, but from the point of view of their "clique morality."

The concept of the strategic clique has not been developed merely because it follows the traditions of Communist parties; it also implies for us careful evaluation of the so-called institutionalized counter elite. At the highest level of the party apparatus this counter elite includes the 1963 Politburo candidates, with the exception of Sindermann, Axen, Georg Ewald, and Grüneberg. The fact that this specific counter elite registered advances even in the Politburo between 1958 and 1964 can be confirmed by a comparison with candidates elected to the Politburo in 1958. None of the 1958 Politburo candidates can be regarded as an economic expert associated with the party or state. For the most part they did not issue from the younger generation. Consequently, the changes in the social composition of the SED extended only to the threshold of the Politburo, and that only in 1963. At this point a safety barrier blocked all further advances; this can be explained in terms of an isolated "in-group" mentality of the leadership: No member of the counter elite is a full member of the Politburo.

At the Thirteenth Plenum of the Central Committee in September 1966 Günter Mittag was appointed a member of the Politburo (*Neues Deutschland, September 18, 1966, p. 1*). He has thus become the first representative of the institutionalized counter elite admitted to the Sanctum Sanctorum of the strategic clique. It is still impossible to decide whether this constitutes an integration and thus a loss of power on the part of the opposition. Nevertheless, it is remarkable that Günter Mittag publicly aired, in various speeches since the Thirteenth Plenum, questions of ideology and foreign policy rather than economics.

THE FIRST SECRETARIES OF THE SED *Bezirk* EXECUTIVES REPRESENTED IN THE CENTRAL COMMITTEE
Among the *Bezirk* secretaries of 1958, ten can be regarded as veterans and all have held their positions since 1952–1953 (cf. Table 39):
1. Hans Kiefert from 1953–1959 has been First Secretary in Erfurt and then in Berlin.
2. Bernard Koenen started as First Secretary of the KPD or SED *Land*[66] executive for Sachsen-Anhalt and since 1958 has been First Secretary of the SED *Bezirk* executive for Halle. From 1953–1958 his activity as First Secretary was interrupted while he served as chief of the East German diplomatic mission (later, the embassy) in Czechoslovakia.
3. Walter Buchheim was First Secretary of the SED *Bezirk* executive for Karl-Marx-Stadt from 1952 to 1959.

[66] In the GDR, from 1945 to 1952, the administrative units below the national or state level were called *Länder*. There were five such *Länder* in East Germany: Brandenburg, Mecklenburg, Sachsen, Sachsen-Anhalt, and Thüringen. In 1952 the *Länder* were dissolved and merged into 15 *Bezirke:* Cottbus, Dresden, Erfurt, Frankfurt-on-the-Oder, Gera, Halle, Leipzig, Karl-Marx-Stadt, Magdeburg, Neu-brandenburg, Potsdam, Rostock, Schwerin, and Suhl; East Berlin also was assigned the status of a *Bezirk*. Besides these 15 *Bezirke* there is the *Gebiet* Wismut, which is sometimes referred to as an additional *Bezirk* of the GDR. The SED was first organized along the lines of the *Länder;* in 1952 it established one *Gebiet* and 15 *Bezirk* party executives.

Table 39
First Secretaries of the SED *Bezirk* Executives Represented in the Central Committee (1958 and 1963)

Bezirk	Central Committee 1958	Central Committee 1963
Berlin	Kiefert	P. Verner*
Cottbus	—	Stief
Dresden	Reuter	Krolikowski
Erfurt	Bräutigam	Bräutigam
Frankfurt-on-the-Oder	Götzl	Mückenberger
Gera	—	Ziegenhahn
Halle	B. Koenen	Sindermann
Karl-Marx-Stadt	Buchheim	Roscher
Leipzig	Fröhlich	Fröhlich
Magdeburg	Pisnik	Pisnik
Neubrandenburg	Steffen	—
Potsdam	Seibt	Seibt
Rostock	Mewis	Tisch
Schwerin	Quandt	Quandt
Suhl	Funke	Funke
Wismut	Weihs	—

* Verner is also a CC secretary, not belonging to the upper middle, but to the very top of the party apparatus.

4. Paul Fröhlich has been First Secretary of the SED *Bezirk* executive for Leipzig since 1952.

5. Alois Pisnik has been First Secretary of the SED *Bezirk* executive for Magdeburg since 1952.

6. Max Steffen was First Secretary of the SED *Bezirk* executive for Neubrandenburg until 1960.

7. Kurt Seibt was First Secretary of the SED *Bezirk* executive for Potsdam from 1952 to 1964.

8. Karl Mewis was First Secretary of the SED *Bezirk* executive for Rostock from 1952 to 1961.

9. Bernhard Quandt has been First Secretary of the SED *Bezirk* executive for Schwerin since 1952.

10. Otto Funke was First *Bezirk* Secretary for Gera from 1952 to 1955 and for Suhl since 1955.

The youngest among these veterans is Otto Funke, born in 1915. Only Bernhard Quandt can be regarded as having acquired expertise, during his brief stint as Minister of Agriculture from 1948 to 1951. In 1958 only four other cadres who were promoted to second or first SED *Bezirk* secretaries in 1954 and 1955 joined the group of veteran functionaries. These include two members of the younger generation: Rolf Weihs (born in 1920) and Eduard Götzl (born in 1921). Götzl was long active in the steel industry; from 1951 to 1954 he was plant manager of the Steel Rolling Mills in Brandenburg.

Among the group of first secretaries represented in the Central Committee in 1958, six still occupied this post in the Central Committee of 1963: Paul Fröhlich, Alois Pisnik, Kurt Seibt, Bernhard Quandt, Otto Funke, and Alois Bräutigam. All are veteran functionaries. Among the other eight, who were not admitted to the Central Committee until 1963, four were born before 1920 and four between 1920 and 1929. Among these, Harry Tisch rates mention. He may have acquired expert knowledge while Secretary for Economic Policy in the SED *Bezirk* executive for Rostock. Two other functionaries were active in agriculture within the party: Erich Mückenberger, Central Committee Secretary for Agriculture from 1953 to 1960, and Paul Roscher, Secretary for Agriculture of the SED *Bezirk* executive for Erfurt, 1955-1958.

The first secretaries of the SED *Bezirk* executives represented in the Central Committee have thus not been affected in the general rejuvenation and professionalization of the party apparatus. A similar trend can be observed when comparing all party functionaries of the upper middle belonging to the Central Committee (primary function 12): of a total of 28 with primary functions, 14 belonged to the younger generation in the 1963 Central Committee (cf. Table 17), while among the comparable group of 13 *Bezirk* secretaries[67] only four can be regarded as belonging to the younger group. Professional training or specific economic, technical, or agricultural knowledge could not be established for any of the first *Bezirk* secretaries. Only two of these officials represented in the Central Committee in 1958, and four in

[67] Except Paul Verner, who belongs to the top level of the party apparatus (primary function 11).

1963, could have acquired expert knowledge by virtue of previous activity in economics or agriculture.

The results of this analysis demonstrate that the first secretaries of the SED *Bezirk* executives—like Politburo members—should be regarded as members of the strategic clique. This subgroup appears even less "open" than the Politburo to the dynamics of economic and technical development.

A comparison of Politburo members and first secretaries of the SED *Bezirk* executives reveals a number of characteristics common to both groups. With regard to the fact that many first secretaries are represented as members or candidates in the Politburo, and that ascent from the executive of a *Bezirk* secretariat to the Politburo is relatively easy, the heads of the *Bezirk* secretariats and the Politburo can be regarded as the main subgroups of the strategic clique in this context.

8. The Relation between Party and State Apparatus in the Light of Social Change (1954 to 1965/1966)

In section 7 of this chapter it was established that the difference between the party and state apparatuses must be sought primarily in the increasing "professionalization" of the latter organizational system. A phenomenon apparent throughout East German society can therefore be observed with particular clarity at certain focal points. How do these differences affect the traditional relationships between party and state apparatuses in the GDR? This problem is dealt with below. The scope of this study limits analysis to overlapping memberships in the Peoples' Chamber and the Central Committee, in the Council of Ministers and the Central Committee, and in the State Council and the Central Committee.

MEMBERSHIP IN THE PEOPLES' CHAMBER AND THE CENTRAL COMMITTEE
In this section the Central Committees of 1954, 1958, and 1963 are related to the respective Peoples' Chambers for each year (cf. Table 40). Of the 135 Central Committee members and candidates in 1954, 49 (19 percent) were also members of the Peoples' Chamber in that year. In both 1958 and 1963 the proportion of Central Committee members and candidates in the Peoples' Chamber rose to 26 percent. The

Table 40
The Number of CC Members and Candidates in the Peoples' Chamber (1954, 1958, and 1963)

	Members including the Berlin representatives Total	of these SED Members	of these CC Members and Candidates	
			absolute number of members and candidates	% in reference to the SED fraction
Peoples' Chamber of October 1954	466	258	49 (41 + 8)	19
Peoples' Chamber of November 1958	466	258	68 (61 + 7)	26
Peoples' Chamber of October 1963	500	292	76 (68 + 8)	26

absolute number of Central Committee members and candidates in the Peoples' Chamber rose in 1963, compared with 1958, since after the Peoples' Chamber was enlarged the SED fraction as a whole rose by 34 to a total of 292 persons. When the Council of Ministers is included in this comparison a counter trend is apparent with regard to overlapping membership: Only in the Peoples' Chamber did the number of members and candidates rise between 1954 and 1963 from approximately 11 percent (1954) to 15 percent in 1958 and 1963.

It is impossible to characterize exhaustively the group of members and candidates who hold overlapping memberships in the Central Committee and the Peoples' Chamber. Since the latter is constitutionally classified—although not in reality—among the political decision-making bodies of the GDR, our analysis can be broken off at this point.[68]

MEMBERSHIP IN THE COUNCIL OF MINISTERS AND
THE CENTRAL COMMITTEE

In recent years the Council of Ministers has gained in importance. In the formal sense it is the second-ranking body and subject to the

[68] For the detailed development of the Peoples' Chamber, especially in contrast with the Bundestag, see Mersch, "Volksvertreter in West und Ost."

decisions of the Peoples' Chamber. Since the introduction of the "new economic system" in 1963, the Council of Ministers has been restructured and has become one of the most important executive organs of the Politburo and the State Council in all economic affairs. The tasks of the Council of Ministers and its presidium have been repeatedly redefined. Recently, its sphere of activity was outlined in detail in the State Council decree "On the Planning and Direction of the National Economy by the Council of Ministers," in the "Law on the Council of Ministers," and in the "Directive for the New Economic System of Planning and Direction of the National Economy."[69] In his speech to the Seventh SED Congress, Prime Minister Willi Stoph demanded that the Council of Ministers concentrate "primarily upon economic prognostications for the decisive branches, upon the further development of planning and direction, as well as upon fulfillment of the overall program of the plan and the annual plans in the most important spheres."[70] Ulbricht emphasized three primary functions of the Council of Ministers in his speech to the Second Central Committee Plenum in July 1967: The Council of Ministers was to develop an "economic strategy for the GDR" and set up economic prognoses; it was to "completely mold the economic system of socialism"; and it was to control the implementation of its strategy in detail.[71] These primary functions by no means exhaust the sphere of activities of this body. In its decree of December 22, 1965 the Council of Ministers set forth its functions as follows:

Ensuring the highest possible increase in the national income as well as its suitable usage; developing science and technology of the greatest economic use for society and its purposeful and systematic application to the national economy in order to raise the productivity of labor in society.

[69] "Erlass des Staatsrates der Deutschen Demokratischen Republik über die Planung und Leitung der Volkswirtschaft durch den Ministerrat," dated February 11, 1963, in *GBl. der DDR. Teil I* (1963): 1 ff: "Gesetz über den Ministerrat der Deutschen Demokratischen Republik," dated April 17, 1963, in ibid., pp. 89 ff; and "Richtlinie für das neue ökonomische System," dated July 11, 1963, in *GBl. der DDR. Teil II* (1963): 453 ff.

[70] "Die Durchführung der volkswirtschaftlichen Aufgaben. Aus dem Referat des Genossen Willi Stoph, auf dem VII. Parteitag der Sozialistischen Einheitspartei Deutschlands," *Die Wirtschaft* 22, no. 17 (1967): 5.

[71] Konstituierung der staatlichen Organe und Probleme ihrer wissenschaftlichen Arbeitsweise. Referat des Genossen Walter Ulbricht auf der 2. Tagung des ZK," *Neues Deutschland,* July 8, 1967.

Determining the optimum structure of the economy.

Developing foreign economic relationships, particularly with the USSR and other COMECON countries, as an economically and technically integrating component of planned and proportional productive processes, the economically most effective direction of investments as the core of expanded socialist production.

Embodying the uniform socialist educational system for developing personalities with high general qualifications

Developing the material and cultural conditions of life for the people in accordance with the requirements of increased socialist reproduction.[72]

The most important individual decisions of the Council of Ministers between 1963 and 1966 dealt almost exclusively with problems of economic organization. This applies, for example, to the October 1963 decision "Development of the Chemical Industry in the GDR, Particularly Crude Oil Processing and Petrochemistry," the January 1964 decision "On the Directing of Chemical Plant Construction and Establishing Relevant Committees," and, furthermore, to the guidelines established by the Council of Ministers for developing the following branches of industry: metallurgy, electronic components and instruments, techniques of plant management, indices, programming and regulation, the program for developing machine tool construction, the glass and ceramic industries, and the potash industry.[73]

In accordance with these duties, the Council of Ministers had to cooperate closely with the most important executive organs in the economy. Thus, regular consultations were held with representatives of the National Economic Council and, after the dissolution of the latter, with the industrial ministries,[74] as well as with the Ministry of Construction. A close relationship also exists between the Council of Ministers and the State Planning Commission, as well as the Central Administration for Statistics. The influence of the latter on the Council of Ministers has probably increased since the Seventh SED Congress, whereas the

---

[72] See Rudi Rost, "Die führende Rolle der SED bei der Entwicklung des sozialistischen Staates und Rechts in der Deutschen Demokratischen Republik," *Staat und Recht* 15, no. 5 (May, 1966): 739.

[73] In connection with the decisions of October 1963 and January 1964, see Willi Stoph, *Aufgaben and Arbeitsweise des Ministerrates im neuen ökonomischen System der Planung und Leitung der Volkswirtschaft* (Berlin, 1964), pp. 17 ff. In the present context, see *Handbuch der Deutschen Demokratischen Republik* (Berlin, 1964), p. 210.

[74] See Chapter One, note 5 (p. 9).

role of the State Planning Commission as "the economic general staff for the Council of Ministers" (Ulbricht) should be regarded as weakened after Ulbricht's sharp criticism of this body at the Second Central Committee Plenum in July, 1967.

The functional description of the Council of Ministers will be followed by discussion of the membership of this body and the Central Committee. Before analyzing these overlapping memberships, we propose to survey the Central Committee members and candidates represented in the Council of Ministers. Table 41 shows that the proportion of Central Committee members and candidates in the Council of Ministers has not changed substantially between 1958 and 1963. Barely half the members in the Council of Ministers were also represented in the Central Committee. In contrast, the ratio changed suddenly for the restructured and expanded Council of Ministers at the beginning of

Table 41
The Number of CC Members and Candidates in the Council of Ministers (1954, 1958, 1963, and 1965/66)

	Members of the CM	of these SED Members	of these CC Members and Candidates	
			absolute number of members and candidates	proportion in the CM
Council of Ministers November 1954	27	19	11 (9 + 2)	41%
Council of Ministers December 1958	23	19	11 (11 + 0)	48%
Council of Ministers November 1963	38	30	19 (19 + 0)	50%
Council of Ministers after 11th plenum of the CC 1965/1966	49	43	19 (16 + 3*)	39%

* Of these three candidates in the 1963 CC two advanced to full membership between 1963 and 1966: Löschau and Wittik were thus already members of the CC when admitted to the Council of Ministers.

1966. At present, a bare 39 percent of the membership of the Council of Ministers also belong to the Central Committee, despite the fact that the proportion of SED members has increased in the Council of Ministers.

A detailed investigation of this phenomenon made it advisable to analyze Central Committee members and candidates who belonged to the Council of Ministers, as well as those in the Council of Ministers who belonged to the SED, but not to the Central Committee. Changes in 1967 are included.

CENTRAL COMMITTEE MEMBERS IN THE COUNCIL OF MINISTERS

Table 42 reveals that of the 19 functionaries who are members both of the Council of Ministers during 1965–1966 and of the 1963 Central Committee:

Six have been members of the Council of Ministers and the Central Committee for a long time: Alexander Abusch, since 1961 Deputy Chairman of the Council of Ministers; Dr. Hilde Benjamin, Minister of Justice, 1953–July 1967; Dr. Erwin Kramer, Minister of Transport since 1954; Erich Mielke, Minister of State Security since 1957; Willy Rumpf, Minister of Finance, 1955–December 1966; and Willi Stoph, since 1952 Minister of the Interior, then of National Defense, later active in other leading government positions, and since 1964 Chairman of the Council of Ministers and Deputy Chairman of the State Council.

Ten newcomers to the 1963 Council of Ministers, who had become ministers between 1959 and 1963. Of these, five had belonged to the Central Committee for a longer period as members or candidates: Heinz Hoffmann, Minister of National Defense since 1960; Margot Honecker, Minister of National Education since 1963; Alfred Neumann, Chairman of the National Economic Council (dissolved in 1965) from 1961 to 1965, since March 1965 Deputy Chairman of the Council of Ministers, and since December 1965 Minister for the Supply Economy and Deputy Chairman of the Council of Ministers; Dr. Herbert Weiz, State Secretary for Research and Technology since 1962, and Deputy Chairman of the Council of Ministers since July 1967; Dr. Margarete Wittkowski, since 1961 Deputy Chairman of the Council of Ministers, previously Deputy Chairman of the State Planning Commission, and since July 1967 President of the Central Bank of (East) Germany and no longer a member of the Council of Ministers. Another five entered the Central Committee in 1963 and the Council of Ministers between 1959 and 1963: Julius Balkow, since 1961 Minister for Foreign and Inter-German Trade, and since March 1965 Deputy Chairman of the Council of Ministers; Georg Ewald (Minister and) Chairman of the Agricultural Council of the GDR since 1963; Heinz Matthes, since 1963 (Minister and) Chairman of the Committee of the Workers' and Peasants'

Table 42
The Members and Candidates of the Central Committee in the Council of Ministers (1954–1965/66)

CC Members and Candidates who also belong to the CM	Central Committee*			Council of Ministers†			
	1954	1958	1963	1954	1958	1963	1965/66
Abusch		M	M		X	X	X
Apel		C	M			X	
Balkow			M			X	X
Becher	M	M		X			
Benjamin	M	M	M	X	X	X	X
G. Ewald			M			X	X
Grotewohl	M	M	M	X	X	X	
Hoffmann	M	M	M			X	X
M. Honecker	C	C	M			X	X
Kramer	M	M	M	X	X	X	X
F. Lange	C			X			
Leuschner	M	M	M	X	X	X	
Löschau			C				X
Maron	M	M	M		X		
Matthes			M			X	X
Mielke	M	M	M		X	X	X
Neumann	M	M	M			X	X
Rau	M	M		X	X		
Rumpf	C	C	M	X	X	X	X
Schürer			M			X	X
Selbmann	M			X			
Sölle			C				X
Stoph	M	M	M	X	X	X	X
Ulbricht	M	M	M	X	X		
Weiz		M	M			X	X
Winzer	M	M	M				X
Wittik			C			X	X
Wittkowski	M	C	M			X	X

* M = Member of CC; C = Candidate of CC.
† X denotes membership in the Council of Ministers.

Inspectorate; Gerhard Schürer, since 1963 Deputy Chairman and since December 1965 Chairman of the State Planning Commission, and since July 1967 also Deputy Chairman of the Council of Ministers; and Johann Wittik, since 1963 First Deputy Chairman of the National Economic Council and since December 1965 Minister of Light Industry. Three functionaries were first represented in the Council of Ministers since 1965–1966. They include two Central Committee candidates, one of whom (Löschau) became a member, as well as a longtime Central Committee member (Winzer): Dr. Siegbert Löschau, since December 1965 Minister of the Chemical Industry and a member of the Presidium of the Council of Ministers, was replaced in May 1966 by Günther Wyschofsky and in September 1966 ousted from the Central Committee of the SED for reasons of "disreputable conduct"; Horst Sölle, since 1965 Minister of Foreign and Inter-German Trade, and since July 1967 Minister of Foreign Economy; and Otto Winzer, Minister of Foreign Affairs since June 1965.

The seven new 1963 Central Committee members and candidates who became ministers between early 1959 and 1966[75] belonged to the younger generation, except for Balkow. They were all born in the 1920s. The five state officials in this group are known to be professionally qualified. The other two, Schürer and Wittik, distinguished themselves by extended activity in expert bodies: Gerhard Schürer, originally a mechanic, has been sector chief for planning in the planning and finance section of the SED Central Committee Apparatus since 1955. From 1961–1962 he was the director of this section, and until 1962 Deputy Chairman, and from 1963 First Deputy Chairman of the State Planning Commission. At the Seventh SED Congress (April 1967) he was presented as a social sciences graduate. Johann Wittik, originally a weaver, was with the Ministry of Light Industry as the director of the technology division in 1952, then the First Deputy Chairman of the Head Office for the Textile Industries, and later Deputy Minister. From 1958 to 1961 he was First Chairman of the *Bezirk* Economic Council in Gera, and in 1961 he became Deputy Chairman and in November 1963 First Deputy Chairman of the National Economic Council. He recently obtained his diploma as a textile engineer. Consequently, the state functionaries who were admitted to the Central Committee in 1963, and to the Council of

---

[75] These are Balkow, G. Ewald, Matthes, Schürer, Wittik, Löschau, and Sölle, all of whom except Löschau also sat on the reduced Council of Ministers of 1967 and, again with the exception of Löschau, became members or a candidate (Sölle) of the Central Committee at the Seventh SED Congress.

Ministers between 1959 and 1965–1966, can for the most part be regarded as professionally qualified representatives of the younger generation, engaged mostly in technical or economic activities.

SED MEMBERS IN THE COUNCIL OF MINISTERS

The rise of the younger, professionally qualified generation in the Council of Ministers during 1965–1966 becomes clearer upon examination of the age, acquired occupation, primary function, or professional career of the 24 members of the Council of Ministers during 1965–1966, who were members of the SED without belonging to the Central Committee. All of them had joined the Council of Ministers between 1963 and 1966. Of these 24 ministers, 18 belonged to the generation born in 1920 and after. Among them 8 were actually born between 1929 and 1931, and were approximately 35 years old when admitted to the Council of Ministers.

Five of the eighteen younger SED members in the Council have economic or technical training at the technical college or university level and therefore can be regarded as economic functionaries in the narrower sense:

Arno Donda, born in 1930, member of the Council of Ministers from July 1963 to July 1967, long-time employee, since 1963 Director of the Central Administration for Statistics, graduate economist and Dr. rer. oec., since 1959 Director of the Institute for Statistics at the University of Economics, Berlin-Karlshorst, and since 1963 Professor of Statistics.

Rudi Georgi, born in 1927, since December 1965 Minister for the Construction of Processing Machinery and Vehicles, formerly General Director of VVB Iron, Sheet Metal and Metal Wares, graduate of industrial commerce, correspondence graduate of economics, and Dr. rer. oec.

Karl Grünheid, born in 1931, from March 1963 to July 1967 member of the Council of Ministers, formerly Director General of Equipment for VVB Heavy Industry and Gear Works, First Deputy Chairman of the State Planning Commission (responsible for annual planning), and a graduate of economic training.

Wolfgang Junker, born in 1929, since February 1963 Minister of Construction, formerly director of VEB Excavation and Conveyance in Berlin, as well as director of VEB Industrial Construction in Brandenburg, since 1961 State Secretary in the Ministry of Construction, and by profession a mason and construction engineer.

Helmut Lilie, born in 1923, since December 1965 Minister and First Deputy Chairman of the State Planning Commission (responsible for project planning), for many years a chemist in the German Office for Testing Materials and Product Analysis, since 1961 President of this authority, graduate chemist, Dr. rer. nat. habil., and since 1967 no longer in the Council of Ministers.

Among the younger ministers who were not members or candidates of the Central Committee, but who belonged to the SED in 1963 or 1965–1966, a further subgroup rates emphasis. This is composed of economic functionaries in the narrower sense who are not graduates of universities, but who qualified for economic tasks in the course of their professional careers:

Otfried Steger, born in 1926, since December 1965 Minister of Electro-Technical Industries and Electronics, rose from skilled blue-collar worker to electrical engineer and labor economist, since 1959 General Director of the VVB Electrical Planning and Construction, and in 1963–1965 head of the electrotechnical division of the National Economic Council.

Gerhard Zimmermann, born in 1927, since December 1965 Minister of Heavy Machinery and Plant Construction, formerly General Director of the Shipbuilding VVB in Rostock, a professional shipbuilder who acquired his foreman's papers and in July 1967 completed courses in marine engineering.

The economic functionaries in the narrower sense are reinforced by state officials of the younger generation who deal largely with economic and technical affairs. Most of them have had professional training.

Walter Halbritter, born in 1927, since December 1965 member of the Council of Ministers and director of its Office for Price Control, active for many years in the party and state apparatuses (Ministry of Finance, State Planning Commission) and graduate economist.

Erhard Krack, born in 1930, since December 1965 Minister for the Bezirk-directed Industries and Foodstuffs, previously (since 1963) Chairman of the Economic Council in the Rostock Bezirk, and graduate economist.

Wolfgang Rauchfuss, born in 1931, since December 1965 Deputy Chairman of the Council of Ministers, since 1962 Deputy Minister of Foreign and Inter-German Trade, by profession a mechanic, and a graduate economist.

Fritz Scharfenstein, born in 1925, since December 1965 Minister of the Guidance and Control of Bezirk and Kreis Councils, previous activity in the State most recently as Deputy Chairman of the State Planning Commission, white-collar worker, during 1952–1956 studied the economics of domestic trade; in July 1967 graduate economist.

Klaus Siebold, born in 1930, since December 1965 Minister of the Raw

Materials Industry, started as a party functionary, was for many years director of the GDR coal industry (State Planning Commission), by profession a miner and mining engineer (Freiberg Mining Academy).

The following economic functionaries (in the broader sense) have no formal training but have had extensive experience in economic or technical affairs within the state apparatus:

Helmut Dietrich, born in 1922, a long-term employee, and President of the Central Bank of (East) Germany from 1964 to 1967, when he was replaced by Dr. Margarete Wittkowski.

Helmut Koch, born in 1928, from February 1963 to 1967 a member of the Council of Ministers, long-time agricultural functionary in the state apparatus, and from 1962 to 1967 Chairman of the State Procurement Committee for Agricultural Products in the Council of Ministers.

Günther Sieber, born in 1930, since March 1965 Minister of Trade and Food Supply, a long-time co-worker of Erich Apel in the State Planning Commission, and by profession a forestry expert.

Another functionary entrusted with agricultural tasks, who has risen via the party apparatus, belongs to the group of younger SED officials in the Council of Ministers entrusted with economic problems. He is Heinz Kuhrig, born in 1929, First Deputy to the Chairman of the Agricultural Council, with a degree in agricultural economics, and in the Council of Ministers from June 1963 to 1967.

Another qualified functionary with roots in the FDGB is Hellmuth Geyer, born in 1920, from December 1965 to 1967 in the Council of Ministers, Director of the State Office of Labor and Wages, and graduate in the social sciences.

Among the eighteen younger SED members admitted to the Council of Ministers between 1963 and 1966, and not in the Central Committee in 1963, only one has no economic or technical task or corresponding training or experience. He is Joachim Herrmann, born in 1928, since December 1965 State Secretary for All-German Affairs (now West German Affairs), formerly editor-in-chief of the FDJ publication *Junge Welt* and of the *Berliner Zeitung,* and since 1967 no longer in the Council of Ministers.

Some of the remaining six SED members admitted to the Council of Ministers between 1963 and 1966 and born between 1910 and 1919 should also be regarded as experts. They include three economic functionaries: Dr. Kurt Fichtner, Minister of Ore Mining, Metallurgy, and Potash from December 1965 to July 1967 (replaced at that date by Dr.

Kurt Singhuber), and promoted in July 1967 to Deputy Chairman of the Council of Ministers. For many years he was the expert on the potash industry at the National Economic Council. Erich Markowitsch, since December 1965 Director of the newly established State Office for Professional Training, is an expert in mining and foundries. He belonged to the State Planning Commission and the National Economic Council, and was last active as First Deputy Chairman of the National Economic Council. He did not join the diminished Council of Ministers of 1967. Dr. Gerhard Weiss was from 1955 to 1965 Deputy Minister in the Ministry of Foreign and Inter-German Trade, since March 1965 Deputy Chairman of the Council of Ministers. He was formerly a white-collar worker with a higher degree in economics. Aside from the two experienced functionaries in cultural affairs. Ernst-Joachim Giessmann and Klaus Gysi, only one older SED member cannot be regarded as an expert in this sense: Minister of the Interior and Commander of the Peoples' Police Friedrich Dickel, who joined the Council of Ministers in November 1963.

Among the 24 members of the Council of Ministers in 1965–1966 who belonged to the SED but not to the Central Committee, 19 can thus be regarded as economic experts. Most of them joined the Council of Ministers only in 1963 and 1965–1966 and, except for two, were members of the younger generation.

Although the proportion of SED members in the Council of Ministers has risen compared with 1954, 1958, and 1963, the percentage of state or economic functionaries simultaneously represented in the "parliament" of the SED has dropped. The previous analysis (which distinguished Central Committee members from other SED members in the Council of Ministers formed in 1965-1966) revealed that the group of state officials newly admitted to both bodies in 1963 was composed almost exclusively of those who had professional training and talents and who belonged to the younger generation. On the other hand, among SED but not Central Committee members (who were accepted into the Council of Ministers in 1963 or 1965–1966), the younger qualified economists and technicians predominate too. Indeed, in contrast to the younger Central Committee members, a considerable proportion of the latter were born only in 1929, 1930, or 1931. Altogether, 25 of the

43 members of the Council of Ministers in 1965–1966 who were simultaneously members of the SED and in part of the Central Committee, belong to the group of younger professional functionaries.[76]

Since the Council of Ministers was proclaimed the "leading economic organ" at the beginning of 1963, and as a consequence of its continuing enlargement, a rise in the representation of largely younger economic managers has occurred. For the most part, these individual careers are not based in the party apparatus. Consequently, the Council of Ministers gained considerable independence vis-à-vis the Central Committee as a special bureaucracy in a class by itself.

At first sight this line of development seems contradicted by the pattern of appointments to the Council of Ministers in July 1967. Among the 39 members of the reduced Council, 25 are members or candidates of the Central Committee. The proportion of Central Committee members and candidates thus rose to approximately 65 percent. Fewer personnel changes occurred in the Council of Ministers itself. The high proportion of Central Committee members and candidates in the 1967 Council of Ministers should rather be attributed to the fact that seven ministers from the years 1965 to 1966 were accepted into the Central Committee in 1967: Dickel, Georgi, Halbritter, Junker, Rauchfuss, Steger, and Weiss. Furthermore, the two new ministers who had been appointed in the meantime also belonged to the 1967 Central Committee. Siegfried Böhm (since December 1966 Minister of Finance and successor to Willy Rumpf, a member of the Central Committee first in 1967) and Günther Wyschofsky (since May 1966 successor to

[76] These are the following eight Central Committee members or candidates: M. Honecker, Weiz, G. Ewald, Matthes, Schürer, Wittik, Löschau, and Sölle. Except for Löschau, they are all taken over into the 1967 Central Committee and the Ministerial Council of July 1967. To these should be added the following seventeen SED members: Donda, Georgi, Grünheid, Junker, Lilie, Steger, Zimmermann, Halbritter, Krack, Rauchfuss, Scharfenstein, Siebold, Dietrich, Koch, Sieber, Kuhrig, and Geyer. Seven of them (Donda, Grünheid, Lilie, Dietrich, Koch, Kuhrig, and Geyer) were not renominated when the Ministerial Council was cut down in 1967, nor did they become members or candidates of the 1967 Central Committee. Of the remaining ten ministers, five (Georgi, Junker, Steger, Halbritter, and Rauchfuss) became members or candidates of the Central Committee in April 1967 while the remaining five (Zimmermann, Krack, Scharfenstein, Siebold, and Sieber) were not admitted.

Siegbert Löschau, candidate member of the Central Committee in 1963 and full member since 1964). The following members and candidates of the Central Committee in 1963 no longer sit in the Council of Ministers of 1967: Hilde Benjamin (retired due to age), Siegbert Löschau (simultaneously excluded from the Central Committee because of "disreputable conduct"), and Margarete Wittkowski. Before the formation of the Council of Ministers in July 1967 all the Central Committee members or candidates represented in it were already members of the Council of Ministers.

The shift to greater representation of Central Committee members and candidates in the Council of Ministers of 1967 did not take place at the expense of the economic functionaries. Rather it appeared an extension of the trend already indicated by the rise of Günter Mittag to full membership of the Politburo: The strategic clique endeavored to "integrate" the representatives of the institutionalized counter elite. It remains to be seen whether the process of increased independence for the state apparatus vis-à-vis the party will be confirmed by these recent developments. The finding to which we shall limit ourselves at this stage (from analyzing the Council of Ministers within the framework of investigating the Central Committee) is that since the dissolution of the National Economic Council, the economy of the GDR has been increasingly directed by economic experts.

MEMBERSHIP IN THE STATE COUNCIL AND THE CENTRAL COMMITTEE

The relationship between the Central Committee and the State Council further illustrates the relationship between the Central Committee and the state apparatus (Table 43). Of the 155 Central Committee members and candidates in 1958 (and 1960), nine were also represented in the State Council in 1960,[77] i.e.: the majority of the thirteen SED members in the twenty-four-member State Council also belonged to the Central Committee in 1960.

Of the 181 Central Committee members and candidates in 1963, 10 were simultaneously members of the State Council that year—i.e.,

[77] The State Council was not established until September 1960. See the decree of September 12, 1960, "Gesetz über die Bildung des Staatsrates der Deutschen Demokratischen Republik," in *GBl. der DDR. Teil I* (1960): 505 ff.

Table 43
The Number of CC Members and Candidates in the State Council (1960 and 1963)

State Council Membership	Central Committee 1958			Central Committee 1963		
	Members	Candidates	Total	Members	Candidates	Total
Members in State Council 1960	3	0	3	3	0	3
Members in State Council 1960 and 1963	5	1	6	6	0	6
Members in State Council 1963	1	1	2	2	2	4

the overwhelming majority of the 14 SED members in the State Council, which once again numbered 24. The number of full Central Committee members in the State Council changed little with the number of SED members in this body. The death of State Council members Bernard Koenen and Otto Grotewohl—both simultaneously Central Committee members—reduced the group of members and candidates in the State Council in 1964. The new Council members, Brunhilde Hanke and Anni Neumann, both belonged to the SED, but were not in the Central Committee. In the 1967 State Council, from which Christel Pappe (FDGB) and Christian Steinmüller (NDPD) resigned, and to which Maria Schneider (FDGB) and Hans-Heinrich Simon (NDPD) were newly admitted, there were no new entries from the Central Committee. Likewise, no SED member belonging to the State Council was newly elected to the Central Committee in April 1967, so that among the 24 members of the 1967 State Council—14 of whom belonged to the SED—the following most important members are still represented: Ulbricht, Ebert, Gotsche, Mittag, Rieke, Rodenberg, Schumann, and Stoph.

The relatively advanced amalgamation of the Central Committee with the State Council membership is understandable in view of the Council's political functions. Formally an organ of the Peoples' Chamber, the State Council has to guarantee the "unity of state." In contrast to the Council of Ministers, whose tasks have increasingly shifted to the organization of the economy, the competence of the State Council is now more comprehensive. In the wake of implementing the second stage of the "new economic system," the State Council has also increasingly dealt with establishing "scientific principles of guidance." Consequently, as regards organizational policy this body can certainly be compared with the Council of Ministers. Furthermore, like the Council of Ministers, the State Council is a continuously functioning authority, which also meets between sessions of the Peoples' Chamber. According to article 106 of the GDR Constitution, the State Council "issues generally valid interpretations of the laws"; promulgates "decrees having the force of law"; makes "fundamental decisions in questions of national defence and security"; confirms the "basic ordinances of the National Defense Council of the German Democratic Republic," etc.[78]

In view of Ulbricht's strong position in the Politburo, the Secretariat of the Central Committee, and the State Council, it is evident that the latter body has more political influence than the Council of Ministers and its Presidium. Its connection to the Politburo and the Central Committee is to a considerable extent established, both directly and indirectly, by Ulbricht and the long-time director of the State Council secretariat, Otto Gotsche. The State Council is an instrument of Ulbricht whereby the decisions of the Politburo are implemented.

With the exception of Günter Mittag, formerly a candidate member of the Politburo and director of its Bureau of Industry and Construction, the majority of the State Council members in 1963 may be regarded as an Ulbricht team (cf. Table 44). Among the members of the State Council who also belonged to the Central Committee, the following Ulbricht supporters can be identified: Friedrich Ebert, long-time Mayor of Berlin; Otto Grotewohl, Chairman of the Council of Ministers who died in 1964; Bernard Koenen, who also died in 1964, was a long-time First Secretary of the SED *Bezirk* executive for Halle; Hans Rodenberg, Deputy Minister of Culture until 1964; and Horst Schumann, First Secretary of the FDJ. These men had all belonged to the State Council from its inception. In 1963 the Council admitted Otto

---

[78] These comprehensive authorities of the State Council are comparable to the formal authorities of the Presidium of the Supreme Soviet. See Siegried Mampel, *Die Verfassung der Sowjetischen Besatzungszone Deutschlands, Text und Kommentar* (Frankfurt-on-the-Main and Berlin, 2nd ed. expanded, 1966), pp. 291 ff.

Table 44
The Members and Candidates of the Central Committee in the State Council (1960–1963)

	Central Committee*		State Council†	
	1958	1963	1960	1963
Friedrich Ebert	M	M	X	X
Luise Ermisch	M	M	X	
Otto Gotsche		C		X
Otto Grotewohl	M	M	X	X
Bernard Koenen	M	M	X	X
Bruno Leuschner	M	M	X	
Karl Mewis	M	M	X	
Günter Mittag	C	M		X
Hans Rodenberg	M	M	X	X
Horst Schumann	C	M	X	X
Willi Stoph	M	M		X
Paul Strauss		C		X
Walter Ulbricht	M	M	X	X

* M = member; C = candidate.
† X designates membership in the State Council.

Gotsche as its secretary and also Willi Stoph, who replaced Grotewohl as the Chairman of the Council of Ministers.

The most interesting social and political findings of the preceding analysis can be summarized as follows (cf. the section on the Council of Ministers): Younger managers and technologists who are not career functionaries of the party or the mass organizations have not entered the State Council. Ulbricht has secured his position in the State Council by the same technique of careful selection of full members that he used in the Politburo. The institutional barriers which he established have hitherto prevented younger technologists from directly influencing basic political decisions.

9. The Interconnections between the Central Committee and the Central Leadership Bodies of the Mass Organizations

An analysis of the SED power system from the perspective of its social structure could hardly omit a study of the personal connections between the Central Committee and some of the most important mass organizations in the GDR. The following organizations are examined in detail below:

Free German Trade Union Association (FDGB)
Free German Youth (FDJ)
Democratic Womens' Association of Germany (DFD)
National Front (NF)
Cultural Association (KB)
German Writers' Union (DSV)
Association for Sport and Technology (GST)
Young Pioneers (JP)
Association of German Journalists (VDJ)
Peasants' Mutual Aid Association (VdgB)

Because of incomplete data we were unable to consider a professional association which is very important for the aims of this study, namely, the scientific and technical-economic intellegentsia's Chamber of Technology (KdT). In 1963 this comprised 119,000 members and in 1965 approximately 135,000.[79]

It seemed best to include in our analysis members and candidates with primary functions in the mass organizations, as well as those in secondary positions. In accordance with the limits of this study, only the central leadership bodies of the mass organizations were included. The following are regarded as "central": the respective presidium (including the secretariat, if separate), which is also called "executive board" (DSV), "bureau" (FDJ), etc.; and the full board from which the presidium is elected, also called "central council" (FDJ), or "national board" (FDGB, DFD), "central administration" (JP), etc. The individual mass organizations were investigated for periods comparable to those of the 1958 or 1963 Central Committees.[80]

[79] According to the *Statisches Jahrbuch der DDR* (1966), p. 594. No comprehensive description of the Chamber of Technology exists in the East or the West. Material for the earlier years may be found in the various volumes of the *Jahrbuch der Deutschen Demokratischen Republik,* apart from the Statistical Yearbook. The 1964 Handbook of the GDR also contains a short section (pp. 347–351) on the Chamber of Technology.

[80] Like the Central Committee the chief executive bodies of the various mass organizations are elected about every four years. Their congresses are usually held shortly after the Party Congresses, so that possible sociopolitical changes

The results appear with specific names in Table 45. For the rest, membership in 1958 and 1963 in the presidiums (Table 46) and in the boards (Table 47) of the most important mass organizations were compared numerically.

THE SITUATION IN 1958

In 1958 altogether 42 Central Committee members and candidates occupied 56 secondary functions in one or several of the given mass organizations. Twelve of the 1958 Central Committee members and candidates occupied primary functions in a presidium. They include the following first chairmen:

R. Lehmann   (JP)
H. Schumann   (FDJ)
I. Thiele   (DFD)
Herbert Warnke   (FDGB)
F. Wehmer   (VdgB)

---

decided upon and announced at the Congress can immediately be carried through. Particulars of the main mass organization congresses, held in connection with the two SED Congresses of 1958 and 1963, and investigated in this study are shown in Tables 46 and 47. For this purpose the personnel card index of the Institute for Political Science and the following sources were used:

For the FDGB: *Tribüne* 15, no. 253 (1959): 1 ff; Proceedings of the Sixth FDGB Congress, *Protokoll des 6. FDGB Kongresses vom 19. bis 23. November 1963 in der Dynamo-Sporthalle zu Berlin,* published by the FDGB (Freier Deutscher Gewerkschaftbund) (Berlin, 1964).

For the FDJ: *Junge Welt* 13, no. 115 (1959): 4, and 17, no. 128 (1963): 3 ff.

For the DFD: *Frau von heute* no. 2 (1961): 3, and *Für dich* no. 29 (1964): 26.

For the National Front: *Stimme des Patrioten* no. 19 (1958): 5 ff.

For the Kulturbund (Cultural Association): *Sonntag* no. 7 (1958): 9, and no. 24 (1963): 2.

For the DSV (German Writers' Union): *Sonntag* no. 7 (1957): 4; and *Neue Deutsche Literatur* 9, no. 8 (1961):158, and 11, no. 7 (1963): 188 ff.

For the GST (The Association for Sport and Technology): *Sport and Technik* 4, no. 7 (1960): 9, and 8, no. 5 (1964): 4.

For the Young Pioneers: *Junge Welt* 11, no. 290 (1957): 1; and *Der Pionierleiter* 15, no. 18 (1964): 5.

For the VDJ (Association of German Journalists): *Neue Deutsche Presse* 13, no. 6 (1959): 2, and 16, no. 1 (1962): p. 3.

For the VdgB (Peasants' Mutual Aid Association): *Jahrbuch der Deutschen Demokratischen Republik* (Berlin, 1957), p. 94.

The 1958 Central Committee members and candidates with primary functions in the presidiums of the mass organizations are distributed throughout the individual mass organizations as follows, including first chairmen:

FDGB   4
FDJ   3
JP   2
DFD   1
VdgB   2

An exact analysis of the secondary functions excludes Central Committee members and candidates with primary functions in the mass organizations. The group investigated here comprises 38 members and candidates who exercise 51 secondary functions in the top-level bodies of the mass organizations. They are distributed as follows:[81]

in the presidiums

FDGB   0
FDJ   1
JP   no data
DFD   3
NF   6
KB   1

in the boards (except for presidium members)

FDGB   8
FDJ   3
JP   4
DFD   no data
NF   13
KB   6
DSV   5
VDJ   1

Excluding the less important mass organizations (NF, KB, DSV, VDJ), 16 of the 1958 Central Committee members occupy altogether 19

[81] For those functionaries of the mass organizations who were principally employed on one presiding board (executive) but also were members of another presiding board on a subsidiary, part-time basis, the latter occupation was not taken into account.

Table 45
CC Members and Candidates with Main and Secondary Functions in the Mass Organizations (1958–1963)

| Name | CC* 1958 | Main Function in the Mass Organizations | | Secondary Function in the Mass Organizations | | CC* 1963 | Main Function in the Mass Organizations | | Secondary Function in the Mass Organizations | |
		In the Presidium	In the Board	In the Presidium	In the Board		In the Presidium	In the Board	In the Presidium	In the Board
Abusch	M				KB/DSV	M			KB	DSV
Adameck	—					M			VDJ	
Barthel	M				DSV	M				DSV
Baumann	M		DFD		JP	M				
Becher	M				NF/KB/DSV	—				
Benjamin	M		DFD			M				DFD
Berger	—					M	FDGB			
Biering	C	VdgB				—				
Bredel	M				DSV	M				
Buchheim	M	FDGB				—				
Burghardt	C			KB	NF	M	KB			
Ebert	M				NF	M				
Geggel	—					C				VDJ
Gotsche	—					C				DSV
Grotewohl	M				NF	M				
Grüneberg	M				NF	M				
Hager, K.	M				KB	M				KB
Handke	M				NF	—				
Heintze	—					M	FDGB			
Hempel	—					C	FDJ			
Hennecke	M				FDGB	M				
Hertwig	M	JP				M	JP			
Honecker-Feist	C				FDJ/JP	M				
Jendretzky	M				NF/FDGB	M	FDGB			
Kaiser-Gorrish	—					C				DSV
Kayser	—					M				KB
Kern	M		DFD			M		DFD		
Kessler	M				FDJ/JP	M				
Kirchner	C				NF/FDGB	—				

Koenen, W.	M		NF		M		
Kurella	M			KB/DSV	M		KB/DSV
Kuron	—				C	FDGB	
Lehmann, H.	M		NF		—		
Lehmann, O.	M	FDGB			—		
Lehmann, R.	M	JP	FDJ/NF		M		FDJ
Matern	M		NF		M		
Mette	M			KB	—		
Minetti	C			FDJ	C		
Mittag	C				M		FDGB
Modrow	C	FDJ			C		
Mückenberger	M		NF		M		
Müller, F., II	—				C	FDGB	
Namokel	M		NF		—		
Naumann, K.	—				C	FDJ	
Neugebauer	M			JP	M		
Neumann, A.	M			FDGB	M		
Norden	M		NF	VDJ	M		VDJ
Reichert	M		FDJ	NF	—		
Rienäcker	M			KB	—		
Sakowski	—				C		DSV
Schön	M		NF		M		
Schumann	C	FDJ			M	FDJ	
Sindermann	C			NF	M		
Steinke	C	FDJ		GST	—		
Strauss	—				C		FDGB
Svihalek	M			FDGB	—		
Thiele	M	DFD	NF		M	DFD	
Tille	M	FDGB			—		
Ulbricht	M		NF	FDGB	M		
Verner, P.	M			NF	M		
Warnke, Herb.	M	FDGB	NF		M	FDGB	
Wehmer	M	VdgB			M	VdgB	
Wende	M			FDGB	—		
Wenig	M			FDGB	M		FDGB
Wolf, C.	—				C		DSV
Zimmering	—				C		DSV

* M = member; C = candidate.

† See footnote 80, pp. 309–310 and Table 46 or 47 for the exact period of comparison between the bodies of these mass organizations and those of the respective Central Committees.

Table 46
The Number of CC Members and Candidates with Main and Secondary Functions in the Presidiums of Selected Mass Organizations (1958 and 1963)

Mass Organizations	Period of Comparison (1958)	Total of Members	Main Function in MO Presidium	Secondary Function in MO Presidium	Total	Period of Comparison (1963)	Total of Members	Main Function in MO Presidium	Secondary Function in MO Presidium	Total
FDGB	5. National Congress October 1959	25	4	0	4	6. National Congress November 1963	29	5	1	6
FDJ	6. Parliament May 1959	21	3	2	5	7. Parliament May 1963	20	3	1	4
DFD	7. National Congress November 1960	31	1	3	4	8. National Congress June 1964	33	1	1	2
NF	3. Congress September 1958	33	0	9	9	(The 4th Congress has not yet taken place)				
KB	5. National Congress February 1958	Incomplete data on composition of Presidium				6. National Congress June 1963	18	1	1	2
DSV	Delegates' Conference February 1957	Incomplete data on composition of Executive Board				Delegates' Conference May 1963	6	0	0	0
	5. Congress May 1961	17	0	0	0					

Table 47
The Number of CC Members and Candidates with Main and Secondary Functions in the Boards (including the Presidiums) of Selected Mass Organizations (1958 and 1963)

Mass Organizations	Period of Comparison	1958				Period of Comparison	1963			
		Total of Members	of these CC Members and Candidates				Total of Members	of these CC Members and Candidates		
			Main Function in MO Board	Secondary Function in MO Board	Total			Main Function in MO Board	Secondary Function in MO Board	Total
FDGB	5. National Congress October 1959	199	4	8	12	6. National Congress November 1963	233	6	3	9
FDJ	6. Parliament May 1959	141	3	5	8	7. Parliament May 1963	141	3	1	4
DFD	7. National Congress November 1960	Incomplete data on composition of Board				8. National Congress June 1964	125	1	2	3
NF	3. Congress September 1958	220	0	22	22	(The 4th Congress has not yet taken place)				
KB	5. National Congress February 1958	87	0	7	7	6. National Congress June 1963	84	1	4	5
DSV	Delegates' Conference February 1957	40	0	5	5	Delegates' Conference May 1963	54	0	8	8

secondary functions in the FDGB, the FDJ (JP), and the DFD. Of this group, four Central Committee members are associated with mass organizations according to their primary function and must therefore be considered specially. They are:

R. Kirchner, main functionary of the FDGB, delegated for study during the period under comparison and relieved of all his functions.

R. Reichert, whose main function is President of the DTSB.[82] As such, he probably entered the Presidium of the FDJ in this capacity, rather than as a Central Committee member.

K. Svihalek, whose main function is Chairman of the Farm and Forestry Laborers' Union (but who is not a member of the Presidium or of the FDGB National Board).

A. Wende, whose main function is Chairman of the Central Board of the Union of Scientists in the FDGB (but who is not a member of the Presidium or of the FDGB National Board).

In the narrower sense, twelve Central Committee members were entrusted with secondary functions in 1958 (cf. Table 48).

THE SITUATION IN 1963

Thirty-two Central Committee members and candidates occupied primary or secondary functions in one or more of the relevant mass organizations in 1963. Compared with 1958 the number is low, because the National Front was excluded for lack of comparable data. Twelve of the 1963 members and candidates exercised primary functions in the presidiums. (Another, Kuron, exercises a primary function in the National Board of the FDGB.) The following first chairmen exercised primary functions in the presidiums:

M. Burghardt	KB
H. Schumann	FDJ
I. Thiele	DFD
Herbert Warnke	FDGB
F. Wehmer	VdgB

The members and candidates of the 1963 Central Committee with primary functions in the presidiums—including the first chairmen—are distributed throughout the mass organizations as follows:

FDGB   5

[82] The DTSB (German Gymnastics and Sports Association) was not taken into consideration here.

FDJ	3
JP	1
DFD	1
VdgB	1
NF	no data
KB	1

The 1963 Central Committee also included 19 members and candidates with no primary functions in the central apparatuses of the mass organizations, but with 21 secondary functions (including those in presidiums):

FDGB	1
FDJ	1
JP	0
DFD	1
NF	no data
KB	1
DSV	0
VDJ	1

Of those in boards (including presidium members):

FDGB	2
FDJ	0
JP	0
DFD	1
NF	no data
KB	3
DSV	8
VDJ	2

If the less important mass organizations are excluded (NF, KB, DSV, and VDJ), 5 members plus 1 candidate of the 1963 Central Committee with a total of 6 secondary functions remain. Table 49 shows their distribution.

PRIMARY AND SECONDARY FUNCTIONS IN CENTRAL LEADING BODIES OF SELECTED MASS ORGANIZATIONS

The findings of the preceding analysis can be summarized as follows: The relation between the party apparatus—represented by the Central

Table 48
Members and Candidates of the 1958 Central Committee Entrusted with Secondary
Functions in Selected Mass Organizations

	Main Function	Name	Mass Organization	Leading Body
High Party Functionaries	11	A. Neumann	FDGB	Executive Board
		Ulbricht	FDGB	Executive Board
	12	Baumann	DFD/JP	Presidium/ Executive Board
		Neugebauer	JP	Executive Board
High State Functionaries	21	Benjamin	DFD	Presidium
		Honecker-Feist	FDJ/JP	Executive Board/ Executive Board
		Jendretzky	FDGB	Executive Board
		Kessler	FDJ/JP	Executive Board/ Executive Board
	22	Hennecke	FDGB	Executive Board
		Kern	DFD	Presidium
Others	32	Wenig	FDGB	Executive Board
	53	Minetti	FDJ	Executive Board

Table 49
Members and Candidates of the 1963 Central Committee Entrusted with Secondary
Functions in Selected Mass Organizations

	Main Function	Name	Mass Organization	Leading Body
Party Functionary	11	Mittag	FDGB	Executive Board
High State Functionaries	21	Benjamin	DFD	Executive Board
	21	Lehmann, R.*	FDJ	Presidium
	22	Kern	DFD	Presidium
High to Medium Economic Functionary	32	Wenig	FDGB	Executive Board
	33	Strauss	FDGB	Presidium

* It is not clear whether R. Lehmann remained a member of the FDJ Central Council
after surrendering the chairmanship of the JP.

Committee—and the central leading bodies of the main mass organizations (FDGB, FDJ, JP, DFD) has become relatively weakened. Sixteen, or perhaps as few as twelve, of the functionaries who belonged to the 1958 Central Committee exercised secondary functions in the central bodies of these mass organizations during this period, while in 1963 there were only six (including one Central Committee candidate), despite a considerable enlargement of the Central Committee. The difference between 1958 and 1963 is not quite so clear, if we compare those members and candidates who exercised primary functions in the presidiums or in the boards of the mass organizations. Twelve functionaries for 1958 contrast with thirteen for 1963. The numerical representation of full-time functionaries of the mass organizations in the Central Committee of the SED has thus remained approximately constant; however, when taking into account the enlargement in the leading bodies of the mass organizations, we record a relative decline. Among the influential mass organizations this applies primarily to the DFD and the FDJ; it does not apply to the FDGB (cf. Tables 46 and 47). Among the leading mass organizations it has the strongest representation in the Central Committee, both with full-time and sideline functionaries.

The chairmen of the most important mass organizations are represented in both Central Committees. Herbert Warnke, long-time Chairman of the FDGB, was a full member of the Central Committees of 1954, 1958, and 1963. Horst Schumann, since 1959 First Secretary of the Central FDJ Council, was a Central Committee candidate in 1958 and a member in 1959. Ilse Thiele, since 1952 Chairman of the DFD, has been a member of the Central Committee since 1954. Robert Lehmann, since 1957 Chairman of the Pioneer Organization "Ernst Thälmann," has belonged to the Central Committee since 1958. He gave up the chairmanship of the Young Pioneers in 1964 and became Deputy Minister of Culture. His successor, Werner Engst, is not a member or candidate of the 1963 Central Committee. Since the resignation of Robert Lehmann from the Pioneer Organization, the latter is represented only by its Deputy Chairman, Hans-Joachim Hertwig.

These results lead to the conclusion that these mass organizations were not systematically controlled by the party via membership in the Central Committee, even for the years 1958–1963. Although the chairmen of the leading mass organizations are represented in the

Central Committees of 1954, 1958, and 1963, no uniform principle of infiltration or control can be established. This interpretation is born out by a consideration of those Central Committee members and candidates who exercised secondary functions in the mass organizations. The proportion of Central Committee members and candidates working full time or on the sideline in the presidiums of the mass organizations in no case exceeded 30 percent (cf. Table 46). Sideline functionaries in 1958 appear (apart from the Presidium of the National Front) only in the Presidium of the DFD.[83] In 1963 only three sideline functionaries occur in the presidiums: one each in the FDGB, the DFD, and the FDJ.[84] However, both the low proportion of those functionaries in the presidiums, and a more exact examination of the Central Committee members and candidates exercising secondary functions in the boards (i.e., the expanded leadership bodies of the mass organizations) appear to confirm our conclusion. Among the 1958 Central Committee members and candidates exercising secondary functions in the boards of the mass organizations, 5 to 6 of the 10 incumbents hardly figure as wielders of control, since their secondary functions could hardly have been fulfilled, or they merely retained them in the formal sense, as demonstrated by the situation in 1963.[85]

An accumulation of high party and state functions on the one hand, with functions in the leading mass organizations on the other, could not be established. In leading positions the individual functional areas appear largely insulated from each other. The top-level bodies are not linked via overlapping memberships.[86]

[83] These were E. Baumann, H. Benjamin, and K. Kern. Although R. Lehmann and R. Reichert were subsidiary functionaries in the Free German Youth, they were not taken into account since they were at the same time principal functionaries in the Pioneer organization (Lehmann) and the German Gymnastics and Sports Association (Reichert).
[84] These were P. Strauss (FDGB), K. Kern (DFD), and R. Lehmann (FDJ).
[85] For the Free German Trade Union Federation: Ulbricht, Neumann, and Jendretzky; for the German Youth: Honecker-Feist, Kessler, and Minetti. Note in this context that H. Benjamin left the Presidium of the Democratic Women's Association and has since 1963 been an ordinary board member.
[86] With the reorganization of the party apparatus in 1963 it became unnecessary for *Bezirk* presidents of the FDGB, the FDJ, and the DFD to be members of the SED *Bezirk* headquarters, as they had been required to be until then. However, this new regulation was revoked in 1967. (See Chapter Two, pp. 103 ff.)

10. Summary

Further concrete confirmation of the thesis established in this study was obtained by empirical analysis of the biographical data for Central Committee members and candidates in 1954, 1958, and 1963. Our statistics established a number of differences between the 1963 Central Committee and those of 1958 and 1954. These changes appear to confirm the existence of a social transformation in the GDR, which includes the Central Committee. The main tendencies of this change may be stated as follows:

The Central Committee elected at the Sixth SED Congress is much younger. This trend is particularly noticeable compared with the Central Committees of 1954 and 1958.

The Central Committee established since 1963 is undergoing a general process of "professionalization." Graduates of trade and technical schools, colleges, and universities have increased to a remarkable degree. Furthermore, the Central Committee has been "professionalized," even in the specific sense, by an increasing proportion of members and candidates exercising technical–economic and leading administrative functions.

The repeatedly noted trend toward change in the party apparatus could be exactly established to the degree that the bearers, or centers, of stability were distinguished from those which changed. Despite this mobility which we have generally established for the 1963 Central Committee, the strategic clique (mainly the Politburo and the first secretaries of the SED *Bezirk* executives) must be regarded as comparatively stable. Nevertheless, the very center of the state executive—the Council of Ministers—was also a main focal point of the dynamic. This conclusion was established by analysis of the Council of Ministers represented in the Central Committee and by a study of all SED members in the Council of Ministers.

The growing importance of state organizations as a result of functionalized guidance of society can also be concluded from their increased participation in the SED Central Committee. In 1963 far more high-level state functionaries are represented in the Central Committee than in 1958. The constitutional amalgamation of state and party apparatuses typical for totalitarian systems was established in this case.

On the other hand, the findings of our analysis of the Council of Ministers revealed an incipient independence on the part of the state apparatus vis-à-vis the party. Such trends were established primarily for the economic and agricultural apparatuses formerly attached to the state. Cadres active mainly in the economy or agriculture—i.e., economic functionaries in the narrower sense—show greater representation in the 1963 than in the 1958 Central Committee. These cadres are the outstanding representatives of the trend toward rejuvenation and professionalization. However, it was also shown that from the group influencing the economic process—the general directors of the VVBs—only three were accepted into the 1963 Central Committee. This also illuminated a general process evident in the GDR, based on analysis of the Central Committee: namely, the ever-widening distance between political and economic functional areas.

The differentiations that have been emphasized in the party apparatus and East German society as a whole prove that developments in the professional and political spheres for Central Committee members and candidates are no longer clearly parallel. It was established that Central Committee members or candidates had risen professionally upon leaving the Central Committee, or descended professionally upon entering it. Given the strong desire to achieve upward mobility, and the considerable upward mobility of this group of persons, it is clear that the attractions of the party apparatus have waned, since professional ascent via the party apparatus is characterized by greater upward mobility difficulties than in other functional areas. Nevertheless, the rise of Günter Mittag appears to indicate the contrary: There are not enough trained veterans for the constantly enlarged, newly established professional bodies in the party apparatus. The younger party experts therefore have an opportunity for rapid upward mobility. Although this argument is highly plausible, it does not take into account the resistance of veteran functionaries to their replacement at the centers of power.

Available data for mass organizations permits the conclusion that the representatives of these bodies show a lower trend toward election to the Central Committee, and that Central Committee members and candidates tend to exercise fewer secondary functions in the central bodies of the mass organizations.

Consequently, the evident restructuring of GDR society forced by the requirements of universally competing industrial systems has also affected the center of the party apparatus, the Central Committee. Taking into account the results of Chapter Two, our empirical analysis permits us to conclude that the structure of the Central Committee has been substantially changed by enlargement, rejuvenation, and professionalization. The Central Committee of the SED is no longer an organizational focal point for the "old guard" of Communist functionaries, whose political mores were established in the struggles of the 1920s and 1930s and who were therefore frequently unable to adapt themselves to the reality of a highly mobile industrial society. New and younger groups of functionaries are entering the Central Committee, mostly via key positions in the state apparatus. They have considerably altered the profile of the leading groups in the party apparatus.

This change in the social composition of the Central Committee has many consequences in the social sphere. The permeation of society by means of terror and compulsion that was typical of the first fifteen years of the SED regime is being replaced by greater consideration for social realities, primarily social differentiations and new social conflicts. The partial identity of the interests of the party and society, observed in some social spheres, is presently expressed by the SED's greater "openness" toward social realities as well as by a reduction in the gap between the party elite and the people, and differentiations within the party elite itself. The Central Committee itself can no longer be regarded as a center for the incumbents of political positions, to whom the decisions of the Politburo are submitted only for acclamation. The Central Committee is developing into a coordinated organ of transmission for social interests and social differentiations within the SED. The consultative authoritarianism which is an increasing feature of the political system of the GDR in its present form appears to have found one of its expressions in the Central Committee of the SED.

4

Major Trends of Change and Inertia in the Ideological System

1. Utopian and Ideological Aspects of Institutionalized Revisionism
The dialectics of change and inertia peculiar to the organizational system
and social composition of the SED Central Committee are paralleled in
the party's ideological system. (Indeed, the underlying concept of this
study would almost necessitate such a conclusion.) Changes in the
ideological sphere of an authoritarian Communist industrial society,
besides being indicators of actual social conflicts, have a dynamic of
their own and therefore can be viewed as independent variables in the
processes of social change. This aspect of ideology is an important
consideration in any systematic sociopolitical study.

The methodology of analysis in this chapter differs from that
employed in Chapters Two and Three. Theory of knowledge (in the
sense used by Karl Mannheim) is taken into account, and consequently,
the method known as immanent-critical interpretation is applied. Also,
differences in the ideological sphere have been related to the sociopolitical aspects of this study.

The SED ideological system will be analyzed in three sections: (1)
the ideological and Utopian roots of institutionalized revisionism; (2)
aspects of systems theory in modern revisionism—especially cybernetics;
and (3) the transformation of the systems approach into Marxist
organizational theory—i.e., the development of a theory of "self-
organization" of economy and society.

THE CONCEPT OF ALIENATION
Institutionalized-revisionism's ideological and Utopian ancestry is best
demonstrated by its receptivity toward and further development of the
concept of alienation. Interpretation of Karl Marx's concept of alienation
is intended to revive the original universal and Utopian character of
Marxism itself. Currently, the universalist form of Marxist philosophy is
increasingly assuming the pronounced features of a Utopian concept of
man. This is particularly so in Yugoslav discussions where it is stated
that man is

that, which he has not yet become. . . . He is facing his future, which he is realizing and verifying by achievement, today, now, here, at every moment. Man, as man, lives and already now is acting in the future. since he negates the present by the future. Only thus is man a truly authentic historical being, who transforms the existing (indigenous and social) into (full) human potential, which is fraught with meaning and rich in possibilities.[1]

This phenomenological historicization of man seems to have been influenced largely by Alexandre Kojève's interpretation of Hegel. Kojève conceives of man as

negating *Action,* which transforms given Being and, by transforming it, transforms itself. Man *is* what he is only to the extent that he *becomes* what he is; his true *Being* is *Becoming, Time, History,* and he *becomes,* he *is* History only in and by *Action* that negates the given.[2]

Thus, man is constantly in the process of "becoming," conceived of only insofar as he openly confronts his future potential; this receptivity to the future and the negation of the existing is essential to man's freedom.

Variations of this evolutionary Utopian view of mankind are also to be found in the works of the Polish philosopher Adam Schaff, the Czech Karel Kosík, and the East Germans Wolfgang Heise and Georg Klaus.[3] The two principal assertions that characterize this philosophy of man are contradictory: On the one hand, the alienated ego is to be disengaged from reconciliation with the world of product, one form of which, in an industrial society, is that of party and state bureaucracies. The free restoration to an unalienated state of the ego and the species, accomplished by cleansing the ego of alien elements, is the backbone of this concept in which strains of ethical purism are evident. (Robert Havemann's normative Utopia, with its ideals of asceticism and frugali-

---

[1] Milan Kangrga, "The Problem of Alienation in the Work of Marx," *Praxis, Revue Philosophique. Edition Internationale,* 3, no. 1 (1967): 21.

[2] Alexandre Kojève, *Introduction to the Readings of Hegel: Lectures on the "Phenomenology of Spirit,"* edited by Allan Bloom and translated from the French by James H. Nichols, Jr. (New York and London: Basic Books, Inc., 1969), p. 38.

[3] Russian philosophers still find differentiation of the concept of alienation problematical. *Otchuzhdenie* and *ostranenie* are the only words used to denote "alienation," "externalization," "distantiation," and "disposal." The use of *ostranenie* is confined to the literary technique of "distantiation." This concept will be discussed later, particularly with reference to Bertolt Brecht.

ty, retains this concept.[4]) On the other hand, future-oriented man finds his "true human time" only in the "sphere of production," i.e., in Hegel's terms, in the concretization of "labor." This second idea focuses mainly on the establishment, development, and modernization of social systems in Eastern Europe. Thus, current discussions of the Marxist philosophy of man are characterized by two mutually exclusive, incompatible approaches to the problem of alienation.

Adam Schaff confronts the abstract analyses of Fichte, Hegel, and the younger Marx with Polish postwar existential experience. He concludes that, even in a socialist industrial society, the division of labor cannot be abolished.

When faced with the broader issue of Marxism's approach to the human individual, we must—in the presence of experiences unknown to Marx—restate this problem as follows: is it true that private property is at the basis of all alienation? And, consequently, does the end of capitalism mean the end of all alienation? Is alienation impossible under socialism?[5]

This revival of interest in the basic problems of alienation should be juxtaposed with Schaff's simultaneous interest in the continuity and stability of the Communist leadership. His political involvement clearly imposes restraints on his intellectual search—an ambivalence manifest in Schaff's desire to "fight the alienation of ideology." In other words, although he raises fundamental questions, he is also concerned with maintaining the unity of ideological dogma. This formulation clearly reveals Schaff's intention to leave unquestioned the interrelation between ideology and the political system. That institutionalized revisionism politically accepts the existing system of rule is clear from the outset. Unlike the many Western formulations in discussions of "freedom and alienation," neither total negation of the ruling system and the power structure, nor critical assessments of the concept of "alienated leisure," have featured in Schaff's Marxism.

---

[4] For details see Peter Christian Ludz, "Freiheitsphilosophie oder aufgeklärter Dogmatismus? Politische Elemente im Denken Robert Havermanns," in Leopold Labedz, ed., *Der Revisionismus* (Cologne and Berlin: Kiepenheuer & Witsch, 1965), pp. 424 ff.

[5] Adam Schaff, *Marxism and the Human Individual* (New York: McGraw-Hill, 1970), p. 108.

The intensive discussion of "freedom and alienation" that has been going on in the GDR in recent years may be viewed as additional evidence of conflict between the respective forces of pragmatism and inertia in the SED. Since each group—revisionist and dogmatist—cites Marx to make its point, it is appropriate to examine Marx's concept of alienation.

ALIENATION AND ITS ELIMINATION IN MARX'S THOUGHT

Alienation, estrangement, and externalization[6] are central categories of Marx's early work and concepts essential to all his subsequent thought. The concept of alienation lays bare the basis of Marx's philosophy of man, his vision of a future classless society, and his view of the early industrial world. However, to interpret Marx's concept of alienation is not to explain his philosophy of man in toto. The goals of this study require only that his concept of alienation be described with regard to its implications for current East German ideological discussion.

Marx developed his concept of alienation in part from a dispute with Feuerbach, Hegel, and Moses Hess, as well as from a critique of the classical British economists, especially Adam Smith and David Ricardo. These men were motivated by a common intellectual experience. Each was sensitive to the impact of the "material world," i.e., the socio-economic sphere; each was concerned with the apparent preponderance of material reality over the world of ideas. This outlook is basic to Marx's concept of alienation, just as it is the foundation of his general theory of society and of a revolution that would eradicate all alienation. Marx's theory of revolution was influenced by the idealistic, romantic pathos of the Promethean "deed"—the glorification of "human will" found in the thinking of many philosophers of "young Germany" (*Junges Deutschland*) and "young Hegelianism" (*Junghegelianismus*). Activism and voluntarism have survived, to a lesser extent, in present-day Marxist philosophy. The will to create a changed, i.e., technically

---

[6] From a variety of texts the following translations of the German philosophical terms have been chosen: "alienation" and sometimes "estrangement" for *Entfremdung,* "externalization" and sometimes "estrangement" for *Entäusserung,* "objectification" for *Vergegenständlichung,* "reification" for *Verdinglichung,* and "distantiation" for *Verfremdung.*

perfect, world can be found today in the writings of Georg Klaus. However, progress is now considered evolutionary, a constant, "positive" progress rather than a "leap" or total liberation of man by universal spontaneous revolution.

Feuerbach's and Hegel's definitions of alienation throw light on the concept that Marx was to develop. In his criticism of Hegel's definition of alienation Feuerbach maintained that "spirit" does not externalize itself in "nature"; instead, nature "externalizes" or "alienates" itself in the form of thinking man; man derives from himself the sensual–spiritual being, God. Consequently, the "object" of human thought—God—establishes an identity between man, God, and nature. Simply out of human need man abstracted and transferred his own omnipotence and universality onto the concept of God. Consequently, to reappropriate his "alienated" universality man must devalue religion and recast it into the everyday terms of his mundane motives and weaknesses.

Marx opposed Feuerbach's anthropotheism while accepting his critique of religion and theory of man's self-projection onto God (a theory influential up to Freud's time). Nevertheless, Marx was influenced by Feuerbach's anthropocentrism, although he rejected the latter's exclusive emphasis on human subjectivity. Feuerbach's concept of man was bound to appear unhistorical to Marx, who held a more dynamic concept.

Hegel's concepts of externalization and alienation are more important to Marx's philosophy. For Hegel, nature is only an estranged form of the spirit. Thus, he cannot—as Marx criticizes—conceive of the "humanity" of nature, i.e., nature produced by history, or its humanization. Externalization, objectification, and objectivation of the spirit cannot be distinguished from the human act of creation. Labor as both a negating and an objectivating activity coincides. In contrast, the dynamic identity of man and nature in a historically forming society constitutes the central concept of Marx's philosophy of man. His critique of Hegel's concept of alienation is directed primarily against Hegel's failure to trace alienation to its "material" core. For Hegel, human nature is only "abstract" self-consciousness. Correspondingly, Marx interpreted the concrete activity of man in the philosophy of Hegel as purely "abstract–spiritual."

Marx also derived his concept of alienation from a philosophical interpretation of the division of labor. In his philosophy of man, various criteria are assembled into a composite image of alienated man. The capitalist division of labor is the concrete manifestation of man's alienation; the division of labor itself develops from a gradual increase in population. In addition to the division of labor, which grows with increasing rationalization and specialization, there "is given simultaneously the distribution, and indeed unequal distribution (both quantitative and qualitative), of labor and its products, hence property."[7]

Through private ownership of the means of production the division of labor gradually penetrates all of society; it separates "industrial" from "commercial" work and the latter from "agricultural" work, causing a separation of town from country. However, for Marx, the division of labor is present in ultimate brutal clarity, only when a distinction between "material and mental labor" occurs, and when man's "consciousness" becomes separated from his "being" and his original integrity disintegrates. These separate human entities were typified by Marx as "the worker," "the capitalist," and "the intelligentsia." Alienated man, divided in the process of the division of labor, becomes the symbol of only individual partisan interests. The original unity of individual and collective interest disintegrates into the particular interests of individuals and groups within society. Finally, the division of labor creates artificial castes and classes. Thus, the capitalist division of labor destroys not only the original social order but also the original human entity—man's natural relationship to the process and products of his labor, himself, and his fellow human beings.

Implicit in this visionary philosophical view of the division of labor, and especially man's alienation from the products he creates, is Marx's ambivalent attitude toward technology—an attitude no less ambivalent for later Marxists and thinkers including Georg Lukács and Georges Sorel. On the one hand, Marx glorifies heavy industry and the dynamics of industrial labor. On the other, his concept of the worker's alienation involves a comprehensive critique of technological development per se: The worker is reduced to the level of a machine, and human relationships become relationships between mere objects. "In short, by

[7] Karl Marx and Friedrich Engels, *The German Ideology*, R. Pascal, ed. (New York: International Publishers, 1947), p. 21.

the introduction of machinery, the division of labor inside society has grown up, the task of the worker inside the factory has been simplified, capital has been concentrated, human beings have been further dismembered."[8] "In short, the machine has so great an influence on the division of labor that when, in the manufacture of some object, a means has been found to produce parts of it mechanically, the manufacture splits up immediately into two works independent of each other."[9] Thus, in his early writings Marx views the machine primarily as a "unification of tools," which both advances the division of labor and encourages new technical discoveries. This concept of technology contains the seeds of Marx's later "concentration theory" of capitalism, formulated particularly in *Das Kapital*. The division of labor and the concentration of capital ultimately destroy the "whole man" and can be counteracted only by a total revolution. Marx's definitely ambiguous attitude toward technology and the technical world—in keeping with his idealistic, romantic view of man—differs radically from the positive philosophy of technology now being propagated by numerous Soviet and East European revisionists and dogmatists and has in effect been ignored by present day ideologues of technocracy. The unidimensionality of the technological Utopia asserted by the revisionist interpreters of dialectical and historical materialism is based on a purely optimistic view of society, history, and the industrialization process. Nevertheless, as particularly evident in the "system concept" of Georg Klaus, this optimistic endorsement of technology obscures an organic, multi-dimensional image of human nature. This latter view has its origins in a romantic almost bucolic type of thought basically hostile to technology and organization.

The concept of division of labor has revealed the historical and philosophical dimensions of alienation as seen by Marx. These are also essential to the Marxian "dialectic of labor." As Herbert Marcuse points out, the positive aspects of Marx's concept of labor (derived from that of Hegel and the classical British economists) were derived as "counter concepts" to alienated labor.[10] The central motif of the Marxian

[8] Karl Marx, *The Poverty of Philosophy,* in the series *World Marxist Library,* vol. 26 (New York: International Publishers, no date), p. 119.
[9] Ibid., p. 118.
[10] See Herbert Marcuse, "Neue Quellen zur Grundlegung des historischen Materialismus," *Die Gesellschaft* 9, 2nd half-volume (1932): 145.

philosophy of man is "self-realization": Man creates himself and realizes himself only through labor. Basically, labor is the only means by which man can live in society and understand his own history. Furthermore, only through the process of working can man transcend his alienated state. "Labor is *man's coming-to-be for himself* within *externalization* or as *externalized* man."[11] Marx regards this "externalization" or "estrangement" in an entirely material sense: "The first historical act is thus the production of the means to satisfy these needs, the production of material life itself."[12] Marx thus regards work as an act of self-generation by man, the defining activity by and through which man realizes his true nature.

Marx regards labor, production, and performance as ceaseless actions. Labor, the constant relation of man to an object, becomes the absolutely defined activity of man. Marx therefore evaluates all society from the perspective of the sphere of labor. It seems to follow that he should have viewed the concepts "man," "worker," and "proletarian" as identical: Man is only conceivable as a worker, for work is "the determinant by which all men are governed." In addition, work has an absolute value, since it and it alone creates a constant, proliferating stream of "instrumental values," of concretely conceived and measurable performances. In *Das Kapital,* Marx states:

So far therefore as labour is a creator of use-value, of useful labour, it is a necessary condition, independent of all forms of society, for the existence of the human race; it is an external nature-imposed necessity, without which there can be no material exchanges between man and nature, and therefore no life.[13]

For Marx "creative action" and "labor" mean a struggle with the two great forces determining human life: nature and divided capitalist society. Through labor, man grows beyond his "pure naturalness" and "originality"; he loses his "herd" or "tribal instinct" and becomes distinguished from "mere nest-building animals." In an industrial world freed of political power drives man relates to his labor in a conscious and free fashion and can thus re-establish his identity with nature. Hence, for

---

[11] Karl Marx, "Economic and Philosophical Manuscripts," in Lloyd D. Easton and Kurt Guddat, *Writings of the Young Marx on Philosophy and Society* (Garden City: Doubleday and Co., Inc., 1967), p. 322.
[12] Marx and Engels, *The German Ideology,* p. 16.
[13] Karl Marx, *Capital* (New York: Random House, 1906), p. 50.

Marx man is free only when he performs his own work within an historically determined nature. Man is free when he relates to himself "as to a universal being." The concept of a "universal being" utilizes, in addition to Feuerbach, interpretations of others drawn from Rousseau. Rousseau in his *Social Contract* calls for the total relinquishment of individual rights in society by all parties to the contract. *Gemeinschaft* can be constituted only by such a relinquishment or externalization of personal rights.

The self-realization of man in and through the process of work includes his loss of identity, his alienation in capitalist society. The positive aspects of the labor concept are inseparably bound with the negative ones; for the "realization of labor is its objectification."[14] By "objectification" Marx meant "alienation," under conditions of capitalist labor, or—as formulated by Lukács and Marcuse—"reification." The moment the worker manufactures his product, the latter becomes an "external" object and man loses his original connection to it.

The product of labor is labor embodied and made objective in a thing. It is the *objectification* of labor. The realization of labor is its objectification. In the viewpoint of political economy this realization of labor appears as the *diminution* of the worker, the objectification as the *loss of and subservience to the object,* and the appropriation as *alienation* [*Entfremdung*], as externalization [*Entäusserung*].[15]

This "dialectical" concept of liberating creative work and alienated labor of man in an industrial society once again reveals the ambiguous attitude of Marx towards a world determined by economic and technological reality:

The more the worker *appropriates* the external world and sensuous nature through his labor, the more he deprives himself of the *means of life* in two respects: first, that the sensuous external world gradually ceases to be an object belonging to his labor, a *means of life* of his work; secondly, that it gradually ceases to be a *means of life* in the immediate sense, a means of physical subsistence of the worker.[16]

Consequently, man "consumes" nature in the true sense under capitalism and thereby loses his identity. In industrial society, alienation has become the basic element of the human condition.

These concepts indicate that for Marx nonalienated existence is

[14] Karl Marx, "Economic and Philosophical Manuscripts," p. 289.
[15] Ibid.
[16] Ibid., p. 290.

possible only in a society not yet or no longer determined by technology—
i.e., in preindustrial primary groups of the classless society (the future
projected ideal of a large primary group). In a nonalienated community,
an association of equals, the "original (material) inadequacies of the
natural situation" still permit a certain type of "Communist individual-
ism."[17] It is an agrarian, physiocratic world where "man is not yet
socially consolidated."

Marx's early writings often emphasize the organic unity of the
preindustrial world. Here one man can still be "a hunter, a fisherman, a
shepherd or a critical critic."[18] Consequently, the earth is "still recognized as a natural entity independent of man; it is not yet the capital or
the object of labor itself."[19] The instruments with which the earth is
worked are still within the range of man's comprehension. His tools—the
focus of production—have not yet become "alien" instruments.

Marx never tires of describing the intensified process of alienation
associated with the loss of man's original integrity, and thus of human
identity, in the industrial working environment. Man not only becomes
alienated from the products which he creates and from work as such,
but also from his own original ideal nature and from his species.
Gradations of alienation, from "indifferent alienation" to "actually
hostile alienation," were developed by Marx, though implicitly, as a
"scheme" of alienation.

However, total alienation contains the basis of its own overthrow:
The conscious, universal, and revolutionary action of every social group
deeply enmeshed in the dialectics of self-realization and self-alienation
leads to a universal reappropriation of self and thus of the objective
world. Marx states that general human emancipation is identical with
that of the worker ". . . because the whole of human servitude is
involved in the relation of the worker to production, and all relations of
servitude are only modifications and consequences of the worker's
relation to production."[20] According to Marx, alienation can be over-

---

[17] See Herbert Marcuse, "Über die philosophischen Grundlagen des wirtschafts-
wissenschaftlichen Arbeitsbegriffs," *Archiv für Sozialwissenschaft und Sozial-
politik* 69 (1933): 269.
[18] Marx and Engels, *The German Ideology*, p. 26.
[19] Marx, "Economic and Philosophical Manuscripts," p. 293.
[20] Ibid., p. 299.

come only by total revolution. The necessity for *total* revolution becomes obvious from Marx's ultimate goal of changing the nature of human activity and thus of man himself. This visionary emancipation of mankind contains clearly apocalyptic and eschatological elements. In contemporary Marxism-Leninism in the GDR, by contrast, these elements are more and more replaced by a Utopia restricted within the limits of technology.

REVISIONIST ATTEMPTS TO INTEGRATE THE CONCEPT OF ALIENATION WITHIN IDEOLOGICAL DOGMA

Many East European Marxist philosophers (primarily in Poland, Czechoslovakia, Hungary, Yugoslavia, and East Germany) have attempted to raise the concept of alienation from its subordinate position in official Marxist-Leninist doctrine, particularly since the Twentieth CPSU Congress in 1956. The majority treat historical and dialectical materialism as their basic, unquestioned philosophical framework of reference. Often critical of Marxist-Leninist dogmas and stereotypes, the revisionist philosophers have revitalized the ideological system by insisting that a Marxist philosophy of man and ethics deal comprehensively with the concept of the alienation of man. This demand is understandable only if it is interpreted as meaning that the new metaphysical historical view is to be used as a model for a technical civilization, a model pregnant with new implications for a specific newer kind of socialist order. Since such normative analysis of necessity implies the existence of positive impulses in industrial society, these philosophers reject the theory of total negation. Consequently, they are unable to accept Herbert Marcuse's basic thesis that alienation has become complete, and that the human subject is consumed by his alientating surroundings.[21] Ernst Bloch laid bare the metaphysical core of such a "positive" philosophy of man—i.e., one based on total negation—when he stated at the International Conference of the Philosophical Section of the German Academy of Sciences in Berlin, February 1958: "The truth liberates, since freedom has one thing in common with truth: both

---

[21] Herbert Marcuse, *One-Dimensional Man: Studies in the Ideology of Advanced Industrial Society* (Boston: Beacon Press, 7th pr., 1968), p. 11.

deny alienation."[22] This call for freedom necessarily included a demand for the reformulation of the spiritual basis of the social order in Eastern Europe. Alienation, as defined above, has its correlation in the concept of "the totality of man" and still reflects the abstract Utopianism of the 1920s, which left its imprint on Bloch's thinking. Bloch was able to retain this type of thinking more easily than men of the next generation, such as Kołakowski, Schaff, Klaus, and Heise. His philosophy of man has not yet capitulated—or did not yet have to—to the imperative of becoming an all-encompassing system of ethics, a philosophy of man, and thereby a "positive" Marxist theory that would point the way for the future of socialist societies. The inner contradictions of the classical tensions between critique and Utopia, apparent in outline in Bloch's definition of alienated man, become quite clear in the thinking of Leszek Kołakowski and Adam Schaff on the one hand,[23] and Wolfgang Heise and Georg Klaus on the other.[24] It took the rapid industrialization of the Eastern European countries to bring about a confrontation between the vision of man advanced by these theorists and the realities of a technical society. The contradictions in Utopian visions of man were clearly perceived by Schaff:

The estranged man, living and acting in a world of alienation, is curtailed in his development, and mutilated in his personality. The ideal type of man in the age of communism is one who has liberated himself from the rule of alienation; the total, universal man. This ideal may be unattainable, like the limit of a mathematical series, but even so one can and should try to reach it.[25]

The realism of a philosophy confronted with the conditions of a

[22] *Das Problem der Freiheit im Lichte des wissenschaftlichen Sozialismus. Konferenz der Sektion Philosophie der Deutschen Akademie der Wissenschaften zu Berlin 8–10 März 1956. Protokoll* (Berlin: 1956), p. 347.

[23] See Leszek Kolakowski, *Marxism and Beyond: On Historical Understanding and Individual Responsibility*, trans. J. Z. Peel, with an introduction by Leopold Labedz (London: Pall Mall Press, 1968), or the American edition, *Toward a Marxist Humanism* (New York: Grove Press, Inc., 1969); and Schaff, *Marxism and the Human Individual*.

[24] See especially Wolfgang Heise, "Über die Entfremdung und ihre Überwindung," *Deutsche Zeitschrift für Philosophie* 13, no. 6 (June 1965): 684 ff; Georg Klaus, *Kybernetik in philosophischer Sicht*, 2nd ed. (Berlin: 1962), 4th ed. (Berlin: 1965); and *Kybernetik und Gesellschaft* (Berlin: 1964).

[25] Schaff, *Marxism and the Human Individual*, p. 137.

developing industrial society becomes clear only in the formulations of Schaff.

Many prominent Marxists are currently concerned with these problems. The East Germans include, besides Wolfgang Heise, Robert Havemann and Georg Klaus; the Poles, Leszek Kołakowski, Adam Schaff, and the sociologists Stanislaw Ossowski and Andrzej Malewski; the Czechoslovakian Karel Kosík; the Hungarians György Lukács, Agnes Heller, and András Hegedüs; and finally, in Yugoslavia, Milan Kangrga, Gajo Petrovíč and Pedrag Vranicki. While Heise, Kołakowski, Kosík, Heller, Hegedüs, and Lukács represent a historico-philosophically oriented view of man—and thus of historical material-ism—Klaus, Schaff, and Havemann have dealt largely with the theory of cognition and problems of ontology. Consequently, their theories fit more closely within the framework of dialectical materialism. Nevertheless, the outlooks of the revisionist *histomat* and *diamat* philosophers coincide in their basic recognition of alienation even in a "socialist society" leading to a commitment to achieving the liberation of the individual, and a call for a rationalized bureaucracy and a system of planning. On these points Heise, Klaus, Havemann, Kołakowski, and Schaff not only differ fundamentally from the ideological dogmatists, but are in mutual agreement, despite individual differences. Their theories are consonant with those of many Western Marxists, e.g., the Austrian Ernst Fischer and the Frenchman Roger Garaudy. However, they diverge in their attempts to adapt Marx's concept of alienation to historical and dialectical materialism.

Chapter Four of this study is limited to an interpretation of Karl Marx's concept of alienation as it has been viewed by revisionist thinkers in the GDR. Wolfgang Heise[26] and Georg Klaus[27] were selected as

[26] Wolfgang Heise has been full professor of the History of Philosophy at Humboldt University in Berlin since December 1963 and is director of the Division for the History of Philosophy at Humboldt University's Institute for Philosophy. Born in 1923, Heise attained his "Habilitation" with the publication of *Aufbruch in die Illusion. Zur Kritik der bürgerlichen Philosophie in Deutschland*, published by VEB Deutscher Verlag der Wissenschaften (Berlin: 1964).

[27] Since 1968 Georg Klaus has been Professor of Logic and director of the Division for Logic and Epistemology at the Institute for Philosophy at Humboldt University, Berlin. He holds the posts of director of the Institute for

prototypes. The statements on "freedom and alienation" of Schaff, Kołakowski, Havemann, et al., are included only for the sake of rounding out our analysis. The principle questions posed by these interpretations within the context of differentiation and change in the organizational system and social composition of the SED can be formulated as follows: (1) What does this re-examination of Marx's concept of alienation contribute to a critique of ideological dogma within the framework of the philosophy of history, as opposed to a cybernetic theory of the system? (2) In what way does this particular re-examination of Marx enrich dogma with a positive social theory? To further concretize these questions: Which form of Utopia is more adequate to a critique of a social system affected by basically irrational decisions made by the GDR's strategic clique? The question of criteria for adequacy presumes the recognition of the positive nature of an industrial society, as well as the "concrete subjectivity" of socially active man. These terms preclude regarding as an alternative criterion for the adequacy of a Utopian social critique the transcendental subjectivity which is found at the core of Herbert Marcuse's thought.[28] In Marcuse's view every positive action is evaluated as "external" or "alien" to the subject, and thus as an emanation or form of alienation. An answer to this question is attempted in the section below, through use of the frameworks of aesthetics and social philosophy.

Philosophy of the East German Academy of Sciences, chairman of the Academy's Section for Philosophy, and deputy chairman of the Section for Cybernetics of the Academy since its establishment in 1962. Born in Nuremberg in 1912, Klaus studied mathematics, physics, and philosophy at Erlangen. In 1933 he was arrested for anti-Nazi activity and spent six years in the Dachau concentration camp. In 1948 he received his doctorate at Jena University and in 1950 attained his "Habilitation" at Humboldt University with a paper on the early writings of Kant. After holding a professorship at Jena he took over the Chair for Logic and Epistemology at Humboldt University in 1953. He was director of the Institute for Philosophy at Humboldt until his appointment as director of the working group on philosophy (later renamed the Institute for Philosophy) of the East German Academy of Sciences.

Klaus was a member of the KPD or KJV prior to 1933. Between 1945 and 1947 he was active as a *Kreis* secretary of the KPD or SED in the *Kreis* executive of Sonneberg. He holds many high East German decorations.

[28] Marcuse, *One-Dimensional Man*, esp. p. 139.

REMARKS ON THE AESTHETIC INTERPRETATION OF MARX'S CONCEPT OF
ALIENATION: ALIENATION AND DISTANTIATION

In the social theory of revisionist Marxism—in its historical or dialectical form—the interpretation of Marx's and Hegel's concepts of alienation, as well as the attitude adopted by different thinkers toward this
concept, must be currently regarded as fundamental to the renovation of
the key dogma of Marxism-Leninism. Moreover, even in Marxist
aesthetics and in discussions of the history of literature, the concept of
alienation as Marx formulated it is assuming increasing significance in
the East European countries. This is demonstrated by Bertolt Brecht's
theory of distantiation (*Verfremdungstheorie*), the more recent interpretations of Franz Kafka,[29] and the interpretation of certain aspects of
Hegel's theory of aesthetics.[30] Since a complete discussion of recent
thought in aesthetics and literary history is beyond the scope of this
study, only a summary of East European discussion of alienation will be
attempted. The essential theory of distantiation and its relationship to
Marx's concept of alienation will be covered.

The Brechtian theory of distantiation may be regarded as an
attempt to transpose to the theatre the alienation that Marx thought
universal for man and society. "The theatre must engage itself with
reality."[31] Brecht, like Marx, assumes that rationalized, specialized
labor in industrial societies can truly be understood only through the
"perspective" of an alienated human being, and his certitude, which
results from a knowledge of historical processes. This assumption was
carried over in his theory of the theater: "The world today can only be
described to the man of today if it is described as a changeable world."
The Marxist concept of the relation between theory and practice has

---

[29] See the protocol of the Kafka Conference, *Vědecká konference věnovaná dílu
Franze Kafky, Liblice, 1963* (Prague: Nakl. Československé akademie věd; 1963).
For the dogmatic counterargument to such positive interpretations of alienation
in the works of Kafka, see Klaus Hermsdorf, *Kafka. Weltbild und Roman,*
(Berlin, 2nd rev. ed., 1966).

[30] See also Wolfgang Heise, "Hegel und das Komische," *Sinn und Form* 16, no.
6 (1964): 811 ff.

[31] Bertolt Brecht, "Kleines Organon für das Theater," in his *Schriften zum
Theater. Über eine nicht-aristotelische Dramatik,* zusammengest. von Siegfried
Unseld (Berlin and Frankfurt-on-the-Main, 1960), p. 141.

thus been applied by Brecht to drama. This metamorphosis of alienation to a theory of distantiation must be understood in the light of Karl Korsch's interpretation of Marx, with its examination of "reified structures" in an "age of science." It should also be seen as an outcome of both a philosophy of "great passion for creativity" and a critical and Utopian view of man and the world. "Indeed, personal interrelationships have become more unfathomable than ever before." Brecht calls this state "alienated," and claims that it can be shown only through a "distantiated portrayal." Actual experience is to be rendered impossible by distantiation, or by man's "provoked" consciousness. Brecht's theory and technique of distantiation attempts to remove "objects" and processes of social life from their familiar environment and to transform them to unexpected remarkable events in need of additional explanation. He holds that things and situations "known" to us are mere appearance and actually epitomize human alienation—a theory based on Marx and on the distinction made by Hegel between the "familiar" and the "known" or perceived.[32] Only when known things are truly discerned can human alienation in an industrial society be overcome by art. According to the Brechtian theory of distantiation these things are discerned by being shown on stage as incomprehensible and grotesque, while simultaneously being explained and thus "distantiated." Brecht endeavors to tear things and events out of their usual environment and insert them into an artificially created reality by means of distantiation effects. The clear aim of these effects is to create a distance between them and the audience, thus permitting criticism of what is presented "from the social point of view."[33] The Brechtian theory of distantiation is closely connected in one particular aspect with the Marxian concept of alienation: Brecht's view of the nature and role of social criticism is closely related to the Marxian concept of revolutionary criticism. For Marx, critical consciousness, as the discerning power which destroys the "false consciousness" of man, guides work, deed, action, and finally revolution. In Brechtian theory of the drama, the artificial distantiation of social

[32] In his introduction to *The Phenomenology of Mind* Hegel states: "What is 'familiarly known' is not properly known, just for the reason that it is 'familiar.'" See G. W. F. Hegel, *The Phenomenology of Mind* translated with an introduction and notes by J. B. Baillie (New York: Macmillan, 2nd rev. ed. 1931), p. 92.
[33] Bertolt Brecht, "Die Strassenszene," in *Schriften zum Theater*, p. 99.

processes is intended to "remove the stamp of the familiar which now preserves it from interference."[34] The theater is thus meant to teach the audience to assume a critical distance by establishing a clear border of consciousness between the audience and estranged objects or events. The audience is not meant to enjoy the play but to follow it in a conscious and critically distant fashion in order to change society along the lines of the new consciousness gained from this distance.

Rendered politically and literarily effective, Brecht's theory draws attention to the potentials of social criticism in its aesthetic version. This aesthetic form of political criticism continued to perform certain functions under Stalinist conditions. Social criticism within an aesthetic medium was often the sole expression of the individual will to survive. Under the present conditions of a dynamic industrial society, aesthetically disguised political criticism no longer appears to have its formerly unique importance. Its critical and Utopian features are not entirely free of hints of resignation and aesthetical pessimism. Nevertheless, the powers that be still fear this type of criticism.

ALIENATION AND SOCIALIST INDUSTRIAL SOCIETY FROM THE
PERSPECTIVE OF HISTORICAL PHILOSOPHY (WOLFGANG HEISE)
Heise treats Marx's concept of alienation from the point of view of two pragmatic postulates: On the one hand, he recognizes the functional efficiency of the division of labor in an industrial society, even in socialist systems. On the other, he calls for concrete empirical analysis of "alienated human situations" in society. Both postulates presume the existence of alienation in a socialist society. Like Roger Garaudy, Adam Schaff, Georg Klaus, and Ernst Fischer, Heise proceeds from the basic conviction that as long as the "law of value" can be applied, and various types of property—e.g., cooperative property—coexist with state property, the economic roots of alienation are not overcome, even if "socialist" alienation differs basically from the type prevalent under capitalism. In response to a question put during the course of a public discussion, "Do we have alienation in our society?," Heise stated:
Alienation does not exist here in the general sense, i.e., in that society is powerless in the face of its own life processes. This situation has been

[34] Ibid.

eliminated by the creation of socialist conditions. However, it does exist in several other forms, since it springs also from economic and political processes, as a sort of birthmark of former society in a period of transition. Its manifestations include bureaucratization, the exclusion of individuals from the conscious formation of the overall social process, or attitudes of strangeness vis-à-vis our state.[35]

This acknowledgment of alienation in East German society is based on Heise's interpretation of Marx's concept of alienation.

Heise's social philosophy of alienation comes close to interpreting Marx's concept from the point of view of its origin in Hegel's thought. To a certain degree, this reflects the Marxist school of cultural and social criticism represented by Adorno and Horkheimer. In contrast to Schaff —who emphasizes the philosophy of man contained in the Marxian concept of alienation—Heise rejects all psychological, existential, and personalistic "anthropologization" of Marxism as "without valid precedent."

Heise clearly realizes the pitfalls that face many "critical" Marxists operating within the norms and categories of a preindustrial society: "In the outlook of historical materialism is the demand for a 'philosophy of man' justified, one which a priori regards a certain degree of dogmatic impoverishment of historical materialism as absolute, while repeating pre-Marxian positions?"[36] At first sight this question indicates a double intellectual pattern: first Heise's proximity to the ideological dogmatic position adopted in the GDR by the younger philosophers, such as Manfred Buhr.[37] The latter also rejects all demands for a Marxist philosophy of man. However, Buhr bases his rejection on not very convincing arguments. He describes attempts to formulate a philosophy

---

[35] Wolfgang Heise with Wolfgang Eichhorn II and Klaus Korn in a forum on "Empiricism—Theory—Perspective," *Forum* no. 23 (1963): 2.

[36] Wolfgang Heise, "Produktivkräfte und Produktionsverhältnisse und die subjektive menschliche Tätigkeit," *Deutsche Zeitschrift für Philosophie* 13, Sonderheft (1965): 140.

[37] Despite all the differences between Buhr and Heise, and Buhr's sharp criticism of Heise, certain similarities in their thought exist. Buhr also characterizes the concept of alienation developed by Marx in his "Economic and Philosophical Manuscripts" as basic to further discussion of this phenomenon in Marxism. In contrast to Heise, Buhr claims that Marx's concept of labor constituted an economic category "even in his earlier writings." See Manfred Buhr, "Entfremdung—philosophische Anthropologie—Marx-Kritik," *Deutsche Zeitschrift für Philosophie* 14, no. 7 (July 1966): 817.

of man as characteristic of "bourgeois" philosophy in the epoch of imperialism.[38] Compared with Buhr, Heise makes much finer distinctions. On the other hand, his posing of the problem reveals a methodological outlook whose substance lies primarily in the fact that every point of view detached from the historically and philosophically conceived course of human society (and not anchored in the dynamic subject–object relationship) must be regarded as obsolete in respect to *Geistesgeschichte*. Here we can detect the basis of Heise's criticism of culture, which runs parallel to the dialectical social theory of Theodor W. Adorno, Max Horkheimer, and Herbert Marcuse. These thinkers criticize a philosophy of man from a similar perspective, as a science of "positivistic" disguise of "reified subjects" in society. Heise's specific arguments criticizing "late bourgeois capitalist society" reveal a structure identical to those advanced by the Frankfurt school of social and cultural Marxism. The same also holds true for Heise's concept of "consciousness," which he formulates as follows: "The nonconceived appears as an alien power. . . ."[39] However, relying on his concept of a subject–object dialectic, "progressively" oriented and optimistically attuned, Heise differs ultimately from the Frankfurt school while at the same time reinterpreting the Hegelian scheme of activist voluntarism. Though hesitant and indecisive, Heise reflects the almost classical Marxist relationship between theory and practice, which in no way negates every power relationship.

This dissociation springs from two motives: First, Heise reacts strongly against all attempts to abandon the dialectic of subject and object—basing his position on the philosophical interpretation of Marx's earlier writings that Lukács schematically expressed in his *History and Class Consciousness*. On the other hand, Heise argues in a directly political fashion, relying on the dogmatic position of the Marxist theory of the class struggle. On Horkheimer and Adorno's *Dialectics of Enlightenment* Heise writes:

The technical integrating function of positivism is indeed hit by [the authors'] criticism, as is the inhumanity of the social apparatus. But in the *Dialectics of Enlightenment* this inhumanity appears as a product of "enlightenment," as the mechanics of an absolutely independent,

[38] Ibid., p. 831.
[39] Heise, Über die Entfremdung und ihre Überwindung," p. 709.

spontaneous process and as the total objectivization and total subordination of individuals. Consequently, the determinant dialectic of the class struggle—the struggle of the working classes—and indeed the possibility of its active influence on the course of history, have been sacrificed to the inborn dialectic of this impersonal mechanism. Consequently, the uncompromising negation of all phenomena associated with capitalistic alienation has only one abstract criterion for its overthrow, in which religious elements and philosophical ideas taken from Rousseau coincide. This negation of the existing under capitalism is thus accompanied by an intransigent negation of the only true alternative: socialism.[40]

In the light of historical experience of recent decades such an alternative hardly constitutes a real choice. Indeed, the trite, stark counterposition of capitalism and socialism also illustrates a remarkable penchant for ideological naiveté. However, this passage succinctly summarizes the Eastern bloc's critique of the leading schools of Western Marxism. Numerous other East European revisionist thinkers besides Heise, to the extent that they are related to the tradition of Hegel and Marx, have followed this line. For both Heise and Kołakowski, this critique focuses on a specific programmatic set of aims: the aim of creatively transforming the inner tension between analysis, critique, and Utopia that pervades Marx's work into a positive theory of socialist society, rather than into a totalitarian philosophy. Such an approach calls for recognition of the historical necessity of a functional industrial society, recognition of the untenability of Utopian aims, and, finally, an emphasis on the primacy of "practice." However, in practice the implementation of this program involves "revolutionary construction and the consolidation" of an existing society; in no case does it invoke revolutionary destruction or total negation of the present system by marginal social groups claiming a monopoly on the interpretation of "historical reason" and its "imperatives" (the hallmarks of that thinking prevalent among the conspiratorial secret societies of the past).

Heise's interpretation of the Marxian concept of alienation and his demand for an empirical analysis of it are derived from the original concept: "The analysis of alienated labor became for Marx the primary interpretation of the total structure of capitalism."[41] Heise leans almost

---

[40] Heise, *Aufbruch in die Illusion,* p. 405.
[41] Heise, "Über die Entfremdung und ihre Überwindung," p. 689.

exclusively on the analytical feature of the complex structure of Marx's concept of alienation:

In this way Marx enriched historical materialism by his analysis of alienated labor . . . a general category of alienation is thus replaced by his concrete delineation of empirical activity and circumstances.[42]

At first sight Heise's interpretation of Marx's earlier work appears to remain within Marx's original ideological and dogmatic interpretations. Heise posits an unconditional preeminence for the economic aspects of the alienation concept which he derives even from Marx's earlier writings. Following this line of reasoning, Heise criticizes as "idealistic" the elements related to Marx's philosophy of man within the alienation concept; he attempts in similar fashion to close the interpretive gap between the views of the younger and the mature Marx by a one-sided elaboration of economic postulates and concepts in the latter's thinking. Finally, he remains consistent with this approach in his further criticism of the merely "apparent" abolition of alienation in the "bourgeois–capitalist" world.

Bourgeois labor sociology and psychology aim at the abolition of "alienation of the worker," without being able to or indeed desiring to remove the source of true alienation—namely the separation of labor power from the conditions of its objectification and full realization.[43]

How does Heise tie in his basic view that alienation also exists in "socialist" systems, with his interpretation of Marx's concept of alienation and his demand for an empirical analysis of alienation? How can he introduce the analytical element of Marxian alienation into an empirical analysis and the same time enrich the latter? How does he avoid the contradictions and obscurities inherent in his attempt to upgrade and at the same time downgrade the Marxian concept of alienation? How does he justify his simultaneous recognition and denial of alienation in socialist systems? Heise attempts to solve these problems by using a theoretical framework characterized by elements of historical and dialectical materialism, and endeavors to incorporate elements of functionalism and behaviorism. However, his analyses from the perspective of purely Marxist philosophy ignore the behavioristic formula. Thus he states:

[42] Ibid., p. 693.
[43] Ibid., p. 696.

The concept "alienation" remains pertinent, (even) if we analyze the transition from capitalism to communism [i.e., in the Socialist period, P.C.L.]. Indeed, it is the more necessary in order to direct interpretations of the residue of class society toward an understanding of general correlations—just because this very process of transition is featured by the abolition of alienation.[44]

This argument is remarkable insofar as it conceives alienation in the sense of Hegel's "synthesis," or rather as a process encountered both in the West and East. Heise argues that the "capitalist class society," which has been abolished in the GDR in the historical and dialectical sense, still exerts its aftereffects in the form of surviving values and mores. Capitalism is thus generically connected with socialist society by an "overlapping" process in which alienation is eventually eliminated. In the course of his interpretation Heise puts decisive emphasis upon the attempt to resurrect the Marxian vision of alienation for historical materialism by advocating a program of behavioral analysis which is both "critical" and "dialectical." It is of little use to look for or assert the existence of alienation, since as a concept "alienation becomes practicable only in determining concrete relationships, conditions, and behavior patterns. . . ."[45] In his attempt to integrate the Marxian concept of alienation within historical materialism, Heise combines these two divergent points of departure by expanding the economic analytical component in Marx's concept of alienation into the general social sphere. This is a heuristically productive interpretation. It enables Heise to relegate the originally revolutionary Bolshevik party to the level of a bureaucratic apparatus poorly adapted to society in a dynamic industrial phase of consolidation. He can also expand the margin of freedom of the individual. Finally, this analysis permits greater differentiation within the concept of alienation, although Heise's call for Marxist behavioral research never assumes concrete proportions.

The primary significance of Heise's position seems to lie in the fact that he can assume a comprehensive social and historical perspective without abandoning the Marxist scheme of periodicization. He can postulate, so to speak, a dogmatically unreconciled social and historical continuity from early bourgeois society to late bourgeois and socialist

[44] Ibid., p. 699.
[45] Ibid.

industrial societies. Utilization of actual historical examples allows Heise to depart from the rigid scheme of historical materialism and to develop a relatively open conception of Marxist social history. The general consequences of this step for the dogma of historical materialism are of considerable importance. Once he has acknowledged that "history" is far from a unidimensional subject for Marxists, Heise can demand the application of empirical—i.e., sociological—behavioral research. In thus expanding his frame of reference, Heise, at least in the programmatic sense, can bypass the fruitless discussions of "socialist ethics" conducted for decades within a rigid ideological straitjacket; he has at least set the stage for dogma to incorporate the contributions of the behavioral disciplines, in particular those of sociology. This approach also gives Heise the opportunity to criticize, within the ideological system, the large bureaucratic organization of the party apparatus for its failure to adapt to the dynamics of a modern industrial society. His evaluation can be regarded as an attempt to regain the unit of theory and practice, which have at present become divorced in Marxism–Leninism.

The threat of Heise's thought becomes even clearer in his treatment of the subject–object dialectics of Hegel and Marx. His interpretation of this concept avoids an unconditional acceptance of a personalistic and/or existentialist philosophy of man, an absolutely tabooed approach in the classical Marxist tradition. At the same time he surrenders the claim for greater freedom for the "subject" in history, working man. In opaque terms and in convoluted fashion, since he is advocating for ultimate freedom for the individual, Heise states: "We are dealing with the subject–object relationship, which (by definition) includes the individual subject; thus we deal here with the general structure of that which we express in our thesis of the necessary growth of the subjective factor."[46] This search for an expanded margin of human freedom, based on the historical dynamism of the subject–object dialectic, is reminiscent of Bloch's views, which are crystallized in the concept "freedom of decision and action."[47] Like Bloch, Heise affirms the spontaneity of man as an *acting* being. This "spontaneity" is regarded

[46] Ibid., p. 702.
[47] Ernst Bloch, "Freiheit. ihre Schichtung und ihr Verhältnis zur Wahrheit," in *Das Problem der Freiheit im Lichte des wissenschaftlichen Sozialismus*, p. 22.

less as spontaneous action within the framework of the class struggle than as a concrete expansion of man's individual freedom of decision within a functionalized society. Heise constantly links this spontaneity to man's alienation as defined by Bloch and Marx: ". . . this concept [alienation] can be used to eradicate all that which hampers active socialist relationships and the development of the individuals."[48] However, his concern for the "subjective factor," i.e., the concrete individuality of man, is not consistent. His thinking is also prompted by the dogmatic slogan "the consciousness of the masses is the strength of the socialist state." This ambiguous attitude toward the concept of "human spontaneity" is one of the typical contradictions of his thought and, for that matter, of institutionalized revisionism as a whole. On the one hand Heise asserts that spontaneity lies at the base of man's inborn desire to attain freedom. In so couching his argument, he can claim a direct connection with the thought of Marx. On the other hand, he joins Lenin in relegating spontaneity a priori to the status of "mere" spontaneity.

Heise characterized the SED ideological action program as one dominated by the categories of subject–object dialectics. Man's spontaneous will to achieve freedom is thereby denied. (This constitutes the decisive difference between Heise and Bloch.) This position is socially and politically basic to his thought—and not merely of *Geistesgeschichte* significance. On the other hand, Bloch's definition of Marxism as a "system of open correlations" is in stark contradiction to the social and political realities of East Germany. Bloch's Marxism followed the lines of Hegel's and Schelling's thought, and thus never had to pose as a "theory of society," much less as a sociological theory. Consequently, from the perspective of our sociological analysis of Eastern European revisionism, Bloch is an "outsider." He may properly be aligned with those thinkers of the older generation who in the 1920s glorified the Utopian image of the revolution. These "partisans," such as Lukács, did not undermine the dogmatic foundations of Marxism–Leninism from within. Thus, Bloch belongs to the revolutionary tradition of idealist philosophy. Up to the "Polish October" and the Hungarian revolution in 1956, these thinkers may be regarded, for the most part, as representative of those who attempted to revise Marxist thought in Eastern Europe.

[48] Heise in the *Forum* discussion on "Empirie—Theorie—Perspektive," p. 3.

In contrast to Bloch, Heise—like Klaus, Havemann, and Schaff—is more closely attuned to the ideological and political realities of the society in which he lives and which he criticizes. Like Klaus and Havemann he also has recourse to Hegelian concepts, but in his thought Hegel is reinterpreted as a major contributor to the theory of evolution. Thus, Heise has been selected for this study as a prototype of the newer revisionist, "schooled" in his own social and political system. He has directly applied the Utopian theory of total revolution to the vision of a socialist society under construction. His thinking is a fundamental critique of Marxism–Leninism in its dogmatic form, and places him firmly in the institutionalized revisionist school. The endorsement of the party and state, typical in this variant of revisionist thought, is an attempt to "relegitimize" the roles of these institutions in society and to dissolve their "reified" bureaucratic structures. This approach allows Heise to regard man as the invariably socially and politically determined *homo faber,* i.e., man who fully realizes his potential in society through his work. The affirmation both of a concrete, historically based view of man and of human coresponsibility for state and society lead Heise to a devastating criticism not only of bureaucracy per se, but of the SED party apparatus specifically. This type of thinking can be regarded as a basic point of departure for a social philosophy of "consultative authoritarianism." Thus, Heise states:

Under certain conditions a central power apparatus, surveillance, and information gathering may be necessary—for example, in the presence of a powerful internal class enemy, when there exist underdeveloped productive forces, and low [political] consciousness of the masses or a shortage of cadres. However, this centralization must be abolished in a socialist democracy after the short-term need has disappeared, and replaced by development of conscious mass activity, so that democratic centralism becomes the active form of [the society's] will, growth, and integration.[49]

In order to elucidate his criticism of the bureaucracy further, Heise's reinterpretation of the economic aspects of Marx's concept of alienation is again emphasized:

Alienation characterizes the social form of human production relations, i.e., [it is comprised of] both the independence of the products of activity and reciprocal relationships of individuals in society to the power

[49] Heise, "Über die Entfremdung und ihre Überwindung," p. 706.

which regulates their activities, their bondage under this power, and their information and shaping by this power. . . .[50]

By interpreting the economic aspects of the Marxian concept of alienation as a social and historical feature of early bourgeois and "socialist" industrial society, Heise can affirm, with fundamental consistency, the need for overall social organization and at the same time criticize bureaucratic overcentralization in society. He has reached this outlook, however, only by a redefinition of alienation, which for decades had been viewed by ideological doctrine purely in terms of Marxist political economy.

It would thus be nonsense to demand or expect direct democracy in the production process or to foresee a weakening of authoritative central economic planning and decision making as a condition for eliminating alienation, or indeed to demand a reduction in social organizational forms as a precondition for individual freedom. This would contravene the real necessity for rationalized production and its (innate) economic and technical logic.[51]

Heise criticizes the irrational decisions of a residual and exclusive political ruling clique, as well as their system of organization, which has been rendered obsolete by social and economic developments.

The elimination of arbitrariness from the basic decisions of our social life is a precondition for functional efficiency. . . . Consequently, one-sided centralization must be overcome by . . . the reduction of bureaucratism.[52]

Heise's call for the abandonment of arbitrary political decisions and his view of democracy point to major differences between his thinking and that of Klaus. While Heise maintains that a relationship exists between dialectical theory and practice (albeit hesitantly accepting the analysis of behaviorist sociology), Klaus aims at purely technical rationality, at a developed cybernetic theory and, thus, at a purely conceived technical Utopia.

As a consequence of his analysis, which he derives from Marxist social criticism, Heise projects a future image of East German society:

Once socialist property relationships have been established, the eradication of alienation ensues as a positive development caused by individual and social forces in the Socialist way of life. [This is accomplished] on the one hand through the rapid development of the forces of production

[50] Ibid., p. 705.
[51] Ibid., p. 706.
[52] Ibid.

—i.e., through technical revolution—in objective and subjective, technical and organizational relationships, and on the other, through the development of Socialist democracy and the progressive adaptation of the social and political organizational structures to newer subjective and objective conditions, as well as through a comprehensive cultural development which takes place in both structures while at the same time extending beyond them.[53]

Even in his Utopian view of history, the demand for "adaptation" of the party organization to newer industrial conditions remains primary. It is evident that Heise's thought is more open toward the experience of the industrial world than that of the ideological dogmatists.

Nevertheless, the resurrection of Utopian concepts undermines the applicability of Heise's conclusions. Both the strength and the weakness of his position lie in his idealization of the situation he analyzes, under the rubric of the Utopian image, and his recourse to a subject-object dialectic. The reference to freedom and human "spontaneity" corresponds to his well-substantiated, politically effective criticism of bureaucracy. Thus far, this pattern of analysis implicit in institutionalized revisionism is quite up to date. However, the critical and Utopian concept does not lead to any systematically elaborated, positive theory of society (or even to an abstract system of reference) that could point to the future path of development of a dynamic industrial society. Heise's call for behavioral research remains merely hortatory. This renunciation of any attempt to tackle the problems he poses or to apply the findings yielded by the behavioral sciences to the problems he analyzes, indicates the dogmatic cast of this type of thinking. Since his behavioral model is made up of mere abstract postulates it cannot directly incorporate results of behaviorally oriented research. Such puristic, Utopian thinking can hardly be reconciled with the institutionalization of this revisionist position. Heise's significance within the framework of institutionalized revisionism should be seen in his philosophy of history, as well as his aesthetically based political criticism, rather than in any design for a new theory of society.

ALIENATION AND SOCIALIST INDUSTRIAL SOCIETY FROM THE PERSPECTIVE OF THE PHILOSOPHY OF TECHNOLOGY (GEORG KLAUS)

The "philosopher of cybernetics," Georg Klaus, like Wolfgang Heise takes

[53] Ibid., p. 707.

as his point of departure a basic recognition of alienation in socialist systems. Like Heise, he demands the abolition of human alienation in a socialist society, a condition which has not been remedied despite the destruction of capitalist property relationships. For Klaus "synthesis of a socialist order and socialist consciousness with modern technique and organization"[54] forms the empirical basis of his philosophical approach. He too calls for an "empirical" analysis of alienation in an industrial society. However, he differs from Heise when he demands empirical analysis of "alienated situations," since he is less oriented toward the axioms of Marxist subject-object dialectics. Indeed, he is more concerned with the problems posed by the findings of mathematics and physics, the general philosophy of science, physiological behavioral research, and bionics. This basic outlook is expressed in a peculiar combination of cybernetic speculations with several basic categories of dialectical and historical materialism.[55] In agreement with Hilbert and Ackermann's work, *Logik*,[56] Klaus strives for the "mathematization" of philosophy and the social sciences, as well as for the modeling of social processes. Klaus follows Heise in establishing a direct connection between the demand for functional efficiency and the empirical analysis of human behavior and alienation in a socialist order: Since the technology that primarily conditions the functional efficiency of society is in a constant stage of development and has not yet reached its ultimate possible stage, working man is still subject to the "necessity" of an industrial environment in his work. This "necessity" conditions the alienation of man; to the extent that man can define it in empirical terms, the process of rationalized human action and behavior becomes more feasible.

Before analyzing Klaus's view of the various aspects of alienation, it would be well to indicate the philosophical postulates upon which it is based. Klaus's view can be summarized by the formula of A. A. Liapunov and A. I. Kitov: man-machine symbiosis. Harking back to the basic cybernetic principle of the feedback control system, Klaus

[54] Georg Klaus, "Schematische und schöpferische geistige Arbeit in kybernetischer Sicht," *Deutsche Zeitschrift für Philosophie* 9, nos. 2–3 (February–March 1961): 353.

[55] See section 3 of this chapter, pp. 391 ff.

[56] D. Hilbert and W. Ackermann, *Grundzüge der theoretischen Logik* (Berlin, 2nd rev. ed., 1938).

maintains that man increasingly assumes the function of a "regulator," whereas the magnitude controlled—the "controlled system" of the machine—becomes ever more independent in its functions. In the course of progressive technical development man is still the "installer and regulator" of the feedback control system, but in the further course of history he increasingly will only set "the aims of production and feed the most general evolutionary principles recognized by him into these automatic systems."[57]

The concept of symbiosis is borrowed from biology. As applied to men and machines in its transference to cybernetics, it is based on the concept of a comprehensive system consisting of two subsystems, man and the machine. For Klaus man is thus described in terms of the machine and vice versa. The human brain can be regarded as the feedback control center, while components of the machine are seen as his artificial organs. The machine is then not regarded as simply the "unorganic product" of man, but also as a separate environment, restructured and changed by him. Consequently, the machine not only becomes a transfer machine, but also an adapting machine. Thus, it is not just controlled by man in accordance with a rigid program, but can adapt its functioning to the most varied inputs. Both man and machine can thus mold and change certain sectors of overall reality. This interpretation renders the central thesis of Klaus's philosophy of man comprehensible: "There is a reciprocal process of adaptation between man and machine. . . ."[58]

This hypothetically postulated symbiosis of man and machine implies a further series of assumptions which have by no means been verified in cybernetics research, although they have been fused by Klaus into his philosophy. Klaus not only assumes that in borderline cases men can behave like automatic machines, but that automatic machines can react like men. Indeed, Klaus is also convinced that human action, and consequently all behavior, can be algorithmically described and controlled. In principle he views cybernetics, biology, and anthropology as algorithmic theories. Indeed, an algorithm can be correlated with cybernetically interpreted biology and anthropology when human conscious-

[57] Klaus, *Kybernetik und Gesellschaft*, p. 124.
[58] Ibid., p. 119.

ness is regarded as the regulator of man's practical actions. In a linked feedback control system consisting of several interconnected control circuits, disturbances of the controlled system can be recognized and eliminated by the regulator's monitoring device. Instruments for eliminating disturbances can be conceived as algorithms, i.e., as various means of controlling actions in progress, or also as a system of conversion rules, whereby certain behavior can be described and determined. Since in the theory of algorithms it is assumed that every process describable by an algorithm can be taken over by an automatic device, the actions and behavior of man could be algorithmically controlled or regulated.[59]

The social and political implications of this cybernetic Utopia and its consequences for ideological dogma are of special interest for the correlations of this chapter's analysis. To focus on the constriction of the concept of society inherent in Klaus's reduction of the Marxian view of alienation: For Klaus society is an intermeshed control system of gigantic proportions without either "practice" or "history" in Marx's sense. Klaus's view of society is further elucidated by two ratios: the differentiation of the concept of alienation and the "dialectical ratio of creative and mechanical activity." The latter complex is reminiscent of Marx, and even more of Hegel. Man's Promethean power—activity, action, work—and the actual nature of man—his character as a "generic entity"—are correspondingly interpreted by Klaus as man's capacity, willingness, and opportunity to learn. In this the Marxian concept of deed and work—indeed, of revolutionary action—is reinterpreted as a process of constant learning, as a relearning of the original process of learning.[60] In Klaus's thought a further original elaboration, derived from the Marxian heritage, is encountered in the division of alienation into "social" and "technical" (or "instrumental") alienation. What, in fact, does Klaus mean by these concepts?

The social alienation of man and his work is caused by the need for man to sell his labor and abandon its products to whoever may buy it. Without being identical, technical alienation is indeed closely connected to social alienation. The technical alienation of man is the need,

---

[59] The theory of algorithms is thus relevant to all other aspects of cybernetics, i.e., systems theory, control theory, information theory, and theory of games. In this context we have specially in mind control algorithms.

[60] Klaus, *Kybernetik in philosophischer Sicht*, 2nd ed., p. 398.

inherent at a specific stage in the development of the forces of production, to perform monotonous physical or mental labor and subject himself to the pace of the assembly line.[61]
The concept of technical alienation is further elaborated by the definition of "instrument alienation" (*Geräteentfremdung*). By this Klaus means a "state in which the individual serving a machine knows only its entire or partial functions, without understanding its [total] structure."[62] Klaus's view of technical and instrument alienation clearly goes back to the basic characteristics of alienation and alienated labor that the younger Marx repeatedly emphasized. However, in his definition of technical alienation, Klaus characteristically changes the original focus of the Marxist interpretation of alienation. In the Klausian concept of technical alienation only man's alienation from the "product" of his labor and his alienation from the production pattern are considered of basic importance. Thus, Klaus has deemed expendable the many aspects of Marx's concept of alienation, which all hark back to the concept of reification—i.e., of man himself becoming an object or article of trade and commerce. The narrowing of Marx's concept of society is once again evident.

The use of political hermeneutics in Klaus's analysis precludes the necessity for a legitimate interpretation of the ideological heritage. Rather, he is faced with the problem of how the historical materialism officially propagated by the party can be revised in light of the concept of technical alienation. By distinguishing between social and technical alienation Klaus clearly establishes a more solid initial position than Wolfgang Heise, or those thinkers who retain the basic perspective of historical materialism. First, the criticism of capitalism implicit in the concept of social alienation can be harmonized with the official doctrine of "state monopolistic capitalism and imperialism."[63] Klaus can thus avoid the most common accusations of ideological dogmatists against the institutionalized revisionists, namely, that the latter blur the differences

---

[61] Ibid., p. 430.
[62] Ibid., p. 205.
[63] For the official doctrine see *Imperialismus heute. Der staatsmonopolistische Kapitalismus in Westdeutschland,* published by the Institute of Social Sciences of the SED Central Committee (1st and 2nd eds., Berlin, 1965) (3rd ed. Berlin, 1966) (4th rev. and exp. ed. Berlin, 1967).

between capitalism and socialism in their interpretation of the concept of alienation. For Klaus "social alienation . . . is overcome with the victory of socialism."[64]

Unlike Lukács or Heise, Klaus, because of differentiation between technical and social alienation carefully avoids conflict with ideological orthodoxy by refraining from a frontal attack on the party apparatus or the total ruling system of the SED. According to Klaus, alienation does exist in socialist societies, but only "technical" alienation. Under conditions of technical progress it can be abolished. By reducing Marx's complex concept of alienation to just one of its dimensions, Klaus is enabled to endorse the ruling system of the SED in clearer terms than Heise. Klaus has often openly affirmed the power interests represented by the strategic clique. For example, on the problems involved in providing comprehensive objective information to the Politburos, currently under discussion with the disciplines of sociology and social psychology, Klaus states:

The way in which events are reported expresses the interests, aims, and intentions of a social class stratum. The most important function of this pragmatic practice in the sphere of public information consists of expressing the interests of the ruling class in the state. These interests ultimately determine what is regarded as important or expedient and what items are selected from the available information.[65]

Apparently Klaus also emphasizes the control aspect of information, i.e., the view much reiterated by Ulbricht that information constitutes an essential form of political control. Klaus's statements demonstrate the lengths to which he is prepared to go in order to establish the ideological dogmatist assertion that "philosophy" or "science" is in agreement with (or reflects) "politics." Such statements also indicate the self-image of this manifestation of institutionalized revisionism: Klaus conceives his philosophy of technology as a basis for the rational planning of society's activities by the strategic clique of the SED.[66] Finally, he succeeds— through his careful differentiations within the Marxian concept of alienation—in projecting a Utopian image of man and society, whose outlines largely coincide with those of the future Communist society

[64] Klaus, *Kybernetik in philosophischer Sicht,* 2nd ed., p. 430.
[65] Georg Klaus, *Die Macht des Wortes. Ein erkenntnistheoretisch-pragmatisches Traktat* (Berlin, 1965), p. 109.
[66] See section 3 of this chapter, pp. 400 ff.

often described by Khrushchev and Ulbricht, and which can be regarded as Klaus's attempt to transmit the visions held by these Communist leaders into the sphere of reality.

These reflections lead to the problem of the connection between cybernetics, a philosophy of man, and the interpretation of Marx's concept of alienation. Klaus's analysis of the Marxian view relies upon the so-called Paris manuscripts of 1843–1844 (as does Heise's). In contrast to the latter, who attempted to solve the economic aspects of alienation in a general social fashion, and thus to construct an evolutionary subject–object dialectic relationship, Klaus includes the "dialectical relationship of creative and mechanical labor" in his concept. He resorts to Hegel's philosophy of "externalization" in order to define the difference between creative and routine labor, justifying this procedure as follows: "Although this concrete aspect of Marx's alienation theory is undoubtedly the basis for all other aspects of alienation, it must not be forgotten that the Hegelian concept of alienation—as well as that of Feuerbach—are reflections of actual circumstances in their respective cases."[67] Thus, neither Marx's concept of labor nor the development of his thinking from the early period up to *Das Kapital* constitute the actual spiritual points of departure for Klaus's conception of creative work. Instead, his point of reference must be sought in the Preface to the *Phenomenology of Mind* and in Hegelian philosophy as a whole. Hegel demands in his Preface that "the particular individual, so far as content is concerned, has also to go through the stages through which the general mind has passed."[68] Klaus has connected this thought with his reflection that the intellect "becomes externalized into nature." Accordingly, he concludes that "every product of human labor is a form of externalization into nature of a specific part of the human spirit."[69]

The Hegelian concepts of "creativity" and "externalization" account for Klaus's differentiation of labor into the "creative" and "routine" categories. Creative labor is a form of "externalization" of the human spirit into nature. However, the active spirit does not become lost in nature; externalization of the spirit is not transformed into *social*

[67] Klaus, "Schematische und schöpferische geistige Arbeit," p. 167.
[68] Hegel, *The Phenomenology of Mind*, p. 89.
[69] Klaus, "Schematische und schöpferische geistige Arbeit," p. 167.

alienation. Indeed, externalization constitutes a means for development of the infinite creative potential of man. The constant repetition of this negating, but simultaneously creative, activity—i.e., the constant negation of the existing—continually leads man back to himself, back to his original identity. Consequently, in this context any type of labor that is not solved by algorithms can in principle be regarded as creative. However, for Klaus nearly all creative labor performed once can be translated into terms of an algorithm. Because of its "historical" character this activity becomes routinized so that in the future machines can perform it. The historical relativity of what Klaus calls the creative thus becomes apparent. However, the creative process is not directly affected by mechanization and automation (and therefore by alienation). This is one of the essential differences between Marx and Marxists such as Bloch, Marcuse, and Heise on the one hand, and between Marx and Klaus on the other.

Klaus has established a coherent connection between the automatic control theory and concepts of routine labor and technical alienation by directly linking routine labor with technical alienation. This type of alienation has not yet been eliminated, even in socialist societies. However, technical alienation will be increasingly limited in its effects by cybernetics and automation. In order to understand this interconnection it is necessary to examine Klaus's views on the forms and possibilities of labor in contemporary socialist societies:

We must distinguish between three types of labor within a cybernetic machine environment: first, labor pertaining to this environment—i.e., work in an automated plant with its control personnel and maintenance brigades, etc.; second, the creative labor performed by the designers of this machine environment, and those who guide and direct the system— the planners. Third, there is a sphere of labor in which the fundamentals of science, engineering, and production technique are so underdeveloped that automation cannot yet start its path to victory.[70]

In socialist societies the last two types of labor will become increasingly important. The creative element in the work process will grow and ultimately man will exit from the direct work process to become a creator of control systems, in the sense of the man-machine symbiosis.

Klaus thus adapts the concept of alienation, but only ambiguously.

[70] Ibid., p. 347.

In narrowing the scope of Marx's formulation of the problem, he returns to Hegel. Resort to the *Phenomenology of Mind* provides two points of departure for his cybernetic theory. These are the reflexive nature of Hegel's concept of externalization ("man understands how his spirit functions") and the infinite development implicit in the Hegelian concept of the creative. Unlike Marx, Hegel maintained that the creative is not exclusively determined within the frame of reference of the subject-object dialectic in concepts of action and revolution. Consequently, the creative does not necessarily end in complete social alienation. Although Klaus accepted Hegel's concept of the creative in the sense of a universal dynamic (so designated by Hegel himself), the critical subject in Klaus's view of world history, which is reduced exclusively to aspects of technical development, cancels itself. By ignoring the role of the subject Klaus is being consistent with his interpretation of the human organism, which interpretation is in turn influenced by Klaus's view of projected research in bionics. Nevertheless, this theory retains traces of Hegelian elements.

Klaus refers to the concept of the organic formulated by Hegel in his *Phenomenology of Mind*. Hegel regards the organic as motion as such.[71] That is, he conceives of the organic as a substance which preserves itself and—in terms of dialectical philosophy—always returns to itself. This view of the organic influenced Klaus's concept of man. Man—although equipped with some creative impulses and a controlling consciousness—is bound to stay within the limits of the control system. Man and system are interpreted as an organic whole. By this, however, the subject–object dialectics—basic to Hegel's thinking—have been overthrown by Klaus. The totality of the historical subject is left behind. For Klaus, man—as subject—is completely fitted into the system.

THE DOGMATIST'S REJECTION OF THE ALIENATION CONCEPT

Analyzed systematically with respect to its reinterpretation by Heise and Klaus, the Marxian concept of alienation is significant in two aspects: first, alienation is an integral element of Marx's philosophy of history as well as his philosophy of man. His vision of a universal human revolution is based on the concept of alienation. On the other hand, for

[71] Hegel, *The Phenomenology of Mind,* p. 298.

Marx the concept of alienation in the framework of his philosophy of history constitutes an analytical instrument. Using the concept of alienation, Marx probes the structure of early capitalist society by formulating various manifestations of alienation (classes), the worker, the capitalist, etc., and finally, the lowest social layer affected by alienation, the proletariat. To the latter Marx promises a path of suffering and victory through historically determined society. The proletariat, a class laboring in total alienation, is invoked as the simultaneous subject and object of history. Its historic role is seen as the achievement of universal human emancipation—i.e., it is to represent all mankind—through its revolutionary action and the struggle against other classes.

Besides containing a typology of different kinds of alienation, the Marxian concept of alienation is tied to the vision of the "whole," "complex," or nonspecialized man. For Marx alienation remains connected to the original Hegelian concept of estrangement. Man himself becomes estranged in the flow of never-ending development in nature, and his creative activity reveals ever new opportunities for realization and objectification. Seen against the rapid development of industrial societies in the West and East, this point of view should be given emphasis, since the experience of an industrial environment is increasingly replacing the classic Marxist vision of total man, even in the East; this is graphically demonstrated by the development of experimental "polytechnical education" in the Soviet Union and Eastern Europe. The experience gained from this type of education by Marxist pedagogy, psychology, and sociology could contribute to a gradual elimination of the taboos on the discussion of freedom and alienation—taboos which are evident even in revisionist thinking.

The experiences of an industrial society and the revisionist efforts of many prominent Marxist thinkers heightened the defensiveness of ideological orthodoxy. This is manifested in the definition of alienation worked out by the ideological dogmatics and given in *Philosophisches Wörterbuch*:

As a philosophical and sociological category, the concept of alienation reflects a universal social and historical situation, in which relationships between men appear as relationships between objects and things, and in which the products created by the material and intellectual activity of man stand in opposition to social conditions, institutions, and ideologies of man as alien, dominant powers. This social and historical circum-

stance is evident primarily in economic fetishism and political, ideological, and religious alienation. Alienation assumes a comprehensive character under capitalism.[72]
This definition of alienation is remarkable for several reasons, not the least of which is its formalization of Marx's thought. The metaphysical dimensions, and thus the transcendentally related elements in the concept of alienation, are a priori relegated to an equal level of analysis. Thus they lose their multidimensionality. The totality and apocalyptic force of alienation—dominant for Marx—is subdivided into economic, political, ideological, and religious alienation and thus deprived of its revolutionary force, for the revolutionary force of Marx's concept of alienation lies in its universality and uniformity. Thus, the ideological dogmatists introduce positivistic thinking into their ideological dogma.

Alternately, alienation is conceived of as the "reflection" of an already historically determined situation. This view is espoused by Horst Ullrich, a leading specialist in the SED Central Committee's Institute for Marxism-Leninism. Ullrich defines alienation as a *historical* category.[73] When associated with the philosophy of history, alienation assumes the character of a historically and socially limited totality. It is associated solely with "capitalist" society. The theory of the class struggle maintains that alienation has been abolished in socialist systems since the October Revolution. The dictatorship of the proleteriat has not only ended the private ownership of the means of production and gradually abolished the class struggle in the social sphere, but has also abolished all types of alienation associated with the former. The dogmatic counterargument on alienation is not conditioned solely by a positivistic interpretation of traditional ideological tenets—a tactic usually associated with "bourgeois" Marxology—but is also characterized by a remarkable differentiation and a wide range of justifications and unconvincing arguments. This lack of conviction has many psychological causes. In the context of this study, one of the most outstanding is that the "refunctionalization" of ideological tradition is the common goal of both revisionist and dogmatist Marxists in the GDR.

---

[72] "Entfremdung," in *Philosophisches Wörterbuch*, Georg Klaus and Manfred Buhr, eds. (Leipzig, 1964), p. 137.
[73] Horst Ullrich, "Klerikalismus und Entfremdung," *Deutsche Zeitschrift für Philosophie* 12, no. 6 (June 1964): 693.

In the dogmatic argument about the "real" meaning of alienation in Marx's writings one basic contradiction is evident. On the one hand, the dogmatists (inter alia, the East Germans Alfred Kurella, Gottfried Stiehler, Hans Koch, and Horst Ullrich; and the Soviets I. N. Davydov, T. I. Oizerman, and E. M. Sitnikov) claim that the most fully elaborated version of Marx's concept of alienation was formulated in his later works, primarily in *Das Kapital*. In this connection, Kurella comments:

. . . in the concept of alienation Marx reveals the basic contradiction between the capitalist mode of production and society, the contradiction between social production and private acquisition. . . . It is not difficult to see that these thoughts constitute the very kernel of what we generally describe as Marxism. Here Marx has found his way to a labor theory of value; he has discovered the concept of surplus value—the essential element of the system of capitalist exploitation—and gives a new economic, political, and historical content to the class concept originated by Guizot; he uncovers as well the root cause of cyclic crisis. . . .[74]

Kurella regards the metaphysical version of alienation in Marx's early writings as a "passing stage." Davydov and Ullrich, however, see alienation in Marx's early writings—particularly in the Paris manuscripts—as an already distinct, separate category of political economy.[75] Consequently, they reject all reinterpretations of Marx's views on alienation that stress its nature as a philosophy of man. On the other hand, Kurella regards the

objectification [and, thus, alienation] of the socially determined, essential powers of man . . . as an infinite process, a constant and necessary condition of human development.[76]

Similarly, Oizerman sees the "process of overcoming alienation of personality" not as a unique act, but as a continuous process of man's realization of his human potential.[77] Kurella's and Oizerman's interpretations refer back to the Hegelian concept of externalization. Thus, the

---

[74] Alfred Kurella, "Was verstand Marx unter Entfremdung?," *Sonntag* no. 14 (1964): 4.

[75] See J. N. Dawydow (= I. N. Davydov), *Freiheit und Entfremdung* (Berlin: Dietz Verlag, 1964), p. 45 (translated from the Russian *Trud i svoboda* [Moscow: Vysshaia shkola, 1962]); and Ullrich, "Klerikalismus und Entfremdung," p. 693.

[76] Alfred Kurella, *Der Mensch als Schöpfer seiner selbst. Beiträge zum sozialistischen Humanismus* (Berlin, 1961), p. 48.

[77] T. I. Oiserman (= Oizerman), *Die Entfremdung als historische Kategorie* (Berlin, 1965), p. 132.

historical validity, or applicability, of the Marxian concept of alienation or the essential human determinants of man's nature are not explored as elements of dogma. However, these considerations are indispensable to the interpretation of Marx and to the validity of all the fundamental assumptions of both historical and dialectical materialism. Furthermore, the problem of whether, and/or to what degree, the Marxian concept of alienation can be applied to concrete historical social entities in the present and future remains unanswered.

However, this view of the problem of alienation widens the possibilities for interpretation of the Marxian concept. Even the guardians of orthodoxy have been compelled to take into account in their discussions its more humanist and ontological components developed by Sartre and Camus. According to Schaff, this is necessary since "philosophical anthropology must solve the problem of the individual's ontological status and thereby provide a link between anthropology and the whole view of the world."[78] This more positive interpretation of the ideological heritage is accompanied by the call to develop a philosophy of man and ontology within the framework of dialectical materialism. The call for a Marxist philosophy of man—currently being raised even by dogmatists—can be regarded as an attempt to adapt ideological dogma to the realities of an industrial society. However, what does adaptation mean in this context? The demands for a positive philosophy of man under the political conditions of an authoritarian society can be interpreted only in the sense of a code of conduct, i.e., an attempt to implement the nominal claims of the party more effectively vis-à-vis the population.

Faced with this situation the guardians of ideological orthodoxy have developed rather bold interpretations. Rejecting the theories of Roger Garaudy and Ernst Fischer, Kurella does, indeed, deny any connection between alienation and the division of labor in Marx.[79] Nevertheless, he endeavors to separate the division of labor in its mechanical or technical emanations from its more essentially human features, and to maintain the former for the theory of a socialist industrial society. Although he rejects the interconnection of technical

[78] Schaff, *Marxism and the Human Individual*, p. 99.
[79] Kurella, "Was verstand Marx unter Entfremdung?," p. 4.

and social alienation propounded by Klaus, he approximates Western sociological interpretations in his call to "de-demonize" the concept of "alien": "In practical life this alien quality need not be repulsive or hostile."[80] This sentence could have been written by a Western organizational sociologist. It assumes an integration of society, as well as a voluntaristic conception of human individuality. Although man is enmeshed in a net of institutions and organizations, he repeatedly creates new areas of freedom by his voluntary actions. This interpretation of the "alien" fits man into the existing organizational system and removes the revolutionary tension between freedom and necessity. In the view of the dogmatists, man under a socialist order must devote his creative powers to building and consolidating the social system, though this demand has not been derived directly from the posing of the problem by dialectical materialism.

Analysis of Kurella's arguments reveals a dogmatically unconvincing line. This watchdog of ideological orthodoxy is on the defensive, and has been forced to adopt a narrow eclectic position. This position tends to stifle all possibility of the kind of penetrating analysis of historical and dialectical materialism developed by Klaus and Heise. A comprehensive analysis of possible revisions in dogma (impossible here) would reveal the close connection between the securing of the strategic clique's power and specific changes of dogma. Kurella's reflections should be seen in this light. His "harmonistic" interpretation of the "alien" conceals the structural conflicts in a technical society by declaring them reconciled. The reconciliation of social conflicts that he postulates demonstrates the will on the part of the SED's ideologues to maintain a closed ideological system—even when their arguments are self-contradictory—while granting occasional concessions in the sphere of its operating ideology.

SUMMARY AND CONCLUSIONS

The varied degrees of approval and disapproval accorded to the Marxian alienation concept by ideological dogmatists on the one hand, and different revisionist philosophers of history and technology on the other, might be summarized briefly as follows: The Marxian concept of alienation has not been included in the rigid ideological dogma. In

[80] Ibid., p. 3.

contrast, the concept of alienation plays a central role in revisionist thought.

One philosopher who represents institutionalized revisionism, Wolfgang Heise, attributes decisive importance to the Marxian concept of alienation. Basing himself on Marx, he goes on to assume the existence of alienation in "socialist" societies. His interpretation of the Marxian concept of alienation allows him to castigate, within the framework of historical materialism, the excessive centralization of the party and state apparatus, and to lambaste arbitrary decisions made by the strategic clique. Furthermore, Heise succeeds in rescuing the subject–object dialectics of Hegel and Marx from the empty formulas of ideology through his criticism of bureaucracy, which he has substantiated by his acceptance of alienation even under socialism. Finally, Heise fits this dialectic into a relatively open conception of historical Marxist thought, and demands an increased margin for human freedom. By so accepting and interpreting the Marxian concept of alienation, Heise is able to increase the margin of freedom for the "subject" in history. Although the expansion of individual freedom and criticism of bureaucracy can be regarded as politically relevant elements in Heise's philosophy, he provides no convincing consistent alternative to the social theories of historical materialism. His views on this issue remain highly abstract. Furthermore, we are dealing with a thinker who has resigned from his role of *effective* critic of the system; this becomes even clearer in his theory of aesthetics.

The philosophy of Georg Klaus represents the attempt to revise dialectical materialism in the GDR. Although this school purports to deduce the concept of alienation from Marx, in actuality it takes its point of departure from the similar concept of Hegel. Klaus also recognizes a "partial" alienation—of a technical sort—even for socialist societies. By resorting to the Marxian concept of alienation Klaus can posit the presence of total (i.e., social and technical) alienation only for capitalist societies and on the other hand, infuses the exhausted promise of communism with new vitality. By going back to Hegel's concept of externalization, Klaus is enabled to go on to formulate a dynamic philosophy for an "open" society—i.e., one extremely reactive to technical progress.

It becomes evident that the analogy between human and mechanical activity advanced by Klaus in his cybernetic theory of society has more pertinent content—despite its epistemological and logical weaknesses—than Heise's concept of man and society. Although the tension between creative and routine labor is quite as unidimensional, under the conditions of reduced totalitarianism in society a gain in technical rationality must be given higher priority than the arbritrariness which Heise's resignation cannot escape. Heise desires to eliminate alienation in the subject–object dialectics. This concept, however, seems to imply that the subject is more or less singled out. Society, the economy, and politics—i.e.,the objective world—serve only as background. Klaus, on the other hand, is primarily interested in the dynamics of the economic and technological development. In his views the expansion of technology absolutely constitutes the foreground, and man—the subject—becomes less important. For Klaus man is just an element fitted into the system; the historical subject is reduced to an unhistorical and abstract subject equipped with such faculties as "impulses," "will," and "control."

The dogmatist rejection of the Marxian concept of alienation is characterized by a very broad range of arguments, which itself is symptomatic of both a decomposition and refunctionalization of ideological dogma. In order to characterize the arguments of the ideological dogmatists, the following points of view have been emphasized. First, Marx is still interpreted in simplistic fashion purely as a political economist. The unity of the Marxian intellectual synthesis is to be preserved even at the risk of a complete devaluation of its content. However, even defenders of ideological dogma—such as the institutionalized revisionists—no longer completely reject a realistic view of modern industrial society—as can be seen in their positive acceptance of the concept of "alien." Nevertheless, this acceptance remains formal, and the concept is applied in disjointed fashion, rather than integrated into dogma.

The consequences of such thinking can hardly be disregarded. Both revisionists and dogmatists acknowledge a desire to lead the SED out of its isolation from society and to approve certain larger types of social organization with their forms of functional authority. The history of power politics has demonstrated that those in power and their subordinates—the dogmatists—have invariably learned from their critics. The present intellectual climate within the SED has not been ultimately affected by the fact that the ideological system has become more receptive and more open to criticism from the marginal zones of the party.

2. Systems Theory in Institutionalized Revisionism

The theoretical postulates of institutionalized revisionism go beyond historical and philosophical Utopianism. The "man-machine symbiosis" of Marxist systems theory is a modification of the classical Marxist Utopia couched in cybernetic terminology. The model of cybernetic systems analysis incorporates the elements of hope and promise; yet this thinking is rational and more amenable to verification than the official stereotypes of contemporary Marxism-Leninism.

Discussion of the "correct" interpretation of the Marxian concept of alienation centers on criticism of outmoded ideological dogma, and contains only the vague outlines of a positive social theory. The formulations of the systems theory version of revisionism are much more ambitious in scope. Its terminology and categories include extensive areas of dialectical and historical materialism, while the structure and subject matter of Marxist-Leninist dogma often do not correspond to systems theory. Traditional Marxism-Leninism, including its political economics, is to be made more functional through a theory of cybernetic systems. However, certain basic axioms are retained, such as the "dialectic structuring" of matter and its reflection in consciousness. The major theoretician of the cybernetic systems concept and ideologist of technocracy in the GDR, Georg Klaus, has attempted to apply the findings of logic and epistemology and other fields of the philosophy of science to both dialectical materialism and Marxist social theory.

Klaus is an ideological representative of the institutionalized counter elite, just as the party experts, Mittag, Jarowinsky, and Kleiber are economic representatives. Klaus's thought is more relevant to the contemporary ideological changes in the GDR than, for example, Robert Havemann's marginal thinking, which is based on the normative Utopia of aesthetic communism.[81] Klaus is a spokesman of "adaptation"—i.e.,

[81] See Ludz, "Freiheitsphilosophie oder aufgeklärter Dogmatismus?," pp. 380 ff.

the adaptation of thought and action to an advanced industrial civilization in which alienation has been eliminated completely and there exists a symbiosis of man and machine.

REMARKS ON CYBERNETICS

According to Klaus, cybernetics is the "science of all possible behavior patterns in all possible structures." These structures are dynamic, with built-in processes dependent on the time factor. Klaus has defined cybernetics more precisely as the "theory of the connection between all possible, dynamic, and self-regulating systems with their partial systems."[82] Here, "dynamic" obviously means "functioning."[83] "System" denotes a self-contained entity made up of partial systems and their reciprocal relationships. These reciprocal relations, or interactions, can also be regarded as "internal" inputs (to be distinguished from "external" inputs) when they originate within the system. The system is further characterized by its specific connection with the environment. Finally, the cybernetic systems concept implies that all total systems contain partial systems, which are analogous to the larger system. Klaus assumes that every dynamically self-regulating system is a "technical model [or expression] of specific dialectical contradictions." He proceeds from the further assumption that all conflicts in a society (in his terms, all dialectical contradictions) can be mathematically modeled— i.e., "technically imitated"—and, thus, solved. In other words, Klaus defines a system concept a priori in terms of dialectical logic and Marxist epistemology—i.e., theory of reflections.

For Klaus, Heinz Liebscher,[84] and the Westerners Helmar Frank[85] and Stafford Beer[86] the system aspects are the most important elements of cybernetics. On the other hand, Norbert Wiener,[87] Louis

---

[82] Klaus, *Kybernetik in philosophischer Sicht,* 4th ed., pp. 35 and 41.

[83] Georg Klaus and Heinz Liebscher, *Was ist, was soll Kybernetik?* (Leipzig, Jena, and Berlin, 1966), p. 10.

[84] Heinz Liebscher, *Kybernetik und Leitungstätigkeit* (Berlin, 1966), p. 10.

[85] Helmar Frank, "Was ist Kybernetik?," in Helmar Frank, ed., *Kybernetik. Brücke zwischen den Wissenschaften. 29 Beiträge namhafter Wissenschaftler und Ingenieure* (Darmstadt, 5th ed., 1965), p. 10.

[86] Stafford Beer, *Cybernetics and Management* (New York: John Wiley & Sons, Inc., Science editions, 1964), pp. 20 ff.

[87] Norbert Wiener, *Cybernetics* (Cambridge, Mass.: MIT Press, 1962), p. 24.

Couffignal, et al.,[88] hold that the control and communication aspects are the most essential, while the Soviet mathematician A. M. Kolmogorov[89] maintains that the information aspect is most important.

An extensive discussion of the problems of cybernetics is beyond the scope of this study. A brief survey of three of the five principal aspects of cybernetics distinguished by Klaus and Liebscher must suffice.[90] These are "system," "control," and "information."[91] Under the systems aspect of cybernetics, man and society are regarded as dynamic, self-regulating systems—hence its primary importance for Klaus. Cybernetics can most easily be transposed to society by emphasizing the systems aspect. This society—invariably a socialist industrial society—is regarded as a complex probabilistic system. The future of man and society (as a whole) cannot be completely predetermined, nor can the effect of individual partial areas on the developments of the total system. Klaus regards society, in terms of biological organisms, as a "dynamic self-regulating system" which is ultra-stable. The concept of ultra-stability implies that systems of this type can maintain their stability against multiple types of interference.

The second aspect integral to Klaus's cybernetic theory is that of control. The concept of control and/or regulation is fundamental in

[88] Louis Couffignal, *Kybernetische Grundbegriffe* (Baden-Baden and Paris, 1962), p. 57.

[89] See A. M. Kolmogorov's introduction in the Russian edition (Moscow, 1959) of William Ross Ashby, *Introduction to Cybernetics*. Kolmogorov states that "cybernetics is concerned with the study of optimal systems capable of receiving,, accumulating, and processing information for guidance, with the [ultimate] purpose of control and regulation." (Quoted from V. Stoljarow and K. H. Kannegiesser, "Zu einigen philosophischen Fragen der Kybernetik," *Deutsche Zeitschrift für Philosophie* 10, no. 5 (May 1962): 605.

[90] Referring to William Ross Ashby, Klaus and Liebscher place particular emphasis on the following instruments of cybernetic analysis: the black-box model, the analogy model, and the trial-and-error method. "Black-box" denotes a system whose structure is only partially known. While Ashby describes the black box in terms of no prior organization of the inputs by the experimenter, Klaus regards the black box and the experimenter as a feedback system. See Georg Klaus, *Kybernetik in philosophischer Sicht,* 4th ed., p. 225; and Heinz Liebscher, *Kybernetik und Leitungstätigkeit* (Berlin, 1966), pp. 18 ff.

[91] Klaus and Liebscher also distinguish between aspects of the theory of games and the algorithm theory, both of which can be disregarded in this context. See Klaus and Liebscher, *Was ist, was soll Kybernetik?*, pp. 16 ff.

cybernetics. "Regulation" is invariably tied in with the achievement of changes; it means man's control of his actions and behavior through his central nervous system, man's guidance of these activities and his behavior, and finally the control of automated equipment or machinery by human beings or by these machines themselves.

A basic principle of cybernetics is the control circuit and its associated feedback function. The control circuit consists primarily of the regulator and the system to be controlled. The regulator uses a regulating unit in order to change or secure the control unit against interference, depending upon the given function. Regulator A and controlled system C are connected by feedback to the extent that any changes at point C are recorded at point A. At times, isomorphism exists between the regulator and the controlled system, at least in ordinarily determined systems. The main characteristic of organic mechanisms of control is the fact that they are homeostats—i.e., control circuits—in which a random variable is maintained within predetermined limits. The basic cybernetic principle of dynamic self-regulation by systems is derived from the principle of homeostasis.

Laws formulated in the automatic control theory are not related to specific bases of matter, energy, etc., as regards their validity—according to cybernetic abstraction—but apply to all systems in all areas in which feedback processes occur.[92]

In the Marxist theory of organization the control aspect of cybernetics is of central significance, since the application of concepts relevant to economic and social planning, such as "command" and "control," pertain directly to the sphere of the theory of automatic control.

The third distinct aspect of cybernetics, its ramifications for the theory of information, is also important to Klaus, mainly in his attempts to establish a link between cybernetics and dialectical materialism. This is also essential to the Marxist theory of organization. Information and organization can be brought into homologous connection through cybernetic theory. To do this the syntactic and semantic element of information is considered, on the one hand, and, on the other, the structure and function of organization. Information, in the sense of the theory of communications, can be regarded as processes taking place within

[92] See Liebscher, *Kybernetik und Leitungstätigkeit,* p. 13.

cybernetic systems: "Processes taking place in complex cybernetic systems are by nature information processes—i.e., processes which generate, record, transmit, accumulate, release, and process information."[93] Indeed, East German discussions on these aspects of cybernetics tend to attribute one-sided pre-eminence to the data and communication aspects.[94] Thus, information is regarded as symbols transposed from one type of signal to another by a source of information via selection from a store of information. Consequently, the syntactic aspect of information as a section of general semiotics (i.e., the simple or complex relationship between symbols or signals) is especially emphasized. However, symbols are not merely related to other symbols, but also to the meaning of these symbols. Consequently, as Klaus emphasizes, information can also be conceived from a semantic perspective. Correspondingly, he defines information as "an entity consisting of a semantic and a physical carrier."[95]

According to Klaus, the signals are given both meaning and significance by their receiver. A "signal" becomes "information" for its receiver only when it has been assigned a clear meaning by the receiver. These associated possibilities both of interpreting and determining the meaning of signs and signals are of well-nigh decisive relevance to Klaus. His semantic interpretation of information theories opens new possibilities for verifying the internal consistency of the major relationships of dialectical materialism, and for renewing the discussion of previously unsolved basic Marxist philosophical problems associated with the theory of cognition and ontology. Emphasis upon the semantic aspects of information theory undoubtedly facilitates a more flexible approach on the part of the receiver to the interpretation of the information. However, one of the cornerstone theories of Marxist philosophy, the theory of reflection, is thus thrown open to doubt. Can we still assume isomorphism between the reflective consciousness and the reflected being, if the receiver of a signal has to transform the latter into information by giving it a content of signal? Repeated strong emphasis

[93] Ibid., p. 14.
[94] See, for example, Helmut Metzler, "Information und Leitung," *Deutsche Zeitschrift für Philosophie* 13, Sonderheft (1965): 240.
[95] Klaus, *Kybernetik in philosophischer Sicht,* 4th ed., p. 136.

upon the semantic aspects of information nevertheless ignores a further series of questions: Is information a tertium beyond "consciousness" and "matter"; must it therefore be associated with a third sphere of being? The last question will be explored later on in another context.

THE PROGRAM OF CYBERNETIC SYSTEMS THEORY

Cybernetics was not regarded as a serious science[96] by Soviet ideologists until after Khrushchev's address to the Twenty-Second CPSU Congress in 1961, in which he described cybernetics as the "fundamental science of the coming age." Ulbricht called for the setting up of mathematical models for political economics at the Twelfth Plenum of the SED Central Committee in 1961 and made favorable mention of cybernetics at the Fourteenth Plenum.[97] After this Klaus made great efforts to justify the new science vis-à-vis the dogmatic representatives of historical and dialectical materialism.

However, Klaus was publicly defending cybernetics as early as 1958,[98] after Fritz Selbmann in 1957 (then deputy chairman of the Council of Ministers and divisional director of the State Planning Commission) pointed out the significance of cybernetics for automation, optimum planning, and rationalized administration.[99] It is worth noting

[96] For the Soviet Union, see Mark B. Mitin, "Der XXII. Parteitag der KPdSU und die Aufgaben der wissenschaftlichen Arbeit auf dem Gebiete der marxistisch-leninistischen Philosophie," *Deutsche Zeitschrift für Philosophie* 10, no. 5 (May 1962): 535 ff. For the early development of cybernetics research in the GDR, see Heinz Liebscher, "Kybernetik und philosophische Forschung," *Deutsche Zeitschrift für Philosophie* 13, no. 2 (February 1965): 188 ff.

[97] Walter Ulbricht on the Twenty-Second CPSU Congress and its bearing upon the GDR, in *14. Tagung des Zentralkomitees der Sozialistischen Einheitspartei Deutschlands, 23. bis 26. November 1961* (Berlin, 1961), p. 82.

[98] Georg Klaus, "Zu einigen Problemen der Kybernetik," *Einheit* 13, no. 7 (July 1958): 1026 ff.

[99] See Fritz Selbmann, *Ein Zeitalter stellt sich vor* (Berlin, 1957). He states that "in the process of mechanization, production machines invariably assumed the function of manual labor. Moreover, we are now confronted by a completely new phenomenon: machines are performing mental work. Insofar as this phenomenon obtains in the production process, it is termed 'cybernetics,' a definition which was coined by the American cyberneticist Norbert Wiener, and which has already been accepted in Soviet terminology." (p. 13)

For the political aspects of the gradual acceptance gained by cybernetics in the GDR, see Klaus Siebert, "Hürdenlauf der Kybernetik," *SBZ-Archiv* 17, nos.

that Klaus had emphasized only the practical usefulness and application of cybernetics while propagating this science in a highly charged political context. His 1962 article contained very little on the theoretical implications of cybernetics for ideological dogma. Instead, he emphasized the function of cybernetics for economic and social planning, the rationalization of the output structure of industrial enterprises, the acceleration of technical progress in the automation and mechanization of the economy, and the establishment of new forms of labor organization—particularly within the framework of socialist competition and technical innovation.

It is undoubtedly Klaus's main purpose to apply cybernetic systems theory to economic and sociological problems. However, his attempt to use cybernetics within the framework of philosophical Marxism-Leninism is no less notable. Klaus does not see cybernetics as a mere theory of the connection between possible dynamic, self-controlling systems. As a philosopher of dialectical materialism, he also attempts to revitalize Engels' dictum relating to the production process: namely, that "things as things must be transformed into things for us." For Klaus they become "things for us" when they can be duplicated and are thereby subordinated to the will of man.[100]

Klaus's program for renovating the tenets of historical and dialectical materialism is outlined below:

1. Cybernetic systems theory is meant to define the categories of historical and dialectical materialism "by mathematical principles, particularly those of mathematical logic."[101]

2. The systems theory is intended to "perfect and consolidate the systematic categories of historical materialism."[102] For example, certain concepts with little current relevance, used in historical and dialectical materialism (such as "antagonistic contradiction" and "nonantagonistic contradiction"), could be reformulated by means of cybernetics.

3. Cybernetics as a "theory of dynamic self-regulating systems" is to be

---

15 and 17 (August and September 1966): 232 ff, 264 ff.; idem. "Hoffen auf die Kybernetik," *SBZ-Archiv* 18, nos. 10, 11–12, and 13 (May, June, and July 1967): 156 ff, 173 ff, and 195 ff.
[100] Klaus, *Kybernetik in philosophischer Sicht,* 2nd ed., p. 112.
[101] Georg Klaus, *Semiotik und Erkenntnistheorie* (Berlin, 1963), p. 23.
[102] Klaus, *Kybernetik und Gesellschaft,* pp. 3 and 4.

used for defining in more precise terms the "dialectic of the individual and the social system" that constitutes "social reality" for Klaus.[103]

4. Systems theory is intended to close, or at least narrow, the gap between concrete existing situations and concepts relevant in pure philosophy and social philosophy.

5. In this capacity as "a productive force of the first order," the systems theory will serve as the rationale for automation and influence the general methodology of technology, medicine, biology, etc. This postulate can be fully understood only in light of Klaus's conception of "automated production," which, for him, constitutes a unity between matter, energy, and structure in the production process.

6. Systems theory is to enhance the effects of economic planning and the planning of production campaigns (e.g., socialist competition), and to increase labor productivity. This also pertains to the rationalization of management and guidance structures in the factory, party, and state, as well as to solutions of problems of transportation, optimum location, etc.

7. Systems theory is intended to allow extensive "self-control" within social organizations. Klaus thus advocates a reduction of interference by central organs of control—i.e., the planning organs of the party and state. In accordance with the cybernetic theory of society, which uses the concept of "network of regulation systems," social organizations are to administer themselves in a rational, optimally efficient fashion.

8. The systems theory is to lead to the adoption of "collective work patterns," particularly in science. The SED's agitprop network has demanded this for years, but it has been hardly, if ever, achieved in any of the social sectors.

Some questions arise here. How does Klaus make his program palatable to the ideological dogmatists? What arguments does he use to reduce the dogmatists' mistrust of the introduction of automation techniques and—by inference—of the class of managers and technologists? How does he renovate and to some extent redefine the categories of dialectical and historical materialism without abandoning them?

Klaus invariably endeavors to assert the usefulness of his version of the systems theory both to ideological dogma and the operating ideology

[103] Ibid., pp. 3 ff.

of the Communist leadership. He repeatedly emphasizes that the application of cybernetic techniques would strengthen the political power position of Communist parties. His cybernetic investigations and speculations, and his attempts to establish the validity of his findings in terms of the ruling dogma lead to the conclusion that Klaus regards himself as a philosophical "innovator" within a fundamentally Marxist framework. Accordingly, he can be regarded as a representative of institutionalized revisionism in the GDR.

THE CYBERNETIC ASPECTS OF CONTROL AND INFORMATION AND OF DIALECTICAL MATERIALISM

Klaus attempts to confirm the tenets of dialectical materialism mostly by posing questions and findings developed by theories of control and information. A prerequisite of this procedure is the recognition of dialectical logic in the dialectical theory of cognition and the theory of reflection. Like his major opponent Havemann, Klaus repeatedly calls for a "conscious and systematic" application of dialectical logic. Like Havemann, Klaus also regards formal logic as merely "one aspect of the human environment." In accord with the axiom of the dialectical structure of matter and its reflection in consciousness, dialectical logic alone conceives the full breadth and depth of the human environment. Dialectical logic and formal logic thus stand in the relationship of the whole to one of its parts.[104]

In acknowledging this thesis, Klaus had hardly advanced beyond his basic position of 1951. At that time (as had A. D. Alexandrov in the USSR) he stated in his address "Dialectical Materialism and Mathematical Logic" that a "limited sphere of applicability for formal logic does not exist," but that "its application was limited in itself."[105] Following the Soviet model, Klaus described formal logic as "formalistic," with very little applicability. At the same time he noted that formal logic was

---

[104] See Georg Klaus, *Einführung in die formale Logik* (Berlin, 1958), pp. 11 ff; idem, "Der dialektische Materialismus und die mathematische Logik," in *Protokoll der philosophischen Konferenz über Fragen der Logik am 17. und 18. November 1951 in Jena* (Berlin, 1953), pp. 7 ff; idem, "Zur Soziologie der 'Mensch-Maschine-Symbiose'," *Deutsche Zeitschrift für Philosophie* 10, no. 7 (July 1962): 893; and idem, *Kybernetik und Gesellschaft*, p. 130.
[105] In *Protokoll der philosophischen Konferenz*, p. 11.

designed to eliminate contradictions. After other authorized interpreters of dialectical materialism had accepted the thesis of "the independence of language of class," advanced by Stalin in *On Marxism and Problems of Linguistics* (1950), Klaus gradually expanded the field of applicability for formal logic. He, too, recognized it as being "independent of class." However, then, as previously, the sphere of applicability for formal logic remained limited in principle. The actual philosophical implications of this position—namely, the relationship between dialectical and formal logic on the one hand, and between logic and ontology on the other—were not confronted squarely by him. Klaus was interested primarily in the connections between cybernetics and dialectical logic. He proceeded on the assumption that all "cybernetic formulations of terms . . . are by nature similar to those of dialectical materialism." He thus claimed that the dialectical pairs of categories "appearance and essence," "cause and effect," "necessity and chance," "possibility and reality," etc., either become "crystallized" and "specialized" or are further developed by cybernetics.[106] In this sense he described cybernetics as the theory of "dialectically contradictory reciprocal actions."[107]

Essentially, Klaus attempts to clarify three major problems in dialectical materialism by using the cybernetics theory concepts of control and information. These problems are: (1) how to define, more precisely than dialectical materialism has done, the pair of categories "change and necessity"; (2) how to clarify the relationship of causality to reciprocal action, and of causality to teleology, by using the cybernetic category of feedback; and (3) how to deal with the problem of the materialist interpretation of cybernetic information concepts.

Klaus uses the instability of organic control systems to support his thesis, based on a statement by Engels in the *Dialectics of Nature,* that "the accidental is necessary; necessity determines itself as chance; on the other hand, chance is . . . absolute necessity."[108] In principle, the theory of control signifies that the "inner necessity of the system totally overcomes external chance."[109] The ability to control ultra- or multi-

---

[106] Klaus, *Kybernetik in philosophischer Sicht,* 2nd ed., p. 96.
[107] Ibid., p. 157.
[108] Frederick Engels, *Dialectics of Nature* (Moscow: Foreign Language Publishing House, 1954), p. 292.
[109] Klaus, *Kybernetik in philosophischer Sicht,* 4th ed., p. 342.

stable systems is one of the great achievements of cybernetic control theory. The systems' guiding automatic devices, to be constructed on models of control theory, distinguish them from organic systems by the fact that the ratio of necessity and randomness is stabilized, and random influences upon the system are thus sharply reduced. This also applies to "flow equilibrium" in open systems, as first discovered in biology by Ludwig von Bertalanffy. Klaus's cybernetic control theory is now adapted to the basic axiom of dialectical materialism, namely, that chance and necessity are in a relation of constant dialectical reciprocity—i.e., they are both dynamic categories. Klaus uses this axiom to postulate "a unique form for the solution of the contradiction between necessity and chance." The incompatibility of the intellectual concepts juxtaposed by Klaus becomes evident upon examination of his attempts to transpose the category pair "chance and necessity" to the social and political spheres. According to his philosophy of man, in which man is defined as a controller, Klaus is forced to conclude that the accidental in society can be gradually eliminated by controlling actions that are dictated by necessity. Although the accidental cannot be entirely "eliminated," it can be "organized" or "controlled." Accordingly, chance and spontaneity of action in the sociopolitical sphere are reduced by means of the control system. On the other hand, the dialectics of chance and necessity are to be preserved, ad infinitum, in nature. Even if we disregard the inner contradictions, such a view—resulting from the vision of a technically perfected society—is incompatible with the Marxist concept of an abstract social stratum based on the dialectics of chance and necessity, spontaneity and consciousness.

Klaus assumes a similarly logically obscure position in his interpretation of the concepts of causality, reciprocal action, and teleology. His lack of precision is due primarily to the fact that, like Havemann, he has derived his concept of reciprocal action (or reciprocal determination) from Hegel's *Logik*. Yet unlike Havemann, Klaus advances the thesis that reciprocity is synonymous with a basic concept of cybernetic control theory, feedback. This alleged identity is based on the view that Hegel's concept of reciprocity can be defined and expanded in terms of physics and cybernetics theory.[110] Klaus assumes that reciprocal actions can be

[110] See also Herbert Hörz, *Atome, Kausalität, Quantensprünge. Quantentheorie— philosophisch betrachtet* (Berlin, 1964), p. 98.

observed throughout the universe. All processes in nature and society are thus interpreted as being constituted of reciprocally acting structures. In this definition causality itself becomes reciprocal action. The definition of reciprocity is correspondingly shallow: "The result invariably acts back in some fashion upon the cause." Consequently, Klaus defines reciprocal action as a "general philosophical category . . . which cannot be reduced any further."[111] Klaus's arguments are not convincing in this connection either. Furthermore, in other contexts in his works, reciprocity and feedback are *not* used synonymously. Feedback is declared to be "in a systematic dependence" with reciprocity.[112] Finally, the concept of reciprocal action is merely defined as an "aspect" of feedback.[113] This last definition excludes a direct identity of both categories.

This contradictory analysis of the reciprocal principle in the context of cybernetics is not clarified by Klaus's further reflections on the relationship between causality and reciprocity. Although he alleges that "in the framework of cybernetics an illumination of the various forms of causality and the possibility of a mathematically exact systematization of the various forms of causal connections can be achieved,"[114] he casts no new light on the problem of causality as it is defined in the official Marxist-Leninist doctrine. As do orthodox proponents of dialectical materialism, Klaus regards linear causality as an exceptional, or "borderline" case of reciprocity (feedback). In this case we can speak of a feedback having a zero value.

In connection with his analysis of the concepts reciprocity, feedback, and causality, Klaus also attempts to establish a new "materialistic" teleology. Based on the thought that systems with feedback behave in a systematic or purposeful fashion, Klaus recognizes only two classes of aims or purposes: a class of possible aims which are to be within the system's capacities to attain, which implies the choice of a system's possible future state. This concept of predetermination enables Klaus to establish a dialectical pair of categories, "possibility and reality": "All future states of a system are at least potentially or implicitly present in

[111] Klaus, *Kybernetik in philosophischer Sicht,* 4th ed., pp. 323 and 328.
[112] Ibid., pp. 330 ff.
[113] Ibid., p. 113.
[114] Klaus, *Kybernetik und Gesellschaft,* p. 19.

the state of the system at any given time, but not all possibilities of a system are normally realized."

Klaus goes on to distinguish a second class of aims. These contradict the laws of nature and, therefore, are so constituted that they can effect no change in the initial situation of a system. Klaus traces this position on the determination of the future configurations of systems with feedback to Hegel. Hegel's thesis that history is a progressive realization of freedom is interpreted by Klaus to mean a constant expansion of areas for controlled or regulated action: "The category of purposiveness thus embraces the dynamics of action. It is the purpose of all our science and research to control specific natural or social systems. To control the system means to ascribe specific states to it, states to be realized only in the future."[115] This "materialistic" purposiveness is seen as inherent in systems with feedback. It need not be elevated to the level of a chiliastic principle. Such a teleology is hardly consistent with Klaus's views on various aspects of the dialectic of chance and necessity.

Interrelations between causality, reciprocity, and teleology remain unestablished, since no distinction has been made between reciprocity and feedback. Reciprocity can be interpreted as feedback only in the narrow sense that certain symbols, signals, or information are sent back to the regulator in a feedback control system. A feedback control system is characterized by the fact that it is not "closed" in the causal sense alone, but also in the sense that it gives repeating reply signals. The regulator continuously sends out new pulses based on the response signals he receives; these pulses pass on information, and thus immunize the control circuit against outside interference. Cybernetic feedback can thus at most be regarded as a single special instance of reciprocal action.

Thus, Klaus has failed to solve this problem, partly because he conceives of reciprocal action, in a relatively vague fashion, as a comprehensive structural principle within the broader range of his evolutionary metaphysics of technology. His expansion of the concept of reciprocal action and disregard of information aspects have made it more difficult for him to confront the problem of defining the essence of "information." Is information to be characterized as matter, according to Lenin's concept of matter, or as consciousness? Or can information

[115] Klaus, *Kybernetik in philosophischer Sicht,* 4th ed., p. 338.

also relate to a third dimension of existence? Klaus claims that information is neither matter nor energy. Here he is in agreement with Western cyberneticists such as Norbert Wiener, Helmar Frank, et al. However, in order to clarify his concept of information, Klaus reverts ultimately to the syntactic aspect of information—i.e., he regards it merely as a connected, orderly arrangement of data and, by doing so, philosophically places it in the context of matter. Thus, Klaus is unable to solve the problem in terms of Marxist ontology and epistemology, which state, on the one hand, that the concept of information is closely tied to a material entity and, once created, can exist beyond and independently of consciousness; but, on the other, that it must be created by a conscious intelligence. Like many other East German cyberneticists (for example, K. H. Kannegiesser and W. Stoljarow), Klaus views the cognitive aspects of the information problem in purely ontological terms. As a result, his interpretations of the syntactic and semantic aspects of information assume the status of arbitrary assumptions.

THE PROBLEM OF ANALOGY

Historical and dialectical materialism has long recognized that the reasoning from analogies is different from induction and deduction, and from analysis and synthesis. Attempts to achieve agreement between cybernetics and dialectical and historical materialism have, however, greatly enhanced the opportunities to employ analogies. Klaus avails himself extensively of these possibilities. Following Louis Couffignal, he expressly defines analogy as a scientific working method which is basic to the "methodology of cybernetics."[116] Couffignal distinguishes between analogies in the numerable and innumerable sense. The former are described as "common functions of two organs which are found in two analogous mechanisms," and the latter as "the properties of two analogous mechanisms."[117] Couffignal—like Norbert Wiener, the biologist Warren S. McCulloch, and the neurologists William Ross Ashby and Grey Walter—has specified primarily those specific biological processes which he believes are transferable to automation processes by means of

---

[116] Klaus, *Kybernetik in philosophischer Sicht*, 2nd ed., p. 53; and *Kybernetik und Gesellschaft*, p. 171.
[117] Couffignal, *Kybernetische Grundbegriffe*, p. 77.

analogies. By analogies in thought we mean generally that historical and/or empirical data are seen as having relationships on the basis of mutually shared attributes. In such a way the specifics of certain data or interconnections between them can be explained from one or the other. The empirical dimensions related by means of analogy which Klaus and cyberneticists in general focus on, are patterns of behavior in the biological and physiological sense on the one hand, and the behavior of machines on the other. In the words of Wolfgang Wieser, we are dealing with "technical-biological analogies," an attempt "to reflect the same function in various material realms by means of different principles."[118] Many cyberneticists have formulated the principle that all biological functions—to the extent that they can be clearly defined—can be reflected in models; in other words, they can be used as analogies. This view does not yet permit us to speak of the "physiology" of a machine; such a term would lead to one of the major pitfalls of indiscriminate use of analogies, the uncritical use of metaphors.

Klaus has accepted, for the most part, the principle of reflecting biological functions in modes. His thesis of the importance of analogies to the progress of empirical science is undoubtedly correct: As emphasized by Herbert Stachowiak, an essential part of scientific progress is the "continuous transfer of known ordinal properties of the objective world to phenomenological fields which remain as yet inaccessible to causal analysis."[119] However, Klaus does not limit himself to the frequent use of biophysiological-technical analogies, but applies refined analogical relations to dialectical and historical materialism through the application of cybernetic concepts of analysis.

Nevertheless, his views had changed between 1958 and 1964. In 1958 he was still emphasizing that "the analogy between man, animal, and machine . . . leads us to the creation of the concept of cybernetics."[120] Yet, at this time he merely assumed "certain" analogies between the functioning of a machine and that of the human brain were possible. He posited no analogies between machine processes and

---

[118] Wolfgang Wieser, *Organismen, Strukturen, Maschinen. Zu einer Lehre vom Organismus* (Frankfurt-on-the-Main, 1959), p. 20.

[119] Herbert Stachowiak, *Denken und Erkennen im kybernetischen Modell* (Vienna and New York, 1965), p. 139.

[120] Klaus, "Zu einigen Problemen der Kybernetik," p. 1033.

dialectical thinking; at best they could hold merely for a general comparison of machines and the techniques of formal logic. At present, the Klausian application of analogies has become more diversified, although only in certain specific areas. In the 1965 edition of his *Kybernetik in philosophischer Sicht* Klaus expressly emphasizes the limitations of analogies. He defines the formal structure of analogy and distinguishes between four different levels, or stages, in models of analogy. Analogies exist at the "level of results attained by systems, the level of behavior leading to these results, the level of structures, and, finally, the level of matter."[121]

This differentiation in the use of analogy is very important for the definition of the different categories of dialectical materialism. The precipitate transformation of analogies between different systems (particularly between physiological and electronic processes) into identities has been avoided by the use of these distinctions. Klaus now claims that "a necessary prerequisite for analogy to become identity . . . is agreement at these four levels."[122]

Klaus has recently used this insight against his former teachers. He accuses Couffignal and Wiener in particular (as well as the representatives of neopositivism and behaviorism) of "constantly misapplying analogies." For example, he alleges that Norbert Wiener uses erroneous analogies in claiming a relation between "mechanisms" and "vitalism." Klaus's position has been occasioned to a great extent by the increasingly bitter disagreements between Marxists and logical empiricists.

Nevertheless, Klaus himself continues to use analogies quite loosely in order to establish the basic axioms of dialectical materialism. When he claims that cybernetics is concerned with the "study" of control processes, with the precise relationships between structure and function —relationships which have by no means been established—and when he uses the abstraction principle of mathematics as an analogy to support this contention, one is forced to regard this as an abstruse use of this methodological aid. Such vague use of analogies is particularly noticeable when Klaus fails to apply the four levels of analogy he himself distinguished, when he projects from laboratory experiments to large-

[121] Klaus, *Kybernetik in philosophischer Sicht,* 4th ed., p. 267.
[122] Ibid.

scale pilot runs, and when he relies instead on the Hegelian interpretation of the "dialectical unity of quantity and quality." In this context, Klaus asserts that when analogies are drawn in the technological field, the "dialectical law" of the transformation of quantity to quality applies.[123] Given his qualified affirmation of the principle of analogy, Klaus's criticism of its unsubstantiated, unverified application to general social processes seems clear. He criticizes the transposing of social or psychological empirical findings to more universal social situations, and he objects to the "direct transferral of facts from electronic computers to social events."[124]

Since Klaus has rejected the transferral of unsubstantiated analogies from the physiological, biological, or technological fields to social processes (and vice versa), it is paradoxical to find him adopting certain principles of historical materialism, first in the field of technology and then—claiming greater methodological precision—feeding them back to analyze general social and historical situations. This second step is particularly important in his interpretation of society in terms of cybernetic concepts. "We thus find at the level of society—in modified fashion, according to its specific character—conditions analogous to those established in physics for the behavior of microparticles."[125] There are many subsequent derivations of the intellectual outlook expressed in this quotation: There are similar control mechanisms in man's social relations. For example, class solidarity is a feedback process through which a certain social class attempts to assert its class consciousness by opposing outside factors that inhibit the process. Here, Klaus violates one of the basic tenets of modern empirical science, which allows the use of analogies only when functions, for example in the realm of biology, are clearly definable—i.e., when they can be subjected to rigorous logical and/or empirical controls. Thus, he is guilty of the very methodological sin that he attributes to Karl Steinbuch and Peter Hofstätter, with whom he engages in frequent controversy. Klaus has also expanded his use of analogies to apply to universal historical relations. Thus:

[123] Klaus, *Kybernetik und Gesellschaft,* p. 172.
[124] Ibid., p. 30.
[125] Ibid., p. 57.

Horse-drawn vehicles did not need streamlining. The form of a buggy would be exceptionally dysfunctional for cars moving at speeds above 100 kilometers an hour; streamlined features are appropriate in their case. This analogy may be transferred to the relationship between previous technological development and technology in the age of automation. Technology from the Stone Age to the middle of the twentieth century was adapted to man's subjective capacities. A certain symbiosis between man and machine existed, which in its machine aspect was adapted to man with all his imperfections and, thus, in many aspects subordinated man to the machine. This relationship of man and machine was conditioned primarily by its social setting. Members of the oppressed and exploited class that served the machine suffered from this historical variant of the man-machine symbiosis. Members of the ruling classes did not. In the world of the future, the machines will cease to establish social and technical barriers.[126]

Extended to history and society, analogies like these cannot avoid pictorial comparisons and metaphors. The historical Utopia is "concretized" by analogies from the present state of technical development, but it is doubtful that Klaus's arguments thereby become more exact or convincing. His excessive use of analogy, and the fact that he has yet to accomplish a true clarification of the categories of his thought accentuates the problem of this approach. Here it will suffice to mention briefly his views on the relationships of analogy to model, homomorphy, and isomorphism.

Klaus's use of analogies transposed to historical metaphysics is an example of a scientifically obsolete interpretation of reality. His utilization of universal historical and biological comparisons parallels the thinking of the late nineteenth century, which assumed the existence of analogous relationships between organic and inorganic "basic processes." Thus, Klaus continually runs the risk of reverting to empty formulas, such as those defined by Ernst Topitsch.[127]

REFERENCE TO HISTORICAL DOGMA: REVERSION TO FRIEDRICH ENGELS
AND ERNST MACH

Discussion of the influence of historical dogma on institutionalized revisionism will help to illuminate the general outlines of the latter type

---

[126] Ibid., pp. 121–122.
[127] Ernst Topitsch, *Vom Ursprung und Ende der Metaphysik. Eine Studie zur Weltanschauungskritik* (Vienna, 1958), pp. 221 ff.

of thinking. By establishing the manner and degree of revisionist deviations from the dogmatic, more traditional philosophical orientation, it is possible to determine the relative position of revisionist thought both in history and in terms of historical and dialectical materialism.[128]

Klaus makes extensive use of Marx's and Lenin's thought to support his social philosophy. Marx is repeatedly described as the "first cyberneticist."[129] Lenin is cited as the fountainhead of "creative work" with respect to his achievements after the period of war-time Communism following the October Revolution. Klaus also uses the arguments against modern positivism and behaviorism that are found in Lenin's work *Materialism and Empirio-Criticism.* Klaus bases himself on Lenin's polemic against Ostwald and Mach, especially his arguments against the "idealistic behaviorism" that aims at "reducing all phenomena of nature to motion or energy."[130]

Yet Klaus's thought is fundamentally influenced by Hegel, rather than Marx or Lenin, and is supplemented by Engel's later works and Ernst Mach's philosophy. Reliance on Engels is standard for a philosopher who represents dialectical materialism; reversion to both Hegel and Mach is most atypical.

Here, it will be appropriate to analyze Klaus's utilization of concepts derived from Engels' later writings, because contradictions arise in Klaus's interpretation of the actual founding principles of dialectical materialism. At a scientific conference on cybernetics, philosophy, and society in April 1961, sponsored by the journal *Einheit,* Klaus interpreted Engels as a natural scientist, quoting a sentence from the *Dialectics of Nature* to the effect that "the form of development of natural science . . . is the hypothesis."[131] Recognizing hypothesis as the "only" scientific method, Klaus called for a separation of the forms of thought from "their content." To support his thesis he cited Engels: "In order to investigate forms and relationships in their total purity it is

---

[128] For Klaus's relationship to Hegel, see p. 359. Among other thinkers who influenced Klaus—apart from the physiologist and cyberneticist William Ross Ashby—Engels and Mach are the most important.

[129] Klaus, *Kybernetik in philosophischer Sicht,* 2nd ed., p. 219. See also his *Kybernetik und Gesellschaft,* pp. 158 and 175 ff.

[130] Klaus, *Kybernetik in philosophischer Sicht,* 2nd ed., p. 186.

[131] Cf. Engels, *Dialectics of Nature,* p. 318.

necessary . . . to separate them completely from their content. . . ."[132]
While the principle of the separation of forms of thought from content
holds true for scientific logic, it does not apply to dialectical materialism.
Klaus's interpretation made Engels an empirical scientist whose thinking
strictly followed the sequence: ask, observe, formulate hypotheses, and,
finally, experimentally test and control these hypotheses. On the other
hand, Klaus postulated—again citing Engels' concept—that functions
must be "representations of qualities," and that "dialectics had entered
the realm of mathematics with the introduction of functions and
differential calculus."[133] This interpretation represented Engels as the
founder of dialectical materialism or, more precisely, of dialectical logic.
The arbitrary application of logical and cognitive categories, characteristic of Engels, is also found throughout Klaus's thinking. This is particularly noticeable when Klaus identifies key concepts such as "function"
and "dialectics."

In reverting to Engels, Klaus seeks the kind of support for his
logical and cognitive position that can only be found by openly accepting
the principles of formal logic. His eclectic position—involving, as it
does, the adoption of principles both from formal and dialectical
logic—had been criticized as early as 1951 at the Philosophical Conference on Problems of Logic, primarily by the philosopher Paul F.
Linke and the mathematician and logician Karl Schröter.[134] Klaus's
application of a basic idea of Mach (or Richard Avenarius) is, if
anything, even more revealing than his contradictory position vis-à-vis
Engels. In this context we should once again note Klaus's reinterpretation of the Hegelian estrangement concept in his elaboration of the
concept of the creative and his analysis of creative activity in terms of
algorithms.

Klaus has similarly transformed Mach's principle of "thought
economy." Like Mach and Avenarius, he begins formally by regarding
the principle of "thought economy" as an "economy . . . [only] in the
context of a specific purpose." But, whereas Mach and Avenarius had

[132] Cf. Rainer Thiel's notes on the 1961 conference in *Einheit* 16, no. 7 (July 1961):
Supplement, p. 12.
[133] Ibid., p. 17.
[134] These discussions are in *Protokoll der philosophischen Konferenz über Fragen
der Logik,* pp. 26–29 and 30 ff (cf. note 104).

not used the term "economical" to mean "useful" or "practical" in the clearly material application of the word,[135] Klaus has reverted to interpreting the principle of thought economy in terms of an "ideal image" of the "economy of behavior and cybernetics systems." Following this line of thought, Klaus states that "we describe that manner of thinking as economical, which attains specific results with a minimum of effort." [136] He has thus merely abstracted patterns of concrete behavior from the concept of economics. He goes back to Lenin to substantiate his materialistic reinterpretation of "thought economy" in two ways: He applies Lenin's derogatory application of "subjective idealists" to Mach and Avenarius, and he chooses to regard economy of thought in the framework of the theory of reflection almost solely as an "ideal image" of optimum behavior in cybernetic systems.

Klaus's use of Mach's concept of "sensation" is also open to criticism. In taking over this concept Klaus abandons both Mach's subjective idealism and logical empiricism more in word than in fact. For Klaus sensation is "the psychic experience which occurs when a complex of physical stimulations is received by our sensory organs."[137] Sensations are mutually comparable on the basis of their specific attributed qualities and quantities. However, comparability implies reduction to a single identical basic element. But Mach attributed these purely basic elements to his concept of sensation. For Mach all things, including the ego, are mere sensations: "The primary fact is not the I, the ego, but the elements [sensations]." By sensations Mach therefore means "perceptions, ideas, volition, and emotion—in brief, the whole inner and outer world composed of a small number of homogeneous elements connected in relations of varying evanescence and permanence."[138]

Klaus extends the application of Mach's and Avenarius' concepts of sensation and perception to those parts of his systems theory in which he

---

[135] Klaus, *Die Macht des Wortes*, p. 117. For Mach, see Hans Henning, *Ernst Mach als Philosoph, Physiker und Psycholog. Eine Monographie* (Leipzig, 1915), p. 133.

[136] Klaus, *Kybernetik und Gesellschaft*, p. 297.

[137] Georg Klaus, *Spezielle Erkenntnistheorie. Prinzipien der wissenschaftlichen Theorienbildung* (Berlin, 1965), p. 114.

[138] Ernst Mach, *Contributions to the Analysis of Sensations*, trans. by C. M. Williams (Chicago: The Open Court Publishing Company, 1897), p. 18.

analyzes information and language. After establishing these concepts as images in Lenin's sense, and having made his point of departure dogmatically secure, Klaus goes on to use them in support of his own theory of "ideal language."[139] A full discussion of this aspect of instrumentalization in Machian philosophy is beyond the scope of this study. Some mention of Mach's view of sensations is helpful in clarifying the basic tenets of Klaus's thinking—i.e., Klaus's attempts at direct practical application of systems theory and concepts from the philosophy of history to human activities.

According to Klaus, sensations can be subjected to empirical analysis and can be regarded as manipulatable data—i.e., *not* as transmitters of information having the character of truth. This view of sensations is at odds with Klaus's repeated emphasis in other contexts of the purely semantic aspects of information. On the problem of "agitation and the effect of truth" he states that

truths can only be regarded as such if (as stated by Marx) they affect the masses. For agitation, the truth of an assertion is indeed a necessity, but not a sufficient prerequisite. For assertions of truths the most effective linguistic formulations must be chosen. Social empirical analysis must be used to establish probable reactions (which are also dependent largely upon the general political and economic situation) of people to very specific verbal formulations in the process of propagating certain truths by agitation.[140]

In his view of semantic analysis agitation should be "scientifically implemented." In terms of the Marxian relation between theory and practice, or Hegel's concept of synthesis, agitation (but not information theory supported by the analysis of sensations) is conceived of as a "synthesis of the pragmatic and semantic aspects which reflect reality in our consciousness."[141]

This reliance on concepts derived from Hegel and Mach does not seem purely accidental. Both philosophers encompassed concrete material in vast system concepts, although Hegel took as his point of departure his views on the philosophy of history, while Mach bases his thought primarily upon psychological concepts. Within the framework of the history of philosophy Marxists classify Hegel as an "objective

[139] Klaus, *Spezielle Erkenntnistheorie*, pp. 118 ff.
[140] Klaus, *Die Macht des Wortes*, p. 123.
[141] Ibid.

idealist" and Mach and Avenarius as "subjective idealists" and, therefore, as representatives of idealist philosophy. Indeed, traces of idealist
philosophy may be said to appear in Klaus's systems theory.

If we expand this study of Klaus's intellectual origins to include the
founders of idealist systems, the basic structure of his formulations
becomes clearer and the following observations may be made: First, in
resorting to Hegel, Mach, Avenarius, et al.,—philosophers who have
developed idealist systems of thought—he has abandoned the principles
of unity of theory and practice categorically demanded by dialectical
and historical materialism at every stage of its development. Thus,
Klaus's interpretation of the concept of reality, plus his resort to political
action on behalf of the SED's strategic clique, are not consistently
related with his cybernetics theory, which is rooted in his philosophy of
history.

Thus, theory and reality exist side by side and become neither a
single totality nor a synthesis. Second, man, in Klaus's systems theory,
becomes nonhistorical, material, viewed abstractly. Since Klaus has
professed his intention to construct a "mechanical imitation," a pure
mechanism as the image of "cognizant acting man," this result is highly
consequential: In cybernetic models man is regarded on the one hand as
a "functional entity," and on the other as a "systems component." However, the concept of rational action implicit in this view of man—i.e.,
those anticipated actions which aim at "optimum solutions of problems"
—has nothing in common with the Marxist theory of man, apart from
its emphasis on man's purely practical activities. With the introduction
of the concept of the predictability of human actions, the theory of
consciously directed "spontaneity" of action, which is faintly reminiscent
of the Marxian concept of "action," loses its traditional content for the
study of man and his behavior.

SUMMARY AND CONCLUSIONS

The Marxist systems theory aimed at by Klaus is more closely attuned
to the problems and experiences of an industrial society than that of
many revisionist thinkers, primarily those who base their analyses on
historical materialism. Cybernetic categories undoubtedly facilitate a
more exact analysis of economy and society than do the dogmas of

historical materialism, even when the latter have been refurbished in revisionist style. On the other hand, cybernetic systems theory once again betrays the inherent weaknesses of certain major categories of dialectical materialism, such as necessity and chance, and causality and reciprocal action. Nevertheless, without clearly establishing the dogmatic basis for their claim, the ideological dogmatists have accepted cybernetics as the most important "productive force of science." Indeed, such formal justification has not been necessary. The pragmatic application of science to the control of economy and society invariably developed as a result of the recognition of a specific science's utility by the party elite; it did not, therefore, demand rigorous ideological substantiation.

The change in the ideological system as well as limitations of such change in the GDR have become more evident in the process of Klaus's interpretations of essential problems in Marxist philosophy. Over recent years it has become clear that certain long-standing problems of the Marxist philosophical concept of matter, dialectical logic, and the theory of cognition cannot ultimately be resolved, even by the application of cybernetic concepts. By the same token, this confrontation of cybernetics with dialectical materialism has left many problems in cybernetics theory unsolved. Primary among these are the connection between dialectical and formal logic, the still unclarified relation between syntactic and semantic aspects of information, the potentialities and limitations of analogy, and, finally, the hardly convincing identity posited between the concepts of reciprocity and feedback. The cognitive connections between the concepts of causality, reciprocity, and feedback advanced by Klaus are also not substantiated in strict logical fashion. Here, Klaus has tried to revise official ideological dogma by expanding the "subjective factor," i.e., the latitude of human spontaneity.

It is especially important at this point to note his emphasis upon the semantic aspects of information. The implications of his interpretation for the pragmatic aspects of information— and, thus, for communication and interaction—have not been pursued thoroughly here. Nonetheless, the relevance of Klaus's information theory to Marxist organizational theory and organizational reality in the GDR is unmistakable. The following section will treat certain themes common to theories of cybernetic systems and the Marxist theory of organization.

3. The Cybernetic Systems Concept and the Marxist Theory of Organization

The practical relevance of Klaus's systems theory is most evident in the fields of organizational concepts and politics. From this arise two questions: How did he establish and substantiate the connection between systems theory, organizational theory, and politics? What are the consequences of the confrontation of ideological dogma with cybernetics for an improvement in the technique of exercising political power and the attendant stabilization (or subversion) of the strategic clique's position of power?

The answers to these questions rest on three basic assumptions. First, the ideologists of technocracy have declared their intention of using cybernetics to serve established political power, to strengthen and secure this power, and simultaneously to develop rational justifications for the decisions of the strategic clique. Second, the comparability of certain cybernetic principles and categories with the basic axioms and categories of historical materialism is posited. Third, it is assumed that the cybernetic theory of systems and automatic control has not been without influence upon the Marxist theory of organization, in particular, upon the "science of management."

THE CYBERNETIC ASPECTS OF SYSTEM, CONTROL, AND INFORMATION
THEORY AND OF HISTORICAL MATERIALISM

It is the intent of those who propound cybernetics both to expand and complement the categories of historical materialism. In this context, Klaus assumes that "the method of cybernetics . . . adequately meets the demands of the cognitive method of historical materialism."[142] Insofar as "cognitive method" denotes Marxist-Leninist theory of reflection, the reader is referred to section 2 of this chapter. In addition, Klaus has applied black-box analysis to the operations of GDR society. This methodical approach is intended primarily to analyze the latter in terms of structures and functions of complex stochastic and/or probabilistic systems. Klaus regards the industrial society of the GDR as such in terms of a system. Even in a socialist society, at best only the inputs and outputs that influence this system can be analyzed, not its

[142] Klaus, *Kybernetik und Gesellschaft*, p. 35.

inner structure, or the functions of the elements that constitute that structure. Klaus thus searches extensively for the "response" of society to external inputs. However, this response by the society implies a clarification of its inner structure, or at the very least a clarification of the language in which its social interactions are to be formulated or described.

In order to clarify his view of the inner structure of society, Klaus elaborates upon certain key concepts. He prefers to use (though not really convincingly) the concepts of "social practice," "social labor," "production conditions," and "class"—categories derived from historical materialism.[143] However, this limits in advance the utility of his black-box analysis, since the concepts of function, structure, system, and relation, which are fundamental to black-box analysis, cannot really be reconciled with the empty formulas of historical materialism from which Klaus proceeds. Indeed, it is all the less feasible because Klaus applies the major concept of historical materialism in uncritical fashion, alternating, as does official East German dogma, between Marx's and Lenin's interpretations. One example will suffice to illustrate the attendant ambiguity. For Klaus, "class solidarity [is] a feedback process by means of which a certain social class attempts to assert its [class] norms by counteraction against impeding external factors. This is meant to involve the maintenance of a nominal value (e.g., the retention by the ruling class of a specific standard of living, certain privileges, property conditions, etc.) or a changeable leadership factor, if a newly rising class is to maintain the developing trend."[144] This example, which relies on the concept of feedback, gives rise to the suspicion that cybernetic concepts have indeed been used to legitimize dogmatic facts, but that we are hardly dealing with an actual elaboration and analysis of socially relevant historical material through the application of cybernetic categories.

As Klaus sees it, the categories of historical materialism are characterized by the attribute, "qualitative."[145] They thus apparently stand in opposition to the quantitative categories of cybernetics and have a clearly superior utility for evaluation. Consequently, the nineteenth and early twentieth century experiences contained in Marx's and Lenin's

---

[143] Ibid., pp. 34–35.
[144] Ibid., pp. 22 23.
[145] Ibid., p. 35.

formulations of the categories of historical materialism have been appropriated in a far from critical fashion and unsystematically combined with the operational and/or operative terminology of cybernetics. However, they have been applied to a complex organizational reality which must be controlled, but cannot be conquered. Even Klaus's occasionally advanced claim that the "essential control conditions" of a complex industrial society must be viewed in terms of cybernetic concepts does not really offer additional insights into society's operations, for Klaus regards these control conditions, "which determine what is specific to the behavior of all partial systems,"[146] as synonymous with "correct" perceptions of Marxist historical philosophy. In his view, the analysis of organizational systems effected through cybernetics theory has merely "supplementary" functions.[147]

The purpose of the rationalization of scientific activity aimed at by Klaus (inter alia by means of black-box analysis) is in the end defeated by his ideological and political prejudices. Thus, Klaus proceeds from the traditional Marxist assumption that social practice determines social consciousness, which in turn determines individual consciousness. He also identifies social practice with the "practice of the class struggle"—an assumption that does not hold for the present stage of development of GDR society because its ideological dogma does not permit such an interpretation. At this point Klaus not only knocks out the main underpinnings of his own analysis, but even manages to lose sight of the empirical reality which he initially sought to reveal. He has based his program on the consolidation or stability of an existing society, not upon an analysis of the specific historical conditions of the class struggle in that society. Under these circumstances it is not surprising that the social, psychological, and sociological factors which determine the behavior of social groups remain merely on the periphery of the issues identified by him as negative factors.

THE CYBERNETIC CONCEPT OF "SELF-ORGANIZATION" AS APPLIED TO THE STATE, SOCIETY, AND ECONOMY IN THE GDR

In socialist societies, which are conceived by Klaus as dynamic self-organizing systems, the concepts of "stability" and "organization" occupy

[146] Ibid., p. 28.
[147] Ibid.

prominent roles. Stability of a dynamic system means its return to a state of equilibrium which had existed prior to a given disturbance. However, the degree of "stability" attained is always relative and must be constantly re-established over time. A return to the state of equilibrium is effected by controls and/or regulations—more precisely through feedback circuits which counteract the disturbances and reinstitute stability. The latter, as well as certain other distinct tendencies of systems behavior which occur in the process of the given system's self-regulation are related by analogy in Klaus and certain Western authors (e.g., Stafford Beer) to physics, or related theoretically to the law of entropy. In such a system, described in terms of an analogy model, "order is more 'natural' than chaos"[148] just as in a single control circuit or a system of such circuits.

Klaus clearly distinguishes between the functions of open-loop and feedback control. He regards open-loop as a stage of influence no longer applicable to the "new economic system" in the GDR. Its effect is said to be distinctive in that it is not connected to a closed circuit as with regulation, but runs through a linear directional path, or control chain. By way of social analogy, this part of the analysis relates to an earlier form of "democratic centralism," whereas feedback appears as a more mature manifestation of the power principle. The key distinction between open-loop and feedback processes lies in the fact that an open-loop system is organized and stabilized externally, whereas a feedback system is organized and stabilized by means of internal, self-generated feedback. "External" disturbances in GDR society—i.e., the effects of a class enemy—can no longer be envisaged in the concept of the feedback control system.

The concept of "self-organization," central to cybernetic systems theory, has its roots in the concept of organization. In cybernetics in general, and for Klaus in particular, organization—rather *being* organized—primarily denotes generally the state of a dynamic system in which the elements are interconnected by certain relations which are subject to definition and control. The relations are conceived of as couplings or feedbacks in a black box. However, such relationships are also regarded as functions in a structural context. Moreover, the

---

[148] Beer, *Cybernetics and Management,* p. 41.

cybernetic concept of organization resembles that of the structuralists, and both are often used synonymously. However, here "structure" would appear to describe, more accurately than the term "organization," the isomorphic character of *all* the relationships and elements that appear in the system.

The cybernetic concept of organization, in Klaus's view, has two roots, which upon closer examination reveal two additional variants to which Klaus applies the term "organization." On the one hand, the organization concept reverts to views of self-reproducing and self-stabilizing organic systems, as described by Ludwig von Bertalanffy. The latter emphasized two characteristics of such self-organizing systems: namely, their dynamic and "open" character. "Whereas the order of organic events was previously attributed to fixed and mechanical structures, we are now dealing with a different type of order, which without rigid mechanical characteristics arises from the interplay of dynamic forces in the system."[149] This characterization of a dynamic self-organizing system already seems to provide evidence that we are not dealing with an imitation of the theory of machines developed by Descartes (which was based largely on the classical model of a mechanism as an individually closed and isolatable system), but with "open" systems of the biotechnical type. The "openness" of the dynamic self-organizing system is derived from analogy with a biological organism. This concept was later refined by Norbert Wiener, Ludwig von Bertalanffy, et al.: "The organism is an open, not a closed system. We term a system closed if no material can enter it from outside and none from it can extrude. In contrast, an open system involves the material inputs and outputs."[150] These characteristics of a self-organizing system are frequently represented by cybernetics in an ideal model form. The homeostat is a relatively simple model. This model can both neutralize certain disturbances in its structure caused by inputs, and invariably return to its initially constituted values. It can thus continue to fulfill its original functions. The concept of openness of organization also regards

[149] Ludwig von Bertalanffy, *Das Gefüge des Lebens* (Leipzig and Berlin, 1937), p. 13.
[150] Ludwig von Bertalanffy, "Der Organismus als physikalisches System betrachtet," *Die Naturwissenschaften* 28, no. 33 (1940): 521.

as open a system that "organizes and exploits external influences, regardless of whether they are useful or not."[151] Organization in this variant is regarded by Klaus as a systematic elaboration of inputs. His concept of organization thus allows an alternative variant.

The concepts of organization and self-organization used by Klaus are still characterized by the Marxist version of the biological theory of organization. This goes back to Darwin and has influenced many other Marxist thinkers, via Engels and Lenin. In particular, Alexander Bogdanov attempted at a relatively early date to apply the theory of the dynamic self-organizing system drawn from biology and physiology to the Marxist theory of organization.[152] He had already applied the concept of organization to biological, technological, and sociological processes, and used the concept of relative stability in his *General Theory of Organization*. By including the concept of organization in systems theory Klaus succeeded in reviving the concept of organization, so important to Marxism. Bogdanov, as well as many other Marxist thinkers from Marx and Rosa Luxemburg to Lukács, Bloch, and Havemann visualized the organological concept of a social structure and its functional relationships when they spoke of "society." Society is viewed as a living organism, a "totality" which is at the same time more than the sum of its components. Like a living organism, society can die (as with capitalism), but can also unfold and develop (as with socialism). Here, a third variant of the Klausian concept of organization becomes evident.

Klaus attempts to place GDR society and economy within the framework of this stratified concept of organization or self-organization. In applying the cybernetic concept of organization to the operations of the state, Klaus distinguishes the state in a bourgeois class society from that in a socialist society. In a class society the state assumes the functions of controlling society. Thus, the state has the function of a repressive control mechanism—as does the entire superstructure—instituted primarily to stabilize the position of power of the ruling class. In contrast, in a socialist society the state is "refunctionalized" as regards

---

[151] Klaus and Liebscher, *Was ist, was soll Kybernetik?*, p. 35.
[152] A. Bogdanov, *Allgemeine Organisationslehre*, 2 vols (Berlin, 1926, 1928), 2: 19–20, 122–123 and passim.

its operations in society. The guiding principle of democratic centralism is now foremost. During the "period of transition from capitalism to socialism" the state or party apparatus largely continues to retain the function of a control mechanism. However, Klaus maintains that throughout the entire period of transition the controlling state institutions are no longer identical with the superstructure in its totality, as opposed to the state of affairs in capitalist society. The State Council the Presidium of the Council of Ministers (and for the party apparatus the Politburo) are regarded as the main control units, or regulators.

By adapting the cybernetic theory of organization to the Marxist concept of the state Klaus attempts to solve a problem that has troubled Marxism for decades—i.e., the precise definition of the state and its role vis-à-vis society:

If we apply the cybernetic apparatus of concepts to these most general categories of historical materialism—base and superstructure—we receive an immediate answer, which has been highly controversial at times. We often hear the question: what does it actually mean when we say that the state is a component of the superstructure?
Do we mean that the state as both an institution and as an ideology pertains to the superstructure, or do the police and courts also properly belong to it, etc.? Cybernetics provides a simple answer. The state pertains to the superstructure in two fundamental ways: first, in terms of information theory—as an ideology structured in a specific fashion—and second, as a specific state and administrative structure, a special form of order.[153]

Klaus thus distinguishes various functions of the state by analyzing the latter in terms of the cybernetic theory of organization. In accordance with cybernetics' basic distinction between informational and regulating functions, he distinguishes between the ideological elements of the superstructure and those of the state executive. However, this view leaves several questions unanswered. What does Klaus understand by "ideology structured in a specific fashion"? Is it the syntactic, the semantic, or the pragmatic consideration which is the most decisive here? Furthermore, what is the character of the "order" posited by Klaus? The last question is of particular significance in view of the reinterpretation—particularly by Uwe-Jens Heuer—of the power principle in a system governed by democratic centralism.

[153] Klaus, *Kybernetik und Gesellschaft,* p. 63.

Despite these limitations, several distinctions established by application of the cybernetic theory of organization can point the way to a specifically Marxist theory of society. For example, viewing social processes in terms of the concepts of structure and function could introduce a certain flexibility in the ideological doctrine of "democratic centralism." Klaus retains Stalin's definition of the primary function of the state during the "period of transition," namely, the economic-organizational function. However, this conception of the state is opposed to that of a social system described in terms of the concepts of structure and function. Thus, the state as regulator is the guarantor of the dialectical unity of structure (in this case the economic structure of society) and function (the development of productive forces) and thus maintains the conditions for the existence of the social system in question.[154]

The state as the central control unit of society is to be replaced gradually by a self-regulating or self-organizing social system. Thus, control of society by the state is to be replaced by the feedback system of a socialist society. In a dynamic self-regulating system the regulator (Politburo or State Council) is increasingly influenced by the controlled system (society) via feedback, i.e., the flow of information from the controlled system back to the regulator. Thus, the Politburo and/or State Council are limited in the scope of their decisions. These limits gradually become narrower, until the growing social consciousness of the laboring masses ultimately replaces central regulation in a Communist society.

Although Klaus has not expressly stated it, this transformation of cybernetic control to feedback not only implies the replacement of the State Council and the Politburo by other political mechanisms, but also the gradual replacement of central social organizations by alternate instrumentalities. In accordance with the concept of the feedback control system, a longer period of transition could thus involve workers' councils (soviets). However, Klaus does not explicitly draw this ultimate conclusion. Indeed, he rarely expresses in openly political fashion the clear-cut predominance of feedback or control mechanisms. A sentence like the following is rarely encountered in his works: "In a certain way the degree of democracy or dictatorship permitted in a specific state indi-

[154] Ibid., p. 35.

cates the pre-eminence of feedback (regulating) or open-loop relation-ships."[155] However, a more indirectly political position is more fre-quently expressed in the frame of reference which discusses the set of relations between "social existence" and "social consciousness" in terms of cybernetics—i.e., parallels it to a feedback control system. Marxist terminology is here less conspicuous. Existence and consciousness form a dialectical dynamic unit in the sense that social consciousness develops gradually and limits the compulsory all-pervading character of existence.

The third area, aside from state and party, interpreted in terms of cybernetic theory of organization is the economy. The interpretation intended for application of cybernetic theories of system and control to planning the national economy and the economic system as a whole are the most original in Klaus's thought. Many economists in the GDR have realized in the course of time that a centrally controlled planned system is unable to react with sufficient speed to new basic goals defined by the Politburo or to the new inputs generated by technological and economic developments. Klaus, along with many economists, jurists, and organiza-tional theoreticians (e.g., Werner Kalweit, Uwe-Jens Heuer, and Horst Tröger) raises the demand for self-regulating systems—primarily in the economic sphere—in the form of relatively autonomous VEBs and VVBs:

If correctly applied cybernetic principles of organization lead to exten-sive self-regulation at the lower levels in the sense that interference by the central regulator—the state planning organs—is rarely necessary in the system of internal factory organization, and would be limited to cases where the corresponding subprogram, as announced, is not fulfilled, or where it does not fit into the framework of the overall program.[156]

In the economic sphere Klaus proceeds initially from the concepts of a network of regulating systems and a hierarchy of control circuits, which are initially self-regulating at the factory level within the frame-work of a "new economic system." This concept involves both rational-ization of the planning system and the delegation of decision making, a view that corresponds to the acceptance of the large VVBs and VEBs as numerous relatively stable systems:

The regulator of the multi-stable social system is not concerned with its

[155] Klaus, *Kybernetik in philosophischer Sicht,* 4th ed., p. 507.
[156] Klaus, *Kybernetik und Gesellschaft,* p. 95.

individual ultra-stable partial systems. The regulator is exclusively concerned with the way and manner in which these partial systems are fitted into a whole, i.e., with the reciprocity that exists between the entire system and its components, but not with processes in these partial systems themselves, or with the relations of these partial systems to corresponding aspects of their overall environment. Basic decisions are thus decisions referring to the reciprocity between the overall system and its parts.[157]

Klaus thus tries to nip a new bureaucratism in the bud, primarily in the economic and administrative spheres.

CYBERNETIC SELF-ORGANIZATION AND SOCIALIST DEMOCRACY

Several younger scientists have interpreted the "new economic system" as a cybernetic system of regulation and control in a somewhat more clear-cut, fundamental fashion than Klaus. For example, Klaus Dieter Wüstneck states that "the new economic system has a cybernetic character down to all its details and can thus only be understood in its entire theoretical breadth by a conscious consideration of the laws and categories of cybernetics."[158] Wüstneck calls both for the delegation of decision making to the factories, and for a clarification of confused concepts in the Marxist theory of management through the application of cybernetic terminology. Going beyond Klaus, he also attempts to take account of the "material interest" of the workers in the regulating process. Finally, Wüstneck deems it necessary to replace the State Planning Commission by the Research Council,[159] since learning systems correct themselves by direct application of their own experience and no longer require control mechanisms of the traditional type.

For learning systems, adaptation to a given or merely quantitatively changing environment should take place. In contrast, in a system planned and perspectively guided, not only should adaptation to a future

[157] Georg Klaus and Gerda Schnauss, "Kybernetik und sozialistische Leitung," *Einheit* 20, no. 2 (February 1965): 99.

[158] Klaus Dieter Wüstneck, "Der kybernetische Charakter des neuen ökonomischen Systems und die Modellstruktur der Perspektivplanung als zielstrebiger, kybernetischer Prozess," *Deutsche Zeitschrift für Philosophie* 13, no. 1 (January 1965): 6.

[159] The GDR Research Council *(Forschungsrat der DDR)* is the highest national body in charge of the planning and direction of all research in the natural sciences to be carried out at universities and other institutions. The Council was founded in 1957; according to its statutes it is an organ of the GDR Council of Ministers.

situation, known and assumed only in ideal form, take place but this desired situation is to be gradually shaped in accordance with the plan by concentrating on overcoming the present environment. This is the essential difference expressed in the functioning of the planning and directing apparatus in the new economic system. The learning process which previously involved changes in the model by planning on the grounds of current experiences is now replaced by the process of prognosis formation. In this process we learn to predict the future and adapt present activity to future requirements.[160]

The most interesting elaboration of the Klausian cybernetic model in recent years appears to have been made by the East Berlin jurist Uwe-Jens Heuer, in his study *Democracy and Law in the New Economic Systems of Planning and Direction of the National Economy* (1965). Heuer has also evaluated the pertinence of numerous contributions from Soviet discussions of cybernetics in recent years. He does not limit himself to reinterpreting society and economy in the GDR (although he gives scant treatment to the party and state apparatus). Indeed, by means of systematic political analysis Heuer tries to account for the emergent phenomena of differentiation and pluralization in East German society.[161] For example, he clearly distinguishes between society, state, and party and regards the relationship of party to society as by no means "one-sided or leader-led." His analysis to date is more political in character than Klaus's philosophy.

Heuer devotes far less space than Klaus to grounding cybernetic systems theory in the dogma of dialectical and historical materialism. He thus disregards Klaus's indecisive abolition of differences established in the concept of "basis" vs. "superstructural" sciences. Heuer's freedom from bias and dogmatic ideological concerns is expressed in his analysis of the categories of chance and necessity.[162] The accidental is by no means regarded as a mere disturbance in the social or political spheres:

Individually speaking, creativity, whether it be innovation, invention,

---

[160] Wüstneck, "Der kybernetische Charakter des neuen ökonomischen Systems," p. 24.

[161] See Heuer's contribution to a reader's discussion, "Afraid of Steep Paths?," published under the title "Neue Ökonomie verlangt neues Recht," *Neues Deutschland*, January 21, 1967, p. 10.

[162] Uwe-Jens Heuer, *Demokratie und Recht im neuen ökonomischen System der Planung und Leitung der Volkswirtschaft* (Berlin, 1965), pp. 102–103.

economic experiment, or the bold exploration of new markets, is accidental by nature. The ability of a partial system to overcome the effects of disturbances on its own depends also upon its capacity to encounter the environment in an independent and creative fashion.[163]

Heuer's analysis serves to establish a new basis for determining the relationship between political decisions and economic or social structures. "The thesis of the primacy of politics alone answers the question: What is the role of political forces in social change? However, it gives no reply to a second question: What are the aims of these forces and what criteria apply to their activity?"[164] Heuer does not content himself with citing the "dialectical unity" of central guidance and self-organization, but seeks new "forms of movement" in the economy and society. He proclaims an open society. In designing such new organizational forms, Heuer has not hesitated to draw upon the experiences of Western societies: "The critical acceptance of bourgeois experience will contribute towards reinforcing our position in the sphere of economic competition."[165]

The cybernetic concept of self-organization occupies a central place in Heuer's analysis. Following the insights of the Russian natural scientist V. S. Nemchinov—but also basing himself upon Horst Tröger and Kurt Braunreuther—Heuer has formulated a number of constituent elements basic to the concepts of self-organization and systems. Like Klaus, Heuer deduces the cybernetic organization concept from that of organisms. However, he goes further than Klaus. Self-organization assumes not only reciprocal actions between the individual elements of a system or a rationalization in the division of labor, but also cooperation and conflict. This applies for various sectors of the economy, as well as for the whole society of the GDR. "Thus, self-organization not merely unquestionably applies to the total social system, but to its partial systems as well (and even to partial systems of these partial systems, etc.)."[166] Heuer's description of "the material interests of the individual as the inner driving force of . . . self-organization" is not confined to the factory level but holds throughout society.[167] In keeping with this tenet,

[163] Ibid., p. 106.
[164] Ibid., p. 154.
[165] Ibid., p. 161.
[166] Ibid., p. 109.
[167] Ibid., p. 130.

his most important demand thus emerges more clearly; it is to move the working man closer to the center of the reform process. This is combined with a demand for expanded enterprise autonomy. In the economy the maximization of profits, the principle of economic accountability, and the greater recognition of both more general and more specific economic factors are the ultimate expression of self-organization on the factory level. "The self-organization of enterprises (and VVBs) under our conditions ultimately assumes the form of economic accountability."[168]

However, this is far from Heuer's final demand with regard to the self-organization of the economy and society. He calls for fixed rules and norms in GDR society under the rubric of the "new economic system" and reduction of the arbitrary nature of authoritarian rule: "Self-organization in the economy—the prime motivating force of which we characterize as material interests and democratic requirements—requires at present, and for the foreseeable future, both general and abstract rules of behavior and subjective rights and duties."[169] At this stage the analysis of GDR society in terms of the cybernetic system and the theory of regulation becomes most politically pertinent. Heuer's categorical demand for expanded democracy for the individual is not confined to the sphere of labor. He expands this concept to the economy as a whole. "In the social sphere self-organization ultimately implies self-decision, the individual or collective decision affecting one's own affairs."[170] On this point he becomes even more explicit in a specific reply to his critics. Here, he once more combines a demand for self-organization in society with freedom for the individual in decision making:

Organization of the socialist system necessarily involves the relative self-regulation and self-organization of partial systems. Self-organization in the social sphere ultimately means self-decision. The self-decision of one's own affairs, either individual or collective, is a necessary prerequisite for the unfolding of a socialist personality.[171]

[168] Ibid., p. 134. For problems of enlarging the decision-making discretion of VVBs and enterprises, see also Uwe-Jens Heuer, "Neues ökonomisches System und Entwicklung der sozialistischen Demokratie," *Wissenschaftliche Zeitschrift der Humboldt Universität zu Berlin. Gesellschafts- und sprachwissenschaftliche Reihe* 15, no. 4 (1966): 490–491.
[169] Heuer, *Demokratie und Recht*, p. 217.
[170] Ibid., p. 180.
[171] Uwe-Jens Heuer, "Gesellschaft und Demokratie," *Staat und Recht* 16, no. 6 (June 1967): 915.

An essential characteristic of the democratization process for the individual is the "co-decision of the producer."[172] The concept of socialist democracy has thus been reduced to self-decision on the part of the working man in society.

Heuer has refused to limit the cybernetically given potentials of scientific factory production to rational economic criteria. By adducing these criteria he has established a basis for thoroughly rethinking "socialist democracy" in the GDR. Heuer rejects the "higher development" of democracy based on purely ideological grounds. However, he too is unable to decide to make democratic self-decision the "sole criterion of social organization under socialism."[173] Following the Czech jurist Zdeněk Mlynář, he assumes that every group and subsystem must also have freedom of action in a given situation, even if this action has not been previously legitimized by democratic voting procedures.[174]

Expanding upon a reflection by the jurist Karl Polak (who as early as the 1950s had endeavored to clarify the concept of democracy in socialist systems[175]), Klaus has attempted to minimize the totalitarian-authoritarian features inherent in the concept of democratic centralism, a tendency still evident in his more recent works. Polak had already distinguished the principle of democratic centralism from the bureaucracy of party and state. In his interpretation of the "Law on the Improvement and Streamlining of Work in the State Apparatus of the GDR" (1958) Polak recommended expanded privileges for local peoples' representatives at the communal, city, and *Kreis* levels. On the other hand, his concept of socialist democracy was burdened by the more traditional interpretations of Lenin and Ulbricht. "Democracy is the unfolding of the power of the masses against older forces. This battle can be fought only under the hegemony of the proletariat and by taking into account the dialectics of development, the uncovering of contradictions, and the advance of the new as against the old."[176] In contrast, Heuer regards

---

[172] Heuer. *Demokratie und Recht,* p. 174.

[173] See ibid., 179.

[174] Zdeněk Mlynář. "Demokratie und Disziplin," *Staat und Recht* 14, no. 1 (January 1965): 131.

[175] See, for example, Karl Polak, *Zur Dialektik in der Staatslehre* (Berlin, 1963).

[176] Ibid., p. 166.

socialist democracy as having real content in the sense of expanded initiative, social independence, and greater independence of the individual. This applies to the new technologists and experts who implement economic and scientific decisions reached by consensus, as well as to individual workers in collectives.

The consequences of this view of democracy extend beyond the Marxist theory of law. Heuer has stripped the concepts of social democracy and democratic centralism of their nonobligatory nature. He distinguishes socialist democracy as an ideological postulate from democracy, defined by him as self-organization. For him the latter variant of the democratic concept is in the foreground. Correspondingly Heuer reduces the concept of democratic centralism to its very foundations in the process of production and labor. Thus, democracy is not merely made clearly distinct from centralism and therefore from the central party and state apparatuses. Indeed, the principle of democratic centralism is "subordinated" to that of socialist democracy.[177] Heuer's plea for the settlement of social conflicts is thus coupled with precisely such a definition of the concept of socialist democracy. He expressly recognizes the "unity of scientific economic guidance and democratic cooperation as a contradictory entity, but certainly not as a dead letter."[178] Heuer correspondingly regards GDR society as an organizational structure consisting of numerous partial systems, far from uniform or complementary. He thus also rejects the concept of a uniform social and/or individual subject that has plagued and continues to plague dogmatic Marxist-Leninist analysis of human development, ethics, and organizational theory. For him, man is defined by his roles in society. In society he distinguishes between social groups, strata, classes, and individuals.[179] With this view Heuer, like Kurt Tessmann, attempts to "qualitatively determine man's new position in the production process."[180] This concept also enabled Heuer to combine the cybernetic principle of self-regulation and conclude that partial systems can inde-

---

[177] Heuer, "Gesellschaft und Demokratie," p. 918.

[178] Heuer, *Demokratie und Recht*, p. 215.

[179] See Uwe-Jens Heuer, "Noch einmal: Warum entweder—oder?," *Forum* 20, no. 18 (1966): 6.

[180] Heuer, *Demokratie und Recht*, p. 13; and Kurt Tessmann, "Technische Revolution und Sozialismus," *Einheit* 20, no. 2 (February 1965): 17–18.

pendently eliminate disturbances by an optimum channelling of the information flow within themselves.

The system schema of the East Berlin jurist may be understood as a considerable expansion and concretization of the cybernetic system theory elaborated by Klaus, particularly when Heuer deals with the concept of self-organization. His systematic formulation may be regarded as the first theoretical attempt by a representative of the institutionalized counter elite to analyze the economic and technical potentialities of the "new economic system," while at the same time taking into account overall social desiderata. Consequently, it is a realistic analysis.

When . . . widely differentiated processes take place, when the qualifications and self-confidence of workers increases, when the qualitatively high and thus highly differentiated requirements of millions must be satisfied, when it is necessary to react rapidly to incessant developments in natural science, and when there is a further necessity to adapt to the fluctuations of the capitalist market, self-organization must be accorded major consideration.[181]

Thus, Heuer should be regarded as the most prominent representative of institutionalized revisionism to date, since, regardless of his criticism of the party bureaucracy, he assumes the continued stability and further development of GDR society. He firmly believes that social development in the GDR can lead to a higher form of democracy than that of West Germany. At the same time, Heuer's concepts of self-organization, democracy, and the legal relationships in a socialist industrial society should be regarded as a basic criticism of the centralist bureaucratic organizational and social policy of the strategic clique, as well as an independent attempt to design a positive theory for this society.

SUMMARY AND CONCLUSIONS

Among the various strains of revisionist philosophy the more technological strains of Klaus's philosophy can be described as a system adapted to the need for political and ideological rule of a Communist strategic clique, and which reflects the leadership's outgoing priorities. It is therefore all the more remarkable that this rather organologically based system-oriented way of thinking contains the rational impulse to protest

[181] Heuer, *Demokratie und Recht*, p. 110.

against arbitrary decisions by a residual and isolated strategic clique. Yet the typical limitations and the hesitant, qualified character of this protest, characteristic of the development of institutionalized revisionism, can be seen in the fact that rational decisions are criticized only when they appear to counter the criterion of increased performance. As a philosopher of technology, Georg Klaus has assumed a role common to many party experts in the SED within the framework of the present ideological system: He calls for the adaptation of large social organizations of optimum structure, rational decisions, and functional authority (even for a socialist industrial society) to the exigencies of worldwide economic competition. The representatives of institutionalized revisionism or the institutionalized counter elite seek to rationalize rule and society; only in this sense can they be regarded as critics of a system which they affirm in principle.

In contrast to Klaus, Heuer is less affected by the equivocal implications of the cybernetic theory. Heuer's analysis goes beyond a narrow utilitarian critique. Although it does not flatly negate the SED's ruling system, his demand that the rationalization of society ultimately imply democratization and a reduction of the centralist and authoritarian elements implicit in the principle of democratic centralism represents a rather decisive, politically formulated critique.

General Summary

This study has investigated the process of change in a society evolving from a totalitarian to an authoritarian stage. Empirical data on social structures and processes were subjected to sociological examination and description. The data were systematically classified, arranged according to correlative characteristics, and introduced into a wider frame of reference. This enabled us both to transcend mere presentation of facts and to avoid the empirically unsubstantiated claims and speculations sometimes encountered in research on the Soviet Union and East Germany.

In examining the East German social structure and its main features through analysis of selected substructures of that society, this study used the "critical–empirical" theoretical and methodological approach. Finally, an attempt has been made to fit the individual East German analyses into a frame of reference taking the Marxist-Leninist social theory into account. Thus, the concepts of "conflict," "contradiction," and "deviation" are central to our focus. Social and ideological conflicts and differentiations have been described as precisely as possible. It has been assumed that every industrial society—particularly the variant originating from a totalitarian system—invariably constitutes an entity dominated by conflicting interests; specific social structures and conflict situations have been selected for discussion from this point of view. The SED, which is itself a type of large social organization influenced by the conditions of industrial society, has been compared with a model based on the organizational principles of the political secret societies of the eighteenth and nineteenth centuries. Sociologically, two groups are distinguished: the institutionalized counter elite, including party experts and revisionist ideologists, and the representatives of the strategic clique. In the ideological sphere, official dogma has been contrasted with the published variants of institutionalized revisionism.

The present stage of the ideological and social transformation of East German society—and particularly of the SED leadership groups—has been characterized as "consultative authoritarianism," in terms of a continuum developed by Rensis Likert and Alfred G. Meyer. The conditions of technological society compel the authoritarian–political decision-making elite (unlike a totalitarian elite) to consult experts so that the elite can keep abreast of and acquire information on the complicated processes taking place in a constantly evolving industrial society, and retain control over the system. However, unlike the participatory type of authoritarian elite, the consultative-authoritarian is most hesitant to enlarge the sphere of democratic participation in decision making.

Because this study has confined itself to selected areas of East German society that were thought to be most indicative of change and inertia in the whole system, no account was taken of possible forces seeking the total overthrow of the present GDR ruling system. The results of this study appear to confirm that East German society is a continually self-stabilizing system, albeit one in the process of change. Consequently, sociological analysis of resistance to established rule, which would be appropriate for the forms of totalitarian domination that existed earlier in the GDR, is outside the scope of this examination.

Since 1962 or 1963 the guiding organizational principles have shifted their emphasis from political to social and economic considerations. This change in the organizational system of the SED is apparent in selected sectors of the party apparatus, primarily in the establishment of central and regional bureaus of industry and construction. Although the activities of these bureaus were curtailed in 1964, and they, along with the commissions, were dissolved by the end of 1966, the very fact of their establishment in the party apparatus gave rise to the takeover by party experts of executive functions in the economic, social, and political fields. Moreover, the "operational" style of problem solving in the bureaus led to an increase in "functional" authority and in mobility. Both developments affected the organizational system of the SED as a whole.

Further evidence of restructuring within the party apparatus is provided by analysis of the Central Committee, the "supreme party body between party congresses." After functioning for years as a purely acclamatory and declamatory assembly, it is increasingly undergoing change to an active coordinating and transforming body, in which the Politburo decisions are objectively discussed by party functionaries and experts and prepared for transmission downward. Analysis of the Central Committee appears to confirm the existence of the major outlines of the organizational processes described in Chapter One as leading toward "consultative authoritarianism."

Despite the fact that the leadership itself initiated this process, the strategic clique of the SED made every effort to control or reverse the restructuring of the party apparatus into a large, more "open" social organization. The establishment of the workers' and peasants' inspectorates, production committees, and control organs within the bureaus of industry and construction, and the temporary rise in status of the ideological commission are as important in this context as the dissolution of the bureaus and commissions.

Comparative analysis of the social composition of the Central Committee between 1954 and 1963 was most useful in tracing the process of change in the SED organization. The factors of age, completion of education or professional training, and acquired and actual occupation were the most significant. These limited data sufficed to establish the following essential changes in the overall internal structure of the party: replacement of the older generation, a rise in the number of trained party functionaries, and an increase in professional mobility.

In contradiction to the generally held Western view, our analysis discovered cases of resignations normal under the conditions of an industrial society, even in the Communist party apparatus. Views that disregard this characteristic, essential to a changing party apparatus, are based on an ideally posited type of totalitarian rule which has been superseded in the GDR.

Findings in Chapter Three established the existence of a process of "professionalization," and a clear separation in functional areas of party and state apparatuses in recent years. This is accompanied by the advance of younger, more highly qualified party functionaries. More traditional research has often alleged that interchangeability of position is widespread in totalitarian societies. However, under the conditions of a society in flux this phenomenon does not appear to be as prevalent as was previously assumed.

The increased functional separation among, and increased autonomy of, the large party and state organizations has greatly facilitated the discernment of the centers of power of the strategic clique and the institutionalized counter elite. The strategic clique continues to dominate the real decision-making bodies—i.e., the Politburo and the Central Committee Secretariat—and fills the positions of first secretary in the SED *Bezirk* and *Kreis* executives, as well as in the State Council. Centers for the aggregation of party experts are, for example, the Council of Ministers, the State Planning Commission, the Research Council, and, to some degree, the Central Committee itself.

The profound changes in the Marxist-Leninist ideological system of the GDR may be interpreted variously as decay, inertia, or, finally, a refunctionalization of ideological dogma. Analysis of differences and conflicts in various interpretations of historical and dialectical material- ism was included in this study, since these differences paralleled trends perceived in the organizational and social spheres.

The main question is what conditions would make possible the adoption of an "open" perspective from which current realities could be interpreted, both within the framework of historical and dialectical materialism and with more regard to the dynamics of an industrial society. Chapter Four divided this problem into an outline of the Marxian concept of alienation and a discussion of actual social ideas and historical and philosophical views based on this concept. Aspects of cybernetics theory, including systems theory, regulation, and information theory, were considered the most interesting features of institutionalized revisionist philosophy in the GDR. These were related to the more general phenomena of change and inertia, adaptation to the existing system of power, and criticism thereof.

Basic structural differences between historical and dialectical mate- rialism have been clarified. While interpretations of Hegel's concept of "externalization" and Marx's concept of "alienation," both of which are committed to historical materialism, terminate in either a subject–object dialectic or in an aesthetically transformed variant of fatalistic resigna- tion, dialectical materialism attempts to construct a positive social theory and to interpret the "open dynamic" of an industrial world.

Institutionalized revisionist formulations based on systems and regulation theories contain several major contradictions, which show up most clearly in the work of Georg Klaus and Uwe-Jens Heuer. There are obviously common points of contact with the organologically oriented and Utopian interpretations of Marxism. Even the "dialectical" systems theory begins by transposing whole categories from the philosophy of history to the field of technology, and then applies them to the interpretation of history and society under the pretext of greater exactitude (in the form of feedback). Alternately, this type of thinking often involves analogies, and thereby raises new problems for dialectical logic and the theory of cognition. In the context of official ideology, with its empty formulas, the use of analogies undoubtedly constitutes a step in the direction of recognition of formal logic. Apart from logical and empirical analogies, which are not subject to verifying controls, the use of cybernetics introduces into dialectical logic analogies which can certainly be subjected to logical and/or empirical control.

Systems, regulation, and information theories aim at the refunctionalization, not the annihilation, of ideological dogma. Consequently, their guiding principle is the stability of both the existing system of rule and the social system. Yet this philosophy of adaptation retains an element of rationality, the critical function of which in a nondemocratic society, although marginal, deserves emphasis. It enters the picture when decisions of the strategic clique appear arbitrary, and thus likely to impair the workings of a system which has for a guiding principle the permanent increase in productivity. Institutionalized revisionism differs from the even more marginal phenomenon of revisionism in that its criticism aims at stabilizing society, which is interpreted as a conglomerate of intermeshed control systems. Thus, changes in the organizational system and the social composition of the party elite can be directly related to changes in the philosophical interpretation of society.

The representatives of the institutionalized counter elite—e.g., Mittag, Klaus, and Heuer—seek to strengthen the political and social systems of the GDR. They can therefore be regarded as major spokesmen of a new political elite. Nevertheless, their thought is still based largely on the dogmatic ideology of dialectical and historical materialism. However, it can be definitively stated that there has been a recognition of the priorities of technical and economic progress and an awareness of processes of differentiation and ongoing dynamic changes in the GDR's society, coupled with the vision of a permanent increase in productivity. These developments provide the prerequisites for further processes of rationalization of the new elite's outlook, which could facilitate its further attunement to the needs and realities of GDR society.

Appendix 1

The Central Committee and the Seventh SED Congress

Two major tendencies emerged at the Seventh SED Congress (April 17–22, 1967). The policy of "professionalization" established at the Sixth SED Congress in 1963 was reiterated as a continuing goal of the SED leadership and given even higher priority. On the other hand, some opposition to this was manifested as a reaction to the loosening of political control that followed the institution of the "new economic system." These trends were reflected in the changes in personnel effected at the Seventh Congress, the analysis of which is the subject of this Appendix.

1. Changes in the Central Committee from 1963 to 1967

The total number of both members and candidates of the Central Committee elected at the Seventh SED Congress in April 1967 was the same as the 1963 Central Committee—181. However, the number of full members increased from 121 to 131, and the number of candidates dropped correspondingly from 60 to 50. Compared with the 1963 Central Committee, that of 1967 exhibited the following general profile with regard to length of service:

131 members
of whom:
97 were former members of the 1963 Central Committee
21 were former candidates of the 1963 Central Committee (8 of the latter group were promoted to members in 1967)
13 were newly elected

50 candidates
of whom:
25 were former candidates of the 1963 Central Committee
25 were newly elected

Twenty-four members (including Jäckel and Löschau, promoted to full membership between the Sixth and Seventh Congresses) and fourteen candidates from the 1963 Central Committee were not re-elected to that of 1967.

On the basis of changes published since 1963, the Central Committee on the eve of the Seventh SED Congress consisted of 119 members and 50 candidates. Ten members had died between 1963 and 1967: Dr. Erich Apel (1965), Willi Bredel (1964), Otto Buchwitz (1964), Otto Grotewohl (1964), Hans Kiefert (1966), Bernard Koenen (1964), Wilhelm Koenen (1963), Bruno Leuschner (1964), Helmut Scholz (1967), and Friedrich Wehmer (1964). Furthermore, seven of the 1963 candidates had been promoted to membership at the Seventh Central Committee Plenum in 1964: Fritz Dallmann, Pof. Dr. Hans Jäckel, Ingeborg Lange, Dr. Siegbert Löschau, Günter Prey, Johann Wittik, and Günther Wyschofsky and three at the Thirteenth in 1966: Otto Gotsche, Konrad Naumann, and Herbert Ziegenhahn. The following two individuals were dropped from Central Committee membership between the Sixth and Seventh SED Congresses: Prof. Dr. Karl-Heinz Bartsch (1963) because of his former SS membership; and Dr. Siegbert Löschau because of "unworthy conduct" (*Neues Deutschland,* September 18, 1966).

Of the 119 members and 50 candidates in the Central Committee just before the Seventh Congress, 14 members and 12 candidates were not reelected to the new Central Committee. The full members are: Hugo Baumgart, Fritz Bönisch, Rudolf Dölling, Prof. Dr. Hans Jäckel, Prof. Gerhard Kosel, Karl Krüger, Walter Lassak, Robert Lehmann, Lorenz Lochthofen, Frido Meinhardt, Kurt Seibt, Prof. Maxim Vallentin, Erich Wirth, and Ernst Wolf. The following twelve candidate members of the Central Committee before the Seventh Congress who were not re-elected are: Hans Ernst, Dr. Michael Gehring, Walter Kaiser-Gorrish, Werner Krussk, Ernst Lange, Prof. Dr. Rudolf Lappe, Hans-Joachim Marschner, Dr. Wolfgang Oerter, Anton Plenikowski, Prof. Dr. Wolfgang Schirmer, Friedrich Wesselburg, and Christa Wolf.

MEMBERS AND CANDIDATES OF THE 1963 CENTRAL COMMITTEE NOT REPRESENTED IN THE 1967 CENTRAL COMMITTEE
In order to determine the relevance of these changes to the questions in Chapter Three, the 38 members and candidates of the 1963 Central Committee who were not re-elected in 1967 have been subjected to more detailed analysis. With respect to age, the full members excluded in 1967 belong for the most part to the group born before 1920 (21 out of 24). However, younger groups born in 1920 or later constitute a bare

majority of the candidates (8 out of 14). The total of 11 younger members or candidates of the 1963 Central Committee not re-elected in 1967 are: Bartsch, Meinhardt, Scholz, Ernst, Jäckel, Krussk, Löschau, Marschner, Oerter, Schirmer, and Christa Wolf. With respect to Jäckel and Krussk, it may be assumed that their former membership in the Nazi party resulted in their not being re-elected to the 1967 Central Committee. Both had been candidates in 1963; Jäckel was promoted to full membership in 1964. Presumably, Christa Wolf was demoted for her statements at the Eleventh Plenum in December 1965. Among the younger 1963 group dropped in 1967 there were two NVA members, Ernst and Marschner, whose exclusion has not been publicly explained. As of 1968 the following dismissals remained especially enigmatic: Frido Meinhardt, former BPO Secretary in the Iron Foundry Combine East (*Eisenhüttenkombinat Ost*), who was made group director of socialist economic guidance in the Minstry of Ore Mining, Metallurgy, and Potash in 1966; Dr. Wolfgang Oerter, a functionary in the Ministry of Health; Prof. Dr. Wolfgang Schirmer, as of 1968 still the First Chairman of the COMECON Standing Commission for the Chemical Industry, Professor of Technology at Humboldt University, and Director of the German Academy of Science's Institute for Physical Chemistry in Berlin. Furthermore, Meinhardt had been a Central Committee member of long standing (since 1954), while Schirmer had enjoyed candidate status since 1954.

According to occupation at the time of their exclusion, the members and candidates of the 1963 Central Committee demoted in 1967 break down as given in Table 50. The low proportion of state functionaries not re-elected in the 1967 Central Committee is particularly noticeable. Of the 9 members and candidates who occupied top-level state posts in 1963 and were not re-elected to the 1967 Central Committee, 5 had died: Apel, Buchwitz, Grotewohl, W. Koenen, and Scholz. To these should be added Bartsch, excluded in 1963; Rudolf Dölling, who until August 1965 was the East German Ambassador to the Soviet Union, and whose present function cannot be determined; Dr. Michael Gehring, in March 1964 appointed Secretary of State and First Deputy Minister of Health; Anton Plenikowski, formerly State Secretary and Director of the Council of Ministers' Bureau, and most recently Director of the Inter-Parliamentary Group of the Peoples' Chamber, who may well have been retired on the

Table 50
Members and Candidates of the 1963 CC Dropped in 1967: Functional Areas and Positions

Functional Area and Position in 1963*	CC Members and Candidates in 1963 Excluded in 1967			of these	
	Members	Candidates	Total	Died	Dismissed
1 Party	5	1	6	2	0
of these:					
top	0	0	0		
upper middle	2	1	3		
middle/lower middle	3	0	3		
2 State	11	4	15	6	1
of these:					
top	7	2	9		
upper middle	0	0	0		
middle/lower middle	4	2	6		
3 Economy	2	2	4	0	1
of these:					
top	1	1	2		
upper middle	1	1	2		
middle/lower middle	0	0	0		

35 Agriculture	0	0	0	0	0
4 Mass organizations	2	0	2	1	0
of these:					
top	2	0	2		
upper middle	0	0	0		
middle/lower middle	0	0	0		
5 Culture of Education	3	4	7	0	0
of these:					
top	2	1	3		
upper middle	1	2	3		
middle/lower middle	0	1	1		
6, 7, 8 NVA, etc.	1	3	4	1	0
of these:					
top	1	2	3		
upper middle	0	1	1		
middle/lower middle	0	0	0		
Total	24	14	38	10	2

* See code on pp. 226–227.

grounds of his advanced age. (He was born in 1899.) The two top-level economic functionaries who were not re-elected are Dr. Siegbert Löschau, former plant manager of the VEB Leuna-Werge "Walter Ulbricht," and Lorenz Lochthofen, who was apparently relieved of his function as plant director in the Sömmerda VEB Office Machinery on grounds of poor health.

Among the 38 Central Committee members and candidates not re-elected in 1967, detailed examination of three subgroups—the members of the younger generation born in 1920 or later, and those with either top-level state or economic positions—reveals the following trends: No economically or technically trained member of the younger generation was dropped from the Central Committee in premeditated fashion by the party leadership. Furthermore, there are no other clearly recognizable groups whose representation in the 1967 Central Committee has been systematically reduced. Exclusion from this Central Committee must therefore be viewed as a result of anomalies in the given individuals' personal biographies.

NEW MEMBERS AND CANDIDATES IN THE 1967 CENTRAL COMMITTEE
Among the 13 new Central Committee members in 1967 are 4 veteran functionaries: Eisler, Dickel, Fuchs, and Singer. The other 9 had entered the KPD/SPD or SED after 1945. Except for the writer Bernhard Seeger and the chief propagandist Gerhart Eisler, all the new Central Committee members had received specialized professional training. Eight had received university-level education in the natural sciences or in economics.

The new Central Committee members exhibit the following breakdown as regards actual occupation:

Six are top state functionaries. In addition to Walter Halbritter and Günther Kleiber, also elected to candidate status in the Politburo, we find two experts from the ranks of the younger generation: Siegfried Böhm, was born in 1928 and entered the SED in 1948. He is a commercial assistant, holder of a university diploma in economics, and since 1966 the GDR's Minister of Finance; Wolfgang Rauchfuss, was born in 1931, and entered the SED in 1951. He is also a graduate in economics, and was re-elected to the Council of Ministers in July 1967 as one of its deputy chairmen.

The top functionaries of the state apparatus also include two older officials who were former KPD members: Gerhart Eisler was born in 1897, and entered KPÖ in 1918; he has been a journalist since the early 1960s and succeeded Hermann Ley as chairman of the State Broadcasting Commission. Friedrich Dickel was born in 1913 and entered the KPD in 1931; he is a high-frequency technician, an expert on military affairs, and since 1963 he has been the successor to Karl Maron as Minister of the Interior.

Four new members occupy top or upper-middle positions in the SED. Two are first secretaries of SED *Bezirk* executives: Johannes Chemnitzer was born in 1929 and entered the SED in 1946. He has been an agronomist with a university degree in the social sciences and since 1963 First Secretary of the SED *Bezirk* executive for Neubrandenburg. Werner Wittig was born in 1926 and entered the KPD in 1945. He has been a commercial employee with a university degree in the social sciences and since 1964 has filled the post of First Secretary in the SED *Bezirk* executive for Potsdam.

The 1967 Central Committee thus included all first secretaries of SED *Bezirk* executives (including the Wismut executive, whose first Secretary Kurt Kiess became a Central Committee candidate in 1967). Chemnitzer and Wittig augment the representation of the younger generation of functionaries in this subgroup of the strategic clique. Chemnitzer is a party functionary specializing in problems of agriculture, and may thus only belong conditionally to the strategic clique. Two other functionaries who entered the 1967 Central Committee as members belong to the more select, though not the inner circle, of the strategic clique. Otto Reinhold, was born in 1925 and entered the KPD in 1945. He has a university degree in economics, and is professor of political economy. Since 1963 he has been the Director of the SED CC's Institute of Social Sciences. Rudolf Singer was born in 1915 and entered the KPD in 1933; he worked first in export, then as an editor. He has earned his graduate degree in the social sciences, and in 1966 became successor to Herman Axen as chief editor of *Neues Deutschland*.

Whereas Otto Reinhold belongs to that group of younger representatives in the strategic clique who grew up exclusively in GDR society, the addition of Rudolf Singer may be regarded as strengthening the position of the group of older functionaries within the clique.

One new Central Committee member comes from the top ranks of the FDJ apparatus. He is Günter Jahn, born in 1929, who entered the SED in 1946. He has a university degree in economics and in mid-1966 was made a secretary, and subsequently first secretary, of the Central Council of the FDJ.

Two new Central Committee members are functionaries in education and culture. Klaus Fuchs was born in 1911 and entered the SPD in 1930 and the KPD in 1932. He is a physicist and professor of physics, and in 1959 became Deputy Director of the German Academy of Science's Central Institute of Atomic Research in Rossendorf. Bernhard Seeger was born in 1927, entered the NSDAP in 1944, and the SED in 1946. Originally a teacher, he has for a long time been a free-lance writer.

Among the 25 new candidates in the 1967 Central Committee, 20 are in occupations directly connected with their previous specialized training. Ten had received their education in the natural sciences or economics. In addition, three of the new candidates may be regarded as veteran functionaries (Fechner, Kegel, and Kiess). The remaining 22 entered the SPD/KPD only after 1945. It should be further noted that some of them entered the SED at a date relatively late for their personal biographies.

Of the 22, 12 are party functionaries. Of these, 5 occupy upper-middle positions. Werner Hering was born in 1930 and entered the SED in 1946. He has an advanced law degree and for several years has been head of the Central Committee Section for Health Affairs. Bruno Kiesler was born in 1925 and entered the SED in 1946. He was a mechanic and earned a graduate degree in agricultural economy. In 1959 he was made head of the Central Committee Section for Agricultural Affairs. Kurt Kiess was born in 1914 and entered the KPD in 1932. He was a plumber and in 1960 became First Secretary of the SED *Gebiet* executive for Wismut. Siegfried Lorenz was born in 1930 and entered the SPD in 1945. A mechanic with a university degree in the social sciences, he was made head of the Central Committee Section for Youth Affairs in 1967. Paul Markowski was born in 1929 and entered the SED in 1952. He holds a graduate degree in political and legal sciences and was recently appointed head of the Central Committee Section for International Relations.

Seven of the newly elected twelve party functionaries occupy positions at the middle or lower levels, either in SED *Bezirk* and *Kreis* executives, or in industrial enterprises. Roland Bauer was born in 1929 and entered the SED in 1946. A precision tool maker with a Ph.D., since 1964 he has been with the SED *Bezirk* executive for Berlin, first as head of the Ideological Commission and since 1967 the Secretary for Science, Public Education, and Culture. Heinz Berthold was born in 1924 and entered the SED in 1946. He is a mechanic and Central Committee party organizer in the VVB General Chemistry. Hubert Görlich was born in 1921 and entered the SED in 1950. A former bank employee with a degree in engineering and agriculture, he is now First Secretary of the SED *Industriekreis* executive for the Leuna Chemical Combine. Heinz Schönfelder was born in 1935 and entered the SED in 1960. A carpenter who earned a university degree in engineering and agriculture, he is now the SED Secretary for the Vetschau Power Plant. Edith Weingart was born in 1922 and entered the SED in 1948. She began as a commercial employee and became First Secretary of the SED *Kreis* executive for Arnstadt. Heinz Ziegner was born in 1928 and entered the SPD in 1945. He was an administrative employee and since 1960 has served as Secretary for Agriculture in the SED *Bezirk* executive for Magdeburg. Ursula Zschau was born in 1923 and entered the SED in 1946. She is an industrial economist and since 1962 First Secretary of the BPO for the Flöha VEB Cotton-Spinning Mill.

Eight top-level state functionaries are among the group of 25 newly elected candidates. Apart from State Secretary Herrmann, they all work in specialities directly related to their previous training.

Herbert Fechner was born in 1913 and entered the SAJ sometime prior to 1933 and the SPD in 1945. Originally a telegraph lineman, he earned a university degree in political science. Since June 1967 he has been mayor of Berlin. Rudi Georgi was born in 1927 and entered the SED in 1946. He has worked in industrial commerce and has a degree in economics. In 1967 he was made GDR Minister for Processing Machinery and Vehicle Construction. Joachim Herrmann was born in 1928 and entered the SED in 1946. He was an editor and in December 1965 was made State Secretary for Pan-German (now West German) Affairs. Wolfgang Junker was born in 1929 and entered the SED in 1951. Originally a plasterer, then a construction engineer, he was made

GDR Minister of Construction in 1963. Gerhard Kegel was born in 1907 and entered the KPD in 1931. A lawyer and editor, he was made Ambassador in 1959. Herbert Scheibe was born in 1914 and entered the KPD in 1945. He is a compositor and specialist in military affairs and is presently a Lieutenant General in the Ministry of National Defense. Otfried Steger was born in 1926 and entered the SED in 1952. He has worked as a machine fitter, labor economist, and electrical installations engineer. In December 1965 he was made GDR Minister for the Electrotechnical Industries and Electronics. Gerhard Weiss was born in 1919 and entered the SED in 1948. Originally a commercial employee, he earned a degree in economics and served as a deputy to the Chairman of the Council of Ministers.

Two candidates perform functions in the economic apparatus. Joachim Bialecki was born in 1929 and entered the SED in 1949. He has been a fitter, miner, and mining machinery engineer. He is now the Director of the VEB Lignite "Glückauf" in Knappenrode. Wolfgang Biermann was born in 1928 and entered the SED in 1956. He was a machine fitter, mechanical engineer and is presently Director of the "7th October" VEB for Lathe Construction in Berlin.

Two new candidates practice professions in the sciences and in the apparatus for cultural and educational affairs. Inge Hieblinger was born in 1928 and entered the KPD in 1945. She has a degree in law and is lecturer at the Martin Luther University in Halle-Wittenberg. Klaus Dieter Wüstneck was born in 1932 and entered the SED in 1956. He holds a Ph.D. degree in philosophy and is presently a senior fellow at the Academy of Sciences' Institute for Philosophy in Berlin.

One new candidate is a higher-echelon functionary in the National Front. Werner Kirchhoff was born in 1926 and entered the SED in 1956. He has been a teacher and historian and became First Vice-President and Chairman of the Secretariat of the National Council of the National Front.

DISMISSALS AND COOPTATIONS AT THE SEVENTH SED CONGRESS: SOME COMPARISONS

Comparison of the 38 1963 Central Committee members and candidates not re-elected to the 1967 Central Committee with the 38 new additions yields the following data, which relate most directly to the wider framework of this study.

For those born before 1920, exclusions (27) exceed new appointments (9). Out of those born in 1920 or later, 11 1963 members and candidates were dropped in 1967, while 29 newly elected members and candidates belong to the post-1920 group.

Among the group of party functionaries, there was a significantly higher number of cooptations (16) than dismissals (6), while for state officials the number of newly elected people (14) is slightly less than those who were dropped (15). The same applies to functionaries in culture and education, who had four additions but seven exclusions.

Analysis of individual top-level state functionaries dropped in 1967 has established that natural causes (death and old age) were the predominating reasons for their exclusion. In contrast, a number of top-level state functionaries who were experts with economic and technical training or professional experience entered the 1967 Central Committee. These were Walter Halbritter, Günther Kleiber, Siegfried Böhm, and Wolfgang Rauchfuss. Newer members included Rudi Georgi, Wolfgang Junker, Otfried Steger, and Gerhard Weiss. The trend toward professionalization of the Central Committee that has been consistently observed is further confirmed by these membership data.

Here it should be noted that the strategic clique at the same time attempted to consolidate its position at the Seventh SED Congress. No 1963 Central Committee member who also belonged to the leadership group in that year had left the Central Committee in the interim before the Seventh Congress. Moreover, two functionaries associated with the strategic clique had been newly coopted in that period (Otto Reinhold and Rudolf Singer). Furthermore, among the strategic clique's subgroup of first *Bezirk* secretaries Johannes Chemnitzer and Werner Wittig were made full Central Committee members, and Kurt Kiess was made a candidate in 1967. Even if Chemnitzer is regarded as more closely aligned with the institutionalized counter elite, the increased representation of higher party officials is a significant factor in strengthening the relative position of the strategic clique. Of further significance is the fact that some of these officials are members of the younger generation.

Finally, comparison of developments between the Sixth and Seventh SED Congresses with those between the Fifth and Sixth reveals some leveling off in the representation of the group of economic functionaries. The considerable increase in this group that occurred between 1958 and 1963 was not repeated in 1967. The 1963–1967 period shows clearly defined changes in the party apparatus' representation in the Central Committee. While the number of exclusions and cooptations among functionaries active primarily in the party apparatus were approximately equal for 1958 and 1963 (see Table 12), the absolute and relative proportions of new additions greatly exceed demotions from the ranks of the party apparatus between 1963 and 1967.

CHANGES IN THE POLITBURO

The SED Politburo formed in 1967 had 15 members, as opposed to 14 prior to the Seventh Congress. Former candidates Gerhard Grüneberg and Günter Mittag had been promoted to full membership at the Thirteenth Central Committee Session in September 1966. At the Seventh Congress Politburo candidate Horst Sindermann achieved full membership status. (Sindermann was born in 1915 and was made First Secretary of the SED *Bezirk* executive for Halle.)

At the Seventh Congress in 1967 Walter Halbritter and Günther Kleiber joined the ranks of the four remaining candidates, Axen, G. Ewald, Jarowinsky, and M. Müller. Halbritter and Kleiber were also elected to Central Committee membership. Both men epitomize the younger, professionally trained experts in the state apparatus. Born in 1927, Halbritter has a university degree in economics. He joined the SED in 1949 and in 1965 was made head of the Council of Ministers' Office of Price Control, retaining this function when the Council was reconstituted in July 1967. Günther Kleiber was born in 1932, has a university degree in economics, and joined the SED in 1949. In 1966 he was made State Secretary for Coordinating Electronic Data Processing. Kleiber and Halbritter can be regarded as representatives of the institutionalized counter elite. Their inclusion among the Politburo candidates re-established a voice for the counter elite within the SED apparatus. Between the death of Erich Apel and the appointment of Günter Mittag to full Politburo membership in 1967, Jarowinsky had been the only representative of the counter elite among the Politburo candidates.

On the other hand, the changes in the composition of the Politburo undoubtedly reinforced the position of the strategic clique.

2. Members and Candidates of the 1967 Central Committee

AGE AND DATE OF ENTRY INTO THE PARTY

The changes in the Central Committee membership between the Sixth and Seventh Congresses have had the general effect of further rejuvenating that body (see Table 51). The newer members and candidates elected in 1967 were recruited primarily from younger age groups. Twenty-three of the thirty-eight new Central Committee members (slightly over 60 percent) belong to the group born between 1920 and 1929. Compared with the 1963 Central Committee, the proportion of functionaries in this age group has risen considerably. (In 1963 only 74 persons fell within this age group; in 1967 we find 87.) In contrast, the representation of the age group born between 1900 and 1909 dropped from 43 in 1963 to 30 in 1967. Table 52 shows that the number of members and candidates who entered the party after 1945 increased from 108 in 1963 to 119 in 1967, in almost direct proportion to the increase in the number of younger functionaries. The number of veteran functionaries who had already entered the KPD/SPD/CPSU before 1933 fell from 67 in 1963 to 57 in 1967. However, 7 of the 57 veteran

Table 51
Central Committee Members and Candidates in 1963 and 1967 by Age

Age Group	Year of Birth	1967 Central Committee				Newly Elected in 1967
		1963 CC Total	Members	Candi-dates	Total	
1	Before 1890	4	0	0	0	0
2	1890-1899	12	11	0	11	1
3	1900-1909	43	27	3	30	1
4	1910-1919	40	32	8	40	7
5	1920-1929	74	56	31	87	23
6	1930-1939	8	5	8	13	6
Total		181	131	50	181	38

Table 52
Central Committee Members and Candidates in 1963 and 1967 by Date of Entry into
the Party

		1967 Central Committee			
Date of Entry	1963 CC Total	Members	Candi-dates	Total	Newly Elected in 1967
Into the KPD/CPSU, etc., before 1933	67	52	5	57	7
Into the KPD/CPSU, etc. 1934-1944	3	2	1	3	0
Into the KPD/SPD or SED 1945-1951	97	71	35	106	26
Into the SED after 1952	11	4	9	13	5
Data on entry only into SPD	3	2	0	2	0
Total	181	131	50	181	38

functionaries in 1967 were newly elected to the Central Committee.
Nonetheless, their number was much lower than that of the newly
coopted younger functionaries (7 vs. 31).

ACQUIRED OCCUPATION

There were many changes in acquired occupation in the composition of
the 1967 Central Committee, compared with that of 1963. *Neues
Deutschland* published 318 occupational data pertaining to the 181
Central Committee members and candidates elected in 1967. Thus, an
average of almost two (exactly 1.75) entries for the occupations of each
member and candidate is available. Comparison of acquired occupations
on the 1963 and 1967 Central Committees proves that the party
leadership shows continuing interest in coopting persons with high
educational qualifications to Central Committee membership. As discussed in Chapter Three, GDR society's trend toward higher professional qualification has extended to the membership of the Central Committee. Findings for the 1967 Central Committee reconfirmed this thesis.

Unfortunately, the techniques used in Chapter Three could not be
applied here for deriving a general profile of the characteristic of

"acquired occupation." In Chapter Three the data on the acquired occupation of Central Committee members and candidates in 1954, 1958, and 1963 were verified on the basis of all available sources. Consequently, data relating to the acquired occupation of each member or candidate of those Central Committees was retained and served as the basis for empirical analysis. However, the exceedingly high number of 1967 members and candidates with two or more given occupations, and lack of time to verify the *Neues Deutschland* data precisely have prevented us from using the techniques employed in Chapter 3. For the Central Committees of 1963 and 1967, we have used the occupational data published by *Neues Deutschland* on the occasion of the SED Congresses of those years, regardless of whether these data coincide with data collected and verified for analysis in Chapter 3 of the 1954, 1958, and 1963 Central Committees.

The 1963 Central Committee has a total of 204 occupational data, compared with 318 entries for 1967. Table 53 shows a predominance of 1963 Central Committee members and candidates with one acquired occupation. In contrast, the majority of the 1967 Committee have two occupations, and 20 have three occupations.

The occupational data for both Central Committees are classified by acquired professions (as in Tables 10 and 11 in Chapter Three). Analysis of Table 54 reveals that the number of data entries for occupational groups among top functionaries had increased greatly in 1967, compared with 1963, in the technical and administrative fields

Table 53
Total Data Published In *Neues Deutschland* on Acquired Occupations of Central Committee Members and Candidates for 1963 and 1967

Number of Acquired Occupations for Members and Candidates	1963 CC	1967 CC
With one acquired occupation	158	70
With two acquired occupations	23	88
With three acquired occupations	0	20
With four acquired occupations	0	3
Total	181	181

Table 54
Distribution of Data on Acquired Occupations for the Various Professional Groups of CC Members and Candidates in 1963 and 1967*

Acquired Occupation†	1963 CC	1967 CC
11 Technical occupations in the state, economy, or agriculture	126	154
of these:		
111	24	52
112	86	94
113	16	8
12 Administrative occupations in the state, economy, or agriculture	29	90
of these:		
121	12	58
122	17	32
2 Service occupations	5	5
3 Educational occupations	17	41
4 Free occupations	27	28
Total	204	318

* Based on data published in *Neues Deutschland.*
† For the code to the rankings of occupational groups, see Table 55.

(see code numbers 111 and 121). This holds true (with some limitations) for the educational occupations (see code number 3). In contrast, the situation for the service and free professions has scarcely changed. A breakdown of the individual positions in Table 54 yields the distributions of Table 55. From the official data in this table, the following general characteristics emerge:

Among leading technical occupations (111), representation of the following categories had either risen considerably or had appeared for the first time in 1967: engineer-economist with a diploma, agronomist with a diploma, and military scientist.

In contrast, the situation with respect to the group of middle-level technical functionaries (112) has changed very little; here, the more traditional occupations continue to predominate.

Representation in group 113 has decreased. The number of workers, miners, metal, and agricultural workers appeared in only 8 of the total 318 occupations for 1967; in 1963 there were 16 out of 204.

A comparatively large increase in statistics for top-level administrative functions (121) can be noted. Some of these functions were represented for the first time in 1967. Compare the following increase of figures for 1967 over 1963: from 7 to 12 items for those with university degrees in economics. Those with university degrees in the political and legal sciences (3 items) were represented for the first time; the same holds true for those with degrees in the social sciences (18 times). However, holders of university degrees in the social sciences were not recorded in *Neues Deutschland* in 1963 under the heading of acquired occupation. Ph.D. and Prof. are used as titles in 1963, while in 1967 they appear as acquired occupations. This is a further indication of "hierarchicalization" in the occupational structure of GDR society.

It should also be noted that the number of commercial white-collar workers in middle and lower-level administrative functions (see code 122) has risen disproportionately compared to other categories.

Among the fifteen Central Committee members and candidates who occupy educational functions (code 3), the title "Prof." is used in addition to data on their acquired occupation.

For the service occupations (code 2) and the free professions (code 4) there are no absolute changes between data for the 1963 and

Table 55
Data from *Neues Deutschland* on the Acquired Occupations of Central Committee
Members and Candidates for 1963 and 1967

		1963 CC	1967 CC
1	Technical and administrative occupations in state, economy, and agriculture		
11	Technical occupations		
111	Leading functions		
	Engineer	4	5
	Construction engineer	1	1
	Electrical engineer	1	3
	Railway engineer	—	1
	Mining machinery engineer	—	1
	Mechanical engineer	—	2
	Building engineer	—	1
	Chemical engineer	—	1
	Engineer with diploma	6	5
	Railway engineer with diploma	1	—
	Chemist with diploma	5	3
	Engineer-economist	—	1
	Engineer-economist with diploma	1	6
	Certified agronomist	2	11
	Agronomist with diploma	2	2
	Agricultural scientist with diploma	—	1
	Ph.D. in agricultural sciences	—	1
	Agricultural economist with diploma	1	2
	Military scientist	—	5
112	Middle Functions (artisan, skilled worker, farmer)		
	Locksmith	10	10
	Machinist	14	12
	Auto mechanic	2	1
	Construction fitter	1	1
	Engine mechanic	—	1
	Electrical mechanic	—	1
	Mechanic	1	3
	Typewriter mechanic	—	1
	Precision mechanic	—	1
	Mason	8	9
	Plasterer	1	—
	Polisher	—	1
	Insulator	—	1
	Cabinetmaker	3	3
	Painter	1	—
	Carpenter	4	4
	Tinsmith, plumber	3	3
	Electrician	2	3
	Furnace repairman	1	1

Telegraph lineman	—	1
High-frequency technician	—	1
Roofer	2	2
Heating fitter, technician	1	2
Lathe operator	1	1
Molding operator	—	1
Briquet presser	—	1
Metal stamper	2	—
Iron turner	1	1
Toolmaker, lathe operator	4	1
Machine mechanic	1	1
Nautical machine mechanic	1	1
Riveter	1	1
Welder	—	1
Technician	—	1
Technical employee	1	—
Surveyor	1	1
Textile technician	1	—
Laboratory technician	—	1
Printer	4	3
Typesetter	2	3
Tanner	1	1
Butcher	1	1
Weaver	1	1
Decorator	2	2
Piano maker	1	1
Farmer	3	3
Tractor driver	1	1
Mine inspector	—	2
Ship machinist	1	1
Railroad employee	1	1

113 Lower functions

Laborer	2	1
Metal worker	2	1
Textile worker	1	—
Miner	1	2
Forester	1	—
Agricultural worker	1	—
Farm hand	5	2
Mine worker	3	2

12 Administrative occupations

121 Leading functions

Economic scientist	1	—
Labor economist	—	1
Industrial economist	—	1
Economist with diploma	7	12
Social scientist with diploma	—	18
Legal expert with diploma	—	3
Agronomist with diploma	1	2

Table 55 (continued)

	1963 CC	1967 CC
Agriculturist with diploma	1	1
Legal scientist	—	3
Jurist	2	3
Jurist with diploma	—	2
Ph.D. Political science and economics (Dr. rer. pol.)	—	2
Ph.D. Economics (Dr. rer. oec.)	—	10
Ph.D. Jurisprudence (Dr. jur.)	—	3
122 Medium Functions		
White-collar worker	4	6
Commercial white-collar worker	4	10
Administrative employee	1	3
Merchant	—	2
Insurance salesman	1	1
Exporter	—	1
Shipping clerk	1	1
Industrial salesman	—	1
Agricultural machinery salesman	1	1
Commercial assistant	1	2
Bookkeeper	1	—
Savings-bank employee	—	1
Stenotypist	2	2
Forester	1	1
2 Service occupations		
Hairdresser	1	1
Tailor	3	3
Cook	—	1
Pastry maker	1	—
3 Educational professions		
Professor	—	15
Prof. with Ph.D. (*habil.*) in natural sciences	—	1
University teacher	1	—
Ph.D., natural sciences	—	1
Teacher of agricultural science	2	—
Physicist	1	2
Mathematician with diploma	1	—
Philosopher with diploma	—	1
Historian with diploma	1	2
Historian	—	1
Ph.D., humanities (Dr. phil.)	—	4
Holder of a diploma in philosophy and the dramatic arts	—	1
University graduate in German literature	1	—
Musicologist	1	1
Schoolteacher	9	9
School principal	—	1
Teacher with diploma	—	1
Ph.D. in education	—	1

4	Free professions		
	Physician	2	—
	Writer	4	4
	Journalist	1	3
	Editor	8	11
	Artist	1	1
	Commercial painter	—	1
	Graphic artist	1	1
	Architect	1	—
	Actor	5	4
	Director and producer	3	2
	Composer	1	1

1967 committees. Their relative proportion in the total data, however, has decreased.

These results of our tabulation by acquired occupation are none-the-less subject to various qualifications. The reader is reminded that our analysis takes into account only data published in *Neues Deutschland,* and that no systematic verification via cross-checking was possible. Furthermore, we must be extremely wary in interpreting data in instances where high government functionaries have acquired academic degrees, while simultaneously exercising their occupations. As an example we cite Gerhard Schürer and Johann Wittik. Schürer was still described as a machine mechanic in 1966, when he had already become Chairman of the State Planning Commission. However, at the Seventh Congress in April 1967 it is also stated that he is the holder of a diploma in the social sciences. Johann Wittik (in December 1967 the Minister for Light Industry and before that Deputy Chairman of the National Economic Council) was characterized at the Sixth Congress as a weaver. In the interim, he had achieved the professional title of textile engineer. It can be assumed that such newer designations for persons who simultaneously occupy a high post are not based on genuine academic criteria. Nevertheless, like the previously mentioned use of doctoral and professional titles, they illustrate the premium placed by the SED leadership on expert personnel. The process of specialization in the party's bodies can thus not be interpreted as having penetrated the values of the SED from without, but rather as a consciously conceived and implemented policy of the SED leadership.

ACTUAL OCCUPATION

The trend observable since 1963 has thus not been interrupted as regards the occupational position of Central Committee members and candidates in 1967. A definite rise in the number of party and state functionaries has been noted. In 1963, 109 out of 181 members and candidates were active in major party and state organizations; by 1967 the comparable figure had risen to 115 out of the same total membership. Of the 38 newly coopted members and candidates in 1967, 30 had been active primarily in party or state bodies. In contrast, the absolute number of members and candidates in other functions, namely those within the economy, mass organizational affairs, or in cultural affairs had dropped compared with 1963. No such changes are evident for agricultural functionaries.

In 1967 the preoccupation of the Politburo with the reorganization of the party and state apparatuses and the leadership's attempts to adapt to emergent economic and social dynamic processes are far more notable than in 1963. The same would apply for the tightening of control in the instrumental bodies created under the "new economic system." Their concentration of power corresponds to greater, noticeable emphasis on the party's leading role, compared with 1963. It becomes evident in the enhanced representation of members and candidates active in the party and state apparatuses.

In 1963 there were 55 individuals active mainly in the party and 54 in state organs. In the 1967 Central Committee the number of party functionaries had risen to 67, while those in the state had dropped to 48. (See Table 56.)

Comparison of the distribution of 1967 Central Committee members and candidates occupying positions within various functional areas with those of 1963 (see Table 57) reveals only minor changes for top functionaries and those in the upper-middle range, as we have defined these rankings. In 1963 individuals in top positions numbered 91, while in 1967 there were 93 such persons. The number of functionaries holding upper-middle positions only dropped from 49 in 1963 to 48 in 1967. The group of functionaries with positions at the middle and lower levels of the hierarchy had dropped from 36 to 32 persons by 1967.

Our analysis by functional areas within positions occupied in 1967

Table 56
Primary Functions of the Members and Candidates in 1963 and 1967 at the Time of their Admission to the Central Committee

Functional Area	1963 CC Total	1967 Central Committee			1967 Central Committee (New)*		
		Members	Candidates	Total	Members	Candidates	Total
Party apparatus	55	52	15	67	4	12	16
State	54	35	13	48	6	8	14
Economy	19	9	6	15	0	2	2
Agriculture	10	7	3	10	0	0	0
Mass organizations	17	8	6	14	1	1	2
Culture and education	21	12	7	19	2	2	4
NVA and others	5	1	0	1	0	0	0
Retired and others	0	7	0	7	0	0	0
Total	181	131	50	181	13	25	38

* These constitute members and candidates elected to the Central Committee for the first time in April 1957.

Table 57
Positions of Central Committee Members and Candidates (1963 and 1967) in the Hierarchy of the Functional Areas

Positions*	1963 CC	1967 Central Committee		
	Total	Members	Candidates	Total
Top	91	74	19	93
Party	13	16	0	16
State	37	31	9	40
Economy	10	4	3	7
Agriculture	10	7	3	10
Mass organizations	14	7	3	10
Culture and education	7	9	1	10
Upper middle	49	33	15	48
Party	28	26	6	32
State	4	2	2	4
Economy	5	3	2	5
Agriculture	0	0	0	0
Mass organizations	3	1	3	4
Culture and education	9	1	2	3
Middle/Lower middle	36	16	16	32
Party	14	10	9	19
State	13	2	2	4
Economy	4	2	1	3
Agriculture	0	0	0	0
Mass organizations	0	0	0	0
Culture and education	5	2	4	6
Not taken into account	5	1	0	1
Retired	0	7	0	7
Total	181	131	50	181

* For a breakdown within various positions, see code on pp. 226–227.

also yields a picture similar to that for 1963. In the newer Central Committee we found 16 party functionaries and 40 state officials of the top level, compared with 13 party and 37 state officials in 1963. In 1963, 28 party and 4 state officials held upper-middle positions, while in 1967 there were 32 party and 4 state officials at this level. In the other major functional areas no notable differences exist between the Central Committees of 1963 and 1967. In this context, it is emphasized that party officials are distributed in a relatively uniform fashion throughout the echelons, whereas state officials in 1967 occupy primarily top-level functions.

Analysis of the specific tasks performed by functionaries in the party and state reveals substantial occupational differentiation in an admittedly rough glance of 1967 Central Committee members and candidates. Although the number of members and candidates in primary party positions had grown considerably compared with 1963, and there had been a corresponding drop in the number of state officials in the Central Committee, the group of party functionaries performing specialized tasks had also risen greatly (see Table 58). If, for instance, we compare the number of economic and agricultural functionaries in the 1958 and 1963 Central Committees (see Table 37), we find the following in relation to the proportion of such functionaries (in the broadest sense) for the 1963 and 1967 Central Committees: Of a total of 53 party functionaries with upper, upper-middle, and lower-middle positions in 1963, 34 fulfilled purely administrative tasks, while only 19 performed specialized functions. By contrast, in 1967, of the 66 party officials in comparable categories we find 37 active in administration, while 29 performed more specialized tasks. The number of party functionaries in the Central Committee entrusted with special tasks had thus risen from 19 in 1963 to 29 in 1967 (i.e., by over 40 percent). These findings establish that even in 1967 expertise was not neglected as a goal of the leadership in constituting the Central Committee. To a certain extent, this finding puts the shifts in representation noted in Table 56 in a more relative light—even though the overall number of party functionaries entrusted with economic or agricultural tasks had varied only slightly.

Table 58
Economic and Agricultural Functionaries (in the Broader Sense) in the 1963 and 1967 Central Committees

Party/State Functionaries by Areas of Activity	Position*							
	1963 Central Committee				1967 Central Committee			
	Top	Upper Middle	Middle Middle	Total	Top	Upper Middle	Middle Middle	Total
Party functionaries	13	28	12	53	16	32	18	66
of these:								
party functionaries in the stricter sense	6	22	6	34	6	23	8	37
with specialized party tasks	7	6	6	19	10	9	10	29
of these:								
with economic tasks	2	1	1	4	2	0	1	3
with agricultural tasks	2	0	1	3	1	1	2	4
State functionaries	37	4	11	52	40	4	4	48
of these:								
with political administrative tasks (state functionaries in the stricter sense)	16	1	5	22	19	1	2	22
with specialized administrative tasks	21	3	6	30	21	3	2	26
of these:								
with economic tasks	10	2	1	13	13	2	0	15
with agricultural tasks	2	0	3	5	1	0	2	3

* See code on pp. 226-227.

"VETERAN" WORKERS AND PARTY FUNCTIONARIES

A new phenomenon in the 1967 Central Committee is the emergence of a group of older members and candidates with purely honorific status, who can no longer exercise their primary functions in the party, state, or other bureaucracies—presumably on grounds of advanced age and poor health. In official parlance, they have been designated "veterans" of the party or of labor. This group includes older functionaries who had entered the KPD/SPD before 1933. Retirement from their primary occupational function had in no case led to the loss of their seats in the 1967 Central Committee (this also holds true for certain members and candidates of the Central Committee throughout the 1950s). Furthermore, some Central Committee members retain membership in the State Council or the Peoples' Chamber. This group of veterans, which still has either direct ties to the strategic clique, or enjoys a sympathetic ear among its members, includes the following individuals:

Friedrich Ebert, who was born in 1894, and entered the SPD in 1913; he was replaced as Mayor of Berlin and appointed an honorary Berlin citizen shortly after his re-entry to membership in both the Central Committee and Politburo in 1967. He became a member of the newly constituted State Council in 1967, and a member of the Peoples' Chamber elected in 1967 and of its presidium as a representative of the SED group.

Hans Jendretzky was born in 1897 and entered the KPD in 1920. He was formerly a member of the FDGB National Board, and was elected to the chairmanship of the FDGB group in the 1967 Peoples' Chamber.

Hans Rodenberg was born in 1895 and entered the KPD in 1926. He had already resigned as Deputy Minister of Culture in 1967, when he became a member of the State Council and the Peoples' Chamber.

Hilde Benjamin was born in 1902 and entered the KPD in 1927. She was replaced as Minister of Justice by the young former Deputy to the LDPD's Secretary General, Dr. Kurt Wünsche, upon the reorganization of the Council of Ministers in July 1967. That same year, she also lost her seat in the Peoples' Chamber, and was appointed in September to a professorship at the Walter Ulbricht German Academy for Political Science and the Law.

Willy Rumpf was born in 1903 and entered the KPD in 1925. He was replaced in late 1967 in his long held position as Minister of Finance by a 38-year-old holder of a university degree in economics, Siegfried Böhm, and was not re-elected to the Peoples' Chamber in 1967.

Hans Warnke was born in 1896 and entered the KPD in 1920. He was replaced as Director of the Rostock Port Authority in 1967.

The fact that these functionaries retained their seats in the SED Central Committee in 1967 indicates two interrelated lines of development: On the one hand, a certain stabilization of the SED's rule is indicated, on the other, the organizational system has apparently not been affected by technical and economic dynamics of the society, at least to the extent that traditional party functionaries had to be removed completely from the national political scene.

3. Summary and Conclusions

The Seventh SED Congress heralded the further consolidation of the social and political situation in the GDR, but not solely in terms of the party leadership's conception of what its role should be in that society. The trend toward consolidation was particularly clear in Ulbricht's speech on "Social Developments in the German Democratic Republic up to the Achievement of Socialism." The source of the leadership's evident self-confidence is the increasing identity of its political goals with those of the Soviet Union. Among other things, the strong emphasis placed on improvements in the scientific and technical efficiency of equipment, plus the relatively dramatic increase in the GDR's standard of living, can be regarded as indicators of this consolidation process. Erich Honecker's statements on "The Role of the Party in the Period of Achieving Socialism" also fit into the general emerging pattern of cohesion within the society and its political system, which we find expressed in the slogans of the "new economic system." This has been accompanied throughout by a longstanding call for the intensification of "ideological work," while at the Seventh Party Congress the leadership reiterated its demands of 1963 and earlier for an increased representation of technical and economic expertise within the ranks of the SED.

As both a concomitant of the party leadership's call for increased ideological and propaganda activities and a crystallization of its views on social and political matters, we can observe an enhanced prominence of party functionaries on all levels of administration. This also has held true for the changes traced in the Central Committee's composition. Although both an absolute and relative rise in the number of party functionaries in the Central Committee is due primarily to an expansion in the representation of groups at the middle and lower levels of the SED's hierarchy, the rate of advance by party experts observed for 1963 has dropped quite considerably. Fewer functionaries from the upper or upper-middle levels of the state, economic, and agricultural bureaucracies have moved into the 1967 Central Committee than had been advanced between 1958 and 1963. For state functionaries at the middle or lower levels, we have likewise noted a drop in representation compared with the 1963 Central Committee.

The process of rejuvenation in the ranks of the Central Committee, and a consequent decrease in the number of veteran KPD/SPD functionaries have not been interrupted by the decisions of the Seventh SED Congress. The definite trend toward "professionalization" within the Central Committee's membership noted in Chapters Two and Three has also continued. A rise in the educational qualifications of party cadres has been documented by the statistics on "acquired occupations" for Central Committee members and candidates, published in *Neues Deutschland* on the occasion of the Seventh Congress. In this context, it should be re-emphasized that the number of party officials entrusted with specialized tasks (aside from strictly economic or agricultural functions) within the party apparatus has risen appreciably. Between 1963 and 1967 the strategic clique seems to have aimed systematically at training a group of loyal future successors.

Beyond the rejuvenation and professionalization of the Central Committee's membership, some other trends noted in Chapter Three have been documented in this appendix. Analysis of the 1967 Central Committee's composition established that, on the whole, younger technologists and managers entered the Central Committee only after having risen professionally in the state apparatus. The number of members and candidates who also belonged to the Council of Ministers had increased to 25 by 1967—despite a reduction in the membership of this body in July 1967. This rise can be attributed mostly to the fact that more younger, specially qualified members of the Council of Ministers in 1965–1966 were elected to the Central Committee for the first time at the Seventh Congress.

The strategic clique has undoubtedly attempted to integrate representatives of the institutionalized counter elite into the upper reaches of the political system (notably Mittag). At the same time, however, it seems to have weakened the counter position by using its "own" cadres. This has made both the sclerosis at the top level and the reduction of mobility within the more prominent leadership groups all the more apparent. It is sufficient to say that no member of the 1963 Central Committee with definite ties to the strategic clique at the time of the Seventh Party Congress had been demoted from the Central Committee, either prior to the convocation of the Seventh Congress, or as a result of its proceedings.

Appendix 2

Members and Candidates of the Central Committee and the Politburo, 1950 to 1967

Members and Candidates of the Politburo and Secretaries of the Central Committee of the SED in 1950*

MEMBERS OF THE POLITBURO

Dahlem, Franz
Ebert, Friedrich
Grotewohl, Otto
Matern, Hermann
Oelssner, Fred
Pieck, Wilhelm
Rau, Heinrich
Ulbricht, Walter
Zaisser, Wilhelm

CANDIDATES OF THE POLITBURO

Ackermann, Anton

*Source: *Neues Deutschland,* July 26, 1950, p.1.

Herrnstadt, Rudolf
Honecker, Erich
Jendretzky, Hans
Mückenberger, Erich
Schmidt, Elli

SECRETARIES OF THE CENTRAL COMMITTEE

Ulbricht, Walter (First Secretary)
Axen, Hermann
Baumann, Edith
Dahlem, Franz
Lauter, Hans
Oelssner, Fred
Schön, Otto
Stoph, Willi
Verner, Paul
Vieweg, Kurt
Warnke, Herbert

Members and Candidates of the SED Central Committee in 1950*

Ackermann, Anton
Axen, Hermann
Bauer, Gerda
Baumann, Edith
Becher, Johannes R.
Bergmann, Herta
Bruschke, Werner
Buchwitz, Otto
Bürger, Kurt
Dahlem, Franz
Ebert, Friedrich
Fechner, Max
Feist, Margot
Fischer, Lena
Grotewohl, Otto
Herrnstadt, Rudolf
Hoffmann, Ernst

Holzmacher, Gerda
Honecker, Erich
Jendretzky, Hans
Kern, Käthe
Kessler, Heinz
Koenen, Bernard
Koenen, Wilhelm
Lauter, Hans
Lehmann, Helmut
Leuschner, Bruno
Leutwein, Friedrich
Lohagen, Ernst
Matern, Hermann
Mielke, Erich
Moltmann, Karl
Mückenberger, Erich
Oelssner, Fred
Pieck, Wilhelm
Pisnik, Alois

Rau, Heinrich
Sägebrecht, Willy
Schlimme, Hermann
Schmidt, Elli
Schön, Otto
Steinhoff, Karl
Stoph, Willi
Ulbricht, Walter
Verner, Paul
Vieweg, Kurt
Wandel, Paul
Warnke, Hans
Warnke, Herbert
Winzer, Otto
Zaisser, Wilhelm

CANDIDATES

Barthel, Kurt (Kuba)
Baumann, Georg
Biering, Walter
Birnbaum, Erich
Böhme, Kurt

*Source: *Neues Deutschland,* July 25, 1950, p.1.

Deter, Adolf
Dohlus, Horst
Feist [Honecker], Margot
Götzl, Eduard
Hager, Kurt
Hartwig, Helmuth
Heidenreich, Gerhard
Hoffmann, Heinz
Kirchner, Rudolf
Krebaum, Walter
Kupke, Adolf
Lange, Fritz
Litke, Karl
Mewis, Karl
Neukranz, Gerhard
Rumpf, Willy
Rutha, Erich
Scholz, Helmut
Schuster, Gretl
Seibt, Kurt
Selbmann, Käte
Steinke, Wolfgang
Sztop, Paul
Uschner, Fritz
Wirth, Erich

Members and Candidates of the Politburo and Secretaries of the Central Committee of the SED in 1954*

MEMBERS OF THE POLITBURO

Ebert, Friedrich
Grotewohl, Otto
Matern, Hermann
Oelssner, Fred
Pieck, Wilhelm
Rau, Heinrich
Schirdewan, Karl
Stoph, Willi
Ulbricht, Walter

*Source: "Communiqué of the first plenum of the Central Committee of the SED," *Neues Deutschland,* April 8, 1954, p. 1.

CANDIDATES OF THE POLITBURO

Honecker, Erich
Leuschner, Bruno
Mückenberger, Erich
Neumann, Alfred
Warnke, Herbert

SECRETARIES OF THE CENTRAL COMMITTEE

Ulbricht, Walter (First Secretary)
Mückenberger, Erich
Oelssner, Fred
Schirdewan, Karl
Wandel, Paul
Ziller, Gerhart

Members and Candidates of the SED Central Committee in 1954*

MEMBERS

Alt, Robert
Axen, Hermann
Barthel, Kurt (Kuba)
Baumann, Edith
Baumgart, Hugo
Becher, Johannes R.
Benjamin, Hilde
Blassies, Albert
Bönisch, Fritz
Brandt, Edith
Bredel, Willi
Brust, Richard
Buchheim, Walter
Buchwitz, Otto
Ebert, Friedrich
Engelmann, Friedrich
Ermisch, Luise
Eydam, Kurt
Fabian, Wolfgang
Feist [Honecker], Margot
Fischer, Walter
Götzl, Eduard
Grossmann, Ernst
Grotewohl, Otto
Grünert, Bernhard
Hager, Kurt
Helbig, Kurt
Hennecke, Adolf
Hertwig, Hans-Joachim
Hoffmann, Heinz
Holzmacher, Gerda
Honecker, Erich
Jentsch, Johannes
Kästner, Walter
Kern, Käthe
Kessler, Heinz
Kiefert, Hans
Knoll, Walter
Koenen, Bernard
Koenen, Wilhelm
Kramer, Erwin
Krüger, Karl

Kuhn, Willy
Lehmann, Helmut
Lehmann, Otto
Leuschner, Bruno
Liebknecht, Kurt
Maron, Karl
Matern, Hermann
Meinhardt, Frido
Mewis, Karl
Mielke, Erich
Moltmann, Karl
Mückenberger, Erich
Naumann, Robert
Neugebauer, Werner
Neumann, Alfred
Oelssner, Fred
Pieck, Wilhelm
Pisnik, Alois
Rau, Heinrich
Rodenberg, Hans
Sägebrecht, Willy
Schirdewan, Karl
Schlimme, Hermann
Schön, Otto
Schröder, Christian
Schröder, Walter
Schuppe, Erich
Seibt, Kurt
Seifert, Fritz
Selbmann, Fritz
Steinitz, Wolfgang
Stoph, Willi
Thiele, Ilse
Ulbricht, Walter
Verner, Paul
Wandel, Paul
Warnke, Hans
Warnke, Herbert
Weber, Fritz
Wehmer, Friedrich
Wende, Alfred
Wenig, Josef
Wienecke, Karl
Winzer, Otto
Wirth, Erich
Wittkowski, Margarete

Wollweber, Ernst
Zierold, Kurt
Ziller, Gerhart

CANDIDATES

Albrecht, Hans
Appenrodt, Paul
Arnold, Walter
Bauer, Gerda
Berg, Helene
Biering, Walter
Birnbaum, Erich
Burghardt, Max
Collein, Edmund
Diesner, Erich
Dohlus, Horst
Dunker, Helene
Erler, Eva
Feist [Honecker], Margot
Felfe, Werner
Florin, Peter
Frickmann, Wilhelm
Fritsche, Karl

* Source: Protocols of the Fourth Congress of the SED, March 30 to April 6, 1954, Berlin 1954, II, p. 1082.

Fröhlich, Paul
Frost, Gerhard
Grauer, Gertrud
Heidenreich, Gerhard
Kallas, Paul
Kirchner, Rudolf
Krause, Anna
Kupke, Adolf
Lange, Ernst
Lange, Fritz
Möller, Ewald
Nimz, Eberhard
Plenikowski, Anton
Quetscher, Johannes
Redetzky, Hermann
Rübensam, Erich
Rumpf, Willy
Schirmer, Wolfgang
Scholz, Helmut
Sens, Max
Steinke, Wolfgang
Sternberg, Frieda
Tauchert, Richard
Uhlig, Hans-Joachim
Verner, Waldemar
Wolf, Hanna

Members and Candidates of the Politburo and Secretaries of the Central Committee of the SED in 1958*

MEMBERS OF THE POLITBURO

Ebert, Friedrich
Grotewohl, Otto
Honecker, Erich
Leuschner, Bruno
Matern, Hermann
Mückenberger, Erich
Neumann, Alfred
Norden, Albert
Pieck, Wilhelm
Rau, Heinrich
Stoph, Willi
Ulbricht, Walter
Warnke, Herbert

CANDIDATES OF THE POLITBURO

Baumann, Edith
Ermisch, Luise
Fröhlich, Paul
Hager, Kurt
Kurella, Alfred
Mewis, Karl
Pisnik, Alois
Verner, Pul

SECRETARIES OF THE CENTRAL COMMITTEE

Ulbricht, Walter (First Secretary)
Grüneberg, Gerhard
Hager, Kurt
Honecker, Erich
Mückenberger, Erich

Neumann, Alfred
Norden, Albert
Verner, Paul

*Source: "Communiqué of the first plenum of the Central Committee of the SED," *Neues Deutschland,* July 17, 1958, p. 1.

Members and Candidates of the SED Central Committee in 1958*

MEMBERS

Abusch, Alexander
Altenkirch-Feist, Margot
Axen, Hermann
Barthel, Kurt (Kuba)
Baum, Bruno
Baumann, Edith
Baumgart, Hugo
Becher, Johannes R.
Benjamin, Hilde
Berg, Helene
Bönisch, Fritz
Bräutigam, Alois
Brandt, Edith
Bredel, Willi
Buchheim, Walter
Buchwitz, Otto
Dahlem, Franz
Dölling, Rudolf
Ebert, Friedrich
Ermisch, Luise
Eydam, Kurt
Fabian, Wolfgang
Florin, Peter
Fröhlich, Paul
Frost, Gerhard
Götzl, Eduard
Grossmann, Ernst
Grotewohl, Otto
Grüneberg, Gerhard
Grünert, Bernhard
Gsell, Wilhelm
Hager, Kurt
Handke, Georg
Hennecke, Adolf
Hertwig, Hans-Joachim
Hoffmann, Heinz
Holzmacher, Gerda

Honecker, Erich
Jendretzky, Hans
Kassler, Berthold
Kern, Käthe
Kessler, Heinz
Kiefert, Hans
Knolle, Rainer
Koenen, Bernard
Koenen, Wilhelm
Konzack, Therese
Kosel, Gerhard
Kramer, Erwin
Krüger, Karl
Kurella, Alfred
Lange, Emil
Lange, Erich
Lehmann, Helmut
Lehmann, Otto
Lehmann, Robert
Leuschner, Bruno
Liebknecht, Kurt
Maron, Karl
Matern, Hermann
Meinhardt, Frido
Mette, Alexander
Mewis, Karl
Meyer, Martin
Mielke, Erich
Moltmann, Karl
Mückenberger, Erich
Namokel, Karl
Naumann, Robert
Neugebauer, Werner
Neumann, Alfred
Nimz, Eberhard
Norden, Albert
Pieck, Wilhelm
Pisnik, Alois
Quandt, Bernhard
Rau, Heinrich
Reichert, Rudi

Reuter, Fritz
Rienäcker, Günther
Rodenberg, Hans
Rompe, Robert
Sägebrecht, Willy
Schneikart, Friedrich
Schön, Otto
Schröder, Walter
Schubert, Heinz
Schuckert, Walter
Seibt, Kurt
Sens, Max
Steffen, Max
Stoph, Willi
Storch, Hermann
Svihalek, Karl
Thiele, Ilse
Tille, Walter
Ulbricht, Walter
Verner, Paul
Warnke, Hans
Warnke, Herbert
Weber, Fritz
Wehmer, Friedrich
Weiz, Herbert
Wende, Alfred
Wenig, Josef
Winzer, Otto
Wirth, Erich
Wolf, Ernst
Wolf, Hanna
Wolter, Adolf
Zierold, Kurt

CANDIDATES

Albrecht, Hans
Apel, Erich
Arnold, Walter
Baade, Brunolf
Biering, Walter
Burghardt, Max
Collein, Edmund

Deutschmann, Gertrud
Dohlus, Horst
Erler, Eva
Felfe, Werner
Funke, Otto
Grauer, Gertrud
Heidenreich, Gerhard
Honecker-Feist, Margot
Jürgen, Lothar
Kirchner, Rudolf
Köckeritz-Wollermann, Frieda
Krause, Anna
Lange, Ernst
Lautenschlag, Helene
Minetti, Hans-Peter
Mittag, Günter
Modrow, Hans
Plenikowski, Anton
Rentmeister, Hans
Riemer, Kurt
Rübensam, Erich
Rumpf, Willy
Schirmer, Wolfgang
Schneidewind, Kurt
Scholz, Helmut
Schumann, Horst
Siegert, Maria
Sindermann, Horst
Steinke, Wolfgang
Thieme, Kurt
Thoma, Karl
Verner, Waldemar
Vielhauer, Irmgard
Weihs, Rolf
Wittig, Heinz
Wittkowski, Margarete
Wulf, Ernst

*Source: Protocols of the Fifth Congress
of the SED, July 10 to 16, 1958, Berlin
1958, II, p. 1031.

Members and Candidates of the Politburo and Secretaries of the Central Committee of the SED in 1963*

MEMBERS OF THE POLITBURO

Ebert, Friedrich
Fröhlich, Paul
Grotewohl, Otto
Hager, Kurt
Honecker, Erich
Leuschner, Bruno
Matern, Hermann
Mückenberger, Erich
Neumann, Alfred
Norden, Albert
Stoph, Willi
Ulbricht, Walter
Verner, Paul
Warnke, Herbert

*Source: "Communiqué of the first plenum of the Central Committee of the SED," *Neues Deutschland,* January 22, 1963, p.1.

CANDIDATES OF THE POLITBURO

Apel, Erich
Axen, Hermann
Bartsch, Karl-Heinz
Ewald, Georg
Grüneberg, Gerhard
Jarowinsky, Werner
Mittag, Günter
Müller, Margarete
Sindermann, Horst

SECRETARIES OF THE CENTRAL COMMITTEE

Ulbricht, Walter (First Secretary)
Grüneberg, Gerhard
Hager, Kurt
Honecker, Erich
Mittag, Günter
Norden, Albert
Verner, Paul

Members and Candidates of the SED Central Committee in 1963*

MEMBERS

Abusch, Alexander
Adameck, Heinrich
Albrecht, Hans
Apel, Erich
Axen, Hermann
Balkow, Julius
Barthel, Kurt (Kuba)
Bartsch, Karl-Heinz
Baum, Bruno
Baumann, Edith
Baumgart, Hugo
Benjamin, Hilde
Berg, Helene
Berger, Rolf
Bönisch, Fritz
Bräutigam, Alois

Brandt, Edith
Brasch, Horst
Bredel, Willi
Buchwitz, Otto
Burghardt, Max
Credo, Renate
Dahlem, Franz
Diehl, Ernst
Döhler, Johannes
Dölling, Rudolf
Dohlus, Horst
Ebert, Friedrich
Ermisch, Luise
Ewald, Georg
Ewald, Manfred
Eydam, Kurt
Felfe, Werner
Florin, Peter
Fröhlich, Paul
Frost, Gerhard

Funke, Otto
Grotewohl, Otto
Grüneberg, Gerhard
Grünert, Bernhard
Grundig, Lea
Hager, Kurt
Heidenreich, Gerhard
Heintze, Horst
Hennecke, Adolf
Hertwig, Hans-Joachim
Hoffmann, Heinz
Holzmacher, Gerda
Honecker, Erich
Honecker, Margot
Jarowinsky, Werner
Jendretzky, Hans
Kayser, Karl
Kern, Käthe
Kessler, Heinz
Kiefert, Hans
Knolle, Rainer
Koenen, Bernard
Koenen, Wilhelm
Kosel, Gerhard
Kramer, Erwin
Krolikowski, Werner
Krüger, Karl
Kurella, Alfred
Lange, Erich
Lange, Marianne
Lassak, Walter
Lehmann, Robert
Leuschner, Bruno
Lochthofen, Lorenz
Markgraf, Martin
Maron, Karl
Matern, Hermann
Matthes, Heinz
Meinhardt, Frido
Mewis, Karl
Mielke, Erich
Mittag, Günter
Mückenberger, Erich
Müller, Margarete
Neugebauer, Werner
Neumann, Alfred

Norden, Albert
Pisnik, Alois
Quandt, Bernhard
Rieke, Karl
Rodenberg, Hans
Rödiger, Kurt
Rompe, Robert
Roscher, Paul
Rübensam, Erich
Rumpf, Willy
Schön, Otto
Scholz, Helmut
Schröder, Walter
Schürer, Gerhard
Schumann, Horst
Seibt, Kurt
Sindermann, Horst
Stief, Albert
Stoph, Willi
Storch, Hermann
Streit, Josef
Thiele, Ilse
Tisch, Harry
Ulbricht, Walter
Vallentin, Maxim
Verner, Paul
Verner, Waldemar
Warnke, Hans
Warnke, Herbert
Wehmer, Friedrich
Weiz, Herbert
Wenig, Josef
Winzer, Otto
Wirth, Erich
Wittig, Heinz
Wittkowski, Margarete
Wolf, Ernst
Wolf, Hanna
Wulf, Ernst

CANDIDATES

Beater, Bruno
Dallmann, Fritz
Ernst, Hans
Fischer, Martin
Gallerach, Ernst

Geggel, Heinz
Gehring, Michael
Gotsche, Otto
Hager, Werner
Heinrich, Gotthard
Hempel, Eva
Herber, Richard
Heynisch, Werner
Hörnig, Johannes
Jückel, Hans
Juch, Heinz
Kaiser-Gorrish, Walter
Kamps, Peter
Krussk, Werner
Kuron, Karl
Lamberz, Werner
Lange, Ernst
Lange, Ingeborg
Lappe, Rudolf
Lietz, Bruno
Löschau, Siegbert[1]
Mäde, Hans Dieter
Marschner, Hans-Joachim
Meier, Heinz
Meyer, Ernst-Hermann
Minetti, Hans-Peter
Modrow, Hans
Müller, Fritz I
Müller, Fritz II
Naumann, Konrad
Neuner, Gerhart

Oerter, Wolfgang
Plenikowski, Anton
Pöschel, Hermann
Prey, Günter
Sakowski, Helmut
Schirmer, Wolfgang
Schwarz, Heinz
Skibinski, Willi
Sölle, Horst
Sternberg, Frieda
Strauss, Paul
Thieme, Kurt
Thoma, Karl
Tiedke, Kurt
Traut, Herbert
Waak, Günther
Walther, Elisabeth
Wekker, Rudi
Wesselburg, Friedrich
Wittik, Johann
Wolf, Christa
Wyschofsky, Günther
Ziegenhahn, Herbert
Zimmering, Max

[1] Löschau was admitted to membership of the Central Committee on the seventh CC plenum but was excluded on the thirteenth. See "Communiqué of the seventh meeting of the Central Committee of the SED," *Neues Deutschland*, December 6, 1964, p. 1, and "Communiqué of the thirteenth plenum. . . ." *Neues Deutschland*, September 18, 1966, p. 1.

*Source: Protocols of the Sixth Congress of SED, January 15-21, 1963, Berlin 1963, p. 494.

Members and Candidates of the Politburo and Secretaries of the Central Committee of the SED on January 1, 1967*

MEMBERS OF THE POLITBURO

Ebert, Friedrich
Fröhlich, Paul
Grüneberg, Gerhard[1]

Hager, Kurt
Honecker, Erich
Matern, Hermann
Mittag, Günter[1]
Mückenberger, Erich
Neumann, Alfred
Norden, Albert
Stoph, Willi
Ulbricht, Walter

Verner, Paul
Warnke, Herbert

Axen, Hermann
Ewald, Georg
Jarowinsky, Werner
Müller, Margarete
Sindermann, Horst
*See p. 454 for source and footnotes to the preceding list.

Ulbricht, Walter (First Secretary)
Axen, Hermann[2]
Grüneberg, Gerhard
Hager, Kurt
Honecker, Erich
Jarowinsky, Werner[3]
Mittag, Günter
Norden, Albert
Verner, Paul

Members and Candidates of the SED Central Committee on January 1, 1967*

MEMBERS

Abusch, Alexander
Adameck, Heinrich
Albrecht, Hans
Axen, Hermann
Balkow, Julius
Barthel, Kurt (Kuba)
Baum, Bruno
Braumann, Edith
Baumgart, Hugo
Benjamin, Hilde
Berg, Helene
Berger, Rolf
Bönisch, Fritz
Bräutigam, Alois
Brandt, Edith
Brasch, Horst
Burghardt, Max
Credo, Renate
Dahlem, Franz
Dallmann, Fritz[4]
Diehl, Ernst
Döhler, Johannes
Dölling, Rudolf
Dohlus, Horst
Ebert, Friedrich
Ermisch, Luise
Ewald, Georg
Ewald, Manfred
Eydam, Kurt

Felfe, Werner
Florin, Peter
Fröhlich, Paul
Frost, Gerhard
Funke, Otto
Gotsche, Otto[5]
Grüneberg, Gerhard
Grünert, Bernhard
Grundig, Lea
Hager, Kurt
Heidenreich, Gerhard
Heintze, Horst
Hennecke, Adolf
Herber, Richard
Hertwig, Hans-Joachim
Hoffmann, Heinz
Holzmacher, Gerda
Honecker, Erich
Honecker, Margot
Jäckel, Hans[4]
Jarowinsky, Werner
Jendretzky, Hans
Kayser, Karl
Kern, Käthe
Kessler, Heinz
Knolle, Rainer
Kosel, Gerhard
Kramer, Erwin
Krolikowski, Werner
Krüger, Karl
Kurella, Alfred
Lange, Erich
Lange, Ingeborg[4]

Lange, Marianne
Lassak, Walter
Lehmann, Robert
Lochthofen, Lorenz
Markgraf, Martin
Maron, Karl
Matern, Hermann
Matthes, Heinz
Meinhardt, Frido
Mewis, Karl
Mielke, Erich
Mittag, Günter
Mückenberger, Erich
Müller, Margarete
Naumann, Konrad[5]
Neugebauer, Werner
Neumann, Alfred
Norden, Albert
Pisnik, Alois
Prey, Günter[4]
Quandt, Bernhard
Rieke, Karl
Rodenberg, Hans
Rödiger, Kurt
Rompe, Robert
Roscher, Paul
Rübensam, Erich
Rumpf, Willy
Schön, Otto
Scholz, Helmut
Schröder, Walter
Schürer, Gerhard
Schumann, Horst
Seibt, Kurt
Sindermann, Horst
Stief, Albert
Stoph, Willi
Storch, Hermann
Streit, Josef
Thiele, Ilse
Tisch, Harry
Ulbricht, Walter
Vallentin, Maxim
Verner, Paul
Verner, Waldemar
Warnke, Hans

Warnke, Herbert
Wehmer, Friedrich
Weiz, Herbert
Wenig, Josef
Winzer, Otto
Wirth, Erich
Wittig, Heinz
Wittik, Johann[4]
Wittkowski, Margarete
Wolf, Ernst
Wolf, Hanna
Wulf, Ernst
Wyschofsky, Günther[4]
Ziegenhahn, Herbert[5]

CANDIDATES

Beater, Bruno
Ernst, Hans
Fischer, Martin
Gallerach, Ernst
Geggel, Heinz
Gehring, Michael
Hager, Werner
Heinrich, Gotthard
Hempel, Eva
Herber, Richard
Heynisch, Werner
Hörnig, Johannes
Juch, Heinz
Kaiser-Gorrish, Walter
Kamps, Peter
Krussk, Werner
Kuron, Karl
Lamberz, Werner
Lange, Ernst
Lappe, Rudolf
Lietz, Bruno
Mäde, Hans Dieter
Marschner, Hans-Joachim
Meier, Heinz
Meyer, Ernst-Hermann
Minetti, Hans-Peter
Modrow, Hans
Müller, Fritz I
Müller, Fritz II
Neuner, Gerhart

Oerter, Wolfgang
Plenikowski, Anton
Pöschel, Hermann
Sakowski, Helmut
Schirmer, Wolfgang
Schwarz, Heinz
Skibinski, Willi
Sölle, Horst
Sternberg, Frieda
Strauss, Paul
Thieme, Kurt
Thoma, Karl
Tiedke, Kurt
Traut, Herbert
Waak, Günther
Walther, Elisabeth
Wekker, Rudi

Wesselburg, Friedrich
Wolf, Christa
Zimmering, Max

*From data of the Institute for Political Science at the Free University of Berlin.

[1] Cf. "Communiqué of the thirteenth plenum . . ." op. cit.
[2] Cf. "Resolution of the Central Committee," *Neues Deutschland,* February 18, 1966, p. 2.
[3] Cf. "Communiqué of the fourth plenum . . ." ibid., November 2, 1963, p. 1.
[4] Cf. "Communiqué of the seventh plenum . . ." ibid., December 6, 1964, p. 1.
[5] "Communiqué of the thirteenth plenum . . ." ibid., September 18, 1966, p. 1.

Members and Candidates of the Politburo and Secretaries of the Central Committee of the SED in 1967*

MEMBERS OF THE POLITBURO

Ebert, Friedrich
Fröhlich, Paul
Grüneberg, Gerhard
Hager, Kurt
Honecker, Erich
Matern, Hermann
Mittag, Günter
Mückenberger, Erich
Neumann, Alfred
Norden, Albert
Sindermann, Horst
Stoph, Willi
Ulbricht, Walter
Verner, Paul
Warnke, Herbert

*Source: *Neues Deutschland,* April 23, 1967, p. 3.

CANDIDATES OF THE POLITBURO

Axen, Hermann
Ewald, Georg
Halbritter, Walter
Jarowinsky, Werner
Kleiber, Günther
Müller, Margarete

SECRETARIES OF THE CENTRAL COMMITTEE

Ulbricht, Walter (First Secretary)
Axen, Hermann
Grüneberg, Gerhard
Hager, Kurt
Honecker, Erich
Jarowinsky, Werner
Lamberz, Werner
Mittag, Günter
Norden, Albert
Verner, Paul

Members and Candidates of the SED Central Committee in 1967*

MEMBERS

Abusch, Alexander

Adameck, Heinrich
Albrecht, Hans
Axen, Hermann
Balkow, Julius
Barthel, Kurt (Kuba)

Baum, Bruno
Baumann, Edith
Benjamin, Hilde
Berg, Helene
Berger, Rolf
Böhm, Siegfried
Bräutigam, Alois
Brandt, Edith
Brasch, Horst
Burghardt, Max
Chemnitzer, Johannes
Credo, Renate
Dahlem, Franz
Dallmann, Fritz
Dickel, Friedrich
Diehl, Ernst
Döhler, Johannes
Dohlus, Horst
Ebert, Friedrich
Eisler, Gerhart
Ermisch, Luise
Ewald, Georg
Ewald, Manfred
Eydam, Kurt
Felfe, Werner
Fischer, Martin
Florin, Peter
Fröhlich, Paul
Frost, Gerhard
Fuchs, Klaus
Funke, Otto
Gallerach, Ernst
Gotsche, Otto
Grüneberg, Gerhard
Grünert, Bernhard
Grundig, Lea
Hager, Kurt
Halbritter, Walter
Heidenreich, Gerhard
Heintze, Horst
Hennecke, Adolf
Herber, Richard
Hertwig, Hans-Joachim
Heynisch, Werner
Hörnig, Johannes
Hoffmann, Heinz
Holzmacher, Gerda

Honecker, Erich
Honecker, Margot
Jahn, Günter
Jarowinsky, Werner
Jendretzky, Hans
Juch, Heinz
Kayser, Karl
Kern, Käthe
Kessler, Heinz
Kleiber, Günther
Knolle, Rainer
Kramer, Erwin
Krolikowski, Werner
Kurella, Alfred
Lamberz, Werner
Lange, Erich
Lange, Ingeborg
Lange, Marianne
Markgraf, Martin
Maron, Karl
Matern, Hermann
Matthes, Heinz
Mewis, Karl
Mielke, Erich
Mittag, Günter
Modrow, Hans
Mückenberger, Erich
Müller, Fritz I
Müller, Margarete
Naumann, Konrad
Neugebauer, Werner
Neumann, Alfred
Norden, Albert
Pisnik, Alois
Pöschel, Hermann
Prey, Gunter
Quandt, Bernhard
Rauchfuss, Wolfgang
Reinhold, Otto
Rieke, Karl
Rodenberg, Hans
Rödiger, Kurt
Rompe, Robert
Roscher, Paul
Rübensam, Erich
Rumpf, Willy
Schön, Otto

Schröder, Walter
Schürer, Gerhard
Schumann, Horst
Seeger, Bernhard
Sindermann, Horst
Singer, Rudolf
Stief, Albert
Stoph, Willi
Storch, Hermann
Strauss, Paul
Streit, Josef
Thiele, Ilse
Thoma, Karl
Tiedke, Kurt
Tisch, Harry
Ulbricht, Walter
Verner, Paul
Verner, Waldemar
Warnke, Hans
Warnke, Herbert
Weiz, Herbert
Wenig, Josef
Winzer, Otto
Wittig, Heinz
Wittig, Werner
Wittik, Johann
Wittkowski, Margarete
Wolf, Hanna
Wulf, Ernst
Wyschofsky, Günther
Ziegenhahn, Herbert

CANDIDATES

Bauer, Roland
Beater, Bruno
Berthold, Heinz
Bialecki, Joachim
Biermann, Wolfgang
Fechner, Herbert
Geggel, Heinz
Georgi, Rudi
Görlich, Hubert
Hager, Werner

Heinrich, Gotthard
Hempel, Eva
Hering, Werner
Herrmann, Joachim
Hieblinger, Inge
Junker, Wolfgang
Kamps, Peter
Kegel, Gerhard
Kiesler, Bruno
Kiess, Kurt
Kirchhoff, Werner
Kuron, Karl
Lietz, Bruno
Lorenz, Siegfried
Mäde, Hans Dieter
Markowski, Paul
Meier, Heinz
Meyer, Ernst-Hermann
Minetti, Hans-Peter
Müller, Fritz II
Neuner, Gerhart
Sakowski, Helmut
Scheibe, Herbert
Schönfelder, Heinz
Schwarz, Heinz
Skibinski, Willi
Sölle, Horst
Steger, Otfried
Sternberg, Frieda
Thieme, Kurt
Traut, Herbert
Waak, Günther
Walther, Elisabeth
Weingart, Edith
Weiss, Gerhard
Wekker, Rudi
Wüstneck, Klaus Dieter
Ziegner, Heinz
Zimmering, Max
Zschau, Ursula

*Source: *Neues Deutschland,* April 23, 1967, p. 4.

The Members and Candidates of the Central Committee, 1950 to 1967
(M = Member; C = Candidate)

	1950	1954	1958	1963	1967
Abusch, Alexander			M	M	M
Ackermann, Anton	M				
Adameck, Heinrich				M	M
Albrecht, Hans		C	C	M	M
Alt, Robert		M			
Altenkirch-Feist, Margot	M	M	M		
Apel, Erich			C	M	d.3.12.65
Appenrodt, Paul		C			
Arnold, Walter		C	C		
Axen, Hermann	M	M	M	M	M
Baade, Brunolf			C		
Balkow, Julius				M	M
Barthel, Kurt (Kuba)	C	M	M	M	M
Bartsch, Karl-Heinz				M	
Bauer, Gerda	M	C			
Bauer, Roland					C
Baum, Bruno			M	M	M
Baumann, Edith	M	M	M	M	M
Baumann, Georg	C				
Baumgart, Hugo		M	M	M	
Beater, Bruno				C	C
Becher, Johannes R.	M	M	M	d.10.11.58	
Benjamin, Hilde		M	M	M	M
Berg, Helene		C	M	M	M
Berger, Rolf				M	M
Bergmann, Herta	M				
Berthold, Heinz					C
Bialecki, Joachim					C
Biering, Walter	C	C	C	d.21.4.64	
Biermann, Wolfgang					C
Birnbaum, Erich	C	C			
Blassies, Albert		M			
Böhm, Siegfried					M
Böhme, Kurt	C				
Bönisch, Fritz		M	M	M	
Bräutigam, Alois			M	M	M
Brandt, Edith		M	M	M	M
Brasch, Horst				M	M
Bredel, Willi		M	M	M	d.27.10.64
Bruschke, Werner	M				
Brust, Richard		M			
Buchheim, Walter		M	M		

	1950	1954	1958	1963	1967
Buchwitz, Otto	M	M	M	M	d.9.7.64
Bürger, Kurt	M				
Burghardt, Max		C	C	M	M
Chemnitzer, Johannes					M
Collein, Edmund		C	C		
Credo, Renate				M	M
Dahlem, Franz	M		M	M	M
Dallmann, Fritz				C	M
Deter, Adolf	C				
Deutschmann, Gertrud			C		
Dickel, Friedrich					M
Diehl, Ernst				M	M
Diesner, Erich		C			
Döhler, Johannes				M	M
Dölling, Rudolf			M	M	
Dohlus, Horst	C	C	C	M	M
Dunker, Helene		C			
Ebert, Friedrich	M	M	M	M	M
Eisler, Gerhart					M
Engelmann, Friedrich		M			
Erler, Eva		C	C		
Ermisch, Luise		M	M	M	M
Ernst, Hans				C	
Ewald, Georg				M	M
Ewald, Manfred				M	M
Eydam, Kurt		M	M	M	M
Fabian, Wolfgang		M	M		
Fechner, Herbert					C
Fechner, Max	M				
Feist, Margot, born 1923, see Altenkirch					
Feist, Margot, born 1927, see Honecker					
Felfe, Werner		C	C	M	M
Fischer, Lena	M				
Fischer, Martin				C	M
Fischer, Walter		M			
Florin, Peter		C	M	M	M
Frickmann, Wilhelm		C			
Fritsche, Karl		C			
Fröhlich, Paul		C	M	M	M
Frost, Gerhard		C	M	M	M
Fuchs, Klaus					M
Funke, Otto			C	M	M

Name					
Gallerach, Ernst				C	M
Geggel, Heinz				C	C
Gehring, Michael				C	
Georgi, Rudi					C
Görlich, Hubert					C
Götzl, Eduard	C	M	M		
Gotsche, Otto				C	M
Grauer, Gertrud		C	C		
Grossmann, Ernst		M	M		
Grotewohl, Otto	M	M	M	M	d.21.9.64
Grüneberg, Gerhard			M	M	M
Grünert, Bernhard		M	M	M	M
Grundig, Lea				M	M
Gsell, Wilhelm			M		
Hager, Kurt	C	M	M	M	M
Hager, Werner				C	C
Halbritter, Walter					M
Handke, Georg			M	d.7.9.62	
Hartwig, Helmuth	C				
Heidenreich, Gerhard	C	C	C	M	M
Heinrich, Gotthard				C	C
Heintze, Horst				M	M
Helbig, Kurt		M			
Hempel, Eva				C	C
Hennecke, Adolf		M	M	M	M
Herber, Richard				C	M
Hering, Werner					C
Herrmann, Joachim					C
Herrnstadt, Rudolf	M			d.28.8.66	
Hertwig, Hans-Joachim		M	M	M	M
Heynisch, Werner				C	M
Hieblinger, Inge					C
Hörnig, Johannes				C	M
Hoffmann, Ernst	M				
Hoffmann, Heinz	C	M	M	M	M
Holzmacher, Gerda	M	M	M	M	M
Honecker, Erich	M	M	M	M	M
Honecker (Feist), Margot	C	C	C	M	M
Jäckel, Hans				C	
Jahn, Günter					M
Jarowinsky, Werner				M	M
Jendretzky, Hans	M		M	M	M
Jentsch, Johannes		M			
Juch, Heinz				C	M
Jürgen, Lothar			C		

	1950	1954	1958	1963	1967
Junker, Wolfgang					C
Kästner, Walter		M			
Kaiser-Gorrish, Walter				C	
Kallas, Paul		C			
Kamps, Peter				C	C
Kassler, Berthold			M		
Kayser, Karl				M	M
Kegel, Gerhard					C
Kern, Käthe	M	M	M	M	M
Kessler, Heinz	M	M	M	M	M
Kiefert, Hans		M	M	M	d.29.12.66
Kiesler, Bruno					C
Kiess, Kurt					C
Kirchhoff, Werner					C
Kirchner, Rudolf	C	C	C		
Kleiber, Günther					M
Knoll, Walter		M			
Knolle, Rainer			M	M	M
Köckeritz-Wollermann, Frieda			C		
Koenen, Bernard	M	M	M	M	d.30.4.64
Koenen, Wilhelm	M	M	M	M	d.19.10.63
Konzack, Therese			M		
Kosel, Gerhard			M	M	
Kramer, Erwin		M	M	M	M
Krause, Anna		C	C		
Krebaum, Walter	C				
Krolikowski, Werner				M	M
Krüger, Karl		M	M	M	
Krussk, Werner				C	
Kuba, see Barthel, Kurt					
Kuhn, Willy		M			
Kupke, Adolf	C	C			
Kurella, Alfred			M	M	M
Kuron, Karl				C	C
Lamberz, Werner				C	M
Lange, Emil			M		
Lange, Erich			M	M	M
Lange, Ernst		C			
Lange, Ernst			C	C	
Lange, Fritz	C	C			
Lange, Ingeborg				C	M
Lange, Marianne				M	M
Lappe, Rudolf				C	
Lassak, Walter				M	

Lautenschlag, Helene			C		
Lauter, Hans	M				
Lehmann, Helmut	M	M	M	d.9.2.59	
Lehmann, Otto		M	M		
Lehmann, Robert			M	M	
Leuschner, Bruno	M	M	M	M	d.10.2.65
Leutwein, Friedrich	M				
Liebknecht, Kurt		M	M		
Lietz, Bruno				C	C
Litke, Karl	C				
Lochthofen, Lorenz				M	
Löschau, Siegbert				C	
Lohagen, Ernst	M				
Lorenz, Siegfried					C
Mäde, Hans Dieter				C	C
Markgraf, Martin				M	M
Markowski, Paul					C
Maron, Karl		M	M	M	M
Marschner, Hans-Joachim				C	
Matern, Hermann	M	M	M	M	M
Matthes, Heinz				M	M
Meier, Heinz				C	C
Meinhardt, Frido		M	M	M	
Mette, Alexander			M		
Mewis, Karl	C	M	M	M	M
Meyer, Ernst-Hermann				C	C
Meyer, Martin			M	d.16.9.66	
Mielke, Erich	M	M	M	M	M
Minetti, Hans-Peter			C	C	C
Mittag, Günter			C	M	M
Modrow, Hans			C	C	M
Möller, Ewald		C			
Moltmann, Karl	M	M	M	d.5.2.60	
Mückenberger, Erich	M	M	M	M	M
Müller, Fritz II (born 1918)				C	C
Müller, Fritz I (born 1920)				C	M
Müller, Margarete				M	M
Namokel, Karl			M		
Naumann, Konrad				C	M
Naumann, Robert		M	M		
Neugebauer, Werner		M	M	M	M
Neukranz, Gerhard	C				
Neumann, Alfred		M	M	M	M
Neuner, Gerhart				C	C
Nimz, Eberhard		C	M		

	1950	1954	1958	1963	1967
Norden, Albert			M	M	M
Oelssner, Fred	M	M			
Oerter, Wolfgang				C	
Pieck, Wilhelm	M	M	M	d.7.9.60	
Pisnik, Alois	M	M	M	M	M
Plenikowski, Anton		C	C	C	
Pöschel, Hermann				C	M
Prey, Günter				C	M
Quandt, Bernhard			M	M	M
Quetscher, Johannes		C			
Rau, Heinrich	M	M	M	d.23.3.61	
Rauchfuss, Wolfgang					M
Redetzky, Hermann		C			
Reichert, Rudi			M		
Reinhold, Otto					M
Rentmeister, Hans			C		
Reuter, Fritz			M		
Rieke, Karl				M	M
Riemer, Kurt			C		
Rienäcker, Günther			M		
Rodenberg, Hans		M	M	M	M
Rödiger, Kurt				M	M
Rompe, Robert			M	M	M
Roscher, Paul				M	M
Rübensam, Erich		C	C	M	M
Rumpf, Willy	C	C	C	M	M
Rutha, Erich	C				
Sägebrecht, Willy	M	M	M		
Sakowski, Helmut				C	C
Scheibe, Herbert					C
Schirdewan, Karl		M			
Schirmer, Wolfgang		C	C	C	
Schlimme, Hermann	M	M	d.10.11.55		
Schmidt, Elli	M				
Schneidewind, Kurt			C		
Schneikart, Friedrich			M		
Schön, Otto	M	M	M	M	M
Schönfelder, Heinz					C
Scholz, Helmut	C	C	C	M	d.20.3.67
Schröder, Christian		M			
Schröder, Walter		M	M	M	M

Name						
Schubert, Heinz			M			d.1962
Schuckert, Walter			M			
Schürer, Gerhard				M	M	
Schumann, Horst			C	M	M	
Schuppe, Erich		M				
Schuster, Gretl	C					
Schwarz, Heinz				C	C	
Seeger, Bernhard					M	
Seibt, Kurt	C	M	M	M		
Seifert, Fritz		M				
Selbmann, Fritz		M				
Selbmann, Käte	C					
Sens, Max			C	M		d.6.12.62
Siegert, Maria			C			
Sindermann, Horst			C	M	M	
Singer, Rudolf				M		
Skibinski, Willi				C	C	
Sölle, Horst				C	C	
Steffen, Max			M			
Steger, Otfried					C	
Steinhoff, Karl	M					
Steinitz, Wolfgang		M				d.21.4.67
Steinke, Wolfgang	C	C	C			
Sternberg, Frieda		C		C	C	
Stief, Albert				M	M	
Stoph, Willi	M	M	M	M	M	
Storch, Hermann		M		M	M	
Strauss, Paul				C	M	
Streit, Josef				M	M	
Svihalek, Karl			M			
Sztop, Paul	C					
Tauchert, Richard		C				
Thiele, Ilse		M	M	M	M	
Thieme, Kurt			C	C	C	
Thoma, Karl			C	C	M	
Tiedke, Kurt				C	M	
Tille, Walter			M			
Tisch, Harry				M	M	
Traut, Herbert				C	C	
Uhlig, Hans-Joachim		C				
Ulbricht, Walter	M	M	M	M	M	
Uschner, Fritz	C					
Vallentin, Maxim				M		
Verner, Paul	M	M	M	M	M	

	1950	1954	1958	1964	1967
Verner, Waldemar		C	C	M	M
Vielhauer, Irmgard			C		
Vieweg, Kurt	M				
Waak, Günther				C	C
Walther, Elisabeth				C	C
Wandel, Paul	M	M			
Warnke, Hans	M	M	M	M	M
Warnke, Herbert	M	M	M	M	M
Weber, Fritz		M	M		
Wehmer, Friedrich		M	M	M	d. March 1964
Weihs, Rolf			C		
Weingart, Edith					C
Weiss, Gerhard					C
Weiz, Herbert			M	M	M
Wekker, Rudi				C	C
Wende, Alfred		M	M		
Wenig Josef		M	M	M	M
Wesselburg, Friedrich				C	
Wienecke, Karl		M			
Winzer, Otto	M	M	M	M	M
Wirth, Erich	C	M	M	M	
Wittig, Heinz			C	M	M
Wittig, Werner					M
Wittik, Johann				C	M
Wittkowski, Margarete		M	C	M	M
Wolf, Christa				C	
Wolf, Ernst			M	M	
Wolf, Hanna		C	M	M	M
Wollweber, Ernst		M			d.3.5.67
Wolter, Adolf			M		
Wüstneck, Klaus Dieter					C
Wulf, Ernst			C	M	M
Wyschofsky, Günther				C	M
Zaisser, Wilhelm	M		d.3.3.58		
Ziegenhahn, Herbert				C	M
Ziegner, Heinz					C
Zierold, Kurt		M	M		d.7.3.65
Ziller, Gerhart		M	d.14.12.57		
Zimmering, Max				C	C
Zschau, Ursula					C

Bibliography

A. Newspapers and Periodicals (since 1954)

EAST

Die Arbeit. Zeitschrift für Theorie und Praxis der Gewerkschaften, pub. by Bundesvorstand des FDGB, Berlin.

Beiträge zur Geschichte der deutschen Arbeiterbewegung, pub. by Institut für Marxismus-Leninismus beim ZK der SED, Berlin (since 1961).

Neues Deutschland. Official organ of the Central Committee of the SED, Berlin.

Einheit. Zeitschrift für Theorie und Praxis des wissenschaftlichen Sozialismus, pub. by the CC of the SED, Berlin.

Forum. Organ des Zentralrats der FDJ. Zeitung für geistige Probleme der Jugend, Berlin.

Gesetzblatt der Deutschen Demokratischen Republik, Berlin, Part I (since 1949); Part II (since 1955); Part III (since 1960).

Das Hochschulwesen. Wissenschaftspolitische Rundschau, pub. by Staatssekretariat für das Hoch- und Fachschulwesen der DDR, Berlin.

Statistische Praxis, pub. by Staatliche Zentralverwaltung für Statistik beim Ministerrat der DDR, Berlin.

Sonntag. Wochenzeitung für Kulturpolitik, Kunst und Wissenschaft, pub. by Deutscher Kulturbund, Berlin.

Staat und Recht, pub. by Deutsche Akademie für Staats- und Rechtswissenschaft "Walter Ulbricht," Berlin.

Tribüne. Organ des Bundesvorstandes des FDGB, Berlin.

Neuer Weg. Organ des ZK der SED für Fragen des Parteilebens, Berlin.

Die Wirtschaft. Zeitschrift für Politik, Wirtschaft und Technik, Berlin.

Wirtschaftswissenschaft, Berlin.

Deutsche Zeitschrift für Philosophie, Berlin.

WEST

Jahrbuch für Ostrecht, pub. by Institut für Ostrecht, München-Herrenalb.

Recht in Ost und West. Zeitschrift für Rechtsvergleichung und interzonale Rechtsprobleme, pub. by Untersuchungsausschuss Freiheitlicher Juristen, Berlin.

SBZ-Archiv. Dokumente, Berichte, Kommentare zu gesamtdeutschen Fragen, pub. by Joseph C. Witsch, Cologne.

Vierteljahreshefte zur Wirtschaftsforschung, pub. by Deutsches Institut für Wirtschaftsforschung (Institut für Konjunkturforschung), Berlin.

B. Reference Works, Official Party Texts, Document Collections Including Minutes of Meetings, and Legislation by the SED and the GDR Government.

EAST

Sozialistische Arbeitswissenschaft. Taschenwörterbuch, Berlin 1966.

Berufsbilder für Ausbildungsberufe, pub. by Ministerium für Volksbildung bei der Regierung der DDR, Berlin 1964.

Beschluss des Politbüros des ZK der SED vom. 26. Februar 1963 "Über die Leitung der Parteiarbeit nach dem Produktionsprinzip. Mitteilung des Politbüros des Zentralkomitees," in: *Dokumente der Sozialistischen Einheitspartei Deutschlands. Beschlüsse und Erklärungen . . .,* IX, Berlin 1965, pp. 331ff., also Appendix, pp. 372 ff.

Beschluss des Politbüros des ZK der SED vom 29. Oktober 1963: "Grundsätze über die Aufgaben und Arbeitsweise der Produktionskomitees in volkseigenen Grossbetrieben," in: *Dokumente der Sozialistischen Einheitspartei Deutschlands. Beschlüsse und Erklärungen. . .,* IX, Berlin 1965, pp. 720 ff., also Appendix, pp. 380 ff.

Beschluss des Sekretariats des Zentralkomitees der SED vom 17. Februar 1965: "Grundsätze über die planmässige Entwicklung, Ausbildung, Erziehung und Verteilung der Kader in den Partei-, Staats- und Wirtschaftsorganen sowie den Massenorganisationen und auf dem Gebiet der Kultur und Volksbildung," in: *Neuer Weg,* Vol. 20 (1965), No. 6, Supplement.

Beschlüsse der 13. Tagung des Zentralkomitees der SED vom 17. September 1966: "Direktive des Zentralkomitees der SED für die Rechenschaftslegung und Neuwahl der leitenden Parteiorgane, für die Wahlen der Delegierten zu den Delegiertenkonferenzen, Parteikonferenzen und zu den Parteitagen," in: *Neuer Weg,* Vol. 21 (1966), No. 19, Supplement.

"Beschluss des Zentralkomitees der Sozialistischen Einheitspartei Deutschlands und des Ministerrates der Deutschen Demokratischen Republik über die Bildung der Arbeiter-und-Bauern-Inspektion der Deutschen Demokratischen Republik" vom 28. Februar 1963, in: *Dokumente der Sozialistischen Einheitspartei Deutschlands. Beschlüsse und Erklärungen . . .,* IX, Berlin 1965, pp. 352 ff., also Appendix, pp. 374 ff.

Dokumente der Sozialistischen Einheitspartei Deutschlands. Beschlüsse und Erklärungen . . ., Vols. I–X, Berlin 1948–1967.

Dokumente der Staatsordnung der DDR, pub. by Günter Albrecht, 2 vols., Berlin 1959.

Geschichte der deutschen Arbeiterbewegung, pub. by Institut für Marxismus-Leninismus beim Zentralkomitee der SED, 8 vols., Berlin 1966.

Handbuch für den Gewerkschaftsfunktionär, pub. by Bundesvorstand des Freien Deutschen Gewerkschaftsbundes, 3rd rev. ed., Berlin 1965.

Handbuch der Deutschen Demokratischen Republik, pub. by Deutsches Institut für Zeitgeschichte in conjunction with Staatsverlag der Deutschen Demokratischen Republik, Berlin 1963.

Handbuch der Volkskammer der Deutschen Demokratischen Republik, pub. by Volkskammer der DDR, 2. Wahlperiode: Berlin 1957; 3. Wehlperiode: Berlin 1959; 4. Wahlperiode: Berlin 1964.

Jahrbuch der Deutschen Demokratischen Republik, pub. by Deutsches Institut für Zeitgeschichte, vols. 1956–1961, Berlin 1956–1961.

Statistisches Jahrbuch der Deutschen Demokratischen Republik, pub. by Staatliche Zentralverwaltung für Statistik, Vols. 1—11, 1955–1966, Berlin 1956–1966.

Ökonomisches Lexikon, 2 vols., Berlin 1967.

Der dialektische Materialismus und der Aufbau des Sozialismus. Diskussionsbeiträge der Konferenz des Instituts für Gesellschaftswissenschaften beim ZK der SED über den dialektischen Materialismus, die theoretische Grundlage der Politik der Partei der Arbeiterklasse und seine erfolgreiche Anwendung durch die SED, 5. und 6. Mai 1958 in Berlin, Berlin 1958.

Zur ökonomischen Politik der Sozialistischen Einheitspartei Deutschlands und der Regierung der Deutschen Demokratischen Republik. Zusammenstellung von Beschlüssen der Sozialistischen Einheitspartei

Deutschlands sowie Gesetzen und Verordnungen der Regierung der Deutschen Demokratischen Republik, 3 vols., Berlin 1955–1960.

Protokoll der 1. Parteikonferenz der Sozialistischen Einheitspartei Deutschlands, 25. bis 28. Januar 1949 im Hause der Deutschen Wirtschaftskommission zu Berlin, 2nd ed. Berlin 1950.

Protokoll der Verhandlungen der 2. Parteikonferenz der Sozialistischen Einheitspartei Deutschlands, 9. bis 12. Juli 1952 in der Werner-Seelenbinder-Halle zu Berlin, Berlin 1952.

Protokoll der Verhandlungen der 3. Parteikonferenz der Sozialistischen Einheitspartei Deutschlands, 24. März bis 30. März 1956 in der Werner-Seelenbinder-Halle zu Berlin, 2 vols., Berlin 1956.

Protokoll des Vereinigungsparteitages der Sozialdemokratischen Partei Deutschlands (SPD) und der Kommunistischen Partei Deutschlands (KPD) am 21. und 22. April 1946 in der Staatsoper "Admiralspalast" in Berlin, Berlin 1946.

Protokoll der Verhandlungen des II. Parteitages der Sozialistischen Einheitspartei Deutschlands, 20. bis 24. September 1947 in der Deutschen Staatsoper zu Berlin, Berlin 1947.

Protokoll der Verhandlungen des III. Parteitages der Sozialistischen Einheitspartei Deutschlands, 20. bis 24. Juli 1950 in der Werner-Seelenbinder-Halle zu Berlin, 2 vols., Berlin 1951.

Protokoll der Verhandlungen des IV. Parteitages der Sozialistischen Einheitspartei Deutschlands, 30. März bis 6. April 1954 in der Werner-Seelenbinder-Halle zu Berlin, 2 vols., Berlin 1954.

Protokoll der Verhandlungen des V. Parteitages der Sozialistischen Einheitspartei Deutschlands, 10. bis 16. Juli 1958 in der Werner-Seelenbinder-Halle zu Berlin, 2 vols., Berlin 1959.

Protokoll der Verhandlungen des VI. Parteitages der Sozialistischen Einheitspartei Deutschlands, 15. bis 21. Januar 1963 in der Werner-Seelenbinder-Halle zu Berlin, 4 vols., Berlin 1963.

Protokoll der Verhandlungen des VII. Parteitages der Sozialistischen Einheitspartei Deutschlands: Bis zur Veröffentlichung des Protokolls see *Neues Deutschland,* 17–25 April 1967.

Sozialistische Rationalisierung und Standardisierung. Konferenz des ZK der SED und des Ministerrates der DDR, 23. und 24. Juni 1966 in

Leipzig. Referate, Berichte, Schlusswort, Berlin 1966; *Diskussion,* 2 vols.; *Tafelwerk,* Berlin 1966.

"Richtlinie für das neue ökonomische System der Planung und Leitung der Volkswirtschaft" vom 11. Juni 1963, in: *Gbl. der DDR, II,* 1963, pp. 453 ff.

9. Tagung des Zentralkomitees der Sozialistischen Einheitspartei Deutschlands, 20. bis 23 Juli 1960. Durch sozialistische Gemeinschaftsarbeit zum wissenschaftlich-technischen Höchststand im Maschinenbau und in der Metallurgie. Brief Walter Ulbrichts an die Maschinenbauer und Metallurgen. Brief des ZK zur ökonomischen Verwendung von Rohstaffen und zur strengsten Sparsamkeit. Referate, Diskussionsreden, Schlusswort, Beschluss, Berlin 1961.

14. Tagung des Zentralkomitees der Sozialistischen Einheitspartei Deutschlands, 23. bis 26. November 1961. Der XXII. Parteitag der KPdSU und die Aufgaben in der Deutschen Demokratischen Republik. Bericht des Genossen Walter Ulbricht und Beschluss, Berlin 1961.

14. Tagung des Zentralkomitees der Sozialistischen Einheitspartei Deutschlands, 23. bis 26. November 1961. Diskussion zum Bericht des Genossen Walter Ulbricht über den XXII. Parteitag der KPdSU und die Aufgaben in der Deutschen Demokratischen Republik, Berlin 1961.

7. Tagung des Zentralkomitees der Sozialistischen Einheitspartei Deutschlands, 2. bis 5. Dezember 1964: For individual published contributions see notes to Chapter Two.

Ulbricht, Walter, *Die Durchführung der ökonomischen Politik im Planjahr 1964 unter besonderer Berücksichtigung der chemischen Industrie. Referat auf der 5. Tagung des ZK der SED, 3. bis 7. Februar 1964,* Berlin 1964.

—, *Zur Geschichte der deutschen Arbeiterbewegung. Aus Reden und Aufsätzen,* 10 vols., Berlin 1953 ff.

—, *Dem VI. Parteitag entgegen... Die Vorbereitung des VI. Parteitages der Sozialistischen Einheitspartei Deutschlands. Referat auf der 17. Tagung des ZK der SED, 3. bis 5. Oktober 1962 ... Um wissenschaftlich-technischen Höchststand und ökonomischen Nutzen. Rede auf der 2. Plenartagung des Forschungsrates der DDR, 12. November 1962,* Berlin 1962.

—, *Das neue ökonomische System der Planung und Leitung der Volks-*

wirtschaft in der Praxis. Diskussion zum Referat und zu den vorgelegten Entwürfen der Dokumente, Berlin 1963.

Die Verfassung der DDR (The Constitution of the GDR) Berlin 1949, 1968.

Die Volkskammer der Deutschen Demokratischen Republik . . ., see *Handbuch der Volkskammer . . .*

Wagener, H., *et al., Ökonomik der Arbeit in der DDR,* 3rd ed., Berlin 1964.

"Wirtschaftskonferenz des Zentralkomitees der SED und des Ministerrates der DDR vom 10. bis 11. Oktober 1961. Referate und Diskussionsbeiträge," in: *Die Wirtschaft,* Vol. 16 (1961), No. 42/43, No. 44.

"Wirtschaftskonferenz des Zentralkomitees der SED und des Ministerrates der DDR vom 24. bis 26. Juni 1963. Referate und Diskussionsbeiträge," in: *Die Wirtschaft,* Vol. 18 (1963), No. 26.

Wörterbuch der Ökonomie. Sozialismus, pub. by Willi Ehlert *et al.,* Berlin 1967.

Philosophisches Wörterbuch, pub. by Georg Klaus and Manfred Buhr, Leipzig 1964.

Aus dem Wortprotokoll der 25. Tagung des ZK der SED vom 24. bis 27. Oktober 1955, photographic reproduction of internal party publications.

Aus dem Wortprotokoll der 33. Tagung des ZK der SED vom 16. bis 18. Oktober 1957, photographic reproduction of internal party publications.

C. General Publications Concerning the Elite and Social Systems in the GDR

EAST

Behrens, Fritz, *Ursachen, Merkmale und Perspektiven des neuen Modells der Leitung der sozialistischen Wirtschaft (Sitzungsberichte der Deutschen Akademie der Wissenschaften zu Berlin,* 1966, No. 1), Berlin 1966.

Beiträge zur Zeitgeschichte. Sonderheft zum 10. Jahrestag der Gründung der DDR, pub. by Deutsches Institut für Zeitgeschichte, Berlin 1959.

Berger, Wolfgang, and Otto Reinhold, *Zu den wissenschaftlichen Grund-*

lagen des neuen ökonomischen Systems der Planung und Leitung. Das neue ökonomische System der Planung und Leitung—ein wichtiger Beitrag der Sozialistischen Einheitspartei Deutschlands zur marxistisch-leninistischen Theorie, Berlin 1966.

DDR—300 Fragen—300 Antworten, pub. by Ausschuss für Deutsche Einheit, 6, completely revised ed., Berlin 1964.

Doernberg, Stefan, Die Geburt eines neuen Deutschland 1945–1949. Die antifaschistisch-demokratische Umwälzung und die Entstehung der DDR, Berlin 1959.

—, Kurze Geschichte der DDR, pub. by Deutsches Institut für Zeitgeschichte, Berlin 1964.

Erfahrungen der sozialistischen Gemeinschaftsarbeit. Referat und Diskussionsbeiträge der Konferenz über Probleme der sozialistischen Gemeinschaftsarbeit, 26. und 27. März 1960 in Ballenstedt, Berlin 1960.

Hauk, Roland, et al., Zur Ökonomik der Übergangsperiode in der Deutschen Demokratischen Republik. Die Herausbildung sozialistischer Produktionsverhältnisse, Berlin 1962.

Horn, Werner, Die Errichtung der Grundlagen des Sozialismus in der Industrie der DDR (1951–1955), Berlin 1963.

Zwanzig Jahre Blockpolitik, Berlin 1965.

Kittner, Heinz, and Karl-Heinz Richter, Arbeiter-und-Bauern-Inspektion, neue Qualität der Kontrolle, Berlin 1963.

Koziolek, Helmut, et al., Zu aktuellen Fragen der Ökonomie, Beiträge aus der Forschung. Pub. on the occasion of the twentieth anniversary of the VEBs (Planung und Leitung der Volkswirtschaft, Sonderheft), Berlin 1966.

Lungwitz, Kurt, Über die Klassenstruktur in der Deutschen Demokratischen Republik. Eine sozialökonomisch-statistische Untersuchung, Berlin 1962.

Müller, Richard, et al., Territorial-Planung im neuen ökonomischen System der Planung und Leitung, Berlin 1966.

Neumann, Alfred, Zur Anwendung des neuen ökonomischen Systems der Planung und Leitung der Volkswirtschaft in der Industrie der DDR, Berlin 1965.

Probleme wissenschaftlicher Führungstätigkeit der örtlichen Staatsorgane in der zweiten Etappe des neuen ökonomischen Systems der Planung und Leitung (Aktuelle Beiträge der Staats- und Rechtswissenschaft, Vol. 18), Potsdam-Babelsberg 1966.

Die Deutsche Demokratische Republik auf dem Wege zum Sozialismus. Dokumente und Materialien, assembled and edited by Percy Stulz und Siegfried Thomas, intro. by Walter Bartel, 2 parts, Berlin 1959–1961.

Die Rolle des Staates und des Rechts bei der Leitung der Industrie in der Deutschen Demokratischen Republik. Wissenschaftliche Konferenz der Juristenfakultät der Karl-Marx-Universität, Leipzig am 16. und 17. Oktober 1959, Berlin 1961.

Rost, Rudi, *Der demokratische Zentralismus unseres Staates,* 2nd completely revised ed., Berlin 1962.

Sachse, Ekkehard, *Technische Revolution und Qualifikation der Werktätigen,* Berlin 1965.

Spitzner, Osmar, *Wirtschaftsverträge—sozialistische Wirtschaftsleitung. Rolle und Bedeutung der Wirtschaftsverträge im neuen ökonomischen System der Planung und Leitung der Volkswirtschaft,* Berlin 1965.

Stoph, Willi, *Aufgaben und Arbeitsweise des Ministerrates im neuen ökonomischen System der Planung und Leitung der Volkswirtschaft.* Lecture delivered at the Parteihochschule "Karl Marx" at the CC of the SED, *June 1964,* Berlin 1964.

—, *Die Vorzüge der sozialistischen Staats- und Gesellschaftsordnung besser für den umfassenden Aufbau des Sozialismus in der DDR nutzen. Aufgaben des Ministerrates und der Staats- und Wirtschaftsorgane zur Entwicklung der Volkswirtschaft,* Berlin 1965.

Theel, Jochen, *Technische Revolution und Erzeugnisgruppenarbeit,* Berlin 1965.

Ulbricht, Walter, *Über die Dialektik unseres sozialistischen Aufbaus,* Berlin 1959.

—, *Die Entwicklung des deutschen volksdemokratischen Staates 1945–1958,* Berlin 1958.

—, *Zum neuen ökonomischen System der Planung und Leitung,* Berlin 1966.

Weidig, Rudi, *Neuerer in der technischen Revolution,* Berlin 1965.

Das funktionelle Wirken der Bestandteile des neuen ökonomischen Systems der Planung und Leitung der Volkswirtschaft, pub. by Büro für Industrie und Bauwesen beim Politbüro des Zentralkomitees der SED, Berlin 1964.

WEST

Angestellte in der Sowjetzone Deutschlands. Verhaltensweisen und gesellschaftliche Einordnung der mitteldeutschen Angestellten, pub. by infratest-Institut, München-Hamburg, Mai 1958, mimeographed.

Blücher, Viggo Graf, *Industriearbeiterschaft in der Sowjetzone. Eine Untersuchung der Arbeiterschaft in der volkseigenen Industrie der SBZ,* pub. by infratest-Institut, Stuttgart 1959.

Brandt, Heinz, *Ein Traum, der nicht entführbar ist. Mein Weg zwischen Ost und West,* München 1967.

DDR. Geschichte und Bestandsaufnahme, pub. by Ernst Deuerlein, München 1966.

Demmler, Horst, "Der Rang der Zone als Industriemacht," in: *Frankfurter Allgemeine Zeitung,* April 22, 1967, p. 5.

Duhnke, Horst, *Stalinismus in Deutschland. Die Geschichte der SED,* Köln 1955.

Feddersen, Dieter, *Die Rolle der Volksvertretungen in der Deutschen Demokratischen Republik* (Publications of the *Institut für Internationales Recht an der Universität Kiel,* Vol. 52), Hamburg 1965.

Gleitze, Bruno, *Die Industrie der Sowjetzone unter dem gescheiterten Siebenjahrplan (Wirtschaft und Gesellschaft in Mitteldeutschland,* Vol. 2), Berlin 1964.

—, et al., *Der Osten auf dem Wege zur Marktwirtschaft,* Berlin 1967.

Haas, Gerhard (revised by Julian Lehnecke), *Der Gewerkschaftsapparat der SED. Organisation, Hauptaufgaben und politische Entwicklung der kommunistischen Pseudo-Gewerkschaft in der Sowjetzone,* pub. by Bundesministerium für gesamtdeutsche Fragen, Bonn–Berlin 1963.

Hamel, Hannelore, *Das sowjetische Herrschaftsprinzip des demokratischen Zentralismus in der Wirtschaftsordnung Mitteldeutschlands (Wirtschaft und Gesellschaft in Mitteldeutschland,* Vol. 5), Berlin 1966.

Handbuch der Sowjetzonen-Volkskammer. 2. Legislaturperiode (1954–1958), pub. by Informationsbüro West, 2 parts, Berlin 1955.

Zwei Jahrzehnte Bildungspolitik in der Sowjetzone Deutschlands. Dokumente, pub. by Siegfried Baske and Martha Engelbert (*Osteuropa-Institut an der Freien Universität Berlin. Erziehungswissenschaftliche Veröffentlichungen,* Vol. 2) 2 parts, Berlin 1966.

Köhler, Heinz, *Economic Integration in the Soviet Bloc. With an East German Case Study,* New York–Washington–London 1965.

Ludz, Peter Christian, "Widersprüche im Neuen Ökonomischen System. Organisatorische Probleme der Erzeugnisgruppen", in: *SBZ-Archiv,* Vol. 15 (1964), No. 7, pp. 101 ff.

Mampel, Siegfried, *Arbeitsverfassung und Arbeitsrecht in Mitteldeutschland,* Stuttgart 1966.

—, *Die Verfassung der Sowjetischen Besatzungszone Deutschlands. Text und Kommentar,* Frankfurt/Main–Berlin 1962; 2nd ed., 1966.

Ehemalige Nationalsozialisten in Pankows Diensten, pub. by Untersuchungsausschuss Freiheitlicher Juristen, 5th enlarged edition, Berlin 1965.

Pleyer, Klemens, *Zentralplanwirtschaft und Zivilrecht. Juristische Untersuchungen zur Wirtschaftsordnung der SBZ. Aufsätze aus den Jahren 1961 bis 1965 (Schriften zum Vergleich von Wirtschaftsordnungen,* Heft 7), Stuttgart 1965.

Pritzel, Konstantin, *Die wirtschaftliche Integration der Sowjetischen Besatzungszone Deutschlands in den Ostblock und ihre politischen Aspekte,* Berlin–Bonn 1962.

Richert, Ernst, *Das zweite Deutschland. Ein Staat, der nicht sein darf,* Gütersloh 1964.

—, *Macht ohne Mandat. Der Staatsapparat in der Sowjetischen Besatzungszone Deutschlands (Schriften des Instituts für politische Wissenschaft,* Vol. 11), 2nd revised and enlarged ed., Köln–Opladen 1963.

—, *Die Sowjetzone in der Phase der Koexistenzpolitik,* Hannover 1961.

—, in collaboration with Carola Stern and Peter Dietrich, *Agitation und Propaganda. Das System der publizistischen Massenführung in der Sowjetzone (Schriften des Instituts für politische Wissenschaft,* Vol. 10), Berlin–Frankfurt/Main 1958.

SBZ von A bis Z. Ein Taschen- und Nachschlagebuch über die Sowje-

tische Besatzungszone Deutschlands, pub. by Bundesministerium für gesamtdeutsche Fragen, 1st to 11th eds., Bonn 1953–1967.

SBZ-Biographie. Ein biographisches Nachschlagewerk über die Sowjetische Besatzungszone Deutschlands, assembled by Untersuchungsausschuss Freiheitlicher Juristen, Berlin, pub. by Bundesministerium für gesamtdeutsche Fragen, 1st ed., Bonn–Berlin 1961, 3rd ed., Bonn–Berlin 1964.

Stern, Carola, "Eastern Germany," in: *Communism in Europe. Continuity, Change, and the Sino-Soviet Conflict,* pub. by William E. Griffith, Vol. 2, Cambridge, Mass.–London 1966, pp. 43 ff.

Stolper, Wolfgang F., and Karl W. Roskamp, *The Structure of the East German Economy,* Cambridge, Mass. 1960.

Storbeck, Dietrich, *Arbeitskraft und Beschäftigung in Mitteldeutschland. Eine Untersuchung über die Entwicklung des Arbeitskräftepotentials und der Beschäftigten von 1950 bis 1965 (Dortmunder Schriften zur Sozialforschung,* Vol. 18), Köln–Opladen 1961.

—, *Soziale Strukturen in Mitteldeutschland. Eine sozialstatistische Bevölkerungsanalyse im gesamtdeutschen Vergleich (Wirtschaft und Gesellschaft in Mitteldeutschland,* Vol. 4), Berlin 1964.

Studien und Materialien zur Soziologie der DDR, pub. by Peter Christian Ludz *(Kölner Zeitschrift für Soziologie und Sozialpsychologie,* Sonderheft 8), Köln–Opladen 1964; also additional bibliography. 2nd ed. 1971.

Thalheim, Karl C., "Bedeuten die Wirtschaftsreformen in den Ostblockländern einen Systemwandel?", in: *Wirtschaftsplanung im Ostblock—Beginn einer Liberalisierung?,* pub. by Erik Boettcher, Stuttgart-Berlin-Köln-Mainz 1966.

—, *Die Wirtschaft der Sowjetzone in Krise und Umbau (Wirtschaft und Gesellschaft in Mitteldeutschland,* Vol. 1), Berlin 1964.

Wer ist wer? Das deutsche Who's Who. XIV. edition of Degeners Wer ist's?, Vol. 2, pub. by Walter Habel, Berlin 1965.

Wer ist wer in der SBZ? Ein biographisches Handbuch, Berlin 1958. (Later editions under the Title *SBZ-Biographie.*)

Zauberman, Alfred, *Industrial Progress in Poland, Czechoslovakia and East Germany, 1937 to 1962,* issued under the auspices of the Royal Institute of International Affairs, London-New York-Toronto 1964.

D. Selected Literature Concerning the History and the Social and Organizational Structure of the SED and the Cadre Problem

EAST

Arnold, Inge, and Gerhard Noack, *Wie organisieren die Parteiorganisationen eine richtige Arbeit mit den Kandidaten?*, Berlin 1963.

Arlt, Wolfgang, "Zur Entwicklung der SED von der Partei der Arbeiterklasse zur Partei der Arbeiterklasse und des werktätigen Volkes," in: *Beiträge zur Geschichte der deutschen Arbeiterbewegung*, Vol. 7 (1965), No. 2, pp. 171ff.

Benser, Günter, *Vereint sind wir unbesiegbar. Wie die SED enstand*, pub. by Institut für Marxismus-Leninismus beim ZK der SED, Berlin 1961.

Böhm, Siegfried, *Zu den Aufgaben der Betriebsparteiorganisationen bei der Durchführung des neuen ökonomischen Systems der Planung und Leitung der Volkswirtschaft im Planjahr 1964*, Berlin 1964.

—, "Einige Aufgaben der Grundorganisationen bei der Durchsetzung des Systems der ökonomischen Hebel," in: *Einheit,* Vol. 19 (1964), No. 5, pp. 3 ff.

Im Bündnis fest vereint. Die schöpferische marxistisch-leninistische Bündnispolitik der Sozialistischen Einheitspartei Deutschlands, 1945–1965. Ausgewähltes und überarbeitetes Protokoll der wissenschaftlichen Konferenz des Instituts für Gesellschaftswissenschaften beim Zentralkomitee der SED, des Instituts für Marxismus-Leninismus beim Zentralkomitee der SED und der Parteihochschule "Karl Marx" am 13. und 14. April 1966 in Berlin, Berlin 1966.

Dahlem, Franz "Walter Ulbrichts Kampf um die Leninschen Organisationsprinzipien," in: *Neuer Weg,* Vol. 18 (1963), No. 12, pp. 536 ff.

Doernberg, Stefan, "Zur Bündnispolitik der SED in den Jahren von 1956 bis zur Gegenwart," in: *Beiträge zur Geschichte der Sozialistischen Einheitspartei Deutschlands,* pub. by Institut für Gesellschaftswissenschaften beim ZK der SED, Berlin 1961.

Dohlus, Horst, "Mit den Parteiwahlen die Beschlüsse des 5. Plenums des ZK verwirklichen," in: *Neuer Weg,* Vol. 19 (1964), No. 5, pp. 206 ff.

—, "Produktionsprinzip erfordert höheres Niveau der Organisationsarbeit," in: *Neuer Weg,* Vol. 18 (1963), No. 21, pp. 961 ff.

—, "Für eine höhere Qualität der politisch-ideologischen Führungstätigkeit der Partei," in: *Verwirklichung der Beschlüsse des Zentralkomitees,* pub. by Abteilung Parteiorgane des ZK der SED, Berlin 1965.

Über einige Erfahrungen der Parteiarbeit in den örtlichen Staatsorganen, pub. by Abteilung Staats- und Rechtsfragen des Zentralkomitees der SED, Berlin 1966.

Fröhlich, Paul, "Das Leben unserer Partei," in: *Einheit,* Vol. 21 (1966), No. 4, pp. 419 ff.

Frost, Gerhard, "Die Besten werden Kandidat der Partei. Über einige Erfahrungen der Bezirksleitung Halle," in: *Neues Deutschland,* Oktober 16, 1965, p. 3.

Hager, Kurt, "Partei und Wissenschaft," in: *Einheit,* Vol. 21 (1966), No. 4, pp. 439 ff.

Heitzer, Kurt, "Probleme der Bündnispolitik der SED von 1949 bis 1955," in: *Beiträge zur Geschichte der deutschen Arbeiterbewegung,* Vol. 6 (1964), No. 1, pp. 39 ff.

—, *Geschichtliche Voraussetzungen für die Entstehung der SED (Deutsche Akademie der Wissenschaften. Vorträge und Schriften,* No. 76), Berlin, 1962.

Herber, Richard, "Die wachsende Führungsrolle unserer Partei," in: *Einheit,* Vol. 20 (1965), No. 1, pp. 3 ff.
—, "Wesen und Entwicklung der wissenschaftlich fundierten Leitungstätigkeit der SED," in: *Einheit,* Vol. 21 (1966), No. 3, pp. 291 ff.

Herber, Richard, *et al.,* "Probleme sozialistischer Kaderarbeit," in: *Einheit,* Vol. 17 (1962), No. 8, pp. 51 ff.

Herber, Richard, and Herbert Jung, *Wissenschaftliche Leitung und Entwicklung der Kader,* Berlin 1964.

Honecker, Erich, "Die Vorbereitung der Parteiwahlen 1966/67," in: *Neues Deutschland,* September 19, 1966, p. 3.

Horn, Werner, *et al., 20 Jahre Sozialistische Einheitspartei Deutschlands. Beiträge,* pub. by Parteihochschule "Karl Marx" beim ZK der SED, Lehrstuhl Geschichte der deutschen Arbeiterbewegung, Berlin 1966.

Hümmler, Heinz, "Die Bündnispolitik der SED mit Handwerkern,

Gewerbetreibenden, Komplementären und Unternehmern," in: *Beiträge zur Geschichte der deutschen Arbeiterbewegung,* Vol. 8 (1966), No. 6, pp. 1016 ff.

Köhler, Helmut, und Horst Noack, *Die Leitung der Parteiarbeit nach dem Produktionsprinzip und die Prinzipien der ehrenamtlichen Parteiarbeit,* Berlin 1963.

Koop, Hannelore, und Konrad Gurke, *Die Arbeit der Grundorganisationen mit den Beschlüssen des Zentralkomitees der SED,* pub. by Abteilung Parteiorgane des Zentralkomitees der SED, Berlin 1966.

Kramer, Horst, "Wissenschaft und Partei," in: *Deutsche Zeitschrift für Philosophie,* Vol. 14 (1966), No. 4, pp. 434 ff.

Kühnel, Hans, *Die Parteiinformation im System der Leitung der Parteiarbeit nach dem Produktionsprinzip,* Berlin 1964.

Lange, Alfred, *Die ökonomische Weiterbildung von Wirtschaftskadern. Erfahrungen und Probleme,* Berlin 1965.

Langendorf, Kurt, "Die schöpferische Rolle der SED bei der Ausarbeitung des neuen ökonomischen Systems der Planung ung Leitung," in: *Wissenschaftliche Zeitschrift der Humboldt-Universität zu Berlin. Gesellschafts- und sprachwissenschaftliche Reihe,* Vol. 15 (1966), No. 4, pp. 477 ff.

Matern, Hermann, "Die revolutionären Traditionen der deutschen Arbeiterbewegung leben im Kampf der Sozialistischen Einheitspartei Deutschlands," in: *Einheit,* Vol. 21 (1966), No. 4, pp. 431 ff.

Mittag, Günter, *Aufgaben und Methoden der Parteiarbeit in der Industrie, im Bauwesen und im Handel,* Berlin 1960.

—, *Fragen der Parteiarbeit nach dem Produktionsprinzip in Industrie und Bauwesen,* Berlin, 1963.

—, *Das Parteilehrjahr—entscheidendes Instrument zur Lösung der Aufgaben der Partei. Referat zur Eröffnung des Parteilehrjahres 1964/65 am 12. Oktober 1964,* Berlin 1964.

Müller, H., *Die politisch-ideologische und organisatorische Entwicklung der SED,* Berlin 1964, unpublished dissertation.

Hohes Niveau der Partei- und Massenarbeit—der Schlüssel für gute genossenschaftliche Arbeit. Sechs Beiträge aus der Praxis, pub. by Abteilung Landwirtschaft des ZK der SED, Berlin 1962.

Pisnik, Alois, "Die Perspektiven des Siebenjahrplanes—Grundlage der Erziehung und Qualifizierung der Kader," in: *Neuer Weg,* Vol. 15 (1960), No. 3, pp. 254 ff.

Pöschel, Kurt, und Joachim Tripoczky, *Probleme der Kaderarbeit in der sozialistischen Industrie,* Berlin 1966.

Rost, Rudi, "Die Entfaltung der wirtschaftlich-organisatorischen Tätigkeit der Staatsorgane und die Aufgaben der Parteiorganisationen im Staatapparat," in: *Einheit,* Vol. 14 (1959), No. 6, pp. 754 ff.

—, "Die Kaderarbeit als Führungsaufgabe," in: *Staat und Recht,* Vol. 16 (1967), No. 1, pp. 4 ff.

Schön, Otto, *Über den Inhalt politischer Leitungstätigkeit,* Berlin 1960.

—, *Die höchsten Organe der Sozialistischen Einheitspartei Deutschlands,* Berlin 1965.

Schulz, Gerhard, *Die politische Führungstätigkeit der Parteiorganisation bei der Vorbereitung des Volkswirtschaftsplanes,* Berlin 1963.

Schulze, Erhard, *et al., Die Verantwortung der Parteiorganisationen und der Mitglieder der SED für die Arbeit in den Gewerkschaften,* Berlin 1964.

Söder, Günter, "Die führende Rolle der Partei und das neue ökonomische System der Planung und Leitung," in *Einheit,* Vol. 21 (1966), No. 11, pp. 1372 ff.

Sorgenicht Klaus, "Das gesetzmässige Wachstum der führenden Rolle der SED bei der Lösung der Grundaufgaben der gesellschaftlichen Entwicklung in Deutschland," in: *Staat und Recht,* Vol. 15 (1966), No. 11, pp. 1769 ff.

Sozialismus und Intelligenz. Erfahrungen aus der Zusammenarbeit zwischen Arbeitern und Angehörigen der Intelligenz, pub. by Institut für Gesellschaftswissenschaften beim ZK der SED, Lehrstuhl für Philosophie, Berlin 1960.

Stelter, Klaus, *Die Berufung der Staats- und Wirtschaftsfunktionäre (Arbeit und Sozialfürsorge,* No. 23), Berlin 1958.

Ulbricht, Walter, *Zu Fragen der Parteiarbeit,* Berlin 1960.

Vereint sind wir alles. Erinnerungen an die Gründung der SED, with an Introduction by Walter Ulbricht, pub. by Fanny Rosner *et al.,* Institut für Marxismus-Leninismus beim ZK der SED, Berlin 1966.

Wagner, Horst, *Die Verantwortung der leitenden Parteiorgane für die Kaderarbeit und die Parteierziehung,* Berlin 1963.

Wetzel, Hans, "Die Kampfkraft unserer Parteiorganisation ist grösser geworden (Nach der Delegiertenkonferenz des Bezirks Leipzig)," in: *Einheit,* Vol. 13 (1958), No. 7, pp. 917 ff.

Wrona, Vera, "Weltanschauung und Politik—und die Entwicklung der SED zur Partei neuen Typus," in: *Deutsche Zeitschrift für Philosophie,* Vol. 15 (1967), No. 3, pp. 273 ff.

WEST

Baylis, Thomas,*The New Class in East German Politics,* Ph.D. Dissertation, Department of Political Science, University of California, Berkeley 1963, unpublished.

Croan, Melvin, "Intellectuals under Ulbricht," in: *Soviet Survey,* 1960, No. 34, pp. 35 ff.

Gniffke, Erich W., *Jahre mit Ulbricht,* with an Introduction by Herbert Wehner, Cologne 1966.

Jänicke, Martin, *Der Dritte Weg. Die antistalinistische Opposition gegen Ulbricht seit 1953,* Cologne 1964.

Lange, Max G., *et al.,* "Das Problem der 'Neuen Intelligenz' in der sowjetischen Besatzungszone. Ein Beitrag zur politischen Soziologie der kommunistischen Herrschaftsordnung," in *Veritas, Justitia, Libertas. Festschrift zur 200-Jahr-Feier der Columbia-University New York,* presented by the Freie Universität and the Deutsche Hochcshule für Politik, Berlin, Berlin 1953, pp. 191 ff.

Ludz, Peter Christian, "Funktionsaufbau und Wandel der SED-Führung," in: *Politische Vierteljahresschrift,* Vol. 7 (1966), No. 4, pp. 498 ff.

—, Produktionsprinzip versus Territorialprinzip. Probleme der Parteiorganisation im Rahmen des Neuen Ökonomischen Systems," in: *SBZ-Archiv,* Vol. 17 (1965), No. 1/2, pp. 5 ff.

Müller, Karl V., *Die Manager in der Sowjetzone. Eine empirische Untersuchung zur Soziologie der wirtschaftlichen und militärischen Führungsschicht in Mitteldeutschland (Schriftenreihe des Instituts für empirische Soziologie,* Vol. 2), Köln-Opladen 1962.

Picaper, Jean-Paul, "Le Parti communiste en Allemagne de l'est. Evolution de sa physiognomie et de ses fonctions," in: *Revue Française de Science Politique,* Vol. 16 (1966), No. 1, pp. 35 ff.

Prauss, Herbert, *Doch es war nicht die Wahrheit. Tatsachenbericht zur geistigen Auseinandersetzung unserer Zeit,* 2nd ed., Berlin 1960.

Riklin, Alois, and Klaus Westen, *Selbstzeugnisse des SED-Regimes. Das Nationale Dokument, das erste Programm der SED, das vierte Statut der SED (Aktuelle Studien,* Vol. 1), Cologne 1963.

Schultz, Joachim, *Der Funktionär in der Einheitspartei. Kaderpolitik und Bürokratisierung in der SED (Schriften des Instituts für politische Wissenschaft,* Vol. 8), Stuttgart-Düsseldorf 1956.

Stern, Carola, "Einheitspartei ohne Einheit," in: *SBZ-Archiv,* Vol. 5 (1954), No. 20, pp. 305 ff.

—, "Parteileitung nach dem 'Produktionsprinzip'," in: *SBZ-Archiv,* Vol. 14 (1963), No. 6, pp. 83 ff.

—, *Porträt einer bolschewistischen Partei. Entwicklung, Funktion und Situation der SED,* Cologne 1957.

—, *Die SED. Ein Handbuch über Aufbau, Organisation und Funktion des Parteiapparates,* Cologne 1954.

—, *Ulbricht. Eine politische Biographie,* Cologne-Berlin 1963.
Weber, Hermann, "Die KPD-SED an der Macht," in: *Der deutsche Kommunismus. Dokumente,* pub. and annotated by Hermann Weber, Cologne-Berlin 1963, pp. 10 ff. (reprinted 1964.)

E. Selected Literature Concerning Social Planning in the GDR, Marxist Theory of Organization, and Sociology of Organization

EACT

Apel, Erich, *Aktuelle Aufgaben zur Erhöhung der Qualität der Leitung der Volkswirtschaft durch die Verbesserung der komplexen Planung, insbesondere durch die Beachtung der Wechselwirkung zwischen Organisation und Technik und die Ausarbeitung der Pläne "Neue Technik."* Lecture delivered in December 1961 at the Parteihochschule "Karl Marx" beim ZK der SED, Berlin 1961.

—, *Neue Fragen der Planung. Zur Rolle und zu den Aufgaben der zentralen staatlichen Planung im neuen ökonomischen System der Planung und der Leitung der Volkswirtschaft,* Berlin 1963.

—, *Durch sozialistische Rekonstruktion und Erhöhung der Arbeitsproduktivität zur Erfüllung des Siebenjahrplanes. Referat und Entschliessung der 5. Tagung des Zentralkomitees der Sozialistischen Einheitspartei Deutschlands, 22 and 23 Mai 1959,* Berlin 1959.

—, "Technische Revolution und volkswirtschaftlicher Nutzeffekt," in: *Einheit,* Vol. 19 (1964), No. 9/10, pp. 45 ff.

Apel, Erich, und Günter Mittag, *Fragen der Anwendung des neuen ökonomischen Systems der Planung und Leitung der Volkswirtschaft bei der Vorbereitung und Durchführung der Investitionen,* Berlin 1965.

—, *Wissenschaftliche Führungstätigkeit, neue Rolle der VVB,* Berlin 1964.

—, *Ökonomische Gesetze und neues ökonomisches System,* Berlin 1964.

—, *Planmässige Wirtschaftsführung und ökonomische Hebel,* Berlin 1964.

Benjamin, Michael, "Zur Anwendung mathematischer Methoden in der staatlichen Leitung und Rechtspflege," in: *Staat und Recht,* Vol. 14 (1965), No. 6, pp. 899 ff.

Braunreuther, Kurt, "Die soziologische Organisationsanalyse als eine Gegenwartsaufgabe in der Industrieforschung," in: *Soziologie und Praxis. Beiträge zur Entwicklung der marxistischen Soziologie,* pub. by Günther Bohring and Kurt Braunreuther, Berlin 1965, pp. 13 ff.

—, *Über die marxistische Soziologie und ihren Beitrag zur wissenschaftlich begründeten Leistungstätigkeit (Deutsche Akademie der Wissenschaften zu Berlin. Vorträge und Schriften, No. 99),* Berlin 1965.

—, and Helmut Steiner, "Soziologische Probleme der sozialistischen Wirtschaftsführung," in: *Wirtschaftswissenschaft,* Vol. 12 (1964), No. 10, pp. 1601 ff.

Eichhorn, Wolfgang I, "Wissenschaftliche Leitung, marxistische Ethik und moralische Triebkräfte des umfassenden Aufbaus des Sozialismus," in: *Einheit,* Vol. 19 (1964), No. 11, pp. 54 ff.

Friedrich, Gerd, "Wissenschaftliche Führungstätigkeit stellt hohe Anforderungen an den Arbeitsstil der Leiter," in: *Einheit,* Vol. 20 (1965), No. 4, pp. 104 ff.

—, "Wissenschaftliche Führungstätigkeit setzt klare Zielsetzung voraus," in: *Einheit,* Vol. 20 (1965), No. 2, pp. 84 ff.

—, "Menschenführung und Organisation—wichtige Elemente wissenschaftlicher Führungstätigkeit," in: *Einheit,* Vol. 20 (1965), No. 3, pp. 82 ff.

Frohn, Gerhard, *Rationell leiten. Ratgeber für Analyse und Organisation der Leitungsarbeit der Betriebsdirektoren und anderer Leiter in Staat und Wirtschaft,* Berlin 1965.

Hahn, Erich, "Bürgerliche und marxistische Gruppensoziologie," in: *Deutsche Zeitschrift für Philosophie,* Vol. 13 (1965), No. 4, pp. 405 ff.

Hahn, Rainer, and Hans Hofmann, "Zum komplexen Charakter der Führung der Gesellschaft und zu den Aufgaben der Wissenschaft," in: *Staat und Recht,* Vol. 14 (1965), No. 10, pp. 1636 ff.

Havemann, Wolfgang, "Die Netzwerkplanung und -leitung staatlicher Aufgaben durch die örtlichen Räte," in: *Staat und Recht,* Vol. 15 (1966), No. 8, pp. 1317 ff.; Vol. 16 (1967), No. 3, pp. 433 ff.

Heuer, Uwe-Jens, "Demokratie und Recht," in: *Staat und Recht,* Vol. 16 (1967), No. 6, pp. 907 ff.

—, *Demokratie und Recht im neuen ökonomischen System der Planung und Leitung der Volkswirtschaft,* Berlin 1965. Reviews by Gerd Friedrich in: *Wirtschaftswissenschaft,* Vol. 14 (1966), No. 8, pp. 1383 ff.; by Hans-Ulrich Hochbaum in: *Staat und Recht,* Vol. 15 (1966), No. 6, pp. 1038 ff.; by Karl Mollnau and Werner Wippold in: *Staat und Recht,* Vol. 15 (1966), No. 8, pp. 1271 ff.

—, *Einführungsvorlesung zu neuen Problemen des Staatsrechts,* Berlin 1966, unpublished manuscript.

—, "W. I. Lenin über die Leitung der sozialistischen Industrie," in: *Staat und Recht,* Vol. 12 (1963), No. 1, pp. 32 ff.

—, "Plan, Selbstregelung und sozialistisches Recht," in: *Sozialistische Demokratie,* 1965, No. 1, supplement, pp. 9 ff.

—, "Neues ökonomisches System und Entwicklung der sozialistischen Demokratie," in: *Wissenschaftliche Zeitschrift der Humboldt-Universität zu Berlin. Gesellschafts- und sprachwissenschaftliche Reihe,* Vol. 15 (1966), No. 4, pp. 487 ff.

—, "Zum Verhältnis von Ökonomie, Recht und Administration," in: *Wirtschaftswissenschaft,* Vol. 14 (1966), No. 6, pp. 929 ff.

—, "Wissenschaftliche Wirtschaftführung und sozialistisches Recht," in: *Staat und Recht,* Vol. 13 (1964), No. 6, pp. 985 ff.

Kallabis, Heinz, review of: Wolfgang Kellner, *Der moderne soziale Konflikt. Seine Ursache und seine Überwindung im Betrieb,* in: *Deutsche Zeitschrift für Philosophie,* Vol. 9 (1961), No. 11, pp. 1401 ff.

Kannegiesser, Karlheinz, "Leitungswissenschaftliche Probleme unter dem Gesichtspunkt der Kybernetik," in: *Staat und Recht,* Vol. 14 (1965), No. 10, pp. 1609 ff.

Kannengiesser, Lothar, *Die Organisation der Beziehungen zwischen Wissenschaft und Produktion. Die Koordinierungsvereinbarung zur Sicherung des wissenschaftlichen Vorlaufs und die sozialistische Interessengemeinschaft als Instrument der ökonomischen Leitung der Industriezweige,* Berlin 1967.

Klaus, Georg, and Gerda Schnauss, "Kybernetik und sozialistische Leitung," in: *Einheit,* Vol. 20 (1965), No. 2, pp. 93 ff.

Koziolek, Helmut, "Grundlagenforschung und Ökonomie," in: *Zu aktuellen Fragen der Ökonomie, Beiträge aus der Forschung,* published on the occasion of the 20th anniversary of the VEBS *(Planung und Leitung der Volkswirtschaft,* Sonderheft), Berlin 1966, pp. 7 ff.

Kulka, H., "Betriebliche Leitungsprobleme in psychologischer Betrachtung," in: *Die Technik,* Vol. 19 (1964), No. 5, pp. 321 ff.

Ladensack, Klaus, *Arbeitsorganisation. Probleme und Aufgaben (Sozialistische Arbeitswissenschaft,* Vol. 1), Berlin 1965.

Lange, H., *et al., Grundfragen der Betriebsorganisation,* pub. by the Zentralleitung der Kammer der Technik, 2nd revised edition, Berlin 1962.

Lehmann, Heinz R., *Grundsätze und Methoden der Organisationsarbeit in sozialistischen Industriebetrieben,* Berlin 1963.

Liehmann, Paul, "Wege und Probleme der Vervollkommnung der sozialistischen Demokratie in der Industrie," in: *Wirtschaftswissenschaft,* Vol. 14 (1966), No. 7, pp. 1078 ff.

Metzler, Helmut, "Zu philosophischen Problemen der Entscheidungstätigkeit des Leiters," in: *Deutsche Zeitschrift für Philosophie,* Vol. 15 (1967), No. 2, pp. 152 ff.

Mittag, Günter, *Fragen des neuen ökonomischen Systems der Planung und Leitung der Volkswirtschaft.* Lecture delivered before the *Kollektiv der Parteihochschule "Karl Marx" im März 1963,* Berlin 1963.

—, *Zur Wirtschaftspolitik der SED in der Periode des umfassenden Aufbaus des Sozialismus in der DDR unter den Bedingungen der technischen Revolution (Schriftenreihe des Zentralinstituts für sozialistische Wirtschaftsführung beim ZK der SED in Verbindung mit dem Arbeitskreis "Sozialistische Wirtschaftsführung" des Beirates für ökonomische Forschung bei der Staatlichen Plankommission der DDR,* No. 1), Berlin 1966.

Moschütz, Hans Dieter, and Gerhard Schulze, "Zum Nutzeffekt staatsrechtlicher Forschung," in: *Staat und Recht,* Vol. 16 (1967), No. 4, pp. 614 ff.

Nehls, Heinz, *Aufgaben- und Verantwortungsbereiche in der volkseigenen Industrie,* Berlin 1962.

Oelssner, Fred, *Einige theoretische Probleme der Planung und Leitung der Volkswirtschaft (Sitzungsberichte der Deutschen Akademie der Wissenschaften zu Berlin. Klasse für Philosophie, Geschichte . . .,* No. 4), Berlin 1964.

Rittershaus, Hans-Joachim, *Neuererzentren und Arbeitsproduktivität. Wie können die Bezirksneuererzentren den wissenschaftlich-technischen Fortschritt unterstützen?,* Berlin 1964.

Rudolph, Johannes, "Kybernetische Aspekte des Informationsflusses im Prozess der planmässigen Leitung der Volkswirtschaft," in: *Wirtschaftswissenschaft,* Vol. 12 (1964), No. 16, pp. 882 ff.

Söder, Günter, "Ökonomie, Demokratie und Politik," in: *Einheit,* Vol. 21 (1966), No. 7, pp. 866 ff.

Sozialismus—Wissenschaft—Produktivkraft. Über die Rolle der Wissenschaft beim umfassenden Aufbau des Sozialismus in der Deutschen Demokratischen Republik, pub. by Institut für Gesellschaftswissenschaften beim ZK der SED, Berlin 1963.

Stüber, Richard, "Wissenschaftliche Leitungstätigkeit im sozialistischen Betrieb und konkrete Sozialforschung," in: *Deutsche Zeitschrift für Philosophie,* Vol. 13 (1965), No. 6, pp. 753 ff.

—, "Neues ökonomisches System und sozialistische Demokratie," in: *Staat und Recht,* Vol. 16 (1967), No. 1, pp. 92 ff.

Such, Heinz, "Aufgaben und Verantwortlichkeit der VVB bei der Gestaltung und Organisierung der Kooperationsbeziehungen ihrer Betriebe," in: *Staat und Recht,* Vol. 14 (1965), No. 3, pp. 391 ff.

Thiel, Rainer, "Zur mathematisch-kybernetischen Erfassung ökonomischer Gesetzmässigkeiten," in: *Wirtschaftswissenschaft,* Vol. 10 (1962), No. 6, pp. 889 ff.

—, "Kybernetik und Gesellschaftswissenschaft," in: *Einige Beiträge zu Fragen der Kybernetik,* Berlin 1963, pp. 115 ff.

Tröger, Horst, "Das Organisationsproblem in kybernetischer Sicht," in: *Wissenschaftliche Zeitschrift der Humboldt-Universität zu Berlin. Gesellschafts- und sprachwissenschaftliche Reihe,* Vol. 13 (1964), No. 5, pp. 593 ff.

—, "Die Organisationswissenschaft und ihr Zusammenwirken mit der Soziologie und Sozialpsychologie," in: *Soziologische und psychologische Erfahrungen aus Forschung und Praxis,* pub. by Gerhart Müller, Berlin 1965, pp. 124 ff.

Vorholzer, Jörg, "Wissenschaftlich fundierte Führungstätigkeit—entscheidendes Erfordernis bei der Verwirklichung des Programms unserer Partei," in: *Einheit,* Vol. 10 (1964), No. 1, pp. 26 ff.

Weichelt, Wolfgang, "Das neue ökonomische System der Planung und Leitung und die Volksvertretungen," in: *Staat und Recht,* Vol. 16 (1967), No. 3, pp. 356 ff.

Wüstneck,, Klaus Dieter, "Der kybernetische Charakter des neuen ökonomischen Systems und die Modellstruktur der Perspektivplanung als zielstrebiger, kybernetischer Prozess," in: *Deutsche Zeitschrift für Philosophie,* Vol. 13 (1965), No. 1, pp. 5 ff.

WEST

Blau, Peter M., and Charles H. Page, *Bureaucracy in Modern Society* (*Studies in Sociology*), Vol. 12, 10th ed., New York 1963.

Busse, Gisela von, *Die Lehre vom Staat als Organismus. Kritische Untersuchungen zur Staatphilosophie Adam Müllers,* Berlin 1928 (originally a Ph.D. dissertation, Göttingen 1926).

Dahl, Robert A., *Modern Political Analysis,* Englewood Cliffs, N. J. 1963.

Deutsch, Karl W., "Mechanism, Organism, and Society. Some Models in Natural and Social Science," in *Philosophy of Science,* Vol. 18 (1951), No. 3, pp. 230 ff.

Etzioni, Amitai, *A Comparative Analysis of Complex Organizations. On Power, Involvement, and their Correlates,* Glencoe, Ill. 1961.

Eucken, Rudolf, "Organisch, mechanisch," in: *Eucken, Geistige Strömungen der Gegenwart,* 5th revised edition, Leipzig 1916, pp. 119 ff.

Gouldner, Alvin W., "Organizational Analysis," in: *Sociology Today. Problems and Prospects,* pub. by Robert K. Merton *et al.,* 5th ed., New York 1959, pp. 400 ff.

Hartmann, Heinz, *Funktionale Autorität. Systematische Abhandlung zu einem soziologischen Begriff,* Stuttgart 1964.

Irle, Martin, *Soziale Systeme. Eine kritische Analyse der Theorie von formalen und informalen Organisationen,* Göttingen 1963.

Jonas, H., "Bemerkungen zum Systembegriff und seiner Anwendung auf Lebendiges," in: *Studium Generale,* Vol. 10 (1957), No. 2, pp. 88 ff.

—, "Materialism and the Theory of Organism," in: *The University of Toronto Quarterly,* Vol. 21 (1951), No. 1, pp. 39 ff.

Kaufmann, Herbert, "Organization Theory and Political Theory," in: *The American Political Science Review,* Vol. 58 (1964), No. 1, pp. 5 ff.

Kerr, Clark, *et al., Industrialism and Industrial Man. The Problems of Labour and Management in Economic Growth,* London-Edinburgh 1960.

Krupp, Sherman, *Pattern in Organization Analysis. A Critical Examination,* Philadelphia-New York 1961.

Lieber, Hans-Joachim, "Kants Philosophie des Organischen und die Biologie seiner Zeit," in: *Philosophia Naturalis,* Vol. 1 (1952), No. 4, pp. 553 ff.

Likert, Rensis, *New Patterns of Management,* New York-Toronto-London 1961.

Luhmann, Niklas, *Funktionen und Folgen formaler Organisation (Schriftenreihe der Hochschule Speyer,* Vol. 20), Berlin 1964.

Lukács, Georg. "Towards a Methodology of the Problems of Organization," in: *Lukács, History and Class Consciousness,* tr. by Rodney Livingstone, Cambridge, Mass., 1971, pp. 295 ff.

March, James G., and Herbert A. Simon, *Organizations,* 2nd ed., New York-London 1959.

Modern Organization Theory. A Symposium of the Foundation for Research on Human Behavior, pub. by Mason Haire, 2nd ed., New York-London 1961.

Schmalenbach, Herman, "Die soziologische Kategorie des Bundes," in: *Die Dioskuren, Jahrbuch für Geisteswissenschaften,* Vol. 1, München 1922, pp. 35 ff.

Shils, Edward A., "The Study of the Primary Group," in: *The Policy Sciences. Recent Developments in Scope and Method,* pub. by Daniel Lerner *et al.,* Stanford, Cal. 1951, pp. 44 ff.

Thompson, Victor A., *Modern Organization,* New York 1963.

Whyte, William H. Jr., *Organization Man,* New York 1956.

Young, O. R., "The Impact of General Systems Theory on Political Science," in: *General Systems,* Vol. 9 (1964), pp. 239 ff.

F. Selected Literature Concerning Marxist Theory of Science, Cybernetics, and Ideology

EAST

Arbeit—Gemeinschaft—Persönlichkeit. Soziologische Studien, pub. by Reinhold Miller and Günther Hoppe, Berlin 1964.

Berger, Horst, *Methoden industriesoziologischer Untersuchungen,* Berlin 1965.

Buhr, Manfred, "Entfremdung—philosophische Anthropologie—Marx-Kritik," in: *Deutsche Zeitschrift für Philosophie,* Vol. 14 (1966), No. 7, pp. 806 ff.

—, "Die Philosophie von Karl Marx und der ideologische Klassenkampf. Zur Funktion des Begriffs der Entfremdung im System der bürgerlichen Marx-Kritik," in: *Einheit,* Vol. 21 (1966), No. 11, pp. 1424 ff.

Entfremdung und Humanität. Marx und seine klerikalen Kritiker, pub. by Institut für Gesellschaftswissenschaften beim ZK der SED, Berlin 1964.

Hager, Kurt, *Humanismus und Wissenschaft. Festvortrag anlässlich der 150-Jahr-Feier der Humboldt-Universität zu Berlin und der 250-Jahr-Feier der Charité,* Berlin 1961.

Hahn, Erich, *Soziale Wirklichkeit und soziologische Erkenntnis. Philosophisch-methodologische Aspekte der soziologischen Theorie,* Berlin 1965.

Havemann, Robert, *Dialektik ohne Dogma? Naturwissenschaft und*

Weltanschauung (*rororo Taschenbuch-Ausgabe,* No. 683), Reinbek 1964.

Heise, Wolfgang, *Aufbruch in die Illusion. Zur Kritik der bürgerlichen Philosophie in Deutschland,* Berlin 1964.

—, "Über die Entfremdung und ihre Überwindung," in: *Deutsche Zeitschrift für Philosophie,* Vol. 13 (1965), No. 6, pp. 684 ff.

—, "Zu einigen Grundfragen der marxistischen Ästhetik," in: *Deutsche Zeitschrift für Philosophie,* Vol. 5 (1957), No. 1, pp. 50 ff.

—, "Hegel und das Komische," in: *Sinn und Form,* Vol. 16 (1964), No. 6, pp. 811 ff.

—, "Produktivkräfte und Produktionsverhältnisse und die subjektive menschliche Tätigkeit," in: *Deutsche Zeitschrift für Philosophie,* Vol. 13 (1965), special issue, pp. 136 ff.

Hermsdorf, Klaus, *Kafka. Weltbild und Roman,* 2nd rev. ed., Berlin 1966.

Huth, Gerda, *Produktivkraft Persölichkeit. Philosophische Bemerkungen über Qualifizierung und wissenschaftlich-technische Revolution,* Berlin 1966.

Imperialismus heute. Der staatsmonopolitische Kapitalismus in Westdeutschland, pub. by Institut für Gesellschaftswissenschaften beim ZK der SED, 4th revised and enlarged edition, Berlin 1967.

Franz Kafka aus Prager Sicht 1963, pub. by the Czechoslovak Academy of Science, Prague 1965.

Kannegiesser, Karlheinz, "Die Bedeutung der Kybernetik für den wissenschaftlich-technischen Fortschritt," in: *Einige Beiträge zu Fragen der Kybernetik,* Berlin 1963, pp. 31 ff.

Klaus, Georg, *Einführung in die formale Logik,* 1st ed., Berlin 1958.

—, *Spezielle Erkenntnistheorie. Prinzipien der wissenschaftlichen Theorienbildung,* Berlin 1965.

—, "Hegel und die Dialektik in der formalen Logik," in: *Deutsche Zeitschrift für Philosophie,* Vol. 11 (1963), No. 12, pp. 1489 ff.

—, *Kybernetik und Erkenntnistheorie,* Berlin 1966.

—, *Kybernetik und Gesellschaft,* Berlin 1964.

—, "Die Kybernetik, das Programm der SED und die Aufgaben der Philosophen," in: *Deutsche Zeitschrift für Philosophie,* Vol. 11 (1963), No. 6, pp. 693 ff.

—, *Kybernetik in philosophischer Sicht,* 2nd ed., Berlin 1962; 4th ed., Berlin 1965.

—, *Die Macht des Wortes. Ein erkenntnistheoretisch-pragmatisches Traktat,* 3rd ed., Berlin 1965.

—, Zu einigen Problemen der Kybernetik," in: *Einheit,* Vol. 13 (1958), No. 7, pp. 1026 ff.

—, *Semiotik und Erkenntnistheorie,* Berlin 1963.

—, and Heinz Liebscher, *Was ist—was soll Kybernetik?,* Leipzig-Jena-Berlin 1965.

—, and Rainer Thiel, "Über die Existenz kybernetischer Systeme in der Gesellschaft," in: *Deutsche Zeitschrift für Philosophie,* Vol. 10 (1962), No. 1, pp. 22 ff.

Kosing, Alfred, *Wissenschaftstheorie als Aufgabe der marxistischen Philosophie (Sitzungsberichte der Deutschen Akademie der Wissenschaften zu Berlin: Klasse für Philosophie, Geschichte, Staats-, Rechts- und Wirtschaftswissenschaften, No. 1),* Berlin 1967.

Kurella, Alfred, *Der Mensch als Schöpfer seiner selbst. Beiträge zum sozialistischen Humanismus,* Berlin 1961.

—, "Was verstand Marx unter Entfremdung?," in: *Sonntag,* April 5, 1964, pp. 3 ff.

Lauterbach, Herbert, and Günter Söder, *Planung—Wissenschaft oder Spekulation? (Taschenbuchreihe "Unser Weltbild," Vol. 40),* Berlin 1957.

Neues Leben, neue Menschen. Konferenz des Lehrstuhls Philosophie des Instituts für Gesellschaftswissenschaften beim ZK der SED über theoretische und praktische Probleme der sozialistischen Moral am 16. und 17. April 1957.

Ley, Hermann, *Dämon Technik?* Berlin 1961.

Liebscher, Heinz, *Kybernetik und Leitungstätigkeit,* Berlin 1966.

Loeser, Franz, *Deontik. Planung und Leitung der moralischen Entwicklung,* Berlin 1966.

Löser, Wolfgang, "Zur kybernetischen Darstellung von ökonomischen Systemen," in: *Deutsche Zeitschrift für Philosophie,* Vol. 14 (1966), No. 10, pp. 1276 ff.

Maschine und Gedanke. Philosophische Probleme der Kybernetik, pub. by Georg Klaus, Leipzig-Jena-Berlin 1962.

Die deutsche bürgerliche Philosophie seit der Grossen Sozialistischen Oktoberrevolution, with contributions by W. Heise, G. Klaus *et al., (Taschenbuchreihe "Unser Weltbild,"* Vol. 1), Berlin 1958.

Die marxistisch-leninistische Philosophie und die technische Revolution. Materialien des philosophischen Kongresses vom 22. bis 24 April 1965 in Berlin (Deutsche Zeitschrift für Philosophie, Sonderheft), Berlin 1965.

Protokoll der philosophischen Konferenz über Fragen der Logik am 17. und 18. November 1951 in Jena (Deutsche Zeitschrift für Philosophie, Beiheft 1), Berlin 1953.

Schnauss, G., *Kybernetik und Praxis (Taschenbuchreihe "Unser Weltbild,"* Vol. 36), 2nd ed., Berlin 1963.

Selbmann, Fritz, *Ein Zeitalter stellt sich vor,* Berlin 1957.

Sozialpsychologie im Sozialismus. Bericht vom Internationalen Symposium marxistischer Sozialpsychologen "Der gesellschaftliche Auftrag der Sozialpsychologie im Sozialismus" vom 21. bis 23. Oktober 1964 in Jena, pub. by Hans Hiebsch und Manfred Vorwerg, Berlin 1965.

Thiel, Rainer, "Zur Anwendung mathematischer Begriffe in Gesellschaftswissenschaften," in: *Deutsche Zeitschrift für Philosophie,* Vol. 11 (1963), No. 1, pp. 19 ff.

—, "Kybernetik, Philosophie, Gesellschaft. Zu einer wissenschaftlichen Beratung der Redaktion 'Einheit'," in: *Einheit,* Vol. 16 (1961), No. 1, Supplement, pp. 1 ff.

Welskopf, Elizabeth C., "Entfremdung—historisch gesehen," in: *Deutsche Zeitschrift für Philosophie,* Vol. 13 (1965), No. 6, pp. 711 ff.

Wüstneck, Klaus Dieter, "Zur philosophischen Verallgemeinerung und Bestimmung des Modellbegriffs," in: *Deutsche Zeitschrift für Philosophie,* Vol. 11 (1963), No. 12, pp. 1504 ff.

WEST

Ashby, William Ross, *Design for a Brain. The Origin of Adaptive Behavior,* 2nd revised ed., London 1960.

Barth, Hans, *Wahrheit und Ideologie,* 2nd ed., Erlenbach-Zürich-Stuttgart 1961.

Bell, Daniel, "Ideology and Soviet Politics," in *Slavic Review,* Vol. 24 (1965), No. 4, pp. 591 ff.

—, "Reply," *ibid.* p. 617.

Bertalanffy, Ludwig von, *Das Gefüge des Lebens,* Leipzig-Berlin 1937.

—, "An Outline of General System Theory," in: *The British Journal for the Philosophy of Science,* Vol. 1 (1950), No. 2, pp. 134 ff.

Bocheński, Joseph M., "The Three Components of Communist Ideology," in: *Studies in Soviet Thought,* Vol. 2 (1962), No. 1, pp. 7 ff.

—, "Toward a Systematic Logic of Communist Ideology," in: *Studies in Soviet Thought,* Vol. 4 (1964), No. 3, pp. 185 ff.

Boulding, Kenneth E., "The Structure of Ideologies," in: *Boulding, Conflict and Defense. A General Theory,* New York-Evanston-London 1963, pp. 298 ff.

Brunner, Otto, "Das Zeitalter der Ideologien: Anfang und Ende," in: *Die Neue Rundschau,* Vol. 65 (1954), No. 1, pp. 132 ff.

Burks, Richard V., "A Conception of Ideology for Historians," in: *Journal of the History of Ideas,* Vol. 10 (1959), No. 2, pp. 183 ff.

Comey, David D., "Marxist-Leninist Ideology and Soviet Policy," in: *Studies in Soviet Thought,* Vol. 2 (1962), No. 4, pp. 301 ff.

Couffignal, Louis, *Kybernetische Grundbegriffe (Kybernetik und Information, Internationale Reihe,* Vol. 1), Baden-Baden–Paris 1962.

Dahm, Helmut, *Die Dialektik im Wandel der Sowjetphilosophie (Abhandlungen des Bundesinstituts zur Erforschung des Marxismus-Leninismus,* Vol. 2), Cologne 1963.

Friedrich, Carl J., "Ideology in Politics. A Theoretical Comment," in: *Slavic Review,* Vol. 24 (1965), No. 4, pp. 612 ff.

Günther, Gotthard, *Das Bewusstsein der Maschinen. Eine Metaphysik der Kybernetik,* Baden-Baden–Krefeld 1963.

Ideologie. Ideologiekritik und Wissenssoziologie, pub. by Kurt Lenk *(Soziologische Texte,* Vol. 4), 2nd ed., Neuwied–Berlin 1964.

Jordan, Z. A., *Philosophy and Ideology. The Development of Philosophy and Marxism-Leninism in Poland Since the Second World War,* Dordrecht 1963.

Laszlo, Ervin, "Dynamics of Ideological Change in Eastern Europe," in: *Inquiry,* Vol. 1 (1966), No. 1, pp. 17 ff.

Lichtheim, George, *Marxism. An Historical and Critical Study,* London 1961.

Lieber, Hans-Joachim, *Philosophie, Soziologie, Gesellschaft. Gesammelte Studien zum Ideologieproblem,* Berlin 1965.

Mannheim, Karl, *Ideologie und Utopie,* 3rd enlarged ed., Frankfurt/Main 1952.

Messelken, Karlheinz, "Zur Rolle von Semiotik und Kybernetik in der marxistischen Philosophie," in: *Soziale Welt,* Vol. 16 (1965), No. 1, p. 289 ff.

Meyer, Alfred G., "The Functions of Ideology in the Soviet Political System. A Speculative Essay Designed to Provoke Discussion," in: *Soviet Studies,* Vol. 17 (1966), No. 3, pp. 273 ff.

Naess, Arne, assisted by Jens A. Christophersen und Kjell Kvalø, *Democracy, Ideology and Objectivity. Studies in the Semantics and Cognitive Analysis of Ideological Controversy,* Oslo–Oxford 1956.

Nahirny, Vladimir C., "Some Observations on Ideological Groups," in: *The American Journal of Sociology,* Vol. 67 (1962), No. 4, p. 397 ff.

Siebert, Klaus, "Hürdenlauf der Kybernetik," in: *SBZ-Archiv,* Vol. 17 (1966), No. 15, pp. 233 ff; No. 17, pp. 264 ff.

Stachowiak, Herbert, *Denken und Erkennen im kybernetischen Modell,* Vienna–New York 1965.

Steinbuch, Karl, *Automat und Mensch. Kybernetische Tatsachen und Hypothesen,* 2nd enlarged ed., Berlin–Göttingen–Heidelberg 1963.

Topitsch, Ernst, *Sozialphilosophie zwischen Ideologie und Wissenschaft (Soziologische Texte,* Vol. 10), Neuwied 1961.

Name Index

For further name references, see Tables 22, 23, 26, and 27, and Appendix 2.

Subject Index

Books Published under the Auspices of the Research Institute on Communist Affairs

Diversity in International Communism, Alexander Dallin, ed., in collaboration with the Russian Institute, Columbia University Press, 1963.
A documentary record of the issues agitating the international communist movement in the years 1961–1963.

Political Succession in the USSR, Myron Rush, published jointly with the RAND Corporation, Columbia University Press, 1965.
A theoretical and historical account of the problem of political succession in the Soviet regime.

Marxism in Modern France, George Lichtheim, Columbia University Press, 1966.
A historical study of French socialist and communist theory and practice since World War II.

The Soviet Bloc: Unity and Conflict, Zbigniew Brzezinski, revised and enlarged edition, Harvard University Press, 1967.
Focuses on the role of ideology and power in the relations among the communist states.

Power in the Kremlin, Michel Tatu, Viking Press, 1969, first published in 1967, by Bernard Grasset under the title *Le Pouvoir en URSS,* and also in England by William Collins Sons and Co., Ltd., in 1968.
An analysis of the shifting balance of power within the Soviet leadership in the 1960s.

Vietnam Triangle, Donald Zagoria, Pegasus Press, 1968.
A clarification of the factors governing the relations among the communist parties and states involved in Vietnam.

Communism in Malaysia and Singapore, Justus van der Kroef, Nijhoff Publications, The Hague, 1967.
The first book-length study of the communist movement in the Malaysian-Singapore region today.

Radicalismo Cattolico Brasiliano, Ulisse A Floridi, Istituto Editoriale Del Mediterraneo, 1968.
A discussion of the problems faced by the Catholic Church when it becomes actively involved in the struggle for social justice.

Stalin and His Generals, Seweryn Bialer, ed., Pegasus Press, 1969.
An anthology of war memoirs from Soviet books, journals, and other writings which gives a picture of the Soviet military elite and of Stalin's role during World War II.

Marxism and Ethics, Eugene Kamenka, Macmillan and St. Martin's Press, 1969.
The author examines both Marx's positive ethics of the truly human man freed from alienation and Marx's materialist critique of moralities as class-bound ideologies.

Dilemmas of Change in Soviet Politics, Zbigniew Brzezinski, ed. and contributor, Columbia University Press, 1969.
A collection of essays which appeared in *Problems of Communism* in 1966–1968, discussing prospects for the Soviet political system.

The USSR Arms the Third World: Case Studies in Soviet Foreign Policy, Uri Ra'anan, The M.I.T. Press, 1969.
Using Egypt and Indonesia as case studies, the author analyzes Soviet involvement in the Third World.

Communists and Their Law, John N. Hazard, The University of Chicago Press, 1969.
The author analyzes the Marxian socialist legal system and examines the implementation of policy by law in the communist world.

Fulcrum of Asia, Bhabani Sen Gupta, published jointly with the East Asian Institute, Pegasus Press, 1970.
The author analyzes and documents the relations among China, India, Pakistan, and the Soviet Union during 1947–1968.

Le Conflit Sino-Soviétique et l'Europe de l'Est, Jacques Lévesque, Les Presses de l'Université de Montréal, 1970.
The author examines the impact of the Sino-Soviet conflict on the relations between the U.S.S.R. and Poland (1956–1959) and between the U.S.S.R. and Rumania (1960–1968).

Between Two Ages, Zbigniew Brzezinski, Viking Press, 1970.
The author projects the impact of technology and electronics on the political and social values of the United States, the Soviet Union, and the Third World, and analyzes their implications for the United States.

Communist China and Latin America, 1959–1967, Cecil Johnson, Columbia University Press, 1970.
The author describes the Chinese efforts to become a major force in Latin America. He compares the Chinese theory of revolution with those developed by the Latin Americans, and he analyzes the efforts to establish pro-Chinese parties and movements as well as the strategy of these pro-Chinese groups.

The Czechoslovak Experiment 1968–1969, Ivan Svitak, Columbia University Press, 1971.
This book presents an anthology of personal political documents, written by a Marxist philosopher in the midst of national crisis. It documents in a unique way the manner in which the Czechoslovak New Left touched the raw nerve of Soviet communism by questioning the vanguard, omniscient role of the Communist Party.

Les Régimes Politiques de l'U.R.S.S. et de l'Europe de l'Est, by Michel Lesage, Presses Universitaires de France, 1971.
The author describes and analyzes the principles which govern the relations between the political regimes of Eastern Europe.

Communism and Nationalism in India: M. N. Roy and Comintern Policy, 1920–1939, John P. Haithcox, Princeton University Press, 1971.
Focusing on the career of M. N. Roy, founder of the Communist Party of India, Professor Haithcox traces the development of communism and nationalism in India from the Second Comintern Congress in 1920 to the defeat of the left wing of the Indian National Congress in 1939.

The Bulgarian Communist Party, 1934-1944, Nissan Oren, Columbia University Press, 1971 (sponsored jointly with the Institute on East Central Europe).
A detailed survey of one of Europe's most powerful and original communist parties during the decade preceding the establishment of communist rule in Bulgaria.

American Communism in Crisis, 1943–1957, Joseph R. Starobin, Harvard University Press, 1972.
In 1943 the American Communist Party was a large, politically influential, broadly based movement. In 1957 it was a small, weak, and isolated political sect. The Party's decline in the intervening Cold War years is the subject of this book—an analysis of a significant radical movement.